SOCCER AND HOCKEY

THE NEW YORK TIMES ENCYCLOPEDIA OF SPORTS

THE NEW YORK TIMES
ENCYCLOPEDIA OF SPORTS

VOLUME 8

SOCCER/PROFESSIONAL HOCKEY

EDITED BY
GENE BROWN
INTRODUCTION BY
FRANK LITSKY

ARNO PRESS
A NEW YORK TIMES COMPANY
NEW YORK 1979

GROLIER EDUCATIONAL CORPORATION
SHERMAN TURNPIKE, DANBURY, CT. 06816

Library of Congress Cataloging in Publication Data

Main entry under title:

Soccer and Professional Hockey

(The New York times encyclopedia of sports; v. 8) Collection of articles reprinted from the New York times.
Bibliography.
Includes index.
SUMMARY: Traces the history of hockey and soccer as presented in articles appearing in the "New York Times."
1. Soccer. 2. Hockey. 3. Soccer—History. 4. Hockey—History.
[1. Soccer—History. 2. Hockey—History] I. Brown, Gene. II. New York times. III. Series: New York times encyclopedia of sports; v. 8. GV565.N48 vol. 8 [GV847] 796s [796.33'4] 79-20372
ISBN 0-405-12634-4

Manufactured in the United States of America

Appendix © 1979, *The Encyclopedia Americana.*

The editors express special thanks to The Associated Press, United Press International, and Reuters for permission to include a number of dispatches originally distributed by those news services.

The New York Times Encyclopedia of Sports

Founding Editors: Herbert J. Cohen and Richard W. Lawall
Project Editors: Arleen Keylin and Suri Boiangiu
Editorial Assistant: Jonathan Cohen

Photographs courtesy *UPI* on pages X, 3, 28, 49, 81, 98, 103, 109, 121, 144, 155, 179, 196

CONTENTS

The world's most popular sport is known in most nations as football, in British Commonwealth countries as Association football and in the United States as soccer.

It is played in more than 150 nations and is especially strong in Europe and South America. Major national or International matches abroad often attract crowds of 100,000 and have drawn as many as 200,000. Crowd violence prompted stadium officials in some South American cities to erect high wire fences, and when those proved insufficient they surrounded the playing field with moats.

No international sports competition attracts more attention than soccer's World Cup, played every four years by national teams. It is more important than the Olympic Games soccer because it involves professionals as well as amateurs. Regional eliminations are conducted for more than a year to reduce the field.

The 1978 World Cup competition in Argentina involved 16 national teams—14 qualifiers plus West Germany as defender and Argentina as host. Argentina won, and the government declared the next day a national holiday. In the 11 World Cup tournaments since 1930 (two were wiped out by war), brazil has won three titles, Uruguay two, Italy two, West Germany two, England one and Argentina one.

The United States has seldom done well internationally. Its great moment came in 1950 when it upset England, 10 to one, in an early round of World Cup competition. For years, soccer was scorned in the United States as a foreign sport too tame for a nation that enjoyed the excitement and physical qualities of American football. That attitude started to change in the 1970's with the rise of the North American Soccer League and growing involvement by youngsters who discovered the joy of playing soccer.

In 1964, the American Youth Soccer Organization had nine teams. In 1977, it had grown to almost 9,000 teams. The United States Youth Soccer Association expanded from 30,000 players in 1972 to 228,000 in 1977. More than a million other youngsters play in unaffiliated youth leagues. In addition, soccer is played in more than 6,000 high schools and 450 colleges.

The idea of the game is to put the ball into a goal 24 feet wide and 8 feet high. The ball is usually advanced by kicking. It can also be struck by the head or body, but only the goalkeeper can touch it with his hands. The field, also known as a pitch, is 100 to 120 yards long and 55 to 75 yards wide.

Soccer was known in England as early as the third century A.D., perhaps introduced there by Roman soldiers. From the 1300's to the 1500's, soccer, like most other sports, was frequently banned in England because it took soldiers from the more relevant task of practicing archery.

Soccer grew quickly in 19th-century Britain. The Football association was formed in 1863 and professional soccer was approved in 1885. Britons spread the game around the world, and the international governing body, the Federation Internationale de Football Association, was founded in 1904.

British immigrants brought soccer to the United States in the last half of the 19th century, first to the eastern part of the country and then to large cities in the midwest and far west. For years, most American players were natives of England, Scotland and Ireland. Later, immigrants from other European nations played in America.

The United States Football Association (now known as the United States Soccer Football Association) was formed in 1913. Within months, it staged its first national championship for the National Challenge Cup.

Soccer prospered in the metropolitan New York City area, St. Louis and other American cities with large foreign-born populations. But most players and spectators were foreign-born, and it seemed that the sport might eventually die in the United States. Instead, it grew beyond the dreams of the greatest optimists.

The American sports boom of the 1960's and 1970's gave birth to the American Football League, American Basketball Association and World Hockey Association, all of which were absorbed into older and stronger leagues. The same boom spawned the North American Soccer League.

There were two rival leagues in 1967—the National Professional Soccer League (10 teams of American and foreign players) and the United Soccer Association (12 foreign teams imported in toto). In the associations' championship game, the Los Angeles Wolves defeated the Washington Whips, 6-5 in overtime, but it was really a victory for the Wolverhampton Wanderers of England over Aberdeen of Scotland.

In 1968, the two leagues merged into a 17-team North American Soccer League. Franchises lived and died quickly, and only six teams played in 1970. The next year, the New York Cosmos entered the league and, like the other teams, struggled to survive.

In 1975, the Cosmos, owned by the Warner Communications conglomerate, made a bold move that changed the face of American soccer. They signed Pelé, the most famous player in history, to a three-year contract that guaranteed him at least $4.7 million for playing and promotional work.

Pelé, whose real name is Edson Arantes do Nascimento, was a 34-year-old Brazilian. When he was 15 years old, he signed with the Santos team of Brazil for $75 per month. At 16, he was a starter. At 18, he led Brazil to its first World Cup title.

When foreign teams tried to sign him, the president of Brazil declared him a national treasure and thus ineligible for export. When he visited Biafra, the civil war there was suspended for two days.

At his peak, he earned $700,000 per year for playing and at least $800,000 per year for endorsements and businesses. He paid more income taxes than any other individual in Brazil.

In 1974, after having scored, 1,216 goals in 1,253 games in 18 years, Pelé retired. Julio Mazzei, the Santos coach, said, "Now, people will tell their little babies, 'Too bad. You will not see Pelé play.' "

As it turned out, many people saw him play. The Cosmos lured him out of retirement by convincing him that he alone could make soccer succeed in the United States. For his first NASL game, he arrived in a helicopter that landed in the middle of the field.

Pelé's popularity changed the status of American soccer. He attracted large crowds everywhere, as he had when he played in Brazil. The NASL's product improved year by year, and the league gradually reduced the foreign influence by requiring its teams to play more Americans and Canadians.

The Cosmos (who by this time had dropped "New York" from their name) without him. Playing in the New York City suburb of East Rutherford, N.J., they set league attendance records in 1978 of 71,219 for a regular season game and 74,901 for a playoff game.

In 1978, the Cosmos averaged 47,000 spectators for home games. The league average was 13,000, and average attendance ran as low as 4,000 in Memphis. But the league's 24 teams were making progress, and franchise costs had climbed to $1 million (when the Cosmos joined in 1971, the franchise cost $10,000).

The Cosmos spent hundreds of thousands of dollars in salary for such foreign stars as Franx Beckenbauer of West Germany, Giorgio Chinaglia of Italy, Dennis Tueart of England, Vladislav Bogicevic of Yugoslavia and Carlos Alberto of Brazil. They also benefitted from the enthusiasm soccer had generated among native-born Americans, especially youngsters. Those benefits did not always reach the American Soccer League, a rival 10-team professional organization that averaged 2,500 spectators per game in 1978.

Women play soccer in American colleges, high schools and youth leagues, but the sport is not as important for them as for men. The first women's world championship was held in 1970, and Denmark won.

HOCKEY

Hockey—more precisely, ice hockey—is like soccer or field hockey on ice. It is an important sport in Canada and, to a lesser extent, in the United States. The National Hockey League—the sport's major league—has more American teams than Canadian, but more than 90 percent of the players are Canadian. However, the Soviet national team repeatedly embarrassed the best NHL players in the 1970's.

The outstanding European national teams, especially those from the Soviet Union and Czechoslovakia, are made up of nominal amateurs, and they play in the Olympic Games and other international amateur competition. But they are, in effect, professionals who devote full time to hockey, and they play and train together 10 or 11 months of the year.

For years, NHL teams scouted Canadian youngsters in their early teens, and the players often quit high school when they turned 16 and played junior hockey all winter. In recent years, more players have completed college in the United States or Canada before becoming full-time professionals.

Few Americans play in the NHL. But the sport is popular in colleges and high schools in the northern part of the United States. The introduction of artificial, indoor rinks helped spread interest.

Hockey was invented in Eastern Canada in the last half of the 19th century, but the details are vague. The game may have been first played by Canadian soldiers in 1855 in Kingston, Ontario, or by McGill University students in 1875 in Montreal, or it may have been brought to those cities from Halifax, Nova Scotia. It may have been taken from field hockey or hurley (a game similar to field hockey) or shinny (a game played on ice).

In any event, the game spread across Canada. The first league was formed in 1885 in Kingston. In 1893, Yale University in New Haven, Conn., and Johns Hopkins University in Baltimore, Maryland, formed teams, and in 1896 the American Hockey League was organized in New York.

Canadian hockey received special recognition in 1893 when Lord Stanley, the Governor General of Canada, donated a trophy to be given annually to the national champion. In time, the award, known as the Stanley Cup, became the trophy for the National Hockey League champion.

Professional teams were formed in the early 1900's. The National Hockey Association was founded in 1909, disbanded in 1917, and immediately replaced by a new organization called the National Hockey League. The embryonic league had five teams, all from Canada.

In 1924, the Boston Bruins became the first American team in the NHL. Next came the New York Americans and Pittsburgh Pirates in 1925 and the New York Rangers, Chicago Black Hawks and Detroit Cougars (later Red Wings) in 1926.

By this time, the NHL had 10 teams. In 1942, it was down to six teams and remained that size for a quarter-century. In 1967, it added six teams, doubling its size and sending major-league hockey to the West Coast.

In 1972, the World Hockey Association started playing as a second major league and changed the game in many ways. The people behind the new league realized they needed immediate credibilty. They obtained it by inducing Bobby Hull to jump from the NHL Chicago Black Hawks to the WHA Winnipeg Jets.

The 33-year-old Hull had played left wing for the Black Hawks for 15 years. He had scored 50 or more goals in five seasons, a record at the time. He had the fastest shot in hockey (118 miles per hour) and he was the fastest player on skates (almost 30 miles per hour). And he was unhappy because the black hawks made salary negotiations painful every year.

So when the new league offered, Hull listened. He signed with the WHA for a $1 million bonus, $250,000 per year for five years as player-coach and $100,000 per year for five more years as coach or executive.

The WHA's next big conquest was Gordie Howe. From age 18 to age 43, he had played right wing for the Detroit Red Wings until he retired because of an arthritic left wrist. He still holds the NHL's all-time records for seasons played (25), games (1,687), goals (786), assists (1,023) and points (1,809). He made the all-star team 21 times, another record. In 1973, at age 45, Howe signed with the Houston Aeros of the WHA so he could play hockey with Mark and Marty, his two sons. He was still playing at age 51, earning far more than the $2,500 he made as a Red Wing rookie.

In its first season, the WHA's 12 teams averaged only 5,300 spectators per game, and all teams lost money. But they had signed 68 NHL players, they had established more credibliity than credit and they had changed the salary structure of hockey. The NHL's average salary was $31,000 in the 1971-72 season, $96,000 in the 1976-77 season. WHA salaries averaged somewhat less.

WHA teams lost money annually. Some NHL teams struggled, but the NHL resisted a merger that would have eased the financial burden for all concerned. Finally, the war ended, and in the 1979-80 season the NHL added four WHA teams—the New England Whalers, Quebec Nordiques, Winnipeg Jets and Edmonton Oilers—to the 18 NHL teams. Each WHA team had to pay a $3.2 million franchise fee.

Hull and Howe were only two of the leading players in modern years. Perhaps the best was Bobby Orr of the Boston Bruins, voted the NHL's outstanding defenseman eight straight seasons (1967-68 to 1974-75) until a weak left knee led to his premature retirement.

Orr was recuperating from knee surgery when Team Canada, an NHL all-star team, played its first series against the Soviet Union. It was held in 1972 before the NHL training camps had opened, so the NHL players were not really physically prepared and they did not take the Russians seriously.

They played four games in Canada and four in Moscow. After 6½ minutes of the first game, Team Canada led, 2-0, and the rout appeared on. But the Russians won that first game, 7-3, prompting Johnny Peirson, a former NHL player, to say, "It's nice to be in on history, but I didn't think it would be Dunkirk." Team Canada won the series, 4 games to 3 (with one tie), on a goal with 34 seconds remaining in the last game.

In the 1975-76 season, two Soviet teams played eight NHL teams and emerged with a 5-2-1 record. The next season, Canada won a six-team Canada Cup competition in a field that included a second-string Soviet team. In 1979, in a three-game Challenge Cup series in New York, the Soviet national team routed the NHL all-stars, 6-0, in the deciding game before 250 million television spectators in North America and Europe.

This NHL team comprised the league's outstanding players, including the stars of the Montreal Canadiens, the NHL's dominant team of the 1970's. With such players as Guy Lafleur, Larry Robinson, Serge Savard and Ken Dryden, the Canadiens played fast, smooth hockey. Their teamwork was a triumph of brains over the brawn that had infested the sport.

The Canadiens won four straight Stanley Cups from 1976 to 1979. That raised their career total to 22 Stanley Cups (the Toronto Maple Leafs were second best with 11). Even rivals admired Montreal hockey. As Don Cherry, then coach of the Boston Bruins, once said, "Hating the Canadiens is like hating your mother."

Hockey was designed to be played with the smoothness of the Canadiens. The rink must be at least 160 feet long and 60 feet wide and is usually a little larger. There are six players to a side—a goalie, two defensemen, two wings and a center. All wear skates and padded gloves. They carry wooden sticks no more than 53 inches long with a blade no more than 14 ¾ inches long. The puck is a black disc of hard vulcanized rubber, three inches in diameter and one inch thick.

The idea of the game is to hit the puck with the stick into a net near the end of the arena. A game consists of three 20-minute periods. Normally, a game can end in a tie except in playoffs, when sudden-death overtime is utilized.

Players are well padded and often wear protective helmets. In addition, goalies wear plastic face masks, a practice Jacques Plante introduced in 1959 in midgame after a puck had ripped his nose and necessitated seven stitches. After 150 stitches, two broken noses, two broken cheekbones and one broken jaw in his career, Plante said he was just acting in self-defense.

—Frank Litsky

CHAPTER 1

SOCCER

Pele, who is probably the only athlete in the world
as famous as Muhammad Ali is shown here
having just scored for the New York Cosmos
against the Rochester Lancers of the N.A.S.L.

Want Colleges to Play Football

England Sends Team of Association Players to This Country to Introduce New Style of Game Which Will Eliminate Present Objectionable Features.

PRESIDENT ROOSEVELT'S plea for the elimination of brutality in college football has received support from Secretary of War W. H. Taft, President Eliot of Harvard University, and many heads of the universities and colleges throughout the country. To accomplish the much-needed reform in the sport the President held a conference at the White House which was attended by Prof. J. B. Fine of Princeton, head coach Reid of Harvard, and Walter Camp of Yale. At the conference the entire subject of the discussion was the elimination of roughness in the game and the modification of the present playing rules.

The visit of the English Pilgrim Association football team at this time may have an important bearing on the sport. The British aggregation is composed of the leading English and Scotch exponents of the game, and every member of the team is an amateur in the strictest sense of the word. Their mission to America is to introduce association football to the American public, more particularly to our leading colleges, with a view to its adoption in place of the present modified Rugby game. The project has the support of Sir Alfred Harmsworth, Sir Ernest Cecil Cochrane, Sir Charles Kirkpatrick, and Charles Murray. The three latter named are now in this country and identified with the Pilgrims' tour.

During last season 21 deaths were recorded from injuries received on the football field, and over 200 players were more or less seriously injured, many being crippled for life, though it is true that most of the serious accidents happened to ill-prepared players. This appalling casualty list appealed to the leaders of college football, and a determined effort was decided upon to adopt heroic measures, which would minimize the dangers of the game.

✦ ✦ ✦

As in the recent peace negotiations between Japan and Russia, President Roosevelt took the initiative and invited several of the leading college athletic lights to Washington for a conference. That this is no new idea of the President is shown by the speech delivered by him at the Harvard Alumni meeting last June, when he devoted a part of his long address to college athletics, saying in regard to football:

"I believe in outdoor games, and I do not mind in the least that they are rough games, or that those who take part in them are occasionally injured. I have no sympathy whatsoever with the overwrought sentimentality which would keep a young man in cotton wool, and I have a hearty contempt for him if he counts a broken arm or collarbone as of serious consequence when balanced against the chance of showing that he possesses hardihood, physical address, and courage.

"But when these injuries are inflicted by others, either wantonly or of set design, not of damage to one man's body, but of damage to another man's character. Brutality in playing a game should awaken the heartiest and most plainly shown contempt for the player guilty of it, especially if this brutality is coupled with a low cunning in committing it without getting caught by the umpire. I hope to see both graduate and undergraduate opinion

The Pilgrim Association Football Team at practice. J. Bryning heading the ball in front of the goal

come to scorn such a man as one guilty of base and dishonorable action, who has no place in the regard of gallant and upright men."

With the desire to place college football on a higher and less dangerous plane, the British authorities believe the time is ripe for the introduction of Association football, which during the past decade in England has practically driven out the Rugby game.

✦ ✦ ✦

The Association game presents many attractive features both from the viewpoint of player and spectator. It is directly opposed to the Rugby game. The team consists of eleven players—a goal keeper, two backs, three half backs, and five forwards, two on the right wing, two on the left wing, and one in the centre. No player except the goal keeper may use his hands when the ball, which is round, not oval, is in play, and a ball must be kicked under, not over, the bar of the goal posts. A player may use any part of his anatomy except his arms and hands in propelling the ball. He is offside, however, when there is no opponent except the goal keeper between him and the goal and he is in front of the goal. Interference of any nature when not in possession of the ball is a foul, as is tripping or handling the ball.

The forwards when "dribbling" keep the ball at their feet and must not kick it even a couple of yards in front of them

except, of course, when passing it to another player of their team. The backs should be able to kick the ball without ever making a mistake, with either foot, from any angle, on the fly, the bound, or the volley. The centre forward should be able to put any kind of "English" on the ball with either foot; should be master of kicking a swift, low, raking shot, or one that will curve either way.

✦ ✦ ✦

These are the fundamentals of the Association game which the visiting English players hope to introduce to supersede the American Rugby game in general favor, and eventually lead to great international matches eclipsing in interest any of the great amateur sporting events of the year.

American football is an evolution of English Rugby. The changes in the rules came about gradually, and naturally, because the Americans, having no traditions to fall back upon in cases of controversy, were compelled to establish their own definite playing code. So it was that the fundamentals even were altered, or, according to the American contention, improved.

✦ ✦ ✦

The game as played now is almost exactly the opposite of Association, which must not be confused with English Rugby. In the American game the ball is carried nearly all the time; possession of it in the scrimmage being eagerly sought for. In-

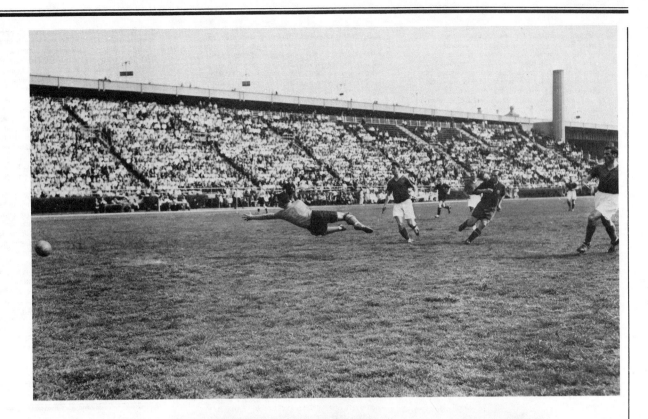

Max Morlock (extreme right) has just booted the ball past the outstretched hand of goalie Peter Wiggins in an all-star game played in New York. Morlock scored seven goals in the final four games of the 1954 World Cup competition for the title.

Lev Yashin of the Soviet Union hugs the ball to thwart West Germany's Uwe Seeler (white shirt) in the 1966 World Cup semi-finals. Yashin is widely acknowledged as the world's best goalie of the 1950's and '60's.

terference for the runner is another important element in the game. Both of these features are considered scandalous by the devotees of Association, and "interference" is also impossible in English Rugby. Kicking in the college game is used principally to work within striking distance for a touch-down, to rest the line and backs, and for other strategic purposes. Lovers of American football believe that just these points of difference from the Association game have put the college game where it is, and will keep it there, not to the exclusion of Association, however, which they believe will serve a purpose entirely of its own.

College coaches naturally give the American game the preference over English Association. While admitting the many advantages of the Association game they do not seriously consider the possibility of a displacement of the present college game.

One of the most enthusiastic promoters of Association football in this country is Charles H. Murray, who is Associate Director of Sir Alfred Harmsworth's many publications in England. He is the financial backer of the present tour of the English Pilgrims, and is traveling with the team in this country. For several years he has devoted considerable time and expense to his endeavors to popularize the sport. His present experiment will cost him fully $10,000, but he considers the money well spent if he accomplishes his object.

+ + +

Sir Charles Kirkpatrick
saving the goal

So eager is he to promote international Association football matches that he proposes to furnish the leading American colleges with the services of the most expert coaches in England free of cost, whose duties will be to give instruction to the students in the Association game. He is willing to spend $25,000 to introduce the sport into American colleges. In addition to being one of the foremost business men in the great English metropolis, he is a recognized authority on the game, and commands the support of the leaders of British sport. His wife is also an enthusiast, and being wealthy in her own right, is willing to lend all the necessary personal aid and financial assistance to further her husband's pet scheme.

The British football team has made a remarkable tour in this country, playing matches in Halifax, Montreal, Ottawa, Toronto, Hamilton, Berlin, St. Louis, Detroit, Chicago, and Philadelphia.

The team will play against an all-New York team on the American League Ball Park next Saturday, when the local lovers of football will have an opportunity of judging the relative merits of the English Association and American college games.

+ + +

Lady Kirkpatrick, wife of the goalkeeper of the Pilgrims, is bitter in her denunciations of the college game. By a curious coincidence the very worst she had been taught to believe was possible in the American game happened at the first game she witnessed in this country. When one of the players was carried off the field with a broken leg she arose excitedly from her seat in the grand stand and cried out, "There! They've done it."

Lady Kirkpatrick is devoted to outdoor life and goes in strongly for rowing, golf, and tennis. In discussing American football she said:

"The game played by American college teams is more of an exhibition of brute force than of genuine scientific skill. It is entirely too 'close' and does not tend to bring out the scientific ability of the players. A man's individualism is lost in the order in which the different combinations are brought into effect. In England each player anticipates what is to be done with the ball and acts accordingly. Tackles are unknown, and if a man is known to have deliberately injured another player he is put off the field immediately and suspended for a month or year, as the seriousness of the offense warrants.

"If we want to see brutalizing sport in England we have prize fights, with or without gloves, and wrestling matches, but in football we play entirely with our feet, and the ball is never in the hands of the player. It is almost a misnomer to call the college game football, when the ball is kicked only on rare occasions. The English Association game is much faster, and it is science, not strength that counts.

"After all, I suppose one's preferences are governed largely by what one is born to. It is apt to be so in religion and politics, and I suppose it is the same in sports. I prefer the Association game because I have always been used to it. You Americans like your game because it is virtually the only kind of football that you know. One of the objects of our visit is to teach you the fine points of soccer, so that the one kind of football will prevail throughout the world. Then international matches can be arranged. I am glad to have had an opportunity to witness your game, but I am not so sure that I want to see another."

+ + +

Sir Charles Kirkpatrick is a type of the pure English country gentleman, passionately devoted to all branches of sport for sport's sake. For years he has been one of the foremost exponents of Associa-

tion football, and is considered one of the best goal keepers in Great Britain. He says it is splendid to see the spirit which is displayed by American college players. "With you," he said, "it is win at all cost, even to the extent of being badly broken up, but we English players are not so keen on winning just for the sake of beating the other side. With us the main point is the feeling that we have played fair."

Sir Ernest Cecil Cochrane, who has offered an international trophy for Association football contests between college teams of England, America, and Canada, is an earnest advocate of the English game. He is at present on a short visit to this country, and has witnessed several college football games. He has a hundred arguments in favor of Association football. Discussing the subject, he said:

"Only a few days ago I was attracted by reports of a football game played at the American League baseball park in this city which characterized the game as brutal. One paper in particular used a big display: 'Wesleyan Team in Football Riot,' Is that sport? Dr. Eliot of Harvard says he does not approve of international matches because they develop many unpleasant incidents. Surely nothing could be more conducive to the promotion of friendly feeling between the two countries.

"I have no desire to attack our American institutions, but to simply point out the advantages of 'socker' football over the game played here. If once properly introduced it cannot but gain a stronghold on the American public, and I feel satisfied that the day is not far off when the sport will become as popular in this country as in England."

October 15, 1905

ENGLISH "SOCKER" TEAM WON FOOTBALL MATCH

Pilgrims Defeated New York by Score of 7 Goals to 1.

LOCAL PLAYERS OUTCLASSED

Good-Sized Crowd Watched First International Association Contest in This City—Play Was Clean.

The English Pilgrim Association football team yesterday defeated the All-New York eleven at the Polo Grounds by the score of 7 to 1. The victory was well deserved, as Capt. Milnes's "Socker" experts were the better all-round players. About 3,000 spectators watched the ninety-minute struggle and cheered the individual stars of both elevens. The Britishers decisively defeated the locals, but the latter at no time were disgraced. They made the Englishmen earn their goals and incidentally brought from Sir Charles Kirkpatrick, the Baronet, who kept the invaders' goal, some of the liveliest moves every credited to the English sportsman.

It was a clean, well-played contest, bristling with clever passing, intricate dribbling, capital dodging, and exceptionally hard kicking. Unlike the American college game, no time was lost in tending the injured, and not an unpleasant incident marred the display. It was a gratifying introduction of the English game to the New York public, and judged by the expressions, during and after the match, it is destined to occupy a high place in American sports. It was an appreciative crowd. In the centre box of the upper pavilion Lady Kirkpatrick was one of the most interested of the spectators, and her gloved hands frequently beat a tattoo as a New York player distinguished himself.

Bearing out the reputation he had sustained in international conflicts at home. Moran Woodward, the Pilgrims' centre, gave the cleverest exhibition of "sockcer" play that the critics had ever seen. He shot two goals, and although the local forwards were busy watching him, he was as elusive as a will-o'-the-wisp, and was in almost every play. Capt. Milnes was not to be denied. He was all over the field, and seldom missed his kick and got it away strong when it came his way. Little James Bryning, the 134-pound outside left, who made a lightning partner for Woodward, shot one difficult goal, but his work bore every earmark of championship. Raine distinguished himself by scoring three goals for the visitors in addition to doing yeoman service on the field.

For the home team Gorman put up a good fast game and scored the only goal for his side. Armstrong, at centre half back, played a consistent game, and Donald's work in the back field was brilliant at times, although erratic at others. McNeill showed more speed than any other player, but he was unreliable and easily beaten by the fast English forwards. Gray, the New York goal keeper, was easily the star of his side, and it was due to his remarkable work between the goal posts that the score was not more one-sided. He stopped almost impossible shots and saved many apparently sure goals.

Sir Charles and his associates, true to their home inclinations, gulped cups of steaming hot tea between the halves, and munched cakes.

New York was beaten by the combination play of the English fast forwards, whose clever foot and head work disconnected the New York back field. The local forward line was fairly fast and showed good combination, but the left half of the team and the back field, with the exception of Gray, the goal keeper, was weak. The local team played fast football for the first ten minutes of the game, but seemed to tire when the Britishers got properly under way. After this it was only a matter of how many goals the Englishmen would score.

Play started promptly at 3 o'clock, the English Captain winning the toss and choosing the south goal. New York kicked off. Bryning shortly afterward tried for a spectacular goal, but Gray saved cleverly. Milnes returned the kick out and New York changed the play, invading the visitors' goal. Gordon and Inglis worked together and by close formation attacked the British goal. Sir Charles Kirkpatrick was not ready for assault, and when Gorman made a low shot, the English Baronet made a poor attempt to save and the ball went into the net, New York scoring the first point in the game. On the kick out Raine and Coopland, by clever dodging and dribbling, tried to equalize matters, but Gray, after an anxious moment, fished the ball away. He again found himself in close quarters from an attack by Walmsley and Fletcher, but he was equal to the emergency and saved again. Woodward and Coopland again carried the ball down the field, when the latter passed to Woodward in front of the goal, who successfully negotiated a difficult shot and the score was even. The New York forwards did not settle and soon Bryning had the ball again for another try, but he shot by. Again did the Englishmen work the ball in the centre for a try, but Gray once more fished. He was so often in the way of the Britishers that they tried every trick in the game to baffle him. A good rally followed in front of the New York goal, but Gray was in waiting and robbed Vivian Woodward of a difficult goal. The leather was returned to British territory, when Barnsdale by clever dribbling carried the ball the entire length of the field. He passed to Fletcher, who headed to Raine, and after an easy shot England led by 2 goals to 1. Gorman and McNeill made distinct gains for New York, but Milnes was in waiting and kicked out of danger. Twice the Britons had corners, but New York rallied strong. Bryning and Walmsley then treated the spectators to some wonderfully clever passing, which resulted in Bryning scoring at a difficult angle, when half-time whistle blew with the score—Pilgrims 3, New York 1.

The teams changed goals and Woodward worked the ball down thirty yards by his individual effort, narrowly missing the net. McNeill kicked to Gorman and the ball traveled toward Sir Charles. McNeill's eagerness cost him the goals as the ball struck the top bar of the goal posts. It was an easy try with no one near him. The Pilgrims again worked the ball back and got a corner. Walmsley kicked to Woodward, who is tall, and heading a goal seems to require little effort from him. The ball shot off his head into the net.

Score: Pilgrims, 4; New York, 1.

The work of the New York backs by this time was so unsettled that the visitors completely baffled their opponents by fast combination plays. With a foul putball Nuttal kicked a fifth goal from the thirty-yard line. It was one of the prettiest kicks of the game. Twice Sir Charles was called upon to jump, and but for Milnes's wonderful work Gorman must have scored for New York. After saving several tries Gray fell a victim to Raines from corner kicks twice in quick succession, when time was called, the final score being 7 to 1 in favor of the Pilgrims. The line-up:

Pilgrims, 7.	Position.	New York, 1.
Sir C. Kirkpatrick	Goal	Gray
F. H. Milnes	Right full back	Martin
C. W. Storrey	Left full back	Donald
E. A. Nuttall	Right half back	Minto
J. D. Barnsdale	Centre half back	Armstrong
T. Fletcher	Left half back	Gordon
J. E. Raine	Outside right	Tait
A. C. Coopland	Inside right	Inglis
V. J. Woodward	Centre forward	Gorman
F. S. Walmsley	Inside left	McNeill
J. E. Bryning	Outside left	Murray

Goals—Raine, (3,) Woodward, (2,) Bryning, Nuttall, Gordon. Referee—Mr. Milton. Linesman—Mr. Wright. Timekeeper H. McKinley. Time of game—Two forty-five-minute halves. Attendance—3,000.

October 22, 1905

POPULARITY OF SOCCER

Gaining Ground on Pacific Coast—Big British Attendances.

Football men are wondering, in the event of changes being made in the rules and tackling and scrimmaging much modified in the American game, if the English Association (soccer) game will ever win the popularity here that it enjoys in the United Kingdom. When American football was abolished in California three years ago, soccer was taken up, and at first did not interest the admirers of the old game. But soccer has grown wonderfully in San Francisco and other coast cities during the past few years. The games in 'Frisco for the city championship in both the junior and senior leagues draw crowds of 6,000 or 7,000 people, which shows that the game is gaining a strong footing out there.

That the soccer game has features which get a firm grip on the sport-loving public is shown by the phenomenal popularity of the game in the United Kingdom. Last year at the annual match between England and Scotland, played at Glasgow, a crowd of 121,452 paid admission to see the battle. The free list brought the crowd up to 125,000. When a University of California co-ed saw the English game for the first time she said: "One can enjoy the game without having to understand it." In the English game it is the running, dodging, kicking, passing and exceptionally clever footwork which keep the crowd interested, and the accidents in England have been only of a minor nature.

Sir A. Conan Doyle defines true sport as "an exhibition of hardihood, without brutality, of good-humored courage without savagery, and skill without trickery."

The assertion of Prof. Clenahan of Princeton that "Leland Stanford and other coast colleges had tried the Association game and that the students would not support it" has brought forth a reply from a well-known follower of the game in Pasadena, Cal. In a letter to THE TIMES this writer says: "Prof. Clenahan's statement is wholly erroneous, as neither Standford nor any other college on the coast plays the Association game, although there are many outside soccer teams. Both Stanford and the State University at Berkley play English Rugby, and also the University of Nevada, with many of the High Schools and smaller colleges. The game is exceedingly popular and is firmly intrenched in the two leading colleges. All over California," says this corespondent, "the Rugby game is surely vanquishing American intercollegiate football. The visits of the Australian and New Zealand players to the coast opened the eyes of the people out that way."

The football season in the British Isles lasts for eight months, and the game is so popular and there are so many participants in the sport, that the newspapers give up pages to it. Papers are published which contain nothing but football news, like The Liverpool Football Echo, a journal devoted almost entirely to the game. Hundreds of teams form leagues, and these different teams play series during the season until the champion team is finally chosen to meet the champion teams of the other countries.

Saturday during the football season is given over almost entirely to the game. It is surprising to note what great crowds these week-end matches draw. For example, in the games played in the First League of London on the first Saturday in November, the Chelsea-Everton match drew 40,000 people, the Woolwich Arsenal-Bradford City match drew 10,000, Newscastle and Tottenham, 28,000; Blackburn-Sunderland, 20,000; Liverpool and Bury, 20,000; Sheffield-Sheffield United, 28,000; Notts-Preston, 10,000. These teams will play every week until April when the season ends; in every city in the United Kingdom the conditions are similar.

Whether the English game could ever win such popularity here, of course, is a question. Among American colleges which play both games, the rougher American game completely overshadows the English game. However, the English game is gaining a foothold here, as was shown in the interest taken in the recent visit of the Pilgrims of England, where much enthusiasm and interest were shown in the clever work of the British kickers.

November 28, 1909

SOCCER'S HOLD AT YALE.

Predicted That American Football Will Be Displaced Eventually.

NEW HAVEN, Conn., March 16.—A prediction that soccer football will displace the American college game, and that the new stadium which will be erected at Yale this Spring will be needed eventually to hold the crowds that flock to the soccer game, as they throng the English championship soccer games, is made by a member of the Stadium Committee in the report of the committee, which assures the beginning of that structure this year. The game has steadily grown in popularity at Yale, and the largest crowds that ever saw the matches will attend the intercollegiate series, which began with to-day's match against Haverford.

The present Yale team is regarded as the strongest the college ever produced, and visions of a possible championship have floated before the players.

Yale adopted the system of graduate coaching in soccer, as in nearly all her other sports, Alexander Timm, 1910, being chosen to direct the coaching system. Dr. Herbert, the former head coach, is a member of the college Faculty, and is available in an advisory capacity.

Yale's Fall schedule brought the team against only one member of the Intercollegiate League, Princeton, which Yale defeated. Spring practice began last week and thirty candidates enrolled. Daily practice has been held on Yale Field. Yale retains eight veterans, including Capt. Gay, Worthington, Chang, the brilliant Chinese player; Gager, Dickey, Dickinson, Cornwell, and Hill. Howard, Clark, and Shepard, who were in fine form in the Fall series, are regulars again this Spring. There are four Chinese players on the squad. Capt. Gay has been shifted from wing to centre forward. He got a rating as all-American wing last season. He has few equals as an all-around soccer player in this country. Hill, who was placed on several all-American combinations last season, will be used in the forward line again. Alexander Anderson Gay, the Captain, hails from West Hartford. He is a member of the senior class in the Sheffield Scientific School and has been on the team three seasons.

SOCCER INTEREST IN COLLEGES INCREASES

Official Recognition by National Intercollegiate Association a Boon for Sport.

Soccer football is arousing greater interest than ever in intercollegiate circles, due to the recent action of the National Collegiate Association in officially recognizing the game, and it is hoped that the time is not far distant when the sport will rank with the American Rugby game.

This season's fight for the intercollegiate championship promises to be close, as each team is keen on gaining premier honors, while the intense earnestness of the numerous candidates for places on their college elevens insures the best available material to participate in the series.

Haverford College, the holder of the championship, is stronger than ever. Nine men on the eleven have been regular first-team players in former years. In addition, the team enjoys special advantages in having the services of Fred Huish, the well-known instructor, who formerly coached Charterhouse School in England.

At Harvard the steady encouragement of the Faculty and the engagement of Charles Burgess, the retired English international player, as coach have given a great impetus to the sport. Although losing heavily by graduation, more than 160 candidates have been playing the

CAPTAINS OF THE LEADING AMERICAN COLLEGE ASSOCIATION FOOTBALL TEAMS

J. C. DAWSON (PRINCETON)

HARROLD PINDAR ZOLLER, CAPTAIN (COLUMBIA)

LLOYD SMITH (HAVERFORD)

W. E. JONES (PENN)

A. A. GAY (YALE)

ROBERT W. DAVIS (CORNELL)

HARRY BYNG, Harvard

game, and while the eleven is inexperienced and undeveloped, the players are full of determination and enthusiasm.

The outlook at Cornell is brighter than in any previous year. About 150 players took part in an intercollege series, and from these men a strong eleven has been chosen, practically made up of American-born players. Some of the most promising men are from New York City high schools.

Columbia University will undoubtedly put up its usual hard fight. Most of the men know the game thoroughly, and although only fifty candidates took part in the trial games, a strong all-around eleven has been got together, which it is believed will thoroughly extend its opponents.

Already this season one honor has been gained by the University of Pennsylvania, namely, the Merion Cup for the championship of the second division of the Cricket Club League. The team is without doubt a better one than last season's, owing to the efficient coaching of D. Stewart, who ungrudgingly gives his services for the good of the game.

Princeton is not in the Intercollegiate League, but will probably join next season. Sixty players took part in the various practice games, and some good material was unearthed. Prospects are decidedly good, and the Orange and Black eleven will be dangerous contestants for highest honors in the near future.

Soccer has also gained recognition by the authorities as one of the regular sports at the Naval Academy, and matches will probably be arranged next season with the teams which comprise the Intercollegiate League. John P. Dalton, Captain of last season's American Rugby team, who is quite an expert at association football, is coaching the players and has a squad of fifty players under his charge.

The following intercollegiate fixtures remain to be played: March 23, Haverford vs. Columbia at Haverford, Cornell vs. Harvard at Ithaca, and Yale vs. Pennsylvania at New Haven; March 27, Harvard vs. Yale at Cambridge; March 30, Haverford vs. Cornell at Haverford and Yale vs. Columbia at New Haven; April 6, Harvard vs. Pennsylvania at Cambridge and Columbia vs. Cornell at New York; April 8, Harvard vs. Haverford at Cambridge; April 13, Columbia vs. Harvard at New York and Cornell vs. Pennsylvania at Ithaca, and April 20, Cornell vs. Yale at Ithaca.

March 17, 1912

YALE WINS SOCCER TITLE OF COLLEGES

Elis Win Every Game in Series and Are Scored Upon Only Once During Season.

Special to The New York Times.

NEW HAVEN, Conn., April 27.—Undefeated in the entire series, and scored against only once, Yale's soccer football players to-day put the finishing touch to a record quite unusual in the annals of intercollegiate matches and captured the championship for 1912 by defeating the University of Pennsylvania eleven at Pratt Field by the score of 2 goals to 0.

Pennsylvania was Yale's chief rival for supremacy and the custody of the Milnes Cup, the gift of Fred Milnes of Sheffield, Captain of the Pilgrims of England, who have twice visited this country.

The Quakers needed to win to-day's game, which constituted a fitting climax to the series, in order to overtake the leaders. In that case, while such a result would have brought about a tie in matches won and lost, Pennsylvania would have had the advantage on the score of goal average. As it is, Pennsylvania finished with a higher aggregate of goal shots in the five matches, having put together a record of 18 goals for and 5 against. Against this stands Yale's tally of 15 goals to 2. On the other hand, whereas Yale has a clean slate, with five straight victories, Pennsylvania, all told, won only three and lost two—to Yale and Haverford.

The ground at Pratt Field was in excellent condition for the match this afternoon, and it did not start to rain until well in the second half. It was a battle royal throughout the entire first period of play and neither side scored. Yale played mainly on the defensive, for a tie was all that was needed to insure retention of first place in the competition. Worthington, Yale's centre halfback, was severely injured and had to give way to Woodruff, who played the game out. D. Gay, brother of the Yale skipper, had his knee wrenched, took off five minutes and then resumed pluckily. Thereafter he played a pretty game to the end.

When ends were changed for the second half, Yale's players adopted different tactics and forced the fighting, after having carefully sized up their opponents. Still, little impression was made upon Pennsylvania's defense until about fifteen minutes after the restart, when one of the fullbacks in warding off an ugly rush accidentally handled the ball. The whistle blew and a penalty was inflicted against the winning team. Capt. A. Gay of Yale took the kick and sent the ball unerringly into the Pennsylvania net.

Hill, playing at inside left for Yale, saved his team from the possible imputation of getting the verdict on a fluke by an exhibition of brilliancy which earned the applause of his adversaries as well as that of the onlookers. Taking the ball in the centre of the field, Hill carried it along with him, dribbling and dodging in a most perplexing way, and succeeded in eluding all of Pennsylvania's backs. Finally, only Goalkeeper Laird confronted the speedy forward, and he proved unequal to the emergency. This ended the scoring, Yale thereby winning by 2 to 0. The line-up:

Yale.	Positions.	Pennsylvania.
Dickinson	Goal	Laird
Dickey	Right back	Sims
Shepard	Left back	Pennell
Gage	Right half	Harle
Worthington	Centre half	Bell
Woodruff		
Summer	Left half	Dunstan
Clark	Outside right	Husband
D. Gay	Inside right	(Capt.) Jones
A. Gay (Capt.)	Centre	McPhee
Hill	Inside left	McFadden
Williams	Outside left	Hopkins

Referee—Mr. Gardner. Goals—A. Gay, Hill, Yale. Time of halves—Forty-five minutes.

Yale, in the series of five games played in the intercollegiate series, was scored against only by Cornell, the score of that match being 3 to 2. Yale won from Columbia by 4 to 0, Harvard, 4 to 0, and Haverford, by 2 to 0. Pennsylvania won from Columbia, 3 to 0; Cornell, 9 to 1; Harvard, 5 to 2, and lost to Haverford, 2 to 1.

April 28, 1912

SOCCER ENTHUSIASTS BUSY.

New Organization Aims to Make Football National Winter Pastime.

By Dr. G. Randolph Manning.

President United States Football Association.

The United States Football Association, the youngest member of the family of national organizations, controls in an international and national sense association (soccer) football in this country. The organization was instituted in April, 1913, as a result of the efforts of enthusiastic followers of the game who by long experience had come to the conclusion that only a co-operative effort among the various minor associations and leagues, culminating in the formation of a national body, could elevate soccer football to that standard which it is deserving of. The success was instantaneous; the entire country joined in the work of forming State and district associations which send one delegate to the Council of the U. S. F. A.

International recognition was obtained from the Federation Internationale de Football Association, with which are affiliated now the national associations of twenty-four countries.

The United States Football Association aims to make soccer the national pastime of the Winter in this country; it assumes jurisdiction over all professional and amateur players, and will represent this country in all national and international matches and questions. A national representative team will be sent to San Francisco in 1915 to take part in exhibition games, and a picked team will for the first time in the history of the Olympic games represent this country in 1916 at Berlin at the Olympic gathering. The U. S. F. A. has entered into articles of alliance with the A. A. U. and has also started out on a vigorous campaign of introducing and furthering the game in all cities where Public Schools Athletic Leagues are in existence.

December 28, 1913

WHY SOCCER GAME IS NOT POPULAR

Many College Athletic Directors Say It Is Too Tame Compared with American Football.

In an effort to increase the popularity of soccer football, the National Collegiate Athletic Association some time ago collected data from various colleges all over the country, which furnished interesting facts about why the game has never reached the popularity of the American Rugby game. The canvass among the colleges, however, showed that the game is growing in interest, not so much as an intercollegiate sport, but as a game in which numerous students may take part among themselves. In this regard, the game is highly regarded among college athletic directors as a valuable adjunct to physical education.

Harvard, where the game is extensively played, furnished the information that the reason that soccer does not stand high as an intercollegiate sport is because it is not a game which appeals to American spectators. The Harvard report states: "It is a great game for thousands of boys and men who cannot for various reasons afford to play the American game. Soccer is well worth cultivating. Eight years ago soccer at Harvard depended upon a few English students who had played the game before. Today we develop each year a score or more new men and have numerous teams."

The physical director at Northwestern University, in explaining why the game has not been popular out there, says: "We do not believe in its success in the ordinary college community. It takes a leaven of good Scotch, English and Scandinavian players to make the game a success. It looks tame to boys after American football and baseball."

The verdict of the Columbia authorities strongly favored the game. The Columbia report stated: "There is no better all around game for college men. The interest seems to grow steadily in clubs and schools here."

At West Point, soccer was never more than a side issue. It is played about one day a week during the regular football season between the football players to keep them in good physical condition. At several colleges in the West it was stated that the interest in the American game was so strong that the soccer game was crowded out.

A. A. Stagg of the University of Chicago, reported on soccer as follows: "I feel that better games are available during good weather. Soccer may be played under moderately bad weather conditions. Another Western college reported: "The game of soccer is a good game and should be played in addition to football, but not to supplant the latter game."

At Nebraska the athletic authorities reported: "There is no interest among the student body in the game as a spectacle. Also at the University of Kansas the authorities stated: "We think it is a good game, but can see no chance for it to supplant the American game."

The Wesleyan authorities reported on the game as follows: "Its only desirable feature with us is that it can be played out of doors after the tennis courts and ball fields can no longer be used because of the weather. It is not a game that appeals to those of our students who are engaged in other forms of athletics. It is not scientific enough. Others do not care to take it up because it requires too much running."

The game, on the other hand, is very popular in many colleges. At Pennsylvania, those who take part in the game are given credit for gymnasium work while practicing the game. Weekly attendance is required at the games to get credit. The report of the Pennsylvania athletic authorities stated: "It fills a place that no other game will ever take in college life and it is invaluable training."

May 23, 1915

HAVERFORD SOCCER TEAM WINS TITLE

Holds Pennsylvania to Tie Game in Final Match of Intercollegiate Series.

Special to The New York Times.

HAVERFORD, Penn., Dec. 18—Haverford won the intercollegiate soccer championship today, when the team played a 1-to-1 tie with Pennsylvania on a field ankle-deep with mud. Weiler of Haverford kicked a goal after twenty-five minutes' play, and Barron of Pennsylvania quickly tied the score.

In the second half Pennsylvania, even with a gale of wind at her back, failed to score. At least twenty-five times the Quakers had chances, but no advantage was taken of the opportunities. Barron, Murphy, Thayer, and Hirst played splendidly for Pennsylvania, while J. Shipley, Carey, and W. Crossman excelled for Haverford.

Haverford won the toss. When the Pennsylvania attack started it carried the ball close to Haverford's net. The Red and Blue had a great chance to score, but Houston slipped, and Carey of Haverford shot the ball down the field. Hardwick, the Quaker goal, made two neat saves, and his kicking was wonderful. Several times he drove the ball fifty yards. H. Busby of Haverford, on a penalty kick, drove the ball into the net, but the score was not allowed.

Haverford kept up a sharp attack, and Weller scored the first point of the contest when he kicked a goal after twenty-five minutes of play.

Barron of Pennsylvania evened the score a minute later. He took a pass at midfield, and headed straight up the field. He tricked three Haverford players, and shot o goal. Twice before Barron and Murphy of Pennsylvania threatened the Haverford goal, but a slippery field blocked them.

Haverford made desperate efforts to tally in the last five minutes of the first half. Edwards and Thayer of Pennsylvania played a great defensive game, and saved the Red and Blue. Hardwick of Pennsylvania left his post several times, and went to the rescue of his full backs. The line-up:

Haverford.	Position.	Penn.
J. E. Shipley	Goal	Hardwick
Gardner	Right full back	Thayer
W. Shipley	Left full back	Edwards
Hallett	Right half back	Mohr
Steer	Centre half back	Hirst
J. H. Busby	Left half back	Busby
Stokes	Outside right	Houston
Weller	Inside right	Wessman
Crossman	Centre forward	Barron
Carey	Inside left	McMasters
G. H. Busby	Outside left	Murphy

Goals—Weller, Barron. Referee—W. E. Hinds. Linesmen—Messrs. Carrigan, Penn., and Thomas, Haverford. Time of halves—Forty-five minutes.

December 19, 1915

MAKES RECORD IN SOCCER

Bethlehem Sets Mark by Winning Double Championship.

Special to The New York Times.

BETHLEHEM, Penn., July 22.—When the sporting annual records for this year are made up the compilers will record for the first time in soccer, or association football, the achievement of a double championship by the same team. The team which did this is the Bethlehem Steel Company association football eleven, which is declared by some to be the greatest soccer eleven that has ever been developed in this country.

The team not only captured the National Challenge Cup, but also the American Challenge Cup. In winning the National Challenge Cup, or Dewar trophy, it repeated its achievement of last year. The winning of the American Cup Championship was not a new experience, for in 1914 the Bethlehem team captured this classic. These titles are to soccer what the National and American League championships are to baseball.

From east to west every soccer eleven of prominence was entered in the contests for the two cups. In the National cup tie there were eighty-eight elevens entered representing Massachusetts, Rhode Island, Connecticut, New York, New Jersey, Pennsylvania, Ohio, Michigan, Illinois, and Missouri. More than 1,200 players participated in the 102 games played. In the American cup tie there were thirty-six elevens entered, covering about the same territory. Both races were elimination affairs in that a defeated team automatically dropped out of the race.

To play these games the different soccer teams traveled distances similar to those covered by the nines in the major baseball leagues. Bethlehem during the past season in a semi-final game for the National Cup went all the way to Chicago to play the Pullmans. That game resulted in a tie and the replay took place at Bethlehem the following Saturday, Bethlehem winning. In the semi-final of the American cup tie and the final of the National cup race, Bethlehem went to Pawtucket, R. I., and Fall River, Mass., winning in both instances from the Fall River Rovers.

The National challenge trophy, or Dewar Cup, and the American Challenge Cup are each worth about $1,000. They are competed for each year. The National Cup was presented to the American Amateur Football Association by Sir Thomas Dewar, Perth, Scotland, for the purpose of encouraging soccer in the United States. This association transferred the trophy to the United States Football Association as the national and governing soccer organization of this country. The Dewar trophy was first won in the season 1912-1913 by the Yonkers, N. Y., team; then in 1913-1914 by the Brooklyn, N. Y., team, and in 1914-1915 and 1915-1916 by the Bethlehem eleven.

The American Challenge Cup's history is much older, dating back to 1884. The past season was the twenty-fifth year it was competed for, because between 1898 and 1905 there were no games. The O. N. T. eleven of Newark, N. J., won it from 1884 to 1887; Fall River, Mass., Rovers, 1888-1889; Pawtuket, R. I., Olympics, 1889-1890; Fall River, Mass., East Ends, 1890-1892; Pawtucket, R. I., Free Wanderers, 1892-1893; Pawtucket, R. I., Olympics, 1893-1894; Newark, N. J., Caledonians, 1894-1895; Paterson, N. J., True Blues, 1895-1896; Philadelphia, Penn., Manz F. C., 1896-1897; Arlington, N. J. 1897-1898; West Hudsons, N. J., 1905-1906; East Newark, N. J., Clark A. A., 1906-1907; West Hudsons, N. J., 1907-1908; Paterson, N. J., True Blues, 1908-1909; Philadelphia, Penn., Tacony, 1909-1910; Pawtucket, R. I., Howard and Bullock, 1910-1911; West Hudsons, N. J., 1911-1912; Paterson, N. J., True Blues, 1912-1913; Bethlehem, Penn., Bethlehem Steel, 1913-1914; Newark, N. J., Scottish-Americans, 1914-1915; Bethlehem, Penn., Bethlehem Steel, 1915-1916.

The rise of the Bethlehem Steel soccer eleven has been rapid. It was not until the season of 1913-1914 that the team became prominent, although the game had been played locally for a few years before then. In many ways the success of the Bethlehem Steel team is due to Charles M. Schwab, the steel magnate. He encourages athletics and has provided a field, on which he has expended $125,000.

The personnel of the Bethlehem Steel team is composed largely of Scotchmen, most of whom have played the game on teams in Scotland. The eleven has played together for several years and it will probably remain intact next season. The players are all employed in the steel plant and are allowed time off in order to practice and make long trips, but they receive no remuneration for playing.

July 23, 1916

Crowds at Soccer Games Lower English Production

LONDON, Jan. 31.—Soccer football, England's national game, is interfering with business and manufacturers are organizing opposition to the playing of cup ties and league games in midweek. Fifty thousand people witnessed a replayed English cup tie between Sheffield Wednesday and Darlington on Monday, Jan. 19, and the loss resulting in the absence from work is estimated at £25,000 in wages and £100,000 in trade loss. It is urged that such loss should not be incurred at a time when every Minister and economist is appealing for increased production as the only means to relieve the country's financial hardships.

February 1, 1920

PENN IS VICTOR IN SOCCER TITLE GAME

Quakers Make Strong Finish Against Princeton Team and Win by 4 to 2 Score.

Special to the New York Times.

PHILADELPHIA, Pa., Dec. 16.—The University of Pennsylvania won the intercollegiate soccer championship for the second successive season when it defeated Princeton on the field of the Marion Cricket Club here this afternoon by the score of 4 goals to 2. Pennsylvania was outplayed in the first half which ended 2 goals to 1 in Princeton's favor, but came back and electrified a truly large crowd by completely outclassing its opponent.

High-pitched rivalry occasioned by two former draw games lent the play a tenseness that communicated itself with the spectators that banked the field. Never has a soccer match in Philadelphia been so cheered or harder fought. The Penn Band gave the atmosphere a football touch and the snake dance after cessation of play further resembled the celebrations of the gridiron.

The first meeting of the teams resulted in a scoreless tie. On second meeting each team tallied three goals and no more, although four extra periods were played. Hence today's game was for blood, and the play was lightning fast at times. Miraculous saves on the part of each goalkeeper probably were the featuring plays, for each in turn was bombarded viciously. Cooper in the last half and Darrow in the first.

Princeton's early scores were made by Stinson and Woodridge. The Tigers were kicking against the wind, but, singularly enough, instead of a hindrance, this seemed almost a help. Penn in its turn against the breeze, which was quite stiff, played with increased success. Spencer scored for Penn just before the half ended.

In the final period Dowlin, Lee and Bingham tallied. Penn appeared far superior in this session, just as Princeton had in the first. It was a revelation to the watchers, who, much as they disliked the thought, for the majority were loyal to Penn, expected a Tiger victory. The line-up:

PENNSYLVANIA (4).		PRINCETON (2).
Bingham	O. L.	West
Pennell	I. L.	Thomas
Spencer	C. F. B.	Stinson
Lee	I. R.	Woodbridge
Dowlin	O. R.	Moore
Neall	L. H. B.	Wood
Binns	C. H. B.	Hunt
Balderston	R. H. B.	McIlvain
Amelia	L. H. B.	Keyes
Darrow	R. F. B.	Fisher
Haywood	G.	Cooper

Goals — Spencer, Pennell, Bingham, Lee, Stinson, Woodbridge.

Substitution—Trewbridge for Moore.

Referee — Scofield. Linesmen — Hines and Addison. Time of halves—45 minutes.

December 17, 1920

FORM NEW SOCCER LEAGUE.

Eight Cities to Be Represented in Football Circuit.

At a meeting of delegates representing eight of the leading soccer football organizations of this country, held at the Hotel Astor Saturday night, it was decided to form a new body to be known as the American Soccer League, the object of which will be to establish a circuit of eight cities.

The clubs represented were the New York F. C., Robins Dry Dock of Brooklyn, Bethlehem Steel F. C. of Bethlehem, Pa., Erie A. A. of Newark, Jersey City F. C., Fall River Rovers of Fall River, Mass., J. & P. Coats F. C. of Pawtucket, R. I. and the Philadelphia F. C.

Luther Lewis of the Bethlehem Football Club was elected Temporary Chairman after the meeting had been addressed by Thomas W. Cahill, Secretary of the United States Football Association, who outlined the scope of the new league. J. Scholefield of New York was appointed Secretary pro tem. It was voted to have the headquarters of the league in New York City. Application will be made to the Council of the United States Football Association for permission to affiliate with the national body.

May 8, 1921

FOOTBALL PASSES CRICKET.

Is New Most Popular Game in the British Isles.

While cricket retains millions of enthusiastic devotees in England it cannot longer hold its position as the national sport of John Bull's island. Football has usurped that rank, and the football association, the big governing body, now has a membership in the neighborhood of 800,000. Baseball crowds here, it is said, are staid and conservative as compared with the crowds that attend British football events. At one of these contests as many as 100,000 fans have assembled, nearly three times as many as could be comfortably seated in the Polo Grounds. The admission fee is usually 6 pence, or about 12 cents, for standing room, so that the receipts are in no way comparable to those of baseball or football games on this side. There are nearly 15,000 clubs affiliated with the football association, about 500 of these being professional organizations.

December 20, 1921

Crowd of 150,000 Turns Out For English Football Final

Copyright, 1922, by Chicago Tribune Co.

LONDON, April 29.—It is estimated that 150,000 persons came in to London from out of town today for the final league football game between Preston and Huddersfield for the British pennant. Fifty special trains were run and thousands came by motor and char-a-banc from as far away as Birmingham and Sheffield, many bringing their own food and beer. The football ground at Stamford Bridge in the Chelsea district accommodates only 80,000, but the rest spent the day in sightseeing, returning at night. Thousands of the excursionists spent two nights on the road and it is estimated that the average expenditure was £5 a head.

April 30, 1922

PRINCETON RETAINS ITS SOCCER TITLE

Defeats Penn in Post-Season Play-Off for League Championship, 3-1.

Special to The New York Times.

PRINCETON, N. J., Dec. 13.—By defeating Pennsylvania 3 to 1 here today, in a post-season play-off, the Princeton Soccer team retained its intercollegiate league championship crown for the second year. This was the third successive year that the Tigers and Quakers have fought it out for the league title and the second time during the three years that post-season play-offs have been necessary to decide the crown. Princeton has won the last two years, but lost in the league tie playoff in 1920.

The game was spectacular from the start, and the few hundred spectators who huddled together in the cold stands of University field were well repaid for braving the biting winds. The Tigers got off to a good start, scoring the initial tally within the first two minutes of play. Soon after the opening of the second half, however, the Quakers evened the count. From then on the battle was nip and tuck between the two rivals. A brilliant finish gave Princeton the verdict over the Philadelphians, both scores coming late in the game.

The use of the head in plays was developed to a high degree on both teams, and during the first half it seemed that the ball was advanced almost as often by means of the head as by the feet. Both teams were too apt to overshoot the goal and essayed long shots from outside the penalty area, when shorter passes would have meant goal shots. Princeton outplayed her rivals and the ball was in Penn's territory during the greater part of the game.

The Tigers got off to a good start in the first few minutes of play. After Penn had taken advantage of the kickoff the Princeton booters drove down the field, with the forward line working like a machine. Cowperthwaite, Penn's goal keeper, was lured away from the centre of his position by one forward, while the ball was neatly passed to Joe Cooper. He shot the spheroid into the cage from a ten-foot distance.

When the second half opened Penn faced a one-point handicap. Undaunted they inerted a bit of speed into their work, and the forward line, playing better soccer than in the first half, ran the ball up to Princeton's goal posts. Then Bill Linglebach, the Quaker centre forward, shot the ball into the cage from the 15-yard line, neatly eluding Princeton's captain and goal tender, Crossan Cooper.

The game then see-sawed, first one side having the advantage then the other. Not until the last few minutes of the titular tilt could the Tigers shove across the necessary tallies. Charlie Woodbridge, diminutive Tiger forward, who replaced Townley at outside right, suddenly shot in between the two Penn backs and caged a pretty goal which the Penn guardian could not handle.

This won the game for Princeton, but the fighting Tigers were not content to rest on their laurels. After a minute of fierce fighting in front of the Penn goal Thomas emerged from the mass and sped the ball squarely between the posts.

The line-up:

PRINCETON (3).		PENN (1).
Jewett	O.L.	McElroy
Thomas	I.L.	Partridge
Stinson	C.F.	Linglebach
J. W. Cooper	I.R.	Blair
Townley	O.R.	Nolte
Davis	L.H.B.	Vollman
Smart	C.H.B.	Amelin
Seidensticker	R.H.B.	Barron
Martin	L.F.B.	Castle
Hurditch	R.F.B.	Donns
J. C. Cooper	G.	Cowperthwaite

Goals—J. C. Cooper, Woodbridge, Thomas, Linglebach.
Substitutions—Princeton: Woodbridge for Townley, Oliver for Jewett, Townley for Woodbridge, Woodbridge for Stinson.
Referee—Hollywood. Linesmen—Hoag and Hunsicker.

December 14, 1922

1,000 HURT IN LONDON IN CRUSH OF 200,000 AT FOOTBALL GAME

Broken Limbs, Ribs and Collarbones Are Result of Mob Swamping Playing Field.

GAME TWICE INTERRUPTED

Police Reserves and Mounted Force Compelled to Charge—Space Meant for 120,000.

KING GEORGE IN ATTENDANCE

He Presents the Association Cup to Bolton Wanderers, Who Defeat West Ham, 2 to 0.

Copyright, 1923, by The New York Times Company.
By Wireless to The New York Times.

LONDON, April 28.—Probably 1,000 persons were injured this afternoon in the crush of an immense mob which sought to witness the final football games for the Association championship in the Wembley Stadium, at which the King was present.

Most of the injuries were minor ones, and were attended at first-aid stations by Red Cross men near the field, but there were many cases of broken arms and legs, broken ribs and collarbones.

It was only with the assistance of the police and a large emergency force of mounted men that the contending teams, Bolton Wanderers and West Ham United, were enabled to play the game for the Association Cup, British equivalent to the last game of a world's series baseball game. Bolton Wanderers won, 2 to 0, and King George presented the championship cup to them in the presence of what was then a gathering of at least 200,000 persons.

Mob Covers Playing Field.

The new stadium at Wembley was used for the first time. It has reserved seats for 30,000 and standing room for 90,000 more, but an hour before time for the kick-off the gates were closed, with 120,000 present, by order of the police to relieve the pressure, with the result that the palings were broken down and from 30,000 to 50,000 more poured in and swamped the entire area, including the playing field. It took the police nearly an hour to clear the space for the teams to play.

Cup Day is one of the annual festivals of the factory districts, and seventy to eighty special trains poured thousands into London in the early hours of today. They amused Londoners by their spirits, as they spent the morning driving in char-a-bancs and specially hired buses through the main streets and then turned toward Wembley.

By 1:30 o'clock all standing room on the terraces was occupied and newcomers were allowed to occupy the running track around the football ground. A big force of police tried to hold them there, but a quarter of an hour later they found their work impossible. The Inspector in charge directed the gates to be closed and then the fun began. Tens of thousands were outside and from all

directions trains, buses and automobiles were bringing up more. Hurried orders were sent for every available policemen to be rushed to Wembley, and the railroad and bus companies were bidden to turn their passengers back.

It was too late, however, and the crowd near the gates simply surged forward, threw down the palings and filled the entire field.

At the height of the turmoil the King arrived. He had a splendid reception as he appeared in front of the royal box, and the tremendous crowd sang the national anthem through, verse by verse.

Then the struggle was renewed, many ugly rushes taking place, with the police displaying amazing patience and forbearance. Eventually, forty minutes after scheduled time, the police, reinforced by mounted men, succeeded in driving the mob from the pitch and the game began in pandemonium.

Meantime an ever-increasing crowd outside the gates came into serious collision; one section, comprising disappointed seat holders, endeavoring to reach the pay box to get their money back, clashed with another section attempting to force their way into the grounds.

Eleven minutes after the game started a mob which had just found a new entrance encroached on the pitch and stopped the play. The police had another difficult time, after which the game was resumed and continued to the finish.

Altogether 200,000 people crammed themselves into the arena, of which less than one-third paid gate money.

Official Statement Issued.

LONDON, April 28 (Associated Press).—Following a riotous football game at Wembley Stadium today, at which about 1,000 were injured, an official statement issued from the field said that by 1:45 P. M. the stadium's capacity was filled and the gates were closed. This information was telephoned throughout London, but thousands of persons still continued to arrive and Scotland Yard was asked to furnish a large force of mounted police. The statement estimated that the total number of persons who paid admission, or who broke in, exceeded 200,000 of whom probably 150,000 had a good view of the match.

The police were obliged to maintain their cordon around the playing field until the end.

April 29, 1923

WILL PLAY SOCCER AT POLO GROUNDS.

Paterson F. C., National Champions, to Stage Games at Home of Giants Next Fall.

MAY GET YANKEE STADIUM

N. Y. S. C. Is Expected to Use American League Park—Also After Ebbets Field.

Professional soccer football is to hold sway in at least one of New York City's big baseball parks when the championship season of 1923 is ended. This was assured late yesterday when officials of the National Exhibition Company, owners of the New York Giants, and Secretary Thomas W. Cahill of the United States Football Association, the body governing the kicking game in this country, concluded negotiations which have been under way many months and which are calculated eventually to establish league soccer in all major league ball parks from the close of each baseball season to the start of the next.

The 1922-23 national soccer champions, the Paterson Football Club, will be the home club at the Polo Grounds, where soccer has not been played since the tour of the famous Pilgrims of England in 1905. Probably renamed more appropriately, the kicking machine owned by Adolf Buslik, will play its home games in the American Soccer League and in the national championships, known as the National Challenge Cup Competition, at the Polo Grounds.

May Get Yankee Stadium.

Following the lead of the Giants' management in establishing the leading Fall-to-Spring team sport at the Polo Grounds, it is expected that the Yankee Stadium will be made available to New York Soccer Club, which has had New York Oval for its home field, and that the Brooklyn National League Ball Park will become the home stand of the Brooklyn Wanderers, who have been campaigning on Hawthorne Field.

President Charles A. Stoneham of the Giants last Fall sought to introduce soccer at the Polo Grounds, but no franchise in the Eastern professional league was available to him and insufficient time remained for him to have developed independently a first-class team for the season then getting under way. New York Soccer Club, with its own park across the Harlem, and protected by territorial invasion restrictions of a clause in the league rules, declined to sell out to the Giants' owners.

In a prolonged reorganization meeting of the League at the Hotel Astor last Saturday night and continuing far into Sunday morning a new set of officers was elected and the territorial protection clause was altered, over the New York Soccer Club's protest, to permit of the transfer of the franchise held by the National title-owning Paterson club to New York City.

In a conference on Tuesday attended by Buslik, Cahill, Stoneham, Jim Coffey, Secretary Tierney of the Giants and Sam Crane, veteran baseball player and writer and professional soccer enthusiast, arrangements were made for the Paterson club's use of the Polo Grounds on Saturdays, Sundays and holidays throughout the Winter season of 1923-24, and articles of agreement were signed by the Paterson club owner and the owners of the Polo Grounds yesterday, according to an announcement made last night.

Ebbets Field May Be Secured.

New York Soccer Club's retaliatory move, it was said yesterday by Manager Hugh Magee, will likely be to arrange to play its home league and cup competition matches in the Yankee Stadium, and Nathan Agar, who heads the Brooklyn Wanderers, expressed the view that Ebbets Field would be procured for the home games of his team.

"I believe soccer is the coming Fall-to-Spring outdoor sport of the nation," said Stoneham yesterday. "It is one of the most thrilling of all team sports and has come to be played with great proficiency by American young men, and dozens of the leading stars of the game in England and Scotland and Sweden have come to this country in the last year. Thus a high standard of play is assured to American fans, and I am confident the game's presentation under suitable conditions in the big league ball parks will vastly increase its public following, which has grown to goodly proportions in recent years."

Fred J. Smith of the Todd Shipyards Athletic Association, Brooklyn, is the newly elected American Soccer League President, succeeding W. Luther Lewis, Auditor of Bethlehem Steel Company; T. W. Cahill of New York City and W. C. Cumming of Pawtucket are Vice Presidents, and M. F. Kelly of New York City, Secretary.

June 28, 1923

SOCCER IN AMERICA GAINING POPULARITY

The various soccer leagues and organizations in this country are turning into the final period for the 1924 championships, and the progress during the season shows clearly the game is established on a firm foundation and that the future of the sport in the United States is assured. Thomas W. Cahill, National Secretary of the United States Football Association, the governing body of the game in this country, says soccer has made its greatest strides here since the war and that in a time not far distant it will rank only second to baseball as the leading professional game.

"I have seen the formation and organization of baseball in this country," said Mr. Cahill yesterday. "I have followed the national game with the closest associations, and soccer in this country is now going through the same formative stages that baseball went through when I was first connected with the game. Every one, practically, knows the organization of professional baseball. They know the National and American Leagues, the Class A leagues and the bushers. In time I believe that soccer will be known just as thoroughly by the public.

"However, soccer is in no way trying to take the place of baseball in the hearts of the public. Baseball is the national sport, and such it will remain. Neither is soccer trying to replace college football in the universities. As baseball is the national professional game, so is American football the national collegiate sport, and the game of soccer is bidding for the place of neither. However, it is gaining popularity, both among the professional and amateur elements, and I feel sure it will soon be followed with as great enthusiasm in the Winter months as the college game is followed in the Fall, or at least nearly so.

"One of the greatest advances made in soccer was immediately after the World War. During the Civil War the soldiers of the North and South were thrown together and when young men mingle in close relationship a game is generally the outcome. In the Civil War it was baseball which received its impetus from the gathering of American youths and the big organization which is established today is the outcome. The World War in the same way brought forward the game of soccer. The sport has long been the national game of England and consequently when the American and British soldiers were thrown together it was inevitable that the United States troops should absorb some of the Britishers' enthusiasm for the game, just as the American soldiers gave to England some of the game of baseball."

Nation-Wide Interest Shown.

The greatest competition in the United States in soccer is the National Challenge Cup Competition, which is held annually and which in some ways corresponds to the big league season, the finals being parallel to the World's Series. This year 134 entries were received from various clubs for the National Challenge Cup, and these entries came from New York, New Jersey, Massachusetts, Pennsylvania, Connecticut, Rhode Island, Wisconsin, Indiana, Ohio, Michigan, Illinois, Missouri and Canada, showing the great national scope of the game.

Both amateur and professional combinations challenge for the trophy, and the preliminary rounds are played in two sections—eastern and Western. In the eastern section the semi-finals have been reached, with the Fall River Football Club of Fall River, Mass., scheduled to meet Abbott Worsted Football Club of Forge Village, Mass., in the upper half of the draw on Jan. 19 at Pawtucket, R. I., and the Bethlehem Steel team slated to clash with the Newark Football Club in the other semi-final at Philadelphia on Jan. 26. The winners of these two matches will meet in the eastern final, and the leading team from this section will then play the winner of the western final for the trophy and championship.

The competition this year is proving to be an open fight, for the Paterson Football Club of Paterson, N. J., which won the title last season was eliminated this season in the fourth round by the Newark Club. Paterson this season entered the play under the name of the National Giants.

In the West, because of the greater number of entries drawn in that section, the play is now in the fifth round.

International competition is planned for this season as in the past. The leading amateur games are played in the National Amateur Challenge Cup Competition for which more than eighty teams entered this season with the increased incentive that the winner is to be sent to represent the United States in the Olympic games. Changes may have to be made because of citizenship qulifications, but it is now planned that the winner of the amateur title will go to Paris as far as it can qualify its members. Those ineligible will be replaced by other players in the amateur ranks who are American citizens.

International Gains Planned.

Another international series which is scheduled for this season is the meeting between the Associated Cricket Clubs of Philadelphia and the Corinthian Amateur Football Club of England. The Philadelphia organization has been granted permission to meet the British combination and the series has been arranged.

The organization of the soccer leagues in this country is vast. As has been mentioned, the United States Football Association is the governing body of the sport and with this association is affiliated the American Football Association, the Municipal Soccer League, the United States Referees' Union and all the State, city and sectional organizations. Associate members include the Amateur Athletic Union, the National Collegiate Athletic Association and the Public Schools Athletic League. In turn the U. S. F. A. is affiliated with the Federation Internationale de Football Association.

It has been estimated that between 65,000 and 75,000 athletes in this country are playing soccer with various clubs, and this number does not include the great army of athletes playing in public schools and colleges. It is to the development of interest in soccer in the public schools that the U. S. F. A. is turning with a great deal of interest, for, as has been pointed out, it is in the youth of this country that any game must be instilled to insure the growth of the game.

Two phases of the development of the game lie in the advancement due to the importation of players from abroad and the progress made in the development of American-born athletes. The game is being played more and more extensively in the schools, and as the youngsters who take up the sport in the schools grow up the American-bred talent is gaining in its quality. There was once a time when a star from England would be met on his arrival in this country by many club officials seeking to obtain his services, but of late there have been occasions when a player from the other side of the Atlantic Ocean has come to this country only to find that the competition was stronger than he expected and has returned again without having gained a position as a player.

January 13, 1924

ENGLAND'S OWN WORLD'S SERIES

They Call It the Cup Finals, It Comes in the Spring, Not the Fall, and the Game Is Football

By CLAIR PRICE

THEY manage these things better in the States.

Take a name like the cup final. No doubt it conveys but little in New York. Yet in England they appear to have coined it as the result of some such reasoning as this: The football association has a cup which is offered every year to the best team in the country. As the season nears its end the eligible teams play a series of elimination games known as semi-finals and the season ends when the two surviving teams meet in the final for the possession of the cup. Hence these English call it the cup final because it happens to be precisely that. It is of course a curious method of reasoning, but it shows how strangely the English mind works.

Needless to say, we manage these things better in the States. We should call it the world's series, and if the name happened to convey nothing to the rest of an unsophisticated world, we at least would know what was going on. We should flock to the Polo Grounds or elsewhere (these things have been known to occur even in such places as Brooklyn) and there spend a series of broiling Autumn afternoons, bouncing up and down in a state of continual scream. For baseball is our national birthright. Baseball has made us what we are today, and since we are undoubtedly the greatest nation in the universe it follows that baseball is a dispensation shut up, sacred and apart.

Still, we have never looked upon the heathen in their darkness with any aloof or self-righteous attitude. We have made every effort to share our great birthright with peoples less fortunate than ourselves. In the case of these English, we have gone to considerable trouble to enable them to share in the generous advantages which we enjoy. Yet to this day they remain a backward people among whom baseball is practically unknown. It is really rather discouraging, for they are not an entirely unpromising people. Given baseball and its concomitant, ability to scream one's self purple about the gills, it is not impossible that in time they might amount to something in the world, say in war or in politics or in finance or in the law or in the arts or in any other realm (if any other realm exists) in which it is worth a nation's effort to amount to something.

At One of the Semi-Finals.
Times Wide World Photo.

Yet even in this enlightened twentieth century such an unbelievable state of things exists among these English that (a) they play football and not baseball, (b) their football season, instead of ending in the Autumn, begins then and ends in the Spring, and (c) instead of becoming incoherent at their football games they contrive in their casual English fashion to remain English. Indeed, if it would not merely heap confusion on confusion, one might add that to this day they have no place called the Polo Grounds. It is true that they do have a place in the outskirts of London where their so-called cup final is played each year; but although it is quite a handsome place —and so new that it was used last year for the first time, it is hopelessly inadequate. Just how inadequate it is you might have seen last year when great crowds had to be turned away because it was already so overcrowded that a question had to be asked about it in the House of Commons. No doubt it will also be crowded next Saturday when this year's cup final is played there, despite an emergency arrangement under which no tickets will be sold on the grounds this year, but only those who have bought tickets in advance will be allowed to enter. They call the place the Wembley Stadium and it holds no more than a mere 125,000 spectators. It is all very bewildering.

Not only do they refuse to play baseball, but the game which they call football is wholly unlike what we regard as football. In the first place, it is played with bare knees.

It seems to be the fact that persons who are born in England are almost invariably born with bare knees, and while most of them recover upon reaching their years of discretion, football players never recover. With the single exception of Scotland, there are more knees in England than in any other country I know about—the dimpled knees of infants, the round and red knees of schoolchildren, and the angular and obvious knees of men who are old enough to know better. The knee is, of course, a useful and friendly member of the human frame, but when a man has attained to his adult stature I doubt whether it continues to be the comeliest part of his being. It is true that most Englishmen, both in England and abroad, sooner or later banish their knees to the darkness and decency of long trousers, but so many knees still remain in England that Englishmen in long trousers seems to me to be sometimes reminiscent of Turks in hats. Having renounced the Nordic knee, they have foresworn an essential part of their native tradition. Football, however, remains faithfully English. It remains a little bit of England, complete with knees.

In the second place, football is played with a round ball like that used in the indoor game which we call basketball, but of the eleven players on a team only the goalkeeper is permitted to touch the ball with his hands. No doubt this statement sounds rather meaningless, but if you have ever seen a fast bit of play interrupted by the steep shrill of the umpire's whistle and a great roar of "Hands!" from 100,000 throats, you will realize that the use of hands, whether accidentally or otherwise, really is forbidden. The ten players besides the goal-keeper are restricted, as long as the ball is in play, to kicking it or dribbling it or passing it with some part of their bodies besides their hands, usually their feet or their heads. What a man can do with a football by bouncing it off his head is one of the unforgetable lessons, not only of English football, but of life in general. A man who can pass the ball out of a scrambling crowd to a teammate waiting for it near the sidelines by jumping his bare head into a fifty-yard kick, is my notion of a fairly hard-headed citizen. With the very important exception that the use of hands is permitted only to the goal-keeper, the game might be broadly described as a sort of large-scale basketball played outdoors on a football field. If you know the several varieties of football, you may succeed in recognizing it from this tabloid description, as association football or soccer.

Once it occurred to somebody that it might be a good idea to modify association football by permitting a player to take the ball in his hands and run with it and so Rugby football or rugger was invented, which lies possibly half-way between association football and the American collegiate variety of football. But Rugby football has never supplanted association football in England. With the possible exception of racing, association football remains the most widely popular of English sports. Both amateurs and professionals play it, the latter of whom sometimes receive the British equivalent of as much as $25 a week, so that naturally it pays a good football player to secure a day or two off from his regular job every week during the season. Professional teams are grouped under the football association into a first division league, a second division league, Northern and Southern third division leagues, Scottish, Welsh, Irish, London and a long list of lesser leagues. Beside the greatest of the trophies, the football association's cup, which is won each year at the cup final, there are also English, Scottish, Welsh, Irish, amateur, army, navy, London professional and London amateur cups to be won. Besides these fixed annuals of the football season, there are also a million or more small-sized, middle-sized and full-sized boys who spend their Winter play time kicking footballs about the streets and the commons of these islands. Your idea of the average English lad in bare knees is an accurate one as far as it goes, but it is by no means complete unless you supply him with a ball to kick. It need not be of regulation football size, it may be no bigger than a tennis ball, but where the American boy throws a hard ball, the English lad kicks a soft ball. He goes to school in the mornings kicking his ball along the street and he comes home in the afternoon kicking the same ball along the street. And so he grows up, nurtured on football, factory smoke and tea. And so they make Englishmen.

So essentially English is football that it has become as universal as Englishmen. I have myself seen English seamen kicking footballs on the Embarcadero in San Francisco where British ships were tied up, English saloon stewards and bakers and pantrymen kicking footballs in front of the Chelsea pier in New York when the quiet of a Sunday morning opened out the spaces of West Street to them, and English soldiers in khaki drill and shorts playing a full game with forty-five minute halves on the flatlands of upper Mesopotamia before 8 o'clock in the morning when the temperature of the July sun was still below 110.

Football has become an English deposit and, especially since the days of the war, when English regiments were scattered in camps where English regiments had never camped before, it has struck its roots down into the local soil and is continuing to grow long after the English regiments which planted it have gone home. In France, football has gained so firm a hold that the word "footballeur" has become a recognized part of the language. In Spain, "el futbol" has acquired a popularity which rivals that of bullfighting. In Northern Italy, its hold dates back to before the war, for football appears to be one of the pleasanter consequences of industrialism. By this time, however, it has taken hold in southern Italy as well and on the Brindisi-Rome and the Naples-Rome trains you may occasionally see Italian football teams looking for all the world like English teams do when they travel. Further east, a Turkish team last year played Rumanian and Czechoslovakian teams at Constantinople, and still farther east to Angora itself Turkish soldiers can usually be found playing the English variety of football, complete with bare knees.

It seems possible that time may endow with a certain amount of real importance this new and wide interest in football which the war has left behind it. Before the war, the continental nations were accustomed to regard the Englishman as a phlegmatic person, by which they meant, without ever quite understanding it, that the Englishman possessed a degree of self-control which they lacked. Man is possibly the only one of the animals who exercises the habit of self-control and self-control in the day-by-day presence of the large number of neighbors who make up a modern city, is the very foundation of any attempt at an ordered and enduring civilization. Incidentally, self-control is the very foundation of football, for 100,000 spectators could hardly sit through the excitement of a game of football and go unharmed away unless their conduct was marked by that self-control and restraint which distinguishes the average football crowd in England. Is there any essential relationship between English self-control and English football? If there is, what is it? Is one the cause and the other an effect? Or do they work upon each other, each fortifying and strengthening the other?

Not long ago, not any longer ago than the days when the notion of the phlegmatic Englishman was growing up on the Continent, the Englishman was accustomed to look upon Continental peoples as haunters of cafés, who talked with their hands as much as with their lips and were utterly devoid of that instinct for restraint and decorum which is native to the Englishman. If the Continental peoples continue to play football, is it apt to give rise on the Continent to that self-control which has hitherto typified the Englishman? And if

the Continent is to turn from its cafés to football, if it is to acquire that Nordic self-control with which football appears to be allied, what results will the history of the Continent reveal when the new generation of "footballers" grows to manhood?

These are questions which time alone can answer. Meanwhile, we may as well get on with the rest of the story.

The holy of holies of the widening world of football is still to be found among the factory chimneys of industrial England. It is still the English Cup final which this year winds up the season at the Wembley Stadium in the outskirts of London next Saturday afternoon. As this is being written the teams which will meet at Wembley are still unknown, for the semi-finals are not yet through. Even if they were known, I doubt whether their names would mean much to us. What do names like Aston Villa, Tottenham Hotspurs and Huddersfield Town mean in New York? Probably as much as names like the Giants, the Cubs and the White Sox mean in London.

What is known at the moment is that, barring tornadoes and typhoons, which are not being anticipated, there will be no standing room left in the Stadium next Saturday (and precious little immediately outside it); that as much of the crowd as is not already on its feet will rise when a little man in a derby hat and with a flower in his buttonhole enters the royal box; that twenty-two small figures in bare knees and colored jerseys will dash out onto the floor of the field immediately afterward, and that the cheers will still be rolling up from 125,000 English throats when the twenty-two small figures line up on the field just below the royal box to be introduced to the little man. Possibly you have seen his photograph more often than you have seen the man himself.

For the rest, you might wait for next Sunday's papers. All we can attempt here is a brief comparison of the spectacle of English football to the more familiar (to us) spectacle of American baseball. For the man in the bleachers, baseball is a waiting game whose attraction lies in the fact that anything may happen at any moment. In baseball at its best, there is little for the man in the bleachers to see. What draws him to the bleachers and holds him there, what draws him again and again, is the fact that at any moment there may be something for him to see. He may wait for one or two or three innings with the outfield loafing, the bases empty and nothing happening which can be seen from the bleachers. This is not the case with football. As long as the ball is in play, it can be seen every minute of the time. It has its thrilling moments when the ball is worked down toward one of the two goals, but these moments are only a tightening of the tension which marks the entire game. Baseball, on the other hand, consists of lightning thrills which break across an otherwise waiting and empty afternoon. Football satisfies the sober and disciplined temperament of England and apparently of an increasing

area of the rest of the world. The more explosive American temperament feeds on baseball.

However, this attempt to compare baseball to football is made only in the strictest confidence. If it ever leaked out that we had attempted a proceeding so grossly unpatriotic, we should certainly be blown from a gun at dawn as soon as we dared set foot in New York again. Alongside the pastimes in which the heathen engage, baseball is of course a high dispensation shut up, sacred and apart. Sport is one of the things which we manage better in the States.

April 20, 1924

105,000 PAY TO SEE BRITISH CUP FINAL

LONDON, April 26.—Newcastle United won the annual football classic today, defeating Aston Villa, 2 to 0. The official paid attendance at Wembley Stadium was 105,000. The match was for the English Association Cup. It is the second time Newcastle has won the coveted trophy.

Both Newcastle's scores were made in the second half. Cowan scored the first goal and Seymour netted the second three minutes from the end of the match.

A light but persistent rain fell all morning. This turned into a regular downpour with thunder around midday. The stadium gates were opened shortly after noon, when about 1,000 entered.

There were plenty of puddles in the running track around the field, but the turf itself was free from them. The rain stopped at 2 o'clock and this brought out a rush of people from the city. The stoppage, however, was only temporary and rain fell very heavily for several hours. Fortunately it stopped just before the start of the game. At that time only 70,000 were present.

The teams had a wild reception as they came out and there was more

enthusiasm when the players were introduced to the Duke of York.

Match Unable to Play.

The Newcastle team was without the services of its regular goalkeeper, Mutch, who was injured in a game with Birmingham last Monday. He was the only man on the club with previous cup-tie experience.

The teams lined up as follows:

Newcastle—Bradley, Hampson, Hudspeth, Gibson, Spencer, Mooney, Low, Cowan, Harris, McDonald, Seymour.

Ashton Villa—Jackson, Smart, Mort, Moss, Milne, Blackburn, York, Mirton, Capewell, Walker, Dorrell.

Moss beat Hudspeth on the toss, but gained little advantage., The ground was very slippery at the commencement of play. The first incident of note was the fine dash through by Harris, who tricked Milne nicely. Harris was fouled, and free kick resulted. This, however, was easily cleared by Smart.

The Newcastle forwards were thrice placed offside by Mort in the first few minutes of play. Walker went through the Newcastle defense and passed to Dorrell, who had a good opening. He centered weakly and a good opportunity to score passed. Cowan and Harris then troubled the Villa defense, Seymour finally shooting right across the goal mouth with nobody home. Immediately afterward Seymour tested Jackson with a terrific shot. Then followed a splendid passing run between Walker and Dorrell, ending by Kirton, who headed over the bar.

Walker started another offensive when he deceived Mooney, and going on, shot hard. It was a low ball and bounced off the goal keeper's chest. In the next minute, Low, after a run, passed to Cowan. The latter centered to Seymour, who headed the ball just wide of the post. The struggle until the end of the first half was a brilliant affair, both goals having narrow escapes on several occasions.

After the resumption Villa made a bold bid for victory and staged a vigorous attack. Mooney charged Capewell off the ball as the centre forward was in the act of shooting. Next Kirton sent in a beautiful low shot which Bradley then dealt in fine style with an awkward effort from the Villa left winger.

Villa Stages Vigorous Attack.

A free kick taken by Hudspeth caused some excitement in the vicintiy of the Villa goal, Mouth and Harris, beating Smart in a dash through, kicked forward for Cowan to head into Jackson's arms. Newcastle continued to press, but the Villa halfbacks prevented Jackson from being seriously troubled from these shots.

The game at this stage developed into a very strenuous display, both sides putting up a brilliant exhibition. As the defense divisions seemed sound, everything pointed to a draw as the end of the match approached. With four minutes to play, Newcastle tried desperately for a goal. After some fine work by the forwards the ball was got well into Villa territory. It came across to Seymour and from the left winger's pass Cowan shot at Jackson. The Villa goalie pulled the ball down and Harris, seizing the chance, dashed in and scored at close quarters.

A minute later Seymour went through the disorganized Villa defense and beat Jackson with a line left foot shot.

April 27, 1924

U.S. Eleven Beaten In Olympic Soccer
North Americans
Eliminated by Uruguay
3 to 0, Before
Crowd of 20,000

PARIS, May 29.—With two of its best men, Rudd and Brix, out of the competition, the United States soccer team went down to defeat here today before Uruguay in the Olympic Games series by a score of 3 goals to 0. From the very start the North Americans never looked like winners, for Uruguay sent into this encounter a team which proved itself the equal of the best of the English professional teams in the science of the game.

Within the first ten minutes of play the South Americans had made four attacks on the United States goal, and that together with the fact that their final score totaled only 3, speaks volumes for the defensive play of the Americans. Against the Czechoslovakians five days ago the Uruguayans had scored a 7-to-0 victory, and following their exhibition today there appears to be little doubt now that they will go forward to the championship, for no other team has shown anything like the same mastery of the game. The North American defeat, therefore, was far from being a disaster.

The United States players were outplayed in every department of the game and their superior stature and weight did not count so much in their favor as it did in the rugby competition a fortnight ago. It was only in the second half that they put their full training to good use. The Uruguayans had scored their three goals in the first half, and no men ever fought more gallantly to prevent a bigger score being piled up on them than did the North Americans in the second half. They were then no longer a team, but eleven Americans, each trying his utmost to prevent a trained, disciplined, united and expert team from disgracing them.

Several times the North Americans managed to open a good attack, but it always came to nothing before the strong Uruguayan defense, chiefly because of lack of coolness and skill which come only from long practice as a team. The United States players were warned three times for rough work and indulged somewhat freely in argument with the referee; but they were cleanly defeated, and the French crowd, this time quite impartial, retrieved in part its faulty behavior during the rugby series by giving full measure of applause to the fine work of Goalkeeper Douglas and to all other individuals who did a particularly brilliant piece of playing.

Swedes Cause Surprise.

PARIS, May 29 (Associated Press).—Uruguay today qualified for the quarter finals in the Olympic soccer football competition by defeating the United States 3 goals to 0 in a match, the score of which does not begin to show the difference in class between the two teams.

The other teams which qualified today were Sweden, which electrified the Olympic football world by defeating Belgium, one of the prime favorites in the tournament, 8 to 1. Egypt, which proved another giant killer by sending Hungary back with a 3 to 0 defeat, and Italy, which won from Luxembourg 2 to 0. Thus the day furnished two big surprises and two favorites, Uruguay and Italy, won.

Fine passing, wonderful speed and greater knowledge of the technique of the game own for Uruguay against the courage, vigor and physical strength of the North Americans. The entire South American line played such football as has never been seen in Europe and as has seldom been even equaled by England's best professional teams.

For the United States, F. E. O'Connor of Lynn, Mass., left back, played an excellent defensive game, while A. G. Stradam of Philadelphia, the best man in the line, was poorly supported by his wing men, who were too slow.

Douglas Gives Rare Exhibition.

Uruguayan superiority was unquestioned excepting for goalkeeping, where J. Douglas of Kearny, N. J., gave an exhibition surpassing anything which has been seen since the tournament began. He played a brave game and showed initiative in judging when to run out and when to remain at goal, thereby saving countless scores.

During the second period the Uruguayans played well within themselves, mindful of their future matches. They showed great sporting spirit even when they had the match safely won, refused to kick outside when their goal was threatened or to play for time.

Manager Collins said after the game: "We were defeated by a team which today was superior to ours. I say today not because we are seeking any excuses, but because I am sure there have been days whn our team could have won."

Captain Nasazzi of the Uruguayans complimented the courageous showing of his opponents, especially since they were without the services of two of their best men, Rudd and Brix. He said he did not believe the presence of these two men in the line-up would have made any difference, but that he would have preferred to have beaten the North Americans when they were playing a full-fledged team.

The Uruguayan team dominated throughout the game, the South American players holding themselves well in hand. The moment the second half began the Uruguayans reopened their attack, the American goal being protected at times by phenomenal work on the part of the United States players, O'Connor and Davis playing a particularly excellent game.

United States Attacks Fail.

Occasionally the North American advanced into their opponents' territory by pretty passes but their attacks were always checked before they became dangerous. Late in the game Burkhart Jones charged against Naya very near the goal line and the referee called a foul although the crowd shouted its disapproval and clamored for Jones's removal from play. The United States players were contenting themselves with an effort to keep the score low while the Uruguayans were indulging in much fancy work, winning great applause but reducing their efficiency.

The weather was very hot, favoring the South Americans, who are used to this sort of temperature, while the Yankees generally play in more moderate heat.

All the scoring took place in the first half, the first Uruguayan tally crossing the American goal after nine minutes of play and the second five minutes later. The Uruguayans attacked immediately after the Americans kicked off and a moment later had the ball in front of the United States goal, but Davis saved it and the Americans took it up the field. The Uruguayans, however, broke the attack and then for ten consecutive minutes peppered shot after shot at Douglas, who stopped everything coming his way, playing a great game.

Despite the heroic defensive work of the North American team, the two goals were scored and the game slowed up for a while, only to be enlivened by another South American attack after a foul had been called against the United States. The Uruguayans played a beautiful passing game, but were somewhat weak in translating their work into successful goals.

Uruguayans Very Steady.

The United States players ran a few spasmodic attacks down toward the Uruguayan goal, but the Uruguayans were playing a cool, steady game, and were never really threatened. The third goal was scored just one minute before half time. It was a fast shot into the lower left-hand corner by Petrone. Previously the Uruguayans had missed many opportunities directly in front of the United States goal.

The line-ups of the two teams were as follows:

United States—F. E. O'Connor, Lynn, Mass., left back; I. C. Davis, Philadelphia, right halfback; F. Burkhart Jones, Bridgeville, Pa., left halfback; R. A. Hornberger, Philadelphia, captain and centre half; C. N. F. Johnson, Chicago, right half; J. Dalrymple, Tacony, Pa.; H. C. Farrell, Philadelphia; A. G. Stradam, Philadelphia; H. Wells, Brockton, Mass., and W. Findlay, Bayonne, N. J., forwards; J. Douglas, Kearny, N. J., goal. Uruguay—Ariste, left back; Nasazzi, captain and right back; Tomasina, left halfback; Vidal centre half; Andrade, right halfback; Romano, Cea, Petron, Scarone and Naya, forwards; Mazali, goal. M. Barette of Belgium was the referee.

The jury forming the appeal court nominated by the International Association Football Federation for the Olympic tournament met today and suspended for the remainder of the tournament Larraza of the Spanish team and Capek of the Czechoslovakian team, who had been sent off playing fields by referees for rough play. The jury rejected a protest filed by Switzerland against two decisions made by the referee during the match against Czechoslovakia.

Montevideo Cheers Victory.

MONTEVIDEO, Uruguay, May 29.—The City of Montevideo went wild with enthusiasm over the Olympic football victory scored by the Uruguayans against the United States. From early morning hours crowds gathered in front of newspaper offices awaiting bulletins, and there was anxious expectancy as to the showing the Uruguayans would make against their opponents. The final result was greeted with an uproar of cheers, rockets, foghorns and whistles.

The first action taken by the Chamber of Deputies at its session today was to adopt a resolution and send a congratulatory cablegram to Paris. Uruguayans are so fond of football that visitors here say there are only two classes of people in the country—those who play it and those who watch it.

May 3, 1924

URUGUAY IS VICTOR; HOLLAND PROTESTS

South American Eleven Plays Uphill Game to Win Olympic Semi-Final by 2-1.

GAME MAY BE REPLAYED

Jury Must Decide Appeal of Dutch Against Allowing Winning Penalty Kick.

PARIS, June 6 (Associated Press).—The Uruguayan Olympic soccer football team today overcame another obstacle in the way of its victorious career toward the world's Olympic title, disposing of Holland's team by a score of 2 to 1 after one of the most desperate uphill matches seen since the tournament began.

The never-say-die spirit of the South Americans carried them into the finals amid the cheers of the large crowd that had been won over by their clean playing sportsmanship. After trailing 1 to 0 in the first period, the winners refused to acknowledge defeat in the face of abominable luck and tremendous odds in weight.

Uruguay picked out of the fire what for twenty minutes appeared to be a lost match despite the obstructions of the Dutch team, which for a time played a purely defensive game. The winning goal was scored on a penalty kick after the ball struck one of the player's hands. Yet Uruguay deserved to win by a much larger score than it obtained.

Although Uruguay has won the right to meet Switzerland in the final match for the title, this right is not undisputed. After the game the Dutch team officially protested against the ruling which allowed the penalty kick which produced the winning goal. The Olympic jury will decide whether this protest shall be upheld, and if it is Uruguay's hard-fought victory will be nullified and the game will have to be replayed.

During the first half of the game the South Americans were obviously off form and the superior weight of the Dutchmen told heavily. The Uruguayans appeared to lack the dash and spirit they had shown in their previous games and their group play was weak. The only score during this period was made by a Dutch player.

The second half began with the Uruguayans fighting desperately to tie the score. They smashed relentlessly at the players from the Netherlands, who, playing a purely defensive game, earned the vehemently expressed disapproval of the crowded stands by preferring to kick the ball over their own goal line rather than to risk the struggle with the Uruguayan forwards.

A great cry of approval went up from the stands when Cea of the Uruguayan team tied the score. A short time later the driving game of the South Americans carried them through the line again and Petrone scored a second goal for them, but this goal was disallowed by the referee, who declared that another Uruguayan player had touched the ball with his hand.

The Uruguayans were outlucked throughout, and with even breaks should have had at least four goals. With the end of the game in sight Scarone scored the winning goal.

June 7, 1924

Holland Loses Olympic Soccer Protest; Dutch Referee for Final Alarms Uruguay

PARIS, June 7 (Associated Press).—The Protest Committee of the Olympic games today decided that Holland's protest of the soccer game in which that country was beaten by Uruguay would not be allowed. This action officially gives the contest to Uruguay by the score of 2 to [illegible]nd places that nation in the finals against Switzerland. The championship of the 1924 Olympic games in soccer will be decided on Monday in Colombes Stadium.

The Olympic officials today also announced that the referee for the final on Monday would be M. Mutters of Holland. The selection caused no little surprise in the Uruguayan camp, coming as it did on the heels of the rather warm discussion that took place during the meeting on the Dutch protest of Uruguay's victory.

While the Uruguayans do not wish to cast any doubt upon Mr. Mutters's impartiality, they do realize that the very hottest words in the course of the acrimonious debate today were spoken by close friends of M. Mutters's, and that these friends were the ones who prolonged the discussion and were unwilling to have the officials of the jury announce their decision without first listening to a lengthy dissertation on the part of the Dutch committee.

The attitude of Holland was presented and pressed by M. Mutters's friends. They were outspoken in their feeling and brought forward statements that called for a review of the entire game that was under protest. They were thoroughly aroused and their words were heated.

The South Americans feel that M. Mutters, although animated by the most impartial intentions in the world, could not fail to come in for criticism from the Uruguayan players in the heat of a stiffly contested match. They feel that a referee from some other country should be chosen, and they probably will convey this information in the shape of a friendly suggestion to the French Olympic Committee tomorrow.

June 8, 1924

URUGUAY'S PROTEST OF REFEREE UPHELD

Olympic Committee Names Slawick of France to Officiate in Soccer Final.

TITLE IS AT STAKE TODAY

South American Eleven Will Play Switzerland for World's Crown— Both Teams In Fine Shape.

PARIS, June 8 (Associated Press).— The Uruguayan soccer football team, which is to play Switzerland in the final Olympic contest tomorrow, today won its protest against the appointment of M. Mutters of Holland as referee. The French Olympic Committee recognized their protest, withdrew M. Mutters and appointed M. Slawick of France to judge the play. The South Americans enthusiastically accepted him.

The Uruguayans, in making their representations against M. Mutters, said they did not question his impartiality, but that they felt a referee from some other country than Holland should be selected. The Olympic Committee placed the names of four experts—an Englishman, a Belgian, a Hungarian and a Frenchman in a hat and on the draw the name of M. Slawick came out.

Both Uruguay and Switzerland will put their strongest men in the field for tomorrow's game. The South Americans have been resting at Argenteuil, ten miles northwest of Paris, since their defeat of Holland, and every player is said to be in fine physical condition. The Swiss team also went into the country after it defeated Sweden, and the men will not return to Paris until an hour or so before Slawick blows the whistle for the commencement of play in the world's championship game tomorrow.

June 9, 1924

60,000 SEE URUGUAY WIN IN SOCCER FINAL

Record Olympic Crowd Present as South Americans Beat Switzerland, 3 to 0.

PARIS, June 9 (Associated Press).— The national flag of Uruguay tonight floats over the Olympic stadium just above the Stars and Stripes of the United States as a result of the thrilling victory today of the South American soccer football team over Switzerland by the score of 3 to 0. The United States held the much-sought position in the stadium since May 18 by virtue of the victory in the rugby competition. Of the two Olympic events thus far completed North America has carried off one and South America the other, Uruguay being the first South American nation to see its national emblem flying from the Olympic masthead.

Uruguay annexed the world's soccer championship by scientific and fast play. The South Americans were really three goals better than the stalwart

team from Switzerland. The victory was clean-cut and impressive, leaving absolutely no doubt in the minds of the record Olympic crowd that the best team won. The Uruguayan team was undoubtedly the best of any of the teams representing twenty-two nations which competed in the Olympic tournament, and was the only team entered which kept its opponents down to two goals in the five games.

Indomitable courage in the face of tremendous odds was the only thing that could be said for the Swiss. They were outplayed from the goal post to the extreme wings, but they never said die and continued fighting hopelessly a lost battle until the referee's final whistle.

Enthusiasm at High Pitch.

The Colombes stadium was filled to its capacity of 60,000 persons, while several thousand more clamored futilely on the outside for admission. The game proved the greatest drawing card of all the Olympic competitions since the 1924 games began, and the gate receipts totaled 520,000 francs.

Such popular enthusiasm as was seen today has never before been equaled in the annals of international sporting competition in Paris and caused a rush to the stadium comparable only to that directed toward Epsom Downs on Derby Day. Before the match began, the stadium was filled, while more than 3,000 others, trying to gain admittance at the games, caused a crush in which a number of women fainted. Several of the women were trampled and injured by the crowd and had to be rushed to the Olympic Red Cross unit station under the stadium.

The weather for the game was ideal with a mild breeze blowing and bright sunlight flooding the exposed sections of the stand, which were studded with French, Uruguayan and Swiss flags. Squads of police reserves from Paris kept the crowds in order inside and outside the stadium and regulated traffic on the roads from Paris, which were jammed with pedestrians and vehicles of every description.

During the last twenty minutes of play, the Uruguayans uncorked a type of play which had never before been seen in Olympic competition and which swept the Swiss players off their feet.

Uruguayans Nervous at Start.

The game began slowly with the Uruguayans, at first nervous, starting the action by carrying the ball into Swiss territory and keeping it there by excellent passing and kicking. The Swiss, however, unexpectedly began a bitter opposition, which held off the South Americans and kept the ball rushing back from one end of the field to the other. The period ended with the score one to nothing, but with the final result decidedly uncertain.

The Swiss defense crumpled soon after the beginning of the second period and despite their desperate efforts, the Uruguayans advanced to two more goals. The play throughout the game was clean although the referee called many fouls. The crowd was absolutely fair, impartially applauding good playing on the part of both teams.

Sweden, which won third place in the Olympic rating by defeating Holland in the preliminary match, 3 to 1, completely outclassed its opponents, displacing the Dutch team which won third place in 1908, 1912 and 1920. The game was a play-off of the 1 to 1 tie game played Saturday.

Montevideo Celebrates Victory.

MONTEVIDEO, Uruguay, June 9.—The capital of Uruguay indulged in a frenzied celebration today upon the receipt of news that the Uruguayan soccer football team had won the Olympic championship by defeating Switzerland. The steam whistles of all the ships and factories augmented the immense cheering crowds that paraded the streets. Business was virtually at a standstill.

June 10, 1924

Football Teams Play 9 Hours Before Barrow Eleven Wins

What is declared to be a record-breaking endurance test on the football field was the nine-hour struggle between Barrow and Gillingham in the sixth qualifying round of the Football Association Cup competition in England. On four occasions these soccer elevens met, with each game ending in a tie at 0-0, 1-1, 1-1 and 1-1 and it was not until the following replay that Barrow managed to qualify for the first round of the cup competition proper, the score being 2 to 1 in as sensational a battle as the previous ones had been. This Marathon of the gridiron started at Gillingham, and proceeded in rapid succession to Barrow, Wolverhampton and Highbury, finally finishing at Millwall, the last three grounds being neutral.

January 25, 1925

100,000 SEE SHEFFIELD WIN FOOTBALL CUP

Yorkshire Eleven Beats Cardiff City, Welsh Finalists, by 1-0, at Wembley Stadium.

Copyright, 1925, by The New York Times Company.
By Wireless to THE NEW YORK TIMES.

LONDON, April 25.—London's West End this evening was crowded with Welshmen and Yorkshiremen who journeyed up to town to witness the final match for the Association Football Cup between Sheffield United and Cardiff City. Sheffield United won by 1 to 0.

The game was played at Wembley Stadium and was witnessed by 100,000 spectators, among whom were the Duke and Duchess of York, who distributed the medals to the winning team of Yorkshiremen, whose captain, by the way, is a Welshman, while the Welsh captain is a Scot.

This is one of the vagaries of professional football players. As a prominent bishop said the other day, players were bought and sold like slaves. So great was consequent outcry that the ecclesiastic hastened to retract his words. It was better, he admitted, to have great crowds out in the open air watching professionals perform rather than sit guzzling in the saloons.

Unhappily another point in the argument was afforded by the fact that for a day's match the Wembley authorities obtained an "all-day license," which permitted the sale of beer and other liquid refreshments during hours when public houses were closed under existing restrictive regulations.

Nevertheless, in a walk along the Strand, which was crowded with football fans this evening, it was rare indeed to see anyone under the influence of liquor.

April 26, 1925

Rival Fans Carry Guns to Soccer Game, So Bologna-Genoa Match Is Called Off

TURIN, Italy, July 17 (P).—The Prefect has forbidden the football match between teams from Bologna and Genoa, scheduled for Sunday, because the feeling between football enthusiasts of the two cities is running so high that it is feared the match, to decide the championship of Northern Italy, would be responsible for rioting and wholesale bloodshed.

This situation, unprecedented in the annals of Italian sport, has been brought about through the encounter between the Bologna and Genoa enthusiasts on their arrival at Turin last Sunday, where the game was to be played. Unfortunately the trains from the two cities arrived simultaneously, and the rivals hurled insults at each other, from which the players refrained. Before the police succeeded in quelling the disturbance a number of shots were fired, and several persons were wounded.

The game was then postponed until July 19, but the officials of the National Football Federation decided that it would be dangerous to have the crowds meet again, and that it would be best to hold their games in secret, not admitting the public. A storm of protest was aroused, football lovers insisting that the games are played only for the benefit of the public and not merely to decide a championship. The plans again were changed to admit the public, but the Prefect, on hearing of this, issued his order forbidding the match.

July 18, 1925

Bullfighting Is Doomed as Favorite Sport In Spain; Soccer's Popularity the Cause

LONDON, Sept. 21 (P).—Soccer football is playing havoc with bullfighting in Spain. Señor Alcaraz, captain of the Madrid football team who has been playing matches in England, says the astonishing progress soccer is making in Spain is having a humanizing effect upon lovers of the spectacular, and that it will not be long before bullfighting is ousted as the sport of the nation.

"I feel sure," said Señor Alcaraz, "that football eventually will supersede bullfighting. If it were not for the fact that the bullfighting season is in the Summertime and the football season comes in Winter this would have happened long ago. We have evidence, both in Madrid and Barcelona, the two principal football centres, that football is proving the more attractive sport to the people. Where football games have clashed with events in the bullring the latter have been postponed owing to poor attendance."

Señor Alcaraz added that up to now only amateurs had played football in Spain, but he predicted that in two years the leading clubs would be made up of professionals. American and English coaches are training the players.

September 22, 1925

SCOTLAND FEARS END OF REIGN AT SOCCER

Says English Clubs Buy Its Players for Large Sums as Soon as They Become Stars.

Copyright, 1925, by The New York Times Company.
By Wireless to THE NEW YORK TIMES.

LONDON, Dec. 19—The sale of professional soccer players is becoming a feature of Great Britain to the same extent the sale of baseball players is in America. As high as $33,000 has reputed to have been paid for the transfer of a player to the Newcastle club, and Scotland is very much excited. She sees a steady drain of her best men either to America or England and fears her national prestige in association football is seriously threatened.

Soccer never has been as popular in Scotland as in England, where it is the national game during the Winter and where the annual contest for the Football Association Cup draws tens of thousands of spectators to see the final in the Wembley Stadium. Scotland fears she inevitably will be beaten in international matches if her best players are attracted by high salaries and big bonuses to the English clubs.

The steady growth of professionalism in association football caused a curious debate at this week's conference of headmasters of the great English schools. A large number of the best known schools have been giving up soccer for rugby with the result that soccer is played now only by such schools as Westminster, which has a traditional connection with the kicking game. Consequently each year it is harder to find amateur soccer players fit to cope with professional and even the standard of such a famous amateur club as the Corinthians is steadily falling.

This is greatly regretted, as nobody wants to see a great popular sport completely professionalized, and so the headmasters adopted a resolution hoping that the big schools would be faithful enough to soccer to maintain a good nucleus of amateur players.

December 20, 1925

KING AMONG 90,000 AT SOCCER FINAL

Copyright, 1926, by The New York Times Company.
Special Cable to THE NEW YORK TIMES.

LONDON, April 24.—London today was turned over to visitors from Lancashire, who came here in thousands to attend the cup final, which determined the British soccer champion. The game, is the biggest event of its kind of the year between two Lancashire teams, the Bolton Wanderers and Manchester City.

King George was present at the exciting contest, which was won by Bolton, 1 to 0.

Another spectator was T. K. Quirke of Philadelphia, a native of Bolton, who came to London for the sole purpose of seeing the game, and by the time he gets back to Philadelphia he will have spent $3,000 to gratify the desire to see the idols of his boyhood, the Bolton Wanderers, in action once more.

The game was played in the Stadium at Wembley, which holds 90,000, and seats brought fancy prices. At one gate the crowd became so angry with the ticket speculators that it stormed past the ticket takers and hundreds gained admittance before the police regained control.

After the game thousands of beribboned, merry Lancashiremen and women thronged the London streets, rivalling Americans in visits to the Tower and other historic places. Most of the men wore caps and some women wore clogs and gay shawls.

More than 150 excursion trains reached London between 5 and 7 o'clock this morning and one railway brought 15,000 fans here in thirty-eight special trains. A tourist agency had 100 charabancs at the Saint Pancras station at 5:30 to meet the incoming trains. Some of the soccer enthusiasts brought flowers which they deposited at the foot of the cenotaph, erected in memory of the British World War dead.

April 25, 1926

SOCCER

When the Hakoah soccer team deserts the training stable for the festive board at the Hotel Pennsylvania tomorrow night, the greatest soccer tour ever made in the United States will come to a close. The Vienna players will sail for home the next day and they will derive great satisfaction from the fact that they performed their mission to this country more creditably perhaps than even they had hoped.

In about a month the Hakoah team has played nine games, today's in Philadelphia being the tenth. So far it has won five of those contests and has performed before 165,000 persons. The Vienna players' second game in New York drew 36,000. This stands as a record for soccer in this country. They have carried the game to the West and have done missionary work of the most effective type for the game. Perhaps they did not play as well here as their record in Europe indicated they would, but it is pretty much of a certainty that they did perform better than they had expected.

Styles of Play Differ.

The Hakoah eleven came to New York with only eight defeats in close to 200 games. The team had conquered the best in Europe, but no one was more apprehensive of success here than the Vienna players themselves. They knew that conditions here are not what they are in Europe; the styles of attack differ and the modes of defense make the game look like two different sports. In Europe the eleven on the defensive does not jam the goal mouth and that style of play here went far to explain the Hakoah team's lack of a scoring punch in its first few games. Toward the close of their campaign, the visitors did develop a will to serve and none can testify better to this than the New York Giants of the American Soccer League.

Masters at Controlling Ball.

Soccer in this country, with the exception of the brand played in the East, has been marked by a hit-and-miss style of play. The system of controlling the ball and advancing it to the rival goal through a series of intricate passes was unknown west of Pittsburgh. Seldom has such mastery over the ball been seen as when the Hakoah eleven started its attack on enemy goals. In midfield the defense always has stood powerless against the clever and fast passing of the invaders and the only

respect in which the visitors failed to measure up to American standards of play was a ferocious attack in front of the goal.

LAURENCE J. SPIKER.
May 31, 1926

KING AND 90,000 SEE WELSH ELEVEN WIN

Cardiff City Beats Woolwich Arsenal for the English Soccer Cup, 1 to 0.

SCENES LIKE WORLD SERIES

Fans Sleep at Gates Through Night — 250,000 Surround Stadium During Game.

Copyright, 1927, by The New York Times Company.
By Wireless to THE NEW YORK TIMES.

LONDON, April 23.—King George and 90,000 of his subjects crowded into Wembley Stadium here this afternoon to see the English Football Association cup final between Cardiff City and Woolwich Arsenal, London's oldest professional football team, Cardiff City winning, 1 goal to 0. The King presented the cup to the captain of the Welshmen and medals to both teams.

The weather was perfect and apparently all Wales journeyed here to root for its first Welsh eleven ever to win in the long history of the soccer football championship cup.

250,000 Around Stadium.

The crowd which gathered around the stadium during the game, which is to England and Wales what the world's series is in baseball is to the United States, was estimated at fully 250,000. Many slept outside the gates during the night waiting for admission.

Arsenal won the toss, which gave it the goal from which the wind was blowing, but the advantage availed it little. Before the game it was thought that Arsenal would be superior to the Welshmen on attack, but the latter soon disproved this. Almost from the start it was practically obvious that the best player on the field was Hardy, Cardiff left half, who blocked Arsenal time after time.

The first half closed with the score 0 to 0, but when the second half began things looked more sensational, and more than once the crowd was or its toes as both sides narrowly missed goals several times.

Cardiff Gets the Break.

The break went to Cardiff when Ferguson shot hard along the ground. Lewis, Arsenal goalkeeper, jumped and smothered the drive, but as he attempted to evade the onrushing Welshmen by crawling around while on the ground he turned in the direction of his own net and lost the ball.

It rolled slowly over the line, giving Cardiff a lead which Arsenal never overcame. Once Arsenal got the ball into the net, but the try was ruled offside. Ferguson's winning shot was made after twenty-eight minutes of the second half.

April 24, 1927

10,000 SEE SOCCER IN NIGHT CONTEST

Large Crowd at Polo Grounds Sees Hakoah and Picked Team Play Scoreless Tie.

BALL IS PAINTED WHITE

Both Teams Use Fast Attack, but Defenses Hold—All-Star Team Forces First Corner.

That soccer by artificial light, other conditions being favorable, is entirely feasible was clearly shown to the satisfaction of a crowd of 10,000 enthusiasts at the Polo Grounds last night when the Hakoah eleven from Vienna encountered a combined team representing two American Soccer League clubs, the New York Giants and Bethlehem Steel, holder of the league championship. The game ended in a scoreless tie.

It already had been demonstrated with fairly complete conclusiveness a week earlier that the lights were highly satisfactory and judging by the favorable comments heard on all sides last night and by the size of the audience, the way has been paved for night soccer on a large scale.

The field of the classic playground for baseball lovers was bright as daylight, the rays from the dozen 1,000-candlepower arc lights, perched on the roofs of the high pavilions and clubhouse, reaching every nook and corner of the enclosure. So accurately had the lights been placed that there was not a shadow within the space, 110 yards by 80.

Lights Are No Handicap.

The illuminating units were high enough to permit the players' eyes to follow the ball, painted white, no matter how high it was kicked in the air. As the sphere descended they had no trouble in intercepting, and, when favorably placed, trapping it.

For all practical purposes the conditions were precisely the same as though the sun were shining brightly overhead. The play was just as fast, the individual efforts quite as spontaneous and the team work all that could be reasonably expected under normal conditions.

Hakoah kicked off at 9:19 o'clock and worked down the ball on the left. Wortmann crossed to Schwartz, who drove over the bar. The first corner came to the picked team in five minutes as Brown forced Fabian to allow the point, but Stark's try went too high. A minute later Schwartz gained a corner for Hakoah on the right. It was cleared by Tandler.

Guttman Forces Corner.

A second corner resulted from Guttman's long shot to Douglas, who touched it behind. Wortmann's try then sailed over.

A fresh ball was thrown out after 15 minutes. Fabian, pressed, came far out to save the situation and did it well. The home goal was in real danger as Schwartz crossed. Hakoah's goal was standing up manfully, and a storm of applause greeted his fine work. Shortly after, the half ended, 0 to 0.

The second half started at 10.25 o'clock with both teams on their mettle, each side prepared to give and take. In three minutes Hakoah gained a corner on the right, but the picked team cleared in a jiffy. The All-Stars in turn had one on the

right wing but Fabian fisted out. Schwartz kicked Vienna's second corner behind. The going was fast but the defenses held and the game ended in a scoreless tie.

The line-up:

HAKOAH (0).	PICKED TEAM (0).
Fabian ....G..........	Douglas
Scheuer ....R. B..........	Tandler
Gold ....L. B..........	Moorhouse
Fried ....R. H..........	Herd
Guttman ....C. H..........	Carnihan
Hess ....L. H..........	McKinney
Schwartz ....O. R..........	Jaap
Haeusler ....I. R..........	Stark
Gruenwald ....C..........	Brown
Wortmann ....I. L..........	Rollo
Fischer ....O. L..........	Goldie

Referee—J. Hume. Linesmen—S. Day and J. Hayes. Substitutions—Strohs for Fried, Mausner for Guttman, Guttman for Mausner, Hess for Wortmann, O'Brien for Rollo. Time of halves—45 minutes.

June 9, 1927

U. S. Centre of Soccer Activity, Though Not a Leader in Sport

Austria, Czechoslovakia, Uruguay, Palestine, Canada and Ireland Send Teams Here as a Gesture of Friendliness—England, Spain, Norway and Sweden May Join Invasion Next Season.

Perhaps it is strange, and then it may not be, that the high road of soccer should lie through the United States, but developments in recent months have proved this to be the case. This country certainly is not rated as one of the world leaders in the kicking game, yet this season has seen the invasion of four world-famous teams.

First there came, from that little South American country of Uruguay, the Olympic championship team. Then followed a second tour by the famous Hakoah eleven from Vienna. While the Austrians were still here a team from far-off Palestine arrived, and then Ireland sent over its representative, the Kerry fifteen, champion of all Ireland in Gaelic football. Kerry and Palestine still are here, but their tours are drawing to a close.

Naturally the close followers of soccer showed the greatest interest in the Uruguay eleven. The club that had carried off the Olympic title in so convincing a style, enthusiasts said, must have a system of high-geared passing. All wanted to see how soccer teams here would stand up against the brand which had brought victory to Uruguay in all parts of the world.

Anxious to Prove Merit.

Uruguay was anxious to show its wares in the American sector. The country was no different from many others in that it wanted attention attracted to itself. It had a very fine soccer team and the next step was logical—the team was sent out on a world tour. The players all remained amateurs, but carried on their diplomatic work in a thoroughly capable manner.

It is obvious that if the players were to spend their time traveling around, and were not wealthy, they would have to receive remuneration. If they were paid they were professionals, so they all were appointed to Government positions, most of them serving as clerks when not away playing.

They invaded Europe and trimmed every team they met. They returned home and then began planning a tour of the United States. It was readily arranged and the club played its first game here five days after getting off the boat, and then close followers of the sport saw why Uruguay won the Olympic crown. The team is one of the fastest in the world and certainly no combination ever boasted a surer and faster attacking style of play. And Uruguay also presented probably the finest back ever seen here in the powerful Andrade, who smashed every play that came within half the width of the field of him.

Major Share of Honors.

Playing the leading professional elevens of the country, the visitors came off with the major share of the glory and then, when it came to playing in the West, where the players are home-breds and not imported stars, there was expected to be a great exposure of native players—and there was, but the resulting discovery was that the young stars of the West are just about on a par with the internationalists of the East, and in bringing out this fact alone, Uruguay did a great service to the game of soccer in this country.

Palestine presented a colorful eleven, one that attracted wide attention because it was the first athletic team ever sent out from the new home of the Jews. It came out on the high road that led to the United States because, its leaders said, "the United States has done so much for Palestine that Palestine wants to show the United States that the Jews are gaining the highest development possible in not only the arts and sciences, but in the realm of athletics."

Last season there also was a team "with a mission" traveling through the United States playing the great international game. Prague, the capital of Czechoslovakia, sent its best eleven here, not to try to trim the American teams, but to "prove to the United States that when President Wilson fought for and secured the independence of the Csechs he accomplished something real, something more than idealistic, for the Csechs have found it possible to enlarge their lives. Where they once found only time for labor they now go in for recreation on a large scale, and thus the team was sent to show that America's faith was well repaid."

"Ireland," the Rev. Father Fitzgerald, in charge of the Kerry fifteen, said, "has a friendly feeling toward the United States. The country wanted to get in close touch with the Americans and what better way could there be than through the medium of a common sport?" Of course Gaelic football is not soccer. It is a combination of basketball, volleyball and soccer in that the ball can be kicked, headed, fisted and caught, but it is a game that is readily understood and, if anything, is a little faster than soccer.

Australia May Compete.

It is planned by Father Fitzgerald to return next year with another Gaelic team and also to have Australia send its football team here to play for the championship of the world, allowing American fifteens also to enter the tourney. The Australian game is very much the same as the Irish brand and the Ameri-

cans would have no trouble in learning either kind.

And, while all these countries have sent teams to the United States during the season that has just come to an official close, the prospects are that next year our soccer fields will see an even greater invasion of foreign clubs. Negotiations already are under way to bring here the British and Scottish Cup winners next year, and plans have progressed very far toward having the national Spanish eleven come here. In addition, the team of American Swedes that now is playing through the Scandinavian countries is anxious to have its visit returned and it may be that both Norway and Sweden will be represented here next season.

Canada and the United States have been playing each other for the last few years and it now is the custom to send a United States team on a short tour of Canada which is followed by a limited engagement through the East of a Canadian eleven.

Workingmen to Play.

Early in the Fall an eleven composed entirely of workingmen will come here from Worcestershire, England, to meet a workingmen's team from Worcester County, Mass. Again the invasion is being made by a team "with a mission"—the purpose of getting the workingmen of the two countries acquainted in an athletic way.

Thus, the United States has been visited by soccer teams from South America, Austria, Czechoslovakia, Palestine, Canada and Ireland, and in the future will see others from Spain, England, Scotland and perhaps Norway and Sweden. The outstanding factor back of these colorful invasions is that the teams come here always in a spirit of friendliness, generally to show what they have been able to accomplish with the help of the United States.

That is why the United States is on the high road of soccer. That is why the greatest elevens of the world come here to play when soccer is not our national sport, when the average man is more interested in Babe Ruth, Jack Dempsey, Sande, Hagen or Tilden than the fast forwards of Uruguay, the neat passing of Hakoah, the clever booting of Palestine or the fiery attack of Kerry.

July 20, 1927

U. S. SOCCER FINAL ENDS IN A 1-1 DRAW

New York Nationals and Chicago Bricklayers Fail to Break Tie in Overtime.

ACTING MAYOR STARTS GAME

Record Cup Tie Final Crowd of 16,000 Sees Thrilling Game at Polo Grounds.

CUTHBERT FIRST TO SCORE

Wortman Then Tallies, Knotting Count—Replay in Chicago Next Sunday.

Battling fruitlessly for two full hours, after a late start, the New York Nationals, Eastern finalists, and the Bricklayers of Chicago, champions of the West, were dead locked when the final whistle blew to mark the close of the second of the extra periods required for the national final for possession of the Challenge Trophy of the United States Football Association, at the Polo Grounds, yesterday afternoon. The score was 1—1, both goals being obtained in the first regular period.

Throughout the second half and the two supplementary periods, the well-matched teams fought to gain the ascendency, but to no purpose. There were plenty of narrow escapes, but always the defenders held the whip hand. A re-play of this soccer classic is now necessary and will take place in Chicago next Sunday.

Record Crowd Present.

It was a gala day for soccer enthusiasts at the famous baseball park. The weather drew an attendance of more than 16,000. This surpassed the record for a cup final in the East at Ebbets Field, two years ago.

With the Yonkers Bagpipe Band leading the way, the two teams marched out on the field soon after 3 o'clock, but, because of the unexpectedly large attendance, with the crowd still coming through the gates, the start was delayed until 3:25 o'clock, with acting Mayor Joseph V. McKee putting the ball in play. There were two Walkers on the field, one on each team, but Mayor Walker was unavoidably absent.

The visitors won the toss and the New York Nationals kicked off, defending the goal near the club house. In the beginning the Bricklayers, playing with the wind, were full of pep and distinctly set the pace. Henderson broke through for New York and headed to McEwan, but the Bricklayers quickly took command of the situation and attacked strongly on the left. Warden blocked a good attempt by Phillips. Walker of New York was stopped by Thompson and McLean drove past. Donald nipped the next shot in the bud by heading to one side.

Walker of Chicago tested Renzulli, who made good. The first foul was given against Slaven who tripped Cuthbert. Renzulli then took care of Cuthbert's drive. Henderson, following the ball, was tumbled by Woods. Next Wortman passed out to Walker, whereupon Henderson again obtained possession and, as he hit the turf, his shot was splendidly taken by McEwan. Next Wortman shot past.

Chicago Takes the Lead.

Chicago took the lead after eight minutes of play when Slaven of New York missed connection with the ball. Cuthbert, backed up by Phillips, dodged Warden and landed the ball in the New York net for the first goal of the game.

As Quinn back-charged Wortmann, a free kick was allowed the Nationals. Donald shot wide. McGhee went through on the left, but his try failed. The Nationals were displaying nervousness as Martyn passed back to Slaven, who in turn got rid of the ball to Donald. Two fine stops by Donald marked the Nationals' play, and in addition he barely saved a corner.

Walker of the Bricklayers started a passing combination with Cuthbert and Phillips, but Walker was declared off-side. Millar, taking Wortmann's pass, sent in a low one which missed its mark. Warden drove far up the field to Henderson, who saved the ball from going over the line, but Wortmann kicked it too high. Two fouls were given against Cuthbert and Scott.

The first corner of the game was given against the New York Nationals after twenty-five minutes, as Walker drove Millar's pass hard at McEwan. The latter made a good stop, the ball glancing off his hand over the net. Next McGhee tried his luck, but again I. Ewan intervened. Phillips went down for Chicago and got by Slaven, but Renzulli saved the day.

Wortmann Ties the Score.

The score was tied at thirty minutes, after much heading of the ball by the Nationals and two good tries by McGhee and Millar. Wortmann, who gained fame as a Hakoah star, suddenly got possession and a beautiful low drive went sailing past McEwan into the Bricklayers' net for the equalizing tally.

The Bricklayers resumed the attack and Chatton brought off a fine save for New York. Thomson was fouled by Walker of New York and another free kick was given. McGhee, nearly tripped by Scott, got through a good one, which McEwan negotiated. McLean was hurt in a scramble, but quickly resumed amid applause. T. Hill took a free kick. A foul given against Warden gave Thomson a free try, but once more Renzulli made the most of his opportunity.

In the second half the Bricklayers started off with a corner on the left, but the New Yorkers came right back with two on the opposite wing. For most of this half the New Yorkers held the upper hand. Play was in the Chicago end of the field, and the goal tender was kept busy as the Nationals attacked with all their strength. On several occasions the Nationals were right down at the goal, but failed to net the ball.

Henderson, who was playing a sterling game, was dogged by misfortune and what seemed sure goals were turned aside, once by a strong gust of wind which curved the ball away from the net and another time when his kick struck one of the posts and glanced back on the field.

There were moments when the Bricklayers got command, but these instances were fleeting. It seemed that fortune was against New York and the home side could not get the ball into the net.

The two extra periods, fifteen minutes each way, found the players in an exhausted state, although they kept the ball flying from one end of the field to the other. Always the defense was strong enough to turn back the attacking side's thrusts.

Hughie Hill, at inside right for the Bricklayers, showed himself to be a lionheart. He was the only one to be badly injured during a game in which there were many fouls. Midway in the second extra period he was forced to leave the game for first-aid treatment. In two minutes he was back and, limping badly, soon was leading a charge on his wing.

In corners the Nationals had a big edge, getting ten to their opponents' three. Honors were even in the first half, each side being credited with one. Three out of four were earned by the Nationals in the second. They added two more in the first of the extra periods, and the tally in the second and last was 3-1.

U. S. SOCCER TITLE TO NATIONALS, 3-0

Special to The New York Times.

CHICAGO, April 15.—The New York Nationals of the American Soccer League defeated the Chicago Bricklayers by 3 to 0 at Soldier Field before a crowd of 15,000 persons here this afternoon and won the national open soccer championship of the United States.

Georgie Henderson, scoring ace of the New Yorkers, accounted for two of the goals, both in the first half, and Siegfried Wortmann made the third.

This is the first time that a New York team has won the national crown, although twice Brooklyn elevens have gained the highest honor in soccer. This also is the first year the Nationals have been playing as a club under the ownership of Charles A. Stoneham.

In the second half, after Wortmann had scored his goal, Bob Millar and Tom Scott were barred from further play by Referee Walder. Millar, the playing manager of the Nationals and a veteran of many years of soccer, was upset near the Chicago goal and Scott, fullback, fell over him. They came to blows. Police rushed on the field and separated the players, who had begun to fight in groups, and when order was restored Millar and Scott were sent off the field.

Mayor Thompson Absent.

There were two more fights among players but no other banishments were ordered. Mayor William Hale Thompson was to have made the ceremonial kick-off but was unable to be present because of business. He was represented by Phil S. Graver, Park Commissioner, who made the kick-off. There were seven members of the Board of Aldermen present.

After the ceremonial kick, a coin was tossed. The Bricklayers won and elected to defend against the wind. The Nationals kicked off and worked the ball down the field, but Scott of the Bricklayers met a flying ball with his toe and the home side took up the attack. The ball went down the right side of the field and a corner was marked against Donald. The kick was cleared, but two more came to the Bricklayers in rapid succession. This, with still another, made four in the first three minutes for Chicago.

Coutte, a fast centre forward, received the ball down at the New York goal shortly after a pass from Cuthbert. The Nationals were thrown off their guard and only Renzulli stood between Coutte and the goal. His kick was hurried and while the crowd stood to yell he kicked too high and the ball soared over the crossbar.

Henderson First to Score.

The Nationals took up the attack and sent the ball down the field to Henderson. Alone he raced for the goal. Two Chicago men took up a futile pursuit. Without diminishing his pace, Henderson timed the shot and sent the ball scurrying into the lower left corner of the net. McEwan had no chance to save and the first goal was registered for New York in twelve minutes.

For the next fifteen minutes the Chicago passing game worked to perfection and the Nats were forced to play a purely defensive game. The Bricklayers gained three corner kicks, but all were cleared. The ball was sent down the field only after Renzulli had been spilled in the net and Chatton had kicked out. Chicago seemed to have spent itself in the heavy going and the Nationals opened a brilliant passing attack that swept the opposition before it. Finally a free kick was awarded to New York about ten yards from the goal but close to the touchline. Walker kicked the ball to Wortmann, who passed to McGhee. The latter lifted the ball back across the field to Walker who promptly centered to Henderson.

Without a second's delay Henderson accepted the chance. As the ball touched the ground he met it with his toe and sent it into the net, leaving McEwan without a chance. The time was thirty-nine minutes and made the score 2 to 0 in favor of the Nationals.

Bricklayers Go on Attack

The Bricklayers returned to attack and gave a remarkable demonstration of clever and effective passing, but it produced nothing more than an additional corner. McLean, who took all of Chicago's corner kicks, centered well on this one, but Renzulli fisted the ball out and the Nationals went back on the attack. They were keeping the play in their rival's half of the field when the half ended.

In the initial period the Bricklayers rang up eight corners to none for the Nationals and had five free kicks, while New York had seven. However, the Nationals scored two goals which more than offset the difference in corners.

Promptly with the opening of the second half the New Yorkers went on the attack. Walker, Henderson and McGhee took turns bombarding the Bricklayers' goal, but Ewan turned aside every threat. Finally, Wortmann got clear and took the ball on a fine pass from Martyn. He beat the two fullbacks with a swift kick that sent the ball into the net for the Nationals. McEwan tried to stop it but couldn't. The time was fifteen minutes.

Chicago resumed the attack after this and the going got pretty hot. Miller was upset when driving the ball to the Chicago goal and Scott fell on him. Fists flew and the two were banished.

From this time on the players were ready to strike blows on slight provocation, and twice more the police were called upon to separate players engaged in pugilistic combat. There was no further scoring and the game ended with New York the victor, 3-0.

In the second half there were no corners on either side, and the fouls were eight against the Chicago club and seven against New York. The totals for the game were eight corners for Chicago, none for New York; thirteen free kicks for Chicago and fourteen for New York.

The line-up:

Nationals (3).		Bricklayers (0).
Renzulli	G.	McEwan
Warden	R.B.	Scott
Donald	L.B.	Woods
Chatton	R.H.	T. Hill
Slaven	C.H.	Quinn
Martyn	L.H.	Thompson
Walker	O.R.	McLean
Wortmann	I.R.	H. Hill
Henderson	C.	Coutte
Millar	I.L.	Cuthbert
McGhee	O.L.	Walker

Goals—Nationals: Henderson 2, Wortmann. Referee — James Walder, Philadelphia. Linesmen—A. Shalcross and J. W. Wood, Chicago. Times of halves—45 minutes.

April 16, 1928

EIGHT CLUBS FORM NEW SOCCER LEAGUE

President Armstrong of National Body Promises All Possible Aid to Eastern Circuit.

WHITWELL IS PRESIDENT

New Yorker Elected, With Wilcox of Philadelphia Vice President— Play Opens Saturday.

With eight clubs, including three which withdrew from the American Soccer League and were suspended by that body, as charter members, the Eastern Soccer League was organized last night at a meeting of delegates held in the grill room of the Hotel Cornish Arms. The name was agreed upon shortly before midnight.

The name of the United States Football League had been chosen tentatively, but was withdrawn at the request of Armstrong Patterson of Detroit, President of the United States Football Association, who was present and was invited to address the gathering. He assured the delegates of the support of the national body, which, he said, at all times would back it up in a legal manner.

Cahill Is in Charge.

Thomas W. Cahill, Secretary of the U. S. F. A., presided over the meeting during the early portion of the evening and later, in the absence of the newly elected President, W. Luther Lewis of Bethlehem, conducted the proceedings.

The line-up:

N. Y. Nationals (1),		Bricklayers (1).
Renzulli	G.	McEwan
Warden	R.B.	Scott
Donald	L. B.	Woods
Chatton	R. H.	T. Hill
Slaven	C. H.	Quinn
Martyn	L. H.	Thomson
Walker	O. R.	McLean
Wortmann	I. R.	H. Hill
Henderson	C.	Phillips
Millar	I. L.	Cuthbert
McGhee	O. L.	Walker

Referee—J. Walder, Philadelphia. Linesmen—Charles E. Creighton, New York, and Alfred White, Auburn, R. I. Goals—Cuthbert, Briklayers; Wortmann, N. Y. Nationals. Time of halves—45 minutes; two extra periods of 15 minutes each.

April 9, 1928

Next Saturday the eight clubs will begin a series of week-end double-headers.

The clubs follow:

New York Giants, Bethlehem, Newark, Philadelphia Centennials, New York Celtics, New York Hakoah, I. R. T. Rangers of New York and the New York Hispano Soccer Club.

The making of a schedule for this week was left in the hands of the secretary. The following officers were elected:

Captain E. W. Whitwell, New York, President; Levi P. Wilcox, Philadelphia, First Vice President; Joseph J. Barriskill, New York, Second Vice President; James Armstrong, New York, Secretary; Allan Cahill, New York, Treasurer.

Hopes of Success Expressed.

Chairman Lewis expressed the hope that in time the new league would be second to none in this country and instructed the clubs to make application for permission to play their league games to the New York State Football Association as a preliminary step.

Announcement was made by Secretary Cahill of the U. S. F. A. that the action of President Patterson in suspending the American Soccer League had been formally ratified by the National Commission and that notices to that effect had been sent to the various State associations in this country and to the International Federation.

October 9, 1928

93,000 SEE BOLTON WIN FOOTBALL CUP

Wanderers Beat Portsmouth, 2-0, in English Title Test as Prince of Wales Looks On.

BUTLER, BLACKMORE SCORE

Wembley Stadium Mecca for Fans From All Parts of England— 40,000 Arrive on 80 Trains.

Special Cable to THE NEW YORK TIMES.

LONDON, April 27.—The Prince of Wales and a crowd of 93,000 in Wembly Stadium today watched the Bolton Wanderers beat Portsmouth, 2 to 0, in the English Soccer Cup final.

Portsmouth, which never before had reached a cup final, put up a gallant fight, but Bolton's experience and airtight defense were too much. So tonight the cup goes back to the North of England, where it has stayed almost without interruption since the war.

Once, when Wembley Stadium first was opened, a crowd of 125,000 stormed the gates and stood around the field and swarmed across the sidelines. Since then the cup final crowds have been admitted only by ticket, and to judge from today's orderliness the system is a complete success, except for a few ticket speculators, who tried to sell 50-cent seats for $10.

Groups of Bolton supporters rushed at the speculators and drove them off.

In the crowd there was no organized cheering and no noisemaking except the clanging of bells, the tooting of tin horns and the roar of cheers

whenever a brilliant play was made. Before the game began the vast crowd stood bareheaded and sang "Abide With Me."

Tonight London belongs to Bolton and Portsmouth. A fleet of buses took thousands sightseeing around the town, while the sidewalks near Piccadilly Circus and Charing Cross were black with crowds. Eighty special trains were needed to take the triumphant Bolton fans back to Lancashire.

Both Goals in Last Half.

LONDON, April 27 (AP).—The Bolton Wanderers won the historic English Football Association cup today from Portsmouth by two goals to none. Both tallies were made in the second half and were scored by the forwards, Butler and Blackmore.

Prince Paul of Greece was among the spectators. King George expressed his regrets that he was unable to attend.

Bolton monopolized the first few minutes of play. Cook and Gibson combined in one pretty movement, which broke down just when it looked like getting somewhere. Weddle, Portsmouth, then gathered his forward line together for a combined assault on the Bolton goal, but the Bolton defense broke up the run. Later Howarth cleared a corner kick luckily, the ball taking a favorable bounce.

When the game had been in progress for thirty minutes the Bolton backs were beginning to waver under persistent attacks. To relieve them, the Bolton forwards became more aggressive, but Bell robbed Blackmore of the ball when he was about to shoot at close range.

Just before the interval McIlwaine saved Portsmouth from a goal by clearing only a yard from the goal line, while Gilfillan, the Portsmouth goalkeeper, lay on the ground.

The great Bolton half and forward lines, with their group of international stars, who had been playing a waiting game, now came into action.

McClelland took a shot which would have gone in, but Gilfillan flung himself lengthwise on the ground to save. Gilfillan saved again brilliantly after a corner, when Gibson put in a hot grounder.

Portsmouth Weakens.

Bolton was obviously asserting a superiority and the character of the match underwent a complete change. The Portsmouth side looked spent and their offensive work was only spasmodic. Bolton richly deserved its first score, which came in the thirty-fifth minute of the second half. Butler shot and Macjin on the goal line desperately attempted to kick the ball away. It hit the goal post and rebounded into the net.

Clever work by Butler and Gibson then enabled Blackmore to shoot into an empty net. Gilfillan having been lured out. The final phase of the match saw Portsmouth struggling fiercely to stave off defeat, but the Bolton defense, confident and comparatively fresh, checkmated their efforts.

A babel of dropped aspirates, Welsh polysyllables and Scotch burrs resounded at Wembley Stadium as partisans of the Bolton Wanderers, representing the North, and of Portsmouth, representing the South, discussed the merits of their favorites.

Replying to a message to King George from the editor of The Sporting Life, in which regret was expressed on behalf of the teams engaged in the English Football Association Cup tie today that his Majesty could not attend the game as usual, Lord Stameordham, private secretary, telegraphed:

"I am commanded to convey to you the King's sincere thanks for your message. The King is glad that the Prince of Wales is able to be present at the cup final. His Majesty will be thinking of all at Wembly with feelings of regret at his enforced absence, coupled with the hope that nothing will prevent his Majesty's attending in future years."

April 28, 1929

SAYS SOCCER WAR IS OVER.

National Secretary Cahill Announces Peace Has Been Declared.

Peace has been declared in the soccer war by the delegates of the United States Football Association and the American Soccer League who have participated in the peace congress here, according to Thomas W. Cahill, secretary of the United States Football Association, who gave out a statement to that effect at the headquarters, 311 West Twenty-third Street, yesterday.

The documents in the case, he said, had been signed and it remains now merely to obtain the signatures of the individual club owners to this document in order to effect a binding and permanent peace.

October 9, 1929

ARSENAL CAPTURES BRITISH CUP FINAL

Defeats Huddersfield Town, 2-0, Before Crowd of 100,000 in Wembley Stadium.

KING GEORGE SEES MATCH

He Presents Trophy, Emblematic of Soccer Championship, to Winning Captain.

EVENT REBROADCAST HERE

Special Cable to THE NEW YORK TIMES.

LONDON, April 26.—In a frenzy of excitement such as seldom is associated with British playing fields, a vast crowd of approximately 100,000 saw the Arsenal football team defeat Huddersfield Town, 2 to 0, in the English Football Association cup final in Wembley Stadium today.

The encounter, which attracted King George and the Duke of York from Windsor Castle and the Graf Zeppelin from its direct course from Germany to London, was followed, thrill by thrill, over the radio by probably 100,000,000 British subjects in all parts of the empire.

The crowd would tolerate no interruption of this game by visiting airships, and, could Captain Ernest A. Lehmann in the Zeppelin's control room have heard above the din of his engines the imprecations that were hurled at him from the ground beneath, it is doubtful if he would have remained long enough to dip the nose of his silvered ship in salute at the royal box. Lehmann came so low that the gondolas of the Zeppelin appeared almost to scrape the tops of the flagpoles surrounding the huge concrete basin, which was filled to the brim with a tightly packed mass of humanity.

Appealed to Air Ministry.

Appeals had previously been telephoned to the Air Ministry by the team managers and ground officials to warn Lehmann from following his intended plan. Officials held that

the noise of the engines would distract the players and possibly cause a break at a critical stage of the game, and no English Cup final, they declared, should be won or lost as the result of an airship's visitation.

The Graf Zeppelin swooped down just as C. J. Preedy, Arsenal goalkeeper, was taking a clearing kick, but there was no pause in the fast-moving game.

The visitors received a lasting impression from the demonstration given when King George stepped on the smooth playing field just before the start of the match and shook hands with the members of both teams, and from the cheer he was given afterward when he presented the famous trophy, emblematic of the British soccer championship, to Tom Parker, Arsenal captain, with a warm handshake and the remark, "I am glad you are keeping the cup in London after nine years."

James Scores First.

Arthur James scored the first goal for Arsenal after fifteen minutes of play and J. Lambert scaled Huddersfield's doom with a terrific shot into the net a few minutes before the close of the contest.

LONDON, April 26 (Canadian Press).—The line-up of today's English Cup final soccer match between the Arsenal and Huddersfield Town, played at Wembley Stadium, follows:

Arsenal (2).		Huddersfield (0).
Preedy	G.	Turner
Parker	R.B.	Goodall
Hapgood	L.B.	Spence
Naylor	R.H.	Baker
Seddon	C.H.	Wilson
John	L.H.	Campbell
Hulme	R.O.	Jackson
Jack	R.I.	R. Kelly
Lambert	C.	Davies
James	L.I.	Ray
Bastin	L.O.	Smith

Goals—Arsenal: James, Lambert.
Referee—J. Crew, Leicester.

Match Rebroadcast Here.

For the first time, one of England's outstanding sports events was brought to the ears of American listeners yesterday morning, when the National Broadcasting Company rebroadcast the cup final of the British Football Association, which was witnessed by more than 92,000 persons, including King George, in Wembley Stadium.

The reception of the play-by-play account of the game and the King's speech was very distinct. The commentator, who did not give his name, gave a fine description of the match. He spoke in the same rapid and enthusiastic manner, as Graham McNamee. His English accent and rugby football terms, such as "has it," "hurls it," "kills it" and "nooks it," were apparent and perhaps somewhat confusing to the American listener. As an American would say in describing a football touchdown, "O, boy, it's over," the English commentator exclaimed, "They are lashing it up the field. Obviously, it will be a goal. It is a goal, surely."

April 27, 1930

U. S. Soccer Team Beats Belgium by 3-0; 20,000 See World's Tourney in Montevideo

MONTEVIDEO, Uruguay, July 13 (AP).—The United States team, entered in the world's open soccer championship tournament, disposed of its first opponent, Belgium, 3 to 0, today.

Twenty thousand persons saw the game despite threatening weather. James Brown of New York and William Gonsalves of Fall River, Mass., were the outstanding stars for the Americans while the Belgian goalkeeper starred for the losers.

In the only other match today, France defeated Mexico, 4 to 1. Tomorrow, Peru will meet Rumania and Jugoslavia will play Brazil.

Hakoah Team Beaten, 3-1.

BUENOS AIRES, July 13 (AP).—The New York Hakoah soccer team was defeated, 3 to 1, today by a picked Argentine aggregation.

July 14, 1930

Argentina Beats France, 1-0, In World's Title Soccer

BUENOS AIRES, July 15 (AP).—Argentina defeated France, 1-0, in the only match in the world's soccer championship tournament today. Monti's free kick after 36 minutes of play in the second half accounted for the only score of the game.

The game was bitterly contested, with the spectators voicing their emotions without particular restraint. Cherro of the Argentine team, became so upset by the shouts and boos that he suffered a nervous collapse and had to be withdrawn.

Tomorrow only one game will be played, Mexico meeting Chile. The United States will play its second match on Thursday against Paraguay.

July 16, 1930

United States Soccer Team Turns Back Paraguay, 3 to 0, in International Play

By The Associated Press.

MONTEVIDEO, Uruguay, July 17 —The United States soccer team today scored its second victory in two starts in the international tournament, defeating Paraguay, 3 to 0. In the only other game of the day, Yugoslavia defeated Bolivia, 4 to 0.

The United States line-up comprised James Douglas, Kearny, N. J.; Alexander Wood, Detroit; George Moorhouse, Long Beach, N. Y.; Jimmy Gallagher, New York; Raphael Tracy, St. Louis; Andy Auld, Providence, R. I.; James Brown, New York; William Gonsalves and Bertrand Patenaude, Fall River, Mass.; Thomas Florie, Harrison, N. J., and Bart McGhee, Philadelphia.

The North Americans played with great confidence and in a business-like way. Their South American opponents exhibited considerable enthusiasm and spirit but could not solve the Yankee defense.

Florie scored the first goal for the United States after nine minutes of play. Five minutes later Gonsalves added another, and the half ended with the North American team on the long end of a 2-0 score.

The Paraguayans made a desperate effort to rally at the start of the second period, but were unsuccessful. Their opponents then assumed the attack and Patenaude added the final goal.

July 18, 1930

Argentina Defeats U. S. Team In World's Title Soccer, 6-1

MONTEVIDEO, Uruguay, July 26 (AP).—The United States soccer team was today eliminated by Argentina, 6 goals to 1, in the world's soccer championship tournament. The United States trailed by 1—0 at the half.

Argentina will meet next week the winner of tomorrow's Yugoslavia-Uruguay match in the final.

July 27, 1930

URUGUAY ANNEXES TITLE AT SOCCER

70,000 Spectators See Argentina Lose Contest for World Honors by 4-2.

By The Associated Press.

MONTEVIDEO, Uruguay, July 30.—Uruguay today won world supremacy in soccer football for the third time, defeating Argentina, 4 to 2, in the final of the international tournament after trailing, 1 to 2, at the end of the first half.

The Uruguayans, winners of the Olympic titles in 1924 and 1928, again proved their right to championship recognition by emerging victorious in this newly established competition in which thirteen teams representing countries of Europe and North, South and Central America have been competing since July 13.

A crowd of 70,000 excited spectators, mainly Uruguayans and Argentinians, saw the home team come from behind in an irresistible second-period attack that scored three goals and brought victory. Argentina, conqueror of the United States entry last week, was powerless to stem the tide.

July 31, 1930

90,000 See West Bromwich Win Soccer Cup; MacDonald Among Notables Who Brave Rain

By The Associated Press.

LONDON, April 25.—Before a crowd estimated at 90,000, West Bromwich defeated Birmingham by 2 goals to 1 today and won the historic English Football Association Cup.

The Duke of Gloucester, third son of King George, and Prime Minister MacDonald headed a company of distinguished persons who braved a downpour of rain. The Duke presented the cup and individual medals to the successful team at the conclusion of the match. It was the third time the West Bromwich Albion Club had won the English cup.

Near the Prime Minister sat Stanley Baldwin, chief of the Conservative party. One of the most excited of all the spectators was Chief Klingage, who rules 75,000 natives in Kenya. Philip Snowden, Chancellor of the Exchequer, left his sick room for the game. He sat with Arthur Henderson, the Foreign Minister.

The West Bromwich team, after an uncertain start, exhibited brilliant strategy. It scored first in the twentieth minute of the first half through its centre forward, W. G. Richardson.

Birmingham drew even in the seventeenth minute of the second half when Bradford, its scoring ace, registered a goal. Before the cheers had died away Richardson again galloped through and put Albion ahead again.

The last minute of the match produced one of the tensest situations in the annals of the cup games, as Birmingham fought to wipe out the slim deficit. A few seconds from the end it attempted a corner kick but it went awry.

The great, gray amphitheatre in the midst of which the rivals were to engage in their soccer tussle by noon was a babel of noise and a blaze of blues and whites. Thousands were armed with rattles and bells, which drowned out the organized community singing.

With the arrival of the band of the Welsh Guards amateur noisemakers were themselves drowned out in a flood of popular airs.

The band had just ranged in formation to play the national anthem when the Duke of Gloucester arrived. He had to face an army of photographers before he walked down and shook hands with members of the teams.

"God Save the King" was rendered in a burst of heavy rain and, to a round of cyclonic applause, the match started.

The line-up:

Birmingham		West Bromwich.
Hibbs	G.	Pearson
Liddell	R.B.	Shaw
Barkas	L.B.	Trentham
Cringan	R.H.	Magee
Morrall	C.H.	W. Richardson
Leslie	L.H.	Edwards
Briggs	O.R.	Glidden
Crosbie	I.R.	Carter
Bradford	C.	W. G. Richardson
Gregg	I.L.	Sandford
Curtis	O.L.	Wood

April 26, 1931

250,000 at Football Field, 55,000 See Buenos Aires Game

Special Cable to THE NEW YORK TIMES.

BUENOS AIRES, Nov. 20.—Two hundred and fifty thousand persons tried to get into the football field this afternoon to see the season's final championship game. Fifty-five thousand were admitted.

Three persons were wounded in a shooting and stone-throwing roughhouse with which the supporters of the losing team resented defeat.

BUENOS AIRES, Nov. 20 (AP).—River Plate won the Argentine professional soccer football championship today, defeating Independiente, 3-0.

Police twice were forced to fire over the heads of a crowd of 200,000 outside the field to keep order. Three persons were wounded by shots fired from among the crowd. Stones and bottles were thrown freely.

November 21, 1932

ARGENTINA ORDERS SOCCER SUPERVISION

Government to Police Grounds and Search Crowds to Avert Recurrence of Disorders.

BUENOS AIRES, April 15 (AP).—Federal supervision of professional soccer games in Buenos Aires to prevent disorders such as occurred last Sunday when spectators hurled missiles and fired shots at the players and even attempted to burn one stadium, will be imposed for the balance of the season, the government announced today.

Easter crowds at tomorrow's games, expected to reach 200,000, will be heavily policed and will be searched for arms and missiles before being allowed in the grounds. The Ministry of the Interior announced it would close indefinitely any stadia where the home clubs were found responsible for inciting outbreaks.

Similar curbs had to be adopted last season, but they had been suspended this year.

Most of the riots have resulted from the belief of partisan crowds that injuries to players on the field were unnecessary or deliberately inflicted.

Camilio Bonelli, of the River Plate team, is under $5,000 bail awaiting trial on a charge of assault and breaking the jaw of an opponent. Another River Plate player, Basilico, escaped prosecution when Delguidice of the Racing Club refused to prosecute after the police had arrested Basilico on a

charge of kicking the Racing Club player in the stomach. Delguidice said he believed the kick was accidental.

The new Federal restrictions affect eighteen teams in the major soccer league.

April 16, 1933

102,000 See Celtic Soccer Team Defeat Motherwell, 1–0, to Annex Scottish Cup

By The Canadian Press.

GLASGOW, Scotland, April 15.— More than 102,000 persons who didn't mind the rain saw the mighty Celtic team take the Scottish Football Association Cup today by defeating Motherwell, 1–0, in a battle of spotty soccer on a muddy field.

Celtic took the laurels for the fourteenth time on a freak play. The ball bounded off a Motherwell player right at the feet of Jack McGrory, Celtic's leading sniper, and McGrory lost no time in shooting it past the bewildered McClory in Motherwell's goal.

That was the only goal scored in the Scottish soccer classic, but in the play many seemingly sure shots

went amiss. Motherwell was considered unlucky in not getting at least a draw, but Celtic had the breaks and made the most of them.

Exactly 102,391 fans crowded into Hampden Park for the ultimate battle between the two teams. Two years ago they clashed in the final and the game was drawn, Celtic winning the replay. In league games this year they had broken even.

After the goal was scored, two minutes after the interval, Celtic definitely had the advantage, but was worried by occasional Motherwell sallies that threatened to tie the score.

April 16, 1933

93,000 IN LONDON SEE SOCCER FINAL

Duke of York in Vast Throng That Watches Everton Beat Manchester City, 3-0.

By The Associated Press.

LONDON, April 29.—Everton today defeated Manchester City, 3–0, in the final of the English Soccer Cup, blue-ribbon event of the season.

Wembley Stadium was filled to the last seat for the event, 93,000 persons being present.

It was the first championship for Everton since 1906. Manchester City last won the cup in 1904.

The pitch was heavy and a bit greasy after several days of rain, but a warm sun came out to make the green field and the packed stands a picturesque setting.

King George was unable to be present, but was represented by the Duke of York, who shook hands with the players and wished them luck before the start.

Manchester City played without the services of its star forward, F. Tilson, who was scratched from the line-up just before game time. He has been nursing an injured leg and his team felt he would be of less use than a fit inferior player.

Everton scored first after 40 minutes of play and just before half time, and then sent the ball winging into the goal twice during the final period.

Everton's attack and brilliant combination sallies kept the play in Manchester City territory most of the game. J. Stein, outside left, Dixie Dean and J. Dunn scored the three goals for the victors.

Since early morning excursion trains had been bringing soccer

fans from all over England, and at game time police estimated that no less than 200,000 persons were crowded in and around the big stadium. Many came from long distances with no hope of seeing the play, but merely to be close to the scene of action.

It was the fourth time in history that two Lancashire teams have competed for the cup in the final, and the Lancashire dialect was heard most often in the crowds.

The line-up:

EVERTON (3).		MANCHESTER (0).
Sagar	G.	Langford
Cook	R.B.	Cann
Crew II	L.B.	Dale
Britton	R.H.	Busby
White	C.H.	Cowan
Thomson	L.H.	Bray
Geldard	O.R.	Toseland
Dunn	I.R.	Marshall
Dean	C.	Herd
Johnson	I.L.	McMullan
Stein	O.L.	Brook

Goals: Stein, Dean, Dunn.

April 30, 1933

King and Queen Among 93,000 Who Watch Manchester City Win English Soccer Cup

By The Associated Press.

LONDON, April 28.—Before a capacity crowd of 93,000, which included King George, Queen Mary and Prime Minister Ramsay MacDonald, Manchester City today defeated Portsmouth, 2 to 1, in the final match of the English Football Association cup competition at Wembley Stadium. The receipts were $122,950.

S. Rutherford scored for Portsmouth after twenty-seven minutes of the first half, but Sammy Tilson, centre forward, booted the tying goal through fifteen minutes before the final whistle and then scored the winning goal just before the end.

After a foggy morning the sun shone at the start of the game, but before it was over lightning was flashing and the rumble of thunder joined with the roar of the mighty crowd inside and outside the stadium.

Since early morning 100 special trains had been pouring fans out at the stadium gates and every seat was filled long before starting time, with thousands more massed outside and unable to get in. There were 400,000 applications alone for the 93,000 available seats.

The King and Queen arrived half an hour before game time, which was 3 P.M. (Eastern standard time). His Majesty was accorded a great cheer as he walked on the field and shook hands with the players of both teams. He also presented the cup after the match.

The Australian cricket players, here for a test series with England, also were roundly cheered as they took their places in the stands.

It was the fourth cup final for

Manchester City and the second for Portsmouth. Manchester City won in 1904, but lost in 1926 and last year to Everton.

Both of Portsmouth's starts have been losing ones, to Bolton Wanderers in 1929 and today to Manchester City.

Twelve hundred special police were drafted under special instructions to track down the sellers of forged tickets to today's game. Thousands of these tickets were known to have been printed and circulated, and $10 to $15 was being asked by the sellers.

London during the morning was jammed with sight-seers wearing the rosettes of the rival clubs. The field at Wembley was in good shape, drying from rain during the week.

The tiers of seats were colorful with a crowd that included a large proportion of women. Manchester's maroon and white colors seemed to predominate, but there were plenty of bluejackets for Portsmouth, the Pompeys being big favorites in the naval station.

The crowd passed the time before the kick-off in community singing. The line-up:

Portsmouth—J. Gilfillan, goal; J. Mackie and W. Smith, backs; J. Nickol, J. Allen and Captain D. Thackeray, halfbacks; F. Worrall, J. Smith, Sam Weddle, J. Easson and S. Rutherford, forwards.

Manchester City—F. Swift, goal; L. R. Barnett and W. Dale, backs; M. Busby, Captain S. Cowan and J. Bray, halfbacks; E. K. Toseland, Bob Marshall, Sam Tilson, Alec Herd and Ernie Brook, forwards.

April 29, 1934

U. S. SOCCER TEAM BEATS MEXICO, 4-2

Mussolini Among Spectators at Game in World Title Tournament at Rome.

Wireless to THE NEW YORK TIMES.

ROME, May 24.—The United States team participating in the world's championship soccer tournament today defeated Mexico, 4 goals to 2, thus gaining the right to meet Italy next Sunday. A moderately large crowd watched the game and cheered both teams impartially.

Premier Mussolini, among those present, warmly congratulated United States Ambassador Long, who sat on his right, on the success of his countrymen.

The Mexican players appeared to be technically superior to the Americans, but they were all of much slighter build and were obliged to yield to the more vigorous game of their heavier opponents.

Game Is Keenly Contested.

Both sides played with great keenness, but in a very sporting spirit and the game was marred by only very few incidents worthy of note. The match was refereed not altogether satisfactorily by an Egyptian player, Yussuf Mohamed.

The American team began attacking immediately and was rewarded

after 15 minutes of play by a beautiful goal scored by its centre-forward, Florie. The Mexicans counter-attacked with great precision and equalized the score in the twenty-second minute with a goal by their centre-forward, Meija. Before the end of the first half Florie again scored to put the Americans ahead.

Mexican Player Banned.

The play at the beginning of the second half was very much more evenly balanced, especially after the referee expelled the Mexican right back, Camerena, for fouling the American left wing, MacLean.

In the twenty-third minute the American inside right, Nilsen, scored. Mexico replied immediately with another goal by Meija, but a few minutes before the end Florie made the game quite safe for the Americans, scoring his team's fourth goal.

May 25, 1934

ITALY SUBDUES U. S. IN SOCCER TOURNEY

Americans Eliminated From World's Title Event at Rome —Score Is 7-1.

MUSSOLINI SEES MATCH

Play Is Constantly in Losers' Territory—Argentina and Brazil Also Defeated.

ROME, May 27 (AP).—The United States all-star team was summarily removed from the world soccer championship today, thoroughly outplayed by Italy in a first-round match, 7—1.

Although play was constantly in American territory, the invaders held Italy scoreless for the first 18 minutes of the game but thereafter it was procession of Italian goals.

Italy led by 3—0 at half time and although Aldo (Buff) Donelli of Curry, Pa., netted the first goal in the second half to make the score 3—1, the Americans really had no chance against the fine team play of their rivals.

Hjulian Plays Well.

Schiavio and Orsi combined to score all Italy's goals, the former getting four and Orsi three. Only fine goal-tending by Julius Hjulian of Chicago kept the score as low as it was.

Schiavio began the scoring in 18:00 of the first half and Orsi followed with the second Italian goal three minutes later. Schiavio's tally in 29:00 ended the scoring for the first half, Italy thus leading by 3—0 at the intermission.

After Donelli had given the United States its lone tally in 12 minutes of the second half the Italians broke loose with another four-goal splurge to decide the issue definitely.

A crowd of 30,000, including Premier Mussolini, saw the match.

South Americans Lose.

Both South American entries in the championship likewise were eliminated, Argentina bowing to Sweden, 3—2, at Bologna, and Brazil to Spain, 3—1, at Genoa.

At Turin, Austria was carried to two extra periods before it could eliminate France, 3—2, while Germany was given a great tussle by Belgium before winning, 5—2, at Florence.

In other first-round games, Czechoslovakia defeated Rumania at Trieste, 2—1; Hungary conquered Egypt, 4—2, at Naples, and Switzerland won from Holland at Milan, 3—2.

The line-up of the American team: Goal, Hjulian, Chicago; right back, Czerkiewiz, Pawtucket; left back, Moorehouse, New York; right half, Pietras, Philadelphia; centre half, Gonsalves, St. Louis; left half, Florie, Pawtucket; right wing, Ryan, Philadelphia; inside right, Nilsen, St. Louis; centre forward, Donnelli, Curry, Pa.; inside left, Dick, Pawtucket; left wing, McLean, St. Louis.

May 28, 1934

ITALY GAINS FINAL BY UPSET IN SOCCER

Beats Austria, 1-0, in World's Title Tournament Before 45,000 in Milan.

CZECHOSLOVAKIA A WINNER

Conquers Germany by 3 to 1 and Qualifies for Next Sunday's Deciding Round.

By The Associated Press.

ROME, June 3.—Upsetting expert predictions, Italy and Czechoslovakia advanced to the final round of the world's soccer championship tournament today. Italy defeated Austria, 1—0, while Czechoslovakia conquered Germany, 3—1. The final will be played in Rome next Sunday.

Italy's victory over Austria, European champion, was achieved before a crowd of 45,000 in Milan. The arena was jammed many minutes before game time and thousands milled around outside vainly trying to get in.

The only score of the game came in the nineteenth minute of the first half. Schiavio booted accurately at the Austrian goal, but Platzer, whose goal-tending bordered on the miraculous all day, punched it out. As he did, Guaita ran in and his hard drive beat the Austrian goalie.

Austria Attacks Briskly.

Austria attacked desperately in the second half in an effort to gain the equalizer, but the Italian defense was entirely adequate. Combi played brilliantly in the Italian goal, although he did not have nearly as much work to do as Platzer.

Germany's downfall at the hands of Czechoslovakia at Rome was a distinct upset. The fury of the Czech attack caught the Germans by surprise and although they matched the first half Czech goal with one of their own seventeen minutes after the second half started, they could not stop the winners' closing rally.

Only about 5,000 spectators were in the stands when the game began and most of them were more interested in the returns from Milan.

Makes Sustained Drive.

Germany's only sustained drive came in the second half when Siffling took the ball on a corner pass and booted through a drive that Planicka could not touch. A minute later the Germans attempted to repeat, but Planicka fell on Lehner's drive and smothered it.

In the twenty-seventh minute Svoboda scored what proved to be the winning goal on a corner kick, and the result was definitely decided in the thirty-fifth minute, when Sobotka scored on a cross kick from Junek, driving home a liner which Kres was barely able to touch with his fingertips.

June 4, 1934

Italy Tops Czechoslovakia in Overtime By 2 to 1 and Takes World Soccer Title

By The Associated Press.

ROME, June 10.—Italy captured the world's soccer championship today, defeating Czechoslovakia, 2 to 1, after a furiously fought engagement which went two extra periods.

Schiavio, Italy's crack centre forward, scored the deciding goal in the fifth minute of the half-hour overtime session, split into two periods of 15 minutes each.

Sole survivors of the big field which started the championship tournament two weeks ago, Italy and Czechoslovakia found themselves well matched in the final.

After a scoreless first half, Puc, who played a brilliant game all day at left wing for the Czechs, tallied the first goal in 21 minutes of the second half. His hard shot from the extreme left angle had Combi, Italian goalie, beaten all the way.

Italy immediately came back with a surging attack that finally netted the tying goal in the thirty-seventh minute. Orsi's hard shot, also at a sharp angle, beat Planicka cleanly, and the crowd, strongly partisan, went wild.

Shortly after the extra period opened the Italians carried the ball down into Czech territory and Meazza passed to Schiavio, who kicked high but just beneath the goal-post past Planicka for the winning goal.

Following the game Premier Mussolini presented awards to the Italians and Czechoslovaks and also to the third-place German team.

June 11, 1934

Remarks Made by Ruth in London May Help Star English Athletes Get Salary Rise

By The Associated Press.

LONDON, March 2.—Babe Ruth, the man who did more than any other to make baseball salaries what they are today, has started a red-hot movement to improve the financial lot of England's professional athletes.

The Babe doesn't know it, but a few of his remarks during his recent visit here may prove the inspiration for a new and better deal for the soccer player and the cricketer. His visit and his remarks, at least, have awakened both public and players to a realization that $40 a week is not an enormous salary.

"Forty bucks a week top pay?" ejaculated the Babe. "What a racket that is. What's chances of me buying into one of those football or cricket clubs?"

While the assembled newspaper men were not too impressed with the Babe's diplomacy, they were forced to admit that he had hit the nail somewhere near the head. Ever since, as though it had just occurred to them, they have been suggesting in print that a man like Alex James, the "Babe Ruth of soccer," might be worth a trifle more than $40 every Saturday.

That, of course, is the maximum salary a player in the British Football Association may be paid, though some of them, like James, add anywhere from 20,000 to 30,000 to the size of the crowd every time they play.

A star cricketer who works at his job twelve months of the year can make around $3,000. The Babe's remarks might result in getting him a slight rise. Who knows?

March 3, 1935

BETTING POOLS HIT BY SOCCER LEAGUE

English Schedule Shuffled to Block Printing of Slips for Forecasts of Results.

MILLIONS TRY THEIR LUCK

Football Authorities Angered by Promoters' £20,000,000 Take Without Benefit to Game.

Special Cable to THE NEW YORK TIMES.

LONDON, Feb. 21.—Betting pools on the results of league soccer football matches on Saturdays which are known to have yielded £16,000 for a one-penny stake and to have attracted between £20,000,000 and £30,000,000 in the course of a year are to be suppressed if possible by the action of the football league management committee.

Football betting pools in which a proportion of the stakes go to those making the best forecasts of results and a proportion to the promoters are one of the most popular forms of gambling in Great Britain. Millions of school children, servants, housewives and others who have never seen a football pitch spend hours during the week poring over forms mailed by the promoters of football pools, calling for forecasts of the results from numbers of Saturday's eighty-eight league games in England, varied by selections of home or away wins or drawn games.

Resents Huge Profits.

The football league committee is not concerned with the morals of the case but is angered that promoters of pools all over the country are growing rich on the game of soccer without contributing to it or increasing attendance. As the promoters are dependent on the publication of league schedules of games early in the season, so that forms may be printed, the league commit-

tee decided today to reshuffle the schedules for the remainder of the season. Clubs in the future will not know against whom they are playing on Saturday until two days before the match, which will give the promoters of pools no time to print forms and to circulate them among clients.

It is known that more than 10,-000,000 persons contribute weekly to the pools. The promoters are to meet immediately to frame retaliatory measures.

Records show more than 10,000 persons, chiefly women, are regularly employed by the promoters in classifying results. The postoffices in Liverpool, Glasgow and Edinburgh, where some of the principal pool offices are located, have special staffs to deal with the extraordinary mail.

Occupies Five Warehouses.

One pool in Liverpool occupies five former shipping warehouses and runs its own printing works, using twenty tons of paper a week.

The pool promoters, unable to broadcast announcements of winning dividends in England after Saturday's matches, take over several Continental radio stations, which are virtually continuously engaged throughout Sunday afternoons broadcasting the pool results for English listeners.

In the face of tremendous public opposition to the soccer league's plan to kill the pools, the league tonight announced it was also contemplating the promotion of a bill in Parliament to declare the pools illegal. It is understood to be seeking the aid of churches and the government to achieve this. With millions in money involved in the short football season of thirty-two weeks, it is feared the results of the matches may be influenced by bribes to players.

Already tonight hostility to the league action is growing. The public, players' clubs and railways (the latter unable to arrange and advertise their hundreds of weekly football excursions at two days' notice) are communicating with the newspapers, protesting against what they describe as "the most dramatic war in the history of British sport"

The government's revenue from the pools is startling. It is officially stated that 80 per cent of its postal order revenue emanates from pool orders, to which must be added the cost of stamps. The Daily Mirror says the profits to pool promoters during the season amount to a total of £6,000,000 and their personal profit £2,000,000. One girl employe of a Liverpool firm, the Mirror says, handles £25,000 worth of postal orders daily.

February 22, 1936

CUT IN ATTENDANCE MARKS SOCCER PLAY

Half a Million Decrease in English League Attributed to Ban on Listings.

GLASGOW RANGERS SCORE

Defeat Aberdeen by 1-0 as Four 4th-Round Scottish Cup Tests Draw 100,000 Fans.

LONDON, March 7 (Canadian Press).—Half a million soccer fans who stayed away from the week-end fixtures are the newest argument against the English League's ban on advance listing of the games. Only 416,000 attended today's forty-four matches which would normally have drawn about 1,000,000. The card brought no upsets in the standings.

The heavy decrease in attendance will be advanced by critics of the league's action when they attend a special general meeting of the clubs at Manchester Monday. The delegates will investigate the whole question of the league's campaign against betting pools, and many clubs have announced their intention of pressing for restoration of the original fixture list.

Although held to a 3-3 draw by Everton, Sunderland retained an 8-point advantage over Huddersfield at the top of the First Division standing.

Present champions and cup-holders, the Glasgow Rangers are favored to capture the Scottish football cup competition for the tenth time. The famous Ibrox Park squad eliminated Aberdeen in the feature game of the fourth round of the series that saw two upsets.

Falkirk, Clyde and Third Lanark are the other teams to enter the semi-finals. Leader of the second division, Falkirk performed brilliantly at home to smash Dunfermline's hopes, 5-0, while Clyde provided the other upset, halting Motherwell by 3-2 at Shawfield Park. Third Lanark defeated Morton, 5-3.

Nearly 100,000 persons turned out for the four games, with Rangers again proving the drawing card when 41,000 spectators—a record at Pittodrie—jammed the enclosure to witness one of the best games of the season. The Dons lost, 1-0.

March 8, 1936

614,000 FANS SEE SOCCER FIXTURES

Increase of 200,000 Follows Lifting of Listings Ban by the English League.

60,000 AT LONDON GAME

Witness West Ham's 3-1 Victory Over Tottenham—Chelsea Wins for First Time Since Dec. 26.

LONDON, March 14 (Canadian Press).—Scoring its first league victory since Dec. 26, Chelsea provided the feature of today's football program that saw a great increase in crowds at all matches. As a result of the lifting of the ban on football listings by the English league, the forty-four games played drew a total of 614,000 spectators.

This represented an increase of nearly 200,000 over the previous week, when league authorities delayed announcement of fixtures in its efforts to stop football pool betting.

Chelsea's 3-2 victory at Bolton lifted the Pensioners out of the danger zone at the bottom of the league, temporarily at least. The leading Sunderland squad had its margin cut to seven points when a weakened Leeds United eleven drew 3-3 at Roker Park. Huddersfield went into second place over Derby County by defeating Liverpool, 1-0.

The second division match between Tottenham Hotspurs and West Ham United, two London clubs, attracted 60,000 persons, the largest crowd of the day, to White Hart Lane. A fast and exciting game saw the Hammers victorious, 3-1.

March 15, 1936

Scotland Takes International Soccer Title By 1-1 Tie With England as 90,000 Look On

By The Canadian Press.

LONDON, April 4.—Scotland added another cup to its soccer trophies today. Drawing 1—1 with England in a thrilling encounter at Wembley Stadium, as 90,000 persons looked on, the Scots won the international championship outright for the seventeenth time and became the first possessors of the trophy awarded by the Football Association in commemoration of the late King George's silver jubilee.

On nine other occasions Scotland has tied for the championship, and the draw was the fifteenth in which the two countries have participated since the series started in 1872. Twenty-seven games have resulted in victories for Scotland, while England has won eighteen times.

The two strong teams staged a brilliant and thrilling game and the deadlock was a fair representation of the play. The visitors might have won had their forwards displayed a scoring punch comparable to their skill in the field. England's attacks were fewer than its opponents, but the home booters had more chances in front of the goal.

The game was thirty-one minutes old when G. Camsell, Middlesbrough Centre forward, put the finishing touches to some fine combination by notching an easy goal. England led by this margin until twelve minutes from the end of the game, when Tommy Walker, Heart of Midlothian star, converted on a penalty against J. Barker, Derby County halfback.

D. McCulloch, Brentford, fell as he was about to shoot, the referee deciding he had been tripped by the English half. Many spectators held, however, that he stumbled and Barker was guilty of no offense.

C. S. Bastin, Arsenal inside forward, was the star of the game. The Gunner was a constant source of trouble to the Scottish defense and his combinations with E. F. Brook of Manchester City, on the left wing, were much appreciated by the crowd.

J. Crum, Celtic, and Walker were the best men on the visitors' vanguard. Playing in his first international match, Crum, who usually takes the inside position for the Glasgow team, enjoyed much success at outside right, delighting the Scottish selectors.

The visitors, with the exception of Alex Massie, Aston Villa, did not play up to expectations.

Injuries necessitated two changes on the English team and one on the Scottish. Hibbs, Birmingham's custodian, was replaced by Sagar of Everton in the English nets, while Barclay, Sheffield United, filled in for Bowden, Arsenal star, on the forward line.

McPhail, Rangers' veteran international, was another casualty and his place in the Scottish front line was taken by Venters, another Rangers player.

The line-ups:

ENGLAND

Goal, Sagar (Everton); backs, Male, Hapgood (Arsenal); halfbacks, Crayston (Arsenal), Barker (Derby County), Bray (Manchester City); forwards, Crooks (Derby County), Barclay (Sheffield United), Camsell (Middlesbrough), Bastin (Arsenal), Brook (Manchester City).

SCOTLAND

Goal, Dawson (Rangers); backs, Anderson (Hearts), Cummings (Aston Villa); halfbacks, Massie (Aston Villa), Simpson, Brown (Rangers); forwards, Crum (Celtic), Walker (Hearts), McCulloch (Brentford), Venters (Rangers), Duncan (Derby County).

FINAL STANDING OF TEAMS

	W.	L.	D.	Goals F.	A.	Pts.
Scotland	1	0	2	4	3	4
England	1	1	1	5	5	3
Wales	1	1	1	5	5	3
Ireland	1	2	0	5	7	2

April 5, 1936

SIXPENNY RIDES TO FORTUNE

Millions of Britons Are Trying Their Luck With Them Every Week in the Gambling Pools, and Parliament Is Told There Ought to Be a Law

By CLAIR PRICE

LONDON.

ABROAD rustling river of big and little money which The Economist estimates at "perhaps more than £500,000,000" pours into betting every year in Britain. Every few years some offshoot of that never-ending river bursts its banks and goes cascading in some new direction toward the pots of gold at the end of some new rainbow. Just now pool betting on professional football is Britain's newest method of winning £1,000 for sixpence. During the football season now closing a total of £30,000,000 is estimated to have poured into pool betting. Six million Britons, it is said, are seeking to endow their declining years by "investing" sixpence or a shilling every week in the pools.

Hence the unusual spectacle of the House of Commons turning aside from wars and rumors of wars, as it did recently, to debate football pools. A month or two ago the governing authorities of professional football fired their first shot in a war to kill the pools. About the same time the churchmen started a war of their own on pool betting, and the result has been the introduction into the Commons of a private member's bill abolishing pool betting except as already legalized in connection with race-track totalizators—machines which are in principle like the pari-mutuels in that they make the calculations according to which the money staked by backers of the horses is pooled and then shared by the backers of the winning horse. Under existing laws tote betting on "approved race tracks" is strictly supervised, but so far the law knows nothing of football pools.

• • •

IT might conceivably be said that Britain has always been one of the heaviest of the heavy betting countries and there is nothing new in British betting today, except some of the forms it takes—dog-racing,

for example, and football pools. This would be true enough as far as it goes, but it would overlook the immense increase in betting which "the dogs" and the pools have brought about. The man who bets up to £50 a week with a bookmaker still supplies the bulk of the betting turnover, but he has always been outnumbered by the little men who bet up to five or ten shillings a week, and these are now themselves outnumbered by the millions of Britons who flutter their shilling a week on football.

You can see some of them streaming out of the gates of any big factory at noon. They are the people who grab the early sporting editions of the evening papers and walk away to their dinners with their faces buried in racing tips and football "form." They all know somebody who has won a few shillings or a few pounds in return for "a penny in the pool." They know all the big prizes which the pools have paid, for there is a flourishing weekly press devoted to pool coupons and prizes. They know that one Liverpool promoter paid £16,000 for a penny on Jan. 18 last year. Another paid £3,405 for a penny on Jan. 9, 1935. Still another paid £628 for threepence on Dec. 22.

True, the mathematical chances against all-correct forecasts in some of the pools have been stated to be as high as 14,000,000 to 1. But that is neither here nor there. The great thing about this class of betting is that the "investment" is so small that any kind of "dividend" looks handsome. The result is that everybody who is dissatisfied with his lot tends to fix his eyes on the blue sky where the windfalls come from rather than on the good brown ground

© PUNCH.

Football pools are England's latest gambling issue—Neville Chamberlain is pictured as saying, "I almost wish I could throw a line here myself."

Betting at Epsom Downs.

beneath his feet. Because of the perpetual dazzle of money for nothing, a considerable part of the population seems to be getting a crick in the neck.

* * *

FOOTBALL pools are only the latest and greatest development in a steady growth of gambling which the existing laws, complicated as they are, have never succeeded in overtaking. As a whole, the laws tend to adhere to the old view that gambling is a luxury reserved for the rich, and this view seems to be responsible for the distinction which they draw between cash betting and credit betting.

Cash betting in Britain is legal only at race tracks, presumably because all race tracks used to be in the depths of the country and the man who treated himself to a day's racing had to be able to catch one of the morning race trains and take the whole day off. Credit betting has remained legal everywhere, presumably because only well-to-do men could afford to bet on credit.

This distinction is fundamental. It has not prevented betting among the poor. Far from it. But it has made the poor man's traditional bet—the little cash bet with the street bookmaker waiting outside his factory gate—illegal.

Ten years ago dog-racing came in and since then gambling has rapidly shot out of its legal clothes. About the dog tracks there has never been anything remote or rural. When they came in they came bang into the most crowded parts of the big towns. Being race tracks, they were entitled to their betting rings. The gambling laws may not have intended cash betting to be carried on openly in the big towns, but so it was.

The dog-tracks held their meetings under the blaze of the arcs at night when everybody could attend. Their oval stands were filled by men and women who had finished their day's work in factories and shops, and there seemed to be no legal reason why they should not run wide open every week-night the year around if they wanted to. At this point, however, Parliament sewed a few extra buttons on its gambling laws. The result has been to limit all the tracks in any one district to 104 nights a year.

* * *

THEN about eight years ago the totalizator came in and the gambling laws ripped again. It is beyond the wit of ordinary mortals to explain these peculiar laws, but their various idiosyncrasies may be noted as they become relevant. It is illegal in Britain to carry on betting at any "house" or "place" with "persons resorting thereto," and that is why British race-track bookmakers never put their signs on posts stuck in the ground. If they do they become a "place" and so are liable to arrest and conviction. It may perhaps be asked why the betting ring is not itself a "place." It can only be said that the Lords have decided otherwise.

But the tote is a machine much heavier than any bookmaker and much more difficult to move about. Undoubtedly it constituted a "place," and a large new patch was accordingly sewn into the gambling laws to cover it. Once the tote was legalized on "approved race tracks," tote clubs presently sprang up like mushrooms all over the towns. But the life of this particular racket was not a long one. The gambling laws neither burst a button nor

ripped. They held firm, and the tote clubs went out as suddenly as they had come in.

* * *

POOLS on professional football may have been running for twenty or thirty years, but their real chance did not come until the tote clubs went out and the Betting Bill of 1934 came in. In this bill the Mother of Parliaments put a few more stitches into her well-patched gambling laws.

When she first drafted the bill she intended to abolish all pool betting except at race-track totes, for these are run under strict supervision. They deduct their legal 10 per cent of the pool and pay out the rest. No other pools are subject to compulsory supervision nor is there any legal limit on their deductions.

But the men who played the football pools bombarded their M. P.'s with sackfuls of frantic mail and so seem to have frightened Parliament out of its original intentions. Pool betting off the track was taken out of the bill and left to the existing laws, which legalize betting on credit everywhere. This is the basis on which the football pools are run. You bet on credit. You mail your forecast of next Saturday's games this week and your shilling next week. If you mailed them both in the same envelope you would be guilty of cash betting and your bet would be illegal.

Since 1934 the popularity of the

pools has spread like a prairie fire. Pennies, sixpences and shillings pour into the pools to an amount reputed to be £700,000 a week. As all bets are transmitted by mail, the postage and the charge for postal orders are said to be worth £4,000,000 a season to the post-office. Most of the big promoters run six-shilling-a-unit pools and a penny pool. All are weekly pools decided by forecasting the results of various selections of the Saturday games. The amount of the penny pool in a single office has been known to run as high as £31,-000—more than 7,000,000 pennies.

* * *

IN such fantastic finance nobody seems to care how the pools are run. All the promoters say their pools are "audited by a firm of chartered accountants." Some of them say they deduct 5 per cent as their profit, but say nothing of the percentages they deduct for expenses. Others guarantee to return 80 per cent of the pool in dividends. As long as there is no outside supervision there is no means of knowing what they take.

Most of the big offices are in Liverpool, where football betting has become one of the city's biggest industries. A total of twenty-eight pools now employ more than 20,000 people in Liverpool alone. The biggest of them began eight or nine years ago with six employes and has grown so rapidly that today it occupies five warehouses. Its printing department is said to consume twenty tons of paper a week. Every week it is said to mail an average of 300,000 postal orders as dividends and more than 5,000,000 coupons bearing selections of next week's games to be forecast.

On busy days the red postoffice vans draw up at its doors at the rate of three or four an hour, for such an office receives well over 1,000,000 coupons a week, and practically all of them come in on Friday and Saturday. They pour from the mail sacks in a broad white waterfall of envelopes. Machines open them by cutting a thin strip off the top of each envelope. Belt conveyors take them up to the sorting floor. More conveyors take the coupons up to higher floors, where hundreds of girls sit in long rows, recording bets with adding machines and checking and filing the coupons.

Opposition to the pools first became public early in February when a deputation of churchmen requested Sir John Simon, the Home Secretary, to introduce "legislation abolishing all betting on the pool or pari-mutuel principle except as provided for by the Racecourse Betting Act of 1928 and the Betting and Lotteries Act of 1934"—in other words, to carry out the original intention of the 1934 bill to restrict pool betting to the supervised totes on "approved race tracks." This is the aim of the Russell bill which has now been introduced in the House of Commons.

Meanwhile the football league has opened its war on the pools with a resounding first shot. With no preliminary warning the league a few weeks ago scrapped its entire remaining schedule of games and substituted a rearranged schedule which was to remain secret until Thursday morning of each week, when only the games for the following Saturday were to be announced.

Because the pool promoters have to mail their coupons a week in advance, the withholding of the games until two days in advance threatened to kill the existing type of coupon, but the expectation was that the promoters would have little difficulty in devising some new type. Both within and outside football circles there was an expectation that sooner or later Parliament would have to pass some new bill either to abolish or to control the pools.

April 12, 1936

93,000 SEE ARSENAL TAKE ENGLISH CUP

Pay $125,000 to Witness 1-0 Triumph of Gunners Over Sheffield United.

DRAKE SCORES ONLY GOAL

Tallies After 74 Minutes' Play in Spirited Soccer Final at Wembley Stadium.

LONDON, April 25 (Canadian Press).—The extra touch of finesse that so often marks the difference between first and second-division English football league teams gave Arsenal supporters plenty to enthuse over today.

In the English cup final at Wembley Stadium, the Gunners' cleverness and experience finally told in a rousing battle with Sheffield United, plucky and youthful second-division squad, and the Londoners scored the only goal of the game to win the trophy for the second time.

Ends Northern Hopes

Ted Drake, idol of London crowds, netted the winning goal after 74 minutes' play. The counter sent most of the huge crowd of 93,000 wild with delight, but it was the death-knell for the hopes of an excited and large contingent from Sheffield and the North of England.

For the whole of the first half and part of the second the Yorkshire players had fought a spirited battle, but the Gunners were not to be denied once they had assumed control of the game.

Cup final day, always an event for the English sporting world, saw thousands brought to London from all parts of England. The various railways operated 130 special trains and large crowds came by motor car and airplane. Receipts at the stadium amounted to nearly $125,000.

Notables in Stands

Members of the royal family were absent on account of the court being in mourning for the late King George, but there were a large number of notables in the stands, including the Indian cricketers who arrived a few days ago for a tour of the British Isles.

After the match Sir Charles Clegg, president of the Football Association, presented the cup and medals to the winning team.

The line-up:
. ARSENAL—Goal, Wilson; backs, Male, Hapgood; halfbacks, Grayston, Roberts, Copping; forwards, Hulme, Bowden, Drake, James, Bastin.
SHEFFIELD UNITED — Goal, Smith; backs, Hooper, Wilkinson; halfbacks, Jackson, Johnson, McPherson; forwards, Barton, Barclay, Dodds, Pickering, Wilson.

April 26, 1936

FUROR OVER REICH DEFEAT

Gloom in Press Follows Shock From Norway's Soccer Victory.

BERLIN, Aug. 8 (P).—Gloom pervaded the German morning papers today over the event in the Post Stadium yesterday where, in the presence of Chancellor Hitler, Germany's soccer eleven lost to Norway, 2—0.

"How could it ever happen?" the sports press cries bewildered. Germany's hopes actually centered on winning the gold medal in this event. With the crack Uruguayan team out of the competition, they figured themselves the Olympics' best. Norway, on the other hand, was figured as a minor contender.

So sure was Germany of victory that Hitler for the first time failed to appear in the Olympic Stadium. All German victors until now have told the German press in interviews that they think only of the Fuehrer when competing and outdo themselves when he's there to watch them.

August 9, 1936

Peruvians Leaving Berlin Today As Protest on Football Decision

All Members of Nation's Olympic Squad Ordered to Depart for Paris—Colombians Join Exodus in Demonstration of Latin-American Solidarity—Chileans Mark Time.

Wireless to THE NEW YORK TIMES.

BERLIN, Aug. 11.—The Peruvian Olympic soccer team, which has withdrawn from the games because the football authorities decided it should replay its match with Austria, is leaving tomorrow morning for Paris.

The Colombian team also is going in response to an appeal from the Peruvians for a show of Latin-American solidarity. The head of the Peruvian delegation to the games claims the Peruvian Minister here has received a message from the Lima government fully approving its stand and the decision to leave Berlin and urging the athletes to depart as soon as possible.

Teams Fail to Compete

The whole Peruvian representation is being withdrawn, although the dispute is confined to football. The Peruvian swimmers were scheduled to compete today and the Peruvian basketball team had an appointment on the Olympic courts, but neither appeared. All of the Peruvians ceased training and devoted themselves today to packing up their effects.

There is considerable indecision in the Chilean camp. Chilean sportsmen would like to show their friendship for their Latin-American neighbors by leaving, but they have not yet made up their minds and have received no orders from home. The Chilean Olympic Committee has been asked for advice, but has not yet reached a decision.

It will be recalled that a crowd of Peruvian enthusiasts was charged with breaking up the football game between Peru and Austria on Saturday and even with attacking some of the Austrian players. The fact is that this alleged breach of the rules is still in dispute. The Peruvians hotly question the version of the affair accepted by the International Football Federation.

The German press stresses in prominently headlined reports today that Germany is in no way responsible for the decision taken by the Football Federation, which is an international body, and that the anti-German demonstrations in Lima consequently are way off the track.

August 12, 1936

100,000 SEE ITALY TAKE SOCCER TITLE

Beats Austria in Olympics by 2-1 in Overtime—Both Victors' Goals by Frossi.

BERLIN, Aug. 15 (P).—A capacity crowd of 100,000 packed the main Olympic Stadium today to see Italy capture the Olympic soccer championship in a bitterly contested final-round battle with Austria, 2—1.

Annibale Frossi, Italy's right wing, scored the first Italian goal late in the second period and then counted the deciding tally in the first minute of the extra session after Karl Kainberger, Austria's inside left, had tied the score two minutes before the end of regulation time.

With Italy taking the gold medal, Austria won the silver and Norway the bronze.

August 16, 1936

SUNDERLAND WINS SOCCER FINAL, 3-1

LONDON, May 1 (Canadian Press).—A football quest that started fifty-seven years ago ended today when Sunderland won the English Cup. Before a crowd officially recorded as 93,495 at Wembley Stadium, the North of England team emerged victorious for the first time in its long history, taking a 3-1 decision from Preston North End.

In many ways the final for soccer's blue ribbon was a memorable event. The King and Queen, accompanied by King Farouk of Egypt, watched the thrilling tussle from the royal box, surrounded by a brilliant assembly of empire notables, including many Indian Princes. The British Government was represented by Right Hon. Ramsay MacDonald, Sir John Simon and Sir Philip Sassoon. The occasion marked their Majesties' last public appearance before the coronation, their arrival at the huge bowl being the signal for a great outburst of cheering. Undaunted by a busmen's strike, the huge crowd made its way to Wembley, all kinds of vehicles being pressed into service.

146 Special Trains Operated

While thousands came to London in motor conveyances, it was estimated the railways poured approximately 70,000 excursionists into the capital from all over England, the majority from the counties of Lancashire and Durham, home shires of the contending teams. To accommodate the visiting crowds, railways operated 146 special trains. Sunderland deserved to win. Class eventually told, but there was little difference between the finalists until the second half, although Preston finished the opening forty-five minutes with a 1-0 lead. The game was fought at a terrific pace, Sunderland's robustness proving the deciding factor.

Ragged play featured the opening exchanges after Preston won the toss and elected to play with wind but faced by a strong sun. Although bottled up most of the game by Johnston, Sunderland's center half, Frank O'Donnell, Preston leader, gave a flash on his real form to give the Lancastrians the lead after thirty-seven minutes.

After the cross-over Burbanks, Sunderland's outside left, paved the way for Gurney, in the center, to equalize. Midway through the period Sunderland ran in two counters in rapid succession to make victory certain. Gurney sent a pass to Carter, International inside-right, who made no mistake. Five minutes later the fast-traveling left-winger Burbanks sent the ball into the net for a third goal.

Presents Famous Cup

Following the game the teams lined up in front of the royal box, where the Queen presented the famous cup to Carter.

Final English League games saw Manchester United and Sheffield Wednesday relegated to second division status. Leicester City finished ahead of Blackpool for the second division honors but both teams will play in the major league next year.

The championship of the league went to Manchester City last week, the squad achieving the honor for the first time in history. Charlton Athletic, with fifty-four points, finished as runner-up three points behind the Mancunians and two ahead of Arsenal.

Goal-scoring honors go to third division players. J. Payne, Luton Town center-forward, netted fifty-five goals for the southern section champion, and E. Harston bagged a similar number for Mansfield Town in the northern circuit.

The line-up in cup game:

PRESTON NORTH END—Goal: Burns. Backs: Gallimore, Beattie. Halfbacks: Shankley, Tremelling, Milne. Forwards: Dougal, Beresford, F. O'Donnell, Fagan, H. O'Donnell.

SUNDERLAND—Goal: Mapson. Backs: Gorman, Hall. Halfbacks: Thomson, Johnston, McNabb. Forwards: Duns, Carter, Gurney, Gallagher, Burbanks.

May 2, 1937

AUSTRO-ITALIAN GAME IS AGAIN A BATTLE

Genoa Team Greeted by Howls at Vienna—Blood Flows When Score Is Tied

Wireless to THE NEW YORK TIMES.

VIENNA, July 4.—Once more the dislike of Italy among large sections of the population was demonstrated on the Vienna football field this afternoon, when violent fighting and kicking wound up the Central European Soccer Cup match in the Stadium between the Genoa team and the Austrian Admira eleven.

The Italians entered the field with the Fascist salute, which had the effect of a red rag on a Red bull for the still largely Socialist crowds of Vienna. The visitors were greeted with howls of "Away with the cat-eaters!" a term of contempt here for Italians.

There was no violence, however, until just before the close of play, when Vienna tied the score through conversion of a penalty against the Italians.

A young Austrian player, Schall, made the goal, and celebrated it by turning around and thumbing his nose at the opponents. At once an Italian player, Andreola, hit him in the face with his fist.

This was the signal for a free-for-all between the two teams. Austrians and Italians kicked each other. Several were knocked down, trampled on and more or less badly hurt.

Although the spectators roared defiance at the Italians, strong police cordons, in readiness for such an emergency, managed to keep them from joining the fight.

After the fighters had been separated the referee got another two minutes of play without further violence.

July 5, 1937

Mussolini Expels Austrian Soccer Team; Vienna, Match Banned, to Protest to Rome

Wireless to THE NEW YORK TIMES.

VIENNA, July 11.—A diplomatic protest will be made to Italy concerning the expulsion of an Austrian soccer team from that country, this correspondent learns.

The incident is a sequel to the free-for-all fight last Sunday in the Vienna Stadium between the Austrian Admira team and the Genoa eleven, which were competing for the Central European Cup. Four Italians were severely hurt.

The match, which ended in a tie, was to have been replayed in Genoa today, and the Admira team left Vienna Thursday, but Friday it was learned that the Italian soccer authorities refused to allow the match to take place.

The Admira players returned to Vienna tonight, announcing that they had been expelled from Italy by order of Premier Benito Mussolini.

"We telegraphed Il Duce yesterday," a member of the team declared, "to ask him to intervene with the Italian football authorities and allow the match to occur.

Mussolini's reply was to order us to leave Italy within twenty-four hours. We wished to stay on in Venice to appeal to the committee of the Central European Cup contests, which is meeting tomorrow."

Dr. Geroe, the president of the Vienna Football Association, left tonight for Venice to enter an energetic protest at the meeting. One representative each of Italy, Austria, Czechoslovakia and Switzerland constitute the committee under a Hungarian president.

Baron Hornbostel, permanent head of the Austrian Foreign Office, tonight telephoned the Italian Minister of the Interior to ask for an explanation of the expulsion. He also spoke with Francesco Salata, the Italian Minister to Austria.

The Austrian Minister in Rome, Egon Berger-Waldenegg, has been instructed to make representations to the Italian Government.

A fight among the players, carried on to the accompaniment of shouts of defiance from spectators who were held in check by strong police cordons, marked the closing moments of play in the European Soccer Cup match between the Genoa team and the Austrian Admira team at Vienna July 4, according to cabled dispatches.

The free-for-all began after a young Austrian player, who had tied the score by conversion of a penalty, thumbed his nose at his opponents, and was knocked down by one of the Italian players.

July 12, 1937

FOOTBALL SEEN BY TELEVISION

British Find the Gridiron Eminently Televisable

WITH three electric cameras trained on the field, the British Broadcasting Corporation recently attempted to televise twenty-two football players in action at Arsenal Stadium during rehearsal.

The test was not successful because of darkening skies of an approaching rainstorm, which dulled the television scene, although earlier experiments were rated "very promising."

The Football League does not sanction televising the actual games because it is argued that attendance might be reduced.

More Cameras Are Needed.

"On the whole, the promise of the demonstration is high," reports "The Listener" of the British Broadcasting Corporation. "It seems clear that football, like lawn tennis, is to become an eminently televisable game.

"The figures and actions of the players stood out clearly on the screen, and the ball, being bigger than a tennis ball, can be seen more clearly when it is within reasonable distance of the camera.

"It seems likely, however, that successful television of football matches will call for a far greater number of cameras, disposed at key positions around the grounds, than are necessary for tennis. It should be remembered also that football, being an Autumn game, cannot expect such satisfactory conditions of light as are obtainable during the Summer."

October 3, 1937

93,000 AT LONDON SEE PRESTON SCORE

LONDON, April 30 (Canadian Press).—The English Football Cup rests in Preston North End's clubrooms today after a lapse of forty-nine years. The famous Lancashire team, one of the originals of the football league, won the trophy for the second time today, vanquishing Huddersfield Town, 1—0, in the most exciting finish to a cup final ever seen at Wembley Stadium.

George Mutch, clever Preston forward, scored the match-winning goal from a penalty in the last minute of a game that went 119 minutes without a score. The two first division teams played through the regulation ninety minutes, displaying a brand of soccer that at no time appeared likely to produce goals.

With excitement at high pitch the players fought desperately to break the deadlock in overtime and it was a bad mistake by Young, Suddersfield center-half and captain, that led to Preston's victory.

King Presents Trophy

When Mutch seemed set to score, Young charged him illegally and Referee A. J. Jewell pointed to the penalty spot with hardly a protest from the Huddersfield players. Mutch took the kick and sent a high shot into the net that scraped the crossbar in its flight.

Ninety-three thousand persons, including the King and Queen, saw Preston avenge the 1-0 victory scored by Huddersfield in the 1922 final.

Following the match His Majesty presented the cup to the Preston team while the Queen gave cup medals to the members of each team. The ceremony was televized for the first time.

It was estimated 50,000 visitors came to London by more than 100 special trains for the annual classic. Fully 20,000 were from the rival counties of Lancashire and Yorkshire.

Triumph First Since 1889

It was the fifth appearance in a cup final for each side. When the Lancastrians last won the trophy in 1889 they were also returned league champions and they have an outside chance to repeat the feat this year. Last season they reached the final only to be defeated, 3—1, by Sunderland.

Gaining a point on the Wolverhampton Wanderers in the English League, Arsenal contiuued at the top in the standing. The Gunners, at home, defeated Liverpool by 1—0 and the Wolves were held to a 1-1 draw at Molyneux Park against Chelsea. Arsenal now has 50 points, Wolverhampton one less.

The line-up in the cup game:
PRESTON NORTH END—Goal, Holdcroft; backs, Gallimore, A. Beattie; halfbacks, Shankly, Smith, Batey; forwards, Watmough, Mutch, Maxwell, R. Beattie, O'Donnell.
HUDDERSFIELD TOWN—Goal, Hesford; backs, Craig, Mountford; halfbacks, Willingham, Young, Boot; forwards, Hulme, Isaac, MacFadyen, Barclay, Beasley.

May 1, 1938

ITALY TAKES SOCCER CUP

Downs Hungary, 4-2, in Final at Paris—Brazil Wins

PARIS, June 19 (AP).—Italy won the World Cup soccer championship today, defeating Hungary, 4 to 2, in the final match before a great crowd. Italy was the defending champion.

In a play-off for third place, Brazil beat Sweden, 4 to 2, at Bordeaux.

June 20, 1938

King and Queen Among 100,870 at Wembley As Portsmouth Takes English Soccer Cup

By The Canadian Press.

LONDON, April 29.—Outclassing the famous Wolverhampton Wanderers before 100,870, at Wembley Stadium today, Portsmouth triumphed by 4—1 to capture the English Cup for the first time in the club's history. The King and Queen and Ambassador Joseph P. Kennedy of the United States were among the spectators.

Seldom, if ever, has any team played better football on the big Wembley field. Surviving a trace of nervousness in the opening 10 minutes, the Fratton Park eleven developed an attack that carried all before it and led 2—0 at halftime.

The young Wolves, regarded as the most improved team in England this year, at no time flashed the form that carried them to the runner-up position in the major league table.

Showery weather prevailed but the dampness had no effect on the spirits of the huge crowd drawn to London from all parts of the country.

In high good humor the spectators, led by three military bands, sang while they waited for the game to start and cheered mightily on the arrival of the King and Queen who were accompanied by the Earl of Harewood and Lord Halifax, the Foreign Secretary.

Before the start the vast gathering swung to attention while the national anthem was sung, the King then shaking hands with the twenty-two players. Later His Majesty presented the cup to the winning players and the Queen presented the cup medals.

Thirty-two minutes had elapsed when R. Barlow, ironically enough a former Wolverhampton player, crashed the netting for Portsmouth's first goal. From then on the issue was never in doubt and J. Anderson made it 2—0 a moment before the whistle stopped play at halftime.

Scores for 3-0 Lead

After a minute's play in the second half C. Parker put his side 3 up. A few minutes later T. Dorsett netted the Wolves' only goal in one of his team's rare raids. The last goal of the game went to Parker's credit.

Although the Wanderers were the strongest favorites in years, Portsmouth's victory was the biggest since Bury routed Derby County, 6—0, in 1903. The Southerners appeared twice before in cup finals being beaten each time. Wolverhampton, playing in its sixth final, won the cup in 1893 and again in 1908.

The teams:
PORTSMOUTH—Goal: Walker. Backs: Morgan, Rochford. Halfbacks: Guthrie, Rowe, Wharton. Forwards: Worrall, McAlinden, Anderson, Barlow, Parker.
WOLVERHAMPTON WANDERERS—Goal: Scott. Backs: Morris, Taylor. Halfbacks: Galley, Cullis, Gardiner. Forwards: Burton, McIntosh, Westcott, Dorsett, Maguire.

April 30, 1939

WEST HAM UNITED WINS SOCCER CUP

Beats Blackburn Rovers, 1-0, in English Wartime Final Before 45,000

LONDON, June 8 (Canadian Press)—West Ham United won the English Football League's War Cup this evening, defeating the Blackburn Rovers by 1—0 in the final at Wembley Stadium. The Hammers scored in the first half.

Forty-five thousand saw S. J. Small whip the ball into the net following smart play in which Goalkeeper Barron saved a drive from J. Foreman.

At the conclusion of the game the Right Hon. A. V. Alexander, First Lord of the Admiralty, presented the wartime trophy to C. Bicknell, captain of the winning East London team.

West Ham lined up with Conway, goal; Bicknell, C. Walker, backs; Fenton, R. Walker, Cockcroft, halfbacks, and Small, Macaulay, Foreman, Goulden, Foxall, forwards. Blackburn had Barron at goal;

Crook, Hough, backs; Chivers, Pryde, Whiteside, halfbacks; Guest, Clarke, Weddle, Butt, Rogers, forwards.

The contest brought to a close England's soccer campaign. A few afternoon matches were played in various regional groups.

Oldham Athletic surprised Blackpool in the Northwest section, winning by 4—2; Grimsby Town gained a 4-3 victory over Notts Forest in an East Midland tussle. In South D Bournemouth beat Aldershot, 2—1; Brighton blanked Clapton Orient, 3—0, and Southend United and Watford drew, 2—2.

Everton took the Lancashire Cup, defeating Bury, 4—2, in the final on the latter's ground.

June 9, 1940

Atlanta's player-coach Phil Woosnam (#17) watches Miami's Novak Tomic put his head to the ball in a 1967 game. Woosnam later became head of the North American Soccer League.

SOCCER ALL-STARS TRIUMPH IN GARDEN

Subdue Scots Americans, 3-2, After St. Mary's Celtic Downs Hispano, 4-1

TWIN BILL DRAWS 9,000

Surface of Sand Ends Problem of Injuries—Free-For-All Enlivens First Game

Indoor soccer, tried as an experiment and found wanting because of dangerous playing conditions several months ago, was brought back to Madison Square Garden last night, and to a crowd of 9,000 persons the change in the surface from a cement floor to smoothly rolled sand appeared to be just right and evoked much favorable comment.

Unlike last February, when spills and slides slowed the action and a number of players were injured, the double-header staged last night produced fast and interesting competition throughout. There was a rousing free-for-all in the opener between St. Mary's Celtic and Brooklyn Hispano, but there was enough action and excitement without the fight, which lasted about one minute.

A three-goal attack in the opening half brought Celtic a 4-1 triumph over Hispano, and in the afterpiece the Scots Americans of Kearney, N. J., for five years champions of the American Soccer League, lost to an all-star combination made up of players from the New York Americans and Brookhattan by a 3-2 count.

League Plan Is Cheered

Judging by the enthusiasm of the crowd, the indoor version of the old game of soccer has an excellent chance of being successful. Plans are being discussed for the formation of an intercity league and when this fact was made public over the loud speaker the announcement was greeted with cheers.

Indoor soccer differs from the outdoor game in that the pitch is only 230 feet long and 110 feet wide. The goals are seven feet high and twelve feet wide. Instead of eleven men, each side is limited to seven and there is less whistle blowing.

Of last night's games the second was the faster and more interesting, though there was nothing slow about the first. Some spectacular goal-tending by Bob Yingling of the Scots Americans and Stan Chesney of the All-Stars kept the first half of the second encounter scoreless. Alex Rae tallied for the Scots, but the goal was disallowed because one of his mates was in the net.

Fisher Puts Scots Ahead

Early in the second period the Scots staged a flurry in front of the All-Star goal, winding up with Frank Fisher scoring on a pass from Rae.

Within two minutes the All-Stars evened the count on a fluke when John Bassett of the New Jerseyites accidentally kicked the ball past his own goalie. George Stamatis, the last All-Star to touch the ball, was credited with the point.

Rae converted a perfect pass from Russell Brown, ten minutes before the final whistle, but this was followed by a marker by Joe Boyle on a pass from Stamatis. With five minutes remaining Boyle scored again, this time on a pass from Rudy Kuntner.

In the first engagement Eddie Ostrowski and Duke Nanoski each tallied twice for Celtic, while John Rodriguez averted a shut out for Hispano.

The line-ups:

CELTIC (4)	HISPANO (1)
Smith ....G............ Jusse
Brandolini ........F.B........ Compton
Weir ..........R.H.......... Anderson
McGuire ........L.H.......... Skiba
Laverty ........O.R.......... Aitken
Naneski ....C.......... Salcedo
Ostrowski ......O.L........ San Anton

Goals—Ostrowski 2, Nanoski 2, Rodriguez. Substitutes—Celtic: Lloyd, O'Neill, Stark, Black, Martinelli. Hispano: Rodrigues, Fernandez, Reavie, Gianotti, Othen, Ruddy, Altemose, Boulos.
Officials—Triano and Donahue. Time of halves—25 minutes.

ALL-STARS (3)	SCOTS AMER. (2)
Chesney ....G........ Yingling
Sternberg ........F.B...... Wolstencroft
Briscoe ........R.F........ Shields
Eisrer ........L.H........ R. Aitken
Stamatis ........O.R........ Brown
Lawrence ....C.......... Rae
Boyle ..........O.L.......... Conn

Goals—Fisher, Stamatis, Rae, Boyle 2. Substitutes—All-Stars: Bryndza, Currie, Jennette, Greinert, Barr, Brady, Kuntner, Herman, De Rostaing. Scots-Americans: Bassett, Fisher, Wojciechowicz, Cooper, S. Aitken, Peters, Dente.
Officials—Triano and Donahue. Time of halves—25 minutes.

May 7, 1941

BRENTFORD TAKES LONDON WAR CUP

Smith's Two Goals Turn Back Portsmouth in Final, 2-0, Before 75,000 Fans

WOLVERHAMPTON WINS, 4-1

Tops Sunderland for Football League Cup—Circuit Title to Manchester United

---

LONDON, May 30 (Canadian Press)—Brentford and Wolverhampton gained England's major wartime soccer trophies today as the season's largest crowds turned out for the finals of the cup competitions.

Brentford took advantage of every break to beat Portsmouth, 2-0, to take the London war cup before a crowd of 75,000 at Wembley. The Portsmouth booters had the better of the play from start to finish, but a defensive lapse put them a goal behind in the first half, and Brentford fought off every attack, winning on a pair of goals by Smith, the International left-winger.

Wolverhampton, held to a 2-2 draw by Sunderland last week in the first game of the football league cup final, scored an easy 4-1 victory. More than 45,000 spectators watched the replay.

The cup finals marked the close of major football in England for this season.

Manchester United got the football league championship although the team finished 4 points behind Blackpool in the final standings. Because of wartime conditions all teams are not able to play the same number of games, so a complicated "bonus" system decided things.

Blackpool had some consolation, however, in a 7-1 victory over Blackburn to annex the Lancashire cup.

May 31, 1942

Observation of European soccer players, like the Norwegian fliers in camp in Toronto, again illustrates that Europeans use different methods from those of American players.

The boys from overseas are so careful to be sure to get a good kick near the goal post that they seem to lose many chances for an easy kick.

The American method is to get near the goal posts and then bang away. Compared to the players of other countries, American soccer players work too hard for a goal.

That is apparently in keeping with American psychology—to work excessively in order to be sure to achieve victory. CARL PETERSON.
Chicago, June 14, 1942.

June 20, 1942

Largest British Wartime Crowd of 90,000 Sees England Rally to Beat Scotland, 6-2

By The Canadian Press.

LONDON, Oct. 14—Britain's greatest wartime sports crowd—90,000—watched a crack England team score six times in the second half to beat Scotland, 6—2, in a thrill-packed international match at the Wembley Stadium this afternoon.

Scotland led 1—0 at half time, but its defense wilted under terrific pressure in the second half.

The mass gathering, the largest allowed by security officials since the first air-raid sirens wailed more than four years ago, included one King (Haakon of Norway), six Cabinet Ministers, scores of foreign diplomats and many Allied service chiefs.

Everton's Tom Lawton played one of his greatest internationals and scored three goals while leading the English team. Len Goulden of West Ham United, silver-haired Horatio Carter of Sunderland and Les Smith of Brentford each scored once.

Scotland took the lead within three minutes of the opening whistle. Art Mille, Hibernian forward, drove into the net from close quarters. From then until the end of the first half, Scotland gave its best exhibition of the war, keeping England at bay with clever defense work.

Scotland's other goal was scored by its star, International Tommy Walker, and came in the seventieth minute following a center from 21-year-old Smitty Smith of Hibernian.

England's first three goals all came within nine minutes, shortly after the second half opened. Lawton scored the first and beat three men to do it, then repeated the dose five minutes after on a corner by Les Smith.

Goulden began and finished the best piece of teamwork in the game in scoring his third tally. Both Stan Matthews, making his thirty-seventh appearance in an international and his twentieth since the war began, and Lawton joined with Goulden in a great combination play.

Matthews and Carter worked an opening for Lawton to score the fourth goal, and Carter kicked England's fifth a couple of minutes later. Smith slammed in the sixth.

Before the match both teams were presented to King Haakon of Norway. Among the notables in the royal box were Deputy Premier Attlee and Labor Minister Bevin.

The BBC, in addition to giving the game a full hour broadcast at home, told it to the world in six other languages—French, Dutch, Portuguese, Norwegian, Swedish and Finnish.

The game, with its pageantry of pre-opening parades and bands, gave thousands of workers and men on leave from the fighting fronts a tonic return to the full panoply and ceremonial of peacetime Wembley.

For the players, it was a unique international. For the first time the Scottish players wore numbers on their backs, six years after England adopted the innovation. Charity benefited by £23,000 from gate receipts.

The Scots have now been beaten eight times by England in twelve wartime internationals. Of the others, Scotland won two and drew two.

October 15, 1944

BOLTON GAINS CUP IN BRITISH SOCCER

MANCHESTER, May 26 (Canadian Press)—The Bolton Wanderers won the League North Soccer Cup today by holding Manchester to a 2-2 tie in the second game of a two-game-total-point series. The Wanderers took the first match, 1—0, a week ago.

May 27, 1945

STRIKE CALLED OFF IN BRITISH SOCCER

New Agreement Announced, Lifting the Wage Ceiling From $32 to $36 Weekly

MANCHESTER, England, Nov. 12 (P)—Britain's professional soccer players and club owners reached a compromise on wages and other issues today, averting a strike that threatened to tie up the sport.

Under the agreement, reached in a three-hour conference, the maximum pay for players will be increased immediately from eight pounds ($32) to nine pounds ($36) weekly and match play payment will be increased from four pounds ($16) to five pounds ($20).

The strike, based on demands for an increase to 12 pounds ($48) weekly, had been set for Saturday.

A joint statement said that under the terms of the new agreement the payment of compensation for injuries will be made on the basis of the Workman's Compensation Act for the time being and "the league will supplement these payments at their discretion as individual cases warrant."

"These conditions apply for this season only," said Frank Howarth, secretary of the Football League, who added that further conferences were planned for March and April when "we hope to be better able to see the position more clearly" regarding arrangements for next season.

November 13, 1945

100,000 SEE DERBY WIN SOCCER CUP, 4-1

Charlton Athletic Beaten in Overtime at Wembley as Royal Family Watches

By Wireless to THE NEW YORK TIMES.

LONDON, April 27—Before King George, Queen Elizabeth, Princess Elizabeth and 100,000 other soccer fans from all parts of Britain, Derby County defeated Charlton Athletic, 4 goals to 1, in the first post-war cup final at Wembley Stadium today.

All the pre-war spirit and color of Britain's premier sports event was apparent in the huge stadium, which was sold out of seats weeks ago. Scalpers asked and got $50 for $8 seats.

Once again there were the rattles and bells as well as rosettes and favors in the teams' colors. And once again, with all the old peacetime abandon, the lucky ticket holders lifted their voices in songs, catcalls and cheers. There have been many vast crowds in Wembley, but none of them could equal the din that was raised by today's 100,000.

The Royal Family was given a tumultuous welcome as they appeared in the Royal Box. There was another ovation for the King as he walked out on the field to shake hands with all the players.

The teams took some time to get over their initial nervousness. At the end of the regulation 90 minutes the score stood at one goal apiece. Derby scored three times in the 30-minute overtime session.

April 28, 1946

LIVERPOOL ELEVEN ROUTS STARS, 10-1

8,000 Brave Rain at Ebbets Field to Watch Unbeaten Soccer Team End U. S. Tour

Displaying a clear superiority over its opponents in every department, the visiting Liverpool soccer team of England brought its ten-game tour of the United States and Canada to a triumphant close by routing an American League All-Star team, 10-1, before 8,000 persons at Ebbets Field last night.

Unmindful of the incessant rain which started to fall forty-five minutes before game time and continued unabated throughout the encounter, the English team went about its task with a vigor which was not to be denied. Once attuned to the uncertain underfooting and slippery ball, the Britishers let loose with all their fury and the locals were compelled to remain on the defensive virtually all of the way.

Too much credit, however, cannot be given to George Davis, the Kearny Celtics' great goalie, who tended the nets for the losers. Davis came up with one sensational save after another.

So deadly was Liverpool's forward line that all five of its members were able to break into the scoring column at least once. Cyril Done, the center-forward, walked off with high-scoring honors, making four goals, but he was closely followed by Capt. Willie Fagan with three. Bob Priday, Jack Balmer and Harry Eastham each came up with one.

The only counter made for the Americans was accounted for by Al Jennette, Brookhattan's outstanding inside left, who registered after twelve minutes of the second half at a time when the Great Britain team was leading, 6—0. In the first six minutes the Americans displayed a surprising amount of strength and appeared to hold an edge over their foes. An indication of what was happening lay in the fact that the home team earned corner kicks three times to one for the British.

The Liverpool squad finally broke loose seventeen minutes after the game had started. Priday, a South African, caught the American defense unawares and booted a quick pass to Fagan, which the latter promptly converted.

From that point on the visitors sent drive after drive into American territory. Priday came up with his tally on a follow-up of a shot which bounded off the crossbar. Fagan registered on a pass from Priday, and Balmer took a boot from Eastham to tally and make the score; 4—0, at the intermission.

The line-up:

LIVERPOOL. (10)		LEAGUE STARS (1)
Sidlow	G	Davis
Jones	R. B.	Laverty
Ramsden	L. B.	Harris
Taylor	R. H.	Skiba
Hughes	C. H.	Gonsalves
Spicer	L. H.	Altemose
Eastham	O. R.	Hynes
Balmer	I. R.	Elsner
Done	C.	Salcedo
Fagan	I. L.	Jennette
Priday	O. L.	Conn

Goals—Liverpool: Done 4, Fagan 3, Priday, Balmer, Eastham. League Stars Jennette. Referee—M. Pirl. Linesmen E. Kopf and M. McCartney. Time of halves—45 minutes.

June 12, 1946

99,000 See Charlton Down Burnley by 1-0 In Overtime Soccer Cup Final at Wembley

Special to THE NEW YORK TIMES.

LONDON, April 26—A crowd of 99,000 fans from all parts of Britain saw London's Charlton Athletic battle to a 1-0 victory over the Burnley Lancashire club in the final for the Football Association's Cup at Wembley Stadium today.

As neither side had scored at the end of ninety minutes' play the soccer rivals had to play on in an extra period. It was in the last few minutes of the thirty-minute overtime session that Charlton scored the goal that gave the team possession of the cup for one year.

The goal came after the Charlton wingmen had forced the ball down to the corner flag where it was squared across the field into the Burnley goal-mouth. Chris Duffy, Charlton left-winger, trapped the ball and with a lightning shot that left the Burnley goalkeeper helpless, registered the deciding point.

From the start play was sharp. Burnley made the first threat and had hard luck in not scoring on an effort by its center forward. In the second period Burnley forced another opportunity, but Charlton's goalkeeper, Sam Bartram, managed to send the ball against the crossbar from where it rebounded into play.

Generally, however, scoring chances were few and Charlton deserved to win if only because it seized the one opening for which the forwards worked.

Before the start of the game scalpers outside the Stadium were asking and getting $28 for a 60-cent standing room ticket. The opening price was $4, but the ticketless fans snapping them up the price began to mount. Some profiteers were saved from manhandling only by police intervention. Local shopkeepers, too, cashed in. Pineapples sold for as much as $5 each.

April 27, 1947

Fans Kick Official to Death
BUENOS AIRES, March 29 (UP)—Soccer official Salvador Naredo was kicked and beaten to death today by players and fans who had disagreed with a penalty he had called during a game.

March 30, 1948

King, Queen, 99,000 See Manchester United Defeat Blackpool in Soccer Classic, 4-2

Special to THE NEW YORK TIMES.

LONDON, April 24—Ninety-nine thousand soccer fans from all over Britain, together with their King and Queen, packed into the Wembley Stadium today to see Manchester United battle through to a 4-2 victory over Blackpool in the final for the Football Association Cup.

King George and Queen Elizabeth, who are celebrating their silver wedding anniversary on Monday, were accompanied on the drive from Windsor Castle by Princess Margaret and the Duke of Edinburgh. People lined the streets throughout the drive to the stadium, where thousands flocked around the main approaches to give a roaring welcome to the royal party.

Ticket scalpers mingled with the crowds outside the stadium offering $5 tickets at $60 to $80. They were snapped up.

The game was played at a tremendous pace and Blackpool, which looked the more composed at the kick-off, scored first on a penalty kick. The penalty was awarded when Blackpool's center forward, Stanley Mortensen, was pulled down inside the penalty area. Immediately after this goal Manchester broke away and penned Blackpool in its own territory for fifteen minutes, during which it frittered away several scoring chances.

Manchester's first goal came from a high center kick with which the Blackpool backs dallied when trying to clear. Then the Manchester forwards seized their chance and from a simple pass Center Forward Jack Rowley almost walked the ball into the Blackpool net.

Blackpool attacked again and just before half-time scored its second goal, following a free kick awarded for handling the ball.

In the second half neither side spared any effort in defense or attack. The Manchester forward line began clicking with accurate passes, and the equalizer came when a high ball was headed into the corner of the Blackpool goal by Rowley, his second tally.

Manchester continued to press strongly, and its efforts were rewarded by two more goals which came after some spectacular passing. The scorers were Stanley Pearson and John Anderson. Blackpool had one or two chances during this period, but inaccurate kicking prevented any chances they had of adding to their score.

Before the game started the crowd whiled away the time with community singing to music provided by the bands of the Life Guards and Grenadier Guards. During the interval instructors and men of the Army Physical Training Corps gave a display of gymnastics. Bells, rattles and bugles added to the din of Lancashire voices as supporters from the home towns of the two finalists bedecked with club colors cheered their teams.

April 25, 1948

SWEDEN SOCCER WINNER

Downs Yugoslavia in Olympic Final, 3-1, Before 40,000

●WEMBLEY, England, Aug. 13 (AP)—Sweden, pre-Olympics favorite, stormed through Yugoslavia tonight, 3 to 1, to win the soccer championship of the 1948 games.

Although the score was close, there never was much doubt among the 40,000 spectators as to the outcome.

In a preliminary game, Denmark defeated Great Britain, 5 to 3, for third place.

Two of Sweden's goals were scored by Inside Right Gunnar Gren—one from a penalty—and the third was registered by Gunnar Nordahl, regarded by many as the greatest center forward in European soccer.

The Yugoslav tally was made by J. Mitic, inside right.

August 14, 1948

sion and are in danger of relegation to the third division.

The cup final day opened with an invasion of London by 40,000 followers of the two clubs from the Midlands. Ticket scalpers were out early and raked in enormous profits as ticketless fans snapped up 3-shilling (60-cent) tickets for 30 shillings, while 42-shilling tickets fetched more than £10 ($40). Money, whisky, cigarettes and nylon stockings also were offered for tickets.

Inside the ground the waiting crowds were entertained by the band of the Coldstream Guards, followed by community singing. Before the start the players were presented to the Dukes of Edinburgh and Gloucester.

This was the third time Wolverhampton has won the cup and Leicester's first appearance in the final.

May 1, 1949

Rio Builds Soccer Field Moat to Protect Players From Crowds in World Title Games

By the Canadian Press.

RIO DE JANEIRO, Jan. 28—The world soccer championship will be decided here in July—on a field surrounded by a moat.

This medieval barrier is considered a highly modernistic improvement in the world cup stadium now under construction. The water-filled nine-foot ditch is to "prevent standing spectators from encroaching upon the players."

It replaces the usual high wire fence which keeps the excitable public off other South American soccer fields.

The new stadium will seat 120,000 fans and accommodate 30,000 standees. Brazilians claim it will be the world's largest sports ground and not a bit too big to care for the huge crowds possible in this soccer-mad country.

The football plant, equipped with bars, restaurants and sleeping space for fifty players, is only the centerpiece of a huge sports development which eventually will include facilities for swimming, tennis, athletics, cycling, basketball, and gymnastics. The layout has a car park for 25,000 vehicles.

One of the biggest problems for Brazilian ground-keepers is to lay down a decent carpet of grass on the playing surface. It is necessary to plant the grass root by root and water it until it "knits"—instead of just throwing down grass seed and waiting for rain.

The result is a fast-growing, harsh, tufty growth which sometimes makes a soccer ball bounce crazily. The field itself is baked ironhard by the sun and even a heavy rain won't soften it much. The water just lies on top and evaporates without penetrating the turf.

On this type of surface, South American teams play a lightning-fast game, in sharp contrast to the British squads which may form their chief competition in June and July.

England and Scotland—both already assured of places in the final sixteen teams which will visit Brazil—are used to heavy fields and a soggy ball. Experts here favor Brazil to win the world cup by capitalizing on their experience of the faster fields.

Local teams sacrifice protection for speed in their soccer equipment. Shin guards are discarded, shorts are ultra-brief and even the boots are cut down to something closely resembling a baseball shoe.

British authorities have been trying to develop a lighter type of boot for use at Rio but so far the project remains in the hush-hush stage.

The Brazilian style of soccer is extremely individualistic. Team play is not as highly developed as in some countries, but crowds give their biggest cheers to the flashy dribblers who can control the ball as they dance the length of the field.

January 29, 1950

Wolverhampton Trips Leicester City, 3-1, In English Soccer Cup Final Before 100,000

Special to THE NEW YORK TIMES.

LONDON, April 30—Princess Elizabeth, the Duke of Edinburgh and the Duke of Gloucester were among the 100,000 soccer fans who saw the Wolverhampton Wanderers battle through to a 3-1 victory over Leicester City in the final game for the Football Association Cup at Wembley Stadium today.

The Wolves deserved their victory if only because they were cooler in the opening minutes, during which Leicester suffered from Wembley "nerves." During this part of the game the Wolves' winger, Johnny Hancocks, ran the ball almost the length of the field to put across a perfect pass which Forward Jesse Pye rocketed into the net with a beautiful header.

Leicester began to fight back, but poor work in front of the goal spoiled the team's chance to even the score.

Then the Wolverhampton forwards began to click. Following a series of corner kicks from which the Leicester defenders could not scramble the ball away, Pye scored again. He collected a lob from Captain Billy Wright and slammed the ball in the net from ten yards out, giving Goalkeeper Gordon Bradley of Leicester no chance.

Leicester rallied gallantly after the halfway interval and in an all-out attack Malwyn Griffiths, their outside right, brushed through the

Wolverhampton defense to open Leicester's account with a drive that rebounded into the goal from a side post.

Wolverhampton refused to be rattled and set up a new series of attacks. Under this persistent pressure the Leicester defenders were forced to kick the ball aimlessly away.

The cup winners put the issue beyond doubt when Sam Smythe, inside right, dribbled through Leicester's defense and scored the final goal in the corner of the net.

Leicester never gave up trying, but the difference was too marked between the winners, who are in the first division, and the losers, who stand low in the second divi-

Arsenal Conquers Liverpool to Take British Soccer Cup

GUNNERS WIN, 2-0, AS 100,000 WATCH

LONDON, April 29 (Reuters)—London's mighty Arsenal Gunners today overcame a stubborn Liverpool squad, 2—0, before 100,000 rain-soaked fans in Wembley

Stadium to capture the Football Association Cup, premier prize of British soccer.

King George presented the famed trophy to the Highbury team.

Arsenal opportunism plus the stoutest of defenses, which refused to crack before a sustained second-half drive by the Merseysiders won the day for the local club.

It was Arsenal's third cup tri-

umph, the Gunners also winning in 1930 and 1936. Liverpool has yet to gain the honor.

Scoring hero of the game was Inside Left Reg Lewis who counted both goals. They came 17 minutes after the start of each half and both were built up in moves initiated behind the Gunner forward line.

Sets Up the First Score

Fullback Walley Barnes started the first score on its way, shoot-

31

ing a forward pass to Inside Right Jimmy Logie, who in turn relayed to Lewis. Lewis drove his shot low into the corner of the net.

A similar maneuver accounted for the second-half goal. Captain Joe Mercer slid the slippery ball up from the halfback line to Outside Left Denis Compton who slipped it across to Freddie Cox, the other winger. Cox wheeled it to Lewis and again Reg picked the corner from 15 yards.

Liverpool threw caution away and moved right into the Arsenal end for much of the rest of the game. But Arsenal's defense, led by Center Half Leslie Compton, with Barnes and Laurie Scott playing strongly in front of Goalie

George Swindin, held on to the finish.

Outstanding in attack for the losers were Bert Stubbins at center and Billy Liddel on the wing. Both tried desperately, but it just wasn't their day.

Sharp Pace Continues

The Wolverhampton Wanderers, with a 4-2 victory over the Bolton Wanderers, ranged alongside Portsmouth as the race for English League honors continued at the sharpest pace for years.

With only a week of the season left, four clubs still have a mathematical chance of winning the championship.

Portsmouth, idle today, has two

games left in the locker and appears favorite for the honor, but the Wolves' victory left the two clubs tied in points with the Wolves due to play one more game. Blackpool, drawing by 1—1 at Stoke City, and Sunderland, whipping Everton by 4—2, retained outside chances. The first five clubs now stand: Portsmouth and Wolverhampton 51, Sunderland and Manchester United 50, Blackpool 49. The United has completed its schedule.

The key game in Scotland between the Rangers and Hibernians was scoreless and left the teams still deadlocked.

April 30, 1950

U. S. Upsets England in World Soccer Tourney

SOUZA'S GOAL BEATS BRITISH ELEVEN, 1-0

Fall River Man Scores After 39 Minutes of Soccer Game and U. S. Protects Lead

AMERICANS GET OVATION

Fans at Rio de Janeiro Carry Players Off Field—Spain Shuts Out Chile, 2-0

RIO DE JANIRO, June 29 (AP)— The United States today defeated England, 1—0, to add the latest and biggest upset in the world soccer championship.

The favored British team and the spectators were stunned by the result. The goal was scored by Ed Souza of Fall River, Mass., after 39 minutes of the first half.

It was the second game of the tournament for both teams. The Americans last Sunday gave Spain a bad scare before bowing, 3—1. England won its opener from Chile the same day, 2—0.

Today's surprise was even bigger than last Sunday's Swedish triumph over Italy, 3—2, or Switzerland's holding Brazil to a 2-2 tie yesterday. Brazilian fans swarmed on to the field after the United States victory and took the Americans on their shoulders while the players received an ovation.

British Forwards Uncertain

The British forwards were uncertain in aiming for goals but their general play appeared superior to that of the winners except on the scoreboard. The

Americans made many long-range passes and showed improvement in their game.

During the second period, England attacked fifteen times to the Americans' ten. The United States, under pressure, yielded six corners to England's two.

Spain defeated Chile, 2—0, at Curitiba, for its second straight victory.

It was a rude shock for the English team to lose. It must now beat Spain in their Rio de Janeiro match on Sunday to stay in the race.

Chile Out of Running

Spain has 4 points to England's and America's 2 each. Chile is out

of the running in this four-team bracket.

Even if the Chileans defeat the United States at Recife Sunday, the result will not affect the outcome of the preliminary bracket. However, if the Americans defeat Chile and England beats Spain, that would throw the bracket into a triple tie which would have to be played off.

Sweden tied Paraguay, 2—2, at Curitiba, practically assuring itself of victory in its bracket. Sweden now has 3 points, Paraguay has 1 and Italy, only other team in the bracket, has none. The Italians are out of the running.

June 30, 1950

U. S. Team, Beaten by Chile, 5-2, Eliminated in World Cup Soccer

RIO DE JANEIRO, July 2 (Reuters) — Four countries — Brazil, Spain, Sweden and Uruguay—today won berths in next week's play-offs for the world soccer championship.

England and the United States were among the five that lost in a day's play which sorted out the teams that will meet in the round robin series to determine the titleholder.

Italy, present cup holder, had lost its grip much earlier in the series by bowing to Sweden. Sweden added points by tying Paraguay and Italy won over the Paraguayans today.

England lost, 1—0, to Spain today and the United States, 5—2, to Chile. Other scores showed Italy winning, 2—0, over Paraguay, Switzerland beating Mexico, 2—1, and Uruguay whitewashing Bolivia, 8—0.

Round-Robin Basis

Play has been on a round robin basis in four pools, leaders of which now go into championship stage.

Of the originally favored teams only Uruguay and Brazil remain. England's elimination today completed Thursday's surprise 1-0 reversal by the United States which

had sent British sport writers into a spin.

Uruguay won the first world cup competition in 1930 and entered the lists well favored, as did Italy, which won the trophy on the only other two occasions it has been at stake—1934 and 1938.

Spain, favored from the first, enters the final stage strongest after winning all three games played.

Same Team Fielded

The United States loss to Chile was on wet, heavy ground, sodden by heavy rains that had fallen continuously for some hours.

The Americans fielded the team that beat England, tacitly disposing of rumors current among British supporters that they had used an ineligible player to win on Thursday.

Gino Pariani of the St. Louis Simpkins was the questioned player, although English officials since have been quoted as saying they never had "the slightest thought" of protesting his status.

United States officials said that Pariani was on the American Olympic team in London two years ago and added it would be strange for his eligibility to be questioned now.

July 3, 1950

URUGUAY ANNEXES TITLE

Upsets Favored Brazil, 2-1, in World Soccer—Sweden 3d

RIO DE JANEIRO, July 16 (AP) —Uruguay upset highly favored Brazil today, 2 to 1, and won the world soccer championship with a defense that choked off all threats but one before 170,000 spectators.

The first half was scoreless but it was evident that Uruguay had found the way to handle the confident Brazilians, who had demolished Sweden last Sunday by a 7-to-1 score, and Spain by 6—1 last Thursday.

At Sao Paulo the Swedish players showed a reversal of form to defeat Spain, 3 to 1, and take third place behind Brazil.

The final standing:

	W.	L.	T.	Pts.
Uruguay	2	0	1	5
Brazil	2	1	0	4
Sweden	1	2	0	2
Spain	0	2	1	1

RIO DE JANEIRO, July 16 (Reuters)—People wept in the streets tonight after Brazil's world cup soccer defeat by Uruguay. The whole city was plunged into gloom.

Stadium doctors said they treated 169 persons. Six fans were taken to hospitals.

July 17, 1950

8 SOCCER FANS DIE AS URUGUAY SCORES

MONTEVIDEO, Uruguay, July 17 (UP) — Eight persons died yesterday as Uruguay won the World Championship at soccer from Brazil.

Three fans died of heart attacks while listening to the radio broadcast of the game played in Rio de Janeiro. The others succumbed when the Uruguayans ran wild last night celebrating the victory.

In Rio, where Brazilians had been sure of a victory, a "mass funeral" was held because, according to the Brazilian press, "soccer died." Plans for a mass celebration were scrapped, flags flying from nearly every rooftop and window were taken down, firecrackers were discarded without being set off.

July 18, 1950

Newcastle United Beats Blackpool to Take British Football Association Cup

100,000 SEE RALLY BRING 2-0 VICTORY

Milburn Gets Both Goals for Newcastle in Second Half to Defeat Blackpool

KING AND QUEEN PRESENT

LONDON, April 28 (UP)—Newcastle United today won the Football Association Cup, Britain's most-prized soccer trophy, for the fourth time by beating Blackpool, 2—0, at Wembley Stadium before a crowd of 100,000, including the King and Queen.

Two spectacular second-half goals by center-forward Jack Milburn decided England's "world series" of soccer in a game that ended in a heavy rain. Newcastle previously had won the cup in 1910, 1924 and 1932.

The Tottenham Spurs clinched the first division championship by edging Sheffield Wednesday, 1—0, in regular season competition.

King Greets Players

Before the start of the cup game, King George shook hands with members of both teams. When it ended, he returned to the field despite the rain to present the coveted trophy to the victorious Newcastle team.

Seated in the royal box with the King and Queen were Princess Margaret Rose; the Duke of Gloucester; his son, Prince William; Foreign Secretary Herbert Morrison, and other members of the royal household and prominent Government and diplomatic officials.

Long before dawn, thousands of British soccer fans had jammed railroads and buses to London for the big game. By midday the streets of the West End were thronged with gaily bedecked fans wearing rosettes and scarves bearing the colors of their favorite team.

Newcastle dominated the first half. Milburn kicked the ball into the net at the nine-minute mark, but the score was disallowed because of a Newcastle penalty and Blackpool received a free kick.

Milburn Scores Goal

Milburn put Newcastle ahead after six minutes of the second half on a brilliant solo effort. He gained possession of the ball near mid-field, outmaneuvered the Blackpool defense, and booted a shot past goalie George Farm.

Four minutes later Milburn scored again on one of the finest combination plays seen in a cup final in many years. Outside right Tommy Walker raced along the wing and turned the ball over to inside right Ernie Taylor, who back-heeled a pass to Milburn. The Newcastle star then unleashed a blazing left-footed kick which rocketed past goalie Farm from 30 yards out.

The defeat was a bitter disappointment for Blackpool's Stanley Matthews, known as the "Joe DiMaggio" of British soccer. At the age of 36, when most soccer players are in retirement, Matthews was seeking a cup medal to go with his sixty-three international trophies.

April 29, 1951

Newcastle Takes Soccer Cup Second Year in Succession

UNITED TEAM TOPS ARSENAL BY 1 TO 0

Newcastle Becomes First in 61 Years to Capture Final Two Seasons in Row

CHURCHILL PRESENTS CUP

Victors Match Blackburn 1891 Feat on Robledo's Goal at Wembley Before 100,000

LONDON, May 3 (AP)—Newcastle United defeated Arsenal, 1—0, on a goal by Chilean-born George Robledo to win the Football Association Cup today for the second straight year.

The cup final, top event of the year for British soccer fans, drew its usual crowd of 100,000 to Wembley Stadium despite rain and chill winds.

It was the first time since 1891 that a team has won the cup two years running.

Arsenal played all of the second half and much of the first with only ten men. Walley Barnes, right back, limped off the field twice with a knee injury and the second time he wasn't able to return. Substitutions are not permitted.

Robledo's goal came six minutes from the end.

Ray Daniel, center half, playing with a broken left wrist encased in a plastic covering, starred for the losers.

Prime Minister Winston Churchill was introduced to the players before the match and presented the cup to Newcastle at the end.

The cup final, along with scattered league games, ended the eight-month soccer season.

Sets Stadium Record

LONDON, May 3 (Reuters)—Newcastle's victory today made it the first club to win the Football Association Cup a second year in succession since Blackburn accomplished the feat sixty-one years ago. The Northerners also gained the honor of being the first team to take the cup four times at Wembley Stadium.

With the soccer season now ended until next August successes and failures in the leagues are: First division champion, Manchester United; runner up, Tottenham Hotspur; relegated to the second division, Fulham and Huddersfield. Second division champion, Sheffeld Wednesday; runner up, Cardiff City, both promoted to first division; relegated to third division, Coventry City and Queen's Park Rangers. Plymouth Argyle, third division south champion, and Lincoln City, third division north leader, were promoted to the second group.

Scottish League Division A, champion, Hibernian; runner up, Rangers. Relegated to Division B, Stirling Albion and Morton. Division B leaders promoted were Clyde and Falkirk.

Misses Good Chances

The cup final was the poorest seen for many years. Arsenal missed good chances in the first minutes while fielding a full team and Newcastle's famed forward line seldom got going.

Among the fans at Wembley Stadium was Gen. Alfred Gruenther, Chief of Staff to General of the Army Dwight D. Eisenhower at Supreme Headquarters, Allied Powers in Europe, who flew over from Paris to cheer Newcastle.

May 4, 1952

U. S. Soccer Team Is Eliminated From Games as Italy Wins, 8-0

TAMPERE, Finland, July 16 (AP) —Italy's soccer team eliminated the United States squad today from the Olympic Games.

In the qualifying tournament, the Italians beat the lightly regarded United States team, 8—0. This removed the Americans from further competition although the games will not begin officially until Saturday.

The large number of entries in soccer, basketball and field hockey required elimination tournaments this week so that the competitions July 19-Aug. 3 period of the games.

Three other nations were eliminated. Brazil's brilliant soccer team whipped the Netherlands, 5—1; Egypt, rallying after a slow start, beat Chile 5—4, and Luxemburg had to play an extra period to defeat Great Britain, 5—3.

The Italian players were clearly superior to the Americans. They were fast, mobile and brilliant and might easily have scored more goals. At half-time the count was 3—0 and the Italians scored five more goals in the second half when a strong wind was at their backs.

The star of the Italian team was Egisto Pandolfini, who scored three goals.

The American team, which upset Britain by 1—0 in last year's world championship in Brazil, consists mostly of young players, who came to Helsinki primarily to gain experience, according to their coach, Walter Geisler.

July 17, 1952

YUGOSLAVIA TIED BY SOVIET ELEVEN

Russians Earn 5-All Deadlock in Olympic Soccer Rally— Play Rough but Clean

By GEORGE AXELSSON
Special to The New York Times.

TAMPERE, Finland, July 20 — Yugoslavia and the Soviet Union both managed to remain in the Olympic soccer football tournament today because the teams of the two rival Communist countries drew, 5—all, after a hectic match.

It was Yugoslavia all the way until the last quarter-hour. The Tito eleven led by 5 to 1, and it looked as though it couldn't lose. The Russians put on a terrific spurt, however, evening the score with a minute to go.

Those who had come to see blood were disappointed, for play was clean throughout, although at imes rough. The fouls, fist fights and stretcher cases that had been predicted did not occur.

The 5,000 fans who had come to watch the encounter in this industrial city, which is regarded as one of the strongholds of Finnish communists, were treated to a good, fair game, and to nothing more. The sympathies of the spectators seemed fairly evenly divided. The deafening cheer that broke out when the Russians drew even would have been accorded to Yugoslavia had their positions been reversed, it is believed.

Yugoslavs Strike Early

The Yugoslavs made the Russians look like bush leaguers in the first half when the Soviet goalkeeper, Ivanov, had to yield three times running. The Yugoslav forwards demonstrated a speed and precision that appeared to disconcert their opponents. The leaders' defense was airtight.

The Russians did not score their first goal until the eighth minute of the second half, after the Yugoslavs had made it 4 to 0. The Russian outside right, Trofimov, picked up a long pass and netted the ball past the Yugoslav goal keeper, Beara.

But Yugoslavia still dominated the field. In the fourteenth minute, the Tito eleven made it 5—1, and kept the ball in U. S. S. R. territory for another fifteen minutes.

Then things began to happen. Perhaps the Yugoslavs were tiring or just became careless, feeling that victory was inevitable. In any event, the Russian team began to play inspired ball. Obviously fighting with a determination born of despair, the Soviet team moved the ball to the Yugoslav side, and there it stayed.

Drop Their Poker Faces

The Yugoslav goal keeper suddenly found himself parrying shots from every angle. Fourteen minutes before the end the score was 5 to 2. Two minutes later it was 5—3 and three minutes before the whistle blew it was 5—4. Then, in the very last minute, a Russian goal scored off a corner made it 5—all and touched off demonstrations of joy probably rare in these cold latitudes.

Even the Russian players dropped their poker faces and danced with glee. The general impression was that the Yugoslavs were tired and a beaten team proved wrong, however. The truth seemed to be that both teams were tired, for neither side could score during the extra thirty minutes of play. If anything, the Yugoslavs had the better of it during the extra period.

After the game, members of both teams shook hands politely, although not cordially, it seemed. As for the Yugoslavs, their chores were not yet over—they went home to answer some 400 wires received from Belgrade during the day, telling them, "You must win."

The referee was Ellis of England. The match will be replayed here Tuesday.

July 21, 1952

YUGOSLAVIA BEATS RUSSIA AT SOCCER

Ousts Soviet From Olympics, 3-1, as Uncomradely Acts Make Referee See Red

By GEORGE AXELSSON
Special to The New York Times.

TAMPERE, Finland, July 22— Yugoslavia knocked the Soviet Union out of the Olympic soccer tournament, 3—1, in a rough-and-tumble match here tonight that, but for the resolute intervention of a British referee, would have degenerated into a brawl between the teams from the two rival Communist countries.

The affair was a replay of their 5-all tie of Sunday, when the Soviet eleven, trailing by 1-5, came from behind in the last quarter-hour of play to level the score.

Tonight no such miracle happened, so the Soviet line-up, an all-Russian eleven drawn mainly from the élite Red Army and Dynamo Club teams, went down to defeat to a team that in the unanimous opinion of objective experts played better and more elegant soccer.

To Play Denmark Next

The price of the Yugoslavs' victory, which qualified them to meet Denmark in Helsinki on Friday, was several badly bruised players, for as the game wore on the Russians noticed that they had little success in going for the ball, they went for the men instead. The Yugoslav inner left, S. Bobek, one of the most effective players, was particularly marked out for fury of the Russians—he was deliberately downed thrice and the last time knocked out cold for three minutes.

The Russian fouling grew so bad that the referee, Arthur Ellis, threatened to send the whole Soviet team off the field. From then on the Russians calmed down but there were only a few minutes remaining to play.

Some 20,000 soccer fans had flocked to see the game at Tampere Field, which is laid out at what appears to be the bottom of a huge sandpit. The interest in this Russo-Yugoslav encounter, already great because of the political antagonism between the two Communist dictatorships and intensified by it being played to settle a draw, was at fever heat.

The unlucky ones who had not obtained tickets were at least as many as those who had the precious pasteboards. Astronomic sums were offered for tickets but there was no scalping because the ticket holders just wouldn't sell.

The story of the match soon was told. For the first ten minutes it was all Russia, then it was all Yugloslavia. Only the uncanny skill of the Soviet goalkeeper, Leonid Ivanov, kept the Yugoslav score down to 3.

The Russian center forward, Vseveolod Bobrov, a Red Army major, made his team's goal after six minutes of play in the first half. Two minutes later he missed a chance to score again.

Penalty Leads to Score

After a few minutes more of Soviet dominance, Yugoslavia went to the fore and stayed there. The second of two Yugoslav goals in this half was the result of a penalty awarded when the Russian center half, A. Bashashkin, used his hands in the penalty area to bat away a shot straight at the Russian goal by Bobek.

Fittingly, Bobek selected a kick penalty and therein made no mistake. The Yugoslavs accomplished the second half's only goal and it was thereafter that the Russians tried to convert the game into something resembling American football. Magnanimous in victory, the Yugoslavs lined up for the customary handshake after the match but the Russian team would have none of that.

The Yugoslav team captain and center half, Ivan Horvat, had to stage a virtual sprint to intercept his Russian opposite number on the latter's way out of the field before obtaining that formal handshake. The Russian accompanied the gesture by giving Horvat the sort of look that a bull supposedly serves for the butcher.

July 23, 1952

HUNGARY SOCCER VICTOR

65,000 See Yugoslavia Booters Lose Helsinki Final, 2-0

HELSINKI, Aug. 2 (P)—Hungary won the Olympic soccer tournament tonight by defeating Yugoslavia, 2 to 0, in a game that never reached the high quality expected by 65,000 spectators.

Hungary thus won the gold medal, with Yugoslavia taking second.

Sweden placed third in the tournament by virtue of its victory over Germany in the consolation final last night.

Germany gained fourth place.

There are no fifth and sixth places in the football competition.

August 3, 1952

Blackpool Wins Soccer Final

LATE GOALS DEFEAT BOLTON FOR CUP, 4-3

Matthews Stars as Blackpool Tops Tourney First Time— Queen Presents Trophy

LONDON, May 2 (P)—Blackpool scored two goals in the last five minutes today to defeat the Bolton Wanderers, 4—3, and win the Football Association Cup for the first time before a crowd of 100,-000 soccer fans in Wembley Stadium.

Although he failed to score himself, Rightwinger Stan Matthews drew the cheers of the crowd —including Queen Elizabeth II and the Duke of Edinburgh—as he set up the goals that brought Blackpool back from a 3-1 half-time deficit.

Bolton, trying for an unprecedented fourth cup, packed its goalmouth with virtually its entire team for most of the second half. But Matthews found an opening for a scoring pass to Stan Mortensen midway through the period, and set Mortensen up with another splendid pass near the finish. Mortensen was fouled on the play and blasted in a free kick from 20 yards out to tie the score.

Sets Up Deciding Goal

Again Matthews brought the ball down the field, eluding the Bolton defenders and getting off a low pass to John Perry in front of the goal. Perry rapped it home and a few minutes later he and his mates were handed the trophy and cup winners' medals by the Queen.

Bolton started with a rush and Nat Lofthouse scored in ninety seconds one of the quickest goals ever in the cup final. Blackpool tied it thirty-five minutes later when Bolton's Chris Hassall headed the ball into his own goal. Bolton scored twice more before half-time, however.

The seven goals scored equaled a 63-year-old record and the gate of 49,900 pounds ($139,720) also was a record.

March 3, 1953

Mexican All-Stars Defeat U. S. In World Cup Soccer Trials, 4-0

MEXICO CITY, Jan. 10 (AP)— The Mexican All-Star soccer team defeated the United States by 4—0 today in a regional elimination match for the Jules Rimet world cup.

William Sheppell of the Americans kicked a goal by mistake for the Mexicans. Sheppell's blunder came at 15 minutes after the first half opened. As things turned out, Mexico would have won easily anyway.

The Mexicans scored two goals in each half before a sell-out crowd of 60,000 at Olympic Stadium to win the first of two games for the North American championship. The second game will be played Thursday.

Jose Luis Lamadrid, Mexican center forward, started the scoring by kicking a goal five minutes after the opening gun.

In the second half, Lamadrid scored again at 3:00 and Jose Chepe Naranjo, Mexican inside right, scored at 19:00.

The victory gave Mexico 2 more points to add to the 4 gained in previous elimination games won from Haiti.

The winning team of the United States-Mexican elimination match will compete in Switzerland for the world title.

Today's game was played under ideal weather conditions — cool but sunny. The altitude bothered the visitors and they were allowed to rest when play was suspended at 29:00 in the first half.

Lack of practice—the players had their first workout as a team only two days ago—and loss of some star players because of immigration difficulties handicapped the United States squad.

January 11, 1954

W. BROMWICH CLUB TAKES SOCCER CUP

Downs Preston by 3-2 With Late Goal in the Final at Wembley Before 100,000

By DREW MIDDLETON
Special to The New York Times.

WEMBLEY, England, May 1— The belief that the English are phlegmatic, dignified and reserved took its annual beating today at Wembley Stadium where West Bromwich Albion whipped Preston North End, 3—2, and won the Football Association Cup.

Four minutes before the end of the game Frank Griffin, slender West Bromwich outside right, booted home a pass from Reg Ryan to score the decisive goal.

Immediately the crowd of more than 100,000 expressed its feelings. Pious non-conformist manufacturers from the north threw their bowlers onto the playing field. Gay young men from London cried aloud for justice. Respectable tradesmen expressed their opinion of the referee.

Earlier in the game two decisions by this official, A. W. Luty, produced comment that would be considered harsh in Brooklyn.

Penalty Goal Decision

One of them gave a penalty goal to West Bromwich on a searing free kick by Ronald Allen, who also scored the winners' first goal.

As there were 100,000 self-appointed officials in the stadium it was hard to get at the rights of the matter. But they are arguing the fine points of the decisions at Saint Martins tavern, a pub around the corner, now and the argument is bound to go on as long as the one about why Heinie Zimmerman chased Eddie Collins across the plate in that world series game long ago.

This match, known from Lands End to John o'Groats as the cup final, is a great English festival, equaling the Derby as an expression of sporting fervor.

The crowd at Wembley lacks the austere intellectuality of the mourners at Lords for a cricket match and the middle class pomposity of the English rugby football crowds but it compensates with a free-handed heartiness and fanatic zeal that are overwhelming.

The first trainloads from the north—the West Bromwich team is from Staffordshire and Preston from Lancashire — reached London at 3:30 A. M. today.

Fill West End Streets

Until noon the streets of London's West End, usually quiet and even sedate on a Saturday, were filled with groups of strolling men. They wore paper hats. They sported huge rosettes in the colors of two teams. They whirled rattles. They whistled. They drank immoderate quantities of beer.

Just before the game began the crowd had quieted. There was a tenth of a million in the enormous stadium but only 40,000 had seats. The rest stood.

The sun shown on masses of upturned faces as a conductor led the crowd in the singing of "Abide with Me." The fans sang pretty well, not so well as a Welsh rugby crowd, but a good deal better than the Old Blues struggling to remember the words of "Bright College Years."

The Queen Mother came out to shake hands with the players of both teams. There was a pause while ebullient members of the crowd exchanged insults. The referee was getting a pretty bad press even then.

Slow Game at Start

It was a slow game at the start. As in so many cup finals the standard of soccer was below that of a regular season match. There were a number of high kicks and some ragged passing.

Just twenty-one minutes after the start, Willie Cunningham, the Preston right back, tried to kick clear and hit George Lee, the West Bromwich outside left.

It was a gift. Lee rushed forward and then passed to Allen, alone at the moment. Allen kicked low into the net for the first score.

At this juncture a tall man wearing a paper hat on top of a derby pulled another man's hat over his ears and then wrenched away the rim. No one batted an eye.

Exactly a minute later Preston scored. Tommy Docherty got the ball, passed to center, and Angus Morrison headed it home. This tied the score and evoked another tidal wave of jubilation.

Emphasis was on defense. But early in the second half Charlie Wayman, Preston center forward, who to many seemed offside, took the ball calmly, dribbled past goalkeeper Jim Sanders and kicked the goal.

About half the crowd thought Wayman had been offside and said so in a variety of accents. There was nothing confused about the aims of these partisans. All of them wanted the referee to pay the extreme penalty.

In the sixty-third minute of the match Albion drew even when Allen took a penalty kick and scored. Again there were suggestions about the best ways to punish the referee, this time from Preston supporters.

So it was 2-all four minutes before the end. Canny Scots were estimating that in the event of a tie they would get 33 per cent more for their money if an extra half hour had to be played. Then Bromwich went into action.

Griffin got the ball near the edge of penalty area after some heavy pressure by John Nicholls, the inside left, and after Ryan had shaken the Preston defense. Griffin is fast. He dribbled past two defenders and beat George Thompson with a sharp low shot from close range.

That's all there was to it, except for the arguments. They'll go on for years.

Each of the winners will get about £20 ($56) for this afternoon's work.

Albion's First Since 1931

LONDON, May 1 (AP)—West Bromwich Albion's soccer cup victory today was its first since 1931 and fourth since 1888.

The same teams met in the 1888 cup final, with West Bromwich also winning that game, by 2—1. West Bromwich also won the cup in 1892.

Receipts for today's game were £49,883 ($139,672).

May 2, 1954

HUNGARY CRUSHES ENGLAND'S ELEVEN

Olympic Champions Register 7-1 Soccer Victory Before 92,000 at Budapest

BUDAPEST, May 23 (Reuters) —One of the world's hottest athletic combinations exploded behind the Iron Curtain today to hand England a crushing soccer defeat.

Eleven elusive Hungarians, whose soccer knowledge stemmed from the teaching of British coaches, beat the English at their own game and rubbed it in with the paralyzing score of 7—1.

Before a crowd of 92,000 supporters, Hungary's Olympic champions booted the ball through the all-England team's defense, running up a 3-0 lead in the first half.

In the second half, the roof fell in on the demoralized English as Hungary rocketed the ball into England's goal three times within four minutes.

A Slim Consolation

Both teams scored again before the game ended in a storm of applause from jubilant Hungarians. But England's lone goal was slim consolation.

All of Hungary's top leaders were on hand to watch their team add to its Olympic laurels and establish itself as undisputed favorite for the world soccer championship series in Switzerland this summer.

Hungarians paid more than $115,000 for seats in the jammed People's Stadium here.

England had been awaiting today's game ever since the Iron Curtain eleven toppled another English athletic record in London last November.

Bewildered English Team

Then the predominantly-military Hungarian team registered a 6-3 victory. It was the first time a continental soccer combination had beaten an English National team on English soil.

The precision of Hungary's attack left the English defense outpaced, outmaneuvered and bewildered today. England's only comparable defeats were 7—2 and 6—1 losses to Scotland in 1878 and 1881.

Disconsolate British fans found little comfort in the fact that British coaches introduced the game to Hungary. The Hungarians, most of whom are regular army soldiers, plainly had gone beyond their teachers.

A commentator on Budapest Radio noted the fact, remarking that "England seems a little nervous" and had no idea how to play a "fast-moving" game.

May 24, 1954

Fighting Breaks Out as Hungary Eliminates Brazil in Soccer, 4-2

South American Player Slashed by Bottle and 3 Policemen Hurt in Locker-Room Brawl—Germany Upsets Yugoslavia

BERN, Switzerland, June 27 (AP)—A fight broke out between the Hungarian and Brazilian soccer teams in Bern's Wankdorf Stadium tonight after Hungary defeated Brazil, 4—2, to enter the semi-final round of the world soccer championship.

The Hungarians eliminated Brazil after a brawling, wrestling, kick-and-shove encounter that reached its climax with the referee banishing Hungary's Josef Bozsik and Brazil's Newton Santos for fighting.

Germany defeated Yugoslavia, 1952 Olympic finalist, by 2—0 in the other semi-final match.

The fighting between the Hungarian and Brazilian teams increased after the game ended in bottle wielding in the locker rooms. Three policemen were injured in quelling the fight.

Boots, Bottles Used

Irate players fought with soccer boots, fizz bottles, glass from shattered partitions—everything they could lay their hands on.

And late tonight the battle was reopened—verbally this time—at an inquiry by officials of the tournament organizing committee.

Brazilian soccer officials charged the post-match battle started with Hungarian team captain Ferenc Puska, slamming a bottle into the face of Brazil's Joao Baptista Carlos Pinheiro. The Hungarian officials denied this.

They said it started with Brazilian player clasping a Hungarian in an apparent friendly handshake and then clipping him with a left on the jaw.

Ernst Thommen, Swiss president of the organizing committee, said he had summoned both Hungarian and Brazilian officials to an inquiry tomorrow.

In the semi-finals, Hungary will play Uruguay and Germany will meet Austria. Both games are scheduled for Wednesday. Uruguay defeated England, 4—2, and Austria downed Switzerland, 7—5, yesterday.

The Hungary-Brazil game had thrills aplenty—but most came from fouls, not football.

The Hungarians went 2 up in seven minutes as Nandor Hidegkuti, center forward, and Sandor Kocsis, inside right, tallied—and the crowd sat back for the football classic they expected.

But in the eighteenth minute a flying tackle by Mihaly Lantos, left back, on the Brazilian center forward, Indio, started a bout of rough stuff that went on to the end of the game and beyond.

In the seventieth minute, Bozsik, Hungary's right half, and Santos, Brazil's left back, started a fist fight. Referee Arthur Ellis of England told them to break it up. They didn't—so he sent them off the field.

Ellis' decision could bring Bozsik's suspension from the tournament.

After the game Uukas slashed a bottle into the face of Pinheiro. Team-mates rushed Pinheiro into the dressing room, his head bleeding from a wide gash. Hungarian players carried Puskas to their dressing room.

Police Keep Out Fans

Hundreds of Swiss police guarded both dressing rooms to keep out yelling fans, but the fight continued between members of the teams inside the locker rooms. It took police twenty minutes to restore order.

Puskas, normally Hungary's captain, had watched the rough game from the sidelines. He was injured in an earlier World Cup match.

Meantime, Germany, dark horse of the tournament so far, advanced on the strength of its defense. The Germans took a lucky lead in the tenth minute, when the Yugoslav center half, Ivan Horvat, put the ball in his own goal. Then they packed the goal to hang on.

The strategy paid off. Four minutes from the end, a German breakaway ended with the outside right, Helmuth Rahn, racing through the Yugoslav defense to score.

June 28, 1954

Germany Upsets Hungary, 3 to 2, To Capture World Soccer Title

65,000 See Team Rally After Rivals Get 2 Goals in 8 Minutes at Bern—West Berlin Throngs Dance in Streets

BERN, Switzerland, July 4 (UP)—Germany spotted "unbeatable" Hungary two goals in eight minutes and then roared from behind to capture the world soccer championship, 3 to 2, today before 65,000 rain-drenched fans in Wankdorf Stadium.

It was Hungary's first defeat in four years. The Hungarians had beaten Germany, 8—3, in the preliminaries.

Hungary took an early lead on goals by Ferenc Puskas and Zoltam Csibor, but the Germans tied the score before half-time on goals by Max Morlock and Helmut Rahn. Then, with six minutes remaining in the match, Rahn notched his second goal to give Germany her surprise victory.

When the final whistle sounded, the strongly partisan crowd went wild and only repeated loudspeaker warnings and a force of 300 policemen and soldiers kept the spectators from breaking through the fence and pushing on to the field.

Huge German banners were waved and hats were thrown into the air as the German players embraced and kissed one another. Most of the Hungarian players broke into tears at the finish.

Employing a pace that amazed even their most ambitious fans, the Germans matched Hungary's vaunted stars throughout the first half and stood up gamely in the second.

Most teams would have been discouraged after dropping behind by two goals so early in the match, but the Germans kept their heads up, re-grouped and started hitting back with a fury that startled the men from the Iron Curtain country.

The winners were paced by Fritz Walter, their 34-year-old captain and inside left. Walter inspired his team on attack and defense, continually springing his men on fast rushes toward the Hungarian goal. Center Half Werner Liebrich also had a big hand in the upset, blunting the Hungarians' usual power up the middle, while every man of the German rearguard played above normal form.

Following the match, the teams assembled in front of the grandstand where Jakpau Rimet, president of the Federation International Football Association, after a brief speech, handed to Walter the World Cup trophy.

"You have won well," Rimet said. "Guard this trophy carefully for the spiritual value it represents."

Hundreds of Germans who traveled across the border without tickets stood outside the stadium bidding desperately for tickets held by speculators. Some grandstand tickets, normally priced at 36 francs ($8.35), were selling at 500 francs ($116).

In the open spaces outside the ground, radio and television booths were erected to cater to fans who had failed to gain admission. For a franc (23 cents), a fan could listen to a commentary on the game. For two francs, he could watch it on television.

Spectators sitting on uncovered seats inside the stadium were entertained during their long wait before the game by yodelers and alphorn blowers from Nuremberg, Cologne, Duesseldorf and other cities in the West German Republic.

Sports Victories Hailed

BERLIN, July 4 (Reuters)—West Berlin went wild tonight as radio and television newscasters announced Germany's "miracle of the century" upset of Hungary in the world cup soccer final by 3—2.

The Berliners who danced or ran cheering through the streets, also told each other excitedly of a second great sports victory for Germany today. German Mercedes racing cars, entering international racing for the first time since World War II, took first and second places in the French Grand Prix at Rheims.

Crowds had gathered in and outside cafes all over the city to listen to the running commentary. Knots of laughing people pirouetted beside taxis, which had their radios turned on full blast.

Cafe and bar proprietors throughout Germany were besieged by throngs wanting to see the match on television or hear it on the radio.

The radio commentator shouted "tor" (goal) five times when the Germans scored the winning goal.

"Germany is ahead, 3—2," he shouted. "Don't think I'm crazy, don't think I've gone off my rocker."

Afterward, happy and exhausted throngs sank down in restaurants and cafes, determined to "make a night of it" reliving the match.

Theodor Heuss, West German president, who watched the match on television in Bonn, immediately sent congratulations to the team in Bern, Switzerland, and awarded to each player the silver laurel, one of West Germany's highest sports awards.

Chancellor Konrad Adenauer also wired congratulations. He sent congratulations, too, to Juan Manuel Fangio of Argentina and his team-mate, Karl Kling of Germany, the Mercedes drivers who took first and second places in the Grand Prix.

The Communist East Berlin radio reported the West German soccer victory as the first item of its main evening news bulletin. And it added, "the radio network of the (East) German Democratic Republic congratulates the West German players."

July 5, 1954

Morlock Gets a Kick Out of Soccer

Star of Nuremberg's Touring Team Got an Early Start

By MICHAEL STRAUSS

When a New York all-star team helps the Nuremberg Soccer Club of Germany open its seven-game tour on Sunday at Downing Stadium, Randalls Island, the player the Americans will be watching the closest will be Max Morlock. They merely will be following orders.

Morlock is to German soccer what Stan Musial and Willie Mays are to baseball. He sparkles in all departments. He can run, pass, dribble and head the ball with amazing agility. But most important, he can score often.

When the German star arrived with fifteen team-mates at New York International Airport, Idlewild, Queens, yesterday, he was his old chipper self. He joked about a twenty-nine-hour plane trip that should have taken eighteen hours. He marveled at the number of automobiles he saw. He wondered whether he could take one home.

Max is no newcomer to New York. He visited here in 1953, when he led Nuremberg to five victories in six games. His contributions included twelve goals. Against Liverpool, the only team to beat the Germans, he scored both tallies in a 3-to-2 reversal.

Although Morlock has been considered one of the best German forwards for years, he reached his greatest heights last summer. In the world championship games in Switzerland, Max was the big gun.

Feats Set Fans Agog

Morlock's feats in that particular series—forty-six countries were represented—set German soccer fans agog. In the final four games, he scored a total of seven goals. He received much of the credit for his country's success.

There were 80,000 townsmen on hand to greet Morlock when he returned to his native Nuremberg. He was the center of a large parade. It was totally unexpected. His first clue to the ceremonies was the throng of youngsters lining the railroad tracks leading into the city.

Morlock's homecoming culminated a series of celebrations. The high point was the welcome received from 100,000 Germans in Berlin's Olympic Stadium. Each member of the team, made up of players from various parts of West Germany, received a silver leaf. The players also were congratulated by President Theodor Heuss.

That was only part of the picture. Morlock was home only a short time when gifts began to arrive. Manufacturers sent him wardrobes of clothing, complete sets of furniture, a television set, motorcycle, refrigerator and camera.

Morlock reacted with his usual modesty. He rejoiced with his wife, Ingeborg, and his 4-year-old daughter, Ursula. He parried questions about his own

Scandinavian Airlines

Max Morlock as he arrived in New York yesterday.

contributions by emphasizing the fine work of his team-mates. Then he returned to his chores as a shop proprietor.

Morlock Owns Store

In Nuremberg, Morlock owns a general merchandise store that features sporting goods. The business is located on Celtisplatz, opposite the city's main railroad station. It is situated close to the street on which the German star began playing soccer.

Morlock explained that many Germans start to play soccer at a tender age. He admitted he put his foot on a ball for the first time as a 5-year-old. By the time he was 7 he was an old hand at it.

"Like so many youngsters at home, I began playing soccer on Nuremberg's streets. It was against the law because the streets are so narrow and house windows can be broken so easily. I must have broken at least a dozen in my day.

"We would station the smaller boys on the corners to watch for the police," Morlock explained through an interpreter. "If they saw a policeman they would whistle twice with their fingers.

"One day," he continued, "I wasn't fast enough. Unluckily, a policeman showed up just as one of my boots caused a ball to go crashing through a storm window as well as a regular one.

"My father thrashed me. But he didn't discourage me from playing soccer. He insisted that I join the 'Diaper League.'"

Morlock remained in the "Diaper League," the equivalent of our Little League baseball set-up, for only a short time. He worked his way up through the junior and intermediate ranks in quick order. At 18, he was a full fledged senior.

"Will the time ever come

He's Willie Mays of Booters and Takes Acclaim Modestly

when American teams will be able to match the Europeans in soccer prowess?" Murlock was asked.

"Sure," was his ready reply. "Just as soon as youngsters in this country get interested enough in the sport to play it on the streets."

April 29, 1955

80,000 See Russia Top West German Eleven, 3-2

MOSCOW, Aug. 21 (AP)—The Soviet Union's picked national team today defeated West Germany's world football (soccer) champions, 3—2. More than 80,000 spectators, including 1,500 West German fans, watched the game in Dynamo Stadium.

After a 1-1 half-time tie, the Germans moved ahead, 2—1, in the fifty-second minute when their left winger, Hans Schaefer, passed the Russian goalie Jashin, with a narrow-angled shot. Then the Russians put every player into the attack. Their right half, Maslonkin, tied the score in the sixty-ninth minute.

While the Germans defended their goal with all available players, Russia's left winger, Iljen, scored the winning goal in the seventy-first minute.

Several German players insisted that a third German goal by Helmut Rahn should have been allowed. They said Rahn picked up the ball in the German half of the pitch, dribbled through the Russian defense lines but was whistled off-side by Referee Ling when he entered the Russian penalty area.

August 22, 1955

SOVIET IMPRISONS 12 SOCCER RIOTERS

Terms Up to 25 Years Given Armenian 'Hooligans' Who Tried to Lynch Referee

MOSCOW, Nov. 24 — Twelve men have been sentenced to prison for instigating a riot after a soccer match in Soviet Armenia last month. The sentences ranged up to twenty-five years.

This was reported in the edition of Kommunist, organ of the Armenian Communist party's

Central Committee, that arrived here today.

According to the paper, the Armenian Supreme Court said five of the rioters had operated as a criminal gang that attempted to rape a young woman later last month. Such news is rarely reported in the Soviet press.

Under the heading "In Supreme Court of Armenian Republic," the paper said "groups of hooligans and criminals" had started a riot Oct. 12 after a match in Erivan, capital of the republic, between two Class B teams competing for the championship of the Soviet Union. The rioters, "using the dissatisfaction of part of the crowd at the result of the game," tried to lynch the referee and actively resisted the police, the paper added.

"For example," it reported, "one person threw a stone at a militiaman [policeman] and injured him, and then when they tried to arrest him he resisted stubbornly and tried to escape but was caught.

"Another group of hooligans threw stones and other objects into the midst of other citizens and militiamen who were at the stadium."

The Armenian Supreme Court sentenced four rioters to twenty-five years imprisonment each and ordered the confiscation of all their property. Two of these men also participated in the rape attempt Oct. 25.

A. P. Ayrapetyan, who took part in both riot and rape attempt, was condemned to twenty years in prison. Two other members of the gang who participated in both incidents were sentenced to fifteen years each.

Three men who took part only in the soccer disorder were condemned to ten years each, one was sentenced to two years and another to one.

Such severe sentences reflect the Government's growing concern with what is termed here as "hooliganism," especially at sports events. The Soviet press has recently condemned in strong terms drinking and rowdyism at football matches.

Komsomolskaya Pravda recently published a lengthy account of serious disorders at a provincial football match in which many persons, including some of the most prominent figures in town, were seriously injured. The paper bitterly attacked the practice of condoning such outbreaks and demanded that the culprits be dealt with severely regardless of their standing in the community.

November 25, 1955

MANCHESTER CITY TAKES SOCCER CUP

LONDON, May 5—A former German paratrooper, Bert Trautmann, was one of the stars today in the English soccer cup final. Despite a painful neck injury received twenty minutes from the end, he continued to keep goal brilliantly and helped nis team, Manchester City, score a 3-1 victory over Birmingham City.

Football fans looked askance when Trautmann, who had been a prisoner of war in this country, was engaged by the Manchester team. Memories of war were still fresh. Now he is hailed as the "football player of the year."

He received congratulations from Queen Elizabeth when she presented the silver cup of the Football Association and gold medals to the winners.

The presence of the Queen and the Duke of Edinburgh added to the pageantry of the setting in Wembley Stadium. The game drew 100,000 fans who paid £50,000 ($140,000) for admission.

Manchester made its second appearance in the cup final in successive years. Last year it lost to Newcastle.

Manchester crushed Birmingham with second-half goals by Jack Dyson and Robert Johnstone. The goals were scored in the sixty-ninth and seventy-third minutes.

Sharpened by a goal within three minutes of the start, scored by Joseph Hayes, Manchester dominated the early exchanges. Norman Kinsey replied for Birmingham in the fifteenth minute.

Three times in the closing stages Trautmann was hurt in collisions while making daring saves. He reeled about the goalmouth, holding the net for support.

The inspiration for Manchester's attack came from Don Revie, deep-lying center forward.

May 6, 1956

RUSSIAN BOOTERS WIN

Beat Germany, 2-1, in Olympic Contest Marred by Fights

MELBOURNE, Australia, Nov. 24 (UP)—A second Olympic "rhubarb" in as many days marked Russia's 2-1 victory over Germany today in a rough-house opening-round soccer game.

With the Soviets leading, 1-0, in the second half, the game erupted into a slugging match when the Russians were balked time and again by a tough German rearguard. Fist fights broke out among several of the players and the referee, H. G. Mann of Britain, had to halt the game three times to warn the competitors.

The incident followed yesterday's charge by the 10,000-meter champion, Vladimir Kuts of Russia, who claimed Britain's Gordon Pirie repeatedly stepped on his heels during the running of the race.

Pirie admitted he had impeded Kuts' stride but insisted it was "quite unintentional."

November 25, 1956

Indonesia 'Iron Curtain' Shuts Out Soviet Eleven

MELBOURNE, Australia, Friday, Nov. 30 (AP)—The Indonesian soccer team threw an iron curtain in front of its goal in the match against Russia today.

Ten men lined the goal with one man sent out to try and score.

The Russians stood in the middle of the field and wondered how to pierce the rim of grim defenders

Every time they attacked the ball was kicked out.

The match ended in a scoreless draw even after extra time had been ordered.

November 30, 1956

RUSSIA CAPTURES SOCCER FINAL, 1-0

Conquers Yugoslavia in Last Olympic Competitive Test Before 100,000 Fans

MELBOURNE, Australia, Saturday, Dec. 8 (AP)—Russia won the soccer championship, the final competition of the Olympic Games, by defeating Yugoslavia, 1-0, in the final today. A Yugoslav goal was disallowed because of an offside. The victory gave Russia its thirty-seventh gold medal of the Olympics.

The teams were scoreless at the end of the first half.

A crowd of 100,000 in the Olympic Stadium watched the game, which was followed by the closing ceremony of the games.

A light rain fell until the middle of the first half and made the field slippery. Players skidded and fell frequently.

Brilliant Three-Man Play

Russia scored in the forty-ninth minute of the game. Anatolii Iliine headed the ball into the net on a brilliantly executed three-man play.

Yugoslavia put the ball into the goal in the sixty-ninth minute when Zlatko Papec took a pass from Dragoslav Secularec and fired it past the Russian goalie. But Referee R. Wright of Australia had whistled him offside just before the kick.

The game ended in a rough exchange of bumping and pushing as Yugoslavia tried desperately to tie. Yugoslavia's Ivan Santek chased Boris Tatouchine for a few steps after they collided and the crowd booed.

The goal came after Tatouchine had broken through and lobbed the ball into the penalty area. Alatolii Isaaev headed it to Iliine, who in turn headed it into the lower left corner of the goal.

Russia and Yugoslavia were first and second in the final Olympic soccer standing.

December 8, 1956

Aston Villa Triumphs Over Manchester United to Take English Soccer Cup

RECORD 7TH FINAL CAPTURED BY 2-1

By THOMAS P. RONAN
Special to The New York Times.

LONDON, May 4—Aston Villa, the only team in sixty years to win both the Football League championship and the Football Association Cup in one season blocked Manchester United's attempt to match the feat today.

Before a crowd of 100,000 that included Queen Elizabeth, Prince Philip and Prime Minister Harold Macmillan, the Birmingham team defeated Manchester United, 2 to 1, in the cup final, Britain's soccer classic.

Aston Villa, which took the double in 1897, had not won the cup since 1920. But its Wembley Stadium victory made it the first team in soccer history to win seven times. Two other teams, the Blackburn Rovers and Newcastle United, have scored six victories.

The heavily favored Manchester team suffered a disastrous blow six minute: after play began when Ray Wood, its goalkeeper, was injured in a collision with Peter McParland. As-

ton Villa's brilliant outside left.

Wood, who suffered a fractured cheekbone, was out of the game most of the first half and part of the second. Except for the last few minutes when he took over again as goalkeeper, he was at outside right while Jackie Blanchflower, the center half held down his job.

Under British rules, unlike the Continental ones, substitutes cannot be fielded. But the league champions fought the Aston Villa eleven to a standstill in the first half.

Each team drove repeatedly to the other's goal but Blanchflower proved as adept as Nigel Sims, the Aston Villa goalkeeper, in staving off the threats, and neither side scored.

Aston Villa made its first goal midway through the second half when its captain, Johnny Dixon, fed the ball to McParland and the lanky Irishman headed it neatly into the net.

Four minutes later the sharpshooting McParland kicked his second goal to put his team well ahead.

With less than ten minutes of play left, Tommy Taylor, center forward, revived the hopes of Manchester's followers when he headed the ball over Sims' outstretched fingers for a score.

Driving desperately, Man-

chester kept the ball in its opponent's territory most of the rest of the game. But Sims and his team-mates met its repeated threats grimly and prevented further scoring.

After the game, Matt Busby, the Manchester manager, said that Wood had suffered periods of blackout following his injury but that he had insisted on returning to the game. He played an alert, aggressive game when he was in but his injury and the change in the line-up probably cost his team the coveted double.

Manchester United's bid for the second crown against the last team to win both in the same season—only one other team, Preston North End, had taken the double and that was in 1889—gave the game a dramatic flavor.

That and perfect weather brought thousands of fans into London. Before dawn special trains were arriving from Glasgow, Liverpool, Manchester, Birmingham and many other cities.

Many of the fans reached an already sold-out Wembley without tickets and the touts had a merry time. Twenty minutes before the kick-off a ticket worth 49 cents was sold for the equivalent of $8.40, one that cost the equivalent of $3.50 went for

$16.80 and a $7 one went for nearly six times as much.

May 5, 1957

2½c British Pool Ticket Wins Widow $574,658

Special to The New York Times.

LONDON, Nov. 5—A 34-year-old widow won the equivalent of more than half a million dollars on a 2-pence ticket in the week-end soccer football pools. Her winnings of £205,235 ($574,658) were said to be the biggest single prize in the pools' history.

Two pence is about 2½ cents.

Mrs. Nellie McGrail, a $15.50-a-week mail-order clerk from Reddish, near Manchester, came to London today with her two daughters to collect her check from Littlewoods Pools. Three thousand persons greeted her at the railroad station.

Like all gambling winnings in this country, Mrs. McGrail's money is tax-free.

November 6, 1957

7 of Top British Soccer Club Die In Munich Air Crash Killing 21

By The Associated Press.

MUNICH, Germany, Feb. 6—A British airliner carrying Britain s champion soccer team, Manchester United. crashed and burned on its third try to take off here in a snowstorm today.

Twenty-one persons were killed. including seven football men and a member of the plane's crew.

The Munich Police Department announced the official death toll of twenty-one and said twenty-three others. had survived. The department said some of the injured were undergoing emergency operations.

The police feared that two Germans were also killed when the plunging plane struck a house and a gasoline shed.

Seat straps trapped some passengers in the flaming wreckage.

The tragedy plunged the European sports world into mourning.

The twin-engine Elizabethan of the British European Airways had halted here for refueling en route to London from Belgrade, where the Manchester United soccer team played Yugoslavia's Red Star team to a 3-3 tie yesterday and advanced to the semi-finals of the European cup matches.

Eleven sports writers were with the team. Peter Howard and E. A. Ellyard of The Manchester Daily Mail were among the survivors.

But Frank Swift of the London News of the World, a former goal-keeping star who played nineteen times for England before World War II and then became a sports writer, died on the operating. table in a hospital.

Matt Busby, the team manager who is considered one of the great soccer master minds of the world, survived.

Three players, including Manchester's great center forward Tommy Taylor, were among those reported dead.

The British European Airways listed four players and a team coach as definitely among the victims.

It said at least seven—perhaps eight—sports writers died in the tragedy, listing the seven as Mr. Swift, Tom Jackson, Archie Ledbrooke, H. D. Davies, Eric Thompson, George Fellows and Henry Rose.

Sports writer A. Clarke was listed as missing.

Witnesses said the plane brushed some treetops at the end of the runway, then plunged from a height of about sixty feet into a two-story house and a shed in the village of Kirchtrudering. Both wings of the plane were ripped off and one engine was thrown through the air.

The police said the shed into which the plane crashed was stacked with gasoline and oil cans and that these exploded and set fire to the plane.

The British European Airways said that among the survivors were four of the six crew members, Capt. James Thain, the pilot, stewardesses Margaret Bellis and Rosemary Cheverton and the first officer. Capt. G. K. Rayment. The radio officer and a steward were still missing.

February 7, 1958

English Soccer Team Wires Field for Heat

LONDON, April 20 (Reuters)—Everton, a major English soccer club tired of icy and rain-bogged turf, is constructing an underground heating system that will keep its field fit for play at any time.

A system of wires underneath the soil, plus a new drainage system, will enable Everton to play during wet winter months.

Every year when fog, rain and snow closes in on the British Isles, the terrible state of fields forces many postponements. Since the teams play every week from August to May, two or three postponed games can put pressure on a team near the end of the season.

Bad fields also cause many broken bones. Entire teams have become so banged up they have been knocked off stride for weeks.

Everton will keep snow dissolved and frost at bay with its new electric wiring system, which will cost about 13,000 pounds, $36,400).

April 21, 1958

Bolton Wanderers Down Manchester United to Capture English Soccer Cup

LOFTHOUSE GOALS TAKE FINAL BY 2-0

Bolton Captain Tallies in Each Half at Wembley to End Manchester Hopes

By JOSEPH FRAYMAN
Special to The New York Times.

LONDON, May 3—Against a wave of national emotion wishing victory for Manchester United, the soccer prize of the year was taken today by the Bolton Wanderers with a score of 2—0.

Millions of Britons longed for the youthful Manchester side, rebuilt from the champion team shattered in an air crash at Munich three months ago, to win the Football Association Cup. But their hopes broke against the superiority of Bolton and the inability of Manchester to rise to the occasion.

The cup was won for the Wanderers by their captain, Nat Lofthouse. Playing in the key attacking position of center-forward with a silver pin in a damaged shoulder, he scored both goals.

Lofthouse holds the record for goal scoring as an international player for England and has been nominated again for the English side to play in the forthcoming World Cup competition.

In the center-forward position in the Manchester eleven was Bobby Charlton, now beginning an international career. Among team-mates were only three other survivors of the airplane wreck.

The clash of two Lancashire teams added to the drama of England's great sports event. When the crowd of 100,000 in the huge Wembley Stadium sang "Abide With Me" as is done before every cup final, thoughts were on the eight Manchester players who died in the Munich crash.

In addition to spectators, millions more watched the match through television. The receipts for the all-ticket final were nearly £50,000 ($140,000).

Open Ticket Auctions Held

Ticket touts were busy and open auctions were held along all roads leading to the stadium. The average price asked for the cheapest tickets costing three shillings six pence (49 cents) was £4/10, ($12.60).

The teams — Manchester in red shirts and white knickers and Bolton in white and navy blue — were presented to the Duke of Edinburgh before the kick-off. So too were Matt Busby, Manchester's manager, and Prof. Georg Maurer, chief surgeon of Rechts Der Isar Hospital, Munich, where the air crish victims were taken.

On Monday Queen Elizabeth will invest Professor Maurer with the Commander Order of the British Empire at Buckingham Palace.

Play was only three minutes old when Lofthouse struck— before the Manchester defenders had time to settle down. From short range he steered the yellow ball past Harry Gregg, Manchester's Irish goalkeeper.

Manchester, appearing in a cup final for the second successive year, tried desperately to equalize, but could recapture only flashes of the spirit and brilliance that had carried the team to Wembley. United's best forwards, Charlton and Ernie Taylor, were too closely marked to be allowed any openings.

Shaky Under Pressure

In the first half hour, Bolton's goalkeeper, Eddie Hopkinson, was called into serious action on only one occasion. But when Bolton threatened, the Manchester defense looked shaky under pressure.

Early in the second half a cannonball shot from Charlton rebounded from the goalpost into Hopkinson's hands when a goal seemed certain.

Barely had the crowd sim-

mered down when Lofthouse scored again, after ten minutes of the second half. As Gregg reached for a high ball he was shoulder-charged by Lofthouse into the net.

The impact knocked Gregg out and for a few minutes he lay prone as the trainer tried to revive him. Manchester's now-despondent supporters had memories of a mishap in last year's final in which the goalkeeper, Ray Wood, had his jaw broken by a collision in the first few minutes. His retirement cost his side the match with Aston Villa.

However, Gregg was able to play on despite an injured back. Manchester resumed the attack and again went close with a shot that struck Bolton's goal post. But luck was denied Manchester and by the end United's attack faded before a solid defense.

May 4, 1958

German Finds Britain Fair in Love and Soccer

Ex-P. O. W., Wed to English Girl, Is Star Goalie

At her home in England all during the war, Margaret Friar, a blue-eyed blonde, grew up hating German soldiers. So it was natural in 1948 that she should fume and fuss when her father invited to tea a former German paratrooper.

"If that man comes into this house," Margaret warned, "I'm going out." The German came. Margaret went to the movies. Hardly anyone in St. Helens, England, could believe it when, eighteen months later, they were married.

But Bert Trautmann, born thirty-six years ago in Bremen, Germany, got most of what he now has against heavy odds.

He is a tall, straight-spined blend with pale blue eyes and speckled, ruddy skin. The redeeming feature of his life has been that he has never plotted, never planned anything; somehow he manages to move rather breezily through life playing everything by ear.

2 Enemies Capture Him

Five years before Margaret met him, he was fighting with the Luftwaffe on the Russian front, doing and thinking pretty much what soldiers do and think in war novels. Once the Russians captured him. Seventeen days later he escaped.

In March, 1945, he was captured again, this time by the Americans. With other German paratroopers, Trautmann was taken to an English P.O.W. camp in Cheshire where, in time, he became the chauffeur of a British colonel's Hillman-Minx.

With the colonel's permission, Trautmann began to play soccer on the Camp 50 team in the P. O. W. league. Soccer "bugs"

Bert Trautmann, the German-born goalkeeper, in action

from near-by St. Helens often attended these matches, and one such bug was a stocky, amiable Englishman named Jack Friar. When Trautmann was released from Camp 50 in 1948, Friar arranged for him to play goalkeeper on the St. Helens team, and also invited him to tea.

In the year following, Trautmann signed professionally with Manchester City, thereby becoming the most controversial player in England. British soldiers protested; hundreds of letter-writers complained in the press; one local headline reasoned: "City Must Be Mad . . ."

But Trautmann remained, and in 1955 he became the first German to play in England's soccer classic, the cup final at Wembley. There he was congratulated by both Queen Elizabeth and the Duke of Edinburgh, who told him, "Sehr gut."

In 1956, as Manchester City again reached the Cup final, and beat Birmingham, 3—1,

Trautmann was named "Footballer of the Year" by England's soccer writers.

Yesterday over breakfast at the Paramount Hotel, Trautmann relaxed and evoked a series of flashbacks, having nothing better to do until 2 o'clock this afternoon when Manchester City engages Hearts of Midlothian, a Scottish team, at Ebbets Field.

The touring Manchester City team is sponsored in this country by the American Soccer League. Today's match will be the only appearance of both clubs in New York City.

Trautmann said he is perfectly happy living in England, and that British fans, finding him a decent bloke, now cheer him. He lives with Margaret in a seven-and-one-half room house, drives a Volkswagen, and is giving no thought to the future.

'He Flies Through the Air'

Erno Schwarcz, business manager of the American Soccer League, and a man given to grand opinion, said Trautmann is the best goalie in the world. He estimated that in the world there are 2,000,000 goalkeepers.

"Trautmann makes miraculous saves," Schwarcz, said. "He flies through the air, dives, jumps high, and fists that ball away from the danger area. He's exceptionally daring. In 1956, before 100,000 fans in the Cup final, he broke his neck. It was an injury very much like Roy Campanella's. Trautmann was out seven months."

For his efforts, Trautmann, like all soccer players, is not overpaid. He earns weekly about $36 take-home pay, but supplements this with speech-making and writing sports for The Manchester Evening News, where he rarely mentions his own name.

It isn't necessary.

May 25, 1958

Brazil Gains World Soccer Cup, Routing Sweden Before 52,000 at Stockholm

SOUTH AMERICANS WIN, 5-2, AND WEEP

STOCKHOLM, June 29 (UPI) Favored Brazil won the World Soccer Cup today by beating the host nation, Sweden, 5—2, with a dazzling display of football wizardry.

It was Brazil's first victory in what is considered the world's most popular sports event, outside the Olympics, and it leveled the score between Europe and South America at three cup victories each. The defending champion, Western Germany, was beaten by Sweden in the semi-finals.

A capacity crowd of 52,000, including King Gustav Adolf of Sweden and other members of the Royal Family, roared the

Swedish battle cry of "Heja Sverige" as Nils Liedholm, inside left, put Sweden in the lead after only seven and one-half minutes of play.

But Stockholm's Rasunda Stadium became more and more quiet as the Brazilians began to weave the patterns that led to a scoring spree unsurpassed in the 28-year-old history of the World Soccer Cup. The highest previous score in a cup final was 4—2.

Pele, Vava and Didi Star

Outstanding on the Brazilian team were Pele, Vava and Didi, forwards. Didi's great midfield strategy provided uncounted openings from which the 17-year-old Pele — the youngest player in the tournament—and Vava scored two goals each.

Pele's second goal—Brazil's fifth—came only seconds before the game was over, and he remained sprawled in the mud in front of the Swedish goal, beating the ground with both hands in a frenzy of joy.

All the Brazilian athletes wept when the president of the World Football Federation, Arthur Drewry, handed the $6,000 Jules Rimet Cup, symbolic of soccer supremacy, to

Captain Bellini. Firecrackers were still being fired by Brazilian supporters as the Brazilian team drove off in a bus, with police trying to snatch away children who were clinging to the doors and the rear end.

The Brazilians dominated the Swedes in every respect. Their dribbling, surprising changes of pace and direction and their quick-witted passing game often made the Swedes look like schoolboys. The host team—a mixture of amateurs playing

with the Swedish clubs and professionals playing in the Italian League—is considered Europe's best together with France. The French were beaten, 5—2, by Brazil in a semi-final.

June 30, 1958

FLYING SAVE: Gylmar dos Santos Neves, Brazil's goalie, smothers a scoring attempt by the Swedish team during the World Soccer Cup final at Stockholm. The South Americans won yesterday's game, 5-2, to capture championship.

Leftists and Clergy Tie In Soccer Match in Italy

BARDINETO, Italy, Aug. 17 (AP)—The game ended in a 3-3 tie. People will be talking about it up here in the Bornida Valley for weeks to come.

On one soccer team were the black-robed village priests from the little towns around. On the other team, in white shorts, were the Communist and Socialist Mayors and Councilmen of the same villages.

Most of the villages of the north Italian area have Com-

munist or Socialist administrations. And all have Roman Catholic churches. Bantering between village elders and parish clergymen finally led to the challenge soccer match.

It was played before 3,000 spectators yesterday.

The 50-year-old rector of the Parish of Calizzano, Don

Sofia, and Father Leone led the priests' attack. The village elders' defense rallied around the 47-year-old Socialist Mayor of Calizzano and the Communist Mayor of Pareto.

August 18, 1958

Nottingham Forest Triumphs Over Luton Town in English Soccer Cup Final

LATE BID CHECKED FOR A 2-1 VICTORY

Nottingham Loses Key Man but Fights on, Takes Cup First Time Since 1898

By JOSEPH FRAYMAN
Special to The New York Times.

LONDON, May 2—Nottingham Forest, playing brilliant soccer, held on to a 2-1 victory over Luton Town in the English Football Association Cup final

today despite the loss of a key man because of a cracked shinbone.

Until Roy Dwight, who scored the first goal, was carried from the field Nottingham had dominated play. As no substitutes are allowed, the depleted side struggled to hold out for the remaining hour of the ninety-minute match.

Luton seized the advantage to reduce the arrears after being two goals down in the first fifteen minutes. Its attackers besieged Nottingham's goal but were unable to score an equalizer.

The game brought two newcomers to the great bowl of Wembley Arena in the thirty-one-year history of cup finals played there.

Luton had never reached the

final of this knock-out competition before. Nottingham last appeared in a cup final in the season of 1897-98, when it beat Derby County, 3—1.

National Folk Festival

The cup final, culmination of a soccer season of more than eight months, has acquired the character of a national folk festival. The crowd of 100,000 cheered the arrival of the Queen and the Duke of Edinburgh.

The sun-tanned Duke, fulfilling his first public engagement since his return Thursday from his global tour, inspected the players—Luton in white shirts and black shorts and Nottingham in red and white.

Luton's supporters were distinguished by their straw hats, the making of which was once the town's main occupation. Today Luton, thirty miles from London, is far more dependent

on General Motor's Vauxhall plant.

The other stands were splashed with the red and white of Nottingham, Midlands town of lace, cigarettes, bicycles and—so it claims—the prettiest girls in the country. Hundreds of Nottingham girls wore summer dresses in club colors.

The preliminaries to the game have by now become almost a ritual, in which the singing of the hymn "Abide With Me" takes chief place. A proposal this year to omit the hymn as inappropriate on a secular occasion was abandoned after the fans had made it clear that the hymn singing added spiritual satisfaction to an enjoyable outing.

Heavy Pressure From Start

Nottingham exerted heavy pressure from the start and was rewarded when Dwight, the outside right, scored after nine minutes of play.

At this stage Luton was powerless against the polished football of its opponents. The five small, red-shirted forwards of Nottingham formed a perfect attacking machine. Their clean, crisp passing found a man in position every time. They were faster on the ball and bewildered the Luton defenders with their swapping of positions.

This was vintage soccer of the great days of England's soccer ascendancy when Nottingham's team manager, Billy Walker, graced the English attack.

In the fourteenth minute, Billy Gray, the Forest's inside left, chipped over a perfect pass to the center, and Tommy Wilson, center-forward, headed the ball into the goal.

Claims Victim Again

Then, after thirty minutes, the lush Wembley turf claimed a victim, as it had done in previous cup finals. Dwight chased a long toss and went into a harmless-looking tackle. He twisted awkwardly as he fell. After attention from the trainer he got up but fell again, holding his right leg.

Now Luton applied the pressure. But Nottingham, although its pattern of play had been disorganized, hung on grimly to half-time.

In the second half, Syd Owen, captain of Luton, playing his last game before retirement, urged his men to greater effort. They threw themselves furiously into attack, and in the sixty-second minute reduced the margin to 2—1 with a goal by David Pacey, the left half, from a corner kick.

Excitement mounted as Luton strove desperately to gain an equalizer. By sheer weight of numbers—eleven against ten—Luton hammered away. But generally the Luton players' methods had more industry than imagination and they were unable to make full use of the advantage that had been presented to them.

May 3, 1959

Famous Soccer Feet to Twinkle Again

By WILLIAM R. CONKLIN
Special to The New York Times.

BLACKPOOL, England, June 25—On a rubbing table in the dressing room of the Blackpool Football Club, the most famous feet in Association football seemed strangely out of character in their complete relaxation.

An assistant trainer flexed and re-flexed the internationally known Stanley Matthews' right knee. Stiffness in the knee had kept him sidelined most of last season. As the rubber worked smoothly along, Matthews leaned back to talk soccer.

In England, Matthews is acknowledged as the undisputed King of Football. Wherever soccer is played around the globe he is recognized as the greatest stylist the game has produced. To see him play is to witness the perfectionist in action, a past master at moving the ball past his opposition. Usually, he feints opposing backs off balance, moves unexpectedly, and leaves them sprawled on the turf without touching them. How does he do it?

Question of Timing

"It's a matter of timing," he explains in modest tone. "You can never plan your moves before the game. In play, when a situation develops, the player who is quickest off the mark has the best chance of getting the ball. That is why I concentrate on 20-yard sprints in training.

"My right knee is fine now, and I'm looking forward to our opening game against the Bolton Wanderers, another Lancashire team, when the new season opens in August."

Matthews, known as "Stanley Motthews" in Lancashire, has played nineteen years with Blackpool as outside right. He will be a superbly conditioned 45 on Feb. 1.

He began playing with Stoke City, a Staffordshire team from the Midlands, then he was 15 years old. By the time he was 23 he had played seventeen times for England. He was the first player to break all records for international appearances, and has played in three cup finals.

In 1953 he won the cup for Blackpool against Bolton in the

Stanley Matthews trains for the new season under approving eye of Blackpool policeman

closing seconds of play in London's Wembley Stadium before 100,000 screaming fans.

His father, Jack Matthews, was "The Fighting Barber of Hanley" in his featherweight days. In 350 bouts he lost only nine. One of his victories was gained at the expense of a Scotsman, Tancy Lee, who had beaten the great Jimmy Wilde.

Stanley's son, 13-year-old Stanley Jr., held the Lancashire junior tennis championship last year. This year the lad is stepping up into the men's open competition in his home county. His sister Jean, 20, is away at college and plans to become a games mistress, comparable to a head coach's job in all sports.

Mrs. Matthews is the former Betty Vallance, daughter of a football trainer and a superior golfer in her own right.

"Football has given me a passport to the world," says Ston The Mon, who stands 5 feet 9 inches and weighs a tidy 157 pounds. "I played twice in Hong Kong before 32,000 each time. Then there were exhibition matches in Ghana, Australia and Zanzibar. They're mad for football in Zanzibar.

"Three years ago I played against a barefoot team in Kenya, and I took great pains to avoid stepping on their feet. As it turned out, I need not have worried. They could kick a football just as hard in bare feet as I could with my heavy football boots on."

Referee Sees Infraction

A few years back, Matthews played against the Wolverhampton Wanderers, known as a rough lot of customers throughout the First Division. One Wolves' player sought to humiliate the Blackpool winger by pulling his shirt out of his pants. After several pulls, Matthews pushed his tormentor away.

The referee saw the push, but had missed seeing the provocation. He awarded a free Wolves' kick against Blackpool with Stonley as the goat. In terms of rarity, this penalty against Matthews could be compared to Sir Winston Churchill's slaking his thirst with water.

When Blackpool opens against Bolton in August, the seaside-city cohorts will be out in force to set up a roar whenever Matthews gets the ball.

"'Ave a go, Ston", they will urge in keen desire for a rare Matthews goal. Failing that, they will once more admire his precise footwork with the oft-repeated:

"Yon mon — he's real chompion."

June 28, 1959

One Soccer Field for Ten Nations

League to Start Play in '60—Every Game at Randalls Island

By DEANE McGOWEN

A new professional soccer league, with teams from at least ten nations, will begin operations next summer. It will be known as the International Soccer League and will have one playing field—Downing Stadium on Randalls Island.

Plans were announced simultaneously yesterday by Mayor Wagner at City Hall and by William D. Cox in London. Cox is the president of the league's New York entry.

The league will include teams from England, Scotland, Ireland, West Germany, Sweden, Austria, Hungary, France, Italy and possibly Spain. There is also a chance that one or two South American teams will compete.

A split season will be played, with the New York team competing in each half against five foreign teams. The foreign teams will be brought here after concluding their regular league competition at home.

The league games will be played on Wednesday and Sat-urday nights at Downing Stadium. An expenditure of $50,000 to $75,000 is planned to improve the stadium's lighting facilities.

Competition will begin May 25 in the first division and will end June 26. Then the second division will start its round-robin play on June 29 and end with a double-header on Aug. 3. A thirty-game schedule is envisioned, followed by a championship play-off between the division winners.

In disclosing the plans, Mayor Wagner said:

"I'm delighted about the new international professional soccer league. We're very happy about the New York entry. New York is a great sports town, and the games will be an important development in our national program to bring about better understanding between the people of our land and those of foreign nations.

"Many of our citizens in the city are foreign born. They all are fond of soccer and they have instilled that fondness in their children. This new league will give all of us a chance to see the greatest players in the game competing against a New York team. The city will coöperate in every possible way to help this league succeed."

Cox is no stranger to the pro-fessional sporting scene in this country. He operated the Brooklyn Football Dodgers of the All-America Conference in 1945. In 1943, he was president of the Philadelphia Phillies baseball team.

Schwarcz an Official

In addition to Cox, the other officers of the New York club are Blackwell Smith, the secretary - treasurer, and Erno Schwarcz, the vice president and general manager. Both were at City Hall yesterday, together with Justin Purcell, the league's executive secretary.

Schwarcz said that no name for the New York club or a coach had been selected. However, it was learned that Danny Blanchflower was being considered as coach.

Blanchflower is one of England's best players. He plays right halfback for the world-famous Tottenham Hotspurs of the English First Division and is also captain of Ireland's national team.

Schwarcz was extremely optimistic in discussing the new league. A former player for the Hungarian national team, Schwarcz pointed to the success of other foreign teams that had played here in recent years.

Schwarcz said that eleven games in Ebbets Field last season had drawn a total of 114,000 soccer fans.

Optimistic About Chances

"Those games were played between outstanding foreign squads against all-star teams composed of local players from the American Soccer League. If the games were that well attended we feel we can make an even greater success of an international league playing a regular schedule leading to a championship.

"We are prepared to spend $400,000 to $500,000 to get this league in operation. We have to transport the foreign teams from and to their home countries and pay for their upkeep while they are here."

The New York squad will be made up of American players and possibly a few foreign international performers. All games will be played under international rules — forty-five-minute halves and no substitutions for an injured player who has to withdraw from the match.

Randalls Island, which can seat 25,000 persons, will be scaled at $2 for general admission and $3 for box and reserved seats. The Parks Department will install 1,200 box seats, which will be sold on a season basis.

October 29, 1959

St. Louis Trounces Bridgeport to Capture N.C.A.A.'s First Soccer Crown

DUEKER SCORES 3 IN 5-TO-2 VICTORY

St. Louis Wins Title in Its First Year of Competition

Special to The New York Times.

STORRS, Conn., Nov. 28—St. Louis University, in its first varsity season of collegiate soccer, became the first National Collegiate Athletic Association champion by defeating the University of Bridgeport, 5 to 2, at the University of Connecticut field today.

A goal by Mike Shanahan at 12:15 of the second period gave St. Louis a 3-2 lead that they maintained despite an inspired Bridgeport attack in the remainder of the second period and throughout the third period.

Penalties cost Bridgeport dearly in the fourth period as St. Louis scored two more goals to put the game out of reach Tom Richmond, the left halfback, scored on a 22-yard kick that the goalie, Nich Wirth,

was unable to control. Richmond tallied at 3:53. Thirty seconds later, John Dueker registered on a direct kick from thirty yards out.

High-Scoring Effort

Dueker was the star of the contest with three goals and two assists.

Bridgeport opened the scoring at 3:10 of the first period when John Majesko tallied. Dueker then followed with two first period goals for St. Louis. Jon Olsen, a substitute, tied the score for Bridgeport at 4:40 of the second period.

St. Louis finished with an over-all record of ten victories and one defeat. The Billikens beat San Francisco and City College of New York in the championship tournament. Bridgeport had won eleven games before today.

St. Louis	2	1	0	2—5
Bridgeport	1	1	0	0—2

St. Louis scoring—Dueker 3, Shanahan, Richmond.
Bridgeport scoring—Majesko, Olsen.

November 29, 1959

Soccer Fans in Europe Boo With Knives, Guns and Rocks

Home-Town Players Objects of Wrath When They Fail

By ROBERT DALEY

Special to The New York Times.

NICE, France, Nov. 25—At Lienz, Austria, during the heat of a game, soccer player Josef Hintenborner, suddenly pitched forward to the turf — shot through a lung by an irate fan.

At Pleszew, Poland, a player named Dame was stabbed in the kidneys by the manager of the stadium.

At Sedan, France, a time-out had to be called when a player was knocked out by a rock thrown from the grandstand. The rock-thrower, one Cyrille Duplicy, was caught, convicted and fined more than $300. Duplicy was unlucky. Hundreds of rock-throwing fans in France get away with it week after week. Duplicy was one of the few whom police have managed to arrest.

All of which goes to prove

Britain Only Outpost of 'Sanity' Among Sport's Rooters

that soccer is a dangerous game as played on this continent, at least for those who do not play it very well. The significant thing is not so much that players are attacked fairly frequently, but that the attackers are almost always their own "deceived" fans.

Visitors Are Safe

A visiting player can score five goals, destroying the home team single-handedly, then saunter out into the street afterward as if nothing had happened. No one will bother him.

But heaven help the hometown goalie who let those five goals go through if he attempts to leave the stadium without a police escort.

Stars, of course, do not have to worry about being shot, stabbed or brained. Instead they became movie actors, industrial barons or popular crooners. Last week Just Fontaine, high scorer of the Rheims (France) team, made his television debut as a "singer of charm."

Critics reported that he had only a "thread of a voice," but marvelled at his poise and predicted a brilliant future. The player's few records have already outsold those of Jacques Charrier, who is younger, better looking and the husband of Brigitte Bardot.

Soccer is by far the world's most popular game and in a dozen cities in Europe fans fill 100,000-seat stadiums to capacity every time a major match is played. More than 60,000 watched in Karlsruhe, West Germany, as the home team played Nurenberg last week—a third of the population of the city.

Swiss Become Bitter

When the peace-loving Swiss were wiped out, 8—0, by the Hungarians recently, it caused a bitter investigation of the officials who had let such a horror occur. Even Sweden is wild about soccer. Last week the "Swedish Athlete of the Year" was named. Was it Ingemar Johansson, heavyweight champion of the world? It was not. It was Agne Simonsson, a soccer player.

The only sane place where the game is played is Britain. A juicy scandal by British standards, recently erupted when several players were accused of faking kicks at the ball—then letting opponents have it in the shins instead.

It was reasoned that this "deplorable" practice, which is as normal as breakfast on the continent, would soon stop when the players involved realized they were losing the respect of their fans.

Why is soccer, which seems unexciting to the American temperament, so popular? One reason is because there is so much competition, despite differences in style and salary. British players earn $56 a week and German $80 or less a month, while French, Italian and Spanish stars may earn up to $30,000 a year.

In the Soviet zone all teams are "amateur," representing factories or army units. However a player's wage or rank is likely to fluctuate in relation to how many goals he scores.

Despite this variety, teams of all nations seem able to compete on absolutely level terms with one other. Competi-

tion in the half-dozen or so international matches each week is intense. Thus, fans not only follow their team in its own league and if it's powerful enough, in international matches, but also follow the fortunes of their national team. Under such intense stimulus, interest remains taut all season long.

Also, the international character of soccer gives it somewhat the same appeal of a travel in their imaginations to all the exotic places their team plays.

For instance, last week the Nice team, as champion of France, played Istanbul in Istanbul. Fans avidly read reports of the game and its atmosphere: How the Turks packed the stadium hours before the game; how men hung like bunches of grapes from the gas works and other structures outside the stadium that gave a view of the field. A group of nonpaying spectators saw the game from a minaret, one report said, and released a flock of pigeons, flapping and fluttering in the autumn air, after every goal.

It was possible, if a man were fan enough, to imagine that he had been to Turkey and seen the match. In any case, his life was more exciting because of it, and his love of soccer stronger.

November 29, 1959

MADRID TAKES TITLE IN EUROPEAN SOCCER

GLASGOW, Scotland, May 18 (UPI)—Real Madrid won the European Soccer Cup tonight for the fifth consecutive time by defeating Eintrancht of Frankfurt, 7—3, before 135,000 fans at Hampden Park.

The game was a personal triumph for a 33-year-old Hungarianborn exile, Ferenc Pus

kas, who scored four goals for the Spanish club.

A thunderous roar went up as the final whistle sounded. It was Glasgow's — and Scotland's — salute to the wizards from Spain. The famed "Hampden roar" went up again as the victors ran around the field holding the cup aloft.

Real has now won the trophy every year since the tournament's start.

After a shaky opening, Real Madrid settled down, went ahead and almost immediately

moved beyond reach. Challenging Puskas closely for the honors was the baldish Argentine, Alfredo Di Stefano, who scored Madrid's other three tallies.

For the Germans, the center-forward, Erwin Stein, scored two goals and the right winger, Richard Kress, one. It was Kress, teaming beautifully with the inside right, Dieter Lindner, who staggered the Spanish defenders early in the game by opening the scoring in the twentieth minute.

May 19, 1960

Bill Brown, Tottenham goalkeeper, dives to stop Bolton shot on goal in game at London

The Swede Who Bets on Soccer Aids All His Country's Sports

Government's Income From Wagering More Than $23,000,000 Annually— $2,000,000 Goes to Athletics

By WERNER WISKARI
Special to The New York Times.

STOCKHOLM, May 28—When the Swedish Olympic team goes to Rome in August, it will travel on a small part of the profits of a huge Government-owned gambling enterprise.

The Olympic Committee and other Swedish amateur sports organizations are financed with money the Government makes from handling the betting on soccer games. It's a profitable business.

When the state went into it in 1934, the intention was to use all profits to support sports and outdoor recreational activities such as camping. But this intention was quickly diluted as betting — and profits — multiplied beyond all expectations.

It wasn't long before the Government began keeping most of the profits to help pay for social welfare, national defense and other costly programs.

In the year ending last July 1, Swedes wagered more than $35,000,000 on Swedish and English soccer games.

Counting the $4,700,000 in income taxes that were withheld from the winnings, the state benefited from the year's soccer betting by more than $23,700,-000. Only $2,670,000 was set aside to subsidize sports and outdoor recreation in general.

More than 40 per cent of this was used for the upkeep of Stockholm Stadium and playing fields, swimming pools and other athletic facilities across the country. Virtually every conceivable type of sport known in Sweden was subsidized from the remainder.

The Swedish Table Tennis Association, for example, got more than $25,600, while the Lawn Tennis Association drew $16,000 and the Badminton Association $7,000. The Golf Association got $7,200 and $2,900 went to nurture an interest in miniature golf.

Many Sports Aided

Among the other sports that were aided were amateur boxing, archery, basketball, bobsledding, bowling, canoeing, curling, cycling, fencing, gymnastics, handball, hockey, rowing, skating, skate sailing, skiing, swimming and track.

The Olympic Committee received $68,000. For the Olympics in Rome, however, it has obtained an increase. Its budget for sending to Rome a squad of 200—165 of them athletes—runs to $100,000.

All this has been made possible by the weekly rush of Swedes to obtain betting coupons from the 11,000 tobacconists, newspaper dealers and other small shopkeepers who act as Government betting agents.

In the most popular form of betting, the player marks his choices in twelve games. The

smallest amount that will be accepted by the Government-appointed bet-taker is 8 cents, of which 1 cent is turned over to the state as a special tax. The remaining 7 cents has a theoretical chance of winning from $1 to $50,000.

English Games Followed

Swedish soccer games are used in the betting except in the winter, when the weather makes games here impossible. Then the bettor turns his attention to English soccer.

It is from England that this form of gambling spread to

Sweden in the Nineteen Twenties. Although it was against the law here then and strenuous attempts were made to stamp it out, English-directed betting on soccer games swept the country.

And so this gambling was nationalized. As one Swedish official explained it, the state took over to end "the moral injuries that accompany an underground activity" and to prevent "considerable sums of money" from leaving the country.

It was a profitable move.

June 5, 1960

Bangu Conquers Kilmarnock, 2-0, in Soccer

Brazilians Win Title Before 25,440 — Santos Excels

By GORDON S. WHITE Jr.

Bangu of Brazil, Latin America's only entry in the International Soccer League, gained the league championship yesterday at the Polo Grounds. In one of the best-played games of the season, Bangu scored a 2-0 decision over Kilmarnock of Scotland before 25,440 fans for the title.

The game was a fast, well-fought contest. The enthusiastic reception it got by the largest International Soccer League crowd of the year brightened the future of this league, which began operations this season.

A Matter of Prestige

Competition next year is virtually certain. The fans left with the realization that they had seen what was probably the best match played in the United States in many a year.

Bangu and Kilmarnock, the winners of the two divisions in the league, met with something big at stake—the prestige of the league title and the American Challenge Cup.

The teams waged a struggle that could have gone either way for eighty-seven of the ninety minutes of play. It was with three minutes to go that Bangu scored its second goal and crushed any hopes the Scots had.

Bangu had scored its first goal after three minutes in the first half on a fine display of team work. The slim margin kept the Kilmarnock partisans hopeful until the end of the match.

Valter Santos, the inside left for Bangu kicked both goals. But it was a team effort for the first score and much the same for the second.

The New York Times

Kilmarnock players carry Decio Esteves da Silva, captain of the victorious Bangu team

Trailing by but one goal, Kilmarnock pressed the attack at every chance, running with the fast, small South Americans and not letting up until Santos had booted his 25-yard shot and pulled down the curtain.

The first goal was executed after the Bangu squad had laid a trap for Kilmarnock and the latter had fallen into it.

Bangu moved the ball up the left side of the field on the attack, playing a split offensive. Stationing three men on the left to move the ball and the rest of its attack on the far right side, Bangu opened the center as the Scots moved to cover both the right and the left.

Suddenly, Santos broke from the group on the left and headed toward the center, leaving defenders behind. Decio Esteves

da Silva passed well to Santos and he kicked by Jimmy Brown, Kilmarnock's goalie. The ball traveled about 10 yards.

This trap, so perfectly sprung, never had claws again. Once burned, the Scots never fell for the split again, though the Brazilians hopefully repeated the same tactics.

A Concerted Effort

The second shot was the result of a concerted effort on Bangu's part to press the tiring Kilmarnock players. During the last ten minutes, the Scots slowed, playing a defending game. The fast Bangu squad moved in time and time again in these late stages.

With the ball bounding about and Bangu in control, Santos let fly with a strong punt directly in front of the goal, 25

yards away. The ball bounded off the head of Bill Toner, a Kilmarnock defender, and flew high, just out of reach of Brown, for the score.

Throughout the first half, Kilmarnock presented the most concentrated attack. But missed opportunities cost the Scots dearly. Once Hugh Brown slipped by the defenders and was in position to boot at the nets, which were covered only by the Bangu goalie, Ubirajara Motta. But Brown slipped in making a turn.

Bangu, however, fell heir to such chances in the second half and also missed some. Correia Ferreira had an open shot without the hindrance of a goalie defending. But he missed by the narrowest of margins as the ball struck the upright to his right after a 10-yard kick.

45

The New York Times

HOLDING THE LINE: Bangu, in striped shirts, thwarts concentrated attack by Kilmarnock in the second half of the International Soccer League championship at the Polo Grounds. Bangu, star Brazilian club, shut out the Scots.

Kilmarnock presented no excuses for losing, having only high praise for Bangu. In a similar display of sportsmanship, the Brazilians unanimously claimed the Kilmarnock team was the best they had ever played.

Brazilian Stature Rises

By winning, Bangu added considerably to Brazil's growing prestige as an international soccer power. Brazil won the world championship two years ago in the competition held every four years.

One of Bangu's stars, Zozimo Calazaes, was on the Brazilian eleven that won the world title in 1958. Santos, Darcy De Faria and Calazaes are expected to be Bangu's candidates for the team that will defend the world title.

In a preliminary game between American Soccer League teams, Hakoah defeated Newark Portugese, 6–1.

BANGU (2)		KILMARNOCK (0)
Motta	G.	J. Brown
Fonseca	R.B.	Richmond
DeFaria	L.B.	Watson
Calazans	R.H.	Beattie
Cruz	C.H.	Toner
N. Santos	L.H.	Kennedy
Ferreira	O.R.	H. Brown
Silva	I.R.	McInally
Esteves	C.F.	Wentzel
V. Santos	I.L.	Black
B. Macedo	O.L.	Muir

Goals—V. Santos 2.
Referee—James McLean. Linesmen—Harry Nowick and Thomas Callaghan.

August 7, 1960

Yugoslav Team Wins Gold Medal in Soccer

ROME, Sept. 10 (UPI) — Yugoslavia, despite the absence for fifty-three minutes of a star player sent off the field by the referee, beat Denmark, 3—1, in the Olympic soccer final tonight.

Hungary had won the bronze medal last night by beating Italy.

The Yugoslavs were two goals ahead when their center forward, Galic, was given his marching orders for arguing with the referee, Loncetto LoBello. They increased their lead to 3–0 midway through the second half.

The Danes scored in the closing seconds.

The performance of the winner was superb. But the Danes were only a shadow of the team that had delighted Italian fans in the early stages of the tournament.

September 11, 1960

St. Louis Triumphs, 3-2, In N.C.A.A. Soccer Final

By MICHAEL STRAUSS

St. Louis University's soccer team made a three-day 2,000-mile round-trip to New York pay off yesterday when it successfully defended its National Collegiate Athletic Association crown at Brooklyn College Field.

The Billikens, paced by the speedy Don Range and Italian-born Gerry Balassi, defeated the University of Maryland, 3—2, in a fast-moving game. Range accounted for two goals and Balassi the third.

The Blue and White extended its winning streak to fourteen straight games. The string is noteworthy because the Billikens had opened this fall with a 3-to-2 setback by Fairleigh Dickinson. It was their only defeat this season.

In losing, Maryland put up a mighty struggle. Trailing 3-1, at the intermission, the Terrapins hammered away in the last two quarters. Except for one lapse, however, in the waning minutes of the third quarter, the Mound City eleven held on in a sparkling manner.

St. Louis had to start without the services of two regulars, Bill Mueller, the goalie, and Tom McDonnell. McDonnell had done a fine job helping to defeat West Chester Teachers Friday. Both were sidelined with leg injuries.

Mike Quinn, a sophomore, filled in for Mueller in an outstanding manner and made fourteen saves. In the last period he was under tremendous pressure because of a bright sun, low in the skies, shining into his eyes.

Quinn, when he was not scurrying and diving to protect the nets, was busy using his hands as an eye shade.

The game was not of the same high quality seen in the semi-finals Friday. Early in the game, both teams showed

The Line-Up

ST. LOUIS (3)		MARYLAND (2)
Quinn	G.	Williamson
Hennessy	R.B.	Vossenkei
Shanahan	L.B.	Zarabko
J. Klein	R.H.	Greene
Michalski	C.H.	Romino
Richmond	L.H.	Cummins
Balassi	O.R.	Sanders
Ranze	I.R.	Krug
Trigg	C.F.	Martin
Malone	I.L.	Limar
Barry	O.L.	Trigg
St. Louis		2 1 0—3
Maryland		1 0 1 0—2

Goals—St. Louis: Ranze 2, Balassi. Maryland: Martin, Krug.
Substitutions—St. Louis: Griffard, T. Klein, Wincoff. Maryland: Korz, Calvert, Krs.
Officials—Thomas Callahan and James McLean. Time of quarters—22 minutes.

man on the field was Bob Guelker, the St. Louis coach. During the intermission, he had his players eat lots of orange halves. After the intermission, he ate more than a half dozen oranges while standing on the sideline.

After the game, presentations were made by Dr. Nelson S. Walke, president of the Intercollegiate Soccer Football Association of America.

November 27, 1960

HEADS-UP PLAY: Mike Quinn of St. Louis leaps higher than Juan Carlos Martin (9) of Maryland to head the ball away from the net in first period of play in the N. C. A. A. final at Brooklyn College. St. Louis successfully defended its title, winning 3-2.

The New York Times

signs of fatigue. But most hands (a bad word in soccer) managed to turn in their share of fine work.

St. Louis' forward line was particularly effective. The inside men, Range and Bob Malone, did a superb job spearheading the attack. For the Terps, Juan Carlos Martin, a native Argentinean, was the sparkplug.

Martin pushed Maryland into the lead after 3 minutes 8 seconds. Flat on his back in front of the Billikens' nets, he back-kicked a rebound down the middle. Quinn had been pulled out of position stopping Dick Romino's shot from the opposite side.

But St. Louis didn't remain behind long. At the ten-minute mark, Range evened matters with a penalty kick. Four minutes later, St. Louis moved into the lead as Balassi, the Billiken's high scorer and top assist man, clicked on a 35-yard kick from the right side.

Ronnie Williamson, the Maryland net-minder, was partially screened by one of the fullbacks and the boot crashed into the nets without Williamson laying a hand on it. The Blue and White led the rest of the way.

Midway in the second quarter, Range added his second goal on a pass from Johnny Klein. It was routine. Range tore in from the right and arrived just in time to make connection with the bullet pass.

Cliff Krug, who tallied three goals Friday in leading Mary-

land to its semi-final triumph over the University of Connecticut, sent a surge of hope through the Terrapin supporters late in the third quarter.

He registered in 19:35, returning a save by Quinn. Quinn was on the ground at the time.

But, through most of the fourth quarter, many of the Maryland players seemed weary despite frequent substitutions by Coach Doyle Royal.

In the last five minutes, however, the Terps played at a blistering pace. At one time they bombarded the goal with six headers in a melee that provided the game's high spot. Quinn and his backfield, however, were equal to the occasion.

Probably the most nervous

Soccer Stars Advised Not to 'Kiss and Cuddle'

LONDON, Jan. 19 (Reuters) — Britain's professional soccer players were advised today not to "kiss and cuddle" one another every time their team scores.

The English Football Association said that the exuberance of players when a goal was scored was understandable, "but the embracing and mobbing of the goal scorer is entirely unnecessary."

"Shouting on the field—often reduced to bawling—is even less necessary. Voice control as well as ball control is needed."

The association said it did not want to be "unctious" about the embracing—"more colorfully described as kissing and cuddling"—but said it was not doing the game any good.

January 20, 1961

Spurs Beat Leicester for Cup and Complete First Soccer Double Since 1897

LEAGUE WINNERS POST 2-0 TRIUMPH

By SETH S. KING
Special to The New York Times.

LONDON, May 6—Tottenham Hotspur made British soccer history this afternoon when it became the first team

in sixty-four years to win both the League championship and the Football Association Challenge Cup.

With two sudden goals in the second half, the Spurs defeated Leicester City, 2—0, in a swift, surging struggle that provided everything the British expect in a Cup final.

Not since 1897, when Aston Villa turned the trick, had a team registered a league-cup double. Only one other team besides Tottenham has accomplished the feat.

More than 100,000 roaring fans watched at Wembley Stadium as the favored Spurs finally marshaled their impressive talents and wore down their fighting opponent.

Precedent was against the Spurs. But luck was not. Throughout the early part of the first half, Leicester's agile forwards bore in time after time, pressing the attack and penetrating deep into Spur territory.

Then, in a flickering moment, the pattern changed. Len Chal-

mers, Leicester's right halfback, made a dive at the ball, tangled with a Spur player and ripped a shin.

No substitutions are permitted in British soccer. So Chalmers remained on the field most of the match. But he was so badly bruised that he was completely ineffective. For the rest of the contest, Leicester played, in effect, with only ten men.

Even so, the rangy Leicester team hung on for the rest of the first half, warding off several threats, including a Spur goal that was nullified by an offside.

In the early minutes of the second half, Leicester again swung down into Spur territory, with the forward line passing well. But with Chalmers barely able to move, these attacks fizzled.

Smith Gets First Goal

Then the Spurs struck. With a deft swing up the middle, they bore down on the center of the Leicester goal.

There, Bobby Smith, the Spurs' burly center forward, took a pass from Leslie Allen, the inside left forward, and slammed the ball into the net. Sixty-eight minutes of play had elapsed.

Eight minutes later, the Spurs scored their second goal on a header by the fragile Terry Dyson, their small left winger. Dyson took a long kick from Smith.

The London-based Spurs went into the contest as the 9-4 favorites. They had balance, blinding speed and the poise of champions.

They had finished a forty-two-game season with only seven losses. In the single-elimination Cup contests, they had gone through the final five rounds with only one drawn game and replay, against Sunderland. All amateur and professional teams recognized by the English Football Association are eligible to play in the Cup competition.

Leicester, which had beaten Tottenham once during the league season, had improved in its Cup matches. But the team had needed four replays to reach the final.

Field Stays Dry

Yet the awesome splendor of Wembley, with its towering oval stands and manicured field, has so often before worked its spell against the favorite.

A damp, chilly wind was blowing at kick-off time, and a few drops of rain had fallen. But the field stayed dry and the rain stopped during the play in this the world series of British soccer — a match many Britons would sell their birthrights to see.

In the early minutes, the nervous strain was clearly showing on both teams. The Spurs, in particular, missed several chances that they should have made look easy.

But in the second half, their superb conditioning began to show. Leicester never slacked off, but the superior finesse and speed of the Tottenham club gradually became too much for them.

May 7, 1961

ST. LOUIS U. UPSET IN SOCCER FINAL

ST. LOUIS, Nov. 25 (AP)— West Chester (Pa.) State Teachers College scored a 2-0 upset victory over St. Louis University, the defending champion, and won the National Col-

legiate soccer title today. The Billikens had won the championship the past two years and had been favored to repeat.

The West Chester Rams, who gained the final on a 2-0 victory over Bridgeport Thursday, hammered away until their brilliant inside left, Bill Fulk, opened the scoring with a goal at four minutes of the final period.

Fulk connected on a free kick, awarded on a St. Louis

foul, and drove the ball into the right corner.

Four minutes later, with a strong wind at his back, Joe Brownholtz, the inside right, slashed a 45-yard drive that went across the goal into the upper left-hand corner.

St. Louis won its first National Collegiate Athletic Association title in 1959 and won again in 1960. West Chester lost in the semi-finals to Bridgeport last year.

November 26, 1961

Tottenham Downs Burnley, 3-1, And Keeps British Football Cup

By JAMES FERON
Special to The New York Times.

LONDON, May 5 — Favored Tottenham Hotspur overpowered Burnley, 3-1, today to win the Football Association Cup final for the second year in a row.

Tottenham thus became the second club in this century to win the cup, England's world series. More than 100,000 fans filled Wembley Stadium with waves of roars. Newcastle accomplished the feat in 1951-52.

Tottenham, a wealthy London club that is the British equivalent of successful Yankee baseball teams, assembled an array of expensive talent to beat Burnley. It paid off quickly.

Within three minutes, Jimmy Greaves, the Tottenham inside left and the nation's most expensive soccer player, hit a low shot past three defenders and the goalie, Adam Blacklaw.

Greaves Rewards Crowd

The crowd that had come to see Greaves score the way Yankee Stadium crowds came to watch Babe Ruth hit one,

screamed its approval. Tottenham had paid the equivalent of $277,000 earlier this season to buy Greaves from an Italian club. He had gone there from Chelsea, another London club.

Spurred by the quick goal, Tottenham pressed its attack. The Burnley defense stiffened, however, and though the Spurs spent most of the first half in enemy territory, they failed to increase their lead.

The first forty-five minutes saw brilliant defensive and offensive moves by both sides, including several dribbles of thirty to fifty yards.

Burnley, which had only five clean shots at the Tottenham goal in the first half, took the offensive as the second half began. Within minutes, the Lancashire club had tied the score.

The Burnley goal was scored by Jimmy Robson, the inside left. He took a pass from Ray Pointer, the center forward who had seized a loose ball, and banged it into the net with his knee.

Tottenham then took the lead permanently.

Bobby Smith, Spurs' center forward who had provided the crucial pass for Greaves' first-half goal, took a pass from his inside right and rammed the ball home. Smith had discarded his shin pads earlier to provide more movement for shooting.

Burnley, behind again only sixty seconds after scoring its goal, returned to the attack. Robson brought the crowd to its feet with what appeared to be his second goal, but he was ruled offside.

As the match moved through the second half, Burnley slowly lost the initiative. Danny Blanchflower, the Spur's captain and right half, scored the final goal with a penalty shot that caught Blacklaw going the wrong way.

Queen Presents Cup

The cup, which was given to the victors by Queen Elizabeth II, is presented each year at the end of a season-long elimination contest.

The participants are the same football clubs that play for the league championship, as well as a few amateur and nonleague professionals. Cup finalists are rarely the league leaders, though the Spurs performed a unique "double" last year by winning both league and cup championships. Ipswich won the league title this year.

It was noted, in fact, that Burnley and Tottenham, which finished second and third in the league, were two of the highest-ranking clubs to take part in a cup final in decades.

The game set a record, according to London police. Scalpers were reportedly in greater numbers and getting better prices than ever before a cup final. Five-shilling (70 cents) tickets were going easily for £5 to £7 ($14 to $19.60).

May 6, 1962

Brazil Defeats Chile, 4-2, and Reaches World Cup Soccer Final

CZECHS SET BACK YUGOSLAVS BY 3-1

SANTIAGO, Chile, June 13 (UPI)—Brazil, the defending champion, whipped Chile, 4—2, and Czechoslovakia beat Yugoslavia, 3—1, today to qualify for Sunday's title game in the World Cup soccer tournament.

Chile and Yugoslavia will meet Saturday for third place.

Both semi-final games offered tough, exciting soccer. Chile fought bitterly as a highly partisan crowd of 80,000 cheered

the home team at Santiago. This game grew very rough in the final stages and the referee expelled one man from each team—Landa of Chile and Garrincha, who had scored two goals for Brazil.

At Vina del Mar, the Czechs and Yugoslavs battled briskly in a game finally decided by the superior size and defense of Czechoslovakia.

Landa, the Chilean center forward, was sent off for kicking Mauro soon after Brazil got the fourth goal. Three minutes later the brilliant Garrinch got his marching orders for fouling Eladio Rojas, a left half.

Brazil Takes the Lead

Garrincha had put Brazil two

ahead with goals in the eighth and thirtieth minutes, the first from a scramble and the second with a header from a corner. Jorge Toro pulled one back for Chile in the forty-first minute with a twenty-five-meter free-kick.

Vava leaped to head in a Garrincha corner for a 3-1 lead in the forty-seventh minute. But the Chileans rallied again. Leonel Sanchez made it 3—2 from the penalty spot. The clincher came in the seventy-eighth minute when Vava headed in Brazil's fourth from a Zagalo center.

An inside-right, Adolf Scherer, scored twice, once from the penalty spot, in Czechoslovakia's upset victory over the eager but inexperienced Yugoslavs. There was no score up to the interval, but Jose Kad-

West Germany's Franz Beckenbauer (left) stops a Dutch attack in the 1974 World Cup Finals. Beckenbauer later went on to play in the N.A.S.L.

Johan Cruyff (#14) is shown here being stopped by West German defender Bertie Vogts in the 1974 World Cup Final. Cruyff was the star player of a Netherlands team that finished second in 1974 and 1978.

raba, the inside-left, put the Czechs ahead in the forty-ninth minute, heading in a rebound from one of his own shots.

Tempers got the better of players on both teams at this stage, and the referee was forced to call the captains together for a warning.

Yugoslavia's center forward, Drazen Jerkovic, leveled in the seventieth minute by heading backward over the head of Viliam Schroif as the Czech goalie came out of his net.

Scherer restored the margin in the eightieth minute with a shot from ten meters as the Yugoslavs hesitated, expecting the off-side whistle.

The same player made it 3—1 seven minutes from time, scoring from the penalty spot after the Yugoslav center-half, Vladimir Marcovic, had handled a shot by Panich when he could have cleared easily.

June 14, 1962

Brazil Retains World Soccer Cup by Beating Czechs, 3-1

RALLY IN 2D HALF DECISIVE IN FINAL

Goals by Zito and Vava Turn Back Czechs After 1-1 Tie at Half-Time in Chile

SANTIAGO, Chile, June 17 (Reuters) — Brazil today retained the World Soccer Cup with a 3-1 victory over Czechoslovakia.

As a result, Brazil will retain the Jules Rimet Cup for another four years.

Czechoslovakia, a 25-1 underdog when the World Cup competition began at the end of May, held its own much of the time today. The game was tied, 1—1, at half-time.

In the last twenty-five minutes, however, the superb Brazilian forward line gained the upper hand against the well drilled Czech defense.

The right half, Zito, made it 2—1 in the sixty-eighth minute, and the center forward, Vava, added the third goal nine minutes later.

Earlier, Czechoslovakia had surprised the crowd of 55,000 with the first goal after a quarter of an hour. It was scored by the left-half, Josef Masopust.

The lead was short-lived. Brazil hit back two minutes later with a magnificent goal by the inside left, Amarildo, who rounded two defenders and shot into the net from an acute angle.

In the second half, the Brazilians launched a series of strong raids before "Little Bird" Garrincha set up Zito's goal. From then on, it was all Brazil.

In the closing stages, Czechoslovakia deserted its defensive style and did its utmost to fight back. But the Brazilian defense proved too strong.

Rio Celebrates Victory
Special to The New York Times.

RIO DE JANEIRO, June 17— Wild celebrations swept Rio de Janeiro tonight as Brazil won the world soccer championship for the second successive time.

Pandemonium broke loose when the long radio broadcast of the game with Czechoslovakia in Chile ended. Rockets burst, fireworks flashed, flags were waved and a paper storm fell from windows. Frenzied fans heaped paper-confetti streamers in the streets and set them afire—then people raced over a city gone mad, and quickly formed samba bands led hundreds of dancing, jumping celebrants through the streets. Traffic was jammed and horns blared for hours.

Flaming balloons were loosed to rise over a city gone mad, and quickly formed samba bands led hundreds of dancing, jumping celebrants through the streets. Traffic was jammed and horns blared for hours.

June 18, 1962

ST. LOUIS TAKES FINAL IN SOCCER

Defeats Maryland, 4-3, for National College Crown

ST. LOUIS, Nov. 24 (UPI)— St. Louis University won the National Collegiate Soccer championship today by beating Maryland, 4-3. It was the Billikens' third title in four years.

Gerry Balassi, an outside right, scored three times for St. Louis and assisted Joe Hennessey on the winning goal. The Terrapin scorers were Eberhardt Klein, Richard Roe and John Ruhs.

The Bills scored twice in the first five minutes, but Maryland bounced back with three goals for a half-time lead of 3-2.

Balassi tied it in the fourth quarter, then made a corner kick to Hennessey to set up the winning goal.

November 25, 1962

MILAN TOPS BENFICA TO WIN SOCCER CUP

WEMBLEY, England, May 22 (UPI)—Milan of Italy became the first non-Iberian team ever to win the European Soccer Cup when it beat the defending champion, Benfica of Lisbon, 2-1, today, before a crowd of 45,000.

Benfica led by 1—0 at the interval, but two second-half goals by Brazilian-born José Altafini gave the Italians the victory and a reported bonus of $1,400 a man.

Altafini's goals gave him the individual European Cup scoring record with 14 tallies.

Eusebio opened the scoring in the 17th minute when he got the ball about 25 yards out from the right, weaved his way through the massed defense, then fired past Ghezzi.

Altafini's goals came in the 58th and 65th minutes. The first, from 12 yards, gave Pereira no chance and the second was another one from in close which he got home at the second attempt.

On their way to the final, the Italians, who were beaten, 3-2, after extra time in the 1958 final by Real Madrid, beat Union of Luxembourg, Ipswich of England, Galasaray of Turkey and Dundee of Scotland.

Benfica, the winner of the title for the previous two years, beat Norrkoping of Sweden, Dukla of Prague and Feyenoord of the Netherlands in its march to the final.

May 23, 1963

©VOLK

Manchester United Takes Soccer Cup

By The Associated Press

LONDON, May 25 — Manchester United defeated favored Leicester City, 3—1, today in the English Cup final at Wembley Stadium and regained a place in big-time European soccer.

The victory put Manchester in next season's European Cup of Cup Winners. The club has not competed in a major European tournament since its ranks were shattered by a 1958 air crash in Munich, Germany, that killed eight of its players.

A capacity crowd of 100,000, which included Queen Elizabeth II and Prince Philip, paid $249,200 to see the game, record for a British soccer match.

The Queen presented the cup to Manchester's captain, Noel Cantwell.

Denis Law, Manchester's inside left, scored in the 30th minute, connecting from 12 yards away, and Manchester led at half-time, 1—0. Law was outstanding throughout.

David Herd, a center forward, made it 2—0 in the 59th minute. He ran the ball into an empty net after Gordon Banks had blocked a shot by Bobby Charlton, Manchester's left winger.

Ken Keyworth, Leicester's center forward, scored in the 82d minute. In the 86th minute, however, Banks dropped a high shot and Herd was on the spot to make it 3—1 for Manchester.

Following the 1958 disaster, considerable money and effort were sent to rebuild the team. Law, for example, cost $322,000.

United had finished in 19th place in regular-season competition. Leicester finished fourth.

May 26, 1963

300 DEAD IN LIMA AS RIOTING ERUPTS AT SOCCER MATCH

Crowd at Stadium Infuriated by a Referee's Decision— Emergency Declared

Special to The New York Times

LIMA, Peru, May 24 — At least 300 persons were killed today when an unpopular decision by a referee at a soccer game touched off a riot at National Stadium.

Five hundred others were injured.

The Government proclaimed a state of emergency throughout Peru. It said constitutional guarantees would be suspended for 30 days in order to investigate the tragedy.

The angry, screaming mob surged out of bleacher seats, smashed every window in the stadium and then overflowed into nearby streets, overturning cars, sacking stores and setting buildings afire. Most of those killed were trampled to death.

Police Use Tear Gas

Policemen on horseback hurled tear gas bombs and released dogs on the crowd of about 45,000. At least four of the dead were shot by police bullets.

The game was between teams from Argentina and Peru competing for a chance to play in the Olympic Games in Tokyo.

With the score 1—0 in favor of Argentina and less than two minutes to play, a Peruvian wingman booted a goal, but the referee, R. Angel Pazos of Uruguay, nullified it because of rough play by Peru.

While the crowd was still booing, two spectators leaped over a barrier and attacked the referee. They were quickly arrested by a detail of 40 policemen.

The crowd roared in anger, and Mr. Pazos ordered the game suspended because of the tense situation and the lack of adequate police protection on the field.

Referee Flees for Safety

When the decision was announced the crowd screamed in disapproval. Mr. Pazos and the players ran for a ramp under the stadium as spectators jumped over the wire fences surrounding the field.

The referee and the players escaped with their lives only because the small police detail at the stadium rushed them into a steel-doored locker room beneath the stadium, and then piled them onto buses that took them to a remote part of the city.

Mounted policemen attempted to direct the crowd toward the exits, often charging into rioters to disperse them. Other policemen fired shots in the air, and threw tear gas grenades. These tactics seemed to increase the panic.

Rioters hurled stones and bottles at the police, overturning benches, and setting a part of the stadium on fire.

Many of the exits to the stadium were locked, and bystanders were trampled or asphyxiated as people rushed toward open exit gates to avoid the tear gas and fires.

Gangs of young toughs swarmed around the stadium and rifled watches, rings and wallets from the dead and injured.

In the heart of Lima a bus, several cars, two office buildings and a brick factory were set afire. But firemen already at the scene were able to extinguish the blazes quickly and fire damage was said to be light.

The dead and injured were transported to hospitals in ambulances, police cars and commandeered private vehicles. Crowds formed outside hospitals and temporary morgues chanting "Revenge!" and "Down with the police!"

One portion of the mob marched on the National Palace to seek an audience with President Fernando Belaúnde Terry to protest police brutality and to seek his intervention in having the soccer match officially declared a tie.

May 25, 1964

DURING FATAL RIOT: Tear gas shells fired by policemen explode in stands of National Stadium in Lima, Peru. Riot erupted over soccer game between Argentina and Peru.

Hungary Downs Czechoslovakia, 2-1, and Regains Soccer Supremacy

Hungarians, in dark shirts, scramble for ball with Czechoslovak players in soccer final. Hungary won the gold medal.

United Press International Cablephoto

TOKYO, Oct. 23 (AP)—Goals by Tibor Csernai and Ferenc Bene gave Hungary a 2-1 victory over Czechoslovakia today and the Olympic gold medal in soccer.

Czechoslovakia won the silver medal and Germany the bronze in the 14-team field.

The Hungarians, who won the Olympic title in 1952, and the Czechoslovaks were scoreless until the 48th minute, when Csernai, playing inside right, booted in a shot. Bene, playing center forward, then clinched the victory by making it 2—0.

Jan Brumovsky, the left wing, scored for Czechoslovakia with 10 minutes remaining.

The original 16-team field was reduced to 14 when Italy and North Korea withdrew. Italy was upset by charges

that its team included professionals. North Korea quit because of international suspension against some of its track and swimming athletes who competed last year in Jakarta in the outlawed Games of the New Emerging Forces.

October 24, 1964

Navy Captures N.C.A.A. Soccer Title

MICHIGAN STATE BOWS IN FINAL, 1-0

Unbeaten Middies Triumph on Goal by Jim Lewis at 17:38 of Last Period

Special to The New York Times

PROVIDENCE, R. I., Dec. 5 —Undefeated Navy captured the National Collegiate Athletic Association soccer championship today, defeating Michigan State, 1—0, on the ice-encrusted

turf of Brown University Stadium.

Jim Lewis, a junior from Uniondale, L. I., scored at 17:38 of the final period after taking a long pass from Bill Thompson. Lewis picked up the ball 20 yards from the goal after the Spartans' center halfback, Dennis Checkett, slipped and then beat Van Dimitriou, the goalie, from 13 yards out.

Tough Defenses

The goal broke up a tense defensive struggle. Both teams had trouble setting up their offense within 25 yards of the goal. Michigan State had the edge in midfield passing, but the middies were superior in heading and defensive play.

Myran Hura of Irvington,

N. J., paced the tough Navy defense. The Ukrainian-born center fullback saved at least six goals with his timely clearings in front of the middies' net.

Hura, a junior who was chosen all-America as an inside right last season, was shifted to the defensive position late in the season by Coach Glen Warner. For his outstanding efforts, he was chosen the tourney's most valuable defensive player.

Top Offensive Player

Sydney Alozie of Michigan State, a center forward from Nigeria, was selected as the most valuable offensive player.

The middies' over-all height, speed, stamina and aggressiveness enabled them to play a

long-passing game that was better suited to the slippery conditions than was the Spartans' short-passing, ball-controlling game.

Navy, which finished its season with a 15-0 record, gained the final with a 2—1 upset of the defending champion, St. Louis, which had won four of the five previous N.C.A.A. tournaments. Michigan State, which wound up with a 10-1-2 record, moved into the final by edging Army, 3—2, in sudden-death overtime Thursday.

A crowd of close to 1,000 watched the final through a steady drizzle in freezing temperatures.

Navy .... 0 0 1—1
Michigan State ...... 0 0 0—0
Goal—Lewis (Thompson). Saves: Johnson 9, Dmitriou 9. Shots on goal: Navy 14, Michigan State 11.

December 6, 1964

Pro Soccer League Formulated Here
Plans for Nationwide 11-Team

SANCTION SOUGHT FROM U.S. GROUP

New York to Have Entry— Competition Expected to Start in Fall of '67

By DEANE McGOWEN

Plans were formulated yesterday for a proposed new professional soccer league involving 11 franchises from coast to coast. Robert R. Herman, the league's president, made the announcement at a meeting in the New York Athletic Club.

The North American Professional Soccer League, if it receives the approval of the United States Soccer Football Association, will begin competition in the fall of 1967. The U.S.S.F.A. is the ruling body of the sport in the United States.

The new league, according to its spokesman, William D. Cox, already has tentative approval of its operation from the Federation Internationale de Football Association, the governing body of international soccer.

Cox, the president of the Manhattan Soccer Club and operator of the International Soccer League in New York the last six years, is among the owners of the New York franchise in the new league.

The other cities are Atlanta, Boston, Chicago, Hartford, Conn., Los Angeles, New Orleans, Philadelphia, St. Louis, San Diego, and San Francisco.

Blessings From England

There were no representatives of the U.S.S.F.A. at the meeting here.

Cox said, "We simply decided to take the bull by the horns and make our announcement now [prior to approval of the U.S.S.F.A.]."

Cox added, "Several of our club owners flew to England last week for a personal meeting with Sir Stanley Rous of F.I.F.A., and we have his blessing."

If F.I.F.A. does approve the new league over the objection of the U.S.S.F.A., it would be a blow to the prestige and authority of the governing body of the game in the United States.

Cox was unable to determine the immediate future of the I.S.L. He said, "We just don't know what we're going to do. We're still discussing that."

But Cox was specific about the aspirations of the new league. He said: "It is our intention to bring United States soccer to the level where we can enter the World Cup, the Cup Winners Cup and other major international competition on a par with the best teams elsewhere in the world."

Plan College Draft

Cox continued, "At first I would guess that we will have to import 180 to 200 players from other countries. We will not trespass on established leagues. We will concentrate on getting the younger players, and they won't be the best. Then, after our first year of operation, we will have a draft of college players, picking the best from American colleges. In five or six years we would hope to be wholly North American in our personnel."

Herman said the league's tentative schedule would call for 26 games, divided between home and away contests.

The Atlanta games would be played in the new Fulton County Stadium, where the owners of the Atlanta Braves also are involved in ownership of the proposed soccer club. Chicago would play its games in Soldiers Field, Los Angeles in the Coliseum, New Orleans in the Sugar Bowl, New York at Randalls Island and Shea Stadium, St. Louis in Busch Stadium and San Francisco in Kezar Stadium.

Five other cities being considered are Detroit, Pittsburgh and Miami and Vancouver and Toronto in Canada.

May 11, 1966

Everton Rallies to Defeat Sheffield Wednesday, 3-2, in Soccer Cup Final

19-YEAR-OLD SETS PACE IN 2D HALF

Trebilcock Scores Twice as 100,000 Watch Contest— Temple's Goal Decides

WEMBLEY, England, May 14 (Reuters)—Everton rallied from two goals down to win the English Football Association cup today with a 3-2 victory over Sheffield Wednesday in the final at Wembley Stadium before a crowd of more than 100,000.

In 15 minutes of exciting soccer in the second half, Everton scored three times to overcome what had appeared to be certain defeat.

Mike Trebilcock, a 19-year-old newcomer to Everton's team, scored two goals and Derek Temple scored the third to snatch the cup from the Sheffield team.

Everton's victory completed a great cup and League double for the city of Liverpool—its neighbors, the Liverpool club, won this season's league championship. It is the first time in 45 years that the cup and league title have gone to the same city.

Sheffield Wednesday outplayed Everton, the 4-to-7 favorite, in the early stages of the final, and it was not until 57 minutes of play that Everton found its touch.

Then it rocketed into the lead with goals by Trebilcock and Temple.

Not since 1953, when Blackpool beat the Bolton Wanderers, 4-3, after trailing 3-1, in the second half, has there been such a transformation in a cup final.

Wednesday's opening goal was scored in the fourth minute of play, when Jim McCalliog tallied with a left-footed shot—the first goal yielded by Everton in this year's cup competition.

Sheffield took a 2-0 lead in the 57th minute when David Ford, an inside left, fired a shot past the Everton goalkeeper Gordon West, on the rebound.

It appeared as if Sheffield had assured its victory—but 10 minutes later the trophy was Everton's.

Trebilcock got his goals in the 58th and 63d minutes and Temple, an outside left, put Everton ahead in the 77th minute.

May 15, 1966

Brazil Defeats Bulgaria, 2-0, in World Soccer

Pele and Garrincha Score—Soviet and Germans Win

LONDON, July 12 (UPI) — Brazil, the defending champion, opened bid for a third straight World Soccer Cup today with a 2-0 victory over Bulgaria at Liverpool.

In the two other matches on the second day of the 16-team round-robin, West Germany beat Switzerland, 5-0, at Sheffield, and the Soviet Union downed North Korea, 3-0, at Middlesbrough.

Brazil scored its first goal in the 14th minute of play and the second in the 63d minute to outclass Bulgaria.

Brazil won the tourney, which is held every four years, in 1958 and 1962. A victory this year would enable Brazil to retire the cup. Despite four players sidelined with injuries, Brazil had little trouble with Bulgaria.

King Pele (Edson Arantes de Nascimento) and Little Bird Garrincha (Manuel Dos Santos), who have helped Brazil dominate world soccer for the last eight years, scored the goals—both on free kicks.

Franz Beckenbauer and Hel-

53

United Press International Cablephoto

With both feet off the ground, Pele, Brazil's star soccer player, scoring on a free kick in game with Bulgaria.

mut Haller scored twice each to pace West Germany to its victory over Switzerland. The losers dropped two men from their team because they had returned home late from a night out.

Edward Malofeev scored twice to lead the Soviet team to its triumph.

In sharp contrast to the dour defensive play in last night's opening match between England and Uruguay, tonight's matches produced open, fast football. England

and Uruguay played a scoreless tie at London. The four London-group teams had today off.

There are four matches on tomorrow's schedule. Mexico will meet France, Spain will battle Argentina, Portugal traces Hungary and Chile goes against Italy.

106,314 Watch Matches

LONDON, July 12 (Reuters) More than 100,000 spectators wat-

ched tonight's three World Cup matches. The Brazil-Bulgaria game at Liverpool attracted the biggest crowd—47,308.

There were 36,000 at Sheffield and 23,006 at Middlesbrough for a total of 106,314.

London bookmakers cut the odds on favored Brazil from 2-1 to 7-4.

One bookie has made West Germany joint second favorite with England at 6-1.

Bulgarians Are Criticized

LONDON, July 12 (AP)—Pele and the coach of the Brazilian team, Vicente Feola, accused Bulgaria of rough play in their match tonight.

"I received more blows than ever before in tonight's match," Pele said. "The Bulgarians are good and I don't see why they have to use such rough tactics."

July 13, 1966

Hungary Upsets Brazil, 3-1, in Soccer

WORLD CUP LOSS FIRST IN 12 YEARS
Brazil Plays Without Pele—
Uruguay Beats France—
Spaniards Top Swiss

LONDON, July 15 (Reuters)—Hungary ended Brazil's 12-year unbeaten streak in World Cup soccer competition tonight with a 3-1 victory at Liverpool in a magnificently played match.

The upset puts in jeopardy Brazil's chances of qualifying for the quarter-finals from the strong North-West Group 3, in which Portugal and Bulgaria are the other contenders.

Brazil, the Cup winner in 1958 and 1962, and Hungary, twice the runner-up, have 2 points each from two games' and Portugal 2 points from one match. With only the top two advancing to the last eight,

Associated Press Cablephoto

GOING FOR THE BALL: Kalman Meszoly of Hungary, left, trying to beat Brazilian goalie Gylmar to ball last night in World Cup game in Liverpool. Hungary won, 3 to 1.

goal average might decide this section. A victory counts 2 points, a tie 1 point.

All of tonight's matches were played in rain on slippery fields. In Sheffield, Spain gained its first triumph in Group 2 by beating Switzerland, 2-1; in London, Uruguay defeated France, 2-1, to register the first victory of Group 1, and in Middlesbrough, North Korea held Chile to a 1-1 draw in Group 4.

Hungary was the last team to beat Brazil in the World Cup. It happened in the quarter-finals of the 1954 competition in Switzerland, when tempers flared both on and off the field and the match became known as the "Battle of Berne." Tonight's game before 51,387 fans was played in a fine spirit.

Pele Out With Injury

The Brazilians could perhaps attribute their defeat to the absence of their incomparable star, King Pele, who is nursing a knee injury, and the damp conditions to which they are unaccustomed. But even at their best, they would have been hard-pressed to hold the Hungarians.

Hungary, which lost to Portugal, 3-1, Wednesday largely through defensive slips, tightened its rearguard and used faster, more direct methods than the defending champions, who took time to build their attacks. Brazil's aging defense was severely mauled by Hungary's graceful center forward, Florian Albert.

The Hungarians took the lead in the third minute with the best goal seen in the 1966 competition. Ferenc Bene weaved his way past four defenders to score with a left-footed ground shot. Twelve minutes later, Tostao, Pele's stand-in, tied the score with a free kick.

Hungary scored two second-half goals, Janos Farkas tallying in the 64th minute and Kalman Meszoly converting a penalty shot 10 minutes later.

Soon afterward, Meszoly left the field injured but returned two minutes later to finish the match with his left arm in a sling. It was believed he had a broken collar bone.

Uruguay Group Leader

In Group 1 Uruguay has 3 points from two games, England 1 point from one match, Mexico 1 point from one match and France 1 from two games.

In Group 2 West Germany and Argentina are tied with 2 points each from one game, Spain has 2 points from two games and Switzerland is pointless from two matches.

In Group 3 Portugal has 2 points from one game, Brazil and Hungary 2 points each from two games and Bulgaria no points from one game.

In Group 4 the Soviet Union and Italy have 2 points each from one game, Chile and North Korea 1 point each from two games.

July 16, 1966

Rough Tactics in Cup Tourney Put World Soccer on Defensive

Special to The New York Times

LONDON, July 24 — Pele, Brazil's star soccer player, criticized today in an interview the defensive tactics used in the 1966 World Cup tournament.

"I am not sad at defeat," he said, "only that I have not been allowed to play soccer. Ideal soccer has become impossible. This is terrible for the game and for the spectators who want a show."

"From what I have seen, only two teams have played really attacking soccer: ourselves and Hungary," Pele told the Sunday Telegraph. "Only by allowing the other team to attack can you do so yourself. But the present negative trend chokes all this and there are only two ways to beat it: by playing the same way or by having good referees. We just happened to be unfortunate with our referees this time."

Joao Havelange, the president of the Brazilian Soccer Federation, said today he would not allow Pele to play in future World Cup competition so long as the game degenerates into "all ruthless, uncompromising defense."

Style of Play Negative

The most disappointing aspect of the early round-robin qualifying matches in the tournament has been its negative style of play. It has seemed to tarnish what should have been

a brilliant exhibition of soccer at its international best. Defensive tactics have dominated throughout as teams have entered the field not so much to win as not to lose. The collective byword has been "play it safe."

The result of this policy of stalemate has been dull soccer, paltry scores and bored spectators. Some games have risen above mediocrity, but not enough to satisfy the frustrated crowds.

It was not always thus. There was a time (and many fans remember it fondly) when teams lined up in the classic 2-3-5 formation—two fullbacks, three halfbacks, five forwards — and played to win. Formations like this flourished in the 1950 and 1954 World Cup championships. Since then, however, the trend has been to bolster the defense at the expense of the offense and to rely on flash counterattacks for scoring.

First, a halfback was lowered in line with the fullbacks for a 3-2-5 configuration; then another halfback and a forward were brought down and the new line-up, 4-2-4, became fashionable. But this was only the beginning of the defensive complex that gripped the coaches, and formations of 4-3-3, 5-2-3 and even 6-2-2 made their appearances on the fields.

The "padlock" or "blanket" defense had arrived. With it came rough, often violent play, no-holds-barred attempts to keep opponents from entering the goal area at any cost.

All this was painfully evident during the boring scoreless game between England and Uruguay, the unpleasant brawl between Argentina and West Germany, the classless draw between France and Mexico. (A London newspaper calculated that, in the first 24 games, one foul was committed every three minutes.) Surprisingly, or perhaps justly, the two countries that nurtured and developed this defensive style have been its victims: Italy and Switzerland were among the nations eliminated in the early rounds.

The few good games that balance this bleak picture have been played by teams that were not influenced by the cult of defense. Hungary's 3-1 upset victory over Brazil and North Korea's 1-0 deathblow to Italy were refreshing displays of fine soccer in an otherwise uninspired competition.

Overzealous defenses cannot be held entirely responsible for the drabness of most games, however. Ineffective offenses, some bad luck and just plain incompetent playing also led the luckless teams out.

By far the biggest surprise of the tournament was the elimination of Brazil, a leading contender and the favorite to win the Jules Rimet Cup for the third consecutive time. There was never a question of quality with the Brazilians. In their games against Portugal and Hungary they were not outclassed. They were simply outscored.

Just as unexpected was the elimination of Italy, which with the Soviet Union, had been favored to head Group 4 play. That the Italians' hopes should have been dashed by North Korea, the tourney's long-shot outsiders, made their defeat all the more shocking. Again, it was a matter of the Korean players, unfettered by defensive complexes, playing the game to win.

July 25, 1966

ENGLISH BEAT WEST GERMANS IN SOCCER FINAL, 4-2;

2 Goals in Overtime Give British First World Cup

By W. GRANGER BLAIR
Special to The New York Times

LONDON, July 30—England, deprived of a victory by a German goal in the last 15 seconds of regular play, broke through in overtime today and won the World Cup, emblematic of international soccer supremacy, by beating West Germany, 4-2. England's first World Cup victory was witnessed by a crowd of 100,000 in Wembley Stadium. It

was a match marked by the kind of hard, clean play that had been noticeably absent from a number of the earlier games in the tournament.

When it was over and the spectators were shouting "England, England," Bobby Moore, the captain of the English eleven, led his team to the royal box to receive the solid gold cup from Queen Elizabeth.

A lesser team than England might have been demoralized by

that game-tying goal in the last 15 seconds of the regulation 90 minutes, when England was leading, 2-1.

Weber Scores Equalizer

In a skirmish in front of the English goal, Wolfgang Weber, a German halfback, kicked the ball into the net for the equalizer. That the Germans were in a position to score stemmed largely from England's refusal to adopt stalling tactics to keep the ball.

Associated Press Cablephoto

With the score 2-1 against West Germany, Wolfgang Weber, at left, kicks in the tying goal and sends the game into extra time. Trying unsuccessfully to block the shot are Gordon Banks, right, English goalkeeper, and Ray Wilson.

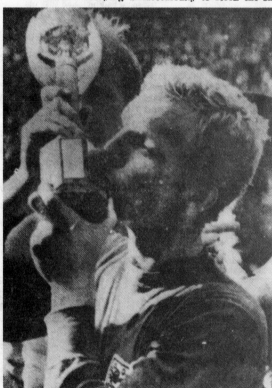

United Press International Cablephotos

Bobby Moore, the team captain, kisses the gold trophy

Only once did the English team stall—about three minutes before the end of regulation play. The crowd began booing and the home eleven quickly swung back to the offensive, thereby giving the Germans their golden opportunity.

Eleven minutes after the 30-minute overtime period began, Geoff Hurst scored for England on a 10-yard shot. He booted in another goal on a breakaway dash in the final seconds. He had scored on a header in the opening minutes of the match.

The scoring began when Helmut Haller, an outstanding German forward, fired a low, powerful shot into the English goal 10 minutes after the opening whistle. Hurst tied it for England nine minutes later, when he headed in a nicely lofted free kick by Moore, who was chosen by soccer writers as the most valuable player of the tournament.

Offensive rushes marked the rest of the first half. Throughout the cup series England had displayed a solid defense, and it was no less so today.

Ten minutes before regulation play was to end, Martin Peters, an English forward, found an opening in a melee in front of the German goal and blasted the ball past the sprawling German goalie, Hans Tilkowski.

Then came the Weber goal that sent the game into overtime. Hurst's first goal in overtime seemed doubtful for a moment. The linesman first indicated that the ball had hit the top bar, but had not gone in. But he and the referee conferred and England was awarded the goal as the crowd cheered.

Whatever doubts German fans might have had about the legitimacy of the English lead were dispelled when, with virtually the entire German team pressing on the English cage in a desperate attempt to score, Hurst broke away with the ball, drove downfield and easily beat the German goalie.

With the exception of 1942 and 1946, the World Cup tournament has been staged every four years since 1930. Brazil, Italy and Uruguay have won the cup twice each and West Germany and England once.

For this eighth tournament, 14 teams besides England and West Germany were entered. The others were Argentina, Bulgaria, Chile, France, Hungary, North Korea, Mexico, Portugal, Spain, Switzerland, the Soviet Union, Italy, Uruguay and Brazil.

STATISTICS OF THE GAME

	Eng.	West Germ.
Goal attempts	47	38
Shots saved	16	12
Shots blocked	10	13
Shots off target	21	13
Fouls	19	13
Handling	2	3
Offsides	1	6
Corners	6	12

July 31, 1966

41,598 See Santos Win in Soccer, 4-1

ITALIANS' DEFENSE CRACKS IN 2D HALF

By GERALD ESLENAZI

Although tripped, mauled and kneed, Pelé led Santos of Brazil to a 4-1 rout of Inter of Milan yesterday before the largest turnout for a soccer match in the United States in 40 years.

The 41,598 spectators at Yankee Stadium — the majority loudly pro-Italian — were attracted by a showdown between two of the world's finest soccer clubs. Inter has held the world

The New York Times (by Barton Silverman)

THAT SELF-SATISFIED FEELING: Pelé of Brazil raises arms in joy after scoring against Inter of Milan, Italy, in Yankee Stadium soccer game. Toninho shares delight.

club title the last two years. Santos held it for the previous two years.

The Italians' vaunted "cement" defense cracked in the second half as the smaller, trickier Brazilians feinted and twisted their way downfield. They passed tiring defensemen and scored three goals.

Pelé should have been the weakest player on the field. Time and again he would press goalward, only to be halted by a knee or elbow. After outmaneuvering the defense he would find an arm locked in his and he would raise his arms high, looking for the referee in vain.

Pelé Starts the Deluge

Finally, soccer's most acclaimed player scored. His goal, midway through the second half, gave the Brazilians a 3-1 lead. He took a pass from Mengalvio in front of the goal, dribbled to his right, taking a defender with him, then raced ahead and smashed the ball in.

The Italians found after only five minutes they could not cope with the Brazilians. After tearing himself away from players who tugged at his shirt, 17-year-old Edu gave Santos

a 1-0 lead at that point by driving past two players and shooting the ball past Giuliano Sarti in the Milan net.

Sandro Mazzola, Italy's premier player, tied the score midway through the first half with a right-footed liner that went past Gilmar, the Santos goalie who was sprawling on the grass after stopping another shot.

The tempo of the game then changed drastically. The Brazilians hit hard, tearing up Inter's forward line, stealing the ball, and setting out on dazzling downfield journeys.

Pelé, who had two goals denied because of offsides, passed to Toninho for an easy score early in the second half. It was the beginning of a bad 45 minutes for the Italians.

Pelé scored next, and Mengalvio made it 4-1 with a goal on a leaping kick. The Brazilians then started to toy, almost cruelly, with Inter, which was making its first United States appearance.

In cat-and-mouse fashion they passed the ball tantalizingly close to the Italians, but always controlling the ball, to the embarrassment of the world champions.

A preliminary American League

game between New York Inter and the Boston Tigers ended in a 4-4 tie.

SANTOS (4)		INTER (1)
Gilmar	G.	Sarti
Oberdan	R.F.B.	Burgnich
Lima	L.F.B.	Facchetti
Carlos Alberto	R.H.B.	Bedin
Zito	C.H.B.	Guarneri
Orlando	L.H.B.	Picchi
Dorval	O.R.	Da Costa
Mengalvio	I.R.	Mazzola
Toninho	C.F.	Vinicio
Pele	I.L.	Suarez
Edu	O.L.	Corso

Half-time score— Santos 1, Inter 1.
Goals—Santos: Edu, Toninho, Pele, Mengalvio. Inter: Mazzola.
Saves—Santos 14, Inter 14. Corner kicks—Santos 2, Inter 1. Fouls—Inter 20, Santos 18. Referee—Felipe Buergo. Linesmen—Aido Clemente and Miro Roguly.

September 6, 1966

SOCCER ACE HIRED TO COACH ATLANTA

Prospect of Raids Is Raised as Woosnam, Briton, Signs

By JOSEPH LELYVELD
Special to The New York Times

LONDON, Sept. 8 — The Atlanta professional team announced here today that it had signed a British soccer star to manage the club it plans to enter in the new National Soccer

League.

The man Atlanta got, Phil Woosnam of the Aston Villa club in the Birmingham that is in England and not in Alabama, is a seasoned inside forward but not a super-star — a Bobby Richardson rather than a Mickey Mantle. His signing seemed to raise the prospect of wholesale raids by American clubs seeking British talent.

A soft-selling official from the Atlanta club, Richard Cecil, disclaimed any such intention. So did the new manager of the unnamed Atlanta club (which won't be called the Braves) in a heavy Welsh accent that will need some time before it sounds even a little bit Georgian. "Everything is above board," Woosnam insisted.

The question of raids arises because the National Soccer League is not recognized by the Federation of International Football Associations, which tends the proprieties of world soccer. (The word "soccer" immediately identifies its user in any British pub as an ignorant foreigner, probably American.)

Question Is Unanswered

Woosnam, who is 33 years old and past his prime as a player, was cagy about whether he would even kick a ball for the fans the team hopes to find for the game in Atlanta. He said it was too soon for him to know.

There was a reason for his caginess. So long as he doesn't play he won't be considered an outlaw from recognized professional soccer here. For Atlanta to acquire him legally as a player it would have to pay Aston Villa what is known here as a "transfer fee." That can be costly: Aston Villa bought Woosnam from the West Ham club in 1962 for $75,600.

If Atlanta were willing to pay a fee—as Cecil insisted it was—Aston Villa could not now accept it because of the National Soccer League's dubious status. Of course, soccer authorities here know that even if the league is not recognized, British clubs may still find themselves losing some of their best players, attracted by the chance to make more money in the United States.

If that has to happen, they would at least like to get the fees—a strong inducement to make the National Soccer League legal.

Salary Is Not Revealed

But there is a snag. Soccer authorities in the United States recognize the rival North American Soccer League, which hopes to have its first season in 1968. The National Soccer League intends to field 10 to 14 clubs next spring.

There was no announcement of the salary Woosnam would earn as a manager for Atlanta. British press estimates put it at $16,800, about $5,600 more than he could get as a player here.

But he insisted that it wasn't money that was drawing him to Atlanta. "This is a challenge to me," he said, in the best tradition of British mission work in benighted parts of the world, "an opportunity to return something to the game. We're really spreading the gospel now."

Cecil acknowledged that the United States has "lagged behind the rest of the world in soccer" in the grim tones an Air Force general might use to warn of a missile gap.

September 9, 1966

Soccer Merger Is Planned

2 NEW PRO LOOPS VOTE NEXT WEEK

Cities of Both Leagues Are to Keep Places Expected in New Circuit

The presidents of the two new and competing professional soccer leagues in the United States have worked out terms for a merger and the circuits will vote on the proposal late this month, the governing body of the sport said yesterday.

James McGuire of New York, the President of the North American Soccer League, which has official sanction, and Robert Hermann of St. Louis, the president of the National Professional Soccer League, which does not have sanction, met in a lengthy closed conference Monday.

"They had a full discussion and talked of getting together," said Joseph Barriskill, the executive secretary of the United States Soccer football Association which governs all soccer in this country." "The two league presidents exchanged ideas and suggestions, and McGuire said his league probably would vote on the merger suggestion at its meeting next Monday, and the other league expects to vote on it a week from today.

Originally, there were three new professional leagues formed on paper. Each sought sanction by the U.S.S.F.A., which said it would recognize only one. The U.S.S.F.A., at its convention on June 25, chose the North American League for sanction.

The other two leagues then merged, under the name of the National Professional Soccer League, and continued efforts to win sanction. Failing that, they said they would start operations next April as an "outlaw" league if need be.

The sanctioned North American League has franchises in New York, Boston, San Francisco, Chicago, Los Angeles, Toronto, Vancouver, Washington, Detroit, Cleveland and Houston.

National League franchises went to New York, St. Louis, Baltimore, Atlanta, Pittsburgh, Minneapolis-St. Paul, Philadelphia, Chicago, Los Angeles, Toronto and Vancouver.

No details of the proposed merger terms were revealed, but it was believed that all the cities that already had franchises in either league would retain a franchise in the final —and probably larger—league.

September 21, 1966

San Francisco Subdues L. I. U., 5-2, for National Collegiate Soccer Crown

HITES OF VICTORS TALLIES 3 GOALS

Hungarian-Born Star Plays With Leg Injury—Launi of L.I.U. Scores Twice

Special to The New York Times

BERKELEY, Calif., Dec. 3—The University of San Francisco won the National Collegiate Athletic Association soccer championship today by defeating Long Island University, 5-2, in Memorial Stadium of the University of California.

The brilliant short passing of the Dons sent them into a 3-0 lead midway through the second quarter. Sandor Hites, a San Francisco forward, got the first of his three goals at 9:28 of the opening period.

The Hungarian-born Hites's shot from 5 yards out caught the right corner of the net. Rudolthus Dekkers scored at 14:22 of the second period and Hites, who played with an injured right leg, made it 3-0 with another short shot at 7:40 of the same period.

The Blackbirds rallied on two goals by their outside left, Marcello Launi. His first tally came at 8:40 of the second period and his second, on a breakaway, at 14:17 of the third quarter.

Hites Cages Long One

But Blackbird hopes were dimmed when Hites slammed in a perfectly placed 25-yard shot at 10:56 of the third period.

Hites, who had scored only eight goals this season going into Thursday's semi-final round, was high scorer for the tournament with four goals. He scored one in the Dons' semifinal victory over Army.

It was the first N.C.A.A. championship for the Dons, who finished the season with a record of 12 victories and one tie. The Blackbirds ended up with a 15-2 mark, their best in history. They were the first L.I.U. team to reach the finals.

This was the first year the tournament finals were held on the West Coast, and the first time that teams from the East and West Coasts met in the title game.

December 4, 1966

U.S. Pro Soccer Loop to Import 12 Top Teams From Abroad

By JOSEPH DURSO

Major league soccer drew a step nearer the United States yesterday.

The owners of the 12 franchises in the new, "sanctioned" professional league ended two days of meetings here and announced that they would import a dozen of the best teams from abroad starting in May.

The teams will represent the following cities: New York, Boston, Washington, Toronto, Detroit and Cleveland in the East and Los Angeles, San Francisco, Vancouver, Houston, Dallas and Chicago in the West.

They will perform in the Astrodome, Kezar Stadium, the Cotton Bowl, the Coliseum in Los Angeles, Tiger Stadium and other arenas. The New York team is still negotiating for a site, it was reported by Bob Wolff, who will direct the franchise here for the Madison Square Garden Corporation.

Sanctioned by World Group

The league has been designated the North American Soccer League, and it has received sanction from the world federation governing soccer in 136 countries. However, it also has a rival, the National Professional Soccer League, which does not possess "sanction" but which does possess a television contract with the Columbia Broadcasting System.

Roy Hofheinz, president of the Houston Astros baseball team and the leader of Houston's new soccer team, said that the North American League planned television, too. But it is still negotiating the questions of where and when and by whom.

The league announced that its 12 teams would play on Wednesdays and Sundays from May to July, which is the off-season for soccer in Europe. Each team will play 16 games, and the top two teams in the eastern and western divisions will play each other to decide who plays for the league title.

The meetings were presided over by James P. McGuire, chairman of the league, and Dick Walsh, former vice president of the Los Angeles Dodgers, who was recently elected commissioner.

In addition to Hofheinz and Wolff, the franchise executives who attended the sessions at the Plaza Hotel included Gabe Paul of Cleveland, Lamar Hunt of Dallas, Weston W. Adams of Boston and Jack Kent Cooke of Los Angeles.

January 27, 1967

How Soccer Is Played: The Techniques and Pitfalls of a Fast, Rugged Game

A glancing kick makes the ball travel in a curve. Effective when shooting at the goal from a distance and from shallow angle.

Side taps make for short, accurate passes. Dribbling, in fact, consists of tapping ball alternately with side of one's foot and toe.

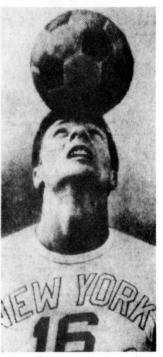

When heading, forehead should meet the ball and hit it forcefully, not the other way around.

For long, accurate passes, the instep kick is best. Approach and follow-through are similar to kicking a football field goal.

The punt propels the ball far but does not guarantee accuracy. It is used mostly when firing point-blank at the goal cage.

The writer of this article is the president of the Metropolitan Intercollegiate Soccer Conference. He is Dean of Students at Long Island University's Brooklyn Center and was L.I.U.'s soccer coach for eight years.

By GARY ROSENTHAL

WITH the start today of professional soccer on a national scale, the American public will see the game played with all of the speed, skill, individual talent and excitement that has made it what many people believe is the world's greatest sport.

Soccer is played with 11 men on a side: a goalkeeper, two fullbacks, three halfbacks and five forwards. The professional game is played in 45-minute halves and each player is expected to play the full 90 minutes.

One point is warded for each goal that is scored by kicking, heading or using any part of the body, with the exception of the arms and hands, to get the ball over the goal line, between the uprights and under the crossbar.

When the ball goes out of bounds over the sidelines, it is put back into play by means of a two-hand, over-the-head throw.

If the ball goes out of bounds over the end lines or goal lines, two methods of returning it to play are possible:

¶If the ball was last touched by a defender, the attacking team is awarded a corner kick.

¶If the ball was last touched by an attacking player, the defending team is awarded a goal kick.

Goalie May Use Hands

The goalkeeper is the only player on the field permitted to use his hands within his own penalty area to prevent goals. He primarily attempts to catch the ball, thereby gaining control of it and bringing the attack on goal to a halt. Once he has control of the ball, he becomes the initiator of his team's attack by means of a pass or kick to a free teammate.

If he is unable to catch the ball he will attempt to "fist" or punch the ball away from the goalmouth. On dangerous passes high in front of the goal, he will attempt to deflect the ball over the crossbar or around the upright to prevent the score.

The fullbacks are primarily concerned with defensive play, specifically with defense against the rival outside forwards. The fullbacks must be adept at taking the ball away from attackers as well as possess the heading and kicking skills necessary for clearing the ball out of the defensive portion of the field.

Modern fullbacks must also possess many of the skills of the forwards. They must dribble and pass well so that they will be able to take part in the attacks of the entire team.

The halfbacks perform three basic functions: they defend against the opposition

The New York Times   April 16, 1967

Diagram of the area defended by each team. A defensive foul in the penalty area calls for a direct shot at the goal from only 12 yards.

A foul is also called when a defender (man at right) goes for rival, not for ball.

Stopping ball with the chest is fair; raising a foot in front of rival is foul.

The New York Times (by Patrick A. Burns)

forwards, they provide midfield liaison between the forwards and the deep defenders and they provide support and depth to their attacking forwards. Good halfbacks are speedy, sure defenders and often gifted, skillful shooters and playmakers as well.

The forwards make up the main attacking force of the team. The forward line is made up of one center forward, two inside forwards (one left and one right) and two outside forwards (one left and one right).

The center forward, because of his central field position, is usually the top-scoring threat on most teams. Along with the inside forwards he forms the basis for playmaking, passing and scoring forays deep into the opponent's defense.

The inside forwards are good passers and playmakers as well as good scorers. They also will go downfield to help when their own defense is under pressure.

The outside forwards are primarily responsible for patroling the outside lines on the field. The defenders must go out to cover them, which prevents the defense from being able to cluster in front of the goal area.

When in possession of the ball, the outside forward will generally attempt to bring the ball down his side of the field toward the corner. When the defense shifts to cover this threat he will send a long pass or cross to the forwards, who have moved into scoring positions.

Spectators will be impressed by the versatility of individual players regardless of designated positions. The game is so fluid, with the ball changing hands (feet) so often that the players are constantly pressed into going from attack to defense and very often from position to position.

Their well developed skills enable them to do this with ease. Defenders can attack when the situation presents itself and attackers can and must be able to defend. This is the essence of modern soccer's strategy.

Styles of play will vary but most teams will employ a variation of a basic four-forward, three-halfback and three-fullback system.

This kind of system allows for defensive security as well as a balanced, closely supported attack. No player, other than the goalkeeper, is confined to his position and it is not surprising to see a forward drop off the forward line into a halfback position and a halfback drop back into a fullback position.

All soccer teams, regardless of the system they employ, strive to upset the delicate balance of their opponents to get scoring opportunities. This is accomplished by long thrusts or deep penetrations through passing or dribbling into one area of the field, thereby drawing the defenders into that area.

Once the defenders feel the pressure put to them in that area and react by commiting themselves to that area's defense, passes will be attempted by the attackers to unguarded players who have positioned themselves in relatively open scoring positions.

Most spectacular move is scissors kick, which is used to intercept ball in mid-air and return it overhead.

Glossary of Soccer Terms

DIRECT FREE KICK from which a goal may be scored directly is awarded as a result of a personal foul such as kicking, tripping, pushing or holding and is taken from the spot of the infraction.

PENALTY KICK is awarded for any personal fouls or intentional handling of the ball by defensive players within their own penalty area. The kick is taken from the designated spot 12 yards from the goal line in the center of the penalty area, with only the goalkeeper defending it.

INDIRECT FREE KICK is awarded for infractions that pertain mainly to violations of playing rules such as ungentlemanly conduct, delay of the game and offside. For a goal to be scored as a result of an indirect free kick, the ball must be touched by another player. The kick is awarded from the spot of infraction.

OFFSIDE. A player is ruled offside if he is nearer his opponent's goal line than the ball at the moment the ball is played *unless:* he is in his own half of the field; there are two opponents nearer to their own goal line than he is (the goalkeeper may be one of them), or the ball last touched an opponent or was played by him. There are no offsides on a corner kick, goal kick, throw-in or when the ball is dropped by the referee.

CORNER KICK awarded to the attacking team if a defender last touched the ball before it went out of bounds over the goal line. The kick is taken from the corner of the field closest to where the ball went out of bounds.

GOAL KICK is awarded to the defending team if an attacking forward was the last to touch the ball before it went out of bounds over the goal line.

THROW-IN is awarded to the team opposite to the player that last touched the ball before it went out of bounds along the sideline. The thrower must use a two-hand over-the-head throw with both feet remaining in contact with the ground and completely out of the field of play. Any player may take the throw-in.

April 16, 1967

Los Angeles Beats New York, 3-2, as Soccer Opens Bid for Sports Dollar

DURANTE SCORES TWICE FOR TOROS

Djukic Also Star in Victors' Attack—Archibald, Mahy Get Generals' Goals

By BILL BECKER
Special to The New York Times

LOS ANGELES, April 16—The Los Angeles Toros defeated the New York Generals, 3-2, today in a National Professional Soccer League opener before a crowd of 9,048 in Memorial Coliseum.

The crowd may have looked smaller in the 93,000-capacity Coliseum, but it showed a surprising amount of enthusiasm. The large and soccer-knowing Latin American population of Los Angeles appeared to have contributed more than half the attendance.

Dragan Djukic, a Yugoslav forward, and Eli Durante, his running mate from Brazil, led the Toros' torrid first-half attack.

Los Angeles led, 3-2, after the offensive-minded first half. Then the second 45 minutes went scoreless, as defenses tightened and tempers flared.

Archibald Tallies for New York

New York was led by Warren Archibald, a flashy forward from Trinidad, who scored one goal and passed to Barry Mahy, the team captain, for the Generals' other score.

But the Generals never could catch up after the Toros took a 2-0 lead in the first 20 minutes.

Djukic opened the scoring with a 12-yard penalty shot in the 15th minute of play. Five minutes later, Djukic passed to Durante, who sliced a 25-yarder in from the left side.

Archibald, a fleet dribbler, booted one in from nearly 30 yards out at 24 minutes to narrow the score to 2-1. Durante's second goal came on a pass from Mehalj Mesaros at 36 minutes, to make it 3-1.

In the final minute of the first half, Mahy, the General halfback from England, took Archibald's pass and scored in a wild melee for the last counter.

The defenses took over in the second half. Both goalies, Geoffrey Sidebottom of New York and Blagoje Vidinovic of Los Angeles, made several sparkling saves.

Heads or Toes: Both Are Weapons for Soccer Players

Associated Press Wirephoto
Gordon Perry (6) of the Atlanta Chiefs and Fernando Azevedo of Baltimore Bays, trying to head ball during match yesterday at Baltimore. Atlanta dropped first game, 1-0.

In the closing five minutes, two near-fights erupted when Henrik Vestergaard, the New York halfback from Denmark, tripped Durante. Barrie Wright of New York flipped Mesaros on his back, but the referees broke things up before blows were struck.

The press box was only one-quarter filled, but sports correspondents for several British, German and Latin-American papers were in attendance.

The game, played under sunny skies with a temperature of about 65, marked the fourth straight victory for the Toros, who had won their first three exhibitions.

The triumph gave them 9 points under the new league's scoring rules. The Generals received 2 points. Each victory is worth a bonus of 6 points—plus points actually scored in the game, up to a maximum of 3.

April 17, 1967

WOLVES CAPTURE U.S. SOCCER TITLE

Defeat Whips, 6-5, Before 17,842 on Coast

LOS ANGELES, July 15 (UPI)—The Los Angeles Wolves beat the Washington Whips, 6-5, with an accidental goal in a sudden-death overtime last night to win the United Soccer Association championship before 17,842 fans at Memorial Coliseum.

At 1:26 in the sudden-death period, Bobby Thomson of the Wolves tried a corner-kick and it bounced off the leg of Washington's Alley Shewan and into the goal.

The teams had played 90 minutes of regulation game and were tied at 4-4, and after a half-hour overtime period were tied at 5-5.

The teams had played 90 minutes of regulation game and were tied, 4-4. At the half-hour overtime period they were tied, 5-5, and were deadlocked, 1-1, at half-time.

Dave Burnside of Los Angeles and Francis Munro of Washington scored three goals each during the prolonged contest.

They were tied still at 4-4 after 15 minutes of regular overtime period. Derek Dougan put Los Angeles ahead, 5-4, in the 113th minute. Then with 10 seconds to play, Munro tied it at 5-5.

The first score of the game was made by Peter Knowles of Los Angeles at 2:30. Jim Smith of Washington tied it, 1-1, in the 21st minute.

Munro scored the first of his three goals in the second half at 63:30 to put Washington into the lead, 2-1.

Burnside struck back with

his first of three to tie it, 2-2, in the 65th minute. Jim Storrie of Washington scored in the 66th minute to put Washington out in front, 3-2, but Burnside made it a 3-3 tie 30 seconds later.

Burnside scored again in the 82d minute for a 4-3 Los Angeles lead, but Munro made it 4-4 to send the game into overtime at 88:30.

July 16, 1967

CLIPPERS TOP BAYS IN TITLE SERIES, 4-2

Djukic Kicks Three Goals in Soccer League Finale

Special to The New York Times

OAKLAND, Calif., Sept. 9— The Oakland Clippers gained the championship of the National Professional Soccer League today by defeating the Baltimore Bays, 4-1, before 9,037 at Oakland Coliseum. The triumph gave the Clippers a 4-2 total-goal advantage in the two-game series that began in Baltimore last Sunday with the Bays posting a 1-0 victory.

The Bays were outclassed today and just didn't seem to be up for the final match. In addition, they played 50 minutes with only 10 men. More important, Dragan Djukic, a Yugoslav forward by way of the Los Angeles Toros, was really on the scoring beam. He booted in three goals in the first half, setting the victory pace.

The pressure initiated by the Clippers after the opening whistle hit its peak midway in the period. Djukic took a pass faom Dave Davidovic, a fellow Yugoslav, and headed it into the far corner of the net from eight yards out. That put the teams even by wiping out the one goal advantage that Baltimore had scored in the first game. Eight minutes later, at 35 minutes, the same combination hit the target again with the same strategic action from 12 yards out.

The two goals that put the Clippers in the lead also unnerved their tense foes. Two minutes later Badu da Cruz fouled Sele Milosevic in a penalty area and Mike Askenazi, the referee, called for a penalty kick.

As Djukic prepared to take the kick, Juan Santisteban walked over and kicked him in the leg. After Askenazi ordered Santisteban off the field, other Baltimore players milled round the referee. When they quieted down, Djukic made good on the kick for his third goal.

Scoring—Oakland: Djukic 3, Marin Baltimore: St. Vil.
Corner Kicks—Oakland 10, Baltimore 9.
Saves—Oakland 6, Baltimore 9.

September 10, 1967

42 Are Killed and 600 Injured In Riot at Turkish Soccer Game

By Reuters

KAYSERI, Turkey, Sept. 17— Forty-two persons were killed and about 600 injured today when a riot broke out among spectators at a soccer game in this provincial capital 165 miles east-southeast of Ankara.

Troops and policemen used rifles with bayonets to break up the battle in the crowd of about 30,000.

Supporters of the local team and the opposing team from Sivas, 110 miles to the northeast, battled with pistols, knives and broken bottles. The fighting spread through the streets.

When news of the riot reached Sivas, at least three cars bearing Kayseri license plates were burned. Troops were ordered to the border between the two provinces.

Premier Suleyman Demirel consulted the Interior Minister, Dr. Faruk Sukan, who was at Izmir (Smyrna). They were reported to be considering putting the two provinces under a curfew.

The riot erupted in the 20th minute of the match—there are two 45-minute halves in a soccer game—when the Kayseri team scored a disputed goal.

Some of the 5,000 supporters

The New York Times   Sept. 18, 1967
A soccer game at Kayseri (cross) led to riot deaths.

from Sivas began throwing stones at the local players.

There have been other battles among spectators at recent matches.

Two weeks ago, at Bolu one spectator was killed and three injured. Last week, 13 persons were injured at Afyon.

Kamil Ocak, the minister responsible for sports, said that he would consider abolishing the Second Division, the minor soccer league in which the recent riots have occurred.

The riot today was the worst at a soccer game since more than 300 people were killed and about 1,000 injured at a match between Uruguay and Peru in Lima in May, 1964.

September 18, 1967

20 CITIES PICKED FOR SOCCER LOOP

New Alignment Eliminates Second Team at 6 Sites

CHICAGO, Dec. 13 (AP)— The merged United Soccer Association and the National Professional Soccer League announced an alignment of 20 cities after an all-day meeting today.

There will be no two-team cities next season. Arrangements were completed with respect to the six two-team cities previously in the two leagues this way:

¶The two New York teams will join to operate as a single team.

¶Boston of the U.S.A., Chicag of the N.P.S.L. and Los Angeles of the N.P.S.L. agreed to move to new cities to be determined.

¶The owners of the Toronto team of the U.S.A. will sell the franchise to the league, leaving Toronto to the N.P.S.L. ownership.

¶San Francisco of the U.S.A. and Vancouver of the U.S.A. have merged and will operate in Vancouver.

The 20-team league will include Atlanta, Baltimore, Boston, Chicago, Cleveland, Dallas, Detroit, Houston, Los Angeles, New York, Oakland, Philadelphia Pittsburgh, St. Louis, Toronto, Vancouver, Washington, relocated Boston of the U.S.A. and Chicago and Los Angeles of the N.P.S.L.

The league will operate with two divisions, the United and National. New York will be in the National and Los Angeles in the United. The rest of the divisional set-up, the new name for the league, schedule details and player personnel will be determined at another joint meeting later.

Dick Walsh, commissioner of the U.S.A., will head the United Division and Ken Macker, the N.P.S.L. commissioner, will head the National. Walsh said the officials of the U.S.A. and N.P.S.L. will meet with representatives of the Federation International de Football Association in Zurich

Dec 16 and as soon as possible thereafter with the Canadian Soccer Football Association.

"The meetings will be to finalize settlement of differences between the two American soccer leagues," Walsh said.

A merger agreement of the two leagues was reached last week. Such a merger appeared close several months ago but failed to materialize.

December 14, 1967

MANCHESTER UNITED WINS EUROPEAN CUP

LONDON, May 29 (Reuters) —Manchester United became the first English club to win the European Soccer Cup by defeating Banfrica of Portugal, 4-1, in overtime at Wembley Stadium tonight.

Manchester United punctured the Portuguese pride with a devastating three-goal spell in the first nine minutes of overtime to shatter Banfrica's of winning the competition for the third time.

Manchester kept the Cup in Britain following Glasgow Celtics' success last season. Manchester will meet Estudiante of Argentina in the world club championship.

Bobby Charlton was the Manchester hero tonight as he scored twice and set up the other Manchester goals. It was Charlton who headed United into a lead after 53 minutes of play before Jaime Graca tied the contest in the 79th minute of play to force the overtime.

Then United rallied. Charlton passed to George Best, who dribbled round three Banfrica players including Jose Henrique, the goalkeeper, to restore Manchester's lead after three minutes of the overtime.

Ninety seconds later Brian Kidd celebrated his 19th birthday as he headed in a Charlton corner pass and Charlton ended the scoring in the ninth minute with a close-range effort.

May 30, 1968

Stadium Stampede Kills 71 Argentines

By The Associated Press

BUENOS AIRES, June 23—A stampede at a soccer stadium exit killed 71 spectators today and injured 130.

Forty of the injured were reported to be in serious condition.

The disaster occurred after 90,000 fans had crowded into El Estadio Monumental to watch Río de la Plata and Boca Juniors play to a scoreless tie.

Guillermo Borda, the Minister of the Interior, said that Gate 12, where the panic occurred, had been open but that the turnstiles had not been removed as usual to make the exit easier.

Many of the injured were found on staircases leading down to the gate, apparently overrun in the panic.

President Juan Carlos Onganía inspected the stadium after the tragedy and Antonio Cardinal Caggiano, Roman Catholic Primate of Argentina, visited hospitals where the dead and injured were taken.

The tragedy is the worst in the history of Argentine soccer. The world's worst soccer stampede occurred at Peru's national stadium in Lima, May 23, 1964. Some 350 people were killed after an amateur match between Peru and Argentina.

A commission began an investigation of the tragedy.

Dr. Mateo Jelisich, chairman of the commission, said most of the dead were at a hospital a few blocks from the stadium in a lower-middle-class residential area in northern Buenos Aires.

June 24, 1968

ATLANTA WINS BY 3-0 FOR SOCCER CROWN

ATLANTA, Sept. 28 (AP)—The Atlanta Chiefs built a 2-0 half-time lead and put up a strong defense in the second half to defeat the San Diego Toros, 3-0, and win the North American Soccer League championship today.

The teams had fought to a scoreless tie in the first game of the two-game championship series at San Diego last Saturday.

The Chiefs' first score was an eight-yard goal by Peter McParland of Ireland with an assist from Brian Hughes of Wales with 22 minutes 34 seconds gone.

The goal was the first by either team in three games and 202 minutes this season. They previously played two 0-0 ties.

The Chiefs scored again with 42:53 elapsed on an unassisted shot by Delroy Scott of Jamaica from 15 yards out. It came on a rebound after Kaizer (Boy Boy) Motaung of South Africa attempted a header.

The final goal came after 79:50 when Motaung took the ball at midfield, dribbled through two defenders and drove it in from about six yards out.

The Chiefs were content to play defense in the second half, shooting only from long range and keeping San Diego out of the penalty area.

September 29, 1968

PRO SOCCER PLANS ONE-TEAM LEAGUE

All-Star Squad to Replace 14 Disbanded Franchises

Special to The New York Times

CHICAGO, Nov. 1—Professional soccer voted today to revolutionize its format in the United States, temporarily disband the 14-team major league and concentrate instead on a single All-America team.

It was proposed that the new team would play perhaps 60 matches next year against international champions in a "glamour tactic to revive interest in soccer in the United States.

The change was voted today by officials of the 14 teams in the North American Soccer League, which played in 17 cities last summer from Vancouver to Atlanta in an effort to establish professional soccer in big-league stadiums.

The decision was prompted by the woes of attendance. During a season that lasted from March to September, the teams averaged as few as 3,000 customers a game (Chicago) and as many as 7,000 (Kansas City and Atlanta). The New York Generals, who needed about 11,000 admissions a game to break even, drew about 4,000.

New Interest Is Aim

However, certain exhibition games were runaway successes. A crowd of 44,000 paid to see the famous Santos team of Brazil play the Napoli Club of Italy in Yankee Stadium. And on the strength of such attractions, the league decided not to go out of business, but to gamble on stirring new interest.

"Soccer won't stop," said Eugene L. Scott, the lawyer and sportsman who is the chief operating officer of the New York team and the chairman pro tem of the league. "We are a league. Each member will own a small part of this new team. If interest becomes big enough, local identity will be engendered and then local operations will be started again."

The decision will be submitted to the two governing bodies for soccer on the continent—the United States Soccer Football Association and the Canadian Soccer Football Association.

If they approve, the teams will place their players on waivers, invite the better ones to tryouts for the all-star team and then maintain skeleton staffs "for the duration." If they do not approve, the owners will meet again to consider what course to follow.

The period of transition will be indefinite. Some of the officials today thought it might last two or three years. Some felt it might last five years. But all agreed the goal was to stoke enough interest to revive soccer on a league basis.

Generals Opposed Shift

The New York Generals led the opposition to the switch at the meeting. They preferred to retain the present format, but they acceded to the decision. The Generals are controlled by a syndicate led by Louis Marx Jr., the toy manufacturer, and three stockbrokers, Neil McConnell, Dan Lufkin and Fred Melkado.

The league contained 17 cities last season: New York, Kansas City, Atlanta, Oakland, Los Angeles, Houston, Washington, Toronto, San Diego, St. Louis, Chicago, Dallas, Cleveland, Baltimore, Vancouver, Boston and Detroit.

November 2, 1968

SANCTION WITHHELD FOR U.S. SOCCER PLAN

The United States Soccer Football Association refused yesterday to allow the North American Soccer League to disband or change its structure unless the league guaranteed that the association would not be responsible for claims by dissident members.

Last month, eight members of the 17-team N.A.S.L. decided to recruit a "national" team from players in the league and match it against foreign competition here and abroad. One club, Houston, dropped out of the league. The eight other members (including the New York Generals) were not in favor of the one team concept, but decided to keep their franchises.

Since the league was formed last year by the merger of the United Soccer Association and the National Professional Soccer League, the U.S.S.F.A. has received more than $250,000 in fees and gate percentages.

The U.S.S.F.A. said that if the one-team concept became a reality, league members would lose their territorial exclusivity, since under the league's contract with the U.S.S.F.A. exclusivity applied only to teams playing in a league.

December 12, 1968

PRO SOCCER LEAGUE WILL FIELD 8 CLUBS

ATLANTA, Jan. 7 (AP)—Professional soccer will be represented in the United States this year by an eight-team league, officials of the Atlanta Chiefs announced today after a meeting here with the owners of seven other teams.

The executives of the eight North American Soccer League clubs appointed Phil Woosnam, Atlanta's head coach and general manager, to a newly created post as executive director of the league.

Cities that will field soccer teams this year are Atlanta, Dallas, Chicago, Oakland, Kansas City, Baltimore, New York and St. Louis.

The owners said there would be an emphasis upon the development of soccer in each league city. In addition, the owners said they were exploring the possibility of bringing top European teams to the United States for a series of league-sponsored exhibitions.

Earlier, the 17 members, who operated within the league last year, had indicated they were considering forming one national team to represent the league until sufficient interest in soccer could be created to make the league's operations profitable.

January 8, 1969

Salvador and Honduras Play Soccer Amicably

MEXICO CITY, June 28 (UPI) Salvador defeated Honduras 3 to 2 in overtime to win their best-of-three World Cup series last night, less than 24 hours after the countries had severed diplomatic relations over incidents triggered by the first two games.

The victory, on neutral turf, ended in embraces and handshakes by both teams. By winning, Salvador advanced to the regional World Cup finals and will play Haiti.

Meanwhile, troops in the neighboring nations were either on maneuvers or had called up reinforcements should the crisis worsen.

Salvador's victory occurred under the watchful eyes of 1,700 Mexico City policemen who feared that fans flown in from the feuding countries once again would clash as they did following the first two games in the series.

Only one outburst marred the match, a brief shout of "Murderers! Murderers!" from the Salvadorean cheering section.

June 29, 1969

Pele Becomes First Modern Player to Reach 1,000 Goals

RIO DE JANEIRO, Nov. 19 (AP)—Pélé, Brazil's soccer ace, scored the 1,000th goal of his professional career tonight.

The 29-year-old inside left of the Santos football club reached the milestone at the huge Maracana Stadium here.

It was the high point of his 13 years as one of the world's top professional booters.

The 1,000-goal mark is a millenium in soccer comparable to the four-minute mile or Babe Ruth's 60 home runs in one season.

The noisy and excitable Brazilians, proud of their soccer heritage (two World Cups and a reputation of having the world's best and most exciting soccer), had followed the countdown on Pélé's bid to reach 1,000.

Newspapers have been blanketed with Pélé stories and some even gave the soccer king more play than the moon landing of the Apollo 12.

Though Pélé is only the third greatest-known scorer in soccer history, the other two—Arthur Freidenreich of Brazil, 1,329, and Franz (Bimbo) Binder of Austria, 1,006—played before professional soccer was organized, leaving Pélé as the undisputed top goal scorer in professional and modern soccer.

The game was televised in many parts of the country.

Santos gained a 2-1 victory over the home team, Vasco da Gama.

Before the game, traffic clogged the roads leading to the famous stadium where the game was played.

More than 100,000 soccer fans crowded the world's largest stadium.

November 20, 1969

Illegal English Soccer Clause
Survives in Different Form

By PAUL GARDNER

It's pretty likely that Curt Flood has no idea who George Eastham is. For that matter, it's a near-certainty that George Eastham has never heard of Curt Flood. Yet, they're almost the same person—well, symbolically speaking—because 10 years ago Eastham did to English soccer what Flood is about to do to American baseball: he took the sport's establishment to court to challenge the reserve clause.

In 1959, George Eastham was one of the top soccer stars in England, a stylish player of considerable intelligence and artistry and the key man in the Newcastle United offense. But between Eastham and Newcastle things were not going well; he was dissatisfied and asked the club to trade him.

The English call this a 'transfer,' and usually there is no player swap, just a straight cash deal. Newcastle, alarmed by the thought of losing Eastham, refused to put him on the transfer list (which would have entitled other clubs to start bidding for him).

Slaves—Not Very Well Paid

Because of the autocratic authority that the clubs had over their players there was little Eastham could do. The conditions then existing made soccer players really little more than slaves—paid slaves, certainly, but not very well paid.

All contracts were of a standard form and lasted for one year only. When the player came to re-sign for the next season, the "retain and transfer system"—which is how the English describe the reserve clause —forced him to deal only with his previous club. The club had several options: it could re-sign the player for another year, it could put him on the transfer list,

release him, or it could retain him without a contract and at a rock-bottom minimum wage of $28 a week.

A retained player could not play, as he had no contract, and could not be approached by another club. As a method of forcing a player to sign a contract on the club's terms, it could hardly have been bettered.

If that sounds bad enough, just wait a minute. When it *did* come to contract time, the player's bargaining rights were almost entirely academic, because of the standard form of the contract and because the Football League imposed a ceiling on wages. No player, no matter how big a star, could negotiate a wage higher than the maximum, which in 1960 stood at the princely sum of $56 a week during the season and $48 during the summer.

A Promise of a House

At the end of the 1959-60 season, Eastham refused to sign a new contract with Newcastle, which placed him on the retained list while it tried to induce him to sign. He was promised a house and told that, if he signed again, he would be transferred at the end of the season.

He was also told by the club manager that he was "big-headed," that he was unpopular with the other players, and that his hands were too short and his pockets too long. ("It's better than saying he's mean," the manager explained.) You can't help wondering what Newcastle wanted with a player like that.

Eastham did not re-sign. He moved to the south of England and, because he was now barred from playing pro soccer, took a job outside the sport. He also, as they say, "sought legal advice." Maybe. Some felt that the legal advice was thrust upon

him by the players' union, the Professional Footballers' Association (P.F.A.). The upshot was that in October of 1960, writs were served on Newcastle United and the Football League that, in effect, asked the courts to declare the league's retain-transfer system illegal.

It had been obvious for some time that unrest was growing among soccer players. What was particularly galling was the knowledge that in other European countries, notably Spain and Italy, top players were being paid 10 times as much as in England. It was no secret that Italian clubs had been scouting English stars.

There was a very real danger that the cream of English soccer would be lured abroad, and that the sport in England would wither to a rather second-rate affair played by people who didn't take it too seriously.

Owners Turn Deaf Ears

Only the club owners seemed impervious to the growing danger. At the beginning of 1960, the P.F.A. asked the Football League to open negotiations on wages and the reserve clause. The league's idea of negotiations was to reject all the association's suggestions. Even the serving of Eastham's writs in October made no impression, and by November the players were calling for a strike as the only way to combat the league's intransigence.

Questions were asked in the House of Commons, where one Member of Parliament called the players "soccer serfs" bound to their employers by "contractual conditions that would have been rejected with a snort of contempt by any intelligent young apprentice in the Middle Ages."

"Who would stand for a contract that tied him after it had expired?" said another.

The owners resisted all through 1960. They really could not believe that the players, *their* players, would strike. Undoubtedly most of the owners were sincerely interested in the welfare of their players, but their paternalistic approach was 100 years behind the times and their

George Eastham

Pictorial Parade

idea of an adequate wage almost equally out of date.

On Dec. 30, with the threatened strike only three weeks away, the league made a major concession—to increase the maximum wage to $84 a week and to abolish it in 1962. But the reserve clause, although modified, was to remain.

"The only safeguard the clubs want," said the league secretary, Alan Hardaker, "is that no player can just walk out at any time on any pretext, however flimsy."

The P.F.A. did not see it that way and insisted the reserve clause had to go. It turned thumbs down on the new offer. The London Times chastised the owners in an editorial: "The players' demands have no doubt all along seemed to the Football League impossible and outrageous in so far as their acceptance means a complete break with the past. But if Association Football (i.e., soccer) is to remain alive, then the past will have to die."

Lull Before the Storm

On Jan. 19, 1961, the league capitulated, and the strike was called off. It seemed that the players had won a complete victory, and that both the maximum wage and the reserve clause were now things of the past.

Had that been so, then little more would have been heard of the Eastham case. But the reserve clause proved a mighty stubborn animal, for the Football League soon

made it clear that it had no intention of abolishing it. It claimed that it had never agreed to do so.

"Freedom of contract to players, as suggested by the union side, would lead to chaos," the league said.

The P.F.A. accused the league of going back on its word. The owners hung on, feeling that with the abolition of the maximum wage and the introduction of two-year contracts they had done enough to take most of the steam out of the players' case, and that the reserve clause dispute would eventually cease to worry anyone.

The P.F.A. would not let the issue drop, but the owners successfully resisted pressure for the next two years. Then, on June 11, 1963, Eastham's case against the Football League and Newcastle United began in the High Court before an impressive assembly of top legal talent, including no fewer than four Queen's Counsels. (Those who felt that soccer players were treated like slaves took hope from the name of the trial judge—Mr. Justice Wilberforce.)

By this time Eastham was playing again, having been transferred (sold for $131,000) to the London club Arsenal in November, 1960. The main thrust of his case, which was backed by the P.F.A., was that once his employment was over—i.e., once his year's contract expired—his club at that point became his former club and he was free to negotiate with any club that he chose. His former club could impose restraints on him, but only those absolutely necessary for its own protection; it was claimed that, under English law, these could not include preventing him from playing for another club.

Players' Lawyer on Offense

"I can think of no industry," said Eastham's lawyer, "which attempts to impose restrictions on its workers after their employment has ended, such as the restrictions imposed on professional footballers."

He also attacked the way in which players were bought and sold and the fact that of the very large sums often paid (the English record at that time stood at $168,000) the player never got more than $840. It was also the only case in which a company paid a lot of money for an asset and did not put it on the balance sheet.

This prompted one of those dry quips that British judges are wont to make. "Livestock at valuation," mused Justice Wilberforce. "It would look a little insulting." But no more insulting, said Eastham's lawyer, than being bought and sold as cattle.

The Football League's defense of the reserve clause was, quite simply, that it was essential if the employers' rights were to be protected. The league claimed that it was lawful and that its requirements did not exceed what was reasonably necessary to safeguard the interests of the clubs and of league soccer. It was repeatedly suggested that without the reserve clause all would be chaos.

"We would not know what to do. Without the system, organized football would be finished," said a Newcastle United director. The transfer system was defended because the development and selling of players was the main source of income for many small clubs. Such clubs would not be able to obtain transfer fees unless they had some reasonable hold on the player, such as that provided by the reserve clause.

Hardaker, in his evidence for the league, said that a large number of clubs would go bankrupt if they could not get transfer fees for selling players, and that many footballers would thus be put out of work.

"Without the retain-and-transfer system there would be complete anarchy in the

football world," he said and, for good measure, threw in another specter that, with its hint of rampant commercialism, was guaranteed to give pause to many sports-lovers: If the reserve clause went, then, instead of being controlled by the governing bodies of football, players would be controlled by agents, as in the entertainment industry.

It was even suggested that the reserve clause wasn't a bad thing for the players, really, because it might have stipulated an unqualified option to extend employment; at least there was the alternative of a transfer.

Reserve Clause Loses Out

The idea that the clause was a good thing as it stood, simply because it might have been worse, evidently did not appeal to Mr. Justice Wilberforce. His judgment, handed down on July 4, 1963, declared that the regulations of the Football League relating to retention and transfer of players were an unreasonable restraint of trade and *ultra vires*. The reserve clause was illegal.

The Football League, after announcing that it was considering an appeal, decided against it. But the owners made it clear that they were not giving up the fight. The judgment, said Hardaker, was given on the basis of regulations in effect three years back. They would be modified, indeed had been modified, but any new system evolved would not include freedom of contract.

"The retain-and-transfer system is fundamental to the league," he said, a statement echoed yesterday by presidents of the Major Leagues: "The reserve clause is the backbone of baseball."

In fact, despite the Eastham judgment, the reserve clause still exists in English soccer, albeit somewhat disguised. Clubs still have the exclusive right to re-sign their players, but that right is now limited to the first renewal of a contract. The player has two added safeguards. If he refuses to re-sign and the club refuses to transfer him, the dispute can be referred to an independent tribunal, which must give a decision within a month. And while the dispute exists, the club must continue to pay him at the rate agreed to in his previous contract.

The disappearance of the maximum wage and the watering down of the reserve clause have not spelled doom for English soccer. Rather the opposite. Since these things happened, the standard of play has risen to the point where the English League is unquestionably the strongest in the world. In 1966, England, for the first time, won the world championship of soccer.

The writer is North American sports correspondent for the London newspaper, The Observer.

January 18, 1970

LONDON, Jan. 19 (Reuters)—Today was ladies' day in English soccer as the Football Association, governing body of the game here, officially recognized women players for the first time.

Denis Follows, association secretary, said after the decision was made by the F.A. council today "some members still think that football is no game for the ladies. However, the council is conscious that many women's football teams are already playing."

The move, first since 1921 when the F.A. first ruled against women's soccer, will allow women to play on grounds of clubs affiliated with the association.

January 20, 1970

Soviet Goalie Is Cited

LONDON, March 22 (AP)—Lev Yashin of the Soviet Union was voted today as the outstanding goalkeeper over the last 20 years in a poll of soccer writers from 35 countries.

March 23, 1970

One-Armed Star Strikes It Rich

The highest paid soccer player in the United States makes $15,000 a year, speaks no English and has one arm.

He is Victorio Casa, a 27-year-old forward form Argentina who weighs only 145 pounds and may be the only one-armed professional soccer player in the world.

A man with bright eyes who combs his thick, dark hair straight back, Casa was signed two weeks ago by the Washington Darts of the North American Soccer League.

Norman Sutherland, the Darts' general manager, said Casa's signing was the "most important this team ever made," and that Casa's salary was the highest paid to a soccer player in this country.

Casa, a professional player since the age of 16, lost his right arm just above the elbow in a freak shooting in 1965. He was a member of the San Lorenzo team at the time and the best outside left in Buenos Aires.

Nervous Sentry Fires at Him

San Lorenzo had an afternoon game rained out and Casa went to meet some of his friends that evening in a club on the Strip in Buenos Aires. The club was situated across from a military installation and as Casa and his girl friend started to get out of a car, a shot was fired by a sentry that shattered his right arm.

It appeared that the shot by the nervous sentry would end Casa's career. Doctors told him they would have to remove the arm and indicated he would never play again. But 22 days later, Casa was back in action, scoring a goal in his first appearance.

"Soccer is not played by the arms and I knew

Victorio Casa

I was going to be back," Casa said through the interpretation of John Muir, a scot who plays for the Darts and studies at the University of Madrid during the off-season.

Casa arrived in Washington two weeks ago.

He had been there in 1968 as a member of the now defunct Washington whips of the National Professional Soccer League. He had some good and bad experiences in America at the time.

Soon after his arrival in Washington in 1968, he became the darling of the Whips' fans but not of his coach, Andre Nagy, who benched him for a while, accusing him of too much dribbling. Like many South American Players, Casa likes to dribble.

Sutherland, however, doesn't worry about the excessive individualism on Casa's part.

"If I didn't think he could fit into the team, he wouldn't be here," Sutherland said in Washington.

Casa, married and the father of two children, returned to Argentina after the Whips folded and played there as recently as last March 20.

"When the Whips and the majority of the national Professional Soccer League teams folded, everyone thought it was the end of soccer in America," Casa said. "When I heard it was coming back, I couldn't believe it."

The Darts are a new franchise in the North American League, which grew out of the merger of the national Professional League and United Soccer association. The league is now operating with six teams. A New York franchise is expected to function next year.

April 26, 1970

Soccer a Rewarding Occupation

By ALEX YANNIS

Many of the soccer players performing in the World Cup in Mexico enjoy incomes larger than the salaries of some heads of state. And this doesn't include income from extra activities such as endorsements, television commercials, newspaper columns and industrial investments.

Edson Arantes do Nascimento of Brazil, better known as Pelé, can claim to be the world's highest paid soccer player. Pelé, 29 years old, who as a young boy shined shoes, makes $144,000 a year from the sport, according to some sources in Rio De Janeiro.

But Pelé is not only a soccer player, he also is a one-man industry. Altogether he earns about $500,000 from different activities and reliable sources report that he owns so much real estate that he allows a number of poor families to reside free at a complex of buildings he owns in Rio. No wonder he is a national symbol.

Plenty to Go Round

A recent survey revealed that Pelé was not the only soccer player who could retire tomorrow with sufficient income. About 30 soccer players in Europe and Latin America could do the same, if they so desired.

In Britain, where young fellows these days either pick up a guitar or kick a straight pass, it is estimated that half a dozen players make more than $47,000 a year. But, as in other countries, the big money comes indirectly from sports.

Bobby Moore, England's captain in the last World Cup tournament and now in Mexico, makes about $60,000 a year from soccer. Moore, however, who was recently accused of stealing a bracelet in Bogota, Colombia, doesn't even bother to figure how much he earns from soccer. Most of his money comes from advertising.

Other players with lucrative incomes from advertising are Bobby Charlton of Manchester United and Geoff Hurst of West Ham United, a teammate of Moore.

Italian officials are reluctant to disclose actual earnings of players there because of income tax considerations. Ten players in Italy, however, are known to earn more than $62,000 a year and six more than $79,200 annually.

Mario Corso and Luis Suarez, a Spaniard who plays for Inter-Milan along with Corso, recently disclosed in New York — they were here to play Santos of Brazil—that they earn "more than enough."

There are other world soccer stars, who are not in Mexico because their countries failed to qualify, who make a "bundle," as a soccer promoter here put it.

Portugal's Eusebio, George Best of Manchester United, Robert Perfumo of Argentina and Amadeo Carrizo of Colombia earn in the vicinity of $100,000 from soccer alone. Best, an Irishman, derives income from, among other things, fashion modeling and the five stores he owns in Manchester.

And Coaches, Too

Other players reputed to lead comfortable lives are Giacinto Facketti of Italy, Jimmy Greaves of England, Jimmy Domazos of Greece, Helmut Haller of West Germany and Uwe Seller, also of West Germany.

Since the retirements of Raymon Kopa and Joseph Piantonni French soccer has not done too well and as a result players there make less than the Poles, the Rumanians, the Czechoslovaks, and even the Greeks, in their respective countries.

The highest paid soccer player in the United States is Victoria Casa, an Argentine with one arm, who makes $15,000 a year with the Washington Darts of the North American Soccer League. However, he earns no money from other activities.

Coaches of the sport also do quite well and apparently working in countries other than their own can be even more lucrative. Helleni Herrera, for example, known as Mr. HH, is an Argentine who works in Italy. As an Italian official here put it, "he pockets more than a hundred grand."

June 7, 1970

Brazil Turns Back England, 1-0, in World Cup Soccer on Goal at 60th Minute

By BRIAN GLANVILLE
Special to The New York Times

GUADALAJARA, Mexico, June 7 — In a superb match that did credit to the competition, Brazil beat England, 1-0, at Jalisco Stadium today and thus became the first soccer team to win against her in the World Cup since 1962.

In other action today, West Germany clinched a quarter-final berth in Group IV, along with Peru, with a 5-2 victory over Bulgaria; Mexico put in three second-half goals to beat El Salvador, 4-0, and Israel and Sweden tied, 1-1.

In 1962, in the quarterfinals at Vina del Mar, Chile, it was the Brazilians themselves who beat England. Their victory today, obtained by a fine goal scored by Jairzinho 15 minutes into the second half, was just about as deserved, but England lamentably squandered her chances.

Not only did Geoff Hurst, usually so penetrative and reliable, dither bewilderingly when, in the first half, the Brazilian defense moved up to leave him free and onside, but late in the game, when Jeff Astle and Colin Bell were substituted for Bobby Charlton and Francis Lee, Alan Ball, from Astle's judicious header, and Astle himself, after a defensive blunder, missed concrete opportunities to score.

Brazil at Disadvantage

Still, it should be emphasized that Brazil played without her most dangerous and effective midfield player, Gerson, who failed to recover in time from a thigh strain, despite intensive treatment.

The English, too, had their problems, including the hot and sapping sun. Under the circumstances, their stamina and tenacity were remarkable. Their slumbers were troubled last night by swarms of noisy Brazilians and Mexicans, who deliberately paraded round the English team's hotel, hooting horns and yelling. The police, despite the appeals of English officials, stayed away in large numbers.

Had it not been for a staggering save by Gordon Banks, the goalie, on Pelé's fine header after 10 minutes, Brazil might have won more easily. Jairzinho, the powerful right winger, beat Terry Cooper and crossed. Pelé dived to head the ball on the bounce, just inside the left post, but somehow Banks got across to sweep it, one-handed, over his bar.

Felix Has 2 Lives

As against that, Felix, a most unhappy goalkeeper and almost a liability to his side, saved on a header from Lee in the first half, and was fortunate in the second when Ball's shot hit the top of the bar.

Jairzinho remains an impressively threatening winger. Pelé, though Alan Mullery played him well, had his usual scattering of glorious moments, and Tostao, until he was replaced in the second half, was wonderfully effective. To him, indeed, belongs the major credit for the goal.

After receiving the ball on the left, Tostao rose through and survived tackle after tackle with amazing balance and dexterity, before slipping the ball across goal, where Pelé moved it on for Jairzinho to score at will.

Now England will have to beat the curiously unfit Czechoslovak team next Thursday to qualify. Brazil is already comfortably in the quarterfinals, and shapes up as favorite. But England has not fired its last shot.

June 8, 1970

Pele Stars as Brazil Beats Italy, 4-1, for World Cup Soccer Crown

FORWARD SCORES, SETS UP 3 GOALS

112,000 in Aztec Stadium See Brazilians Tally 3 Times in Second Half

By JUAN de ONIS
Special to The New York Times

MEXICO CITY, June 21—Brazil, with a crushing 4-1 victory over Italy, won the ninth World Cup soccer championship today and gained permanent possession of the Jules Rimet Trophy, symbol of world supremacy in the sport.

Edison Arantes, better known as Pélé, scored Brazil's only goal in the first half which ended in a 1-1 tie, and set up Brazil's three second-half goals.

The 29-year-old Brazilian forward showed why he is called the King of Soccer, but Brazil's defense, until now the weak spot in a young team, shared the glory with Pélé.

Led by the team captain, Carlos Alberto Torres, the best left fullback in the tournament, the Brazilian defense smothered Italy's counter-attacking offense, except for one moment of confusion.

Moment of Glory

Italy's alert forward, Roberto Boninsegna, stole the ball from the Brazilian defender, Wilson Piazza, at 37 minutes of the first half and with Brazil's goalie, Feliz Mielli, out of his nets, shot home a goal that temporarily tied the game.

The scoring had been opened by Pélé at 18 minutes on a pass from Roberto Rivelino that crossed the Italian defense zone. Pélé, who is only 5 feet 7 inches tall but outjumps most defensemen, headed the ball into the nets past a desperate lunge by the goalkeeper, Enrico Albertossi.

The field at Aztec Stadium, where 112,000 spectators jammed the two-tiered park for the final game, was sodden and slippery from an all-night rain that continued this morning. This hampered both teams during the first half, but at halftime the sun came out and Brazil began to shine.

Associated Press

Carlos Alberto Torres, captain of Brazil's soccer squad, holds Jules Rimet Trophy, now theirs, permanently.

The Italians lost control of midfield to the agile Brazilian defenders and could never set up their scoring ace, Luigi Riva.

At the 65-minute mark (each half is 45 minutes), Gerson Olivera Nuñez, Brazil's great playmaker, took a pass from Pélé on the run at the edge of the penalty area. He drove a left-footed shot deep into the nets past a helpless Albertossi and the game was decided.

Six minutes later, Pélé headed a long pass from Gerson toward Jair Ventura, who beat out Albertossi from three feet out. It was Jair's seventh goal, which placed him second to Gerhard Muller of West Germany, who scored 10 goals before his team was eliminated in the semifinals, in the race for high scorer.

The final goal came at 87 minutes, Pélé, with three Italian players converging on him, rolled a perfect pass to Carlos Alberto, who boomed home a 30-foot shot from the right side of the penalty area.

The victory was greeted with delirious joy by the 10,000 Brazilian fans who came here for the tournament and by the majority of the Mexican crowd. Pélé and the other Brazilian stars were mobbed on the field for 10 minutes after the game.

This was Brazil's third world championship, following earlier triumphs in Sweden in 1958, when Pélé first appeared as a 17-year-old, and in Chile in 1962.

Brazil is the first country to win three times in the competition, instituted in 1930, that is held every four years. Under the regulations, Brazil will retain forever the Rimet trophy, an 18-inch-high gold Winged Victory cup. A new trophy will be presented at the next world championship, to be played in Munich in 1974.

Among the spectators today were President Gustavo Diaz Ordaz of Mexico, Foreign Minister Gibson Barboza of Brazil and Amintore Fanfani, President of the Italian Senate. Also in the stands was Henry Kissinger, President Nixon's national security adviser.

Undefeated in Eliminations

Brazil got to the final undefeated in five games during the elimination round in which 16 national teams participated. Brazil's victories were over Czechoslovakia, England, Rumania, Peru and Uruguay.

Italy had beaten West Germany in the semifinals in the most exciting game of the tournament, a 4-3 overtime victory on Wednesday.

Yet, the Brazilian domination today was so complete that it left no doubt as to the best team in a worldwide tournament that began with 70 teams two years ago. The United States was eliminated in regional competition by Haiti last year.

June 22, 1970

World Cup Gleanings

Brazilian Players' Triumph in Mexico Provides Lift for International Soccer

By BRIAN GLANVILLE

There is an awfully strong case, after the Brazilian's victory a week ago in the World Cup, their third in four years, to say that their football has proved itself definitely the best. With the exception of one sad parenthesis in 1966, when the team was too old and Pelé was actually and literally kicked out of the tournament, Brazil has dominated the World Cup since 1958.

The Brazilians' soccer triumph in Mexico was in many ways a far more convincing and impressive one than that of England, the only country to interrupt their majestic progress, in 1966.

In the first place, it was achieved away from home; England played all its matches not only in London, but also at Wembley.

In the second place, Brazil won all its games. In the third, Brazil won by playing attacking football, rising above a weak defense and a disastrously feeble goalkeeper.

•

What the Brazilians have just shown and done is wonderfully encouraging for football. It has been done in an age of collectivism, negativity, deliberately ruthless tackling and obsessional defense, an age in which the artist, the individual ball player, tends either to be discouraged by his own club or deterred by callous opponents.

But the likes of Pelé Jairzinho, Tostao and Rivelino, not to mention Clodoaldo and the marvelous Gerson, were simply irresistible. Not least, one may ad, because to foul a Brazilian and give away a free kick on the edge of your own penalty area is simply asking for trouble.

The Italians, rather lucky to reach the final, and past masters of all forms of obstruction and prevarication in defense, were simply overwhelmed.

I do not agree with those Italian critics who felt that England, had it reached the final, would have beaten Brazil, but I am sure England would have provided a much closer game than Italy.

•

Italy's drearily negative *catenaccio* methods, with a defender "sweeping up" behind a line of four defenders, and only two strikers (like England, alas) permanently employed upfield, is caution incarnate. The only way to beat Brazil is to attack—or, as Francis Lee of England observed, "you're asking for trouble." Italy, though favored with a very lucky equalizing goal, asked for it, and got it.

Only two members of Italy's team could be properly compared with the Brazilians. Sandrino Mazzola, son of the former captain of Italy who perished in the Turin air crash of 1949, had the game of his life. His display was a compound of so many virtues; courage, high skill, stamina, intelligence.

He ran beautifully, used the ball admirably, and showed that his transition from a striking forward into a sophisticated midfield player is complete.

Nor has he lost, like Bobby Charlton of England, the ability to go forward into attack. Charlton has a good World Cup, and thoroughly deserved to set an international record by playing his 106th game for England, against West Germany, but he showed none of his old flair for getting goals.

•

The other Italian player to distinguish himself was Roberto Boninsegna, the Internazionale center-forward, and it is a commentary on the ineptitude of Italy's preparations that he was not, initially, even named in the party (being picked only when Anastasi dropped out) and that in the closing phases of the final, he was substituted—by Gianni Rivera, a midfield player. No wonder he gestured his disgust, as he came off the field.

Italy's tactical dispositions were, indeed, weired in the extreme. It was most dubious policy to make Pelé with Mario Bertini, an attacking halfback by disposition, whose weakness in the air cost Italy the vital first goal.

And the error was promptly and tacitly admitted when Ferruccio Valcareggi, the team manager, promptly put Bertini at right-back and moved the durable Tarcisio Burgnich into the middle, to take care of Pelé For a country so obsessed with tactics, it all seemed remarkably naive.

Perhaps the true revelations of the Brazilian team was Gerson. For all the 40 cigarettes he smokes a day, hand cupped over them like a man who feels they may be snatched at any moment, he is the motor of his side.

Italy never began to get to grips with him, allowing him far too much space, and the left-footed goal with which he restored Brazil's lead was a perfect joy. He has a fine sense of strategy, the marvelous ball control characteristic of his countrymen (who still, in this dull age, actually love to play) and infinite powers of invention.

In England, meanwhile one hopes that the voice of the winger, the true, specialized winger, the Jairzinho, the Grabowski, the Jimmy Johnstone of Scotland, will be heard in the land again.

England's success in 1966 confirmed her coaches in the heresy that anybody could do anything, that there was no such thing as a specialized winger. So teams at almost every level began to do without them, and the punishment has been condign. Look where you will in England, there are next to no wingers.

By 1974, perhaps we shall have them again. Woe betide us if we don't.

June 28, 1970

Danish Girls Score a First

TURIN, Italy, July 15 (AP) — Denmark won the first world women's soccer championship tongiht when its team downed Italy, 2-0.

July 16, 1970

LANCERS CAPTURE TITLE IN SOCCER

Lose to Darts, 3-1, but Take Series on Most Goals

Special to The New York Times

WASHINGTON, Sept. 13—The Washington Darts defeated the Rochester Lancers, 3-1, today in the second game of the North American Soccer League play-offs, but the Lancers became the league champions. They had triumphed, 3-0, in the first of the two-game, total-goal series.

The Darts dominated the game at Catholic University Stadium, but it was the Lancers who scored first.

After 40 minutes of play, Raul Herrera, the Lancers' center forward, penetrated the Washington defense and scored from close range.

A minute later, the referee, Mike Eshkenasi of New York, awarded the darts a penalty kick. Leroy Deleon, formerly with the defunct New York Generals, converted against the Lancers' goalie, Claude Campos.

Trying to protect their total-goal advantage, the Lancers played defensively in the second half. After five minutes had elapsed, Billy Fraser passed to Nana, who eluded Campos to make it 2-1.

At the 21st minute of the second half, Warren Archibald raced with the ball for about 50 yard and, after avoiding three Lancers, he crossed over the ball in from 10 yards-out.

September 14, 1970

ST. LOUIS RETAINS SOCCER TITLE, 1-0

EDWARDSVILLE, Ill., Dec. 5 (AP)—St. Louis University retained its National Collegiate Athletic Association soccer championship by beating University of California, Los Angeles, 1-0, today.

A goal in the third period by Denny Radican, set up by a Mike Seerey pass, gave the Billikens their 29th straight victory in two unbeaten seasons.

It was the seventh N.C.A.A. soccer title won by St. Louis. U.C.L.A. went into the game with a 16-0 won-lost record this season.

The Uclans had a good scoring chance in the first period when Shoa Agonafer had a long breakaway. Two St. Louis defenders overtook him just before he got his shot off.

Bernardo Ortiz of U.C.L.A. missed a scoring chance also in the first period when he took a foul kick by Agonafer. His boot was just wide of the goal.

December 6, 1970

New York and Toronto Get Soccer Franchises

LEAGUE EXPANDS TO EIGHT TEAMS

Ertegun, Ross and Cohen Head New York Club in North American Loop

By ALEX YANNIS

The North American Soccer League, the offspring of the unsuccessful National Professional Soccer League and the United Soccer Association, expanded to eight teams yesterday for the 1971 season by granting franchises to New York and Toronto.

The New York team will be led by a group of businessmen, headed by Nesuhi Ertegun, executive vice president of the Atlantic Recording Corporation. The Toronto franchise will be run by John W. Fisher, who was the commissioner of Canada's centennial celebrations in 1963.

Other principal owners in the New York franchise are Steven J. Ross and Alan N. Cohen, officers of the Kinney National Service Inc., a group that bid, last year, to buy the New York Jets of the National Football League.

Breakthrough for League

In making the announcement, Phil Woosnam, the executive director of the league, said: "We look upon this as a breakthrough for the league and for soccer in general."

Fisher, who was an aide to Canada's Prime Minister John Diefenbaker in 1963, said that his group was very impressed by the progress the league made last year, when it operated in Atlanta, Dallas, Kansas City, Rochester, St. Louis and Washington.

Norman Sutherland, general manager of the Washington Darts, said, when asked whether his team lost any money: "Let me answer this in another way. Our income went up 100 per cent."

"One can say that the six teams lost a lot less last year than the previous years," Charles Schiano, the manager of the Rochester Lancers, said. Rochester won the title last season.

"This league is run by strong hands who know the business," said Fisher and the owners of the other clubs nodded in agreement.

"We are not joining a United States league. We are broadening the structure of soccer throughout North America," said Fisher. He also predicted that a new sports rivalry would come into existence between New York and Toronto. "Just like the Rangers and the Maple Leafs," he said.

The league will operate in two divisions, the North and the South. As in 1969, foreign teams will be invited to play, with the results counting toward the league standings. Each team will play 20 games against league franchises and about eight games against foreign opposition. The playoffs will be held in the first week of September.

Woosnam said that other cities seeking franchises were Cleveland, Detroit, Montreal, Chicago, Philadelphia, Cincinnati and Pittsburgh.

"These groups are aware of our requirements and we have notified everyone that we are expanding to a maximum of 10. We are more than happy with the eight we have now have," Woosnam said.

December 11, 1970

The Game of Soccer Has Become the Fastest Growing Sport in the United States

By GEORGE VECSEY
Special to The New York Times

FINNEYTOWN, Ohio—Tom Stevens is a husky 40-year-old salesman who used to play guard for his high school football team.

By all the stereotypes of the modern American male, Mr. Stevens should be spending his Sunday afternoons watching professional football on television or, if he's lucky enough to have a ticket, in a stadium.

However, Mr. Stevens spends his Sunday afternoons helping his two young sons and 3,200 other young men in this town's recreation program, play soccer, the game known in 130 other countries as "football," and America's fastest-growing sport.

Although it is not seriously cutting into King Football just yet, soccer is being taken up by more and more people who find that it is less expensive, easier to organize, less injurious and quite often better exercise and more fun for the individual than the sport of helmets and rigid obedience to set plays.

Big Increase in Teams

Until recently, soccer in the United States was mainly played by foreign-born students or by ethnic clubs in big cities, but rarely by American-born athletes.

Five years ago, according to a survey by the Professional North American Soccer League, only about 800 high schools, mostly in the Northeast, had soccer teams. Now there are 2,800 College teams have risen from 225 to 680 in the same span.

Some 3,000 to 4,000 elementary schools have added soccer in the last three years, the league found, while at the sandlot or recreational level, somewhat harder to measure, the number of players seems to have jumped from 50,000 in 1966 to 250,000 in 1970. There are also girl programs in many areas.

Soccer is the world's most popular sport, judging both by the number of people playing it and by sheer crowd appeal. Almost everywhere but in the United States, young boys learn to kick the round soccer ball (smaller than a basketball) when they are still little more than infants. They later learn to advance the ball down a rectangular field in two opposing groups of 10 players, with no tackling or blocking allowed (as in football or rugby), and to try to kick it past the solitary goalie, the only man who may use his hands.

Practice games are played in dusty alleys or muddy swamps, the way Mr. Stevens' two sons grew up playing "catch" in their backyard before they discovered soccer, and championship games from South America to Asia are often played before 150,000 delirious fans.

Trails in Spectator Interest

While soccer in this country is booming on the participant level, it does not approach football or several other sports as a spectator attraction, and perhaps it never will. Soccer, with its low scores and stress on defense, does not have the explosive home run of baseball, the high scores of basketball, the long "bomb" of football or the bone-crunching speed of ice hockey.

However, soccer players rave about running for 60 full minutes in each game (90 minutes for professionals) instead of the 13 minutes or so of action they would see in a football game. And they stress the bravery required in stopping a rocketing ball with their belly or their nose and the challenge to the intelligence of making decisions over and over again during a game. "Every man is a quarterback," is a quote heard around the country.

And the sport has positive physical benefits. David Zimmerman of Seattle had respiratory problems and often visited doctors' offices. Two years ago, when David was 7 years old, a German-born neighbor named Walter Schmetzer began playing soccer with the local boys in Seattle's John Rogers Park, David took to the game immediately. When a winter league was organized this year, David signed up. In his first two games, he has

71

scored six goals — and his breathing problems seem to have subsided. He hasn't been to the doctor in six weeks.

Tom Stevens now wishes he had play the sport in his youth, it looks like so much fun. Mr. Stevens is the secretary of the Finneytown Athletic Association. Three years ago, looking for an inexpensive alternative to football, he discovered soccer at a soccer clinic in Beria, Ky., and since then he has helped about 8,000 boys play the game, most of them for the first time.

The movement has been completely "grass roots," with team rivalries based upon school districts but with no impetus whatever from school systems or recreation departments.

There was some help from the Kolping Society and the Schwaben Club in this heavily German area, but the program could never have grown without the enthusiasm of American-born fathers — and their wives.

"This is a sport that mothers can love," said Mrs. Stevens. "In Little League baseball the score would be 19 to 0 and the mothers would go home because their sons would only get to bat once an hour. But here your son is running all game. He's just as tired whether he wins or loses. He's got to be fast and aggressive and there's plenty of contact for the boys."

Despite the collisions and the bumbles, there have been only two **serious injuries** in the last three years. And mothers like Mrs. Stevens suspect that their smaller-sized sons would be trampled if they ever tried to play football. The oldest Stevens boy, 14-year-old Tom, is 5 feet 3 inches tall and weighs 100 pounds.

"This is for the smaller, sensitive athletes," Mr. Stevens said. "It's not for monsters."

Most Americans are conditioned to watching the "monsters" pound each other in football, of course, and soccer enthusiasts are occasionally teased for getting involved in a secondary sport. But most soccer buffs avoid the heresy of trying to supplant football.

Dr. Joe Guenel of Denver, who has helped form 270 boys' teams with 5,000 members in Colorado in the last 10 years, often advises youngsters to try football first, then switch to soccer if they can't make it.

"I feel there's room for soccer alongside other sports," Dr. Guenel has said.

Some cities try to have the two sports coexist by making soccer a winter sport, as in St. Louis with its massive Roman Catholic youth organization, or in Seattle.

In other areas, soccer supporters have often been frustrated within the traditional football-loving school system. "We can't get too close to educators," said Pete Merovich of the West Pennsoccer Association near Pittsburgh. "They shove us aside." The area is a hotbed of football, and soccer is often resented. However, at a time of defeated bond issues and austerity budgets, soccer is looking better all the time.

"I can outfit a boy for $20 a season," said Bill Clarke, the head soccer coach at Cleveland State University, "and make it $50 if we include warmup jackets and practice uniforms. You couldn't buy one football helmet for that. And we don't have an assistant coach for everybody but the waterboy, the way they do in football."

One convert with a celebrated name is Kyle Rote Jr., son of the football hero from Southern Methodist University and the New York Giants. After meeting a dynamic soccer coach named Ron Griffith, an Englishman, young Rote later gave up a football scholarship at Oklahoma State to play soccer at Suwanee in Tennessee. "I still like football but soccer is the greater game, the greater challenge to an athlete." he has said.

December 18, 1970

ARSENAL WINS CUP IN OVERTIME, 2-1

By Reuters

LONDON, May 8—Arsenal today became the second team in this century to achieve England's coveted soccer double when it scored a 2-1 overtime victory over Liverpool in the final of the English Football Association Cup at Wembley Stadium.

The capacity crowd of 100,000 gave a thunderous ovation to the London club for its performance in capturing its fourth Football Association Cup, only five days after winning the English League championship

[Hundreds of fans went on a rampage, according to United Press International, and scores were arrested by squads of policemen. Outside the stadium before the game, about 300 fans from the working-class districts of Liverpool clashed with hundreds of others supporting London's hometown Arsenal team. They battled with rocks and stones before being dispersed.]

Today's Wembley final, watched on television by an estimated 400 million soccer fans throughout the world, was promoted as the most popular sin-

gle event in sport history.

All three goals came in the 15-minute overtime period.

Liverpool appeared as if it had the game wrapped up when Steve Heighway, who turned professional this season, opened the scoring two minutes into overtime.

Receiving a pass from Peter Thompson, a second-half substitute, Heighway cut in from the left to fire past the goal-

keeper, Bob Wilson, with an angled drive.

Arsenal appeared stunned by this setback, but was given new life when George Graham scored the equalizer nine minutes later following a goal-mouth scramble.

It was now Liverpool that began to lose heart and it was no surprise when Arsenal scored the winning goal with nine minutes to play. The scorer was

20-year-old Charlie George, whose probing passes and powerful shooting had provided some of the game's few bright pieces of play.

John Radford, whose tireless front running had found unsuspected chinks in Liverpool's defense, set George up with a flicked pass. George seized his chance to blast a 25-yard left-footed drive beyond the grasping fingers of Ray Clemence, the goalkeeper.

Not since beating Liverpool,

2-0, at Wembley in 1950 had Arsenal won English soccer's biggest prize.

The only other team this century to win the league championship and the Football Association Cup in the same season was London's Tottenham Hotspur in 1961.

For winning the Cup, the Arsenal club paid each of its players a bonus of $12,000.

The live gate at Wembley was $548,800.

May 9, 1971

Pele Departs World Stage

Associated Press

Pelé at conclusion of yesterday's game in Rio de Janeiro

RIO DE JANEIRO, July 18 (AP)—Pelé, known as the Black Pearl and heralded as the greatest of soccer players, ended his career with the Brazilian national team today before an emotional, highly partisan crowd and an international television audience.

He played the first half of the match against Yugoslavia, then broke into tears as hundreds of admirers mobbed him.

After a short stay in the referee's tunnel, the man who scored 1,086 goals trotted round the field to the beat of his nation's anthem and "Obrigado Pelé" (Thank you, Pelé), which is a national hit.

Tears still running down his cheeks, Pelé stripped off his shirt and twirled it in the air as he jogged around Mar-

cana Field in front of a record crowd of 130,000.

Pelé, whose real name is Edson Arantes do Nascimento, watched the second half from the official box as Brazil came back from a 1-0 deficit and gained a 2-2 tie.

"It is all too overwhelming," Pelé said, his voice choked with emotion. "I had tried to imagine what this would be like, but it surpassed anything I could think."

Soccer fans throughout the world paid tribute to the athlete who completed his 110th appearance with Brazil's national team. But he's not gone forever. He will continue to play, with Santos, his professional club, and will make only occasional appearances in exhibitions abroad.

Officials canceled the bullfights in Seville, Spain, so fans could watch Pelé's farewell on television.

In London, the Daily Mirror described Pelé as "the greatest footballer the world has ever known. Pelé is unique, irreplaceable."

Selection of the Yugoslav team for Pelé's final game was considered a great honor for that country, officials

said in Belgrade. A dozen Yugoslav sports writers accompanied their team to Rio.

The game started slowly with Pelé getting the ball only a few times as teammates attempted to place him in scoring position. Pelé attempted a shot late in the first half but it was blocked.

Pelé made three more scoring tries in the final moments of the half but could not get a goal.

July 19, 1971

Crackdown in Soccer

British Players Mind Their Manners As Referees Enforce Law and Order

By BRIAN GLANVILLE
Special to The New York Times

LONDON, Sept. 4—When British soccer players took the field in the opening matches of the season, they scarcely knew what hit them. The referees for long had been docile creatures who had stood by meekly and complaisantly while the players kicked, tripped and occasionally even punched one another. But now the referees had turned into roaring lions, authoritarians and monsters of pedantry.

Warnings were negligible. As one player, the West Ham center-half, Alan Stephenson, complained, he didn't object to the measures in themselves, but it was a bit too much to be expected to change the habits of a lifetime at 15 minutes notice.

That was approximately the time afforded by the referees of those opening games. They swept into the dressing rooms and, at the behest of the ruling English

Football League, delivered a brief and biting homily.

If a player showed dissent, his name would be taken; or, as it is popularly known, he would be "booked." Three bookings bring him in front of the Football Association Disciplinary Commission (the F.A. is the over-all governing body, with responsibility for clubs outside the 92-team league, as well as those in it) and that can result in a long suspension.

If a player showed dissent, he could be booked. If he deliberately handled the ball, he could be booked. If he deliberately tripped an opponent or tackled (obstructed) him dangerously from behind, he could be booked.

The Floodgates Open

No wonder the result was a flood of bookings, sometimes as many as 30 or 40 in a single day, and a wave of resentful incomprehension among players and managers. The inflammable George Best was sent off for impudence toward a referee in only his second game.

"The day is going to come," said Mike Summerbee, the Manchester City forward who is used to harsh treatment by defenders, "when I shall stand there on the touchline with my hand bag and ask the referee for permission to play."

By general consent, things had gone too far, and the Football Association had been too secretive, holding a series of private, regional meetings at which referees and linesmen had been given the word.

On the other hand, most people agreed that previously things had gone much too far in the other direction, that the intimidatory, ruthless tackle from behind and the so-called professional (i.e., ruthless) foul was making life hell for clever ballplayers and discouraging the artists of the game.

As Francis Lee, the Manchester City center forward, said to me: "The Brazilians don't tackle from behind and they won the World Cup."

Holocaust in Argentina

In countries like Italy and, above all, Argentina, once the leading country in the world for producing ballplayers, things had gone further still. Football in Argentina has, by consent of the more responsible critics there, become a holocaust, by comparison with which British football at its toughest is a veritable garden party.

Clearly it is always hard to find the golden mean in a body-contact sport, but my own feeling is that certain elements of over-compensation are presently at work.

The inference is, and I don't think it an unjust one, that British referees in the past have been ludicrously too permissive. They disgraced themselves in the 1966 World Cup at Everton, England, where they allowed the talented Brazilians and Pelé, to be kicked off the park, as we say, by the Bulgarians and the Portuguese.

They have far too often limited themselves to awarding a mere free kick without a caution (or booking), let along a sending-off, for a cold-blooded intimidatory foul. They have even allowed players to exchange blows without sending them off. Dismissal should be automatic.

Now there is a manifest danger that punishments will not fit the crime, that the salutary shock of the new

measures will be diluted, subverted, because they are so undiscriminating.

If a player can be booked for deliberately handling the ball and booked for brutally felling an opponent, then where the sense of it?

Will the Disciplinary Committee take careful note of the qualitative differences in offenses when those with three bookings are automatically brought before them?

Time will tell. Meanwhile, I hope the Italians and,

above all, the Argentines, are watching us closely. The dreadful experiences of European teams playing in Buenos Aires over the last three years for the world club title caused Ajax Amsterdam, the European Cup holder, to refuse to make the perilous trip to the River Plate this season.

The writer is a British sports columnist.

September 5, 1971

Out of the Wilderness

Hope for U.S. Pro Soccer Envisioned In Growing Strength of College Game

By PAUL GARDNER
Special to The New York Times

MIAMI, Jan. 1—It is no secret that soccer is the fastest-growing college sport, but this week's National Collegiate A.A. games in the Orange Bowl did reveal something new about the sport: the caliber of play is rising along with the number of participants.

The teams involved—Howard University, St. Louis University, the University of San Francisco and Harvard—all showed that college soccer's time in the derness as a deposit for athletes who couldn't make it in other sports is over.

The two semifinals were both decided by one goal, as was the superbly played final in which Howard upset favored St. Louis, 3-2.

The burgeoning strength of college soccer has repercussions for American professional soccer, whose millennium has been oft-proclaimed and equally as oft has obstinately refused to materialize. A major reason for this failure has been soccer's lack of the very thing that gave birth to professional football and basketball: strength in the colleges.

Not too long ago, college soccer was (and in some places, alas, it still is) a crude physical affair of hard running, hefty kicking and that good old sporting standby and panacea, the will to win. Of skill, of artistry, of grace, of subtlety, of all the things that transform soccer from witless kickball into a game of matchless beauty, there was hardly a hint. Whenever one spotted a player who possessed any of the more intricate soccer skills, one could be quite certain he was foreign-born.

Game Is Maturing

One could not be nearly so sure today. The 1971 season has proved to even the most skeptical that college soccer, if it has not yet come of age, is maturing rapidly.

"Every year my new players are of higher caliber than the seniors I lose," says the University of San Francisco coach, Steve Negoesco, "and every year when it comes to playing the games, I find the same is true for all my opponents."

If this were simply a matter of recruiting foreign students it would be of no lasting significance, but the vital point is that more and more American born-and-bred players are beginning to appear in the ranks of the better college teams—and they are a far cry from the old kick-and-run style boys.

The University of Pennsylvania won this season's Ivy League title with a team that played attractive, fast-moving, intelligent soccer, and that included only two foreigners. In the sophomore fullback, John Gribbin, Penn has one of the best American-born players that this writer has yet seen.

In talking of American college soccer players, one ought rightly to begin with St. Louis University, which has for years led the way, fielding teams of exclusively American-born (and furthermore, they will remind you, all St. Louis-born) players and posting by far the most successful college record.

In the N.C.A.A. championship, St. Louis was again in the final four, favorite to repeat its 1969 and 1970 triumphs. It was not to be, but

in the process of losing a magnificent final to Howard, the St. Louis players made it clear that alongside their undoubted fitness and spirit, they possess skills of highly impressive degree.

The heading ability and clever positional play of centerback Dale Harmon and the all-round brilliance of striker Mike Seerey would have been unthinkable in college players of 10 years ago, perhaps even five years ago.

In short, these boys *look* like soccer players, they think and they respond and they move in the ways that boys in a hundred other countries have been doing for so long, and to those who have been waiting to see this happen, it is exciting beyond any telling of it.

The new N.C.A.A. champions, the Howard players from Washington, D.C., represent the other extreme of college soccer: an all-foreign team, with most of the players coming from the Caribbean or Africa. The usual objection to such a squad—that it is suppressing the development of native American talent—is considerably blunted in the case of Howard, an all-black school. American blacks do not, to any great extent, play soccer, and were it not for the foreigners there would be no soccer team at Howard. As it is, the Howard players garnered the first major N.C.A.A. title to go to a black university, and they have created interest in the sport among Howard's American students.

Even so, the problem of foreign players remains a thorny one, with the ominous word "quota" being heard from time to time as a means of making sure that American boys are not pushed aside. The Howard coach, Lincoln Phillips, is, naturally, opposed: "We have American youngsters playing now in Washington who will be challenging for starting spots in four or five years. They will make the team, if they do, because they are good enough, not because they are Americans."

College soccer now stands on the threshold of its most crucial years. As the fastest-growing N.C.A.A. sport, it is beginning to edge up on the big-time glamor. The holding of this season's finals in the Orange Bowl—an arrangement to be continued for at least two more years—is indicative of the trend.

The Standard Counts

Even the recent decision to hold separate university and college division national championships is aimed at long-run improvement though ironically three of the nation's top ranked teams, including Howard, are college-division schools and would therefore presumably be excluded from the major championship.

When all is said and done, it is the standard of play that will be the deciding factor in the future of college soccer. If the game is exciting, the fans will start to gather—as more than 11,000 did when Penn played Harvard last October. Nobody who saw the St. Louis-Howard final last Thursday, described by the North American Soccer League Commissioner, Phil Woosnam, as "far and away the best college game I've seen," will doubt that college soccer is a sport of enormous potential.

When the N.A.S.L. makes good on its decision to hold a college draft this year, another vital link in college soccer's journey to the big-time will be in place. When the next millennium for pro soccer is announced, it will not, as so often in the past, have both feet planted firmly in mid-air, it will have them securely grounded in the college game.

The scores of the N.C.A.A. games here:

Semi-finals
Howard 1, Harvard 0.
St. Louis 3, San Francisco 2.
Final
Howard 3, St. Louis 2.

The writer is North American sports correspondent for the London newspaper The Observer.

January 2, 1972

2-Year Ban Imposed On Glasgow Rangers

BERNE, June 16 (Reuters) —The Glasgow Rangers of Scotland, winners of the European Cupwinners' Cup in soccer, have been banned from European Football Union competition for the next two seasons because of their supporters' misbehavior at the cup final, it was announced today at the union's headquarters.

Moscow Dynamo, beaten, 3—2, by the Rangers in the final May 24 at Barcelona, Spain, had protested the result, charging that its players had been intimidated by Scottish fans who had invaded the playing field.

The result was upheld, even though the ban was imposed. A disciplinary committee said that although events at the Barcelona match were "reprehensible in the extreme," they did not have a decisive influence on the result.

June 17, 1972

Offside Rule Change By Soccer League Cuts Infraction Area

By ALEX YANNIS

The Federale International de Football Association, the world governing body of soccer, granted permission yesterday to the North American Soccer League to change the offside rule, reducing the area in which it is in effect.

A player will be offside now only in the penalty area which extends 18 yards from the goal line, rather than in the whole area to midfield, which is usually 50 yards.

In announcing the change yesterday, Phil Woosnam, the commissioner of the league, said that it would be instituted by extending the line at the edge of the penalty box to the sidelines at the 18-yard mark. He said the rule would go into effect Saturday night, when three league games are scheduled.

Woosnam said that the league had asked F.I.F.A. for the change a year ago, but official permission only came through yesterday.

The Americans will be the first to use the rule just as they were with the rule permitting substitutes, which was introduced here. It is expected that other countries would adopt the change in the offside rule.

"With the evolution of present day defensive systems the game has experienced a reduction in the number of goal-scoring opportunities being created," Woosnam said. "By opening up the play with this change in the offside law, we feel that spectators will be treated to a more exciting and enjoyable brand of soccer."

Goal Average Is Higher

Woosnam was the founder of a point-awarded system in the United States that no other country has yet put into practice. The league awards a team one point for each goal scored up to three, whether it wins or loses. This means that the losers can also get points by scoring. The league awards 6 points for a victory, three for a tie and, of course, no points for a loss.

The point-system has proved to be effective since the teams in this country have the highest goal-scoring percentage. The average here is 3.2 goals a game, elsewhere it is 1.2 goals.

"The entire world of soccer recognizes that changes in the laws that produce greater goal-scoring opportunities must be considered," Woosman said. "It is our belief, shared by many European officials, that the ultimate answer is to make a change in the offside rule and the size of the goal."

June 27, 1972

Goalie Says It Helps to Be Crazy

By ALEX YANNIS

If an athlete took a boa constrictor to practice sessions, ate glass, took a Harvard sociology test in a hotel room in Guadalajara, Mexico, with his coach as proctor, and convinced the Crimson to hire a friend as an assistant coach, he would be no ordinary athlete.

Shep Messing of Roslyn, L. I., an American-born athlete with enough hair to hide a boa in it, has done all these things. But what he does best is play goalie for the United States Olympic soccer team and because of that he has had offers to play pro soccer in Mexico, Guatemala and El Salvador.

"I am very upset about the progress of soccer in the United States. The people in the pro circuit haven't shown enough interest in the American player and if they keep doing that we will just have to play somewhere else," Messing said last Thursday night. "I am talking for a lot of guys and I don't want to sound egotistical, but we are the guys to get."

"The North American Soccer League is our hope at the present time," said Messing, drafted by the Montreal Olympics of the N.A.S.L. in the first round. "But they are gonna have to do better to be able to afford the money to pay us. I am not displeased with their interest in me, but there are others, as good as anybody in the league, who are frustrated at the pace of progress in negotiating contracts."

Messing Is Man to Watch at Munich

Easily identified by his Afro hairdo, the Harvard graduate is a man to watch in Munich, not only for his unorthodox goaltending style but also for his potential at being the center of Olympic controversies.

Even before he brought a boa to practice, Messing was something of a soccer legend "because of my appearance and because I am not a practice player."

Shep Messing

Messing attended New York University for two years. But after they failed to come up with an athletic scholarship as promised, he quit after his sophomore season and became a bartender and a lifeguard for a year.

"During that period, all the good soccer schools contacted me, except Harvard, and that's where I went," he said. "I loved the school but the only thing bad for me was the soccer program."

Messing, a major factor in helping the Crimson to the National Collegiate Athletic Association final in the Orange Bowl, where he was selected as the outstanding defensive player last December, asked the Harvard administrators to replace the soccer coach.

"They wouldn't do it, so we compromised," Messing said. "I agreed to hire a friend of mine as an assistant, and they did." Elliot Klein, Messing's friend, is no longer an assistant coach there, now that Messing has been graduated.

Messing, who was graduated from Wheatley High School where he starred in soccer, wrestling and track and field under Bill Stevenson, his coach in all three sports, is what one would call a "colorful" goalie.

Aggressive, Daring and a Little Crazy

"You've got to be daring and a little crazy to play goalie," Messing said. "You have to be aggressive around the goal, dominate that area. If there is an easy grounder coming in and a forward following it I am not going to just field ¨ and sidestep the guy. I am going to ֊֊ it so I can get the ball and knock his head off, too."

Were it not for Messing, the United States Olympic team probably would not be where it is today, pitted against 15 other qualifiers for the gold medal.

In the first qualifying round the Americans played El Salvador three times and drew all three. So each team was given five penalty shots after the third game.

The Americans converted all five penalty kicks, as easy a task as adding the extra point in football. When El Salvador converted its first two penalty shots, Messing took matters into his own hands to end what appeared an interminable match.

All he did was go slightly beserk. "Nothing was planned," he said. "It was really quite spontaneous.

"Just as the El Salvador player was to take the third kick, I ripped off my shirt and started screaming obsenities in English. I actually left the goal and went out and slapped the guy on the back to encourage him not to miss," Messing said. "Well, the guy was so confused he made the worst penalty kick I have ever seen."

August 6, 1972

COSMOS CONQUER STARS FOR TITLE

Jelinek's Penalty Kick Is Decisive in 2-1 Game

By ALEX YANNIS
Special to The New York Times

HEMPSTEAD, L. I., Aug. 26— The New York Cosmos became the North American Soccer League champions tonight by defeating the St. Louis Stars, 2-1, at Hofstra before 6,102 fans.

The game was decided four minutes before the end, when Josef Jelinek converted a penalty kick to break a 1-1 deadlock.

The kick was awarded to the Cosmos after Johnny Kerr had been fouled within the penalty area by Garry Rensing.

The Cosmos put the Stars under pressure early and scored first. After a corner kick by Roby Young, who crossed the ball nicely in the middle of the Stars' area, Randy Horton jumped higher than anybody else and headed the ball in.

Mike Winter, the Stars' goalie and the league's rookie of the year, made a valiant stretch to stop the shot, which hit the inside of the horizontal bar and landed in the net.

Bombardment Fails

The New Yorkers wanted more of the same and kept bombarding the Stars' goal, but successive shots by Young, Willie Mfum, Horton and Kerr narrowly missed the target.

St. Louis had some sporadic attacks, led by Willie Loy and Casew Franckiewcz, during the first half. But they didn't faze Rich Blackmore, the Cosmos' goalie.

After leading at the half, the Cosmos slowed down momentarily and, after seven minutes of the second half, John Sewell passed to Frankiewcz, who scored a disputable goal.

The referee, Roger Schott, declared the goal illegal, but the Stars' players persuaded him to consult Bill Maxwell, one of the linesmen. Maxwell said the goal was good and so did the referee.

The Cosmos then, and within two minutes, took four shots, one of which hit the post and the others just going wide.

It was not until the last four minutes that the Cosmos found the solution, and Kerr, as he has done all season, took matters into his own hands and made the move that resulted in Jelinek's penalty shot.

August 27, 1972

Rule Change Aids Soccer Offense

By ALEX YANNIS

The United States and Canadian soccer associations and the world governing body of the sport have granted the North American Soccer League permission to change the traditional offside rule, reducing the area in which it is in effect.

A player will be offside now only in the area extending 35 yards from the goal line, rather than the previous 55 to 60 yards to midfield.

"Under the traditional rule, offside applies in the entire half of the field in which a team is attacking," said Phil Woosnam, league commissioner. He called the change a "revolutionary blue-line concept," alluding to hockey's blue-line offside rule.

He went on:

"There is an increasing mood for change throughout the world because the traditional law is being used by coaches and players to restrict the flow of play by congesting the midfield, since an attacking player is offside if he crosses the midfield line ahead of the ball and there are fewer than two defenders between him and the goal."

Woosnam said that the league wanted to overcome the tendency toward defensive tactics and open up the game for the skilled midfield players.

"The change means that attacking players can move to within 35 yards of goal before they concern themselves with being offside," he explained.

Permission was obtained from the United States Soccer Football Association, the Canadian Soccer Association and the international board of the Federal International Football Association, which interprets the rules and regulates the game throughout the world.

The league experimented during the second half of last season by reducing the offside area to only 18 yards—between the goal line and the edge of the penalty area. However, the change resulted in opening up midfield too much and severely restricting the space required to create attacks behind the defense.

May 20, 1973

Sunderland, 250-1, Tops Leeds in Cup Soccer, 1-0

By JOSEPH FRAYMAN
Special to The New York Times

WEMBLEY, England, May 5 —David put on his soccer boots today and slew Goliath. That is to say that Sunderland, a once-derided soccer team in the Second Division of the English League, beat Leeds, one of the best in Europe, 1-0, to win the cherished Football Association Cup.

Soccer fans have waited nearly half a century to savor the satisfaction of the mighty being humbled by the lowly in the greatest of all British sports spectacles. Millions watching on television, as well as most of the 90,000-plus spectators in this oval stadium, cheered Sunderland's victory. The team from the northeast of England made a mockery of the odds of 250-1 that were offered when the elimination contest of hundreds of teams began months ago.

If a minor league team were to reach the World Series and beat the world champions it would convey something of the immensity of Sunderland's achievement.

Three other Second Division teams have played in the Cup Final since World War II. But not since 1931, when West Bromwich, Albion beat Birmingham, has one won the cup.

Sunderland had its heroes on the football field, but the man who made the dream come true was on the sideline, Manager Bob Stokoe. When he arrived at Sunderland last December the team had lost its last 10 matches and was struggling in the lower half of the Second Division.

His effect on the team was astonishing. It won the next 10 and moved up to seventh place. There are 22 teams in the division. A modest man, he says it may take two more

seasons before Sunderland becomes one of the two leaders and wins promotion to the First Division.

The first thing he did was to tell the players to go out and enjoy themselves. "It was the first time we'd ever heard the word," says one of them.

"I didn't bring the magic," Stokoe says. "It's always been there. I came back to find it."

He is a big man of 41, with a touch of Anthony Quinn about the heavy, broad face under thick eyebrows. Sunderland, for him, was returning home. A miner's son from nearby Mickley, Northumberland, he played for 14 years with Newcastle United and was on the team when it won the Cup in 1955.

Fans Are Involved

In the ship-building towns on the Rivers Tyne and Wear, involvement in football is as deeply felt as in soccer-mad Liverpool or Rio. The Sunderland stadium, Roker Park, stands in a sea of gray slate roofs and identical rows of houses.

From them now pour thousands of people to cheer their club, as they did in the palmy days of 1937 when Sunderland, then a First Division side, last won the Cup.

On road to Wembley again, Stokoe's men beat such giants as Arsenal and Manchester City, which with Leeds, Liverpool and a few others have dominated English soccer for years.

Nevertheless, Leeds, which won the Cup last year, was favored to win again. It is an extremely hard side to beat. To a tough-tackling, close-marking defense has been added—under its manager, Don Revie, who once wore the Sunderland colors—the more attractive ingredients of flair and sheer aggression up front. Their very professionalism has incurred some resentment and jealousy.

The white-clad, all-star team kicked off in the downpour that greeted the teams as they came on to the field. Sunderland, in red and white striped jerseys, carefully avoided the storming start expected of them and took a little longer to find their foothold on the slippery turf.

A sturdy Sunderland defense soaked up the blows from the strikers—Allan Clarke, fleet of foot; Peter Lorimer, of the cannonball shot, and Mick Jones, deadly in the air-driven forward by their captain, Billy Bremner.

Dave Watson, supreme in the Sunderland defense at center back, was the rock against which the waves broke. Sunderland took the measure of its opponents, beat them in the air and to the tackle, and launched occasional forays.

From one such raid, 35 minutes into the game, the Leeds' goalie, David Harvey, only just tipped the ball over the bar to concede a corner kick. The ball came loose to Ian Porterfield, standing sideways—on to goal. He juggled with it for an instant and brought his right foot round in an arc to send the ball head-high into the net from 12 yards.

The stadium erupted. Sunderland's fans, in rosettes, fancy hats and scarves jump and roared with joy. The thousands, who had paid as much as $25 for a ticket, $15 for the train ride—and 60 cents for a can of beer on the train—smelled success.

Leeds struck back, but even as Clarke measured his shot the toecap of Watson removed the ball from his foot, and the first 45 minutes ended without further score.

Leeds launched attack after attack in the second half and came desperately close. One shot was brilliantly pushed away by Jim Montgomery, the goalie, only to fall at the feet of Lorimer six yards from goal. His shot sacrificed cool accuracy for force, and the ball somehow hit the body of the seemingly helpless Montgomery, flew up to the underside of the bar and came out for a defender to clear.

Time after time Sunderland's defenders blocked shots, outjumped attackers near the goal and stretched their elastic limbs to smother seemingly inevitable goals.

Growing frustrated, Leeds brought on a substitute, and mounted new offensives. But the storm blew itself out, Sunderland found the strength to counter-attack, and the end came with the Leeds players crowding their own goalmouth to stop Sunderland scoring a second goal.

May 6, 1973

Dave Anderson

'There Is Only One Pele'

Sports of The Times

Throughout the world, beyond the realm of the United States, hardly anybody knows Joe Namath or Hank Aaron or Wilt Chamberlain; some know Jack Nicklaus or Stan Smith or Bobby Orr; many know Muhammad Ali. But the world's most famous athlete is Pelé, the Brazilian soccer player. During the Biafran war, a two-day truce was observed when he appeared there. Political disputes in Algiers and Khartoum were interrupted in his honor. When he was in Macao, some Communist Chinese border guards wandered from their posts to stare at him, even though their country is one of the few he has not performed in. When he was ejected from a game in Bogota, spectators stormed the field, ejected the referee and restored him. Another time, Prince Philip left his seat to meet Pelé, reversing the usual royal protocol. But then Pelé makes more money then Prince Philip does.

"About $1.5-million a year," his business manager, José Fornos Rodriguez, was saying. "About $700,000 of it from soccer."

The other $800,000 is derived from his role as a worldwide ambassador for Pepsi-Cola, his endorsements of a coffee, Café Pelé, and Puma soccer shoes, his involve-

The New York Times

The world's most famous soccer player in game here in 1967.

ments in a rubber factory, a bank, a radio station, a trucking company, an export-import concern and a line of men's clothes. His office in Brazil employs 20 people, including three attorneys. It occupies an

Pele, in midair, kicking the ball backwards over his head

Associated Press

entire floor in a Santos office building.

"Pelé," said one of his attorneys, Romulo Fedeli de Tulio, "is the highest individual taxpayer in Brazil."

The Leopard

On Friday night, the world's most famous and most corporate athlete will be on display with the Santos team against Lazio of Italy in Jersey City's Roosevelt Stadium. But now, in a bedroom of a gold-and-white furnished suite in the Park Lane Hotel overlooking Central Park, he was displaying the graciousness for which he is known.

"He is calling his housekeeper at home," Rodriguez explained. "It's her birthday."

His wife was out shopping on nearby Fifth Avenue and moments later, Pelé appeared. Small and lean at 5 feet, 7 inches and 160 pounds, he moved across the white carpet with the leisurely power of a leopard. He had on a red turtleneck shirt, brown tweed slacks and brown socks, but no jewelry. He understands English a little,

in Portuguese through his interpreter, Julio Mazzei, the Santos trainer, his voice was heavy like José Ferrer's, and he waved his hands expressively.

"He say he doesn't know what means Pelé," the interpreter said. "He has heard lot of stories, but really he doesn't know."

Pelé is not a word in any language. Its origin has been a mystery. Mazzei mentioned one theory, that Pelé means a lucky cat.

"But that is just a story," the interpreter said. "He was born Edson Arantes do Nascimento, but he says he has a memory of when he was 7, 8 years old, the boys in the backyard start to call him Pelé and he wondered why, if his name is Edson, why do they do that. He fight against the name, but it stay with him. Now every black young player, they call him Pelé; now Pelé is a word that means Pelé because there is only one Pelé."

His ability to maneuver a soccer ball but he doesn't speak it well. As he talked

with his feet, his head and his shoulders has resulted in more than 1,300 goals, similar to home runs for a baseball player.

"His ability, he says only God can explain this," the interpreter said. "No smoking, no drinking, a clean life, maybe that is some of the reasons. He says he remembers when he was 11, 12 years old, the other boys would say, 'Why don't you play for us?' and that is when he knew he was good. When he was 14, he went for a try-out with the Santos team. First three or four months, he did not receive nothing but food and room. Then he sign for $140 a year."

'Stay, Stay'

He is the only player to have performed with three World Cup champion teams, but he is 32 years old now.

"He has retired from the Brazil national team. He will play with Santos until October, then he will play exhibitions until the next October, then he will retire. His last game for the national team, in Rio de Janeiro, there were 200,000 people in the stadium yelling, 'Stay, stay,' but he says the most important thing for an athlete is to know the time when you must retire. He prefer to stay out when people want him to stay in, then to stay in when people want him to stay out."

He's worth millions, but when he was asked how many, Pelé laughed and his eyes flashed as he answered.

"He says his father told him, 'During the time you are accumulating money, don't stop to count it.'"

The money is his, but the memory belongs to everyone who has seen him. Because an athlete of his stature appears seldom. Once in a lifetime, if that.

"Now," said Julio Mazzei, "people tell their little babies, 'Too bad. You will not see Pelé play.'"

March 20, 1973

Soviet Union Kicked Out Of World Cup in Soccer

By VICTOR LUSINCHI
Special to The New York Times

GENEVA, Nov. 12 —By its refusal to play in Chile, the Soviet national team has barred itself from the final round of the 1974 World Cup soccer competition, the International Football Federation (F.I.F.A.) ruled today. And that ruling could lead to a boycott by other East European countries.

The ruling, announced by the federation from its Zurich headquarters, automatically gives Chile one of the places for the final round in West Germany in June and July.

After being held to a scoreless tie by Chile in Moscow on Sept. 26, the Soviet team was scheduled to play the return match in the two-game playoff series in Santiago's National Stadium on Nov. 21.

But Moscow balked at playing in a stadium that, it said, had been turned by the military junta into an "arena of torture and execution of patriots" who supported the late President Salvadore Allende. Prisoners were removed from the stadium only last week.

After finding that the Santiago stadium was again back in use as a sports field, F.I.F.A. rejected a Soviet demand that the return game be played at a neutral field in a third country.

But in view of Moscow's continued refusal, Helmut Kaeser, the federation's secretary-general, prevailed in a secret move on the Chilean

Soccer Federation to agree to hold the match in another Chilean city.

However, when disclosing this compromise proposal today, F.I.F.A. also revealed that the Soviet Soccer Federation had rebuffed it in a one-sentence message: "Match in Chile is impossible."

Under F.I.F.A. rules, Moscow thus had to be disqualified. The Soviet federation will also be fined $1,700 and will forfeit its $330 entry fee.

Asked about reports that other Soviet-bloc teams may now boycott the World Cup finals, René Courte, a F.I.F.A. spokesman, said on the telephone, "We will deal with such a situation if we are faced with it."

East Germany and Poland are already qualified for the final round while Bulgaria is also expected to make it.

"This is the first time that a team has disqualified itself for political reasons since the start of the competition in 1930," Courte said.

About 100 nations enter the World Cup tournament, a true "World" Series staged every four years. Teams are divided into groups on a geographical basis, with group winners going through to the 16-nation finals or playing another group victor in a playoff series. Matches are home and away. The Soviet Union won European Group 9 while Chile was the victor in South American Group 3.

The Soviet Union was semifinalist in 1966 and reached the quarterfinals in 1958, 1962 and 1970.

November 13, 1973

4 Coast Cities Awarded Pro Soccer Franchises

By ALEX YANNIS

The North American Soccer League awarded yesterday franchises to four West Coast cities. The league, which operated with 17 teams in 1968 and only five in 1969, will function with at least 12 teams in 1974.

The new teams will operate in Los Angeles, San Francisco, Seattle and Vancouver, British Columbia. And if Atlanta and Montreal, which operated last year but are questionable this season, field teams, the league will have 14 clubs.

"Tremendous progress has been made since 1968, when the league membership dropped suddenly from 17 franchises to five with none remaining on the West Coast," said Phil Woosnam, the commissioner of the league.

"We are looking at today as the most important day in the history of soccer in the United States and Canada," Woosnam said after making the announcement. "Since 1968 there has been an amazing growth in the popularity of the game, particularly in the cities where the new franchises will be located," the commissioner said before the news conference here. Newsmen in the four West Coast cities were tied in by a conference telephone call.

Woosnam seemed certain that Montreal, which has stadium problems, and Atlanta would operate next season. If they do, they join New York, Toronto, Philadelphia, Dallas, St. Louis, Rochester and Miami, the established teams; Baltimore, which was given a franchise last week, and the four new cities.

Baltimore, Los Angeles and Vancouver were originally in the league, but dropped out

after their first year of operation, citing heavy financial losses.

"Three of our clubs just about broke even last season and the others lost in the vicinity of $50,000," Woosnam said. "The new people who have joined the league have done so with the understanding that they will operate for at least three seasons."

The owners of the new teams had to pay $25,000 immediately and a $50,000 deferred payment. When New York, Toronto and Montreal joined three years ago, their admission price was $10,000.

December 12, 1973

St. Louis U. Retains Soccer Title

By ALEX YANNIS
Special to The New York Times

MIAMI, Jan. 4—Dan Counce scored two goals tonight, the second one in the sudden-death overtime, in leading St. Louis University to its 10th National Collegiate Athletic Association soccer championship. The Billikens defeated the University of California, Los Angeles, 2-1.

The Billikens triumph was their third over U.C.L.A. in championship games. They beat the Bruins, 1-0, in 1970 and 4-2, last year.

The Orange Bowl crowd of 5,861 fans saw possibly the best N.C.A.A. final in the last three years. The game was fitting for a championship, with good quality soccer by both teams—one team predominating in each half.

It was marked by sportsmanship as well as fast, aggressive soccer.

St. Louis had problems in the first half, but like the classy team it has been, it gradually recovered its balance and controlled play when it counted.

U.C.L.A. fought desperately to thwart the Billikens in the second half and in the overtime period, but St. Louis was a bit too much.

Counce kicked in the deciding goal with a turn-around shot after four minutes of play in the overtime. His shot ended a well-played collegiate soccer game.

"There were only winners in this game tonight," said Coach Harry Keough of St. Louis after the game. He was right because it was a fine collegiate game to watch and it was a shame it ended so early in the overtime period.

Keough's statement, however, could not give solace to Los Angeles, which played well enough to win in the first half.

The Bruins outran, outhustled and outplayed the Billikens in the first half. The Billikens appeared to be confused and looked sloppy even when attempting to display the fundamentals of the game. They were inaccurate with their passing and way off target with their shooting.

Fullbacks Aid Goalie

St. Louis attempted to regroup its forces in the first half, but was not quite successful. The Billikens originated some good plays at midfield and at the corners of the U.C.L.A. defense. But were unable to penetrate through the middle, forcing themselves to take shots from far out, which didn't bother

Fred Decker, the goalie.

"Decker has been U.C.L.A.'s first real good goalie," said Dennis Storer, the coach. "We've never had a goalie before."

Decker displayed reliability both under his goal posts and away from them. His judgment in coming out of his goal was excellent. He had a lot of help from his fullbacks, especially Terry Lippman, who dominated the middle of U.C.L.A.'s defense in the first half.

The Bruins played without Efren Herrera for most of the game because of a leg injury. U.C.L.A. missed him because his substitute, Hector Salcedo, was of lower caliber, confirming Storer's statement of lack of depth.

Despite Herrera's absence the Bruins led, 1-0, at the half on a goal scored from close range by Firooz Fowzi after four minutes of play. It was scored on a mistake by Bob Matteson. The St. Louis player attempted to pass the ball back to his goalie, Chuck Zorumski, but Fowzi intercepted the pass and booted the ball into the goal.

The Billikens balanced the play early in the second half and tied the game on a goal by Counce, who has been a menace for defensemen all year. He took a long pass from Denny Hadican and lobbed the ball over Decker's head.

St. Louis continued to play better in the second half and were it not for Decker might have taken the lead. Decker made numerous saves.

Regular time ended with the score 1-1.

January 5, 1974

Soccer Final Shatters British People's Image

By ALVIN SHUSTER
Special to The New York Times

WEMBLEY, England, May 4 —For about 56 minutes in the struggle today for the Football Association Cup— the Super Bowl of soccer— there were almost as many "expletives" in the stadium as there were in the transcripts of the White House tapes.

It was a battle of Britain's soccer giants from two seaports; and Liverpool was attacking but getting nowhere and Newcastle United was having trouble staying united and finding the ball at the same time. The fans on both sides were hardly happy.

The 57th minute in the 90-minute contest changed

everything. Kevin Keegan, a man whose timing rivals that of Jack Benny, broke through the Newcastle defense and scored first for Liverpool.

And when it was all over, the Liverpudlians, cheered on by fans who insisted on singing a variety of songs no matter what, emerged with a 3-0 victory, the biggest margin in a Cup final in 14 years. Keegan scored again toward the end of the game and so did Steve Heighway, one of the fastest men on the field and one of the few there with a college education.

That was more than enough for the fans from Liverpool, a seaport about 200 miles northwest of London on the

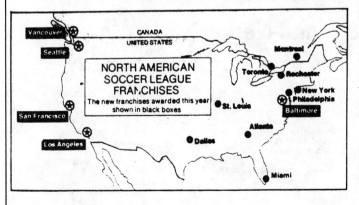

NORTH AMERICAN SOCCER LEAGUE FRANCHISES
The new franchises awarded this year shown in black boxes

The New York Times/Dec. 12, 1973

river Mersey and the town where the Beatles got their start, which doesn't necessarily account for the quality of the singing today. Liverpudlians like to sing "You'll Never Walk Alone," which is a little difficult to do anyway with 100,000 fans in the stands.

Breach in Security

A Cup final, of course, is more than a soccer match. It's a mixture of ritual, scarf-waving, forged tickets, 2,000 policemen and simple pandemonium.

It all combines to shatter the image of the British as a reserved people. All inhibitions disappear and the shouts and the singing are sufficient to make American sports fans appear to be victims of an epidemic of laryngitis.

Another characteristically British touch at these events, too, is the presence of royalty. Princess Anne, daughter of Queen Elizabeth, and her husband, Capt. Mark Phillips, were on hand, shaking hands with all the players at the outset as team members tried and failed to curtsy, and then congratulating the winners.

The royal couple also managed a good look at about the only breach in the security surrounding the field. Two Liverpool supporters broke through the police lines, fell to their knees near the royal box, and kissed the shoes of the team's manager, Bill Shankly, who was jubilant over Liverpool's second Cup final victory in the 102-year-old history of the Cup.

Otherwise, all went smoothly after a year of a surge in disruptions of games by rowdy fans and sometimes streakers. Bookies, who set odds here on just about everything, were even taking bets on whether streakers would dare emerge in the presence of the Princess. None did.

What did emerge was a Liverpool team that lived up to all its advance billing and its role as the favorite. It monopolized the ball in the first 45-minute half, but its passing was off, and the shots to the net were easy lobs quickly hugged by Newcastle's goalkeeper, Iam McFaul, only for his record of success to fade in the second half.

MacDonald Shut Out

Newcastle never appeared to have the ball long enough to mount an offensive. And its fans, who traveled 270 miles from their hometown northeast of London, had no opportunity to cheer "Supermac"—Malcolm MacDonald, the star forward who has scored 27 times during the season.

"They were just all over

us," said Supermac later. "Liverpool was the better team, they didn't allow us a chance."

And so Newcastle, the home of strong brown beer and fans who dress in black and white and thus sometimes resemble escaped convicts, missed its chance for another record. It set one by just turning up—its 11th appearance in a Cup final. But victory would have given it another—the only team to have won four Cups since World War II.

It was not one of those games people will be talking about for years, unless they happen to live in Liverpool. Keegan, clearly able to change direction more quickly than most of his colleagues and as quickly as most politicians, will remember it. So will Heighway, whose score 16 minutes before the end gave Liverpool a 2-0 lead and put it all out of reach for struggling Newcastle.

As the game ended under the gray spring skies, the band of the Royal Marines went home and Princess Anne drove away in a limousine,

Liverpudlian cheering went on into the night. It was the first Cup victory for Liverpool since 1965.

"We tried to play simple football," said Manager Shankly,

in a remark promptly nominated as the understatement of the year.

May 5, 1974

World Cup Finals to Be Expanded

FRANKFURT, West Germany, June 10 (UPI) — The International Football Federation, overruling European objections, has decided to expand the number of teams for future World Cup soccer finals from 16 to an eventual 24, Argentine and Uruguay officials said today. Washington Cataldi, Uruguay's F.I.F.A. delegate, said the executive committee decision would be announced tomorrow at the General F.I.F.A. Congress, two days before the 10th World Cup tourney opens.

Argentina, host of the next Cup finals in 1978, will be allowed to field 18 or 20 teams, according to its organizational ability, the Argentine officials said, and an eventual 24-team tournament in Spain in 1982 and Colombia in 1986 has been approved in principle. European delegates from the European Union of Football Associations voted against the move, which will allow more teams from Africa, South America and Asia to compete in the finals, the officials said.

The basis for qualifying would remain similar to the current system in which the host country and the previous winning team automatically qualify. Cataldi said the system of selection of the other 16 or 18 teams had not yet been decided.

June 11, 1974

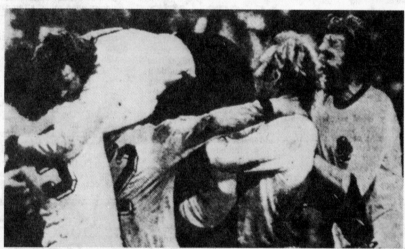

United Press International

Sepp Maier, West Germany's goalie, hurling himself on his teammates after a goal by Gerhard Muller against Poland in World Cup in Frankfurt yesterday. West Germany won, 1-0, and will meet the Netherlands in the final Sunday in Munich.

West Germany and Netherlands Win And Play for World Cup Title Sunday

By ALEX YANNIS
Special to The New York Times

FRANKFURT, West Germany, July 3—Poland's heroics in the World Cup ended here today, while the orange flame from the Netherlands continued to rise and it is now left to West Germany to put it out.

West Germany defeated Poland, 1-0, with difficulty here this afternoon and will

meet the Flying Dutchmen in their orange uniforms in the Cup final in Munich on Sunday. The Dutch advanced by downing Brazil, 2-0, in Dortmund tonight.

In a game delayed for 30 minutes because of thunderstorms, West Germany didn't look impressive in winning on a goal scored by Gerhard Muller 14 minutes before the end.

Muller's goal came after a combination on the left side of the West German attack that involved three players. It was one of the few noticeable combinations by the West Germans, and their only excuse was the wetness of the field.

While the West Germans were not outstanding in their narrow victory, Johan Cruyff's army in Dortmund was the

Sepp Maier, West German goalie, makes a spectacular dive for the ball during the 1978 World Cup competition. This game, against Italy, ended 0-0.

Argentina's Mario Kempes has just scored the first goal against the Netherlands in the 1978 World Cup Final. Later, with the score tied 1-1 in overtime, he booted home the final point that brought Argentina the World Cup.

opposite. The Dutch were held scoreless in the first half, but they stormed the Brazilian defense in the second and got their goals.

The first came from Johan the Second, as Johan Neeskens is known to Dutch fans, and the second goal came from Johan the First.

Poland and West Germany played on a field that would have been more suitable for Mark Spitz.

"This was more of a water polo than a soccer game," Helmut Shoen, the German coach, said afterward, "but you have to give credit to both teams for playing so well."

"The instructions I gave my players at half-time was to move the ball from the fullbacks to the halfbacks a bit faster. I was very pleased to see both teams play offensive football. All my players played well, but I have

to single out Rainer Bonhof for doing a good job at midfield."

Bonhof was instructed by Shoen to keep an eye on Kazimierz Deyna, the Polish captain, who again had a good game despite Bonhof's efforts.

To observers, however, it appeared as if Wolfgang Overath was the man who carried the West German team in the first half. He won all his battles at midfield and fed his forwards with excellent passes. But the forwards had a tendency to come back instead of going forward and trying to set up plays, which gave the Polish defense time to reorganize.

It took the Germans a lot longer to get to the Polish defense than it did the Polish side to reach the other end. The West Germans controlled the game most of the first half, but the red-shirted players were more dangerous

every time they went downfield toward Sepp Maier, the German goalie.

Maier made some spectacular saves in the second half, but the goalie that was admired more this afternoon was Jan Tomaszewski of Poland. Besides a couple of difficult saves, Tomaszewski saved a penalty when the game was scoreless. Uli Honess took the shot, called the death shot in soccer, but Tomaszewski sprawled to his right for the save.

After Honess's penalty was saved, the predominant German crowd in the capacity turnout of 62,000 kept shouting, "Deutschland, Deutschland," but it was obvious it didn't come from the heart.

The Polish team picked up momentum after the penalty and shots by Deyna and Robert Gadocha were saved by Maier, who had his best game in the World Cup. The Polish momentum lasted only

for five minutes, though, and the Germans went back on the attack and shots by Overath and Bernd Holzenbein were saved by Tomaszewski.

Then came Muller's goal and one would think that it would demoralize the Polish players. But Coach Kazimierz Gorski's players didn't give in that easily and staged two final attacks that resulted in shots by Deyna and Gadocha, with Maier saving Deyna's shot while Gadocha's was wide.

It was obvious from the beginning that the players would have problems controlling the ball as it stuck in the water. The Polish players, who like to run a lot, often had to put the brakes

July 4, 1974

West Germans Win Soccer Cup

By ALEX YANNIS

Special to The New York Times

MUNICH, West Germany, July 7—West Germany repulsed a fierce attack to defeat the Netherlands today in the World Cup soccer final, 2-1, and become the champion in the world's most popular sport.

In an electrifying atmosphere at Olympic Stadium here before a capacity crowd, including Secretary of State Kissinger and dignitaries from many other countries, the Dutch exploded like a volcano and scored in the first minute of the game, but the Germans rallied and scored twice before the half was over.

By winning the championship game, West Germany became the fourth host country to triumph since the trophy was put up in 1930. Until the next World Cup is held in Argentina four years from now, the West Germans will be the reigning champions in a sport that is dominant in 142 countries.

World Cup play, which establishes a new champion every four years, is to virtually every part of the world what the annual World Series or Super Bowl is to United States baseball and pro football fans. Interest in Cup competition rivals that of the Olympic Games, also held quadrennially.

The Flying Dutchmen, in their orange uniforms, need-

ed only a minute to score, but they were kept scoreless for the remaining 89 minutes by a stubborn German defense that was impervious to an all-out attack in the second half.

In the very first attack of the game, Johan Cruyff, the heralded Dutch captain, exploited the right side of the German defense and the only way he was stopped was by tackling him from behind a few yards from the goal.

Jack Taylor, the English referee, without hesitation awarded the Dutch a penalty kick that Johan Neeskens converted. The orange flags and umbrellas sprouted in the stands and the possibility of a rout crossed the minds of many of the spectators.

Strangely enough, however, the Dutch slowed the pace of the game instead of taking advantage of the shocked and confused Germans, who gradually started to pick up the pace and even managed to tie the score.

Uli Höeness, who had committed the penalty on Cruyff, made a long pass to Bernd Holzbein, who went at full speed toward the Dutch goal. But as he reached inside the area, Win Jansen brought him down with a fierce tackle and Taylor, who had an excellent afternoon officiating, pointed to the penalty spot nine yards from the goal.

Paul Breitner, the wandering German fullback, got the assignment to execute soccer's death penalty and easily performed his duty, giving the Dutch goalie Jan Jong-

bloed, no chance, just as Neeskens had done to the German goalie 19 minutes earlier.

The game was now even, not only on the scoreboard, but also on the field as both teams exchanged attacks that were easily thwarted by the defenses. This continued from the 20th minute, the time of the German goal, until the 43d minute when the Dutch defense took a nap for a split second. That was all Gerd Mueller needed.

To let Mueller control the ball inside the penalty area is like letting a fox join the chickens in a coop. Naturally, he scored, with a low shot, to put his country ahead to stay.

The decisive goal by Mueller, the highest goal-scorer in Mexico City four years ago when West Germany finished in third place, was a twofold achievement for him and his country.

It was the 100th goal scored by West Germany in World Cup action since 1934 and it was Mueller's 14th, making him the highest scorer in World Cup history. Mueller got four goals in this World Cup, while Grzegorz Lato of Poland took honors as the highest scorer with seven. Poland finished in third place by defeating Brazil, 1-0, on Lato's goal yesterday.

About 80,000 fans, more than 500 dignitaries, 3,000 security men and 2,200 working journalists had taken their seats an hour before the kickoff. They remained there long after the game was over as the West Ger-

United Press International

Franz Beckenbauer, the captain of the West German team, raises trophy after the game.

man players circled the stadium holding the trophy that was presented to them by Sir Stanley Rous, the outgoing president of the international federation.

To earn the trophy, the West Germans had weathered an all-out attack for 45 minutes from the players in the orange uniforms. Their white shirts were as wet with sweat as if they had just come out of a washing machine. The defenders of

Gerd Mueller scores West Germany's second—and winning—goal. The Dutch defenseman at right is Arie Haan.

Associated Press

the German team should feel particularly proud because it was the defense that won the game.

From the beginning of the second half until the end, the Dutch bombarded the German defense with shots from all angles. One of those shots almost killed Sepp Maier, the German goalie, as it came from very close range by Johnny Rep.

But Maier and his teammates, especially Franz Beckenbauer, Breitner, Bertie Vogts, Rainer Bonhof, Hoeness and Wolfgang Overath, kept their fort intact, saving Dutch shots and headers one after the other.

Breitner twice and Beckenbauer and Bonhof once each saved the line for West Germany when the whole Dutch team was on attack. In particular, between the 16th and 25th minute of the second half, the Germans lived moments they wouldn't want to repeat.

During that period, the German team was completely dominated. An indication of how heavy the Dutch pressure was was clearly shown when the Dutch goalie headed the ball about 35 yards away from his goal.

Needless to say, the Dutch did miss a couple of chances when they shot wide. But the fact remains that everything that was shot or headed directly at the German goal

was saved by the heroic German defenders. They deserved all the credit and their coach, Helmut Shoen, was the first who said so in the postgame interview.

"Perhaps the Dutch thought we would be easy after they scored that goal in the first minute," Schoen said. "A soccer match lasts 90 minutes and the better fighters won it."

"Yes, perhaps it was to our advantage that we lost to East Germany," the German coach said. "It forced us to regroup. We thought about today's game after that loss. We decided that if we wanted to make the final we had to

work harder and we did."

"It hurts, but I must congratulate the German team and all German fans," said Rinus Michels, the Dutch coach, who answered questions in German and in English after the game. "We did not understimate the Germans, but we came a long way, too."

He added in jest: "I asked the Germans if they wanted to play another game in another city but they turned me down."

Prince Rainier of Monaco, who was accompanied by his wife, Grace Kelly, said: "The whole atmosphere was really marvelous and the German win was well-earned."

Kissinger, who was there an hour before the kickoff, said: "Truly a great match, a great fight and Germany is a great world champion."

The high standard of soccer played, offensively by the Dutch and defensively by the Germans, made up for some hard-tackling pushing and shoving. Hard tackling and pushing with the body do not mean that the game was dirty. Far from it. It was simply a tough battle and the better fighters won.

July 8, 1974

Aztecs Top Toros, 4-3, for Soccer Title

By ALEX YANNIS

The Los Angeles Aztecs defeated the Miami Toros, 4-3, in overtime in the nationally televised North American Soccer League's championship game yesterday at the Orange Bowl in Miami.

It was not an average league game. It was exciting. But was it exciting enough to convince executives at CBS, which showed the game, or other networks that soccer could be a success on television? The league has been

courting the networks for a contract next season, and the product shown yesterday was not a bad sample.

It was an odd contest in 100 - degree temperatures, offering something for everyone. There was a lot of scoring, the referee went out with heat prostration, a minor fight broke out among players, a player scored against his team and there was the drama of overtime.

The exciting things, however, occurred before the

overtime, in which the teams had to take penalty kicks to determine the winner. The Aztecs, an expansion team, slammed in five kicks to three for the Toros, after regulation time had ended with the score tied, 3-3. The Toros had won all six of their tiebreaker games during the regular season.

Both teams started slowly before 15,507 fans. The Toros scored first when Ralph Wright, a fullback, headed in a corner kick by Ronnie

Sharp after 16 minutes.

The Aztecs tied the score 10 minutes later when Ricardo DeRienzo converted a penalty kick, after a teammate had been fouled inside the penalty area.

With 18 minutes left the Aztecs tried to clear the ball from their area, but it rebounded off Ramon Moraldo, one of their fullbacks, and went into the Los Angeles goal. Undismayed, the Aztecs tied the game again seven minutes later on a free kick by Uri Banhoffer outside the penalty area.

August 26, 1974

Moreover, Moore's fans thought they had seen the last of him in the big time. After al that time with West Ham, a First Division team, and after wearing England's shirt 108 times in international competitions, he moved across London to Fulham, where a good crowd on a Saturday afternoon was a mere 10,000.

For years, everybody laughed when Fulham went out to play. It was famous only because a traveler had to go through Chelsea to get there. It was loved by the diehards, not respected.

When the qualifying rounds began, for the cup final, Fulham was 300 to 1. But with help of Moore, one of the best defenders in the business, Fulham leaped over all the opposition and ended up here today, its first appearance in a final since founded in 1880 by a group of parishoners a St. Andrew's Church Sunday School.

In the first half, Moore showed flashes of his early days and Mellor looked as if he might be up to stemming disaster. West Ham, in its third cup final at Wembley, couldn't pull itself together.

Fifteen minutes into the second half, however, Billy

Jennings fired a shot at Mellor, who allowed it to fall to his left. Taylor was there and scored.

Four minutes later, Graham Paddon tested Mellor with another drive. The goalkeeper let this one fall off his chest and, again, Taylor pushed the ball past the posts. That was it for Fulham's dreams, for Moore's hopes of beating his old team and for suspense in the remaining 26 minutes.

May 4, 1975

West Ham Conquers Fulham, 2-0

By ALVIN SHUSTER
Special to The New York Times

WEMBLEY, England, May 3 —For 15 years, Bobby Moore, was the star of the East London team of West Ham United. Today, in the Football Association's cup final, he took the field against his old teammates and found them just too much to contain.

Bobby Moore, now 34, couldn't do everything for his new team of Fulham, a Second-division team playing in a cup final for the first time. And at the end of the 90 minutes of play, Fulham lost by 2-0, with both goals scored by a player who was 5 years old when Bobby began his career with West Ham.

It was the climax of the English domestic season, with 100,000 fans screaming and singing in the stands, the bands of the Corps of Royal Engineers playing waltzes by Richard Rodgers; the Duke of Kent, Queen Elizabeth's cousin, watching it all, and Alan Taylor a 21-year-old for West Ham, emerging as the hero.

He had a little help. Fulham's goalkeeper, Peter Mellor, dropped two drives and Taylor was right there. There was no doubt that Mellor, who said jokingly before the game that he had bought a tube of glue, should have used it.

These annual classics always seem to manage their little dramas. Six months ago, young Taylor was playing for a Fourth Division Club, an unknown picked up by West Ham for a modest $100,000. He had been an unlikely candidate for the hero's role at Wembley's Empire Stadium.

Pele to Play Soccer Here for $7-Million

By ALEX YANNIS

Pelé, known throughout the world as the king of soccer, agreed yesterday to sign with the New York Cosmos, who will reportedly pay him $7-million in a three-year contract. It is estimated that $2-million of that amount will be to pay the taxes for the Brazilian.

"He will pay his own taxes, just like every American," Clive Toye, vice president and general manager of the Cosmos, said in making the announcement here. Pelé was in Brazil.

The deal makes the 34-year-old Pelé, whose real name is Edson Arantes do Nascimento, the highest-paid team athlete in the world.

Pelé will sign the contract here within the next few days, and will play the remainder of this season and the next two years for the Cosmos. He will be in about 85 games, some of them exhibitions overseas.

It appears that the deal will also allow Warner Communications, owner of the Cosmos, to make use of Pelé's name for advertising and public relations purposes.

Secretary of State Kissinger sent a telegram to Pelé recently in which he said: "Should you decide to sing a contract, I am sure your stay in the United States will substantially contribute to closer ties between Brazil and the United States in the field of sports."

Besides Kissinger's cable, Pelé also received a communique from the Brazilian Foreign Minister, Antonio Azeredo da Silveira, who urged him to sign with the Cosmos. Kissinger is an avid soccer fan who attended the World Cup tournament in West Germany last summer.

Pelé warming up before a game while he was with Santos

Pelé retired from pro soccer last October after an 18-year career in which he played in 1,253 games and scored 1,216 goals. He also led Brazil to three of the four World Cup championships between 1958 and 1970.

The Cosmos play a 22-game league schedule and are expected to take a tour when the North American Soccer League season is over at the end of August. The Cosmos said yesterday that they didn't know when Pelé

would make his debut with the team, but it appeared that he would play next Tuesday night in Philadelphia against the Atoms. His likely home debut would be June 15.

Toye made clear yesterday that Pelé would not play for the Cosmos tonight against the Hartford Bicentennials at Downing Stadium on Randalls Island.

Along with Pelé, the Cosmos also hired his closest

friend and adviser, Julio Mazzei. He was head of the physical education department with Santos, the pro soccer club in Brazil for which Pelé starred until he retired last October.

"With the Cosmos, Mazzei will continue to run clinics with Pelé, in conjunction with the Pepsi-Cola program, and will assist Coach Gordon Bradley in the preparation of the team," Toye said.

To get what Brazil has declared a natural resource, Toye traveled about 75,000 miles. He recalled yesterday that he first asked Pelé to play in New York in 1971.

Commenting on the deal, Phil Woosnam, the only commissioner the N.A.S.L. has ever had, said: "This is the final piece of the jigsaw."

Pelé's last reservation about returning to soccer was said to concern the fear of angering his fans in Brazil, since he had refused to play for last year's World Cup team on the ground that he had made an irrevocable decision to leave soccer.

He overcame that reservation, though, when he said at Downing Stadium last Wednesday night: "I think my countrymen will be proud of me helping soccer in the biggest country in the world."

"It is not a matter of betrayal. I had good reasons not to play in the World Cup last year."

Yesterday in Brazil, Pelé said, "My contract is not to just play for the Cosmos, it is to promote soccer in America."

Pelé's decision to sign has made many people happy in Brazil, according to reports, except for one assemblyman in the southern state of Rio Grande. He has proposed that Pelé's title of honorary citizen be revoked "because he has disappointed millions of Brazilians."

June 4, 1975

TampaWins Crown, 2-0, In N.A.S.L.

SAN JOSE, Calif., Aug. 24 (AP) — Arsene Auguste, a substitute defender, broke a scoreless tie with a second-half goal and Clyde Best scored later to give the Tampa Bay Rowdies a 2-0 victory over Portland for the North American Soccer League championship today.

Paul Hammond, the goalkeeper, kept Tampa unscored upon through the playoffs with several spectacular

saves, and Stewart Jump, a Tampa defender, was named the most valuable player in the nationally televised game.

The Eastern Division champions had allowed only 27 goals in 22 regular-season games and became the third straight first-year expansion team to win the league championship. Portland's Timbers also joined the N.A.S.L. this year, and both finalists were stocked primarily with Britons.

Auguste, from Haiti, scored from about 30 yards out 21 minutes into the second half, 3 minutes after entering the game. Best scored with 2:23 left.

Best, a Bermudan who also plays as a forward for West Ham United of England's First Division, took the ball at midfield, maneuvered around Portland's Graham Day and kicked his goal from about 15 yards.

Derek Smethurst, Tampa's leading scorer, got an assist on Auguste's goal.

Jump, another player in England's First Division, darted in front of the Tampa goal late in the game. to block one of Portland's best scoring opportunities. He was

credited with eight steals.

Hammond registered 13 saves for Tampa, eight in the first half.

A crowd of 17,009, almost capacity, turned out at San Jose's Spartan Stadium.

August 25, 1975

Southampton Wins F.A. Cup Final

WEMBLEY, England, May 1 (UPI)—Southampton, the 5-1 underdog, scored a 1-0 victory today over Manchester United in the 75th English Football Association Cup final. A capacity crowd of 100,000 in Wembley Stadium saw Bobby Stokes score the deciding goal in the 82d minute of play.

The match appeared destined to go into extra time when Peter Osgood slipped a pass to Stokes, who slotted his shot wide of the diving Alex Stepney. It was the first time Southampton has won the trophy, the oldest prize in soccer, and the second time in three years that a Second Division club has upset a First Division rival.

Peter Rodrigues, the Southampton captain, led the Saints up to receive the trophy from Queen Elizabeth.

May 2, 1976

San Francisco Booters Top Indiana in Final, 1-0

By ALEX YANNIS
Special to The New York Times

PHILADELPHIA, Dec. 5—Indiana's heroics at Franklin Field ended today when San Francisco sent the Hoosiers to their first defeat of the season and captured the National Collegiate soccer title for the second year in a row.

With a better defense and a number of experienced forwards, the Dons won, 1-0, before 5,981 fans on a goal by Andy Atuegbu. For the second straight year, Atuegbu was voted the best offensive player of the tournament.

It was the eighth shutout in the last 10 games for the Dons. The defeat was the first in 20 games for the Hoosiers, who were in only their fourth year of varsity competition. Only one foreign-born player was on their roster.

In the consolation game Hartwick defeated Clemson, 4-3. Three Clemson players were ejected in the rough contest. Clemson committed 39 fouls to six for Hartwick. All the scoring, the ejections and most of the fouls came in the second half, in which the Warriors from upstate New York raced to a 3-0 lead.

With superb goalkeeping by Peter Arnautoff, the only American on a defense crowded with Norwegians, the Dons didn't allow the Hoosiers to break through the middle, which Indiana did yesterday in defeating Hartwick in the semifinals.

Coach Jerry Yeagley's players thus had to try from the flanks with long crosses, and that was where Arnautoff exceled. He gathered everything that came his way from both sides.

Indiana missed a chance to tie after Atuegbu's goal nine minutes before the end of the half. The Hoosiers were awarded a penalty kick when Rudy Glenn was tripped inside the penalty area. Charlie Fajkus, who had not

missed such a kick before, sent Arnautoff the wrong way, but his shot hit the post.

"I miskicked it," Fajkus said afterward with tears in his eyes. "I blew it, man, I missed the big one." Fajkus got the only goal in the Midwest final, which sent the Hoosiers to the championship tournament.

"I am very proud of my players because they played an experienced team on equal terms," said Yeagley, who has brought Indiana's soccer program a long way in a short time.

Indiana's problem was that Angelo DiBernerdo, who played with an injury, was ineffective. Steve Negoesco, the San Francisco coach, who saw DiBernardo score both Indiana's goals in the 2-1 victory over Hartwick yesterday, had ordered John Brooks to guard him closely.

Hartwick, which had several hundred supporters in the stands, got goals from Gary Vogel, Angrik Stapanow, Phil Wallis and Art Napolitano. Benedict Popoola scored Clemson's first two goals and Kenneth Illodigwe got the last one.

December 6, 1976

THE SELLING OF SOCCER-MANIA

By Lowell Miller

*You don't have to huddle up and you
don't have to wait for the pitch. It moves, Dad, it
moves all the time.*

—DENNIS MONTALBANO, age 10, fullback.

On the soccer field, your light cleated shoes are really the only piece of equipment. The wind blows through your shirt and around your legs as you run. And you're running all the time, constantly moving, constantly alert. There's an open space. You run into it, creating an outlet for a pass. The ball comes to you. You control it, keep it close, using only your feet, perhaps your chest, never your hands. Hard-running defenders rush upon you and the field becomes a mass of enemy jerseys. You spot a free teammate off to one side, pass to him, run to him, take a return pass behind the defender, pass it back to your man as he comes running by. The motion is fluid, quick, sudden. One moment a serious attack threatens, in the next everyone is running backward, trying to catch up with a reversal of the play. It's a tense game, a game of configurations forming and re-forming, of pressures that build and dissolve, of electric instants and fantastic feats of physical agility. There are no timeouts.

With practically no advance warning, soccer has become a big-time sport in the United States. As recently as 1972 attendance at North American Soccer League games was a paltry 400,000. Last year that figure had risen to 2.5 million, and this year the crowds should exceed 3.5 million—an eightfold increase in only five years—including a sellout in excess of 75,000 for a league playoff game. Today, the Soccer Bowl (the N.A.S.L. championship game being played in Portland, Ore., at 4 P.M., E.D.T.) is sure to be a sellout and millions of people will see the game on national television.

Participation at the grass roots, youth level is expanding just as quickly. While 10 years ago there were perhaps 50,000 registered players in youth leagues, this year there will be close to a million—including boys' and girls' teams. That figure is already half as large as the enrollment for Little League baseball. Soccer is also by far the fastest-growing college sport, there being 429 teams now as against

---

Lowell Miller is the author of "North American Soccer League Complete Book of Soccer" to be published next spring and "Hot Stocks," a book on investing which will appear in February.

---

277 in 1966. Within only five years, at current growth rates, more young people will be playing soccer during the summer than baseball.

□

It is an intermittently rainy Wednesday evening at Giants Stadium, its tons of glistening white concrete perched incongruously atop New Jersey's vast turnpike marshes in the new Meadowlands sports complex. The air is hot, humid, stifling, on the verge of a downpour. Still, more than 30,000 undaunted soccer fans have shown up to watch the Cosmos take on the San José Earthquakes. Pelé, the legendary Brazilian superstar whose presence brought the game into its own in this country, won't be playing tonight. That doesn't matter. The fans don't care. They're here to watch soccer.

The crowd roars with the first kickoff and will not stop responding to the action until the last play is squeezed into the final second of 90 nonstop minutes. The wiry fullback Rildo has been trapped with the ball by three San José players, but he manages to feint and fake and shuffle and eke out a pass to Franz Beckenbauer (the West German star voted the best player in Europe last year and recently imported by the Cosmos). Though the fans are mostly white suburbanites, they chant approval in a Spanish accent: "Reeeel-Do, Reeeel-Do!"

The sport is chic, now, and so is its international flavor. Beckenbauer, a 6-footer and big by soccer standards, moves gracefully toward the San José goal, pushing the ball over to an open Tony Field (an English veteran). Field goes around one defender, fakes another out of position, then lofts the ball far across the Earthquake defense to the Italian star striker, Giorgio Chinaglia. No quarterback calls these plays, no substitute rushes in with instructions from the coach. Soccer's a game of instinct. A groundswell cheer rises as Chinaglia approaches the goal, stalking for a score. Instead of shooting, he flips the ball through two defenders back to Field, who has broken clear toward the far goal post. In a charged moment, Field, free and alone, slams the ball past a helpless Earthquake goalkeeper. The fans go wild. "AWWWWWWR-RRRRIGHT." These foreign athletes have become the new American sports heroes.

The crowd at Meadowlands is surprising in its composition

— not the predominantly male, immigrant or ethnic crowd you'd expect. To be sure, the Italians are here, and the Germans are here (soccer is the major sport in almost every country but ours), but the stands are full of all-American suburban kids — wide-eyed, glued to the action on the field, dressed in jackets covered with patches from the small-town teams they've played on: Scarsdale, Mineola, Poughkeepsie, Short Hills. Many of these kids are girls. In fact, many of the adult fans are women (women account for some 45 percent of league attendance). Soccer's new audience is clean-cut, affluent, "upscale" — as Madison Avenue puts it — and Madison Avenues is now following its progress quite seriously. And neither this new audience nor the phenomenal growth of the game is any accident. There has been a strenuous public-relations effort over the last eight years conducted by the North American Soccer League and its 18 franchised club managements that is now beginning to yield impressive results. League commissioner Phil Woosnam says, in his now barely discernible Welsh accent: "We've had to be soccer missionaries."

His converts do not exactly hail from the nation's inner cities. The new base for soccer is in the suburbs, surrounding what Woosnam calls the "All-American" cities, places like Dallas, Los Angeles, Seattle, even that uniquely American city Las Vegas. Eighty-six percent of the fans are under 44 years of age; 74 percent have attended college, more than half have family incomes over $20,000 annually. In unlikely towns like Tampa, Fla., bumper stickers and T-shirts announce that "Soccer is a Kick in the Grass." In Minneapolis-St. Paul, swarms of suburbanites descend on the stadium parking lot hours before game time for tailgate picnics — it's a family affair — and linger hours after the game when team players come out to mingle with the fans. In Los Angeles, young rooters might be treated to the sight of rock singer and soccer aficionado Elton John cheering on the Aztecs, of which he owns a major share.

The *image* of soccer in this country has changed, has been made to change, and the change in image, like so much else in America, has brought success. As former Cosmos coach Gordon Bradley put it, "We're not offering a fad. This is a genuine sport, the top sport in 147 countries around the world. But we had to create an image to get Americans — the most sports-minded people — to accept soccer."

☐

How did soccer move from the sandlots of immigrant areas into the razzle-dazzle mainstream of major-league professionalism and national television? The real thrust came from a handful of men who love soccer, money and a challenge, in no particular order. (Nothing goes big time without the second item on that list.) Among them are Lamar Hunt, of the rich Texas Hunt family and owner of the Dallas Tornado in the N.A.S.L. (he also owns the American Football League Kansas City Chiefs); Clive Toye, former president of the Cosmos, who brought Pelé to this country (Pelé himself is a member of the group), and the manic, ever-running commissioner, Woosnam. In the mid-60s', the business of sports began to boom on all fronts. Tickets for professional football, basketball and hockey games grew scarce. Weekend tennis and golf players found themselves waiting in line to play. Television had discovered, or rediscovered, professional sports, and began pouring money into broadcasting contracts. At relatively low cost, a network could hold the attention of a large audience for one, two, even three hours while its advertisers sold the fans beer, razors, autos, soap. As TV money juiced up sports income and broadened the ticket-buying base, teams that had been glamour toys for the rich suddenly began making the rich even richer. He who had a sporting event to sell to television had the proverbial goods.

Men already involved in professional sports now saw the opportunity to develop a new sports product for the media. What they had in sight was the behemoth of sport, No. 1 in the world with a global audience of more than a billion: soccer. Never mind that Americans could have cared less about the game. Americans loved sport, and once exposed to the beauties and excitement, they would become hooked. How could a billion soccer fans be wrong?

In 1967, two professional leagues were formed, the United States Association and the National Professional Soccer League. A network contract with CBS appeared with remarkable speed. Having imported rather average professional teams from Europe and South America to provide the action, the new team owners sat back and prepared to savor their slice of the American soccer pie. But the pie proved more of a Pop-Tart. No one came to the games. Sometimes there were more stadium personnel than paying fans. American football was ascendant, and baseball solidly entrenched. Who gave a damn about the immigrant sport?

In 1968, the owners tried again, merging the two leagues into one and renaming it The North American Soccer League. But even one league proved to be one league too many. Twelve of its 17 teams dropped out after the 1968 season, leaving the N.A.S.L. as an operating professional league with an absurd total of five teams. Woosnam, the newly appointed commissioner and a former soccer star himself, was convinced that soccer could still make it. As coach of the Atlanta franchise in 1967-68 he had seen crowds of 20,000 coming to games in a city that had absolutely no soccer background and a negligible immigrant population.

To an outsider, though, the situation in 1969 looked patently hopeless. Most of the original teams were gone, having lost cumulative millions. Only the die-hards remained, the true believers. Among them was Lamar Hunt, who felt he had an obligation to the people he'd begun with, and who, as part owner of one of the great American fortunes, lent credibility to the apparently incredible enterprise. The mere mention of his name caused potential franchise buyers to think again about what seemed a ridiculous investment. Hunt had no special background in soccer. "I was just another businessman, trying to build a show-business attraction," he says.

And the league did indeed build its attraction. The previous CBS television exposure had helped bring soccer out to the American hinterlands, young people had begun to play it, and now, finally, they wanted to see the real thing, in the flesh. While crowds were still relatively small (average attendance was about 8,000, and 20,000 was terrific), the popularity of the sport in the years after 1969 had grown sufficiently to interest other entrepreneurs with eyes on the future. Then too, as communities and schools discovered, soccer was an inexpensive and safe sport that provided great conditioning and athletic opportunities

The Cosmos' new prize, Franz Beckenbauer of West Germany, voted best in Europe last year.

to youths of both sexes and all ages and sizes; what writer Paul Gardner has called "the simplest game" began to appear with increasing frequency on the playing fields of suburbia. By the winter of 1975, with Woosnam covering 250,000 miles a year selling soccer franchises to anyone with money who'd listen, the N.A.S.L. had expanded to 20 teams. In the meantime registered soccer-playing young people had jumped from perhaps 50,000, in 1965, to half a million.

The teams were still losing money, though. Soccer was developing some momentum, but its future as a major professional sport was doubtful to all but the inner circle of soccer promoters. The game needed some kind of push, some oomph, before it could really break into the American consciousness.

Soccer needed what every other sport has, a superstar — someone to capture the imagination of the nation's youth, the broadcast media and the press. In the spring of 1975, after years of cajoling and negotiation, Clive Toye, president of the Cosmos, succeeded in signing the world's most famous, highest paid and perhaps best athlete to play for his struggling New York franchise.

Pele, the Black Pearl, broke soccer wide open in this country. The papers were full of his multimillion-dollar contract. Media executives sat up at their desks. What's this? What's the greatest soccer player in the world doing in America? No one with even the remotest interest in sports could fail to be aware of the presence of a great new athlete. It was only natural that thousands would want to see his act, and the stage on which he played. Wherever he went, attendance more than doubled. Stadiums that had never filled for soccer had to turn fans away.

The signing of Pelé was a coup for the

Cosmos and for the league, but it had been no easy matter. Toye and Woosnam first contacted him at an exhibition game in Jamaica in 1971. At that time he was looking toward retirement and they suggested he might come to play in America as a kind of soccer ambassador. In 1971, no great soccer star could take an American offer seriously, but both Toye and Woosnam are men who don't stop until an issue is utterly and irredeemably dead. Toye met with Pelé again and again, in São Paulo, in Rome, in Munich, in Brussels. The global courtship lasted three years and included more than 100 direct contacts along with countless letters and telex messages. Pelé was the king of the most popular sport on earth, and Toye finally prevailed by appealing to his regal instincts toward immortality. "You can go down in history as the man who truly brought soccer to the United States, the one major country in which it has not caught on," he told him. For a humble man who'd started his career by kicking around a ball of twine, it was an attractive idea. A six-year contract, including three years as a player and three as a public-relations figure for Warner Communications (owner of the Cosmos), a complicated offshore tax-free incorporation deal, and at least $5 million must have helped Pelé decide. Even so, the matter became a delicate problem of international relations. Pelé was Brazil's pride and joy — the Government had already declared him a national treasure —and the Brazilian soccer establishment, Government, soccer fans, and press had to be convinced that this was more than a *norteamericano* buy-out. This task was finally accomplished through a blitz (in Warner's best communications style) of public-relations releases, press meetings, Government announcements, repeated statements by Pelé himself, and even the intercession of soccer fan and then-Secretary of State Henry Kissinger. Kissinger proposed that it would be a great thing for U.S.-Brazilian relations, and the Brazilian Government shortly approved Pele's move to its most important hemispherically.

The growth of soccer that had been some 10 years in the making spurted ahead another 10 years on a single night, in June 1975. Godlike, Pelé descended from the sky in a helicopter at the funky Randalls Island stadium (then the Cosmos' home field). Fans mobbed him, as they have continued to do for his three seasons with the Cosmos, trying to touch him, to see him.

On the field, even an out-of-shape Pelé could toy with ball and opponent like a Harlem Globetrotter. A Greek chorus of oooh's and ahhh's was sung from the stands when Pelé gently and precisely pushed the ball through his opponent's legs, or bounced it seven or eight times on his own thighs as he ran past three defenders, or reached out and plucked a chest-high pass from midair with his foot, laying the obedient ball quietly before him. American soccer had its Joe Namath, its Muhammad Ali, its Babe Ruth. It had gone the other sports one better, in fact, for Pelé

had proved himself on a global scale. His was a name broadcasters could pronounce (it's pay-lay), and his style was sweet, humble; publicly he exuded an almost religious goodness ("Soccer is life," he says; "all men must work together."), the kind of clean-cut hero who has all but vanished since the great liberation from all that in the 60's. And he got his press. Cosmos attendance soared at home and on the road, to an average, this year, of 39,000 per game. People who'd never seen a soccer match before came out to watch the "new" superstar. It didn't matter that he was out of retirement and supposedly over the hill — he popped up everywhere on the field without ever seeming to move his legs. (In this game where running is everything, one imagines Pelé coming back to the locker room cool as a cucumber, dry as a fresh towel.) American schoolchildren and pros alike finally saw how the game was supposed to be played.

Soccer was growing before he came, but it was as the mere starter motor for a jet engine. As a missionary, Pelé has succeeded where no one else could. On June 19 of this year more than 62,000 fans packed into Giants Stadium to watch him and the other 10 Cosmos defeat Tampa Bay. The crowd was a record for soccer in this country, and a record for a summer sporting event in New York. With tears in his eyes after the game, Pelé proclaimed: "This is what I came for." It was no fluke. The following Sunday attendance was 57,000, outdrawing a Yankees baseball game just across the river. And on Aug. 14, for a playoff game against the Fort Lauderdale Strikers, a standing-room only crowd of 77,691 set yet another record, cheering mightily as the Cosmos fired in 8 goals to the Strikers 3.

On existing momentum alone, soccer will soon be a media sport on the order of football, baseball and basketball. Now that Pelé has played here no world-class player can think himself too good to come to the United States (Europeans used to think American soccer was a joke, a circus; but 70,000 paying customers make it a joke no longer). Indeed the league has become littered with great international stars — Beckenbauer, Chinaglia, George Best, Eusebio, Rodney Marsh, Derek Smethurst — players who are living legends in their home countries. Americans play on all teams by league rule but

there are few standouts. It will take quite a few years before our level of play is up to international standards, but Woosnam claims that within 10 years "soccer will not only be the No. 1 sport in the U.S. but also the major soccer center of the world. America will win the World Cup. More people will watch and play soccer here than in any other country. It's a question," he adds, "of better marketing from here on in."

□

Soccer will expand because of its intrinsic attractions (exciting, safe, cheap, open to those of average build and to women) and because club owners stand to make rather large fortunes if they are successful. Franchises are still inexpensive, perhaps the best and only bargain left in sports. Right now you can buy a franchise for only $250,000 cash plus a reserve of about $1 million to cover initial costs and losses for the first few years. As crowds grow to the point where average attendance exceeds 50,000 per game — which is a near reality for a few clubs — a team's average net income from ticket sales, concessions and television might come to $1 million or $2 million each year. That's comparable to what an N.F.L. football club earns, and it represents more than 300 percent in annual return on investment.

The real payoff, though, is in franchise value. Sports franchises such as N.F.L. football clubs sell for 10 to 15 times their annual earnings. This means that in a few years (five to ten years by most projections) a club might be worth $20 million to $30 million, a cool 10,000 percent return. Toye claims the Cosmos would be a quick sale, if they were for sale, at $5 million today. The value in five years, with continued sellouts and postseason European tours, is anyone's guess. The Cosmos could well become the most valuable sports franchise in the world. Yet only six years ago Warner Communications, then Kinney National, purchased the club for $10,000.

Obviously, if the club owners have anything to say about it, every youngster in this country is going to learn how to dribble. They've taken a thoroughly businesslike approach to the sport, modeling their operations on the solid success

of the National Football League. Clinics with team stars are held for kids. Free tickets go out to Boy and Girl Scouts. Bumper stickers appear as if for a political campaign. Public-relations staffs churn out a stream of releases showing how much fun soccer is to play and watch. Local fans learn how to pronounce names like Vitomir Dimitrijevic and Ace Ntsoelengoe. Coca Cola announces a worldwide grant of $5 million for youth soccer, much of the money to go to the U.S. That's not advertising, that's a grant. Henry Brandes, sports manager for Coca Cola, U.S.A., shunning an opportunity for hyperbole, says the sport has "momentum." Now, in high schools, soccer is hip, and kids can star in it without taking on the traditional "jock" image.

Though sports are hardly a high-priority social concern, the swing toward soccer is probably a good thing for everyone. A sport that does not need protective equipment, a sport that does not encase you in armor, has got to take us in a more positive direction than the slamming and banging and snorting and anger of football. As the global village becomes a reality, it seems fitting that we join the rest of the villagers in their free-flowing, nonlinear game.

Finally, soccer may well become the game symbolic of our most crucial social change — the emergence of women. Considering the level of conditioning demonstrated by women in Olympic competition, it is already clear, Woosnam contends, that women can develop sufficient endurance to play soccer at any level, and, as more women learn the necessary ball-control skills, they may well compete on the same playing field with men. Some body contact is inevitable. It remains unknown whether a woman will be strong enough to deal with a man when the ball is contested. But it's entirely conceivable that women and men will play together at the interscholastic and intercollegiate levels. And one day a woman may play alongside the next Pelé or Beckenbauer on a North American Soccer League team. "Time is all it takes," says Woosnam. "Girls are now beginning to show real skills, real ball control." What a gimmick that will be. ■

August 28, 1977

Cosmos Win Soccer Title

By ALEX YANNIS
Special to The New York Times

PORTLAND, Ore., Aug. 28—The Cosmos celebrated Pelé's last North American Soccer League game today by winning the league championship game, 2-1, from the Seattle Sounders.

The finale of the sport's breakthrough year in the United States was shown over national television and in 10 other countries. The attendance at Civic Stadium—35,548—was a record crowd for an N.A.S.L. title game.

This marked the second championship in the league's 11-year history for the Cosmos, the first club to win two crowns. The first time the Cosmos won, in 1972, Pelé was in Brazil and the man who scored today's winning goal, Giorgio Chinaglia, was in Italy.

Steve Hunt, voted the outstanding player, scored the opening goal in the 19th minute, and Chinaglia scored the winner on a header with 13 minutes left in the tense game.

Seattle's goal came four minutes after Hunt's as Tommy Ord blasted a low shot under Shep Messing, the Cosmos goalkeeper.

Messing later made a spectacular save, moments before Chinaglia's winning goal. "Championship games sometimes are decided on key breaks," the goalkeeper said after the match. "Today we created these breaks in a game that could have gone the other way. We proved that we can respond to the pressure."

Werner Roth, the captain of the Cosmos, who played with a slightly injured kneecap, said: "Pelé is No. 1 and now we are No. 1 along with him. This team showed a lot of character in the playoffs."

Shouts of "Pelé, Pelé, Pelé" rang through the overcrowded dressing room.

The Brazilian superstar acknowledged the feeling of his last championship by saying, "God has been kind to me, now I can die."

The 21-year-old Hunt caused the biggest problems for the Seattle defense, especially with his long, diagonal runs in front of the Sounders' penalty area. He also broke up several plays on defense and ran more than any of his teammates.

It was Hunt's hustle, speed and alertness that resulted in the first goal. It was scored at a time no one expected, least of all Tony Chursky, the talented Seattle goalkeeper.

Chursky had come out of his goal and gathered in the ball after Hunt had chased it off a lead pass by Chinaglia. The Seattle goalkeeper held the ball for a few seconds, checking the field around him, then decided to roll it on the ground. Hunt, anticipating the play, moved in and stole the ball, giving it a soft kick toward the goal. The ball rolled into the net, with both men chasing it.

Associated Press

Steve Hunt holding shoe aloft while in arms of Pelé, his Cosmos teammate, after scoring against Sounders.

Commenting on Hunt's goal, Pelé said:

"I tell the players in practice to always look at the ball during the game. You never know what happens—maybe the goalkeeper gets a heart attack and drops it."

Hunt was a little-heralded player when he was signed from the English League by the Cosmos just before the season. He now wants to renegotiate his contract. "I'm very pleased with myself," he said. "I gave 120 percent during the playoffs."

He said of his surprising steal and subsequent goal, "I was watching out the corner of my eye, and Chursky turned his back, so I thought I'd have a go at it."

For Hunt, it was his fourth goal in the playoffs. He also assisted on the winning goal, which was Chinaglia's ninth goal in the playoffs, setting a

Associated Press

Pelé of the Cosmos attacking the Seattle defense.

league record.

The goal came as something of a surprise, since Chinaglia is not known for his headers. His strength is, instead, on ground shots.

The Sounders were somewhat surprising also as they gave the Cosmos a tough match. With a variety of crisp passes, they delighted the crowd, which included many Seattle partisans. The Sounders had sold 8,000 tickets to their fans in three hours after they won their semifinal match on Friday.

Thwarting all predictions that they would attack with high passes from the flanks, the Sounders, coached by Jimmy Gabriel, attempted to penetrate through the middle with the ball on the ground.

All the Seattle attacks originated on the sidelines, in an attempt to draw the Cosmos defenders out, and then broke quickly toward the middle.

The Sounders also threatened in the air a couple of times, and Ord almost put them in front in the early stages, but his header went wide to the left.

For the most part, Chursky was excellent. He stopped the Cosmos several times in spectacular fashion, particularly on free-kicks by Pelé and Franz Beckenbauer.

Coach Eddie Firmani's troops, however, appeared to be revitalized in the second half when Vito Dimtrijevic took Terry Garbett's place in midfield. The Cosmos played with plenty of determination, as indicated by the three cautions — to Beckenbauer, Dimitrijevic and Carlos Alberto—issued by the referee, Tores Kibritjian.

Both squads created many good plays, particularly the Cosmos, but neither team could captitalize on the opportunities. Twice the Cosmos excited the crowd with perfectly executed passes inside the Seattle penalty area, but twice there was a pass too many as they tried to set up teammates for a goal.

At the end, it was the Cosmos who proved to be the better, if luckier, team. And Beckenbauer, the former West German star, summed up the feeling of most of the players when he said: "I am very happy for Pelé and myself. It is a great honor for me to win a championship."

August 29, 1977

Rules Limit Foreigners In N.A.S.L.

By ALEX YANNIS

The club owners of the North American Soccer League have voted to accelerate the league's Americanization program by limiting the number of foreign players on the field at one time and by reducing the number of non-

News of Soccer

citizens on a roster. The roster. The Americanization movement, promoted by Commissioner Phil Woosnam and a number of owners for years, made no progress during the 1977 season.

Under the new regulations, nine non-North Americans will be permitted on the field next year. The quota will not change in 1979, but it will be reduced to eight in 1980, seven in 1982 and six in 1984. Also affected will be the 30-player maximum roster, which only a handful of the teams in the league carried last season.

From its present limit of 15 non-citizens, the new regulation will reduce the total to 14 in 1978, 13 in 1980, 12 in 1982 and 11 in 1984. This will enable more North Americans to at least be on reserve teams, except that very few teams have reserve squads.

October 23, 1977

Soccer Gets New Format: 6 Divisions

By ALEX YANNIS

Phil Woosnam, the commissioner of the North American Soccer League, announced yesterday the realignment of the league's 24 franchises to provide

what he called "excellent television marketing opportunities."

Woosnam's goal is to achieve television packages with the three networks. The league has no national television contract now.

Woosnam, whose 18 clubs competed in four divisions last season, was behind the division of the N.A.S.L. into two conferences, American and National, with each conference featuring three divisions of four teams.

The Cosmos, the defending league champions, were placed in the Eastern Division of the National Conference along with Toronto, Rochester and Washington.

Minnesota, Colorado, Tulsa and Dallas will make up the Central Division of the National Conference, and Vancouver, Seattle, Portland and Los Angeles will compete in the Western Division.

The American Conference has Boston, Philadelphia, Tampa Bay and Fort Lauderdale in the Eastern Division. Detroit, Chicago, Memphis and Houston are in the American Conference Central, and Oakland, San Jose, California and San Diego are in the American Conference West.

Modeled After N.F.L.

Woosnam said that a key ingredient in the success of the National Football League had been the competition between the two conferences, and that the new N.A.S.L. format had been largely based on the N.F.L.'s structure.

"Our new format," Woosnam said, "will provide for a schedule that emphasizes both regional and conference games and also interconference competition in the regular season."

Each team will play the rivals within its division twice, on a home-and-away basis. The 30-game regular-season schedule for each club will feature 18 games against conference rivals and 12 interconference matches.

Of the 12 interconference games, eight will be against teams in the corresponding division of the other conference. For example, the Cosmos will meet Boston, Philadelphia, Tampa Bay and Fort Lauderdale of the American Conference East twice, home and away.

"As long as we maintain the rivalries we have created," Mike Martin, a vice president and the general manager of the Cosmos, said, "we don't mind being shifted to a different conference than Tampa Bay."

Martin indicated that the majority of the Cosmos' games at Giants Stadium in East Rutherford, N.J., would again be played on Sunday afternoon, with a few games on Wednesday nights and on Sunday evenings during the hotter weather in July.

The N.A.S.L.'s regular season will extend from April 1 through Aug. 6, and 16 teams will make the playoffs. The playoff format provides spots for the two top teams in each division along with two wild-card teams from each conference. The wild-card teams will be determined by the greatest total of points among squads that are not in the top two in their division.

The playoffs will culminate in a game between the conference champions on Aug. 27. The championship game, the Soccer Bowl, will be played at Giants Stadium.

January 10, 1978

The Soccer Hooligans: Angry Britain Seeks Answers

By R. W. APPLE Jr.
Special to The New York Times

LONDON, April 20—During a soccer game between Brighton and Tottenham Hotspur on Saturday, the teams had to take refuge in their dressing rooms for 14 minutes while the police cleared cursing, brawling spectators from the playing field.

Last month, a 14-year-old boy was wounded by a dart thrown by a supporter of a rival team during a game between Burnley and Oldham. It penetrated two inches into his skull, just missing his eyes.

Phil Parkes, the goaltender for Queen's Park Rangers, a London team, has been attacked by fans twice this season. One threw a knife at him, and another rushed onto the field and attempted to wrestle him to the ground.

After repeated riots at the home field of Millwall, a team from southeast London, the Football Association, the governing body of British soccer, closed the place down for two weeks. Other teams have been ordered to build wire fences to contain the spectators.

Little Agreement on Remedies

Almost every weekend for months there have been incidents somewhere in Britain—fistfights, arrests, fences flattened. And the growing soccer hooliganism, as it is called here, has been exported to the Continent as well.

After a match in Luxembourg last fall, British fans smashed windows and autos and started brawls in bars. Luxembourg said it would never play Britain again. Two weeks ago, Liverpool fans returning from a match in Düsseldorf wrecked several cafes, stole about $20,000 worth of merchandise from the duty-free shop of a cross-channel ferry and ran amok on two chartered trains.

The police and the soccer authorities have been searching desperately for an answer to the problem, which almost everyone believes reflects the deep frustration among British working-class youngsters. But there is little agreement on how to proceed.

Stuart Hall, the director of contemporary cultural studies at Birmingham University, said:

"Unless one believes that a particular minority of football supporters are gripped or possessed by the devil every Saturday from lunchtime onwards, there must be reasons for their behavior."

Role of Press Cited

"Football hooliganism is only the last, or most recent, in a cycle of moral panics about working-class youth," he said. "The connection between football hooliganism of the 70's and the Teddy boys of the 50's, the mods and rockers of the 60's and the skinheads of yesterday are very complex. But we ignore these sorts of connections at our peril.

"When we understand not only why our society produces such phenomena," he continued, "but why it also treats them in the brutal, shorthand and simplifying way that it does, and the role of the press in generating and keeping alive social reaction, we will be in a better position to unravel the problem of football hooliganism."

When the Den, Millwall's field, was closed last month, the club's chairman, Herbert Burnige, complained bitterly about the action, which cost the club money and perhaps a victory or two.

"It strikes me that what the Football Association has done is given the hooligans the license to close down clubs," Mr. Burnige said. "We want to keep them out at Millwall, but we need help to do it. It's not easy to enforce, especially when the hooligans aren't punished."

Soccer commentators in newspapers have all made suggestions. Michael Hart of The Evening Standard of London went so far as to propose that all fans of visiting teams be barred, an extreme measure in a sport where supporters travel around the country to cheer for their teams. John Oakley of The Evening News proposed that those under 18 years of age should be barred from matches unless accompanied by an adult.

Violence by fans here has generally been more frequent and serious than in the United States, where there has also been concern over an upsurge of spectator rowdiness. One of the first of such incidents occurred during the 1973 National League playoffs between the New York Mets and the Cincinnati Reds, when fans at Shea Stadium in New York showered the field with debris and caused an iinterruption of the game.

In 1974, the Cleveland Indians forfeited a game to the Texas Rangers after hundreds of Cleveland fans charged onto the field in the ninth inning. Then, last year at Yankee Stadium, as soon as the Yankees won the final game of the World Series, thousands of fans swarmed across the field, knocking over some policemen and being clubbed by others. A football game in 1976 between the New York Jets and New England Patriots at Foxboro, Mass. was marred by a melee that led to 49 arrests.

Though these and other incidents, including a series of clashes between black and white students at high school football games, have produced anguish in the United States, the problem has not received the kind of attention it has here, where it has reached Parliament.

In a debate on the problem in the House of Commons this month, Michael Brotherton, a Conservative, called for the use of corporal punishment on young offenders. John Evans, a Labor member, urged more fences and a ban on the sale of alcoholic drinks.

But Michael Butterfield, chief executive of the National Association of Youth Clubs, said there was "little hope of combating football hooliganism if all we can think of is punitive measures."

"Until every inner-city area has facilities for children and young people to have kick-about areas and opportunities for play and adventurous

British policemen subdue an unruly spectator during soccer match.

areas," he said, "we should not be surprised if they respond in ways that are unacceptable to society."

Taxpayers and merchants have protested to the Government about the cost of the hooliganism. Shops and pubs near the main soccer fields have to close on match days, and the hundreds of policemen who try to contain the violence, both on foot and on horseback, are reported to cost between $100,000 and $250,000 a season in each region.

New Committee Set Up

Last week, in yet another attempt to get to the bottom of the problem, the Minister for Sport, Dennis Howell, set up a committee to recommend countermeasures. It is headed by Sir Walter Winterbottom, the former manager of the English national soccer team.

But if the recent past is any guide, it is doubtful that any concrete action will result. As Sir Walter himself said last month, when three reports on soccer violence appeared almost simultaneously, "We are not really doing anything, so I would like to see stimulation to get on with some of these recommendations."

One of the difficulties, understood by most of those who have looked into the subject but acknowledged publicly by few, is that many soccer clubs, whose attendance has been declining, are caught in a dilemma. They need their young supporters to keep gate receipts up, but violence by the youngsters tends to drive adult spectators away.

A study by the Sports Council and the Social Science Research Council, one of the three to appear last month, urged the segregation of rival fans, better security on trains and buses and controls on alcohol. It also said that newspapers and television exaggerated the extent of the problem and helped to spread it.

$140,000 for More Research

At the same time, the Research Council said it was possible that segregation of crowds "produces overheating in certain sections of the crowd, bringing together elements looking for trouble instead of dispersing them among the sobering influences of other groups." To try to find out whether that is true, the Research Council appropriated $140,000 for more research on crowd behavior.

Ted Croker, the secretary of the Football Association, reacted with disdain. He had read the report from cover to cover, he said, "and I don't think it will contribute one scrap to the prevention of football violence." What was needed, Mr. Croker insisted, was less theorizing from the the social scientists and an increased willingness on the part of judges to "hammer" offenders.

Like Papuan Tribesmen?

"I think I can imagine a few chuckles when this is read in police departments and football clubs," he said, "mixed with some concern when they see that we're going to spend $140,000 on another report."

Newspapers ridiculed Peter Marsh, co-director of the Violence Research Center at Oxford University, who had a key role in the other two reports, for his assertion that the rituals of the young soccer fans resembled mating dances of Papuan tribesmen.

But many of those concerned about the problem agreed with his broad conclusions about its origins. In one report, he wrote:

"The reason that the social world of the football terraces [stands] exists and flourishes has a lot to do with the fact that kids are leading boring, routine, often alienated, safe and uneventful lives. Football offers an escape —but what to? Another routine and ordered existence? That's the problem."

Dull, Defensive Game

Other researchers, some of whom have mingled with the young fans during and after matches, make a connection between the increasingly defensive and therefore dull character of British soccer over the last decade and the rise of violence. To compensate for what is not happening on the field, according to this theory, danger and unpredictablity are injected into life in the stands and on the streets and buses after the matches.

The British soccer season has only about a month to run, and the authorities are hoping that the remaining games will be free from major violence. In the last two years there have been at least two deaths and scores of serious injuries, to say nothing of the damage to fields and nearby shops. The feeling among many soccer people is that something beyond research must be done to insure that next season does not bring what many of them privately fear—a disaster in which many people are killed.

April 21, 1978

WORLD CUP— OR WORLD WAR?

The international championships. which begin within two weeks. have traditionally been sublimated warfare with great tactical preparation, excessive nationalism and outbursts of uncontrolled violence.

By Lowell Miller

The year is 1969. In the hills of Central America soldiers march stealthily through the undergrowth. Troops armed for modern warfare by the Government of El Salvador are on a search-and-destroy mission. Reconnaissance planes fly overhead. Walkie-talkies crackle in the mountain air. They seek the forces of the enemy, Honduras. Honduras? El Salvador? At war? Why?

The reason is clear enough to the soldiers. Tensions had been brewing between the countries for years, centering mostly on the plight of ill-treated Salvadorans living in Honduras. Then, only weeks before, El Salvador had triumphed in the World Cup elimination match between the two. Heady with victory, intoxicated by the skills of their national team, the Salvadorans took the typically frenzied passions of international soccer one logical step further—into outright war.

The United States has no sports occasion that engenders the sort of nationalism and pride that soccer mobilizes in the population of most countries on earth. We have three major team sports, perhaps five if you include hockey and now soccer. In most of the world there's only one, soccer. Compared with the World Cup — the world championship of soccer being played next month in Argentina — the Super Bowl and the baseball World Series *combined* add up to rather ho-hum entertainment. The World Cup is really world war, organized, transformed, sublimated.

☐

Everything about the World Cup, from the preparations in the host country to the emotional involvement of fans, exists on a colossal, exaggerated scale. More than a billion fans will watch the final via international live satellite transmission (only the Apollo 11 moon landing came close to that "rating") and estimates of the viewing audience for the whole tournament — 25 games culminating in the championship match on June 25 — range from a conservative 2.5 billion viewers to an exuberantly optimistic 20 billion. In the United States, the matches will be shown on closed-circuit television in theaters and arenas, and plans have been made for the final to accommodate more than a million people, most of whom will cheer their teams on as if the players could hear them. Ethnic groups will cluster together and rise and salute as the national anthems of their countries of origin are played. In 1970, when Brazil won the cup, a spontaneous fiesta arose in sold-out Madison Square Garden. The only way the garden's security forces could empty the hall was to start a conga line, complete with drums, and slowly march the chanting and dancing spectators out onto the street. The feelings can have less joyous results, too, as when, according to soccer writer Nestor Kraly (he claims to have witnessed this incident) a fan at the 1958 cup in Sweden promised to commit suicide from "sheer joy" if Brazil won the World Cup. Brazil did indeed win the cup, and the fan kept his promise.

The money and man-hours that go into preparing for an event of this magnitude are stunning. Not only does the tournament itself require huge resources, it is also the most potent public-relations event most host countries will ever have. Argentina, a country of teeming poverty and breathtaking inflation, has refurbished three stadiums and built three new ones. It has spent some $50 million on a new color TV transmission installation —an effort roughly equivalent to starting a fourth network in the United States. (A country must be able to broadcast in color to win the right to stage a World Cup.) Airports have been enlarged, roads built and rebuilt, new hotels constructed, player accommodations created from scratch and a special armed security force has been organized to protect players as well as fans; despite these precautions, however, a bomb exploded 10 days ago at the cup press center, and a police officer was killed.

Entire new parks have been created "in order that the view make the environment agreeable to a day of sport," and the country will put itself on display during pregame television transmissions: Officials of the police state explained, "If it were necessary to make some correction in our image which exists abroad, the 1978 World Cup will be just the occasion to show the world our real way of life." The tab for all this refurbishment and spring cleaning? Somewhere between $450 million and $500 million, most of which will be unrecouped expenses.

It's a big effort for a sporting event, but it's a big sporting event. After issuing more than 7,000 press credentials, the Government was forced to call a halt. Reporters from cities as large as Chicago are being denied access. At the ceremony for the draw, which is merely a lottery affair to decide who will play whom, there were 350 members of the Brazilian press alone. Room rates have doubled — mediocre hotel accommodation may cost more than $100 dollars per night, if you can find one. A merchant describes the situation tourists can expect; "I am ashamed to see what is happening with prices at stores that sell to tourists. They really have the knives out." There will be an overflow of visitors. One soccer observer predicts an influx of 100,000 Brazilians for the first round. Fans the world over will be coming by hook or by crook. The soccer journals, perhaps eager to prove that this was so, erroneously reported in detail that a stereotypically enterprising and penurious Scot had discovered the cheapest way to go—that 150 Scots had each chipped in $1,000 and chartered a submarine. World Cup fever is reflected throughout

the culture. "Alley's Army," a song rooting for the underdog Scots, is No. 5 on the British hit parade. There's probably no way to measure the true amount of international betting that will be done on the cup, but it's safe to say that nothing in human life keeps the bookies busier. In Great Britain, fans who habitually bet on soccer anyway, will wager more than $50 million. And drink at least that many bottles of ale.

□

The modern game of soccer (known in other countries as football) appeared with relative spontaneity, devoid of any real history, in England during the 14th century. There are records of a game played with ball and foot in ancient China and Rome, and no doubt the earliest cave man must have kicked around a skull, or a bird's nest, but there is no good documentation of anything that could be called soccer until 1314. At that time, Edward II issued a proclamation prohibiting a game featur-

ing "a gret noise in the city caused by hustling over large balls." The sport was played in the streets, interfering with feudal business and injuring valuable serfs. By 1349 the game was officially called "football" by Edward III, who threatened to punish players by casting them in the dungeon.

Despite official disapproval, this early football, which was probably more akin to modern-day rugby, continued to be a popular grass-roots sport. You just couldn't keep them from kicking. There was an intrinsic appeal too strong to be squelched by higher social powers. Ultimately, it was the English schoolboy population that brought the sport legitimacy. In the early 1800's, the country's nonpublic "public

schools" were in turmoil. The offspring of the rich were in a constant state of rebellion, undisciplined, impossible to teach, veddy un-British. Among their complaints was a prohibition against sports, specifically against football. School authorities finally decided legalization and co-optation of the game was preferable to ongoing anarchy. And with legalization came rules. If there must be football, at least it would become orderly, dignified, rule-governed, British. Team size was limited, referees were added, rules against violence instituted. But there was a split between schools who favored use of the hands and those — mainly Eton and Harrow — who opted for "the dribbling game." The original game divided: rugby for the rough and football, or soccer, for the gentlemanly.

As schoolboys became adults and continued to form

A Uruguayan is kicked in the head as he ties the score against Bulgaria in 1974. Injury, insult and sour grapes are common.

football clubs, the game spread throughout the country. In 1862 J. C. Thring of Cambridge University attempted to codify the rules, calling his document the rules for "the simplest game." With few changes, these remain in effect today. By 1871, less than 10 years later, there were professional leagues playing to paying fans. In 1901 no fewer than 110,000 fans came to the English professional-league cup final.

The British, at the time, controlled vast areas of the world under colonial rule, and they took their "new" game with them to the colonies. No one was forced to play soccer, but it quickly became apparent that a sport played with ball and foot touched something powerful, deep within people, no matter what their culture or language. By 1904 soccer had sufficient international participation to warrant the formation of the F.I.F.A. (Fédération Internationale de Football Associations), which remains the world governing body of soccer.

International competition began through the Olympics, but by 1920 there were professional leagues flourishing in virtually every major country, and the amateurs-only Olympics didn't reflect the quality of soccer in any of the countries. The best players were playing for money, not gold medals. Responding to the need for an international competition comprising soccer of the best quality, the F.I.F.A., in the person of visionary Frenchman Jules Rimet, decided to organize the first World Cup.

Italy, Holland, Spain, Sweden and Uruguay all wanted the first matches, in 1930. In effect, tiny Uruguay purchased the rights. The Uruguayans were celebrating the 100th anniversary of their independence, and would have the cup as part of the festivities. (This was not surprising. As the national team manager was to say at the 1966 World Cup, "Other countries have their history, Uruguay has its football.") The Uruguayans offered to build a new stadium at Montevideo *and* pay all traveling and hotel expenses for the visiting teams. It was an offer the financially strapped F.I.F.A. could not refuse.

But the boat trip from Europe to Uruguay took three weeks, and every major European team refused to come. Two months before kickoff there was not a single European entrant. After much haggling, Yugoslavia, France, Rumania and Belgium were cajoled into making the journey, but these countries were hardly among the stronger Continental powers. The snub embittered the Latin American federations, which threatened to withdraw from F.I.F.A. (a threat they would repeat many times in the years to come), and was the first of many insults and rejections the Southern Hemisphere has received from the Northern.

Those 1930 matches also previewed future cups in the frequency of on- and off-the-field violence. When Argentina played France in the round of 16, for example, the referee accidentally blew his whistle, ending the game six minutes before official time was out. Fans stormed the field in outrage. Mounted police were required to restore order. During Argentina's later match against Chile, Monti, Argentina's star forward, gave Chilean left half Torres a wicked kick to the groin as Torres jumped to head the ball. Torres punched Monti, and in seconds both teams and fans were engaged in a chaotic brawl which was broken up only with great difficulty by yet another club-swinging squad of gendarmes.

The Argentine team met Uruguay in the final. Back home, thousands of fans, unable to get places on the boats headed for Montevideo, jammed Buenos Aires, chanting: "Argentina si! Uruguay no! Victory or death!" The Argentine team itself had been frisked and searched for weapons several times upon arrival. At the new stadium, twice as many fans as the 100,000 it could hold stormed fences and smashed ticket booths before the match began, and referee John Langenus requested that soldiers with fixed bayonets patrolled the crowd inside.

Uruguay won. The next day was declared a national holiday. Horns blared, flags and banners flew, sirens wailed, there was dancing and drinking and reveling in the streets. In a typical display of World Cup sportsmanship, an angry mob of Argentines stoned the Uruguayan Consulate in Buenos Aires, shouting and crying until dispersed when police opened fire.

Snubs, insults, threats, fights, retaliations, police actions, celebrations, sour grapes, and the best soccer anywhere. The first cup was a model for those to follow. As Langenus said of the 1934 cup in Italy, "Beside the desire to win, all other sporting considerations were nonexistent."

[ ]

The World Cup, like any other international conflict, is a patriotic affair. When a team survives the two-year ordeal of regional eliminations required to reach the round of 16, it's not the team that competes, it's the *country*. Kurt Lamm, secretary of the United States Soccer Federation (our branch of F.I.F.A.) says, "A man sees his country prove to the rest of the world how good it is. And the victor holds the most prestigious sports prize in the world. It must be a dream for a man to see his country win it. Unlike the World Series of baseball or the Super Bowl of American football, the country that wins the World Cup is a true champion of the world." So with the world watching, national pride is what is at stake to the professional player, far more than money (though the member of a winning team stands to make tens of thousands of dollars in bonuses). Rumor had it that Brazil spent more than $4.5 million to defend its World Cup title in the 1974 edition — quite a sum for a country riddled with poverty and slums. The intensity of World Cup fever is such that fans seem literally able to cheer their team on to victory. The cup has almost always been won by a nation from the continent on which the final is played, and 7 of 10 cups have been won by the host country or a bordering neighbor.

Reaching the final is not easy. There are 146 countries fielding national teams affiliated with the F.I.F.A. Preliminary eliminations for this year's final began back in 1976 in regional playoffs for areas such as Africa, North and Central America, South America, Asia-Oceania, Asia-Middle East and Europe in nine different groups. As with all elimination tournaments, the structure tends to favor the strongest by pitting them against the weakest (the host country and the previous winner both receive byes to the round of 16) — but the process often also results in matching top teams against each other well before the finals. It's not inconceivable to have the world's second- or third-best country fail to reach the final round of 16 at all. In this year's elimination, Italy knocked out England, always a strong team. England may not have had a chance to take the cup this year, but it is likely a better team than Tunisia or Iran, which will at the cup.

Only native citizens of a country may play for its national team. The quality of soccer played in a given country is not reflected, only the quality of its active players. Johannes Cruyff, a Netherlander generally considered among the top players, is a professional on the Barcelona club in Spain. But he can't play for Spain — he plays for the Netherlands or not at all. Since the best players do go where the money is, a nation's star may not play on home turf for years. But he is still eligible to compete for his country in the World Cup. Thus, when players don their country's uniform they become soldiers, nationalistic soldiers. "They're no longer playing football. It's war," as Ferenc Puskas of Hungary said of the 1962 World Cup. He made the statement just before the great Brazilian forward Little Bird Garrincha (thought by many to be Pelé's mentor) was smashed on the back of the head by flying bottles on his way back to the locker room.

The play itself rises to its highest level, athletes putting out the proverbial 110 percent, and so do passions rise. Players become heroes and villains. Teams have been sequestered for months, players prevented from seeing their wives, in preparation. Governments tremble if the cream of their players cannot fuse into a fluid and victorious side. Fans weep, fans roar ecstatic; in Mexico in 1970, some stabbed and killed each other — all over possession of that golden trophy. Alan Ball, a 1966 cup star for England and soon to play for the Philadelphia Fury of the North American Soccer League, put it this way: "Players and teams always rise above themselves and play their best. You feel you are competing against the best in the world. You're a hero to the average fan, and you can't let him down. When I played in the World Cup I didn't feel like I was playing *for* England, I felt I *was* England. . . . I could feel the power of the fans behind me. I win for them; they're a part of me."

The World Cup is not about soccer in the strictest sense. It's about competition. It's an *opportunity* to compete, to feel the feelings of competition that make the blood sing. Athletes and fans find it hard to be articulate except in the most ordinary of clichés. But they know what they like. Even the dour, neutral Swedes have been prey to the rising swell of desire for victory. For the 1958 World Cup played in their country, they brought *cheerleaders* right onto the field: One stern and solemn father figure (white hair, white beard) incited the fans and urged them on, waving his little Swedish flag frantically. All this was a gross violation of F.I.F.A. protocol. If the Swedes can be moved to expressive freedom, imagine what happens to the Latin Americans.

The 1962 cup was held in an ill-prepared Chile, whose facilities were mocked and scorned by European journalists, most notably the Italians: "The capital has 700 bedrooms. The telephone doesn't work. A cable to Europe costs an eye out of your head. An air letter takes five days. . . . The city is filled with prostitution, illiteracy, alcoholism, wretchedness . . . while the inhabitants of African and Asian countries have not progressed, these have *regressed*."

For proud Chile, such remarks were not to be taken lightly. Their match against Italy was a welter of violence, broken bones, expulsions; rancor filled the air. The Chileans were busy spitting in the Italians' faces when the referee's back was turned. The referee himself, Ken Aston, called the match "uncontrollable." L'Equipe called it "a veritable street fight." English forward Jimmy Greaves remarked, "There are some good teams here playing bloody rubbish; they're afraid to hold the ball in case they get killed."

If the European-South American feud was smoldering after 1962, the 1966 quarterfinal match between England and Argentina, played at Wembley Stadium, burst all the tinder into flame. Argentina had come to the games with a great team, but with an even greater machismo and an enormous chip on its shoulder. When poor refereeing was blamed for neighboring Brazil's elimination from the matches, Argentina entered the field against the limeys with tempers already unleashed. Within minutes, the Argentines began committing a series of deliberate fouls. Ordered from the field, Argentina's Antonio Rattin refused to leave. (He finally left, reluctantly, making obscene gestures to the crowd and officials.) Short a man, Argentina held well against the English, but Roger Hunt of England knocked a high, curling ball into Argentina's goal with a beautifully timed header, putting his team into the semifinal.

Then, en masse, Argentina's had eliminated them — first off the field, then on it.

The World Cup war of 1974 in Germany was clean and quiet. Little Holland, led by Johannes Cruyff, ran circles around the major soccer powers, interpassing with a rapidity that left their opponents flat-footed. The Germans, if nothing else, know how to keep order. Security measures were tight — the blood of guerrilla violence at the Munich Olympics was still fresh. In the final, though, the Dutch could manage only one shot on goal in the second half. The German team led by Franz Beckenbauer (now starring for the Cosmos of the North American Soccer League) squeezed out a 2-1 victory over the Dutch.

□

What about 1978? Germany and Argentina look like the powerful teams this year. Pelé thinks Italy and Brazil also have a good chance. But in the World Cup, prediction is a dicey affair. A single player having a magnificent game, or one crumbling under the intense pressure, can make all the difference. "The venue," as Alan Ball says, "is of crucial importance." This would seem to give the edge to Ar-

Sweden's Svensson blocks a Pele goal attempt at the 1958 cup.

gentina, a traditionally strong team in any stadium.

The outcome can also be affected by the everpresent undertone and threat of violence. Indeed, this year's host country, with its police-state control tactics, hardly seems ideal for a competition whose history has been so fraught with outbursts and emotion. Many visits were made by worried F.I.F.A. officials before they finally decided to award the games to Argentina. It's not hard to imagine that the existing tensions there might be exacerbated and stretched to the bursting point by the volatile nature of the cup. It's the sort of country in which a boisterous fan could land himself in jail for months, or in which a demonstration might end in gunfire. One can only hope that this edition remains closer to the exciting international soccer contest it was meant to be than a display of a dictatorship's power.

There's been much talk now of holding a World Cup in the United States, but this will not happen soon. The 1982 site will be Spain; Columbia has been chosen for 1986. Nineteen-ninety is possible, though there are many problems to be overcome. The North American Soccer League (an F.I.F.A. affiliate) has altered the rules of the game to make it, naturally, more "commercial." The tie-breaking shoot-out, the point system and a foreshortened offside line all encourage a higher-scoring, more offensive game without the unsatisfying ties that so often occur in soccer. But the N.A.S.L. is a featherweight in the F.I.F.A., and we will certainly get no World Cup as long as we presumes to change the rules of the game — in typically American fashion — against the unanimity of the rest of the world. Soccer is growing so fast in this country that we may soon field a team that can compete at the World Cup level. But we're Johnny-come-latelys to the soccer community, and even with capitulation to international rules it will be many years before we're allowed to butt in ahead of countries who've been waiting to stage a World Cup for decades. ∎

May 21, 1978

Argentina Captures World Cup in Overtime, 3-1

By JUAN de ONIS
Special to The New York Times

BUENOS AIRES, June 25—Argentina won its first world soccer championship today with a 3-1 overtime victory over the Netherlands that unleashed a massive celebration in this country of 25 million people.

The game at River Plate Stadium, before 75,000 spectators, was a 1-1 draw after 90 minutes of regulation play after the Netherlands barely missed a winning goal in the last minute. In the 30-minute overtime Argentina stormed back for two goals and the World Cup title.

"Argentina, Argentina" the crowd chanted as the blue-and-white-shirted Argentine players received the cup, symbolic of world soccer supremacy. As in Munich against West Germany in 1974, the orange-shirted Dutch team had to settle for second place.

Kempes Argentine Star

The hero of the day was Mario Alberto Kempes, the sturdy, dark-haired Argentine forward who plays for the Valencia club in the Spanish Soccer League. He was the high scorer in Spain this season with 27 goals.

Kempes made the difference in an even game with two goals. The first came at 38 minutes of the first half, when he bulled past a Dutch defender and launched a powerful shot that Jan Jongbloed, the Dutch goalie, could not reach. His second goal was the clincher in the 14th minute of overtime.

Kempes also made possible the third Argentine goal, 24 minutes into the overtime, with a charge into the Dutch goal area that attracted two defenders and left Daniel Bertoni free to score.

Kempes is the equivalent of a power runner like Franco Harris in American football, with the strength and speed to overwhelm defenders. His two goals today made him the high scorer of the 11th World Cup championship with six goals.

Shot Hits Crossbar

But the festivities that exploded at the end of the match could have been different if the fast-moving Dutch team had had an inch of difference on a shot by Rob Resenbrink in the last minute of regulation play.

Ubaldo Fillol, the outstanding Argentine goalkeeper had saved his side on several occasions but he was beaten on Resenbrink's shot. As the crowd gasped in relief the shot bounced off the crossbar and back into play where the ball was cleared by the Argentine defenders.

This set the stage for Kempes in overtime. The deciding goal came on a personal effort. He first drove a hard shot at Jongbloed. When the ball bounced back he tapped it with his outstretched foot past two lunging Dutch defenders into the open goal.

President Jorge Rafael Videla and his fellow-members of the Argentine military junta, Admiral Emilio Massera and Air Force General Orlando Agosti, hugged one another. Henry Kissinger, former United States Secretary of State, invited to attend the final games by the Argentine Government and President Hugo Banzer of Bolivia congratulated their hosts.

This was Argentina's first victory since the World Cup competition began in 1930. The victory over the Netherlands, coupled with Brazil's 2-1 victory over Italy yesterday in the game to decide third and fourth place, restored South American supremacy over Europe in the world's most popular sport.

In the last World cup in 1974, won by West Germany, the Netherlands was second, Poland third and Brazil fourth. This year, the Latin American classic, Brazil vs. Argentina, ended in a scoreless draw, and Argentina went on to qualify for the final with a spectacular 6-0 victory over Peru.

Argentina, which lost to Italy in a quarterfinal-round match, is not regarded as a great team, but it showed a tremendous will to win during this championship. The hometown crowd helped to lift morale in difficult moments.

The Netherlands played its characteristic team game, with all players attacking and defending all over the field. The goal that put the game into overtime was scored by Dirk Nanninga. The goal came at 38 minutes of the second half after a period of Dutch domination that almost produced the winning goal as regulation time ended.

Each team made two changes in the second half. Argentina substituted Moromar Larrosa, a midfielder who was a key man in the 6-0 victory over Peru, for Oscar Ardiles and Rene Houseman, a right wing, came in for Oscar Ortiz.

The Netherlands strengthened its defense by replacing Wilhelm Jansen with Willem Suurbier and brought in Nanninga for Johnny Rep.

This was the first overtime final in the World Cup since West Germany forced England to go into an extra 30 minutes with a tying goal in the 44th minute of their championship match in London in 1966. England went on to win, 4-2.

Dutch Fans Sad

THE HAGUE, June 25 (Reuters)—Gloom filled millions of Dutch homes tonight as the national soccer team lost in the World Cup title game for the second consecutive time.

At the end of the overtime game, a torrential downpour drenched the streets in the Hague, further dampening the spirits of those who had watched the television relay from Buenos Aires.

Queen Juliana and Prince Bernhard, who watched the game at Soestdijk Palace, sent the team congratulations on its second-place finish and the Government sent a telegram saying "The Netherlands is proud of you."

The Dutch team will be welcomed at Schiphol airport on Tuesday by Prime Minister Andreas van Agt and members of his government, and will then be driven straight to Soestdijk, near Utrecht, to be received by the Queen.

June 26, 1978

Tourney Tally: Mediocre Play, Poor Officiating

By ALEX YANNIS

In the past, World Cup tournaments have been known for the emergence of stars such as Pele and Johan Cruyff, new systems such as the Brazilian 4-2-4 formation and the Dutch "total soccer" concept.

The 1978 edition of the quadrennial extravaganza, which ended in Argentina yesterday, will be remembered mainly as having been won by the host country, the fifth time that has happened in the 11 tournaments played. Some persons will recall the tournament for its atrocious refereeing, rugby-like tackles or faked injuries that reached a new height in the championship game.

Argentina won, 3-1, from the Netherlands in overtime. But the Argentines spent most of the overtime on the ground, contending that they had been fouled and pleading with the Italian referee to call fouls. They apparently forgot the main issue—a soccer game that was watched by about a billion people round the world.

Players Kicked Violently

An indication that the referees were misinterpreting the rule about fouls and misconduct came in the first minute yesterday when two players from one side and one from the other were kicked violently and the offenders went uncautioned.

Except for a few games—Italy's 1-0 victory over Argentina, the Netherlands' 5-1 trouncing of Austria, Argentina's 2-1 edging of France, Austria's 3-2 triumph over West Germany and Brazil's victories over Peru and Poland —the quality of play was below cup caliber. Brazil was the only undefeated team among the 16 that participated in the 38-game tournament.

In terms of tactics the tournament was, in the words of France Beckenbauer, "made for the defense." From the opening day, June 1, it was apparent that defense was on everyone's mind.

The West Germans, the defending champions, played Poland to a scoreless tie on opening day. Two days later Brazil set the tempo by playing defensively against Sweden in a 1-1 tie.

For those who admire fluidity and virtuosity, which the Brazilians are capable of producing, their defensive tactics were a big disappointment.

the world in the 1958 tournament in Sweden not only by introducing Pelé, but also by unveiling an offensive-oriented formation that called for four defenders, two midfielders and four forwards. After winning that tournament, they successfully defended their title in 1962 and repeated in 1970, again by playing offensive soccer.

With Cruyff at the helm, the Netherlands introduced a concept in 1974 that called for 10 players to attack when the team had the ball and to defend when possession was lost. The Dutch reached the final that year, defeating Argentina, 4-1, on the way.

They were favored to win in 1974, but the West Germans, with Beckenhaven the dominating figure, withstood a fierce attack and won, 2-1. The two times the Dutch have been in the final they have had the disadvantage of playing the host country.

One unexpected development was the play of Tunisia. The number of superb performances by goalkeepers was also impressive.

Representing Africa, Tunisia defeated Mexico, 3-1, fought West Germany to a scoreless tie and was edged by Poland, 1-0.

Eliminated after the first round, the team nevertheless was authorized by Prime Minister Hedi Nuoira to stay in Argentina until the end of the tournament. He congratulated the squad for "the excellent results it achieved and for the dignity with which it represented Africa, the Arab world and Tunisia."

"Tunisia was one of my favorite teams in the tournament," said Dennis Tueart, the star forward of the Cosmos who watched several cup matches on closed-circuit television. "They had some brilliant individual players and were very sportsmanlike."

Mexico was a big disappointment, allowing 12 goals in the three games it played. Watching the Mexicans lose, 6-0, to West Germany, Beckenbauer, who captained West Germany when it won in 1974, said: "Mexico would not score if the game lasted three days."

Argentina's goalkeeper, Ubaldo Fillol, saved his team from defeat enabled him to save a penalty in the match against the Netherlands, who played the most offensive soccer in the first 35 minutes of the second half.

Sepp Maier of West Germany established a cup record of 499 minutes without allowing a goal. Ronnie Hellstrom turned in a memorable performance against Austria and Brazil in the Swedish goal, but could not avert elimination for his country.

Ramon Quiroga, the Argentine native who played goalie for Peru, had a dubious distinction. He allowed Argentina six goals, thus helping his native country reach the final. After Brazil had defeated Poland, 3-1, it became necessary for Argentina to score at least four goals against Peru to reach the final.

There were reports of money squabbles involving several teams, notably the Argentines, Brazilians and Dutch. A drug incident involving a member of the Scottish team was nothing new. But this World Cup did produce something new—a surprisingly pedestrian tournament, teaching the world of soccer nothing but bad things.

June 26, 1978

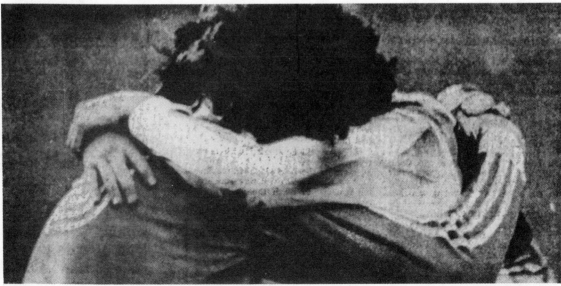

United Press International

Ubaldo Fillol, left, Argentina's goalkeeper, and a teammate, Mario Kempes, embracing after Argentine victory

Cosmos Eliminated By the Whitecaps

By ALEX YANNIS
Special to The New York Times

EAST RUTHERFORD, N.J., Sept. 1 — The Cosmos were eliminated from the North American Soccer League playoffs today when they lost a minigame, 1-0, in a shootout to the Vancouver Whitecaps. The Cosmos had previously won the regulation game, taking a 3-2 shootout victory.

Nelsi Morais failed to get off his kick within the five-second limit, and the Whitecaps took the minigame shootout by 3-2. It was the first time in league play that shootouts were needed in the regulation game and a minigame to decide a winner. The victory sent Vancouver into the Soccer Bowl next Saturday here at Giants Stadium.

Terry Garbett, the Cosmos' reliable midfielder who had not seen action for over a month, converted the decisive kick in the regulation-game shootout to give the Cosmos the victory.

It was the fifth shootout victory for the Cosmos in six attempts this year, the only setback coming here against Seattle on July 11.

Franz Beckenbauer and Seninho were also successful in their shootout attempts, while Vancouver converted only once in four attempts. The Whitecaps did not take their final attempt because they could not have caught up.

Giorgio Chinaglia scored both goals for the Cosmos in regulation play before 44,109 fans. The game was nationally televised by ABC.

The two teams played a scoreless sudden-death overtime of 15 minutes. Vancouver sent the regular game into overtime when Willie Johnston tied the score with 5 minutes 30 seconds to play. Bob Lenarduzzi crossed the ball from the left side and caught the Cosmos napping. Johnstone met the ball and headed it past Hubert Birkenmeier, the Cosmos' goalkeeper.

Chinaglia had put the Cosmos ahead in the 10th minute of the regular game.

Francisco Marinho passed to Vladislav Bogicevic, who pushed the ball through to Chinaglia's right, the way Chinaglia likes to receive the ball.

The center-forward of the Cosmos took a few steps and as Phil Parkes, the Vancouver goalkeeper, came off his line, Chinaglia then blasted the ball in for the goal.

John Craven tied the game in the 27th minute, after a free kick by Alan Ball on the right side.

But Chinaglia put the Cosmos ahead again in the 38th minute with his 20th career playoff goal and sixth in six games this season. Seninho created the goal with a good run and cross from the right side. All Chinaglia had to do was push it into the net as Parkes was out of position.

Style Hurt Cosmos

The Cosmos, who elected to play possession soccer with about 10 minutes left, seemed content to win the regular game by 2-1. The Whitecaps, though, surprised them and tied the game.

The Cosmos played without Carlos Alberto, whom the league suspended last night for the rest of the season. Andranik Eskandarian, suspended yesterday by the league for one game, also did not play.

The Cosmos vehemently protested the suspension of Carlos Alberto to the league and its commissioner, Phil Woosnam. The reason for Alberto's suspension was "violent conduct," which occurred after the first game of the series last Wednesday night in Vancouver.

Julio Mazzei, the technical director of the Cosmos, used Beckenbauer as sweeper in place of Carlos Alberto, and Morais in place of Eskandarian. Dennis Tueart took Beckenbauer's midfield position and Seninho replaced Tueart as striker.

Tueart Injured

Tueart, the most valuable player in the playoffs last year, pulled his left hamstring after playing 31 minutes 36

The New York Times / Larry Morris

Marinho of Cosmos leaping in front of Vancouver's goalkeeper, Phil Parkes

seconds and was replaced by Mark Liveric.

Liveric, at left wing, brought sparkle to the Cosmos' attack. Running endlessly on the left side, he caused panic and confusion among the Whitecaps' defense.

Johan Neeskens also confused the Whitecaps with his non-stop hustling and tackling. Both he and Wim Rijsbergen had missed the game in Vancouver last Wednesday night.

Vancouver used all three of its substitutes in the regular game to rest players for the minigame.

The Cosmos, in order to rest Neeskens, who again got a beating, used Garbett with 17 minutes remaining in the regular game. It was the first time he had played since July 11.

Some Excellent Play

Neeskens, who missed the game in Vancouver because of a pain in his groin area and a twisted left wrist, fell hard on his slightly separated right shoulder.

Rijsbergen did a good job marking Trevor Whymark and Morais did well in his assignment shadowing Kevin Hector, the Whitecaps' leading scorer, with 15 goals in the regular season.

Ricky Davis, the young American, was again assigned to watch Willie Johnston, the Scottish winger who was suspended in the World Cup in Argentina last year for using a stimulating drug.

A measure of the hard playing in today's game had been evident earlier in the season with the Cosmos' loss twice to the Whitecaps. In fact, the Whitecaps were the only team in the league to defeat the Cosmos twice during the regular season. Of the seven meetings between the two clubs since the series began in 1974, the Whitecaps have been the winner six times.

September 2, 1979

The New York Times / Larry Morris

Cosmos' Wim Rijsbergen battling a Vancouver player

CHAPTER. 2

PROFESSIONAL HOCKEY

A couple of hockey greats mix it up: Montreal's Maurice "The Rocket" Richard (white uniform) attempts to score against Detroit in the 1952 Stanley Cup finals. Gordie Howe (#9) and Red Kelly (standing behind Richard) try to deter him as goalie Terry Sawchuk looks on anxiously.

BIG SALARIES FOR HOCKEY PLAYERS

Professionals Receive More Pay for Short Services Than Ball Players.

ONE MAN GOT $10 A MINUTE

Keen Rivalry and Popularity of Sport in Canada Makes Strong Demand for Most Expert Players.

There is a very general impression in this country that baseball players in the big leagues are the highest paid professional athletes in the world, but this is far from correct. Few people know that hockey players of the professional class receive more money than the players of the National game in this country, yet it is a well-known fact that the "pro" players in Canada receive sums far in excess of anything that would be dreamed of by the average person. The actual amount of cash may not be as large, but then the playing season for hockey is very limited, and the men participate in only a few games during even that short period, so that, according to the season of play, the hockey professional gets far more for his services than the baseball man.

As in baseball, there are extra large sums paid to some few players, but the average of the professional Canadian hockey player might be rated at $1,000 for participation in not more than eight or nine games. As against the average stipend of the baseball player, which might be rated at $2,500, the hockey player is much the better paid. He can attend to some other business at the same time that he is engaged for hockey and thus increase his income, and this is, in fact, what many of them do, some even being given sinecure positions which require almost no attention, with big pay attached, so that in reality it might be considered in the nature of a salary for hockey as unless the incumbent of the position were not a first-class chaser of the puck he would not be eligible for such a position.

Aside from what the average professional hockeyist receives, however, there are many instances of exceedingly high salaries being paid to high-class men. Probably the highest salaried player in the Dominion is Fred Taylor of the Renfrew team, who receives $4,000 a year. In addition he holds another position, it is said, because of his hockey ability, from which he receives $1,200 a year, and besides all this he gets a bonus if the Renfrew team wins the championship. It is said that it costs $19,000 to place seven men on the ice to represent Renfrew. On this basis the average salary would be $2,700 for a playing season, which extends over only a few weeks.

The example regarding Renfrew is only an instance of that which prevails with practically all of the other professional teams. Cobalt last year paid Art Ross at the rate of $10 a minute in the match against the Haileybury team. Two halves of 30 minutes each were played, and Ross received for his part in the game $600. It is doubtful if any baseball player ever received an equal sum for participation in a single game. All of the other members of the two teams received big

money for their part in the contest. The match was played at Cobalt in the heart of the silver-mining district, and the miners were willing to make a big outlay in order to get two good teams together so that they might lay heavy wagers. Betting is, in fact, a part of the programme. The towns in which the contests are played are small and could not begin to give in gate receipts anything like the sum necessary to pay the salaries of the members of the teams. It is the chance that the backers of the teams have to lay heavy wagers which holds the sport in a class by itself and makes the Canadian professional hockey player the best paid in the world.

January 30, 1910

WANDERERS WIN HOCKEY SERIES

St. Nicholas Rink Packed for Final Canadian Game Won by Quebec.

The professional hockey series at St. Nicholas Rink came to a rough spectacular close last night, with the Quebecs and the Wanderers in the final jamboree. The Wanderers thereby take the two-game series, 12 goals to 10 goals, but the Quebecs won last night's fray by a score of 5 to 3. It was the weirdest hockey spectacle ever seen at the rink. Much of the time a heavy fog hung like a blanket over the ice, and at times the players were invisible to the spectators who packed the vantage places as they have never been before.

Joe Malone, the Quebec centre, was the headline attraction last night, for he scored all of the goals for his team, his net shooting being really fine art. The great Art Ross ran amuck of another giant named Mummery, and the two came together often, with all the gentleness of a head-on collision on the New Haven road.

Twice Ross was ruled from the ice. Hyland laid Marks of the Quebecs low with a slash, and was sent out of the game. Hall of the Quebecs was also put out of the game. It was the roughest tilt that the rink has ever seen, and the Canadian professionals will go back home with more black eyes, cut heads, and cracked ribs than any teams which have ever played here.

Just before the end of the game, the heavy Quebec players swept down upon the Wanderers' goal like a whirlwind and knocked the goal tender Cadotte unconscious in the net.

He was dragged out and soon got the stars out of his eyes.

The defensive playing was so vicious and bruising last night that neither team could show any team work. The luckiest play of the game was a long shot, half the length of the rink, by Art Ross in the first period. The fog was so heavy that Moran didn't see the puck at all. In the third period Ernie Russell stuck his stick into a cloud of mist while the puck was in the air and drove Sprague Cleghorn's rebound into the net for another lucky goal.

Joe Malone was lightning fast. He glided over the ice phantomlike in the heavy mist. His ghost-like figure seemed to be in front of every Wanderers skater and never did he fail to steal the rubber from an opponent. His hockey stick was like a thing alive, for it poked its way between skates and under falling players in a way which brought Malone the puck every time. He wiggled his way through the roughest scrimmages and always brought up in front of the Wanderers' net. Then he ripped the puck in. Sometimes it didn't go in and hit Cadotte so hard on the chest that it almost knocked him over.

The crowd got as excited as the players. When the scrimmage was lost to view in the fog, they yelled themselves hoarse every time two heads cracked or a player was laid out on the water-

covered ice. The line-up:

Wanderers.	Position.	Quebec.
Cadotte	Goal	Moran
Ross	Point	Hall
S. Cleghorn	Cover point	Mummery
Russell	Centre	Malone
Hyland	Left wing	Smith
O. Cleghorn		
Price	Right wing	Marks

Goals.—First period, first goal for Wanderers, by Russell in 10:30; second goal for Quebec by Malone in 13:17; third goal for Quebec by Malone in 18:02; fourth goal for Wanderers by Ross in 19:20, second period, fifth goal for Quebec by Malone in 10:29; third period, sixth goal for Wanderers by Russell in 5:16; seventh goal for Quebec by Malone in 12:39; eighth goal for Quebec by Malone in 17:48.

Penalties.—Russell, 2 minutes for tripping; Ross, 2 minutes for tripping; Ross, 2 minutes for tripping; Hyland, 5 minutes for slashing.

Referee—Russell Bowie, Montreal. Assistant Referee—William Russell, Hockey Club. Goal Umpires—Frank Ellison, Wanderers, and Gus Hornfeck, Wanderers. Timer—W. J. Croker, Wanderers. Time of periods—Three of twenty minutes each.

March 16, 1913

QUEBECS WIN LAST GAME

But Wanderers Take Championship on Aggregate Score for Two Games.

Three periods of hockey which bristled from beginning to end with a brand of the Canadian game seldom witnessed hereabouts marked the close of the competitive season last night at the St. Nicholas Rink. The game, which was the final of the Canadian professional series for the Dominion championship and a purse of $5,000, resulted in a victory for the Quebecs of Quebec over the Wanderers of Montreal, 8 goals to 6 on the night's play, but resulted in the winners finishing the runners-up.

The final series of two games began on Saturday night last, when the Wanderers were the winners by 9 goals to 4, and as the aggregate goals scored during the two games played decided the championship the honors went to the Wanderers with the total score 15 to 12 of two games in their favor.

The games was probably the fastest and most exciting exhibition of the rink game witnessed here this season and showed the Quebecs entering the final tilt on the short end of the 0 to 4 score coming from behind in the second period and getting within one point of victory only to succumb to an almost superhuman flash by the Wanderers, which gave them a brace of goals, their only tally during the period.

After finding their stride in the second period the Quebecs came on with a rush and took the aggressive, carrying the Wanderers at top speed, and continued until the end with a succession of plays embodying team work, individual attack, and all-around superior work that amazed the spectators and Wanderers as well. The line-up and summary:

Wanderers.	Position.	Quebec.
Lehman	Goal	Moran
Ross	Point	Mummery
S. Cleghorn	Cover point	Prodgers
Kendall	Centre	Malone
Hyland	Left wing	Crawford
O. Cleghorn	Right wing	Harris

Goals: First Period—First goal for Wanderers by S. Cleghorn, 6:28; second goal for Wanderers by Kendall, 13:42; third goal for Quebec by Malone, 18:02. Second Period—Fourth goal for Wanderers by O. Cleghorn, 1:35; fifth goal for Quebec by Malone, 11:25; sixth goal for Quebec by Prodgers, 4:45; seventh goal for Wanderers by Ross, 12:00; eighth goal for Quebec by Malone, 15:00; ninth goal for Quebec by Crawford, 16:00. Third Period—Tenth goal for Quebec by Marks, 2:34; eleventh goal for Quebec by Malone, 7:29; twelfth goal for Quebec by Harris, 14:07; thirteenth goal for Wanderers by Kendall, 16:35; fourteenth goal for Wanderers by O'Grady, 17:03.

Summary: First Game—Wanderers, 9; Quebec, 4. Second Game—Quebec, 8; Wanderers, 6. Total Goals—Wanderers, 15; Quebec, 12.

Substitutes—Marks for Harris, Nighbor for Marks, O'Grady for O. Cleghorn.

Penalties—Ross and Mummery for fighting. Referee—E. Oatman. Assistant Referee—S. Nicholls. Goal Judges—F. Allison and Bud Claffy. Timer—W. Croker. Time of game—Three twenty-minute periods.

March 24, 1914

Hockey Players Under Surveillance.

A novel idea in the method of handling indifferent hockey players was introduced recently by the management of the Wanderers Hockey Club at Montreal. The management is of the opinion that when a player can train—that is, has the facilities and time—and will not train, he should be made to do so. So in this manner, it was rumored recently, and with considerable credence it might be added, that the management of the Montreal hockey seven had engaged detectives, regular, sure-enough private detectives, to keep tabs on the players who in the opinion of the management of the club had not been paying strict attention to the rules governing training methods.

March 14, 1915

WANT NO "PRO" HOCKEY.

Neither New York Nor Boston Would Enter Such a League.

There is no chance for a professional hockey league to enter either New York or Boston, according to a statement made yesterday by Cornelius J. Fellowes, proprietor of St. Nicholas Rink, when he was apprised of a report that the professionals planned an invasion of this city and the New England metropolis. No one has approached Mr. Fellowes on the organization of such a league, which, according to the scheme proposed, would be divided into three sections, West, Central, and East, and Mr. Fellowes would consider no proposition which would involve the playing of professional hockey here.

New York wants hockey played by amateurs only, Mr. Fellowes said, and even in Canada they have become tired of professional hockey. Two franchises in the National Hockey Association, the big league in the Dominion, are now on the market and no one seems inclined to purchase them.

"Professional hockey is in a similar class with professional baseball," said Mr. Fellowes. "High-salaried players are ruining the game financially and it is next to impossible for the holder of a franchise in a Canadian professional league to make money.

"The theory that hockey is a big money-maker in Canada has been exploded," continued Mr. Fellowes. "Few, if any, of the best teams have an account on the proper side of the ledger at the conclusion of the season. It takes $15,000 to run a professional team in ten games, which includes the salaries of the players, some of which run up as high as $3,000 for a season of ten games. The year the Canadians won the N. H. A. pennant they cleared only $6,500 and they attracted large crowds to every match they played.

"The only city in the East which would be likely to accept a franchise in a professional league, if it were formed, would be Pittsburgh. The professional game was played in that city ten years ago and was unprofitable, so in all probability no effort will be made to revive the sport there at this time."

December 16, 1915

MONTREAL CANADIENS CAPTURE STANLEY CUP

Beat Calgary, 3-0, and Win Trophy Emblematic of World's Pro Hockey Title.

OTTAWA, Ont., March 25.—The Montreal Canadiens, champions of the National Hockey League, tonight won the Stanley Cup, emblematic of the world's professional championship. They defeated the Calgary Tigers, champions of the Western Canada League, 3 to 0.

March 26, 1924

NEW YORK ENTERS PRO HOCKEY LEAGUE

Franchise Granted Rickard in National Circuit for Contests in the Garden.

GORMAN TO MANAGE TEAM

Famous Canadian Pilot Will Head Local Six—First Games Are to Be Played Next Winter.

Professional ice hockey will be inaugurated in New York City next Winter. This became definitely established yesterday when Tex Rickard, Madison Square Garden promoter, and Tom Duggin, Montreal promoter and sportsman, announced at the conclusion of a conference in the Garden that they had closed terms whereby a professional sextet will be put in the field next season. The team, which will be known as Tex Rickard's New York Hockey Club, will operate under a New York franchise in an international professional hockey league, which will be a ten-club affair, and will play its home games in the new Madison Square Garden to be erected at Fiftieth Street and Eighth Avenue.

The league will virtually be an enlargement of the present National Professional Hockey League of Canada, which became an international body this season with the entry of the Boston Bruins Hockey Club. Rickard became interested in professional hockey a year ago and at that time obtained a franchise to operate in the National League this season, but changed his plans when it became definitely decided that the present old Garden would be torn down. Rickard figured that the expense for installing an ice plant in his arena would be too great to warrant its construction for only a single season.

The present teams in the Canadian National League are, in addition to the Boston club, the Canadiens of Montreal, present world's champions; the Ottawa Senators, Montreal Hockey Club, Hamilton Tigers and St. Patricks of Toronto. These six clubs will remain in the circuit for next season, and the league already has been enlarged to nine clubs with the addition of the New York club and clubs to represent Pittsburgh and Philadelphia. A tenth club, it is understood, will be located either in Detroit or Cleveland.

It was also disclosed, after the conference between Rickard and Duggin, that the New York club will be managed by Tom Gorman, who recently sold his controlling interest in the Ottawa Senators. Gorman is generally recognized as one of the most successful managers in professional hockey, and during his leadership in Ottawa he piloted the Senators to four world's championships.

February 6, 1925

Lady Byng Gives Hockey Cup For Canada's Fairest Player

Special to The New York Times.

OTTAWA, Ont., March 8.—In a letter to President Calder of the National Hockey Association, Lady Byng of Vimy points out the danger to the future of hockey in the rough play that has become a serious feature of the game. She offers a cup to be presented annually to the fairest and most sportsmanlike player, the selection to be made by the sporting editors of the press in the cities where teams of the National Hockey Association play. The cup has been accepted and trustees appointed.

March 9, 1925

VICTORIA SIX TAKES WORLD HOCKEY TITLE

Beats Canadiens in Final Game of Series by 6 to 1 and Wins the Stanley Cup.

VICTORIA, B. C., March 30.—The Stanley Cup, emblematic of the world's professional hockey championship, was returned to the West tonight when the Victoria Cougars defeated the Montreal Canadiens and won the cup series, three games to one. The Westerners smothered the Cadaniens under a 6 to 1 score.

March 31, 1925

NEW HOCKEY RINK LARGEST IN WORLD

Madison Square Plant, Seating 15,000, Will Have Many Modern Features.

New York's new ice hockey arena, which will be opened to the public this Fall with the completion of the New Madison Square Garden, will be the largest in the world, both in point of playing surface and seating capacity. This will be good news to the lovers of the thrilling and spectacular sport who still can recall the old days at the famous St. Nicholas Rink and the difficulties they encountered in gaining even so much as standing room at the big matches. The new arena will seat 15,000, a matter of 6,000 more than can be accommodated at the arena in Montreal, which, until the projection of the New Madison Square Garden plant, was looked upon as about the last word in hockey arenas.

In the old St. Nicholas Rink the playing surface was barely up to the then existing regulations. Many a jam and crash occurred in the Sixty-sixth Street arena due to the small size of the rink. The new rink here will be 186 feet long and 85 feet wide, dimensions that were decided upon only after practically every hockey expert in this country and Canada had been consulted. The first desire of the builders was to eliminate the old bugaboo occasioned by the small rink, which proved dangerous and often a handicap to speedy teams. Fearing to go to the other extreme and create a rink too large, the builders weighed the matter for many months, going into the subject very deeply, and finally decided upon a rink 186 by 85 feet, and it is agreed among experts that this is the ideal size.

Cooling System Arranged.

The ice plant at the new arena is to have a capacity of 1,000 tons daily, which will permit of creating an ice surface in seven hours. This will be a great advantage, as it will allow the holding of boxing matches, track meets, &c., on one night and a big hockey match the following night. The ice plant will not be confined to making ice for the hockey rink, but will be used for cooling the entire Madison Square Garden. Because of this it is very likely that Summer boxing shows indoors will be held next year with all the advantages of the coolness of outdoors and the safety from rain that always is a hazard for outdoor amusement enterprises.

Of course, with the greatest rink in existence, the new Madison Square Garden will have to furnish a high class of hockey, and to that end this city is to have one of the strongest professional sextets in this country or Canada, and is quite likely also to back a strong amateur club in an amateur circuit which will be organized within a few weeks.

Before hockey lost popular favor in this city both pro and amateur games here were big attractions. There were many leagues in the city among mercantile and banking houses, and plans are under way to revive some of these old amateur circles. The pro. circuit will be the National Hockey League, which had fine success last season, when it placed a team in Boston. The circuit may undergo several changes before the season opens, and it is likely that Pittsburgh and Cleveland will be among the cities represented in the organization.

To Enlarge Amateur League.

The new amateur league, which probably will share amateur hockey in this country with the United States Amateur Hockey Association, is to be organized at a meeting in Springfield, Mass., on Aug. 3, when plans to take in Boston, one of the greatest hockey centres in this country; New Haven, Springfield, Philadelphia, New York and probably Pittsburgh and two other Eastern cities will be considered.

The present plans are to feature the professional game while the new amateur circuit is gaining a foothold. The professional ice sport is the fastest indoor sport in which man indulges, though the amateurs provide a game that is only slightly less speedy.

Tom Gorman, who won three world's hockey titles among the pros for Ottawa, and who will manage the New York arena and the pro team in this city, already has half a dozen stars signed up and is on the trail of others. Gorman is recognized as one of the leaders among hockey promoters and managers and is certain to put a fine team here to inaugurate the pro game.

July 26, 1925

PRO HOCKY BODY COMPLETES LEAGUE

Approves Applications of New York and Pittsburgh at Meeting Here.

An eight-club international hockey circuit was completed yesterday at the meeting of the National Hockey League in the Biltmore Hotel with the approval of applications for memberbship in the league by teams of New York and Pittsburgh. With the favorable action on the applications of New York and Pittsburgh, an eight-club circuit with clubs in Montreal, Toronto, Hamilton, Ont.; Ottawa and Boston is to be completed. Montreal is to be represented by two teams, the Canadians and the Wanderers.

New York's games are to be played at the New Madison Square Garden, beginning Dec. 8. Purchase of the players of the Hamilton, Ont., club by local interests was announced by T. P. Gorman, manager of the Garden team, in the course of the meeting. It also was announced that the Pittsburgh club's games and the team's headquarters will be in Duquesne Gardens in Pittsburgh.

The players who are to make up the New York team were announced last night as follows:

Fordes, Randall, Langois, Spring, Roach, McKennon, Bouchard, the Green brothers and Captain Billy Burch, the latter said to have been purchased from the Hamilton, Ont., club by the New York franchise owners, for a sum in excess of $40,000. Twenty-one dates for the Garden have been alloted, but have not yet been finally settled upon.

September 27, 1925

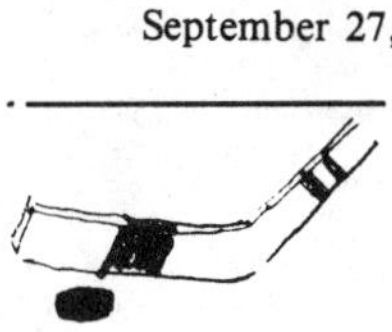

PRINCE OF WALES SPONSORS NEW CUP

Trophy Costing $2,500 Will Be Emblematic of National Hockey League Titlɔ.

TO BE READY ON DEC. 15

Winner of Canadiens' Match With New York in Garden Will Hold It Until End of Season.

At the end of the National Hockey League's season the winner of the league title will receive a trophy new to the ranks of the ice sport, it has been announced by Colonel John S. Hammond, President of the New York sextet of the league. The prize will be known as the Prince of Wales Cup and will be viewed for the first time on Dec. 15 in Madison Square Garden when the Canadiens of Montreal and the New York six go on the ice. The winner of that match, the first to be played in the new Garden, will have possession of the cup until the end of the season.

The cup will be of sterling silver and on it will be the coat of arms of the Prince who is sponsor for it. The fact that four of the seven league clubs are from Canada makes the play for the trophy international and it is expected that in time it will be one of the most coveted cups in competition.

The cost of the trophy, Colonel Hammond announced, was $2,500. Each season the name of the team winning the league title will be engraved on it. The cup will be in competition in perpetuity and will rank only second in importance to the famous Stanley Cup, emblematic of world's championship in hockey.

It was thirty years ago that the Stanley Cup was introduced and now the winner of it is determined when the Pacific champion and the National League champion meet in the play-off. Hockey is a sport that puts great strain on the players and cannot be run off as the title series in many other sports, so an anticlimax necessarily results, but it only serves to add more fire to the true climax.

This year is the first the United States has gone in for hockey on a large scale and the entry of this country has added an international aspect that will do a great deal toward further popularizing the sport.

December 7, 1925

HOCKEY GAMES BOOKED FOR BROADCASTING

THE international hockey game between the Canadian team of Montreal and the New York team will be broadcast by WJY Tuesday, beginning at 8:15 P. M., direct from the new Madison Square Garden. It will be the first game to be played in New York in the newly formed International Hockey League. Music will be furnished by two bands, the Governor General's Royal Footguard Regimental Band from Ottawa and the band of the United States Military Academy at West Point, which will represent the United States.

A hockey game between the Boston Bruins and the Ottawa team will be broadcast by WBZ Tuesday at 8 P. M., direct from the Boston Arena.

December 13, 1925

GARDEN IS OPENED IN BLAZE OF COLOR

17,000 Throng Arena to Attend Formal Inaugural and Greet Pro Hockey.

SOCIETY OUT IN FULL FORCE

Mingles With Sport Celebrities as Ice Carnival Spirit Grips Crowd.

CANADIENS SEXTET VICTOR

Beats New York in First League Game Here, 3-1, and Takes Prince of Wales Cup.

By HARRY CROSS.

From the land of the ice and snow there came to New York last night a new game to celebrate the formal opening of Madison Square Garden. The new arena was thronged with a capacity gathering of 17,000 spectators, which included many society matrons of this city and Canada, who lent their patronage to the occasion in aid of the Neurological Institute Society of this city.

In the tiers of flag-draped boxes was a social registered representation which was something entirely new in New York's long history of the events of sport. Mayor Hylan and Mayor-elect Walker were both there to aid in the dedication of the city's super-structure of athletic pastimes. Park Avenue mingled with Broadway, and in the merry cheers which greeted the inaugural, the voices of the east and west sides harmonized for once in the applause of the city's representative citizenry.

The feature event of the evening, of course, was the opening game of the National Professional Hockey League season here, with New York going down to defeat before the Canadiens of Montreal by a score of 3 to 1. The victory gave the Canadiens possession of the Prince of Wales Cup to remain with them until the close of the season, when it is to be awarded to the team winning the league race. Mayor-elect Walker presented the trophy to the winners.

The Garden was a picture of a temple of sport which, perhaps, has no equal in all the world. There have been preliminary events in the new Garden; the six-day race, some amateur bouts and a championship fight, but last night's celebration was the fashionable start of the city's latest centre of entertainment.

The evening provided not only its fashion show and impressive social soiree and the first game of professional hockey in New York, but between the periods the spectators enthused over exhibitions of fancy skating which furnished more poetry of motion than the ballet. Miss Gladys Lamb and Norval Baptie delighted with a graceful number and Charlotte, who used to perform so beautifully at the Hippodrome when skating was in vogue there a few years back, brought forth volumes of cheers when she gave her first exhibition here since her five-year sojourn on the Continent. Mr. Peterson and Miss Charlotte also gave an impressive exhibition of continental figure skating.

Garden a Riot of Color.

The new Garden was dressed up in its best holiday togs. Festoons of bunting of red, white and blue and gold and blue and light blue and white were draped from the front of the boxes and from the front of the balconies. The arena was flooded with white lights. The Stars and Stripes mingled with the British flag is a glorious splash of color. color.

Just before game time the spacious lobby looked like the foyer at the opera. Fashionably gowned women were there in furs and jewels. It was a hockey crowd de luxe. Flashes of cerise, magenta, Nile greens, scarlets and royal purples colored the boxes. Vendors ambled among the spectators with their apples, oranges and souvenir hockey sticks.

Society caught the spirit of the hockey fans. There was none of the reserve and aloofness of the typical society gathering. The crowd was there to have a good time enjoying the sport of the Dominion. It was a typical sporting occasion with the matrons joining in the cheers and applause of the lovers of the game perched high in the galleries.

The top gallery filled first and then the mezzanine gathered in its thousands of spectators. Last to fill were the promenade seats and boxes, which filled while the West Point Band and the Bugle and Drum Corps from the Academy tooted military airs.

A Perfect Hockey Plant.

The new rink is a perfect hockey plant. The smooth, glassy playing surface is the largest on the National Hockey League circuit and the skaters could be seen from every seat in the arena. The game has changed somewhat since it was seen here years ago at the old St. Nicholas Rink. There are now six players instead of the seven-man teams, the cover-point having been dropped to speed up the game. In the game now there is a neutral zone in the center of the rink in which there is no offside play. This change was also made to increase the speed.

If this impressive gathering at the inaugural of the pro game here is any criterion, New York is going to like its hockey and like it immensely. It was long after the time for starting the game when the Governor General's Foot Guards Band came onto the ice. They were resplendent in their red coats, gold br id and great shakos. They formed on one side of the rink and on the other was the military band from West Point with its trim blue uniforms, the white-lined capes thrown back over their shoulders.

The Canadiens, in their fiery red jerseys, were first on the rink and lined up with the Foot Guards. Then came the New York players in striking hockey suits which were a riot of red, white and blue, with a galaxy of stars sparkling from their manly chests. They were a fine looking lot, these New York players. Each team was led by a color-bearer flying the emblems of both clubs.

Great Reception for Visitors.

The Canadian team paraded around theh rink behind the Foot Guards and got a rousing reception. Then the New York team went through its paces behind the West Point Band. The deep booming brass horns, the cornets, the bugles and the trombones burst forth in a blast of melody which fairly shook the great steel girders which roof over the rink.

The music started the outburst of enthusiasm and then it continued throughout the evening. The two bands with players faced each other across the rink while the Foot Guards played "God Save the King" and the West Pointers played "The Star-Spangled Banner." No sport in any man's town ever got the rousing greeting that Canada's great

How Rival Sextets Lined Up;

CANADIENS (3).		NEW YORK (1).
Joliat	L.W.	S. Green
Boucher	R.W.	R. Green
Morenz	C.	Burch
Coutu	L.D.	Randall
Manthu	R.D.	Langlois
Rheaume	G.	Forbes

Goals, first period—New York: S. Green, 11:55. Second period—Canadiens: Leduc, 12:47; Boucher, 3:55. Third period—Canadiens: Morenz, 8:00.

Substitutes—Canadiens: Lepine, Leduc, Paulhaus, New York; Simpson, Bouchard.

Referee—Cooper Smeaton. Assistant referee—Lou Marsh. Time of periods—20 minutes each.

game got in Rickard's new aphitheatre last night.

This was no common or garden variety of sporting event. It assumed the importance of a momentous event with a capital E. Much water will flow under the Brooklyn Bridge before New York witnesses a sporting carnival with so much fuss and ostentation as that which attended the Garden's gala opening and the introduction of pro hockey in Gotham.

Superior team play won for the Canadiens. The individual efforts of the New York skaters at times was brilliant but they were unable to get the puck past the Montreal defense when it was set for business at the Canadiens' cage.

The Montreal players were superior on the defense and their checking was at times vigorously rough. The game was fast and the crowd was continually roused to a high pitch of excitement. The Montreal skaters assaulted the New York net in formations of two or three players and their passing was far more effective than the long individual shots of the New York players. The game made a great hit with the crowd and, with its swift action, rough checking, speedy skating and skillful stickhandling, is sure to gain popularity.

Hylan Starts Game.

Mayor Hylan came out onto the ice with Tex Rickard, Colonel Hammond and Director Tom Duggan just before the game started and tossed in the rubber puck, which started professional hockey on its merry way.

Captain Billy Burch and Morenz made a wild scramble for the disc and the game was on. Randall first brought the crowd to its feet when he broke forth in a wild chase up the ice right to the mouth of the Canadiens' goal, where the defense bunched and stopped him cold. The skating was swift and the defense tight. Joliat for the Canadiens then took a flying journey around the rink with the disc at the end of his stick. He weaved in and out among the New York skaters until he hit the defense, where his wonderful dash all went for naught.

The play became fast and furious and the checking was so effective that many of the players were upset during the scrimmage. There was a wild demonstration when Burch plucked the disc from Joliat and ran it toward the Canadien goal and made a pretty shot to Shorty Green, who slammed the puck into the net, but the goal did not count, as some of the New York skaters were off side. Groans went up from the enthusiastic New York fans.

There were more groans when a fine side shot by Burch hit the side of the Montreal net and bounded out onto the ice. Joliat, with his black cap, enlivened the period with some remarkable skating. He was fast and slippery.

The Canadiens tried desperately to score. Boucher and Coutu raced right up to the New York goal and tried to jam the disc through, but Forbes was too smart for them and tilted it away.

After Randall made a swift assault on the Montreal net and was spilled for his pains, Coutu again carried the rubber to the Gotham net only to have Forbes carom it over his head.

Green Scores First Goal.

Shorty Green had the distinction of scoring the first goal in the new rink. He carried the puck up the ice, gliding swiftly and gracefully through the Canadiens until he was at the Montreal net, where, by a tricky little shot, he sped the rubber past Rheaume for a goal. The home crowd rejoiced. The first period ended with New York in front by virtue of the lone score.

Bill Cook, who is shown here, was a wing on the great Ranger line of the 1920's which included his brother Bun and center Frank Boucher. Bill led the league twice and tied once in goals scored.

Boucher's sortie on the New York goal opened the second period, but his drive for the net was stopped neatly by Forbes. Down the ice rushed Randall, and his effort at the Montreal net traveled so high that it cleared the wire screen back of the net and sailed into the crowd.

The checking became a bit rough and several of the players were sprawled out on the ice at various times. Randall was laid out for a few moments but resumed playing. Shorty Green and Boucher had a mêlée all of their own and both were ruled off on a penalty.

New York Net Bombarded.

Joliat and Morenz bombarded the New York net with a fusillade of shots when the Canadiens were playing with only four men on the ice. It was only the great goal guardianship of Forbes which saved New York during the furious rally. Forbes gave a fine exhibition of a young Gibraltar.

The Canadiens evened the score after a sharp scrimmage in front of the New York net. Joliat had carried the disk within striking distance and made a nice pass to Leduc, who drove the rubber at Forbes so hard that it bounded past his shoulder into the goal. Boucher of the Canadiens got a terrific bump in one of the scrimmages, but refused to quit.

The Canadiens jumped into the lead when Boucher made a mad dash down the rink, outguessed all the New York players and sent the rubber into the net on a hard drive from a bad angle. The period ended with the Canadiens leading by a score of 2 to 1.

The final period saw the New York skaters trying desperately to tie the count, but their combination play was broken up continually by the hard checking of the Canadians. Burch and Green made fast shots at the Montreal goal which were turned back by Rheaume. Boucher twice came within inches of shooting the rubber into the New York net, for Forbes's great work prevented scores.

Shorty Green was badly shaken up and was helped off the ice. The passing game of the Canadiens was smoother than the team play of the New Yorkers at this period of the match.

The battle at this point became almost torrid in its strife in front of the New York cage and after a hard rough scrimmage in which Joliat's drive was pushed out by Forbes, Morenz got the puck on the rebound and shot another goal for the Montreal sextet.

New York's star skater, Bullet Joe Simpson, went into the game to try to turn it in New York's favor, but he was not able to break through the stubborn defense which banked in front of the Montreal cage.

December 16, 1925

MAROON SIX VICTOR, WINS LEAGUE TITLE

Defeats Ottawa in Stanley Cup Play-Off, 2-1, by Taking Second Game, 1-0.

WILL MEET THE COUGARS

Siebert Scores Goal That Enables Montreal to Enter Series for Pro Hockey Crown.

OTTAWA, March 27 (AP).—The Montreal Maroons won the National Hockey League championship, the Eastern Canada title and the right to meet the Victoria Cougars in the Stanley Cup series for the professional hockey championship of the world by defeating the Ottawa Senators here tonight, 1 to 0, after one of the hardest fought and most bitterly contested games ever seen on Ottawa ice. It was a battle royal from start to finish. The only goal of the game coming from the cleverly handled stick of Babe Siebert after 5 minutes and 45 seconds of the second period.

Seventeen penalties were meted out and the two teams fought to the finish. The Montreal team assumed the defensive rôle immediately after it had gained the lead and baffled the frantic and massed attack of the Senators throughout the final period. Buffeted by weakening body checks at every turn, the Senators never let up and the final period was a rain of flying pucks around Sleepy Benedict, the Maroon goalkeeper. The losers played themselves into exhaustion against the stonewall defence of the Maroons and at the end of the game Clancy was tottering on his feet and had to be helped off the ice.

The series was decided on the total goal basis and Montreal was therefore the winner by 2 goals to 1. The teams tied in the first game at Montreal at 1—1. Ottawa led the National Hockey League during practically the whole season and Montreal won the right to meet the Senators in the final playoff by defeating Pittsburgh, 6—4 total goals, in two games.

Siebert's winning goal was a gem. He took Bill Phillips's pass at centre and swung in on the wing. Smith swung his stick on him but Babe got the shot away and raced in on the rebound. He trapped the rubber and as Phillips attracted attention in centre ice, swept in to bang the disc over Vonnell and into the net.

Game Is Fast and Rough.

The game opened at terrific speed, although both teams were using safety-first methods. The checking was hard and close and they applied the gad unsparingly. Boucher came through alone and took a penalty for piling into Phillips when the latter attempted to block him.

Clancy burned along with hard shots dead on, and one of these Benedict was lucky to clear, the puck lodging in his skates at the net mouth. Stewart gave the Ottawa fans heart failure when he drifted right through alone, and only a magnificent stop by Connell avoided a score.

Clancy was penalized for riding Siebert and Phillips also got the gate for trying to floor Clancy. In the early moments Broadbent attempted to shoot the puck against the fence to go around Boucher and the flying disk hit Denneny in the face. He was considerably cut and had to retire, Kilrea coming on. The period ended without either team having registered a goal.

Some of the heaviest and roughest hockey of the season was seen in the second session. There was no abatement of the pace and penalties came thick and fast. The Maroons broke into the scoring lists in five minutes when Siebert came back off Alex Smith's rush, took Phillip's pass at centre and tore a terrific shot into Connell's pads.

The rebound flew out to the side and quick as a flash, Siebert had pounced on it and driven it back into the net, despite Connell's effort to block it. In a minute the Senators rapped through a goal but it was caught as off side.

Montreal Plays the Defense.

Both goalies had narrow squeaks. Once Benedict stopped a hot one from Nighbor, the puck dropping over his arm but just outside the post. Denneny slipped in a hot one that had the crowd yelling as it shook the net but was on the outside.

Nels Stewart continued his wonderful display and twice more in this period was right in on the net only to have Connell pull a sensational save. The terrific pace was maintained until the end of the period, with the count then Maroons 1, Ottawa 0.

Montreal gave early demonstration of their intention of playing a defensive game in the third period. They packed their defense immediately the period opened and sent one man at a time up on the attack. Rarely throughout the session did more than two Maroon players carry out a rush.

Ottawa pounded right in to force the play and hustled a bundle of shots at Benedict. The long goalie stopped sometimes three or four drives before the puck was sent up the ice again. Spirit ran high and there was no letup in the heavy work. Hooley Smith took a penalty for cracking Phillips and talked himself into a $15 fine with Hewitson.

Clancy was rushing like mad. He burned shot after shot on to Benedict's pads and stick, but could not beat him. Half way through the period the Maroons resorted to shooting the puck the length of the ice and the crowd stood up as both teams strained every nerve to get a goal.

Nighbor was through for a close one, but Benedict footed it to safety. Boucher split the defense and passed to Denneny, but Broadbent blocked his attempt to shoot.

Connell went down to save on a spectacular play. Montreal made little effort to get out and shot the puck up the ice. Clancy burned one past the net inches off the mark. Noble kneed Boucher and went off and Dinsmore followed him for holding Denneny. Benedict saved the Maroons with a wonderful stop. Clancy rushed three times in succession, but his shots were wild. The entire Ottawa team was inside the Maroon blue line, but could not score. Clancy was rushing as the bell ended the struggle.

The line-up:

MONTREAL (1).		OTTAWA (0).
Benedict	Goal	Connell
Munro	Defense	G. Boucher
Noble	Defense	Clancy
Stewart	Centre	Nighbor
Broadbent	Wing	H. Smith
Siebert	Wing	Denneny
Phillips	Sub	Kilrea
Dinsmore	Sub	Gorman
Carson	Sub	A. Smith
Rothschild	Sub	Duggan
Holloway	Sub	Finnegan

First Period.

No scoring.

Second Period.

Montreal, Siebert, 5:45.

Third Period.

No scoring.

Penalties—First period: Boucher, 2 minutes; Phillips, 2 minutes; Clancey, 2 minutes. Second period—Smith, 6 minutes; Phillips, 2 minutes; Clancy, 2 minutes; Stewart, 2 minutes; Siebert, 2 minutes; Boucher, 2 minutes; Broadbent, 2 minutes. Third period—H. Smith, 2 minutes; Noble, 2 minutes; Nighbor, 2 minutes; Dinsmore, 2 minutes.

Referees—Lou Marsh, Bobby Hewitson.

March 28, 1926

PRO HOCKEY TITLE WON BY MONTREAL

Maroons Take Fourth Game From Victoria, 2 to 0, and Capture the Stanley Cup.

STANDING IS 3 OUT OF 4

Final Encounter Played Under Western Rules Finds Cougars Outclassed by Eastern Six.

MONTREAL, Quebec, April 6 (AP).—The Stanley Cup, emblematic of the world's professional hockey championship, will remain in Montreal for at least one year. The Montreal Maroons, National Hockey League champions, defeated the Victoria Cougars, Western Canada titleholders, by a score of 2 to 0 here tonight in the fourth game of the series and thereby clinched the title. The Maroons had won the two first games, but Victoria took the third on Saturday, which made the fourth necessary. Tonight's game was played under Western rules.

A superior defensive system, coupled with an unceasing attack, gave the Maroons their third victory and the title. The Cougars went down fighting to the end, but they were unable to make any headway against the Montreal machine.

Both Slow to Start.

Both teams were slow to start, but as time wore on play speeded up with end-to-end rushes featuring. Stewart and Phillips alternated in rushes on the Victoria net, but were unable to beat the veteran Holmes. The latter was called upon to stop six shots in quick succession from the sticks of the Maroon forward line before the visitors had tested Benedict.

Reg Noble, Montreal defense player, made the first dangerous play on the Victoria goal. He cleared a shot from Oatman at the Montreal end, skated through the Victoria defense, but missed the net by a hair.

Spills were frequent from the heavy body-checking of the two defenses. Frederickson and Halderson were relieved by Foyston and Fraser, but the Westerners were unable to make any impression on the Maroon defense.

The Victoria rear guard showed signs of breaking under the consistent attacks of the Montreal forwards, and only the good work of Holmes saved the situation in the initial period. Meeking was benched for holding Noble and, while short a man, the Cougars made their first dangerous rush when Frederickson split the Montreal defense and burned a hot one at Benedict, the latter just blocking the shot.

Shortly before the end of the first period Stewart and Foyston were chased for renewing their feud. Halderson followed shortly after for holding Siebert. In the last second of play Fraser was also benched for carrying a high stick.

Maroons Finally Break Through.

Montreal took command of the offensive at the start of the second period while Victoria was short of Fraser. Stewart stole the puck from Foyston at the Maroon defense. He went down, flanked by Phillips and Broadbent. A scuffle developed in front of Holmes and he was called upon to make four stops as the Maroon line rained in the rubber.

Stewart finally broke through when he skated around the back of the Cougar net and caught Holmes too slow to make the other corner of the cage. The goal was scored in 1:50.

The Cougars came back after the face off with a vengeance. They rushed in on the Montreal defense, but were unable to penetrate. Benedict was called upon to stop a sizzler from Hart. Meeking missed a great chance to tie the score when he failed to get Frederickson's pass in the Maroon goal mouth and Benedict saved. Meeking came back like a flash, but Benedict was safe. Halderson repeated Meeking's performance a minute later, but he also missed.

Victoria fought hard for the tying goal, but in the closing minutes of the second period Montreal came out of its defensive game and Stewart and Broadbent gave Holmes two hot ones to handle. Finally Stewart scored on one of his own rebounds. The time was 17:30.

Phillips Plays Brilliantly.

Phillips was back at centre fo- the Maroons to start the final session. Loughlin burned one at Benedict and Stewart retaliated with a sizzler at the other end. Phillips went through and almost drove Holmes into the Cougar net, so h avy was the shot. Halderson had thumped Phillips as he went around the Cougar defense and the slim guard was chased.

Phillips was brilliant as time and again he drilled the puck at Holmes. Stewart dashed through the Cougar defense. He was tripped when about to shoot and Fraser was ruled off. The Cougars were fighting like wildcats and the Maroons, with victory, the cup and world title in sight, were matching the Westerners for speed and fight.

Despite the best efforts of the Victoria forward line, Holmes was called upon to stop shot after shot from the sticks of Broadbent, Stewart and Phillips. Benedict had a comparatively easy time in the final minutes of the game, as most of the Victoria rushes were halted at the Maroon defense.

In the last minutes Loughlin began to show signs of temper. He dropped Phillips heavily and was benched. This ended the Victoria hopes to tie up the game.

The line-up:

Montreal (2).		Victoria (0).
Benedict	Goal	Holmes
Noble	Defense	Loughlin
Stewart	Defense	Halderson
Phillips	Centre	Frederickson
Siebert.	Wing	Walker
Broadbent	Wing	Oatman
Carson	Sub	Hart
Dinsmore	Sub	Foyston
Rothschild	Sub	Meeking
Munro.	Sub	Fraser

First Period.

No scoring.

Second Period.

1—Montreal, Stewart 1:50
2—Montreal, Stewart 17:30

Third Period.

No scoring.

Penalties—First period, Meeking, Stewart (2), Foyston, Halderson, Broadbent, Fraser. Second period, Stewart, Meeking. Third period, Halderson, Fraser, Broadbent, Loughlin.

Referees—Billy Bell and Cooper Smeaton. Time of periods—20 minutes.

April 7, 1926

HOCKEY BODY ADMITS CHICAGO AND DETROIT

New York Rangers Official Made Member of National League at Montreal Meeting.

MONTREAL, Sept. 25 (AP).—Chicago and Detroit teams were officially admitted to the National Hockey League at the annual meeting here today.

If the rink under construction in Detroit is not ready for the opening of the season, the Detroit home games will be played at Windsor, Ont. Chicago's home rink will be in the Coliseum, where an ice plant will be installed.

The New York Rangers also were officially admitted into the league. The team is owned by the Madison Square Garden Company and was represented by Colonel Hammond and Wilfred Smythe of New York.

The league is now officially constituted of ten teams, two in New York, one in Boston, two in Montreal, one in Toronto, one in Ottawa, one in Chicago, one in Detroit and on in Pittsburgh.

The following additions to the playing rules were adopted:

1. That the off-side centre ice area be regulated by two lines drawn squarely across the ice surface each sixty feet from the goal line.
2. That uniform goal nets be adopted by the league and installed in each rink; and that goal-posts be squarely fastened in the ice.
3. That the score sheet devised by the President and placed before the meeting be adopted as official, and that an official scorer capable of undertaking the keeping of such official scores be appointed in each city.
4. That the benches for both home and visiting players be situated in each rink on the same side of the rink and as close to the half-way mark as may be possible.
5. That a rider be added to the off-side rule to the effect that "a player cannot be off-side if the puck has last been played by or touched an opponent."

D. N. Gill, manager and coach of the Ottawa team, and A. H. Ross, manager of the Boston team, dissented from Rule 5.

September 26, 1926

CANADIENS ATTAIN GROUP FINAL, 2 TO 1

Down Maroons, 1-0, in Second Game of Montreal Series to Win in Total Goals.

MORENZ ENDS STRUGGLE

Counts From Face-Off Near Net After 12 Minutes of Overtime in Game Packed With Thrills.

Special to The New York Times.

MONTREAL, March 31.—One of the greatest hockey games ever witnessed in Montreal, and there have been many, came to a dramatic end here tonight when the Canadiens, the Flying Frenchmen, eliminated the world's champion Montreal Maroons from the play-offs in the National Hockey League.

The score was 1 to 0. The victors advanced to the final in the international group by a total goal tally of 2 to 1 in the two games, the opener last Tuesday ending in a 1-all draw.

The Ottawa Senators, leaders of the International Group, will come to Montreal on Saturday night for the first game to decide the championship of this sector, while the Canadiens will go to Ottawa on Monday night for the second and final game of this series, total goals to count. The winner of this series will meet the survivor in the American Group for the world's championship and the Stanley Cup.

Only after 12 minutes and 5 seconds of strenuous overtime play did the Canadiens knock the crown off the Maroons. The teams battled through the three regular periods and the first half of the extra session without a score.

With the fans suffering under the strain almost as much as the willing players, the deciding goal came from the stick of Howie Morenz, and no player deserved the winning goal more.

Morenz Thrills 12,000.

The Canadien flash turned in a superman effort. He skated like the wind all evening, and the goal that sent the majority of the 12,000 spectators into raptures of delight ended a great performance.

Morenz is the hero. The story of the game reads like a novel with the hero finally coming into the limelight to realize his ambition.

The better team won. Of that there is no doubt. All the way the Frenchmen carried a distinct edge on the play but only the great work of the veteran Clint Benedict in the Maroon net kept his team in the fight. The break had to come, however, and it was no fault of this grand and courageous man of the heavy pads that he was beaten.

The second half of the overtime session had been on only two minutes when the long-looked for counter entered the net.

From the face-off near the Montreal net Morenz stole the disk while Phillips and Noble were engaged, to flip the rubber into the net from right under Benedict's nose.

The crowd which packed the Forum to the doors and roof, many of whom stood in line outside the building for twelve hours, was spellbound. They did not know what to do.

Maroon Followers Quiet.

Then the French Canadien supporters broke loose with their familiar chant of victory, "Les Canadiens sont la," and for nearly fifteen minutes the cheering lasted. The Maroon followers were quiet, while the loyal followers of the Flying Frenchmen cheered incessantly as they trooped out of the building.

While Morenz was the outstanding player on the ice, he was not the only man who played a big part in the Canadiene victory. Joliat and Gagne, his wings, played great games, while back on the defense, Silvanio Mantha with his face bandaged from injuries in the first game, and his partners, Herb Gardiner and Albert Le Duc, never played better. Hainsworth in goal, as usual, saved many sure-looking goals.

Canadiens Excel on Attack.

The Canadiens displayed a big margin on the playing in the second period, but try as they would they failed to net the disk against the sensational goal tending of the veteran Benedict. The Maroons barely missed a counter shortly after the session got under way when Siebert hit the post with a wicked drive.

Right after this effort the Canadiens set a dazzling pace, Morenz and Joliat scintillating with brilliant rushes and hard drives. Le Duc broke through on a nice rush but fell and the Maroon players pilled up in front of the goal, averting a score. The Canadiens had the advantage on the attack in this session, but the Maroon defense was air tight and again the teams left the ice with both goals clean.

The third period was a repetition of the first. The Canadiens steamed in on the Maroon goal, but Goalie Benedict was always the stumbling block. The Maroons, however, were weakening, but the flying Frenchmen never let up in their pace.

The Canadiens skated down relentlessly, while only occasionally did the Maroon forwards make a break for the goal. They were often dangerous, but the back checking of the Canadiens always interfered or Gardiner and Le Duc or Mantha were invulnerable.

At times the Canadiens would miss on a great play and the same thing applied to the Maroons, and the rival supporters either growled or cheered, but the end of the third period found the teams still scoreless and they went into the first overtime session after one of the most thrilling games of hockey 12,000 fans ever witnessed here.

The Canadiens again carried the attack without result. Changes were made and the substitutes continued the pressing on both sides. The disk went up and down with the rival sixes attacking in turn and it looked like a scoreless game when the first ten extra minutes came to a close.

Play was on only two minutes after switching goals in the extra period when the battle came to an abrupt end. From a face-off to the left of the Maroon net, Morenz got around Noble and Phillips and flipped the disk into the corner of the net, and the Canadiens' supporters went wild with joy.

The line-up:

CANADIENS (1).		MONTREAL (0).
Hainsworth	Goal	Benedict
Gardiner	Defense	Munro
Mantha	Defense	Noble
Morenz	Center	Stewart
Gagne	Wing	Broadbent
Joliat	Wing	Sieber
Cooper	Sub	Phillips
Lepine	Sub	Carson
Hart	Sub	Rothschild
Pelangie	Sub	Oatman
Le Duc	Sub	Donnelly
Larochelle	Sub	Dutton

Firs Period.

No scoring.

Second Period.

No scoring.

Third Period.

No scoring.

Overtime.

1. Canadiens, Morenz, 12:05.

Penalties—First period: None. Second period: Munro, Lepine, two minutes each. Third period: None. Overtime: None.

Referee—Hewitson and Marsh, Toronto.

April 1, 1927

RANGER SIX IS HELD TO SCORELESS DRAW

Battles on Even Terms With Bruins in Opening Game of Group Final.

By SEABURY LAWRENCE.

Special to The New York Times.

BOSTON, April 2.—After three periods of intensive hockey here tonight in the Huntington Avenue Arena, crowded with 9,000 rabid Boston fans, the New York Rangers played the Boston Bruins to a scoreless tie in the first game of the American Group final.

The arena was crowded to the last inch and the fans were strictly partisan, shrieking wildly every time a Boston player performed brilliantly and booing the Rangers generously when they got a bit rough. Play had to be called in the first period because the fans showered papers on the ice and this had to be cleared before the game was continued.

The game was scoreless principally because of the wonderful defense thrown out by the Rangers, who devoted most of their attention to quenching the fiery attacks of Frederickson, Oliver, Galbraith and Shore. The Rangers did not open the dazzling attack that has carried them to so many victories because their manager, Lester Patrick, figured that if they could keep Boston out of the net here they could win on their home ice in Madison Square Garden.

The second game in this two-game series will be played in the Garden on Monday night and as this is a total goal proposition, no overtime was played tonight.

The game was rought as well as fast and fourteen penalties were handed out by the referee for rule infractions.

Action Rough at Start.

Before a rabid crowd that kept up a continuous roar, the teams played through the opening minutes of the game at a hurricane pace. The play was rough and carried along at such a wild clip that several penalties were enforced.

After nine minutes of action, with the disk going up and down the ice at lightning speed, Shore and Herberts were benched, and the crowd roared its disapproval. The fans also threw programs and papers on the ice until Referee La Flamme called the teams off the ice, while attendants cleaned off the surface.

The referee did not let the teams resume play until the Back Bay spectators showed a disposition to quiet down. After play resumed, the brilliance of play continued. The attacks were made at such lightning speed that the eye could hardly follow them. Frank Boucher, Ranger centre, stood out as a superbartist at poke-checking, breaking up many a Bruin attack before it got started.

At one time Boucher was flat on his back after stealing the disk at centre ice and being bumped over by Hitchman. He bounced up, grabbed the rubber again and continued his charge.

Rival Goalies Feature.

Frederickson and Hitchman performed brilliantly for Boston in the first period, and only superb blocking of their heavy drives by Lorne Chabot kept the Ranger's goal clear. Winkler, a former Ranger, also did yeoman service in the Boston net.

A clever save by Chabot on a heavy drive by Frederickson was a luminous feature of the opening part of the second period. Wild attacks by Frederickson, Shore and Hitchman roused the crowd to a wild pitch and when Ching Johnson, big Ranger defense man, was sent off late in the session the spectators shouted approval.

Gorgeous and grilling hockey marked this period, as it had the first. Heavy checking was the order of the day and seven penalties were ladled out during the chukker, the Rangers suffering heavily in this regard.

Lester Patrick threw in the Ranger reserve forward line of Murdock, Thompson and Bourgeault, but the youngsters failed to get very far with the iron-bound defense of the Bruins. Although Bourgeault made some glowing dashes down the left wing he was spilled to the ice by Cleghorn and Hitchman.

Boston Charges in Vain.

The Bruins skated down desperately late in the second period, but could not crash through Johnson and Abel, and the period ended with the game still a scoreless tie.

High-tension hockey marked the first half of the third period, with Boston doing the heaviest attacking and the crowd out of its seats most of the time.

Johnson was kicked in the knee by Hitchman half way through the session and had to leave the ice.

Abel's stick went far down the ice during a melee in mid ice and on a wild attack by Bill and Bun Cook, Winkler only saved himself by gymnastic efforts. Bill Cook, whirling down a minute later, gave Frederickson the stick and was benched.

,Heavy attacks by each side were futile and the game ended in a scoreless tie.

The line-up:

RANGERS (0).		BRUINS (0).
Chabot	Goal	Winkler
Abel	Defense	Cleghorn
Johnson	Defense	Hitchman
F. Boucher	Centre	Frederickson
Bill Cook	Wing	Galbraith
Bun Cook	Wing	Oliver
Murdock	Sub	Meeking.
Thompson	Sub	Herberts
Bourgeault	Sub	W. Boucher
Brown	Sub	Coutu
——	Sub	Shore
——	Sub	Stuart

Penalties—First period: Frederickson, Shore, Abel, Bill Cook, Herberts; Bun Cook, two minutes each. Second period: Bourgeault 2, Stuart, Bill Cook, W. Boucher, Bun Cook, Johnson, two minutes each. Third period: Bill Cook, two minutes.

Referee—Jerry La Flammo and Billy Bell.

April 3, 1927

RANGER SIX BEATEN IN GROUP FINAL, 3-1

Eliminated From Stanley Cup Play-Offs in Rough, Fast Clash in Garden.

CROWD OF 14,000 PRESENT

New York Gains Lead, 1-0, in First Period, but Bruins Count Three Times in Second.

MANY PENALTIES CALLED

Fourteen Are Handed Out in Middle Session—Boston's Defense Halts Desperate Final Charges.

By SEABURY LAWRENCE.

The New York Rangers saw their chances of getting into the Stanley Cup finals against Ottawa go glimmering at Madison Square Garden last night when they were defeated by the Boston Bruins by 3 to 1 in the roughest and one of the fastest games ever seen here. A crowd of 14,000 persons was kept in a constant ferment by the rough play and surging attacks.

As a result of last night's game the total scoring of the two-game play-off between the teams was Bruins 3, Rangers 1. The rivals played a scoreless tie in Boston in the first game last Saturday night.

A total of twenty-seven penalties was handed out by the referees during the game, creating a new American record in this regard, fourteen of them coming in the second period, where the high peak of the wild checking occurred.

This middle period also put the game on ice for the Bruins as they staged a series of superb combination plays which resulted in three goals. The Rangers had been skated into a more or less bewildered condition toward the end of this session and the Bruin forwards skated through with comparative ease in the closing minutes.

Bill Cook had sent the Rangers away to a one goal lead in the opening period and things looked fairly favorable from a local standpoint. Herberts of Boston evened this one up, however, in 7:42 of the second session and ten minutes later came the flying offensive by Frederickson, Hitchman and Oliver, which resulted in two more counters and victory.

Bruins' Defense Impenetrable.

After rolling up a lead the Bruins gave one of the greatest defensive exhibitions ever seen here and constant attacks by the Rangers through the final period were blanked by the hard-fighting back line of the visitors. It can be said, however, that the Rangers missed many close and well-timed shots.

In considering last night's game, it is worthy to note that both Johnson and Abel, the heavy defense men of the Rangers, were both off the ice for roughing when the last two Boston goals were scored.

It was a noisy crowd even before the game started. The Boston players came on the ice first, led by Sprague Cleghorn and were greeted by a thunder of jeers. The New York fans evidently recalled the generous razzing given the Rangers in Boston last Saturday night. The Rangers, led by Bill Cook, got a rousing ovation as they skated out.

The high tiers of the end galleries were filled before game time and these rooters produced the most rabid noise. It was a good betting game and the Rangers, being on their own ice were installed 7 to 5 favorites before play started.

Just before the opening whistle Referee O'Hara called the teams to the centre and gave them some preliminary advice as to rough play.

The action was under way at 8:50 and Bun Cook made the first shot of the game, a long drive from centre ice which went over the Boston net. Play went up and down the ice at terrific speed, with heavy checking and spills rousing the crowd to a frenzy. Frank Boucher, Ranger centre, did some beautiful poke-checking to break up Boston attacks.

Fredrickson Ruled Off.

On a flying-counter-offensive, Boucher was thrown heavily by Frederickson and the latter drew the first penalty. While Frederickson was in the penalty box, Bill Cook caused a wild demonstration by scoring the first goal for the Rangers on a brilliant play. Abel, Ranger defense man, carried the disk down the right wing, took a shot which rebounded off the boards and Bill slashed it in on a lightning shot from a hard angle in 4:51.

The Ranger goal sent the big crowd into a furor and papers and programs were thrown on the ice, causing the referees to halt play until the surface could be cleared.

After hostilities were resumed Ching Johnson and Shore were benched for a clash near the Boston net. Frederickson, Galbraith and Oliver then staged some stirring attacks, Frederickson being prevented from scoring only by Chabot's brilliant stops.

The Rangers reserve forward line, Murdock, Thompson and Bourgeault, came on for the Cooks and Boucher, but they failed to crash through the Bruin back line. When the Cooks came back they staged a seething attack with Taffey Abel and Abel missing another try by inches.

Boston Holds Fast Pace.

In the closing minutes of the period Boston blazed away at a terrific pace. At one time play was stopped with three Boston players piled on top of Chabot and Abel. Disaster for the Rangers was averted only by an almost superhuman defense and the session closed with the Rangers leading by 1 to 0.

Chabot had a busier session in the Ranger goal than did Winkler the opposing goalie, being credited with fifteen stops, while Winkler had eleven.

Boucher of the Rangers was still in the penalty box when the second period opened and Boston immediately started a heavy offensive. Shore was prominent with two brilliant forays which were checked, then Bill Cook took the disk down and was thrown heavily by Frederickson, who was ruled off.

The Rangers started a heavy attack and the play grew rough. Shore and Abel were put off for a tilt and soon afterward Cleghorn carelessly swung on Johnson's nose and also was banned. With two of their defense experts off Boston was down to four men but managed to stem the Ranger drives.

Another Boston offensive broke loose and Sailor Herberts tied the count for the Bruins after a clever dash by Galbraith. Herberts took a flying pass and clapped it through in 7:42.

Penalties Come Fast.

Play went on at a wild, rough clip and Abel, Hitchman and Oliver were quickly banished. Ching Johnson had the house in an uproad with two great dashes, but was finally stopped at the end boards.

Shore and F. Boucher were put off for fighting and Boston for a time was down to three men. It was Shore's third trip to the box for the period and he was off a fourth time almost as soon as he got back.

Hitchman, Frederickson and Oliver then started a crackling session of team play and put two more goals through for Boston. Hitchman counted in 17:33 on a pass from Frederickson and a little over a minute later Oliver put in the third Bruin counter on a pass from the same player.

The second period was the roughest session ever seen in a Garden hockey game, fourteen penalties being handed out by the referees. Of these Shore of Boston had four and Abel of the Rangers three.

Frederickson drove down smartly for Boston opening the third period, but was blocked by Johnson and Abel. The Ranger front line charged almost to the Boston net when Coutu dumped Bill Cook and was banished.

Shore Is Ruled Off.

The Ranger attack blazed fiercely with the Cooks, Boucher and Johnson holding the play around the Boston net and the Bruin defense was lucky to keep the webbing clear. Shore was put off and Bourgeault, Murdock and Thompson came on the New York forward line.

Playing a defensive game, the Bruins kept shooting the disk far down the ice and were razzed by the crowd. Bill Cook and Stuart were benched, and a rush by Abel missed by an eyelash.

Boston banked the defense, and heavy drives by Bill Cook, Johnson and Boucher went for naught. With two minutes to go, the Rangers kept up a continuous drive around the Boston net, but the Bruin defense was too good and the game ended.

Indicating the fire of the Rangers' attack, Winkler, the Boston goalie, was credited with twenty saves in the final period.

The line-up:

BRUINS (3).		RANGERS (1).
Winkler	Goal	Chabot
Hitchman	Defense	Abel
Shore	Defense	Johnson
Frederickson	Centre	F. Boucher
Oliver	Wing	Bill Cook
Galbraith	Wing	Bun Cook
W. Boucher	Sub	Bourgeault.
Coutu	Sub	Murdock
Stuart	Sub	Thompson
Herberts	Sub	Mackey
Shore	Sub	Brown
Meeking	Sub	——

First Period.

1—Rangers, Bill Cook 4:51

Second Period.

2—Bruins, Herberts 7:42
3—Bruins, Hitchman 17:33
4—Bruins, Oliver 18:37

Third Period.

No scoring.

Penalties—First period: Frederickson, Johnson 2, Shore 2, Bill Cook, Stuart, F. Boucher, two minutes each. Second period: Frederickson, Shore 4, Abel 3, Cleghorn, Bun Cook, Hitchman, Oliver, F. Boucher, Johnson, two minutes each. Third period: Coutu, Shore, Frederickson, Stuart, Bill Cook, two minutes each.

Referees—Jerry LaFlamme and Billy O'Hara.

April 5, 1927

STANLEY CUP IS WON BY SENATORS, 6 TO 2

Canadian Six Defeats Boston in Fourth and Final Game of Series by 3 to 1.

2D VICTORY FOR CHAMPIONS

Captured Both Games by Scores of 3-1, While Other Two Title Matches Ended in Draws.

DENNENY TALLIES TWICE

Finnegan Also Counts, While Oliver Gets Bruins' Point—Each Winning Player Gets $1,000.

By SEABURY LAWRENCE.

Special to The New York Times.

OTTAWA, Ont.. April 13.-In a game that bristled with fast, rough hockey, the Ottawa Senators defeated the Boston Bruins by a 3-1 score here to-night in the fourth and final game of the Stanley Cup series and thereby won that historic trophy, emblematic of the world's championship.

The Senators won two of the four games in the title series, while the other two were tied, making the score in points, Senators 6, Boston 2.

The players of the winning team each will receive about $1,000 as their share of the proceeds, while the Boston players will get about $600 each.

The Auditorium again was packed with a crowd of over 9,000, the fans, being of a decidedly partisan nature, roared with glee over the rough play, interspersed with fighting.

Police Separate Players.

The main bout of the evening came along in the third period when Lionel Hitchman, Boston defense man, and George Boucher of Ottawa tossed their sticks away and swung lustily at each other until separated by other players and several Ottawa policemen. Hitchman and Boucher both received major penalties from Referee LaFlamme.

La Flamme had his troubles quelling the rough play, and in the second period was roughly treated himself when Sailor Herberts of the Boston team swung his stick around the official's head after being penalized.

Herberts got a major penalty, as did Hooley Smith in the final period for jabbing Oliver in the face with his stick.

Cy Denneny, the rotund forward of the Senators, was the scoring hero of the occasion, making two of Ottawa's three goals — one in the second period and the other in the third.

The Senators counted twice in the second period when their attack was going at high tension. Frank Finnegan, flashing forward, opened the scoring. Boston was scoreless in both the first and second periods and with a two-goal lead the Senators were content to play more or less defensive hockey in the third session.

Boston's only goal came after all of the third period excitement, when Oliver chopped the disk into the net.

Ottawa's victory gave this great team the Stanley Cup for the ninth time in the history of the club.

The ice had a smooth, glassy surface before play began, a feature that was in Boston's favor. The fact that the Auditorium is not heated probably had a good deal to do with keeping the surface perfect.

The game started at a wild, rough clip, Frederickson breaking up two Senator attacks with strong poke checks. Finnegan and Kilrea started on the wings for Ottawa instead of Denneny and Hooley Smith.

Clancy went down hard in two of his dazzling dashes, but failed to beat Winkler. Shore and Galbraith carried the disk back for Boston, an attack that was shattered by Clancy and George Boucher. Boston's attack grew fiery and Frederickson stick-handled cleverly through the defense, only to have Connell make a great save. It was sensational play.

Clancy went down through right wing again and his long, hard drive almost knocked over Winkler. Herberts and Hitchman carried it back on a nice team play and worked in on Connell, but the latter made another good save.

Hooley Smith Ruled Off.

Following a rough mix-up on the side boards, Hooley Smith was sent off of the first penalty of the game. While Hooley was off the ice the Bruins started like wildfire and Connell stretched out on the ice to keep the net clear. Hitchman came through soon afterward on a torrid drive and Connell again blocked the shot. Herberts was sent off for slashing and then followed a concentrated offensive around the Boston net. Clancy, Denneny and Hooley Smith shot from all angles, but a superfine defense kept the goal clear.

Hitchman finally got the disk away but was checked by Nighbor and the first period ended without a score. It was a sizzling session, Boston staging the more brilliant offensive plays.

Shore got the disk from the face-off, opening the second period and tried a long shot which was wide of the net. Kilrea carried it back on a long, swift run, but was knocked off his stride before he could shoot.

Boston Forwards Excel.

Some lightning play followed, the Boston forwards driving down in a terrific assault on the Ottawa net which set the crowd in a wild uproar. Frederickson, Galbraith and Oliver carried through cleverly time after time, but were unable to dent the net. Then the spectators broke into a mad series of shouts as Nighbor and Finnegan got away, the latter scoring the first goal of the game.

Nighbor carried the disk down on some clever stick handling. He whirled around the Boston net and passed out to Finnegan who slashed it in, the time being 5:10. Ottawa then went into high gear and some of the fastest and roughest hockey of the series was in order.

With Boston attacking, Kilrea and Herberts clashed and Referee La Flamme ordered Herberts off the ice. Herberts enraged, threatened La Flamme with his stick and received a major penalty of five minutes. With the crowd still roaring and with Herberts off, the Senators redoubled their offensive. Their team play was brilliant and the rotund Denneny, flashing out of a mix-up at mid ice, tried a long, hard drive that eluded Winkler for Ottawa's second goal. The time of Cy's counter was 7:55. The house roared its approval of Cy and everything in general.

Senators' Play Is Smooth.

When Herberts returned to the ice the Boston offensive again grew strong, but at this point the Senators were going so well that the Bruins could not keep the play in enemy territory.

Nighbor, Clancy and Hooley Smith took the play away from Boston at times, trying long shots which Winkler blocked and the second period ended with score Senators 2, Boston 0.

The band played that old favorite, "The Gang's All Here," when the Ottawa players came out for the third period. Kilrea tried a run down the left wing, but he lost the disk to Galbraith. The play was carried into Ot-

tawa territory, where Clancy and Cleghorn crashed heavily and both were ruled off the ice.

Frederickson, Galbraith and Herberts staged some fine combination efforts, but Ottawa, playing defensive hockey, closely checked the Bruin forwards. Kilrea finally got away for a brilliant dash, but Winkler blocked his fierce drive with his skate.

Connell Active in Net.

Herberts, Shore and Frederickson drove down heavily, and Connell made a gymnastic stop on a drive by Shore. Shore started down again at a fast clip but was tripped at mid-ice by Nighbor. Denneny then stole the disk, carried it down the left wing close on Winkler and easily beat the Boston goalie with the shot, in 11:55.

With the Boston offensive going strong after Denneny's second scoring effort, bad feeling boiled up between the teams. Hitchman, Boston defense man, and George Boucher, threw down their sticks and indulged in a fist fight and both were put off for five minutes. They were separated by the other players and several Ottawa policemen.

The teams were now down to five men each and played that way until Hooley Smith jabbed Galbraith in the face with the butt of his stick and also was ruled off for five minutes.

Boston still attacked gamely and Oliver, working close on Connell, scored the only Boston goal in 16:45. The game ended without further scoring.

The line-up:

SENATORS (3).		BRUINS (1).
Connell	Goal	Winkler
G. Boucher	Defense	Hitchman
Clancy	Defense	Shore
Nighbor	Centre	Frederickson
Kilrea	Wing	Oliver
Finnegan	Wing	Galbraith
H. Smith	Sub	W. Boucher
Denneny	Sub	Cleghorn
Adams	Sub	Coutu
A. Smith	Sub	Stuart
Halliday	Sub	Herberts
	Sub	Meeking

First Period.
No scoring.

Second Period.

1. Senators, Finnegan 5:10
2. Senators, Denneny 7:55

Third Period.

3. Senators, Denneny 11:55
4. Bruins, Oliver 16:45

Penalties—First period: H. Smith, Herberts, two minutes each. Second period: Smith, two minutes; Herberts, five minutes. Third period: Clancy, Cleghorn, two minutes; Hitchman, G. Boucher, H. Smith, five minutes.

Referees—Jerry LaFlamme and Billy Bell.

April 14, 1927

HOCKEY OVERTIME CUT TO 10 MINUTES

Period Is Reduced From 20 at National League Session Held in Chicago.

GOALIES ARE HANDICAPPED

Hockey Sticks and Pads Shaved Down—Interference and Off-Side Rules Receive Attention.

CHICAGO, Sept. 24 (AP).—At a meeting of officials of the National Hockey League here today, President Frank Calder was authorized to sign an agreement affiliating the Central Hockey Association with the National League.

The officials of the National League made several changes, for the most part in playing rules.

J. Cooper Smeaton of Montreal was

appointed referee-in-chief to supervise all referees in gaining uniform interpretation of the rules.

Significant changes made today follow:

The waiver price for transfer of players was raised from $2,500 to $5,000.

The period of overtime play was reduced from twenty to ten minutes.

The length of hockey sticks was restricted to 53 inches. (There had been no limit formerly.)

The blade of goal-keepers' sticks was limited in length to 14 inches.

The size of goal-keepers' leg pads was reduced from 12 to 10 inches in width.

A new clause was written regarding the question of interference to the effect that "any player not in possession of the rubber shall not interfere with any other player of the opposing side not actually playing the rubber by cross-checking or holding. A player shall be considered in possession of the disc until it has been touched by another player.

The rule regarding off-side play was strengthened to the effect that "A defending player shall not be considered off-side in his own area if he receives the rubber in that area."

A provision was made in regard to goal scoring. "The goal shall not be scored if the rubber is put into the goal by any part of an attacking player or his skates.

A rule was made prohibiting a goal-keeper from holding the disc longer than three seconds or traveling more than four feet out with it.

The anti-defense rule was strengthened by providing a minor penalty for three men being behind the blue line.

The officials voted to use the new Ross net in games this year.

The date of the annual meeting was changed from the last Saturday in September to the second Saturday in May.

Governors of all hockey clubs in the league were re-elected with the exception of the Boston and Toronto clubs. C. F. Adams was elected to succeed Art Ross of the Boston club. On the Toronto club Charles Querie was replaced by J. C. Smythe.

The schedule of games will be announced later in the week.

September 25, 1927

MAROONS BOW, 1-0, TO RANGER SEXTET

New Yorkers Take Whirlwind Game at Montreal and Tie Stanley Cup Series.

By SEABURY LAWRENCE.

Special to The New York Times.

MONTREAL, April 12.—Playing magnificent hockey in a game that whirled along at wild speed all through the sixty minutes of action, the New York Rangers defeated the powerful Montreal Maroons at the Forum tonight by a 1-0 score, and evened the series.

Each team has now won two games in the world's championship series in hockey and a fifth contest will be necessary to decide the possession of the historic Stanley Cup. This will be played on Saturday night.

The Rangers were a great hockey team tonight. They had a world of speed and outplayed the Maroons fairly, although the Montreal players had all their old driving power. The crowd of 13,000 fans was thrilled by one of the greatest exhibitions of hockey ever seen by even the oldest rooters.

All of the Rangers, both the forwards and the defense men, played stellar rôles in a superb victory. To Frank Boucher, whirlwind centre, and the Cooks, also must go great credit for tying the series.

Boucher Whirlwind Player.

Boucher was moving like a phantom all the time he was on the ice, but the Cooks, Murdock and Bourgault were not far behind him. It was Boucher who took Bill Cook's pass early in the second period to score the only goal of the game.

Boucher also sank one in the first period which was disallowed because the play was called offside.

Joe Miller, Ranger goalie, also played a great game. He was as cool as a cucumber and stood up before many a titanic drive. Miller was credited with 32 saves for the three periods, while Benedict, in the Maroon net, who also played brilliantly, scored 25.

President John S. Hammond of the Rangers presented each of the players with a check for $100 after the game as a reward for the great victory.

What is known as the "rush end" of the rink, where the admission is 50 cents, was jammed an hour before play began. It was another sell out, nothing but standing room being available when the rink opened.

Miller at Rangers' Goal.

The crowd was singing and cheering with the band long before the players came on the ice. Joe Miller was once more at goal for the Rangers, again substituting for Lorne Chabot, who is still in the hospital with an injured left eye as a result of being struck by the flying disk in the second struggle.

Paul Thompson of the Rangers and Ive Lamb of the Maroons, substitute forwards, did not get into the action, having received match penalties for a fist fight in Tuesday night's battle.

Boucher and Bill Cook swept through the Maroon defense in the opening play of the game, and Bill's bullet drive bounced off Benedict's chest. Red Dutton carried it back and Miller made a good stop on his low, savage drive.

The Cooks and Boucher then carried the disk down on a hurricane raid and five minutes of the fastest hockey ever seen anywhere ensued. Bill and Bun Cook drove through the defense time after time in whirlwind rushes, only to have Benedict save the situation with magnificent stops.

The crowd was in a mad uproar during the Ranger bombardment. Boucher netted the disk, but after the whistle had blown for an offside the goal was not allowed. Benedict was down three times in front of the net as the Rangers kept charging in.

Bourgault went off for crosschecking, the first penalty of the game, and while the Rangers were down to five men it was the turn of the Maroons to sweep in on Miller. The little goalie made some spectacular saves on his own account and the riproaring first period ended without a score for either side.

The crowd sang and cheered between the sessions and the boys had a lot of fun batting toy balloons around.

Nelson Stewart dashed down to the first shot of the second period, but a bad jolt from Johnson knocked him off his stride. Stewart was in scoring distance again only a few seconds later and only a superb stop by Miller prevented a goal.

Johnson and Ward were penalized, but both were back again before any damage was done. The Rangers then swept down in another hurricane raid, and after a wild scrimmage around the Maroon net Boucher drove the disk into the net over Benedict's prostrate body. The pass was from Bill Cook and the time of the goal was 6:15.

Murdock, Boyd and Bourgault relieved the Cooks and Boucher on the Ranger forward line. Murdock, checking very fast on Nelson Stewart, gave the big boy a bad spill and went off the ice for two minutes.

The Maroons blazed down at terrific speed, but could not score, and the second period ended with the count—Rangers 1, Maroons 0. Miller had eight saves and Benedict eleven in the period.

Ranger offensives broke out at hurrican speed at the opening of the third period. Good combination play by Bill Cook, Murdock and Boucher dashed in on Benedict time and again but could not beat the tall goalie.

Play whirled up and down the ice at wild speed. Johnson and Stewart were put off for a mix-up inside the Ranger blue line. The Ranger defense man was playing with a badly swollen left eye.

Miller and Bun Cook were flat in front of the Ranger net to stem a savage attack by Stewart and Hooley Smith.

With the crowd wildly yelling for a tying goal, players were spilled in all directions around the Ranger net as the Maroons charged in but the Maroons could not beat Joe Miller and the final score was Rangers 1, Maroons 0.

The line-up:

Rangers (1).		Maroons (0).
Miller	Goal	Benedict
Abel	Defense	Seibert
Johnson	Defense	Dutton
Boucher	Centre	Smith
Bun Cook	Wing	Stewart
Bill Cook	Wing	Ward
Bourgault	Sub	Munro
Gray	Sub	Phillips
Boyd	Sub	Oatman
Murdock	Sub	Brown
Callighen	Sub	——

First Period.

No scoring.

Second Period.

1—Rangers, Boucher 6:15

Third Period.

No scoring.

Penalties—First period: Bourgault, Oatman, Johnson, Smith, two minutes each. Second Period: Johnson, Ward, Murdock, two minutes each. Third period: Bun Cook, Smith, Johnson, Stewart, two minutes each.

Referees—Marsh and Rodden.

April 13, 1928

RANGERS WIN, 2-1, OVER THE MAROONS; TAKE WORLD'S TITLE

Throng of 14,000 in Constant Uproar at Stanley Cup Hockey Final in Montreal.

BOUCHER HEROIC FIGURE

Scores Both New York Goals by Brilliant Efforts—Miller, Johnson Hurt, Gamely Continue.

RAGING CROWD HALTS FRAY

Litters Ice With Paper When Offside Ruling Voids Maroon Goal—Phillips Tallies for Losers.

By SEABURY LAWRENCE.

Special to The New York Times.

MONTREAL, April 14.—Amid scenes of wild excitement and in a game of thrills and dramatic play the New York Rangers won the Stanley Cup and the world's championship in hockey by defeating the Montreal Maroons by a 2-1 score before 14,000 frenzied fans at the Forum tonight.

It was a savage and bitter battle all the way, with the Maroons going down fighting, but conquered by a team whose spirit and pluck in desperate circumstances finally won over all obstacles in the fifth and final game of this hard-fought series.

All of the Rangers played the most courageous and spirited kind of hockey, but three figures stood out as supreme in this battle of heroes. Frank Boucher, swift centre, who scored both Ranger goals on thrilling individual plays; Joe Miller, who gave a wonderful exhibition of goal tending with his right eye badly injured, and Ching Johnson, great defense man, who, with leg, eye and nose injuries, kept on body checking the heavy Maroons to a standstill.

Play had hardly started when a flying disk from Hooley Smith struck Miller in the right eye and he fell to the ice. He was taken off and the eye attended by a physician. Miller returned to the fray with the eye almost closed and all through the frenzied action stuck to his guns and saved scores time and again by cool, deft plays.

Boucher Saves Situation.

After the injury the odds turned heavily against the Rangers and it looked as if their cause was tottering. The Maroon fans had not figured on Frank Boucher, however, as a situation saver.

It was a rough as well as a swift game, twenty-one penalties being handed out by th referees in the three periods. Ching Johnson went off four times for penalties and three times for injuries and came back smiling every time.

Lorne Chabot, Ranger goalie, whose left eye was badly injured in last Saturday night's game, sat on the side lines watching his teammates play. Chabot left the Royal Victoria Hospital late today for the first time since the accident, but must return to the hospital after the game. He wore a black patch over the injured eye.

Each team had an additional substitute forward in tonight's game. Paul Thompson of the Rangers and Joe Lamb of the Maroons, who received match penalties for fighting last Tuesday night, returned to the fray.

Standing room only was the order of the night once more, although the streets were deep in slush after today's snowstorm. Speculators were getting as much as $35 for single tickets. It was the biggest hockey night in Montreal in years.

A blizzard of torn papers was thrown at the rush end when the Maroons came out to the chorus of organized cheering. The Rangers were booed. Murdock started at left wing in place of Bun Cook, whose right foot, cut in the last game, was not in good shape. The Maroons started dashing in at high pressure right after the opening whistle, and Miller made several good stops before the game was two minutes old.

Frank Boucher kept poke-checking the disk away from the Maroon forwards as they skated down and twice got through with Bill Cook, only to have Benedict turn the shots aside.

A wild Maroon rally then raged around the Ranger net, and Miller, the goalie, fell, his right eye being cut by the disk driven off Hooley Smith's stick. The goalie was helped up and had to leave the ice, the game being held up while Miller went to the dressing room to receive attention.

Miller Returns, Is Cheered.

After a delay of ten minutes, Miller returned to the game and was cheered by the crowd. Johnson was penalized, and while the Rangers were a man shy the Maroons came roaring down. Miller, despite his injured eye, made magnificent stops on Stewart and Hooley Smith to prevent a goal.

Johnson came back, but was soon sent off again for tossing Smith. Bill Cook followed Johnson off for crashing into Ward and the Rangers were down to four men. It was a rough spot for the injured goalie, as the Maroons came crashing down, but again Miller saved a desperate situation.

With Johnson and Bill Cook back, Frank Boucher staged the most sensational play of the series when he secured the disk inside the Ranger blue line and zigzagged through the entire Maroon team to score the first goal of the game.

Boucher skated in close and had nobody to beat but Benedict. He feinted the Maroon goalie out of position and shot the disk over his shoulder into the left side of the net. The time of Bouche's goal was 10:05.

The Rangers were now going like wildfire and on the next play Siebert crosschecked Boucher savagely and was benched. The Maroons went down for a try. Bill Cook and Hooley Smith crashed on the boards and were sent off.

The Maroons kept driving in but could not beat Miller, and the first period ended with the count—Rangers 1, Maroons 0.

Bill Cook and Hooley Smith were still in the penalty box when the second period opened. A cut was opened on Johnson's eye and he had to leave the ice for repairs.

Abel and Siebert went off for roughing and the teams were down to four men each. Johnson got back and as Smith came dashing down Johnson tossed him and he could not shoot. The crowd was in a wild tumult as the attack raged around the Ranger net.

Stewart and Smith both had chances to score but shot across the goal mouth. Miller was flat on the ice to stop another one from Smith.

Murdock was sent off and the Maroons still came on. With two minutes to go the Rangers played defensive hockey and were booed by the crowd. The bell rang as the New Yorkers ragged the disk and the second period ended with the tally still—Rangers 1, Maroons 0.

Miller was the great hero of the second period, his goal tending under the circumstances being nothing short of marvelous.

Maroons in Wild Attack.

Bourgault and Lamb were still in the coop when the third period opened, but the teams were soon back at full strength with the Maroons staging a wild attack as the crowd roared for a tying goal.

A battle royal raged around Miller, and only more heroic work by the little goalie saved the situation. Twice he came out of the net to bat the disk away, once the whole length of the rink.

Finally the Maroons surrounded the net, and with Miller down, Oatman drove the disk into the webbing. The red light flashed and the crowd was in a frenzy, but the cheers turned to groans as the play was called offside and not allowed.

The crowd went into a rage and a blizzard of torn paper and programs, not to mention several hats and a chair, were thrown on the ice. The play was stopped for ten minutes while the attendants cleaned the ice.

The next faceoff was just to the right of the Ranger net. Bill Cook got it away and into safe territory. Lamb, Oatman and Phillips came on for the Maroon forward line and drove in heavily on Miller. A shot by Oatman missed by inches.

Miller Saves With Hand.

In a wild rally at the Ranger net Miller lost his stick and plunged on the ice to save with his hand. Johnson was sent off and was soon followed by Abel. With both of the

Frank Boucher won the Lady Byng Trophy seven times. He was the playmaker on the great Ranger line that included Bill and Bun Cook.

big Ranger defense men off, the Maroons kept charging down.

It looked like a sure thing for the tying goal, but here Frank Boucher changed the complexion of affairs by scoring a second Ranger goal in 15:15 after another brilliant individual play.

Phillips scored the only Maroon goal in 17:50 on a pass from Siebert. Bill Cook got a major penalty for stick-ending Stewart. The Rangers were down to five men as the game ended, but the Maroons could not crash through for another one and the final count was—Rangers 2; Maroons 1.

The line-up:

Rangers (2).		Maroons (1).
Miller	Goal	Benedict
Abel	Defense	Dutton
Johnson	Defense	Siebert
Boucher	Centre	H. Smith

Bun Cook	Wing	Stewart
Bill Cook	Wing	Ward
Murdoch	Sub	Oatman
Bourgault	Sub	Lamb
Boyd	Sub	Phillips
Thompson	Sub	Munro
Callighen	Sub	Walsh
Gray	Sub	Brown

First Period.

1—Rangers, Boucher 17:05

Second Period.

No scoring.

Third Period.

2—Rangers, Boucher 15:15
3—Maroons, Phillips 17:50

Penalties—First period: Siebert 2, Johnson 2 Bill Cook, two minutes each; Bill Cook, Smith, five minutes each. Second period—Thompson 2, Siebert, Abe, Murdock, Bourgault, two minutes each; Third period: Johnson, Abel, two minutes each; Bill Cook, five minutes.

Referees—March and Rodden.

April 15, 1928

American Fans Not Enthusiastic Over Play-Off System in Hockey

Post-Season Games, in Which First Three Teams in Each Group Compete, Not Popular—Rangers-Pirates Game, Originally Carded for Pittsburgh, to End Season Here March 17.

By GROVER THEIS.

As the days grow longer the hockey season steadily becomes shorter. Indeed, the regular schedule is approaching the vanishing point, with the last game here listed for Sunday, March 17, between the Rangers and Pittsburgh.

This game was originally scheduled to be played in Pittsburgh on March 12, but the switch to New York was decided upon yesterday, the club officials making use of a final Sunday in the Garden before the league play-offs. Incidentally, the contest will formally bring the schedule for the league to a close.

However, the end of the routine schedule is not the end of hockey, and an elaborate system of play-offs must be completed before the winner of the Stanley Cup, emblematic of the world's championship, is known.

A number of changes have been made in the play-offs this season, all intended to expedite the procedure. Many fans on this side of the border are clamoring for a more radical revision of the rules, so as to provide something similar to the baseball world's series, instead of having a post-season merry-go-round of games in which the teams that finish in the first three places all have a chance to capture the trophy.

Ratings Are Puzzling.

Some fans cannot reconcile themselves to seeing a team cantering home in third place and then rating on virtually equal terms with another team that has kept in the forefront over the entire schedule.

With the end of the regular season in sight, the official description of the new play-off system is appended so that the enthusiasts who may be a bit bewildered as they contemplate the impending post-season games may study the ramifications. The Stanley Cup conditions are as follows:

A. The club at the head of the regular league standing in the American section shall play with the club at the head of the regular league standing in the International section a series of best three out of five games, the first two games in 1929 to be played on the home ice of the club leading the American section and the subsequent games on the ice of the club leading the International section.

B. The club finishing second in the regular league standing in the American section shall play home and home games with the club finishing second in the regular league standing in the International section, majority

of goals to count, the first game to be played on the ice of the club of the International section.

Third-Place Teams to Compete.

C. The club finishing third in the regular league standing in the American section shall play a series of home and home games with the club finishing third in the regular league standing in the International section, majority of goals to count, the first game to be played on the home ice of the club of the American section, unless such arrangement shall be prevented by occupation of the ice by a club playing in Series A, in which event the first game shall be played on the home ice of the club of the International section.

Of the games played in B and C the first shall continue for sixty minutes. If the total score is tied at the end of the regulation period in the second, the winner shall be decided by the first goal scored in overtime play.

D. The winner in Series B shall then play the winner in Series C a series of best two out of three games, choice of ice for the first (and third, if necessary) to be at the discretion of the club finishing highest in the combined league standings.

E. Winner of Series D shall then play a final series with the winner of Series A, best two out of three games. Winner of Series A shall have choice of ice for first and third games. Each game shall be played to a finish.

March 7, 1929

RANGERS DEFEATED BY BOSTON, 2 TO 1

Bruins Take Stanley Cup Series in Two Straight Games, Dethroning Champions.

GOAL BY CARSON DECIDES

Breaks 1-1 Deadlock With Two Minutes Left in 3d Period—Oliver Makes First Goal.

KEELING'S SHOT TIES SCORE

Comes in 6:48 of the Last Session —14,000 See Stirring Game in the Garden.

By GROVER THEIS.

The Boston Bruins took the Stanley Cup away from the New York Rangers last night, winning at the Garden by 2 to 1 before 14,000 spectators. With the cup the world's championship went to another American city in the first battle for the hockey title ever fought between two teams from this side of the border.

The Bruins carried off the prize in two straight games, having won on Thursday night at Boston by the score of 2 to 0. The Rangers defeated the Montreal Maroons last year in a grueling series to bring the prize to the United States for the first time after having eliminated the same Boston Bruins in the semi-finals.

It was only after a dazzling third period, however, that Boston wrested the cup from the previous champions. Les Patrick's men went into the final session one goal behind and there seemed to be every likelihood that they would stay there because of the strong Boston defense. Butch Keeling, hero of two of the play-off games that landed the Rangers in the final series, then counted in 6:48 after Harry Oliver had scored in 14:01 of the second period.

The rather slim crowd for a championship game roared itself hoarse at Keeling's achievement and was looking forward to overtime and perhaps sudden death play, when Bill Carson dashed their hopes with a flashy shot with two seconds less than two minutes to go in the final session.

The Bruins were undefeated in the play-offs, defeating the Canadiens in three straight games and then winning two in a row from the Rangers. Only three goals were tallied by the opposition in the five games.

The second defeat of the Rangers, carrying with it the Stanley Cup, makes the record of the Bostonians seven out of eight games over the Rangers since the season started last November. During the regular season the Bruins won five out of six games from the New Yorkers. It seemed impossible by virtue of the law of averages that they would keep up this pace, but they proved they could even upset the law of averages.

On behalf of the Rangers it should be said that their gruelling tests in the play-offs against the Americans and Maple Leafs, together with their long travels, took their toll, but nothing should detract from the Boston victory. The Bruins proved themselves real champions. Their defense again showed itself nearly impervious.

Bruins Favored in Betting.

The Bruins opened favorites in the betting at odds 8 to 5, but just before action started 7 to 5 could be had in favor of Boston.

After the face-off Eddie Shore made the first onslaught on the Rangers' goal, upsetting Taffy Abel on his way. Ching Johnson was bowled over soon afterward. Bill Carson drew the first penalty for elbowing.

The Bruins were full of fight, however, and they made several assaults upon Roach, none of which, however, got far beyond the Blue line. In one of them Hitchman was banished for holding.

Neither side was taking many chances. Bill Cook ventured forth on one occasion, but despite the fact that he got by Shore he could not connect. Abel was sent off a moment later for tripping. While the Rangers' forces were thus reduced the Bruins sent down a sortie, and Gainor made a thrust on which Roach had to jump to complete the save.

The blue shirts were far more animated than the night before in Boston, and as Keeling and Murdoch got out on the ice, the Bruins had all they could do to prevent a score, the pair of them combining neatly to give Tiny Thompson all sorts of trouble. The Bruins were not slow to retaliate, for Bill Carson made a sizzling drive at Roach. Galbraith and Carson again advanced in much the same manner to give John Ross something to worry about.

Hitchman Sent Off Ice.

As the Rangers unloosed a new offensive Hitchman was sent off for tripping as the period ended. A recapitulation of the session showed the Rangers were playing a much faster game than they displayed the night before in Boston. Their defense gave the changing forward line plenty of time to roam even if the Rangers could not penetrate Boston's stalwart defense.

The saves for the period were ten for Thompson to seven for Roach.

The Rangers opened the second period with a lot of pretty skating and passing, but they always found a carefully devised Bruin defense breaking up their efforts.

The action was confined mostly to the blue lines with the first big thrill coming when Oliver crashed down on Roach and the disk almost went in on a rebound that hit Abel's skate. It was not long before Oliver was banished for elbowing. The Rangers tried to take advantage of this and Bun Cook made a daring sortie, but Thompson stopped the flying disk.

Bill Cook a moment later was banished for carrying a high stick, otherwise known as slashing. He had hardly climbed over the boards before Eddie Shore went off for the same offense and then Bun Cook

emulated his brother and also went off for slashing.

The rising tide of penalties reflected the rising speed of the game. The Bruins put themselves in the lead with a sudden dash by Harry Oliver, who stick-handled his way right through the Ranger back lines to score in 14:01.

The red light had barely been extinguished when Dit Clapper took a rebound from Connie Weiland and nearly repeated. Roach saved by less than an eyelash. Then Roach was menaced again when Clapper took Hitchman's rebound off the boards just before the bell sounded. The gallant New York goalie was kept busy and distinguished himself by his work, despite Oliver's shot which got by him.

With three goals scored against them in the second period of the two Stanley series games, things looked dark for the Rangers as they entered the third period. In Boston on Thursday it was Clapper and Gainor who wrecked the Rangers' hopes in the second period. Ranger fans, however, clung to the desperate hope of a Ranger come-back. Nevertheless they feared the solidity of the Bruin defense with a one-goal advantage.

Oliver almost added to the Boston lead at the very outset of the third period when he twisted his way around Abel and Johnson for a quick shot which Roach, however, was able to stop.

Murdoch Tries for Goal.

Out to equalize the count, the Blue Shirts darted forth with all the daring they have and Murray Murdoch lashed a furious drive at Thompson, which the latter had a hard time to stop. As play resumed another flashing Ranger came out of a scrimmage, and again the Ranger hopes ran high, only to find Tiny playing the rôle of nemesis.

Meanwhile, the Bruin defense was always organized, with the Rangers sending man after man up here in an effort to equalize the count. Manager Patrick suddenly shot Butch Keeling into the line-up and right from a face-off Keeling did the trick in 6:48.

Butch got the pass on the face-off on the Blue line, and with a few steps and a short snap put the disk past Thompson. The goal elicited a roar from the crowd comparable to the roars that greeted the Bruin goals in Boston Garden the night before. However, the showers of paper were missing to make the scene the same.

When the shouting had died down, Shore went to the penalty box for two minutes for elbowing. Replacements came out in rapid succession as Ross and Patrick matched their wits. The Bruins and the Rangers swarmed all over the ice in their wild efforts to get an advantage.

As the teams stormed against each other, Bill Carson took a pass from Oliver and put the Bruins ahead in 18:02, while both teams were scattered around the Ranger net. It was a shot that seemed to come from nowhere, but it settled the Stanley Cup issue.

The line-up:

Boston (2).	Rangers (1).
T. Thompson ......Goal...........	Roach
Shore ....Defense...........	Abel
Hitchman ....Defense...........	Johnson
W. Carson ......Centre...........	Boucher
Oliver ....Wing...........	Bill Cook
Galbraith ....Wing...........	Bun Cook
Mackay ....Spare........	Murdoch
Weiland ....Spare........	F. Thompson
Owen ....Spare........	Keeling
Denneny ....Spare........	Vail
Clapper ....Spare........	Oatman
Lane ....Spare........	S. Carson
Klein ....Spare........	Bourgault
Gainor ....Spare........	

No scoring.

Second Period.

1—Boston, Oliver 14:01

Third Period.

2—Rangers, Keeling 6:48
3—Boston, W. Carson 18:02
Penalties—First period: Hitchman 2, W. Carson, Abel, two minutes each; second period: Bill Cook, Oliver, Shore, Bun Cook, two minutes each; third period: Shore, two minutes.
Referees—Mallinson and Hewitson.

March 30, 1929

NEW HOCKEY RULES TO HELP SCORING

National Officials at Meeting Act to Make the Game More Open This Year.

MINOR INFRACTIONS CUT

Forward Passing Now Permitted in All Zones—Referee's Duties Are Lightened.

By GROVER THEIS.

The clamor last year against games was recognized at least in part by new rules when the National Hockey Association gathered yesterday in its semi-annual meeting at the Hotel Plaza. Each action taken yesterday was designed to open up the game and give the offense a better chance than the obvious defensive of the past.

There was speculation as to what the new game might do and some of the old-liners clung tenaciously to hockey as it has been played, but after much discussion it was conceded that the experiment might be worth while. The officials passed two rules as follows:

"The ice shall be divided into three sections known as the defending zone, the neutral zone and the attacking zone. It is permitted to pass the disk forward by one player to another of the same side in each of these zones, but it shall not be permitted to pass the disk by a player from one zone to a player of the same side in any other zone unless the player taking the pass crosses the zone line behind the disk."

"Not more than three players, including the goal keeper of the defending side, may be in their defending zone when the disk is in any other zone. Should a team violate this rule it shall incur a minor penalty for each offense, the penalty being awarded to the fourth player entering the zone. If more than one player offends at the same time the offending player nearest to the play shall get the penalty."

Analyzed, the two rules mean that hockey this year will afford more chances for scoring than in the past. The tight games of recent seasons have been discouraging to fans and the hockey magnates have been considering the newly adopted rules for some time. They have been in effect in various sections of the Coast and Western Canada, but except for a trial game last season between the Pirates and the Rangers they have not been acknowledged in the major circuit. That game produced enough scoring but it hardly proved anything.

The major prospect is that the referees will have less whistling to do than they did in the past with the elimination of so many minor infractions.

Aside from the business pertaining to rules, the officials approved of the annual schedule of games which, however, will not be made public until Oct. 10, and accepted the resignation of Dave McGill as a governor of the organization. He will be replaced by William Foran.

As far as could be ascertained the schedule, which will occupy attention through the Winter, will open on Nov. 14 when the Canadiens will meet the Ottawa Senators, the Rangers facing Montreal, Chicago against Toronto and Boston against Detroit. The New York Americans will open in Ottawa and Pittsburgh will open in Montreal on Nov. 16. The first game in Madison Square Garden will be on Nov. 17, a Sunday.

September 29, 1929

HOCKEY RULE MODIFIED.

League Lifts Defense Restriction Contained in New Code.

MONTREAL, Nov. 13 (By Canadian Press).—On the eve of the inauguration of the 1929-30 National Hockey League campaign, one modification in the new code of rules is announced from the League's headquarters here.

The rule which compels only three defending players, including the goal-keeper, to be in the defense area when the puck is not actually in that part of the rink has been changed and now reads that only three defense players, including the goal-keeper, may be in the defense area "until any member of the attacking side has crossed the blue line."

This will, it is believed, tend to prevent the puck-carrier dashing across the blue line and whipping a pass to an uncovered man who has preceded him into that territory.

November 14, 1929

STANLEY CUP WON BY CANADIEN SEXTET

Montreal Six Defeats Boston, 4-3, for Second and Deciding Victory of Final Play-Off.

WINNERS START WITH RUSH

Score Twice in First Period, McCaffery and Wasnie Tallying Goals.

BRUINS' LATE DRIVE FAILS

Trailing, 4-1, They Count Twice in Last Session—13,000 Pack Montreal Forum.

By JOSEPH C. NICHOLS.
Special to The New York Times.

MONTREAL, April 3.—The Canadiens are the new professional hockey champions of the world. In one of the most surprising form reversals in the history of the rink sport, the local sextet came through tonight to register its second successive triumph over the Boston Bruins, and toppled the American outfit from its championship throne.

A crowd of more than 13,000 persons which filled the Montreal Forum to capacity witnessed the flying Frenchmen score a 4-to-3 victory in a game that was fraught with thrills during almost every minute of play. The achievement brings the Stanley Cup, symbolic of the title, to this city after it had remained in the possession of the Boston team for a year.

Fired by their generally unexpected success at Boston on Tuesday night, when they turned back the Bruins by the score of 3 to 0; the local players showed themselves complete mas-

---

ters of their rivals for two periods tonight.

Taking the lead in the opening session with a brace of goals and accounting for two more tallies in the second chapter while the Bruins counted once, the Canadiens filled their followers with great expectations of an easy victory.

Bruins Easily Repulsed.

Boston seemed dazzled and bewildered by the locals' speed for the first two sessions, and its best efforts were so easily repulsed that the game, despite its plenitude of exciting moments, took on the aspect of a rout.

But the final chapter altered the complexion of the situation entirely, for the Bruins came through with a remarkable spurt that swept everything in its path, and which just fell short of effecting a stalemate. Harried and goaded to a tigerish fury by the ease with which their best early efforts were turned back, the Boston contingent came up for the third round with a power that was entirely unlooked for.

The Bruins battled the local outfit savagely and gradually transformed the Canadien crew from an aggregation of confident stickwielders into a body of grimly determined guardsmen who sought desperately, and in the end, successfully, to preserve their net from the onslaught which would have brought about a tie.

Howie Morenz, sterling centre for the Montreal team, was the big factor in the locals' victory. He played as long as any one on either team and proved a veritable thorn in the side of the Boston outfit. The speedy local star was the main cog in every important Canadien advance and co-operated perfectly with his team-mates in effecting the local scores.

Morenz Also Stars on Defense.

He was ably aided by Sylvio Mantha and Burt McCaffery in bringing about the Bruins' downfall. Morenz also was of great aid to his mates in breaking up Boston's heavy advances and shifting the course of the puck from the direction of Montreal's goal frequently.

Eddie Shore rose to the heights for Boston. The belligerent defense star of the Bruins waged a ceaseless struggle, both in the protection of his own net and the bombardment of his rivals'. It was Shore who scored Boston's first goal, which came at a time when the Canadiens were comfortably leading, and it was his fighting spirit and tenacity that inspired the visitors to approach within an ace of the Canadiens' total. Neither his efforts nor those of his team-mates were equal to the task of spiking the Canadiens' opening guns, however, and it was this inability that spelled defeat for the Bruins.

From the very start the local sextet besieged the Bruins' net and raked the visitors' defense with a steady fire that drove the 1929 champions back in desperation.

Morenz descended upon the Bruins' goal in a blinding dash just after the opening face-off, and he almost got the disk past Thompson in the Boston net on his first shot. The latter repelled the effort, but was kept busy in the moments immediately following, turning back a steady stream of speedy shots.

Canadiens Repeat Attacks.

There was no way open for the Bruins to shift the attack from their territory. The Canadiens persisted in the aggressive and their advances were furious. Boston was handicapped seriously when it lost Galbraith and Oliver on penalties, but the disadvantage was seemingly lessened several seconds later when the Canadiens were deprived of the services of Morenz, who was penalized after bringing the disk to Boston's blue line.

His absence did not cause any diminution of the Canadien attack, however, and Montreal skated through for its first goal when McCaffery scored on a pass from Lepine in 9:08. Nick Wasnie accounted for the second local tally when he re-

STAR WHO HELPED CANADIENS WIN STANLEY CUP.

Howie Morenz, Who Scored Victors' Fourth Goal Last Night, Providing Margin by Which Canadiens Beat Boston, 4 to 3, in Final Game.

ceived a diagonal pass from Burke and shot it past Thompson in 16:46.

The Bruins made several efforts to retrieve these goals as the period drew to a close, but their efforts were feeble, and they found no loophole in the Montreal guard.

In the second session the Canadiens continued to assert their all-round superiority, and they registered their third tally when Sylvio Mantha dashed in to take the rubber from Nick Wasnie and flip it past Thompson in 10:05.

Shore followed this achievement several minutes later by scoring his goal. He guided the disk past the Canadiens' defense, and scored, unassisted, in 16:50. His contribution was discounted a minute later, when Morenz slipped through for a tally after receiving a pass from Leduc.

Boston Makes Late Drive.

Boston took to the ice determinedly in the final session and soon gave evidence that it was still in the fight. Shore paved the way for several of the visitors' advances until he was penalized, but after his return the Bruins took up the aggressive and scored in 5:55, when Galbraith counted on a relay from Oliver.

Dit Clapper and Cooney Weiland made the next Boston score, which the former sent into the net in 8:00. For the rest of the session Boston waged a vicious battle in the endeavor to tally once more, but its efforts were capably smothered, al-

though the red light shone once for the American sextet when it sent the disk into the Montreal net in the final minute. This was disallowed, however, due to an off-side.

The line-up:

Canadiens (4).		Boston (3).
Hainsworth	Goal	Thompson
S. Mantha	Defense	Shore
Burke	Defense	Hitchman
Morenz	Centre	Barry
Larochelle	Wing	Galbraith
Joliat	Wing	Oliver
Mondou	Spare	Weiland
Wasnie	Spare	Clapper
Leduc	Spare	Gainor
Lepine	Spare	Owen
McCaffery	Spare	W. Carson
G. Mantha	Spare	Mackay
G. Carson	Spare	Connor
Desrivieres	Spare	Lane

First Period.

1—Canadiens, McCaffery (Lepine)......9:08
2—Canadiens, Wasnie (Burke)..........16:46

Second Period.

3—Canadiens, S. Mantha (Wasnie)....10:05
4—Boston, Shore 16:50
5—Canadiens, Morenz (Leduc).......17:50

Third Period.

6—Boston, Galbraith (Oliver).......... 5:55
7—Boston, Clapper (Weiland) 8:00

Penalties—First period: Galbraith, Oliver, Morenz 2, Hitchman (2 minutes each). Second period: Mackay, Galbraith, Larochelle (2 minutes each). Third period: Larochelle, Shore 2, S. Mantha, Lepine, Morenz, Barry (2 minutes each).

Referees—Hewitson and Mallinson. Time of periods—20 minutes.

April 4, 1930

HOCKEY CIRCUIT RULES TO KEEP 4 MEN ON ICE

National League Revises Penalty Regulations in Convention at Toronto.

TORONTO, Sept. 27 (Canadian Press).—No less than four players on the ice at one time will be the rule in the National Hockey League this year, following the adoption of a delayed penalty system by the governors of the association in convention today.

If two players are off the ice serving penalties, and a third man is penalized, a substitute will be allowed in the third man's place. At the expiration of the shortest penalty being served by the first two men, the third penalty will begin, it was decided.

Other modifications provide for an automatic ten-minute penalty being given a player who cuts, either accidentally or otherwise, another player across the head or face with his stick; the aggressor in a fight to get a major penalty, while his opponent receives a minor; penalties for players intentionally knocking the stick from an opposing player's hand, and a penalty for a player who has lost his stick and takes part in any play.

The general meeting of the National League will be held in Chicago next Saturday. At next week's meeting the question of the playing schedule will be taken up, and it is expected decision will be reached as to whether or not the Pittsburgh Pirates will play their home games in Philadelphia.

Among the delegates at the meeting were W. B. Dwyer, New York Americans, and Colonel John Hammond, New York Rangers.

September 28, 1930

TWIN MAJOR PENALTY ABOLISHED IN HOCKEY

20-Minute Ban for Deliberate Slashing About Head Voted by National League.

DETROIT, Dec. 1 (AP).—The double major penalty for cutting an opponent with a stick was wiped out of the books today at the regular meeting of the governors of the National Hockey League.

The rule, which had been in force only since the opening of the 1930-31 season, was legislated out of existence, effective with tomorrow's games.

In its place will be a rule distinguishing between intentional and unintentional slashes. Unintentionally cutting an opponent will draw for the offender five minutes in the penalty box, as in former years, while deliberately slashing a player about the head will bring the offender a twenty-minute match penalty.

The rule abolished called for a ten-minute penalty for all cuts, regardless of whether they were intentional or unintentional. Strict enforcement had met with disfavor in most league cities. Representatives of Detroit, Boston and Chicago clubs voted for its retention and New York Rangers, New York Americans, Toronto, Philadelphia and Montreal voted for its abolition. The Canadiens and Ottawa were not represented.

December 2, 1930

POLICE QUELL FIGHT AS BRUINS WIN, 8-0

Squad of 12 Rushes on Boston Ice to Stop Fist Battle Between the Quakers and Rivals.

SEVEN PLAYERS ARE FINED

Also Draw Major Penalties for Mixing in Wild Melee—Detroit Beats Toronto, 10-1.

BOSTON, Dec. 25 (AP).—After the Boston Bruins piled up an eight-goal lead on the scoreless Philadelphia Quakers tonight, the latter players dropped their sticks and engaged in a savage mêlée with their high-scoring rivals.

The battle started when Milks, Philly forward, struck George Owen, who had checked him near the Boston net. Eddie Shore, Bruin defense star, rushed to Owen's aid, but Allen Shields crossed his path and they swapped blows. Every player on the ice with the exception of Petch Cude, the Quakers' goalie, then entered the fray and peace was not restored until a dozen policemen were rushed onto the ice.

Referees Bill Shaver and Mickey Ion imposed major penalties on Owen, Shore, Clapper, Milks, Coulson and Shields, the players most conspicuous in the most disorderly hockey scene ever staged in Boston. The police detail came out again, just before time expired, when Jerry Lowery struck Marty Barry during a mid-ice scrimmage. Lowery, the officials decided, was at fault and he received a major penalty, a minor being imposed on Barry. Fines of $15 accompanied each major penalty. Shore spent 32 minutes in the penalty box.

The line-up:

Boston (8).		Philadelphia (0).
Thompson	Goal	Cude
Shore	Defense	Shields
Owen	Defense	Coulson
Weiland	Centre	Milks
Clapper	Wing	Kilrea
Harris	Wing	Howe

Goals—Clapper 3, Barry 2, Oliver, Weiland, Beattie.

Spares—Boston: Beattie, Oliver, Barry, Galbraith, Pratt, Chapman, Hitchman. Philadelphia: Lowery, Jarvis, Hutton, McCalium, Barton, Lymond, Drury, McKinnon.

Penalties—McCalium, Shore, Jarvis, Coulson 4, Shields, McKinnon 2, Kilrea, Owen, Barry 2, 2 minutes each; Shore, double major; Coulson, Shore, Clapper, Shields, Owen, Milks, Lowery, majors.

Referees—Shaver and Ion. Time of periods—20 minutes.

Detroit Beats Toronto, 10—1.

DETROIT, Dec. 25 (AP).—Goalie Benny Grant of the Toronto Maple Leafs spent an unhappy session in front of his team's net tonight while the Detroit Falcons swept the Leafs off their feet to pile up a 10-to-1 victory and set a season's National Hockey League scoring mark to date.

The Falcons, led by their sharpshooter, Ebbie Goodfellow, took the Leafs, and particularly Goalie Grant, by surprise as the game opened and pounded in two goals during the first minute of play. They kept up the scoring spree in the first period until they had five goals. Two more were added in the second period and three in the third, while the lone Toronto goal came midway in the final period.

Goodfellow increased his National League scoring lead by four goals, while George Hay and Herbie Lewis, Falcon wingmen, got two goals apiece, and Carson Cooper and

Larry Aurie sent home one goal each. The Toronto goal came off the stick of Ace Bailey, wingman, with Jackson assisting.

The line-up:

Detroit (10).		Toronto (1).
Dolson	Goal	Grant
Noble	Defense	Clancy
Rockburn	Defense	Day
Goodfellow	Centre	Blair
Aurie	Wing	Bailey
Sorrell	Wing	Cotton

Goals—Goodfellow 4, Lewis 2, Hay 2, Aurie, Cooper, Bailey.

Spares—Detroit: Hicks, Evans, Cooper, McInenly, McCabe, Steele, Hay, Lewis, Frederickson. Toronto: Horner, Conacher, Jenkins, Jackson.

Penalties—Rockburn 3, Clancy 2, McInenly, Steele, Horner, Conacher, Sorrell, Jackson, 2 minutes each.

Referees—George Mallinson and Jerry Goodman. Time of periods—20 minutes.

December 26, 1930

BOSTON SIX BEATEN IN HOCKEY PLAY-OFF

Loses to Canadiens, 3 to 2, in 19 Minutes of Overtime in Deciding Game.

By The Associated Press.

MONTREAL, April 1.—The Montreal Canadiens beat the rugged Boston Bruins, 3 to 2, in overtime tonight, ending their five-game National Hockey League first-place series, the Canadiens winning the play-off, three games to two.

A smashing cross-shot by Wilder Larochelle, Canadien substitute wingman, ended the battle after nineteen minutes of overtime, and gave the Flying Frenchmen the right to meet the Chicago Black Hawks in the Stanley Cup finals.

The Boston Bruins were great in defeat. They were smothered in the first period under a shifty, hurtling, bewildering attack. They got their stride in the second period and with increasing momentum drove furiously in a terrific offensive in the third to tally two goals and tie the score.

The 13,000 fans were tense and tingling with excitement as Canada's sole surviving hope for the Stanley Cup series fought desperately to stay in the running to defend the historic silver trophy it won last season.

Both teams were leg-weary and battered by the four hard games they had played. Boston won the first encounter at home, coming from behind to win 5—4. The Canadiens next defeated the Bruins at Boston, 1—0. The Canadiens took their first home game, 4—3, and then lost to Boston Monday night, 3—1.

The crippled Canadiens, who played without the injured Al Leduc, defensive star, tore into Boston with a vicious offensive in the first period. Boston did not get a shot on Hainsworth till eighteen minutes went by. In this opening session the Canadiens gained a 2-0 lead.

Johnny Gagnon scored first on a pass from Marty Burke; then Lepine took a short pass from Joliat to drive the puck into the corner of the net.

No further score came until the third period, and then Cooney Weiland drove two shots past Hainsworth. He first beat Hainsworth with a cross-shot; then his second marker came from a scramble in Canadiens' defense area.

Canadiens Miss Goal.

A swarm of Canadiens players around Thompson shoved the puck over the line with two minutes to go, but the play was called back.

In overtime the Canadiens drove toward the Boston goal again and again, the sturdy Shore-Hitchman defense stubbornly resisting. Boston seemed tired and waited for a break. Marty Burke rushed into Boston defensive area through centre and sent a quick pass to Larochelle on right wing. The fiery little wingman sent a whistling drive into the corner of the net and the game was over.

Manager Art Ross of the Bruins ran across the ice to congratulate the Canadiens, who go to Chicago tomorrow to meet the Black Hawks Friday and Sunday, after which they return to Montreal to complete the five-game series, playing the first game here Tuesday, and clashing here again on Thursday and Saturday if necessary.

Canadiens in Early Rush.

The Canadiens started Lepine at centre, flanked by Wasnie and Joliat, and the trio made three quick attacks, but Shore and Hitchman stopped them with heavy body-checking. Hitchman charged Lepine and the latter was hurt. Morenz replaced him at centre and jabbed at Hitchman, drawing a penalty.

Lepine had to fill in until Morenz came back, then stayed in the game. Morenz and Lepine crossed the Boston blue line together, but Thompson handled the resulting shot. Shore went off for upsetting Morenz. Owen was ruled off for charging Morenz, leaving the Bruins two short. This cost them a goal.

The Canadiens rushed the play around Thompson and after three tries Gagnon took a pass from Burke and scored in 6:28.

Boston was at full strength again when the Canadiens scored their second tally in 9:08. Joliat flashed through left wing and Lepine rounded the other wing. Joliat drew Thompson out of his net and passed six feet to Lepine, who poked the disk into the goal.

The Boston attacks fell prey to furious checking at centre ice. The long, sweeping poke of Lepine was working to perfection. Beattie and Owen worked in close for chances at Hainsworth, but missed their shots.

Mantha Is Penalized.

Sylvio Mantha went to the box for upsetting Shore as he crossed the defense line. Then George Owen went off the ice for knocking down Morenz as he broke through left wing.

Beattie and Barry crashed through the Canadiens' defense and drew Hainsworth out of his net. He fell to the ice to check their thrusts. S. Mantha got his stick to the puck in the scramble and drove it down the ice.

Burke was penalized for upsetting Hitchman. Boston attacked strongly while the Canadiens were a man short, but offsides spoiled their chances. Morenz rushed at breakneck speed and was checked heavily by Shore, who drew a penalty. Then Owen upset Joliat behind the Boston net and went to the box to join Shore. Boston stood off the Canadiens until Shore's time was up.

Shore tripped Lesieur and went back to the penalty box. Weiland wasted time by ragging the puck. The Canadiens seemed to content themselves by saving themselves for the next period. Oliver got through right wing for a corner shot on Hainsworth.

Lepine took a quick shot on Thompson and Wasnie rifled a long one at the Boston net. Lepine stick-handled the puck out of danger after a furious scramble in the corner near the Canadien goal.

Boston launched a desperate attack as the third period started. Five men skirmished frantically around the Canadiens' goal. The puck came to Hainsworth from all angles. S. Mantha brought the play back to normal with a lofting shot down the ice.

The Canadiens seemed to have decided on a defensive game. They did not carry their plays past the Boston blue line. Weiland and Clapper broke through and missed. Then Weiland dashed trickily from centre ice.

He drew the Canadien defense to the left and drove the disk past Hainsworth on a corner shot in 4:34.

Oliver received a penalty for crashing Gagnon to the ice. The Canadiens appeared tired. Boston was at full strength again and scored the tying goal on a pretty passing play with Hainsworth out of his net. Weiland took a double pass from Barry and Clapper for the scoring shot in 13:42.

Shore upset Morenz in front of the Boston goal and went to the penalty box. Hitchman spilled S. Mantha and the Canadien player had to leave the ice. Then Chapman received a major penalty for cutting Howie Morenz in the face with his stick as the Canadien star bore in on the Bruins' defense. Boston was two men short for a minute before Shore came back.

Canadien Shot Disallowed.

The Canadiens thrust the rubber into the Boston net in a scramble, but the play was called back because Canadien players were in the goal with Thompson. The Canadiens rushed furiously upon Thompson in the last moments of the period.

The Bruins were still without Chapman as the overtime play started. Gagnon made two shots at Thompson, but the latter handled them carefully. Chapman came back and the Bruins were at top strength again. Beattie rushed, but Burke skated him into a corner.

Shore circled the Canadien goal, but lost the puck behind the cage. Both teams were tired, and Boston played a waiting game, trying to outlast the Flying Frenchmen.

The Canadiens kept up their offensive, while Boston waited for a break. Lepine made a wicked shot at the side of the Boston net. The Canadiens' aggressiveness in the extra period then gave them the victory. Burke passed to Larochelle and the Canadien spare slammed a vicious shot into the net from twenty feet out.

The line-up:

Canadiens (3).		Boston (2).
Hainsworth	Goal	Thompson
S. Mantha	Defense	Shore
Burke	Defense	Hitchman
Lepine	Centre	Weiland
Wasnie	Wing	Clapper
Joliat	Wing	Galbraith
Mondou	Spare	Owen
Morenz	Spare	Barry
Gagnon	Spare	Gainor
Larochelle	Spare	Oliver
Lesieur	Spare	Darragh
G. Mantha	Spare	Harris
Rivers	Spare	Pratt
——	Spare	Beattie
——	Spare	Lyons
——	Spare	Chapman

First Period.

1—Canadiens, Gagnon (Burke).......... 6:28
2—Canadiens, Lepine (Joliat).......... 9:08

Second Period.

No scoring.

Third Period.

3—Boston, Weiland.......... 4:34
4—Boston, Weiland (Clapper, Barry).... 13:42

Overtime Period.

5—Canadiens, Larochelle (Burke)....... 19:00

Penalties—First period: Owen 2, Morenz, Shore, S. Mantha, 2 minutes each. Second period: Shore 2, Owen, Burke, 2 minutes each. Third period: Chapman, 5 minutes; Oliver, Shore, 2 minutes each. Overtime period: None.

Referees—Ion and Hewitson.

April 2, 1931

CHICAGO SIX BEATS CANADIENS, 2 TO 1

Gottselig's Goal in 24:50 of Overtime Decides Thrilling Game on Victors' Ice.

17,000 SEE STIRRING FRAY

Black Hawks Even Stanley Cup Title Series at One Victory Each.

WINNERS SCORE FIRST

Adams's Tally in Second Period Is Followed by Wasnie's in Third.

By The Associated Press.

CHICAGO, April 5.—Setting a blistering pace and maintaining it through 24 minutes 50 seconds of overtime, the Chicago Black Hawks tonight defeated the Canadiens of Montreal, world's hockey champions, and evened the Stanley Cup series at one victory each.

The deciding goal was registered by Johnny Gottselig, the Black Hawks' stellar stick-handler, who skated almost lazily up the ice and pounded a fifteen-foot shot past George Hainsworth. The shot ended one of the most bitterly fought contests Chicago has ever seen. More than 17,000 persons witnessed the match.

The Hawks stuck to their original plan of skating the Canadiens to defeat, and while the Frenchmen looked even better than they did in winning by the same score Friday night, they could not hold off an attack in which a new set of forwards was used every two or three minutes.

Stewart Adams put the Hawks into the lead after 11 minutes 45 seconds of the second session. He raced up the centre, split the Montreal defense pair of Burke and S. Mantha and let fly at Hainsworth.

Hawks Hold Advantage.

The shot slipped between Hainsworth's legs and from there on until better than halfway through the third period the Hawks had the advantage.

The Canadiens, a great team to capitalize on breaks, caught the Hawks taking it easy and Nick Wasnie, Larochelle and Howie Morenz crashed in. Morenz's shot was stopped by Chuck Gardiner, but Larochelle flipped the puck to Wasnie, who drove it into the net.

Penalties gave both teams chances to score, but neither could do it until Gottselig staged his surprising act. The battle produced near-fights, and Tommy Cook received a major penalty for slashing S. Mantha over the head in the third session.

The match opened along the same lines as on Friday night. The Black Hawks, depending on speed, tried to sweep the Frenchmen before them and play was in the Canadiens' end of the ice. Gottselig had a shot, and Couture and March each took a try at the net. The Canadiens were waiting for opportunities. Gagnon and Morenz slipped up the ice, nearly beating Gardiner at the cage.

During the first six minutes Chicago had a wide edge in territorial play but failed to do more than bother Goalie Hainsworth.

Joliat saved Montreal from being

scored on when he raced in to head off a shot by March while Hainsworth was out of the net. The Black Hawks still were carrying the battle to the Canadiens, without being able to break through.

Canadiens' Defense Strong.

The Black Hawks changed front lines so frequently that the pace never abated, but the fine defensive efforts of the Flying Frenchmen thwarted every effort. Morenz gave some dazzling exhibitions of speed skating and stick-handling, while Gottselig almost surprised Hainsworth with a hard side shot. With two minutes left, Wentworth went to the penalty box along with Morenz, and the period ended.

Wentworth and Morenz were still in the penalty box when the second frame opened. A couple of minutes after the teams faced off, Hainsworth made a beautiful save of a hard shot by Gottselig, and a moment later Couture came within an ace of beating the Montreal goalie. Gagnon and Wasnie dashed down the ice and Gardiner made a great stop of a short shot by Gagnon. Morenz kept the puck away from three Black Hawks, but took a hard spill in trying to get around Bostrom. Hainsworth fell in saving Adams's hard shot, and Adams also fell in trying to beat his own rebound.

Gardiner Makes Fine Stop.

S. Mantha and Morenz combined for a try, and only a great stop by Gardiner prevented a score. Gottselig worked back for a short shot that forced Hainsworth to move fast. Lepine swept the puck back to centre ice. Both teams were playing open hockey and the puck flashed from one end of the ice to the other while the crowd roared.

Adams put the Black Hawks in front on a sensational lone effort. He took the puck behind the Chicago net, dashed down the centre and, evading Burke, drove the puck past Hainsworth.

The Black Hawk score spurred the Canadiens to greater efforts and they staged a savage assault, with Lepine, Wasnie and Morenz advancing. The Black Hawks were driven back against their cage and Gardiner had to work feverishly for a few moments.

Gottselig, Couture and Romnes were sent down the ice and the battle became even again. During a furious individual dash Morenz skated into Bostrom and the latter's stick flew into the crowd. Graham was penalized for tripping Morenz and the Canadiens hammered away at the Chicago goal. The contest was becoming rough.

A drive from Joliat's stick struck a woman spectator who was sitting in the press section and the game was delayed while she received attention. A moment later Joliat drove another shot that knocked the Chicago goalie from his feet. Graham came out of the penalty box and the Black Hawks staged a rush.

Wentworth went through alone and had a clear shot at Hainsworth but was sent sprawling by Larochelle, who was banished to the penalty box. The Canadiens kept on attacking and the period ended with Lepine and Morenz trying to break through the local defense.

Each team was a man short as the final period started.

Chicago made another fierce assault, but could not score against a great defense. Cook got set to shoot, but Morenz swooped in and stole the puck. S. Mantha came back on the ice and the Black Hawks attacked viciously.

Gottselig saved a score by intercepting a Canadien pass with Gagnon waiting for a wide-open shot.

The Canadiens attacked again and this time broke through to tie the score. Wasnie, Morenz and Larochelle sifted through the Chicago defense and Gardiner saved a shot by Morenz. Wasnie, however, took a pass from Larochelle and slammed the disk past Gardiner in 12:10.

Cook hit S. Mantha on the head with his stick, and the Canadien defense man was assisted to the bench. Cook received a major penalty and Mantha got two minutes in the box. Mantha was charged with tripping Cook before the latter slashed him.

Morenz was booed loudly for shoving Graham with both hands. The Canadiens sent four forwards down the ice as soon as Mantha had served his penalty, and the puck stayed in Chicago territory, except for a dash by Gottselig, just before the third period closed with the score tied at 1—1.

Word was received that Gagnon's father died tonight at Chioutimi, Que., but the Montreal player was not notified as the clubs came back to continue the long battle.

Cook was still in the penalty box when the overtime period started. March had two tries at Hainsworth before Joliat seized the puck to try for Montreal. Ingram got loose and had a straight shot that nearly slipped between Hainsworth's knees. Morenz attempted to win the match all alone and three of his dashes had the crowd in an uproar. The Black Hawks changed the front line every two minutes in an effort to wear the Flying Frenchmen down. The players were becoming tired and small clashes became more frequent. S. Mantha finally drew a penalty for driving March into the boards during a furious Chicago assault.

A Chicago four-man offense followed and the Black Hawks had shot after shot, but Hainsworth rose to great heights to save them all.

Larochelle fought his way down the ice for a shot, only to have Gardiner make another sensational save. The teams finished the first twenty minutes of overtime and time was called while the attendants swept the ice.

Adams got close enough to shoot but lost the puck and crashed into Hainsworth. The Montreal goalie was badly shaken up and required about a half-minute of rest.

The match ended abruptly when Gottselig skated leisurely down the ice and drove a shot that whistled past Hainsworth's right arm. He made no move to stop it, apparently having failed to see the puck.

The line-up:

Canadiens (1).		Chicago (2).
Hainsworth	Goal	Gardiner
S. Mantha	Defense	Graham
Burke	Defense	Bostrom
Lepine	Centre	Romnes
Koliat	Wing	Gottselig
Wasnie	Wing	Couture
Morenz	Spare	Abel
Larochelle	Spare	Wentworth
G. Mantha	Spare	March
Gagnon	Spare	Somers
Rivers	Spare	Arbour
Lasieur	Spare	Jenkins
—	Spare	Cook
—	Spare	Ingram
—	Spare	Adams
—	Spare	Desjardins

First Period.

No scoring.

Second Period.

1—Chicago, Adams 11:45

Third Period.

2—Canadiens, Wasnie (Larochelle)......12:10

Overtime Period.

3—Chicago (Gottselig) 24:50

Penalties—First period, Wentworth, Morenz, 2 minutes each; second period, Graham, Larochelle, March, 2 minutes each; third period, S. Mantha, 2 minutes each; overtime period, Cook, 5 minutes; overtime period, S. Mantha, Ingram, Larochelle, 2 minutes each.

Referees—Bobby Hewitson and Alex Romeril.

April 6, 1931

Players of the Game

Howie Morenz—Speedy Centre of the Canadiens

By JOSEPH C. NICHOLS.
All Rights Reserved.

HOWIE MORENZ, generally regarded as the best of all contemporary hockey players, is helping the Canadiens of Montreal in their fight for the Stanley Cup and the honor it signifies—the world's hockey championship.

Still flashing the burning speed which earned for him the name the Stratford Streak, and still possessing the hard shot and marksman's accuracy which have enabled him to finish each season among the highest scorers in the National Hockey League, the speedy centre of the Flying Frenchmen is playing his large part in the attempt to subdue the rugged Chicago Black Hawks in the current Stanley Cup series.

Always reliable, and at the same time always colorful, Morenz has succeeded in withstanding the buffets of nine years of play with the fastest professional team extant, yet he gives no indication of losing the speed and dash which have characterized him throughout his entire hockey career.

Continues to Maintain Speed.

Several years ago, soon after hockey was introduced in the United States on a large scale, speculation arose concerning the length of time Morenz would be able to continue playing at the pace for which he had become famous. Predictions were offered freely to the effect that he would soon burn himself out, and that presently he would be forced to take his place in the ranks of the great army of stick wielders of no particular individual distinction.

But so far, the Stratford Streak has confounded the prophets. Not only has he just completed a season which many regard as his greatest, but he has gone on to take part in the grueling five-game play-off series against the Boston Bruins, a series in which Morenz was bumped and bruised considerably, but which he finished standing up.

Morenz broke into professional hockey in the Fall of 1922, with the

Associated Press Photo.

HOWIE MORENZ.

Canadiens, and he has been with the Habitants ever since. As a youth he played on the Stratford Blues, where he attracted attention for his sterling performances on the forward line. He teamed with Frank Carson, now a member of the New York Americans, and the pair long enjoyed the distinction of being known as the best forward combination in amateur hockey.

Morenz was born in Mitchell, Ont.,

in 1902, but his family moved to Stratford while he was still a child and it was there that he learned to play the game which has brought him fame. Curiously enough, Howie's boyhood ambition was to play in the nets. He lost this desire, however, when, in a game at Stratford in 1916, he yielded twenty-one goals. Since that time he has always played a forward position, preferably centre, but quite frequently at either left or right wing.

Leo Dandurand, now one of the directors of the Canadiens Hockey Club, was responsible for Morenz turning professional. Morenz, while learning the machinist trade in the Stratford Shops of the Canadian National Railway, also played on the hockey team representing that branch of the system. The Stratford shop sextet played a match in Montreal, and Morenz turned in a brilliant performance to score nine goals.

Was Success From the First.

Dandurand, then managing the Canadiens, sent Cecil Hart, present manager of the club, to Stratford to sign the young star. Morenz signed for Hart just before a delegate from the Toronto team arrived to offer him a contract and the Stratford Streak became the property of the Montreal organization.

Morenz was a success with the Canadiens from the start. Dandurand gave him the regular berth at centre over the veteran Odie Cleghorn when the 1922-23 season started, and the newcomer carried out his assignments so capably that he never was regarded in the light of a substitute player.

His development was rapid, and in a comparatively short time Morenz became the greatest drawing card in the league. Always has he displayed a dashing, seemingly reckless aggressiveness that has made him a favorite with the crowds in all cities. He was top-scorer at the end of the

1928 season, and again led the league for the campaign just completed.

Like most outstanding players, Morenz prefers to carry the stick left-handed, but he is at no disadvantage when forced to wield it from the right side. His ability to shoot from any angle with blinding speed has made him the most feared forward on the ice, and opposing players never hesitate to try to spill him when he is carrying the puck.

But Morenz is not easy to spill. He breaks from mix-ups perfectly when carrying the disk and with his great speed easily reaches open ice, where he can institute the swift passing advances which are the forte of the Canadiens. Strange as it might seem, Morenz is not often called upon to stick-handle his way through the opposition unassisted. This work is given to Aurel Joliat, the wily Canadien wing, who is the strategist of the team. It is Joliat who makes his way into enemy territory, where occur the dazzling sweeps which result as often as not in Morenz caging the puck.

Studies His Opponents.

Morenz is a keen student of the game he plays so well and is ever seeking to improve his effectiveness. He pays particular attention to the styles of the various defense men in the league and knows how to play against each individual opponent in the manner calculated to bring the best results.

In addition to his unquestioned offensive ability, the Stratford flash is an able defensive player, as he demonstrated only recently in the second game of the Bruins-Canadiens series, when the Frenchmen scored a goal in the first period and held it to the end of the game to win. In that contest Morenz harmonized perfectly with his defense men and interrupted many a sturdy Boston advance by his clever back-checking.

Strong proof of Morenz's greatness lies in the fact that he is kept regularly at centre for the Canadiens over Pete Lepine, who is rated as one of the trickiest and most proficient centres in the league. Lepine would encounter little difficulty in annexing the first-string position on several of the other teams in the league, but with the Canadiens he must remain as the spare for Howie Morenz.

Named Most Valuable on Team.

To those who assert he is slowing up, Morenz can answer that, in addition to leading the league in scoring this year, he has received the Dr. Hart trophy for being the most valuable player on his team and, further, that he is the selection of thirty-seven sports writers for centre on the "all" team picked this past Winter.

Morenz is one of the highest paid players in the game, with a salary of approximately $10,000 a year. He is married and has a son, Howie Jr., aged 3 years. Incidentally, the Stratford Streak is a good golfer and spends most of the Summer on the links.

April 6, 1931

13,000 SEE CHICAGO DEFEAT CANADIENS

Wentworth's Goal in 53:50 of Overtime Decides Stanley Cup Game at Montreal.

GAGNON SCORES IN FIRST

Canadiens Take 2-0 Lead When Mantha Registers in Second Period.

BLACK HAWKS COME BACK

Tally Twice Near End of Third Session—Victors Gain 2-1 Margin in Title Series.

By The Associated Press.

MONTREAL, Friday, April 10.—Mervin Wentworth, right defenseman of the Chicago Black Hawks, flicked a high shot past George Hainsworth's shoulder at 12:20 this morning and broke up the longest National Hockey League game of the season. The game went 53 minutes and 50 seconds of overtime before Chicago beat the Montreal Canadiens, 3 to 2, to take a 2-1 lead on games in their struggle for the Stanley Cup, emblematic of the world's professional hockey championship.

The first sixty minutes of the game were played at a fast clip with the Canadiens holding a decided margin in the first two periods and scoring twice. In the third period Chicago fought to draw even and succeeded in a triumphant eighteen-second burst of speed which saw March and Adams score. The overtime session was a grim, close-checking affair with both teams waiting for the break and missing opportunities through overanxiety.

The end came when Adams, Wentworth and Cook burst in on a tired Canadien defense. A few short passes while jockeying for position and a brilliant shot by Wentworth gave Chicago a hard-earned victory and sent a disappointed crowd of more than 13,000 homeward from the Forum.

Meet Again Tomorrow.

The teams will meet again tomorrow night and the Hawks must be considered the favorites. Provided the Canadiens can tie the round at two games each tomorrow a fifth and final game is tentatively scheduled for next Tuesday night here.

Morenz and Joliat advanced, but were stopped at the defense. The crowd had its first taste of excitement when Morenz led a three-man rush, which drove the Black Hawk defense back on Gardiner.

Marsh and Cook broke through the Canadien defense, but Hainsworth made a difficult sliding save of a hard shot. Adams and Cook went back again, and on Cook's brilliant forward pass, Hainsworth barely beat Adams to the puck.

The first goal came when the Black Hawks sent three men into the Canadiens' territory. Burke broke away fast, flanked by George Mantha and Gagnon. Burke's perfect pass from the left side was just missed by Mantha, whom Gardiner obviously expected to make the shot. Gagnon seized the disk and drove it into the goal on an angle shot.

Chicago Extended on Defense.

For the next two minutes the Black Hawks had all they could do to hold the speedy Canadiens. At full strength again Chicago worked a triple pass inside the Canadien blue line. The attack was halted by George Mantha.

Gardiner was struck in the face by Lepine's stick when the centre lost his balance near the goal. The goalie continued without a rest. A little later Gardiner made a beautiful one-handed stop of a shot from Lepine. He fell to the ice but raised one hand to block the puck.

The second period had barely opened when the Black Hawks drove down the ice and Tommy Cook fired a shot. Hainsworth was struck on the nose, which bled copiously. He retired to the dressing room. After approximately ten minutes had passed, the goalie returned with two stitches closing the cut. Adams stick-handled his way brilliantly between the Canadien defense men but his forward pass to Cook went astray and Gagnon seized the puck. Silvio Mantha could not control a rolling puck and a pretty rush was futile. On the next play Morenz and S. Mantha eluded Abel and Morenz dashed to the goal's mouth, but could not get his shot away.

Then came the Canadiens' second goal. Lepine shot from the blue line and skated fast between the defense to snare the puck. He circled Gardiner's net and, finding no chance to score himself, flicked the puck to George Mantha, who sent it high and true into the net.

Mondou Gets Into Game.

Mondou came on the ice for his first appearance since the last game of the Boston series last week and skated for a couple of minutes to try himself out. Silvio Mantha was penalized for criticizing Referee Hewitson on an offside decision.

Desjardins tried a snap shot from a face-off, but missed. On the next Black Hawk rush Lesieur checked Arbour. Then Adams, Cook and March, the best scoring threat for Chicago, dribbled their way deep into Canadien territory, where again Hainsworth saved from Cook. Then Morenz was upset by Cook, the Hawk going to the penalty bench.

Cook was still off the ice when Bostrom ended a Joliat rush by tripping the little winger. He joined Cook in the penalty box. Just as the period ended it looked as though Morenz was about to tally after being held scoreless for seven straight games, but he overskated the puck when past the defense and in an excellent position.

Each team was one man short when the third period opened, but Bostrom returned after a few seconds to give Chicago the advantage. The Canadiens drove the puck up the ice to keep the Chicago attack out of their defense zone. Cook got away a sizzling shot which Hainsworth caught and threw to one side. The puck hit the side of the goal post on the throw but stayed outside.

The Black Hawks sent waves of men, four abreast, up the ice but they found a Canadien front line that was checking perfectly and a sound defense. Gottselig and Silvio Mantha clashed and exchanged a couple of blows with the butt end of the stick. Both were banished.

The penalized men returned and Hawks changed their whole team except the goalie. Hainsworth's foot covered the corner of the goal in front of March's drive from right wing.

Sylvio Mantha took another penalty, his fourth of the game, for cutting down one of the ubiquitous Hawks who was rushing straight at Hainsworth. Lesieur joined Mantha in the penalty box and Joliat, Burke, Lepine and Hainsworth were left to face a full team.

Hainsworth was the target for numerous shots until S. Mantha came back. He stopped the disk from all angles until the team was complete again.

With eight minutes to go the Black Hawks took off a defense man and shot four forwards into action. Hainsworth was hard pressed on a three-man attack in which he barely grabbed the puck and deflected it before two players crashed into him, carrying him to the ice.

Chicago then tied the score with dramatic suddenness. Gottselig broke away at the blue line and slipped a forward pass to March, who raced right in on Hainsworth and drove home a high shot to the corner.

Eighteen seconds later Cook and Adams split the Canadiens' defense and Adams secured the puck a little to the left of the goal. He drove home a swift shot waist-high to equalize the score at 2—2.

Chicago Checks Attack.

Cook was banished for tripping, but the weakened Hawks held on in the face of a speedy four-man attack, although Gardiner was struck in the ear in a rush on which Joliat missed the net by inches. Gardiner retired to the side of the ice. He returned shortly, and the game went into overtime for the second time in the three games played so far in the series.

Twenty-five minutes of overtime had passed when Morenz made a speedy rush which ended when he was checked into the boards. He was forced to take a rest.

After the game had reached the forty-first minute of overtime Burke netted a high shot, but the whistle had sounded before he shot and the effort was disallowed. Hainsworth was bombarded again as Chicago drove forward. The line-up:

Canadiens (2).		Chicago (3).
Hainsworth	Goal	Gardiner
Burke	Defense	Abel
S. Mantha	Defense	Wentworth
Morenz	Centre	Cook
Wasnie	Wing	March
Joliat	Wing	Adams
Mondou	Spare	Somers
Lepine	Spare	Couture
Pusie	Spare	Graham
Larochelle	Spare	Gottselig
Lesieur	Spare	Ingram
G. Mantha	Spare	Bostrom
Gagnon	Spare	Desjardins
Rivers	Spare	Romnes
	Spare	Arbour
	Spare	Ripley

First Period.
1—Canadiens, Gagnon 5:15

Second Period.
2—Canadiens, G. Mantha (Lepine) 7:29

Third Period.
3—Chicago, March (Gottselig) 16:20
4—Chicago, Adams (Cook) 16:38

Overtime Period.
5—Chicago, Wentworth (Adams) 53:50
Penalties—First period: Graham, S. Mantha, 2 minutes each. Second period: S. Mantha, Wentworth, Bostrom, Joliat, 2 minutes each. Third period: S. Mantha 2, Lesieur, Cook, 2 minutes each. Overtime period: Lesieur, Wentworth, Morenz, Abel, March, 2 minutes each.

Referee—Hewitson and Romeril.

April 10, 1931

CANADIENS WIN, 2-0; RETAIN STANLEY CUP

Beat Chicago at Montreal in Fifth and Deciding Game of Title Series.

MORENZ CLINCHES VICTORY

Scores His Only Goal of 10 Play-Off Contests in the Last Five Minutes.

GAGNON GETS OTHER POINT

Tallies in Second Period on Pass From Joliat Before Capacity Crowd of 13,000.

By The Associated Press.

MONTREAL, April 14.—The Stanley Cup and professional hockey's highest honors stay in Montreal for another year. Tonight, while over 13,000 spectators cheered them on, the Montreal Canadiens scored a clean-cut 2-0 victory over the Chicago Black Hawks, Johnny Gagnon and Howie Morenz scoring in the second and third period, respectively.

In a great finish to a great series which had been deadlocked at two victories each before tonight's triumph for the Canadiens, Howie Morenz scored his first goal in ten play-off matches four minutes from the end of the match.

The Canadiens then staged a magnificent defense in the face of a courageous attack by the Chicago team, which only admitted defeat when the final whistle had sounded. The losers then gathered about the winners in mid-ice and, bumps and tempers forgotten, congratulated them heartily.

Chicago was outplayed tonight by a great team and went down fighting. Failure to capitalize on an advantage they held in the first period cost the visitors the game.

The Canadiens' attack did not reach its full strength until the middle period, but from then on it held a small but distinct margin over the best efforts of the eleven Chicago forwards who were changed in a bewildering fashion and kept tearing in to force the break which never came.

Victors Congratulate Gardiner.

The goal saves tell the story of the attacks pretty well. In the first period Gardiner handled 3, while Hainsworth saved 10. In the second, as the Canadiens opened up, Gardiner had 13 stops, while Hainsworth had 3, and in the last period Gardiner handled 9 to Hainsworth's 4.

Gardiner was surrounded by the Canadien team after the match and was dragged off the ice by players wishing to congratulate him on his magnificent work during the series. He was picked up bodily and carried to the Canadien dressing room, where he was the centre of a demonstration.

The Canadiens' share of the world's series money is expected to be the largest on record, while Chicago will also divide a considerable amount.

Tonight's crowd was the third capacity gathering here within a week. Fittingly enough, in view of the importance of the struggle, the game opened with close play and for the first two minutes neither goalie had a save. Gagnon and Joliat led the Canadiens' best thrusts, while Cook and March were Chicago's spearheads. Twice Joliat raced back to rob March before the winger could shoot from close in. Joliat winged a great shot at Gardiner which the goalie took on his knee pads.

Couture fooled Burke and rounded him, but Sylvio Mantha checked and Burke got back in time. Gottselig and Ripley had a great try, but Hainsworth capably handled Ripley's shot, which came from a long rebound from Gottselig. Lepine and George Mantha swept right back, but Lepine's shot from the pass out was just off the net.

Both Goalies Outstanding.

Desjardins, Romnes and Ingram came on for Chicago. Burke broke up a great rush by Graham and led a return which Bostrum defeated. Wasnie raced back in time to prevent Desjardins shooting. The goalies, behind smart defensive work, had little to do. Sylvio Mantha took March out on a determined Hawk rush. Both players crashed into the boards and Burke cleared. The game was wide open and crammed with excitement for the fans. Desjardins and Ingram broke the Canadien defense, but Hainsworth, who had fallen, made a one-handed save. Abel was penalized for cutting down Mondou. The Canadiens made their greatest bid of the period, with Gagnon, Morenz and Joliat continually in Hawk territory, but Gardiner performed beautifully to keep them out. Graham and Bostrum were everywhere on the defense.

Cook and Morenz clashed in centre ice and the light Hawk player fell to the ice. Both were penalized and Gardiner skated up to protest. The referees ruled that both had been guilty in the minor scrap.

Adams made a play which deserved a tally when he robbed Lepine in the Canadiens' area and ran in on Hainsworth, who fell to save. Two minutes of five-man hockey passed without a score. Careless work by the Canadien defense in leaving a loose puck in front of the nets almost cost Montreal dearly when March dashed in to pick it up. Only Hainsworth's coolness stood between March and a score.

As the second period opened Morenz cut loose with one of his old-time rushes which carried him through the defense and in on Gardiner. The goalie made a perfect sliding save as Morenz's speed carried him past the goal and into the boards.

Canadiens Open Strong Attack.

Gagnon caused an argument when he stopped short at the blue line to make his check break the anti-defense rule. The Canadiens pleaded for a penalty and Coach Hart took the wing off to break up the dispute. The Canadiens were winging in their attacks with much more brilliance than during the first period and held an edge on the play. Desjardins careened the length of the ice but was crowded into the corner by Burke. Larochelle and Mondou sent the crowd into an uproar with a short passing attack. The shot, by Mondou, came from five feet out, but Gardiner stopped the thrust. It was a beautiful play. Again Gardiner played perfectly on a rush by Leduc and a shot by Larochelle.

The rebound from Gottselig's long shot lay on the ice in front of Hainsworth, but no Hawk could get back in time. March cracked Leduc over the shins on the next rush and was penalized. During his absence the Canadiens tallied. Morenz stole the puck from Gottselig and passed to Joliat, who crossed the blue line and sent an accurate pass to Gagnon. The wing moved fast, held his shot, and dented the twine high up on the left side.

Both teams then drove to the attack, but the Canadiens' efforts were

soon halted when Leduc drove into Adams and boarded him. Leduc was penalized. Coach Irvin sent on Gottselig, Adams, Cook and March to force a break. Lepine and Morenz forced them on the front line.

The puck rarely left the Canadien end, and Adams seemed to have the tying goal on his stick when Burke raced back to knock the puck high into the stands. The danger passed with Leduc's return.

Tempers flared briefly and players were being knocked down all over the ice. There were no penalties, and the managers quickly pulled the offenders to the side to avoid punishment. Morenz and Cook were arguing, as were Joliat and Adams, as the session closed.

Burke Breaks Up Drive.

The Hawks began a relentless attack to start the third period, sweeping in three men abreast. Burke forced Cook into the corner, checking the first drive. Joliat broke up two rushes and Gagnon retaliated with a fast rush. Gottselig, Ripley and Couture came on.

Wentworth was checked by Leduc, who went straight down centre ice. When he split the defense the puck shot ahead and Gardiner raced forth. The goalie got the rubber, but he and Leduc crashed heavily and Gardiner was hurt in the chest. He resumed after a short rest.

Attack was the best sort of defense against the Hawks' driving style and each team moved from end to end in fast, open rushes. A penalty against Ripley for knocking down Joliat gave the Canadiens a chance which they quickly lost when Wasnie was benched for high-sticking Bostrum.

Graham made a great play on a lone rush, but Leduc stopped the charge. Ripley returned and all five Hawks went on an attack which had every indication of success, but Graham crashed Morenz and evened the teams.

Gagnon caused another argument when he was dropped by Bostrum and claimed the defence man should be sent off. Chicago sent on four forwards when Lepine was banished for slashing.

Lepine Penalized Again.

Morenz and Joliat worked like Trojans until Lepine returned, turning back the best efforts of Cook and Gottselig. Lepine was hardly on before he slashed again, breaking his stick on Graham's legs. He took another penalty and once more play swept to the Canadien end in seemingly certain scoring plays.

The Hawks met heart-breaking luck at the defense, their efforts being fought aside and many of their plays being spoiled by loose play at the blue line. For thirty seconds the puck was passed to and from one Hawk to the other but none could get a shot.

Then came a play over which the crowds enthused, Morenz, who had been held scoreless for nine consecutive play-off games, grabbed a puck at centre ice and whirled his way around the left defense, hesitating until he was sure of the shot and hammered it home. It was some minutes before play could be resumed as the fans showered the ice with programs, newspapers and hats.

The line-up:

Chicago (0).		Canadiens (2).
Gardiner	Goal	Hainsworth
Wentworth	Defense	S. Mantha
Abel	Defense	Burke
Cook	Centre	Morenz
March	Wing	Gagnon
Adams	Wing	Joliat
Couture	Spare	Lepine
Ripley	Spare	G. Mantha
Gottselig	Spare	Wasnie
Arbour	Spare	Larochelle
Romnes	Spare	Mondou
Desjardins	Spare	Rivers
Somers	Spare	Deduc
Ingram	Spare	Lesieur
Graham	Spare	
Bostrum	Spare	

First Period.

No scoring.

Second Period.

1—Canadiens, Gagnon (Joliat)..........9:59.

Third Period.

2—Canadiens, Morenz (unassisted)......15:27

Penalties—First period: Abel, Morenz, Cook, two minutes each. Second period: March, Leduc, two minutes each. Third period: Wentworth, Wasnie, Graham, Lepine 2, two minutes each.

Referees—Bobby Hewitson and Alex Romeril.

Time of periods—20 minutes.

April 15, 1931

FREE-FOR-ALL FIGHT MARS HOCKEY GAME

Toronto and Montreal Players Battle on Ice—Two From Each Club Finish Contest.

22 PENALTIES IMPOSED

Jackson and Conacher Start the Melee—Maple Leafs Win by Score of 6 to 0.

By The Associated Press.

TORONTO, Feb. 13.—In a game that broke up in the wildest fight scene ever witnessed on local ice, the Toronto Maple Leafs tonight defeated the Montreal Maroons, 6—0, in their scheduled National Hockey League fixture.

Jackson and Lionel Conacher started the fireworks in the last minute of the game and immediately both teams hopped into the free-for-all and officials and players became one wild, entangled mass. The goalkeepers nonchalantly shot the puck to each other while the mêlée lasted.

Finally the affair was straightened out and the few seconds left of the game were played with four members of each team in the penalty box with majors.

Up to the time the fight started it was a fast game, with plenty of bumping. Benny Grant, on loan from Syracuse, played goal for the Leafs in place of the suspended Chabot, and the Maroons found his superb goalwork unbeatable.

The Leafs scored two goals in the opening period, added three more in the second and one in the third. Frank Finnigan and Ace Bailey led the Toronto attack with two goals each, while Bob Gracie and King Clancy each scored one. Earl Miller, recently purchased from Chicago, appeared with Bailey and Cotton and made one assist.

A total of twenty-two penalties were awarded, including seven majors. In addition, Day and Phillips will be dealt with by the league.

The line-up:

Toronto (6).		Maroons (0).
Grant	Goal	Walsh
Day	Defense	Conacher
Levinsky	Defense	Wilcox
Primeau	Centre	Smith
Jackson	Wing	Northcott
Finnigan	Wing	Ward

Goals—Finnigan 2, Bailey 2, Gracie, Clancy. Spares—Toronto: Blair, Bailey, Clancy, Cotton, Gracie, Darragh, Miller. Maroons: Starr, Stewart, Siebert, Trottier, Brydson, McVicar, Phillips.

Penalties—Blair 2, Jackson 2, Trottier 2, Starr 2, Wilcox 2, Brydson, Levinsky 2, Clancy 2, Smith (two minutes each); Levinsky, Clancy, Jackson, Wilcox, Conacher, Stewart (five minutes each).

Referees—Smeaton and Rodden.

February 14, 1932

TORONTO SIX WINS PLAY-OFF BY 4 TO 3

Gains Stanley Cup Series by Beating Maroons, 3 to 2, in 17:59 of Overtime.

By The Associated Press.

TORONTO, April 2.—Hurdling the last obstacle in their path to the Stanley Cup series, the Toronto Maple Leafs tonight defeated the Montreal Maroons, 3 to 2, to capture the two-game total-goal series between the second and third place play-off winners by 4 to 3. Seventeen minutes and fifty-nine seconds of overtime were required before the bitterly fought contest was finally decided.

The Maple Leafs will now journey to New York to engage the Rangers Tuesday night in the first contest of the best three out of five game series for the historic old Stanley Cup and the world's hockey championship. The second game will be played on Thursday at Boston, and the other games, whatever number are necessary to determine the winner, will be held in Toronto, starting next Saturday.

Bob Gracie, flashy left wing spare, decided the issue in the Leafs' favor and sent a capacity crowd of close to 14,000 fans into a frenzy of joy. The game was bitterly contested from the opening face-off. The score was tied first at 1—1, then at 2—2.

Primeau on the Attack.

Primeau made the first offensive move. Walsh stopping his long shot. Smith made a great individual play to get in close on Chabot. Wilcox was penalized for holding Primeau.

A Toronto goal came a minute later on a peculiar play. Charlie Conacher came sailing up the ice, crossed the Blue line and passed to Horner, who lifted a shot which Walsh apparently did not see, the puck bounding over his shoulder into the net without the goalie making a move. The time of the goal was 3:20.

A minute later Lionel Conacher and Siebert of the Maroons combined for a dangerous rush, but it was spoiled when Siebert missed a shot from a few feet out. Darragh was put off the ice for tripping Stewart, and Chabot had to stop a barrage of shots as the Maroons attacked fiercely.

Northcott, speedy Maroon left wing, hurt his leg and had to retire when he fell over Gracie's prostrate figure and crashed into the boards.

Stewart saved a goal when, with Walsh away from the net, he jumped into the breach and took one of Charlie Conacher's hardest shots on his chest. Heavy checking featured the last few minutes of the period, with Chabot keeping out a hard shot by Siebert just as the session ended.

Northcott Returns to Game.

Northcott came on the ice to start the second period, his leg apparently all right after treatment. Both defenses checked the advancing forwards hard. Jackson got through for a hard shot, but Walsh saved nicely. Charlie Conacher was right back with the puck and nearly took Walsh off his feet with a blazing shot.

The checking became heavier as the game progressed, with the Ma-

roons having difficulty getting past the Leaf blue line. Jackson missed a great chance to lengthen the Leafs' lead when he advanced alone on Walsh, only to have the goalie stick out a foot at the last minute and deflect Jackson's shot for the corner. Levinsky drew a penalty.

Smith, Ward and Northcott came on the ice and made things hum around the Leaf net. The Toronto defense and forwards covered well and Chabot handled everything that came his way. Lionel Conacher was penalized just as Levinsky came back and Walsh had some narrow escapes.

As both teams returned to full strength the Maroons tied the count, Ward scoring from a scramble in front of the Leaf net started from Northcott's shot from the right wing. Chabot fell in saving, and Ward raced in to shove the puck past him in 17:27. The Maroons were on the defensive as the period ended.

Maroons Go Into Lead.

Within a minute and six seconds after the start of the third period, the Maroons went into the lead for the first time in the series as Smith lifted a long shot from just past centre ice. The puck struck Chabot's skate and went into the net.

Smith evaded the Toronto defense for a hot shot at Chabot which the goalie took on his chest. Day sent the crowd into a frenzy of delight with a beautifully executed solo rush the length of the ice. He tricked the defense in clever style and beat Walsh with the best shot of the night and the score was tied again at 9:02. The teams were still deadlocked as the period ended.

Lionel Conacher was penalized in the first minute of the overtime period and the Leafs swarmed around Walsh. The goalie, aided by a large measure of luck, saved shots he did not even see. The big Maroon defense man returned before any damage was done. He immediately led a dangerous attack, but Chabot took care of Stewart's shot.

Toronto's youthful line came on the ice and made it interesting for Walsh, the Maroon goalie making a succession of seemingly impossible saves. A penalty to Clancy allowed the Maroons a breathing spell which was short lived, as Lionel Conacher tripped Bailey and was sent off the ice.

Clancy came back and the Leafs had a one-man advantage. Scramble after scramble took place around the Maroon goal. Finally, with both teams at full strength, Gracie won the game for the Leafs in 17:59 after taking a pass from Blair. The speedy wing drove into a corner of the net out of Walsh's reach to terminate the sudden death period.

The line up:

Maroons (2).		Toronto (3).
Walsh	Goal	Chabot
Wilcox	Defense	Horner
L. Conacher	Defense	Clancy
Smith	Centre	Primeau
Ward	Wing	C. Conacher
Northcott	Wing	Jackson
Starr	Spare	Levinsky
Stewart	Spare	Day
Siebert	Spare	Blair
Trottier	Spare	Bailey
Brydson	Spare	Cotton
Haynes	Spare	Finnigan
McVicar	Spare	Gracie
Phillips	Spare	Miller
—	Spare	Darragh
—	Spare	Robertson

First Period.
1—Toronto, Horner (C. Conacher)......3:20
Second Period.
2—Maroons, Ward (Smith, Northcott)...17:27
Third Period.
3—Maroons, Smith.......................1:06
4—Toronto, Day........................9:02
Overtime Period.
5—Toronto, Gracie (Blair)............17:59
Penalties—First period, Wilcox, Darragh, 2 minutes each; second period, Levinsky, Blair, L. Conacher, 2 minutes each; third period, Horner, Siebert, 2 minutes each; overtime period, Clancy, L. Conacher 2, 2 minutes each.
Referees—Rodden and Mallinson. Time of Periods—20 minutes.

April 3, 1932

TORONTO SIX WINS THE STANLEY CUP

Annexes World's Hockey Title in Three Straight Games by Beating Rangers, 6-4.

14,000 FILL LEAFS' ARENA

See Home Club Gain 5-1 Lead, Blair Tallying Twice in First Period.

BOUCHER NEW YORK STAR

Scores Thrice and Leads Late Spurt, but Victors Maintain Safe Margin to End.

By JOSEPH C. NICHOLS.
Special to THE NEW YORK TIMES.

TORONTO, April 9.—The Toronto Maple Leafs brought the Stanley Cup back to this city after a lapse of ten years by defeating the New York Rangers tonight by the score of 6 to 4. The game was the third of the cup series, which decides the hockey championship of the world, and was

the third straight triumph for the speedy local sextet.

Pitting their speed and skill against the generalship and passing strategy which have been the Rangers' outstanding characteristics throughout the season just ended, the Toronto skaters relented not a minute in carrying the attack to their rivals and never during the exciting tussle was the home team headed or even tied.

Urged on by the thunderous cheers unleashed by a crowd of 14,000 which filled the Toronto arena, the young Maple Leaf warriors took the lead before the battle was hardly begun and pressed their advantage continuously and so successfully that the Rangers never had a chance to threaten seriously.

Leafs Off to Fast Start.

Toronto's neatly functioning attack wrought havoc with the Ranger defense early in the game. Andy Blair took a pair of passes to give the Leafs a two-goal lead before the first period was seven minutes old, and from that time on the Rangers trailed always.

Indeed, the Rangers were trailing on one occasion in the third period by four goals, 5—1. Only by a fine exhibition of individual playing by Frank Boucher, the Rangers' veteran centre, did the New Yorkers draw anywhere near the lightning-like home team.

Boucher registered three goals, two of them in the final session, and received credit for an assist on another. It was his work mainly, with some aid from Bun Cook, that enabled the Rangers to whittle the overwhelming margin enjoyed by the Leafs. Boucher garnered the high scoring honors of the game and presented himself constantly as a threat to the Leaf net, while he was on the ice.

Blair was the leading scorer for the victors, by virtue of his two goals, registered within the first few minutes of play.

Rangers Rush to Attack.

The Rangers, going into the game on the short end of the betting, rushed to the attack immediately, in an endeavor to upset the Leafs after the New Yorkers' defeats in the two previous games in the series.

For the greater part of the first five minutes they charged the Leafs with a boundless recklessness and forced Lorne Chabot, the home team's goalie, to extend himself to the limit to repulse the thrusts sent in his direction. But the Toronto defense began to fathom the flashy Ranger attack, and in a short time sent the play back to the visitors' ice.

It was King Clancy who turned the Ranger tide away from the Toronto net and who engineered the advance which resulted in the first Leaf score. Clancy seized the rubber near his own net, following a torrid New York rush, and guided it swiftly to the visitors' sector, where he flashed a neat short pass to Blair. The latter swept around the opposing guards and flipped a difficult side shot past John Ross Roach to count in 5:44.

Twenty-seven seconds after play was resumed Blair swept around the New York defense again, after taking a pass from Bob Gracie, and once more sent the puck into a corner of Roach's net.

Rangers Charge Opponents.

Finding themselves facing a two-goal deficit, the New York outfit was forced to disregard defense almost entirely. They proceeded to charge with four men early in the session, and succeeded in keeping the play

in Toronto ice for a long period.

But penalties received by Ott Heller and Cecil Dillon robbed the New Yorkers' attack of its effectiveness, and the Leaf guards did not find it a difficult task to repulse the bombardments sent against them.

What looked like a fine advantage came the Rangers' way toward the end of the opening session, when Harvey Jackson received a major penalty following an altercation with Referee Mallinson. While their high scoring star was off the ice, the home skaters concentrated wholly on defense and contrived to keep their goal from being pierced.

In the second session Earl Seibert came very close to scoring when he split the Toronto defense neatly, but the big Ranger defense player pushed the disk too hard when he got past the opposing guards and was unable to retrieve it quickly enough to gain direct shot at Chabot.

Jackson Scores for Leafs.

Ace Bailey and Hal Cotton took a leading part in the Toronto advance when the Rangers withdrew to their own territory. Then Joe Primeau and Charley Conacher advanced. The latter relayed the disk to Jackson, located almost directly in front of the cage, and Jackson scored in 10.57 to give the Leafs their third goal.

This effort stirred the Rangers, who responded with an attack so forceful that Chabot let one shot go by. Boucher counted in 15:24, after Heller made a dash from his own cage to the Toronto blue line before passing.

In the third session the Rangers sought to take the play away from their foes, but with little success. Happy Day thrilled the spectators by picking the rubber up beside his own net and streaking to the Ranger zone, where he circled the goal before sending a neat pass-out to Frank Finnigan, who beat the New York goalie in 8:56.

The subsequent charges released by the visitors were capably smothered, and in 15:07 Bailey chalked up another Toronto goal, after taking a pass from Conacher, to give the Leafs a 5 to 1 lead.

Boucher fought hard for possession of the puck in mid-ice, and finally secured it. He rushed over the blue line before relaying the disk to Bun Cook, and Bun beat Chabot with a short shot in 16:33. The effort was soon discounted by Gracie, who garnered a pass from Finnigan and tallied in 17:36.

Boucher Tallies Twice.

Still trying hard, Boucher garnered a pass from Bun Cook and sent the disk past Chabot in 18:24, and he followed this performance by shooting a pass from Bill Cook into the net in 19:27, but the goals, coming with so little time left, failed to disturb the Leafs.

Both goalies were called upon to do more than the usual amount of work in the nets. Roach turned fifty thrusts away from the New York cage, while Chabot received credit for making thirty-two stops. Twenty penalties were called during the struggle, with the Rangers offending eleven times.

The score of the game was the same by which Toronto defeated the Rangers in the opener of the series in New York. The second game, played in Boston, went to the Leafs by the score of 6 to 2.

The line-up:

Toronto (6).		Rangers (4).
Chabot	Goal	Roach
Day	Defense	Heller
Clancy	Defense	Johnson
Primeau	Centre	Boucher
Jackson	Wing	Bun Cook
Conacher	Wing	Bill Cook
Horner	Spare	Seibert
Levinsky	Spare	Miills
Blair	Spare	Gainor
Bailey	Spare	Keeling
Finnigan	Spare	Desjardins
Gracie	Spare	Somers
Miller	Spare	Dillon
Darragh	Spare	Brennan
Robertson	Spare	

First Period.

1—Toronto, Blair (Clancy) 3:44
2—Toronto, Blair (Gracie) 6:11

Second Period.

3—Toronto, Jackson (Primeau, Conacher)10:57
4—Rangers, Boucher (Heller) 15:24

Third Period.

5—Toronto, Finnigan (Day) 8:56
6—Toronto, Bailey (Conacher) 15:07
7—Rangers, Bun Cook (Boucher) 16:33
8—Toronto, Gracie (Finnigan)........17:36
9—Rangers, Boucher (Bun Cook)......18:24
10—Rangers, Boucher (Bill Cook).....19:27
Penalties—First period: Day Jackson, Heller, Blair, Dillon, Gainor, 2 minutes each; Jackson, 5 minutes. Second period: Seibert, 2, Brennan, 2 minutes each. Third period: Keeling 2, Johnson, Conacher, Horner, Cotton, 2 minutes each.
Referees—Mallinson and Cleghorn. Time of periods—20 minutes.

April 10, 1932

NINE HOCKEY TEAMS IN NATIONAL LEAGUE

Ottawa Readmitted After Two Years' Absence—Pittsburgh's Application Denied.

NEW GROUP IS ORGANIZED

American and Western Canada Organizations Become Affiliated as Minor Circuits.

MONTREAL, Oct. 1 (AP).—With the Pittsburgh franchise again not operating and Ottawa back in the fold, the National Hockey League will have a nine-club circuit this Winter, the board of governors decided at the semi-annual meeting today.

The Ottawa Senators, out for two years, succeeded in convincing the governors they could make a go of their franchise, but Pittsburgh's request for readmittance was denied. The governors did not comment on Pittsburgh's application, but it was understood they doubted the city would patronize a team sufficiently.

48 Games For Each Team.

The schedule will consist of 48 games, each team playing three home games and three on the road against each rival team.

As a result of an agreement between the National Hockey League and the American Hockey League, the governors granted the American League affiliation as a minor circuit. Similar action was taken on the recently formed Western Canada Professional Hockey League.

Make-up of League.

The league teams for the coming season will include the Toronto Maple Leafs, Ottawa Senators, Montreal Maroons, Montreal Canediens, New York Rangers, New York Americans, Chicago Black Hawks, Detroit Falcons and Boston Bruins.

Those attending today's meeting were Frank Calder, president; Colonel John S. Hammond, New York Rangers; William Dwyer, New York Americans; Conny Smythe, Toronto; J. F. Strachan, Maroons; Redmond Quain, Senators; J. F. Callahan, Pittsburgh; H. Pfliderer, Falcons; Leo Dandurand, Canediens; Art Ross, Bruins, and W. Tobin, Black Hawks.

October 2, 1932

USE OF TWO REFEREES IN HOCKEY DROPPED

National League Votes Change in Rules—Second Official to Be Judge of Play.

A change in the rules regarding referees was made at a meeting of the board of governors of the National Hockey League at the Hotel Lincoln yesterday.

Heretofore two referees, each with equal power, have officiated at all National League contests. The change, however, provides for only one referee, whose duty it will be to impose penalties and settle disputes. In place of a second referee an official designated as a judge of play will be on the ice. It will be his function to call off-sides at the blue-lines.

Changes in the playing rules also were effected. The penalty against a team having seven players on the ice was reduced from a major to a minor, and the rule applying to handling the puck was clarified. Previously, a player was privileged to hit the puck, provided no other member of his team touched it after him. The revision calls for a two-minute penalty to any player, except the goalie, for handling the puck.

The board accepted the resignation of Colonel John S. Hammond, former president of the Rangers and elected William F. Carey to replace him. Major Fred McLaughlin of the Chicago Black Hawks also resigned from the board, although he has not severed his connection with the Chicago team. His place was taken by William F. Tobin.

January 5, 1933

HAWKS QUIT ICE, FORFEIT TO BRUINS

Gorman Withdraws Team After Protesting Overtime Goal —Maroons Win, 2 to 1.

BOSTON, March 14 (AP).—After violently protesting an overtime goal scored by the Boston Bruins, Manager Tommy Gorman withdrew his Chicago Black Hawks tonight and automatically forfeited one of the wildest games ever played in the National Hockey League.

Before the Black Hawks retired Gorman struck Referee Bill Stewart to start a fist fight that was broken up by the Boston players.

The rumpus started when the Bruins went ahead after three minutes of overtime play. Although they had put on one of the most sustained drives in the history of Boston hockey, they were two goals down until late in the third period. Eddie Shore managed to score the first Boston goal and put over the tying score with only two seconds left to play.

Drive Puck Over Line.

This defense star also started the drive that broke up the game. With four of his team-mates with him, he drove the puck at the Chicago goalie and the five Bruins followed him to the cage. Every player on the ice, with the exception of the Boston goalie, was slashing in front of the Chicago net when Marty Barry drove the puck over the line.

As soon as the red light went on, all of the Black Hawks rushed behind their net to protest to Goal Umpire Louis Reycroft. Defenseman Johnny Coulter was so excited that he rammed his stick through the netting in an attempt to strike Reycroft. Although Stewart forfeited the game, 1—0, the score stood at 3—2 when the Black Hawks left the ice.

Gorman Makes Explanation.

After being escorted to the Chicago dressing room, Gorman quieted down and explained that he was certain the red light had flashed before Barry drove the puck into the Chicago cage. The manager said he grabbed at the referee's sweater when he passed by the Chicago bench and Stewart shook him.

Referee Stewart refused to discuss the incident and the forfeiture of the game, for which the offending team is liable to a $1,000 fine.

The line-up:

Boston.		Chicago.
Thompson	Goal	Gardiner
Smith	Defense	Coulter
Shore	Defense	Burch
Barry	Centre	Cook
Beattie	Wing	March
Clapper	Wing	Gottselig
Goals—Shore 2, Barry, McKenzie, Gottselig.
Spares—Boston: Stewart, Ripley, Land, Owen, Hitchman, Chapman, Oliver, Galbraith, Heximer. Chicago: McKenzie, Jenkins, McFayden, Romnes, Thompson.
Penalties—First period: Lamb, Barry, McFayden (2 minutes each). Second period: McFayden 2, Heximer (2 minutes each). Third period: Shore, Coulter, Lamb, McFayden (2 minutes each).
Referee—Stewart. Goal Judge—Cleary. Time of periods—20 minutes.

March 15, 1933

Maple Leafs Beat Boston in Longest Hockey Game in History of the Sport

OVERTIME MARK SET AS TORONTO SCORES

Leafs Down Bruins, 1-0, to Gain League Title and Stanley Cup Final.

GAME ENDS AT 1:50 A. M.

1:44:46 of Extra Play Beats League Record of 1:08:52 Made in 1930.

GOAL BY DORATY DECIDES

Record Canadian Crowd of 14,500 Sees Long Battle—Leafs Reject Plan to Toss Coin.

TORONTO, Tuesday, April 4.—The Toronto Maple Leafs won the longest hockey game in the history of the sport early this morning, defeating the Boston Bruins by 1-0 after 1 hour, 44 minutes and 46 seconds of overtime.

ken Doraty, smallest player in the grueling battle, broke up the game at 1:50 A.M. when he scored on Andy Blair's pass. A throng of 14,500, the largest that ever witnessed a hockey game in Canada, stayed to the finish.

The triumph qualified the Leafs, defending world's champions, to meet the New York Rangers tonight at New York in the first game of the Stanley Cup series. The Leafs rushed out of the rink to a waiting special train.

Through three regular 20-minute periods, then five extra 20-minute sessions, Toronto fought the Bruins to a standstill. The Leafs maintained an edge in nearly every period but were foiled by the sensational goal tending of Tiny Thompson.

Player Is Offside.

Each team scored a goal that was disallowed. Alex Smith scored for Boston late in the third period, but a player was offside on the play. King Clancy's shot in the fourth overtime period beat Thompson cleanly but the whistle had sounded before he fired.

President Frank Calder of the National League sought to have the teams flip a coin after five extra periods had been played without a score. The Bruins were agreeable but at the last minute the Toronto players decided to play to a finish and they came right back with the winning goal.

The game, the fifth in the play-off series between the first-place winners in each group, carried with

it the championship of the National Hockey League.

The world's endurance record for hockey was set last season when the Springfield Indians and the Boston Cubs of the Canadian-American League played 100 minutes overtime to a 2-2 tie.

The previous National Hockey League record for overtime was 68:52, which the Rangers and Canadiens established in 1930.

The crowd saw the Leafs sail into the Bruins from the start, Clancy leading two fast assaults. On the second, Sands barely missed a rebound in front of the Boston goal. Lamb broke away alone to lay a hard one on Chabot's pads.

Thoms and Conacher combined on the first real scoring opportunity, but Conacher fired inches over Thompson's shoulder. Stewart, Ripley and Lamb returned with a three-man rush that Horner and Clancy broke up just in time.

Conacher's Shots Wide.

The going was rough and the attacks of both teams let down till Conacher and Jackson returned after a five-minute rest.

Twice they raced down together, Conacher firing wide each time. Thompson barely got a foot on another of Conacher's shots. Clancy pulled down Stewart and got a penalty.

Shore led a succession of power plays with four attackers behind him in a vain effort to break through for a goal.

In the second period Jackson and Conacher sent Toronto away again. Jackson slipped around Shore and struck the goal post with his shot. Conacher staggered Thompson with a terrific wing drive.

Chapman drew a penalty for tripping Gracie. Doraty came from behind the Boston net after Day's rush and nearly slipped the disc past Thompson. Clancy belted a low shot that made Thompson hop, but the Bruins hung on till they were at full strength.

Chabot was lucky to block a Smith Lamb attack, the latter shooting into his pads after taking a pass from Smith inside the Leaf defense.

Blair stepped around Shore to fire when Eddie brought him down from behind and was penalized. Then Toronto stormed the Bruins' cage. The Leafs took the puck into Thompson's zone and kept it there, Jackson, Clancy and Conacher peppering the Bruin netman from all sides and from in front.

Opening the third period, Conacher shook the Boston cage with a scorcher after Thoms had given him a pass at the defense.

Chabot made a spectacular save to block Boston's first really dangerous scoring chance of the night. Clapper shot at the goalie from four feet and Chabot saved. Then Lamb gave Shore a pass and Eddie stood in front of Chabot with the net man unprotected. Shore took point blank aim, but the leaf backstop outguessed him.

Lamb Sent Off Ice.

Lamb dumped Gracie to earn a penalty, but before Toronto could capitalize Doraty went out for tripping Shore. It was quiet and safe hockey till Clapper went off for cutting Cotton over the head with his stick.

As Conacher hurtled down the wing, with four mates beside him, Alex Smith suddenly banged the puck clear and raced down alone on the unprotected Chabot to score, but the play was called back for offside.

Thoms and Cotton then were penalized in succession. Shore led Boston on a wild drive. The Bruins piled up in front of the Toronto goal half a dozen times, but there was no scoring, the battle going into overtime.

Starting the overtime play, the Leafs attacked viciously. Conacher had Thompson sprawled in front of the net as he came around from behind to attempt to poke in the rubber.

Levinsky sent Beattie into the boards with a body check and Toronto held off the Bruins with five men while the former served time. Shore, obviously tired, kept going without a rest. Sands tripped Shore and was penalized.

They had played eighteen minutes of overtime when Sands moved to the sidelines. The Bruins ran wild inside the Toronto blue line, storming Chabot during a power play that went full tilt for two minutes. It was still a scoreless tie at the twenty-minute mark, when the teams took a rest.

Just as the second extra session started, Barry tripped Thoms and was banished. The Leafs rushed Thompson at once and Conacher and Jackson pelted the Boston netman with shots. Hardly was Barry back when Shore batted the puck into the crowd trying to clear. That brought him a penalty.

Shore Sent Out Again.

Sixteen minutes of the period had been played when Shore brought down Clancy with a vicious check and he was sent off again.

Opening the third overtime period Alex Smith had Chabot in trouble, shooting from the wing. Then play flashed from end to end. Clancy was in on Thompson after taking Horner's assist. At the other end Oliver sailed right in on Chabot, picking up Shore's perfect pass at

the blue line, only to have Chabot save sensationally.

The fourth overtime period saw Joe Primeau come in after sitting on the bench for most of the night. In the first minute he broke with Clancy and passed. Clancy went in and scored, but the play was called offside by a foot at the blue line.

Bob Gracie was just outside the net on Doraty's long forward in the fourth overtime session. Then Oliver broke away with only Chabot to beat, but the goalie took the short shot on his chest as the game broke the record for overtime.

In the fifth extra session Cotton circled the Bruin net and tried to poke the puck in. The players piled on the goalie and the Leafs appealed unsuccessfully for a goal.

The line-up:

TORONTO (1).		BOSTON (0).
Chabot	Goal	Thompson
Day	Defense	Smith
Clancy	Defense	Shore
Bailey	Centre	Stewart
Cotton	Wing	Ripley
Sands	Wing	Lamb
Horner	Spare	Owen
Levinsky	Spare	Hitchman
Primeau	Spare	Clapper
Conacher	Spare	Galbraith
Jackson	Spare	Oliver
Thoms	Spare	Barry
Blair	Spare	Beattie
Gracie	Spare	Chapman
Doraty	Spare	Heximer

Sixth Overtime Period.

1—Toronto, Doraty (Blair) 4:46

Penalties—First period: Clancy, Shore (2 minutes each). Second period: Chapman, Shore (2 minutes each). Third period: Lamb, Doraty, Clapper, Thoms, Cotton, Day (2 minutes each). First overtime period: Levinsky 2, Sands (2 minutes each). Second overtime period: Barry, Shore 2 (2 minutes each). Third overtime period: Stewart, Conacher 2 (2 minutes each). Fourth overtime period: Smith, Clancy (2 minutes each). Fifth overtime period: None. Sixth overtime period: None.

Referee—Cleghorn. Judge of Play—Daigneault. Time of Periods—20 minutes. Overtime—104 minutes 46 seconds.

April 4, 1933

RANGERS CAPTURE THE STANLEY CUP

Bill Cook Scores on Keeling's Pass in 7:34 of Overtime to Beat Toronto, 1-0.

VICTORY THIRD IN SERIES

Goalie Aitkenhead Plays Brilliantly to Thwart the Defending Titleholders.

By JOSEPH C. NICHOLS.

Special to THE NEW YORK TIMES.

TORONTO, April 13.—The world's hockey championship returned to the United States tonight. The New York Rangers, meeting the rugged Toronto Maple Leafs in the fourth game of the Stanley Cup series, de-

feated the defending champions in a torrid struggle that went 7 minutes and 34 seconds overtime by the score of 1 to 0.

Bill Cook, wily captain of the Ranger forces, drove home the shot that gave the visitors the triumph, beating Lorne Chabot, the tall net guardian for the Leafs, with a blistering side shot after taking a neat rink-wide pass from Butch Keeling. The score came when the Toronto sextet was playing two-men short, Alex Levinsky and Bill Thoms both watching the play from the penalty box.

The battle was a mighty defensive struggle all the way, with Levinsky and King Clancy rising to spectacular heights for the losers and Ching Johnson covering the Leaf rushes in his characteristically crushing style.

Few Chances for Forwards.

The flashy forward lines that the teams boast had few opportunities to display their skillful passing, but when breaks did occur they were followed breathlessly by the crowd of 13,500 persons that witnessed the encounter.

From the outset the Leafs attempted to dominate the attack, hoping to bring about a tie in games won with their adversaries. The New Yorkers entered the bat-

STARS WHO HELPED RANGERS WIN FINAL GAME.

Times Wide World Photo.
Bill Cook.

Times Wide World Photo.
Andy Aitkenhead.

Ranger Goalkeeper Alert.

tle with an advantage of one game over the local skaters, the Blue Shirts having captured the first two games of the series and the Leafs the third.

There was very little, however, the Canadian skaters could do in the face of the solid New York defense. What Johnson and Earl Seibert were unable to cover little Andy Aitkenhead, competing in his first world's championship play, took care of very handily in the visitors' cage.

The Leafs rifled many long shots at the Ranger goalie in the hope of catching him off guard, but the doughty net-minder turned aside everything that was sent at him. He was credited with 48 saves, while Chabot had 34.

The Rangers, who last captured the Stanley Cup in 1928, were very careful in their aggressive gestures, preferring to await the breaks that must arise in such a tense en-counter. They had several opportunities on penalty advantages during the regulation sixty minutes, but were unable to profit on them. But when the one big break came, there was little hesitancy on the part of the visiting stick-wielders.

Lester Patrick, the Rangers' manager, put five forwards on the ice and this quintet battered away relentlessly at the Toronto guardians. Time after time, though, the speedy New York charges were turned aside, and Levinsky's exile was almost up. He was on the point of returning to the game when Keeling garnered the puck in mid-ice.

Takes the Pass Easily.

Breaking away instantly, Butch sped along the left alley far into Toronto's territory. Bill Cook accompanied him on his journey, traveling along the right lane near the side boards. As Red Horner approached Keeling in an endeavor to steal the disk from him, the latter transferred it quickly and precisely to the fast-skating Bill, who took the pass easily.

Not breaking his stride a bit, the Ranger captain swooped in on Chabot, and when the Leaf goalie sought to come out of the cage to topple his adversary Bill lifted the puck swiftly into the far corner, ending the game and smothering the hopes of the Toronto rooters for a second successive championship.

The crowd was rendered silent immediately following this achievement, but after some seconds applauded roundly, showing appreciation for the workmanlike performance of Keeling and Bill Cook.

The Rangers went almost frantic with joy, however, as soon as the puck lodged in the cage. The entire team rushed to Bill's side and patted him enthusiastically, while he, in his excitement, skated back and forth rapidly, waving his arms wildly to the crowd.

Early in the battle Charley Conacher, the Leafs' sharpshooting young wing, swept into New York ice alone and tested Aitkenhead with a blinding shot from the left alley, but the visiting goalie handled the shot in masterful fashion. The Toronto skaters kept the play in the region of the Ranger goal, but an opening like the one that Conacher missed on was not presented.

The Rangers assumed the aggressive more frequently in the middle chapter, and frequently worked far into Toronto ice, only to see the most of the heavy charges smothered by Clancy, Levinsky or Chabot.

A succession of penalties occurred in the third period, but the teams covered up splendidly and there were few good scoring chances.

The line-up:

RANGERS (1).		TORONTO (0).
Aitkenhead	Goal	Chabot
Johnson	Defense	Clancy
Seibert	Defense	Horner
Boucher	Centre	Primeau
Bill Cook	Wing	Conacher
Bun Cook	Wing	Jackson
Siebert	Spare	Thoms
Somers	Spare	Blair
Heller	Spare	Cotton
Osmundson	Spare	Day
Keeling	Spare	Gracie
Murdoch	Spare	Doraty
Brennan	Spare	Boll
Pettinger	Spare	Sands
Dillon	Spare	Levinsky

Overtime Period.
1—Rangers, Bill Cook (Keeling)...... 7:34
Penalties—First period: Primeau, Boucher (2 minutes each). Second period: Day, Levinsky, Somers, Horner (2 minutes each). Third period: Siebert 2, Clancy, Seibert, Bill Cook (2 minutes each). Overtime period: Levinsky, Thoms (2 minutes each).
Referee—Cleghorn. Judge of play—Smith. Time of periods—20 minutes each.

April 14, 1933

WILD SCENES MARK HOCKEY IN BOSTON

Bailey, Tripped by Shore, Is Sent to Hospital With a Brain Concussion.

HIS CONDITION IS SERIOUS

Shore Is Badly Cut in Fight— Police Summoned as Toronto Triumphs, 4 to 1.

By The Associated Press.
BOSTON, Dec. 12.—The Toronto Maple Leafs and Boston Bruins, who have been at swords' points for several seasons, got beyond control of the referees early in the first period tonight and put on a battle that resembled an old-time Bowery gang fight much more than it did a hockey game. The visitors gained a 4-to-1 victory.

Both teams were guilty of almost every crime in the hockey code during the slam-bang first session, during which Vic Ripley scored a fluke goal for the Bruins and Happy Day evened matters for the Leafs.

The game became rougher every minute and the climax came midway in the second session when, after being slammed into the boards by Red Horner, the retreating Eddie Shore tripped Ace Bailey from behind with his stick. Bailey fell heavily and was knocked unconscious when his head struck the ice with terrific force.

Unconscious Ten Minutes.

Bailey was unconscious for ten minutes and after being revived by Dr. C. Lynde Gately of Boston in the dressing room was removed to the Audubon Hospital, where his condition was said to be serious.

Drs. Gately and Martin Crotty, who accompanied him in the ambulance, described his injury as a cerebral concussion with convulsions. They planned to take an X-ray tomorrow.

An hour after his admission Bailey's condition was described as "comfortable."

After Bailey was tripped at the Garden, Shore returned to his defense position in the Boston zone. Horner immediately rushed over and knocked him down with a heavy right to the jaw.

Shore's head was split open when it hit the ice, and Dr. Crotty used seven stitches to close the three-inch gash. Both players were carried off the ice, and while Connie Smythe, the Leafs' manager, was rushing to the side of his injured player, he became involved in a fist fight with several spectators outside of the Toronto dressing room.

Will Apply for Warrant.

One of them, Leonard Kenworthy of Everett, accused Smythe of delivering the blow that shattered his spectacles and injured his eye. Kenworthy, Boston Garden officials said, will apply for a warrant charging Smythe with assault tomorrow morning.

Horner and Shore received match penalties for their part in the exhibition and the teams played short-handed for twenty minutes.

Late in the second period, Hec Kilrea put the Leafs in the lead and he scored again late in the third period, after Joe Primeau counted unassisted.

The Leafs were showered with programs and other débris when they left the ice and a police detail, which was greatly reinforced after the Shore-Horner outbreak, escorted them to their dressing room.

The line-up:

TORONTO (4).		BOSTON (1).
Hainsworth	Goal	Thompson
Clancy	Defense	Smith
Horner	Defense	Shore
Blair	Centre	Barry
Cotton	Wing	Gracie
Sands	Wing	Clapper

Goals—Kilrea 2, Day, Primeau, Ripley.
Spares—Toronto: Conacher, Primeau, Jackson, Bailey, Kilrea, Boll, Day, Levinsky, Thoms. Boston: Stewart, Beattie, Lamb, Ripley, Oliver, Chapman, Galbraith, Hitchman.
Penalties—Horner 2, Day, 2, Blair, Levinsky (2 minutes each), Horner, Shore (match).
Referees—Odie Cleghorn and Eusebe Daigneault. Time of periods—20 minutes.

December 13, 1933

Eddie Shore (#2, on the left), shown here in action against the N.Y. Americans, was as quick with his fists as with his stick. He was voted Most Valuable Player in the league in 1933, 1935, 1936 and 1938.

Patrick to Reinstate Shore Jan. 28

SHORE ABSOLVED IN BAILEY INJURY

Patrick Clears Boston Hockey Player of Deliberate Intent to Hurt Rival.

SUSPENSION ENDS JAN. 28

Assurances Toronto Star Will Recover a Factor in Action of League Director.

By The Associated Press.

MONTREAL, Jan. 4. — Eddie Shore, defense star of the Boston Bruins of the National Hockey League, today was absolved of any deliberate intent to injure Irvin (Ace) Bailey of the Toronto Maple Leafs when he charged into him at Boston Dec. 12. At the same time it was decided to lift Shore's indefinite suspension Jan. 28.

Frank Patrick, managing director of the league, in announcing his action, said a thorough investigation had convinced him the collision of the two players was an accident. He added that, having been assured Bailey's recovery was certain, he was restoring Shore to good standing.

Bailey, who suffered a fractured skull when he was knocked to the ice by Shore, is still in a Boston hospital. He gave evidence of his recovery today by talking to a reporter and said he hoped to be out of the hospital in a week or two. He also absolved Shore of any deliberate action against him.

Action Is Commended.

Mr. Patrick's action was generally commended as fair, but Connie Smythe, managing director of the Toronto Club, said he planned an appeal to the full league directorate of Patrick, Tom Arnold and Frank Calder, on the grounds that compensation should have been granted Bailey and the Leafs.

Toronto already has spent $2,500 on Bailey's hospital and doctor bills, Smythe said, and he argued that the sum the Boston benefit game brought Bailey was not enough, "since he probably will never play hockey again."

Shore's reinstatement will make him eligible to play with Boston against the New York Rangers Jan. 28. He will have missed sixteen games if he resumes play on that night.

Text of Patrick Statement.

The text of Mr. Patrick's statement:

"For the purpose of arriving at a proper decision in the case of Eddie Shore, legal counsel was engaged to act for and on behalf of the National Hockey League, both in Boston and in Toronto. Fifty-one depositions were taken, which included all the players participating in the hockey match on Dec. 12 in Boston.

"A questionnaire was prepared so that the answers could be readily tabulated. Evidence under oath was taken from the Boston sports writers as well as sworn statements from well-known Boston citizens, the idea being to make the investigation as thorough as possible so that a just decision could be arrived at.

"It developed that only five players of the Toronto team and four players of the Boston team actually saw the contact between Shore and Bailey. The attention of the other players having been concentrated on the play, which was at this time some distance away, sharp differences of opinion exist among the players as to whether Shore actually contacted Bailey in an illegal manner.

"There is no doubt that he did contact Bailey with some considerable force, which in itself would be an illegal play, hence Shore must assume full responsibility for his illegal act.

In Dazed Condition.

"Shore sets up that he was in a dazed condition as a result of a fall just prior to the contact with Bailey. He swears that he has no recollection of Player Horner talking to him or hitting him.

"This would indicate that at this time he was dazed, whether by his fall or by the sudden realization that Bailey was seriously injured, I cannot say.

"Players, critics and spectators, in fact every one who gave evidence, state there was no bad blood between these players and there were no incidents in the game itself that would lead any one to assume that something of a serious nature would inevitably occur.

"We must assume then that whatever did occur was of a spontaneous nature with no malice behind it. Shore claims that the contact was accidental, and many support this claim. I am free to admit that I do not know, for there is some conflict of evidence in this respect, although the preponderance of the testimony is that the contact was accidental.

Doubts Mishap Was Intentional.

"I firmly believe Shore had no intention of injuring Bailey, and in the ordinary course or run of play he would have been given a minor or major penalty, which means either a two-minute or five-minute penalty.

"In arriving at this decision Bailey's condition was, of course, of paramount importance. Dr. Munro of Boston assures me that Bailey is now out of danger. This is most gratifying to every one associated with hockey and to the countless thousands of people all over America who have earnestly prayed for his recovery.

"Proper consideration has been given to the mental anguish Shore has undergone and to the fact his playing record does not class him as a vicious player.

"This is established by the fact he has participated in about 400 games in the National Hockey League and he has never been given a match penalty for injuring an opponent, although he has probably contacted four or five thousand players during the progress of these games.

"The Boston club, by paying the sum of $6,741, proceeds of a regular league match, has in effect paid a voluntary fine, and a sum in excess of any amount that I would have been inclined to impose upon them as a fine."

January 5, 1934

HAWKS TOP WINGS IN OVERTIME, 2 TO 1

Thompson's Tally After More Than 81 Minutes of Play Decides Exciting Game.

ROMNES AIDS IN TRIUMPH

Makes Pass Which Leads to Winning Goal as Stanley Cup Competition Opens.

By The Associated Press.

DETROIT, April 3.—A backhand shot by Paul Thompson in 1:10 of the second overtime period tonight gave Chicago's Black Hawks a 2-to-1 victory over Detroit's Red Wings in the first game of their series for the Stanley Cup, emblematic of the world's hockey championship.

Doc Romnes, who fed Thompson a perfect pass, was given an assist on the goal which ended the game.

Thompson's shot, which Wilf Cude in the Wing net found impossible to stop, ended a bitter battle of more than eighty-one minutes of hockey in which the invading Hawks displayed a great close-checking game, which continually gave the Wings trouble. A capacity crowd of more than 14,000 attended.

The Chicago team, aggressively following the puck from the opening bell, jumped into a lead late in the first period on a great solo dash by Lionel Conacher, who raced down centre ice, split the Wing defense, and rammed the puck past Cude. The time was 17:50.

Counts After Double Pass.

Chicago's checking held the Wings until early in the third period when Lewis scored after a double pass, Graham to Aurie. This goal was registered in 4:45.

During the first overtime session the Wings had an opportunity when Conacher was penalized for tripping Williams, but the visitors' defense was stubborn and the Wings could not break through. Then Thompson's accurate flip in the second minute of the second overtime period ended the game.

Cude in the Wing net was brilliant in defeat. The Hawks fired forty hard drives at him as they repeatedly swept down on the cage. Chuck Gardiner in the Hawk net had only twenty-one saves, and was given great support by the Chicago defense men, Conacher, Abel, Coulter and Jenkins.

The game, which gives Chicago an advantage in the three-out-of-five-game series, was fast and hard played throughout.

Only five penalties were called, three going against the visiting team. A vicious back-checking game, however, prevented the Wing attack from getting under way with any consistency. Throughout the game the Hawks raced into Detroit ice to break up plays before they could get started.

The Wings' first line of Aurie, Weiland and Lewis looked as good as did the first line of Romnes, March and Thompson, but the Detroit second and third lines were outplayed most of the game.

In the early minutes of the first period the visitors resorted to a close, defensive style of play, Romnes and Thompson firing long shots.

Weiland's hard shot almost glanced off Gardiner's glove and into the nets as the play grew faster and rougher.

Wings' New Line Goes On.

March and Lewis were sent off the ice for high sticking, but neither team could get through the rival defense. The Wings' kid line of Marker, Carrigan and Moffatt came on, and their presence seemed to add more speed and spirit to the action.

Aurie, Weiland and Lewis returned to the ice, and the first named just missed the net by inches on a pass from Weiland. Goodfellow poked the disk away from Gottselig, raced down the centre ice, and his hard drive made Gardiner reach.

Conacher got the disk and crashed through Young and Graham at the defense posts and lined a hard shot at Cude. The rubber found the net at 17:50 and it was the only score of the session.

Aurie's hard shot from the boards made Gardiner reach as the second period opened. Thompson's long fly was an easy stop and for the next few minutes the Hawks, checking closely, made the Wing attack look weak.

McFadyen poke-checked the puck away from Goodfellow, passed to Gottselig and the Hawk forward made Cude sprawl to save. Conacher missed a great chance when McFadyen's pass in front of the Wing net got away from him. The Hawks were dominating the play.

Chicago Presses on Attack.

Keeping three forwards checking furiously in Wing territory, the visitors made the most of their chances to add to their lead. Goldsworthy's hard shot was taken by Cude on the chest and Cook took the puck away from Carrigan and Marker on three lays and the Wing manager sent his first-string line to the ice.

The Wing first line failed repeatedly to break through the stubborn Chicago defense of Abel and Coulter. With eight minutes to go the Hawks drew their second penalty, when Thompson was caught high-sticking Aurie.

The Wings sent five forwards down the ice, but Gardiner made a great save of Goodfellow's shot and another on Weiland's. Sorrell raced in close and Gardiner kicked the puck out with his skate.

Carrigan swept down the centre and his shot missed the corner.

Williams flipped a high one and Gardiner, taking no chances, dropped his stick and caught the puck with both hands. Young, grabbing a loose puck, fired one at Gardiner which cleared the net.

The Hawks continued their great checking game in the third period. Conacher rode Sorrell into a corner after Weiland fired a long shot and Conacher and Jenkins broke up a play which Goodfellow and Sorrell carried to the net mouth.

Five Wings raced to the attack and the power play produced results at 4:45. Graham passed out to Aurie, who shot the rubber across to Lewis directly in front of Gardiner. Lewis slammed the puck into the net cleanly. Time was called while the ice was cleared of débris.

Weiland took a pass from Lewis and his shot hit the post, the Wing centre crashing into the boards on the play and taking time out to get his breath. Plays frequently were broken up at centre ice and the period closed with the teams still deadlocked and they went into sudden death overtime.

Both sextets played defensive hockey in the first overtime period and at the close of the 20-minute session the teams were still tied at 1-all. Conacher drew the only penalty of the session and though the Wings sent five forwards down the ice they failed to beat Gardiner and a second overtime session was ordered.

The deciding drive by Thompson followed in double-quick order, bringing the game to an end after 21:10 of overtime play.

The line-up:

CHICAGO (2).	DETROIT (1).
Gardiner .... Goal .... Cude
Jenkins .... Defense .... Graham
Conacher ...... Defense .... Buswell
Romnes .... Centre .... Weiland
March .... Wing .... Aurie
Thompson ..... Wing .... Lewis
Coulter .... Spare .... Young
Abel .... Spare .... Goodfellow
Sheppard ...... Spare .... Wiseman
Couture .... Spare .... Sorrell
Goldsworthy ... Spare .... Emms
Cook .... Spare .... Marker
Gottselig ...... Spare .... Williams
McFadyen ...... Spare .... Carrigan
Trudel .... Spare .... Moffatt

First Period.

1—Chicago, Conacher 17:50

Second Period.

No scoring.

Third Period.

2—Detroit, Lewis (Aurie, Graham).... 4:45

Overtime

3—Chicago, Thompson (Romnes).....21:10

Penalties—First period: Lewis, March (2 minutes each). Second period: Thompson (2 minutes). Third period: Buswell (2 minutes). First overtime period: Conacher (2 minutes). Second overtime period: None.

Referees—Bobbie Hewitson and Odie Cleghorn. Time—Three regular periods of 20 minutes each, one 20-minute overtime period and one sudden death session of 1:10.

April 4, 1934

HAWKS SCORE, 1-0; WIN STANLEY CUP

March's Drive After 30:05 of Overtime Beats Detroit and Ends Hockey Title Series.

PENALTY LEADS TO TALLY

Wings, Short-Handed, Unable to Check Chicago Rushes— Romnes Makes Assist.

By The Associated Press.

CHICAGO, April 10.—A blazing shot from the stick of tiny Mush March, after 90 minutes and 5 seconds of savage hockey, tonight carried the Chicago Black Hawks to a 1-to-0 triumph over Detroit to give them the Stanley Cup for the first time and their first world's professional hockey championship.

They had fought through three regular periods and nearly a half hour of overtime before the break came. Ebbie Goodfellow, big, clever Detroit defense man, was sent to the penalty box for tripping Cook as the Hawk wingman was about to shoot.

Both teams were tired, but as Goodfellow skated slowly and dejectedly to the penalty box the Hawks shed their weariness. March, with his two mates on the Hawk ace forward line, Doc Romnes and Paul Thompson, raced onto the ice. Another Wing defenseman was hurriedly ordered into action.

Refuse to Be Halted.

Twice the Wings broke up desperate rushes that carried almost to the cage. But the third time the Hawks refused to be stopped. Romnes gained control of the disk in mid-ice and passed to the right, where March waited. As the little fellow turned to skate for the goal, he was almost cornered. He jerked loose and took a full sweep at the puck.

It sped, about waist high, past young Wilf Cude before the Wing goalie could shift into position and brought to an end 30 minutes 5 seconds of overtime play.

The spectators, 16,500 of them, raised a terrific cheer. They didn't stop yelling until after Frank Calder, president of the National Hockey League, had handed the 42-year-old pewter bowl to Major Frederic McLaughlin, owner of the victorious club, and March had skated around the ice.

The Hawks had a slight advantage throughout the overtime struggle. They fired fifty-three shots which Cude was able to handle and beat him on the fifty-fourth. So well was he protected by his mates that Chuck Gardiner, the Hawk goalie and captain, only had to make thirty-nine saves.

There were only two other penalties, although the battle verged on out-and-out roughness all the way. In the first period Gus Marker, young Detroit forward, was sent away for tripping, and not long after Lolo Couture spent two anxious minutes in the coop for the same offense.

The Hawks won the trophy for the first time by defeating Detroit in three out of four games. In 1931 they reached the finals, only to bow to the Canadiens of Montreal in five matches.

The game opened at a fast pace, with the March-Thompson-Romnes line giving Chicago the better of it. The Hawks bothered Cude but he had plenty of time in which to handle two hard rushes. Detroit tried hard to get started, but Chicago played carefully and kept the Wings from getting out of control.

McFadyen, Gottselig and Couture outrushed Carrigan, Marker and Starr, but most of their drives were pinched into the corners. Marker was penalized for tripping Gottselig and the Hawk first line went on. Romnes slammed one off the post and Cude was hard pressed before Lewis batted the puck up the ice to relieve the pressure. Marker's time was up as the Wings stopped Coulter.

Gardiner had to hustle to save on Marker, and Couture was sent off for two minutes for tripping as the Wing forward shot.

With Couture off, the Wings let loose with a five-man attack. Conacher helped Gardiner out of trouble, and Thompson almost trapped the Wings. Cude, however, came well out and cleared the puck. March flipped a long one up the ice and Conacher almost beat the Wings back. Couture was out in time to break up the next Detroit rush.

Lewis Misses Hard Shot.

Lewis came within an ace of beating Gardiner in the first few seconds of the second period. He slashed a high one which Gardiner took with his hands, and when the puck slipped away, Lewis almost got the rebound. Jenkins cleared the puck in time, however.

The Wings went at top speed and had the edge in the first few minutes.

The teams went back to defensive hockey as the third period opened, and again most of the play was in mid-ice. Each tried long shots, and an easy roller by Weiland almost skipped over Gardiner's stick.

Trudel and Goldsworthy tried twice and had Cude in trouble, but Pettinger and Goodfellow returned the compliment on Gardiner. The players were opening up, and March banged one off the post, but Lewis came back with a shot for Detroit.

The Hawks were skating faster, but most of their drives wound up in the corners, as the Detroit defensemen followed the play closely. Gardiner had his toughest moment when Emms ripped a high hard one at him. The Hawk goalie went down, and only a savage piece of work by Jenkins kept Goodfellow from shooting. Jenkins cleared, and things eased off for a moment. Gardiner took time out, but returned to action after getting his breath back.

Both sets of warriors appeared tired and there was a short siege of mid-ice exchanging of the puck. No scoring followed and the teams went into sudden-death overtime.

The tension was telling on the players and several near fights developed in the first ten minutes of overtime. No penalties resulted, however.

They put in another spell of battling in mid-ice, apparently trying to snatch a little rest. Twenty minutes of overtime passed without a counter and an intermission was declared.

During the intermission John Ross Roach, who started the season as Detroit's goalie, was ordered to report to the Wing bench. Cude, however, was in the cage when the

second instalment of overtime started.

Cautious manoeuvring was still the rule until March broke away and apparently had a great chance. Buswell, however, skated him out of range. Coulter cracked a terrific shot off Cude's stick and the puck bounced clear back to the blue line.

Coulter Clears Disk.

The Wings rushed suddenly with Carrigan, Marker and Goodfellow in the play. It looked serious until Coulter leaped in and cleared the disk.

Goodfellow was sent out for tripping Cook. March, Thompson and Romnes went on and sought savagely to get loose. Lewis golfed the puck away to smash the first rush. Buswell tied Conacher up on the boards to slow the Hawks down again.

Then March drove in from the right, pulling loose from Buswell, and slashed a shot into the cage behind Cude to end the battle.

The line-up:

DETROIT (0).		CHICAGO (1).
Cude .... Goal .... Gardiner
Graham ...... Defense ...... Conacher
Buswell ...... Defense ...... Jenkins
Weiland ...... Centre ...... Romnes
Lewis .... Wing .... Thompson
Aurie .... Wing .... March
Goodfellow ... Spare .... Abel
Starr .... Spare .... Kendall
Young .... Spare .... Couture
Marker .... Spare ...... Goldsworthy
Carrigan ..... Spare .... Cook
Wiseman ...... Spare ...... Gottselig
Sorrell .... Spare ...... McFadyen
Pettinger ..... Spare .... Trudel
Emms .... Spare .... Coulter

Second Overtime Period.

1—Chicago, March (Romnes).......10:05

Penalties—First period: Marker, Couture (2 minutes each). Second period: None. Third period: None. First overtime period: None. Second overtime period: Goodfellow (2 minutes).

Referees—Cleghorn and Hewitson. Time of periods—20 minutes each. Overtime of 30:05.

April 11, 1934

FREE PENALTY SHOT VOTED IN HOCKEY

Officials of National League Also Establish Lower Salary Limits.

Hockey officials from throughout the East and Canada gathered yesterday at the Waldorf-Astoria Hotel for the semi-annual meeting of the National Hockey League and passed two measures. One affects the financial phase of the game and the other brings a new penalty shot into the sport.

The new penalty provides that any player tripped or otherwise roughly interfered with in attempting to shoot what the referee considers a "sure goal" will be permitted a free shot. The free shot will be made from a point 38 feet from the net and from a circle in the middle of the ice. The circle will be 10 feet in diameter and the player may make the shot either standing or in motion but the puck must leave the stick from within the circle.

Any player not in the penalty box may make the shot and the only defense will be furnished by the opposing goal tender.

A reduction in the salary limit of an individual was voted so that the top remuneration will be $7,000 instead of $7,500. The various teams also will reduce their salary budgets to $62,500 instead of $65,000.

September 23, 1934

MAROONS WIN, 4-1; TAKE STANLEY CUP

Conquer Toronto for Third Time in Row as 13,000 Look On at Montreal.

CLINCH ISSUE IN 2D PERIOD

Regain Lead With 2-Goal Surge and Add Another in Final— Connell Stars in Nets.

By JOSEPH C. NICHOLS.

Special to THE NEW YORK TIMES.

MONTREAL, April 9.—The Stanley Cup comes back to Montreal.

The surprising Maroons conquered the sturdy, hard-skating Toronto Maple Leafs tonight in the third game of the world's championship series, and earned the right to keep the famous old trophy in their possession for a year.

Tommy Gorman's close-checking crew, showing little respect for the vaunted Toronto sextet it had beaten twice previously, tore into the Ontario visitors vigorously to register a convincing 4-to-1 triumph.

The manner in which the Maroons swept through the series, in three straight games, constitutes one of the most amazing upsets in the long history of Stanley Cup competition. Against one of the most powerful and sturdiest teams ever organized in the National Hockey League, the Montreal stick-wielders rose to splendid heights, and gave every evidence of being thorough champions.

Game Is Bitterly Waged.

More than 13,000 persons, one of the largest crowds ever to gather in the Montreal forum, sat in on tonight's contest and saw a bitterly waged, bone-crushing battle that held numerous nerve-tingling thrills. No safety-first hockey was displayed by the Maroons, although their style of play all through the National League season leaned toward the close-guarding side.

Instead, the Maroons gave as much as they took. They rushed whenever the opportunity presented itself, and were the first to score. Jimmy Ward made the counter that gave the local team its first lead, in the opening session. The tally was nullified in the second session, however, when Bill Thoms released the only shot that got past Alex Connell all night.

That was the closest the Leafs came to going ahead. For before the middle period had ended, the Maroons rapped home two more tallies and, for good measure, counted a fourth in the final session.

The hero of the game, without question, was Cy Wentworth, the big, watchful defense man for the Maroons. Time and again Wentworth stepped into everything that came his way, and it was his fine play that kept the sharp-shooting Toronto forwards from getting in on Connell more than they did.

In addition to his splendid defensive play, Wentworth took a large part in his team's rushing. He managed to score one goal and received credit for an assist on another.

Connell also rose to heroic heights in his post in front of the Maroon cage. As sturdy as the Montreal defense was, it could not continuously keep such expert snipers as Charley Conacher and Harvey Jackson from getting in on the net.

Connell Alert in the Nets.

When they did get in, they found the veteran guardian too much for them. He worked feverishly in the face of the mad Toronto rushes, and more than once turned in saves that were truly remarkable.

At the start Toronto swept into the Maroons' territory and leveled a number of blistering drives at the goal. They held the aggressive for several minutes, until both teams changed front lines. Then the Maroons assumed the aggressive, and had their first good chance at George Hainsworth, the Toronto net guardian, when Ward drove a long shot from the left lane.

When Red Horner of the Leafs drew a penalty the Maroons put on a five-man power drive that nearly resulted in a score. Allan Shields carried the disk up from his defense position, and let go at Hainsworth. The latter blocked, but Russ Blinco seized the rubber and skated into the crease, where he missed a fine opening.

The teams alternated at rushing throughout the rest of the period, with Toronto the heavier charges. A penalty to Lionel Conacher forced the Maroons to assume a defensive stand, and the Leafs advanced en masse. But their strategy worked to their own disadvantage, for Baldy Northcott intercepted a pass and carried all the way to Toronto ice. There he passed to Ward who, after his first shot was blocked, seized his own rebound and beat Hainsworth, in 19:35.

Trailing when the second period got under way, the Leafs continued their five-man rushes. They assaulted the Montreal defense heavily and had many chances at Connell, who held up well. As often

as they were turned back, however, the Leafs charged again and the fury of their attacks finally told on Connell.

Northcott Breaks Deadlock.

Frank Finnigan made his way around Lionel Conacher and skated almost to the back boards before flashing a long pass to Thoms, far to Connell's right. Thoms took the pass easily and flipped the puck upward past the Montreal goalie to tie the count in 12:59.

The Maroons found this going hardly to their liking and they immediately went on the offensive. They harried Hainsworth and the Leaf guards persistently, and in 16:18 Montreal went into the lead again. Northcott made the score, getting his stick on the puck passed to him by Ward just in time to deflect it into the cords.

On the next face-off, the Leafs got the puck and carried it into Maroon ice. Harold Cotton made an attempt to get around Wentworth, but was spilled, and lost the rubber to Northcott, who quickly turned it over to Wentworth. The latter broke away like a flash, stick-handled across Toronto's line, closed in on Hainsworth, and beat him in with a straight shot, only twelve seconds after Northcott's tally.

Toronto struck back with all its strength following this tally, but could not reach Connell effectively.

When the third session got under way the visitors sent five skaters into Montreal ice, only to find that Wentworth was waiting for them. Wentworth stole a relay, and with an open path to the net ahead of him, he struck out for Toronto ice. Gus Marker accompanied him, and as the pair drew close to the cage, Wentworth shuttled a flat pass to his team-mate, who scored in 1:02.

Leafs Fight to the End.

The Leafs sent five skaters ahead repeatedly in the effort to overtake their foes, but here the stern Maroon defense asserted itself. Wentworth, Shields, Conacher and Stewart Evans braced in front of Connell, and the latter was afforded perfect protection.

As the clock ticked off the min-

utes, and Toronto's chances of winning grew considerably dim, Connell demonstrated the faith he had in his guards by waving to friends in the crowd. When the final whistle blew, he threw his stick into the end arena, and let out a whoop of triumph.

As hard fought as the game was, there were only two penalties, those issued in the first period. The game closed the National Hockey League drive for 1934-1935.

The line-up:

TORONTO (1).		MAROONS (4).
Hainsworth	Goal	Connell
Hollett	Defense	Wentworth
Day	Defense	Evans
Thoms	Centre	Smith
Boll	Wing	Ward
Finnigan	Wing	Northcott
Clancy	Spare	L. Conacher
Horner	Spare	Trottier
Primeau	Spare	Marker
Jackson	Spare	Cain
C. Conacher	Spare	Gracie
Cotton	Spare	Shields
Kelly	Spare	Blinco
Metz	Spare	Robinson
Doraty	Spare	Miller

First Period.
1—Maroons, Ward (Northcott).........19:35
Second Period.
2—Toronto, Thoms (Finnigan).........12:59
3—Maroons, Northcott (Ward).........16:18
4—Maroons, Wentworth (Northcott)...16:30
Third Period.
5—Maroons, Marker (Wentworth).....1:02
Penalties—First period: Horner, L. Conacher, 2 minutes each. Second period: none. Third period: none.
Referees—Stewart and Bell. Time of periods—20 minutes.

April 10, 1935

Boucher Will Keep Cup.

OTTAWA, April 26 (AP).—The trophy chest of Frank Boucher, veteran centre of the New York Rangers, today included the Lady Byng Trophy, emblematic of the cleanest and most gentlemanly player in the national professional hockey league. It was a perpetual trophy, but in view of the fact Boucher won it seven of the eleven years it has been in circulation, Lady Byng decided he was entitled to it outright.

April 27, 1935

St. Louis Drops From National Hockey League

CUT HOCKEY LEAGUE TO 8-CLUB CIRCUIT

Team Owners Buy St. Louis Franchise and Distribute Players on Roster.

The franchise, rights and players of the St. Louis Eagles hockey team, controlled by Redmond Quain's Ottawa syndicate, were purchased by the National Hockey League yesterday, it was announced by President Frank Calder following an emergency meeting at the Waldorf-Astoria Hotel. As a

result the league's roster is now reduced from nine teams to eight.

Financial difficulties of the club, which had been generally known by persons close to hockey circles, were responsible for the urgent meeting called by the board of governors of the league. It was necessary to straighten matters quickly, inasmuch as work on the schedule for the season and arrangements for Stanley Cup play-offs have to be made.

Each Club Donates $5,000.

Although no purchase price was announced, it was reliably stated that the member clubs had contributed $5,000 apiece, making the total price paid to the Ottawa interests $40,000. Eighteen players of the St. Louis team's roster of twenty-three found berth immediately, the clubs participating in the distribution.

The Chicago Black Hawks, however, did not claim any of the players. The choice was given in the selections to the weaker units in the league. The remaining five players will be placed with minor

league teams, it was said.

Commenting on the decision of the league, President Calder said, "We took over the St. Louis club for the best interests of the league. St. Louis was unable to make a financial go of it and we did not think it was sporting to allow the Ottawa syndicate to take a loss after it had made every effort to keep going."

This move by the league marked the first time it has taken such action since it was organized in 1917. If the league had not made the purchase and the Ottawa group had not been able to put a team into the race, the franchise would have been forfeited and the players turned loose.

Americans and Detroit Swap.

The New York Americans drew two players originally. They were Pete Kelly, forward, and Ed Finnigan, centre. After the meeting, however, the Americans swapped Kelly for Carl Voss, who had been shifted to Detroit. It was a pure exchange with no cash involved.

The Montreal Canadiens received three players. They were Bill Beveridge, goalie; Irvin Frew, defense, and Paul Drouin, forward. Detroit's lot after the exchange with the Americans gave them, in addition to Kelly, William Peterkin, goalie. The New York Rangers got two men, Glen Brydson, forward, and Vernon Ayres, defense man. A trio of players, Joe Lamb and Henri Lauzon, forwards, and Bill Taugher, goalie, went to the Montreal Maroons.

Bill Cowley, forward, and Teddy Graham, defense, went to Boston. Toronto took Charles Shannon, Victor Purpur and John Dewey, forwards, and Mickey Blake, defense man.

The Ottawa interests originally headed the old Ottawa Senators, one of the four charter members of the league. When affairs went badly up there the group tried the Missouri city, but met the same fate there. The club had been placed on the block, but there had been no offers forthcoming.

While the officials were still in attendance Beveridge was switched from the Canadiens to the Maroons in exchange for Lauzon.

The schedule will open with the Americans playing the Black Hawks at Chicago on Thursday, Nov. 7. The rest of the teams will swing into action over that week-end.

October 16, 1935

14,000 SEE DETROIT ANNEX STANLEY CUP BY DOWNING LEAFS

Wings Triumph, 3-2, to Take Title Hockey Series by Three Games to One.

SMITH THE DEFENSE STAR

By JOSEPH C. NICHOLS
Special to THE NEW YORK TIMES.

TORONTO, April 11. — Detroit's Red Wings added another championship to the long list boasted by the automobile city in winning the Stanley Cup tonight. The smooth-skating Wing sextet defeated the gallant Toronto Maple Leafs in the fourth game of the cup series by the score of 3 to 2 in what was the best-played contest of the entire round.

While a crowd of more than 14,000 spectators looked on, the teams waged a bitter, spectacular struggle that abounded with thrills. Toronto went into the lead in the first period on a goal by Joe Primeau, but Ebbie Goodfellow evened the count by tallying in the middle chapter. Marty Barry followed Goodfellow with a goal in the same session, and when Pete (Red) Kelly registered in the third period it seemed all over for the Leafs.

Then Bill Thoms broke away to score unassisted midway in the closing frame and from that point on the Toronto skaters tore into their rivals with such force that it looked as though the visitors must wilt.

But Normie Smith, the doughty little net-minder for the Wings, rose to superb heights in withstanding the terrific onslaughts launched at him by the blue-jerseyed skaters representing the Queen City and succeeded in keeping them from tallying the one goal that would have tied the battle.

Smith's work was probably the greatest factor in the victory that moved the Stanley Cup, emblematic of the world's hockey championship, to Detroit for the first time since the organization of the National League. To win the cup, the Wings captured three out of the four games played, Toronto scoring its sole victory here on Thursday night.

Bearing in mind the miracle that happened in the last game, when the Leafs came from behind at 3 to 0 to tie the score and then win in overtime, the spectators hoped most audibly for lightning to strike a second time. Their players tried desperately and more than once broke in past the Detroit defense in that tense last ten minutes, but no amount of rushing on the part of the Leafs could break through Smith.

Primeau Breaks Through

From the very start of the battle Toronto went out to make a rushing game of it. The Detroit defense was hard-pressed to meet their rivals' opening rush, but meet it they did. They received a little respite when Red Horner took a penalty for tripping Howe, but were called on to work feverishly again as soon as Horner's penalty expired.

Almost all through the opening frame the Leafs kept the puck in Detroit's zone, and in 18:10 of the session managed to poke through the first score. Joe Primeau, breaking fast down the right alley, darted around Bucko McDonald, got in on Smith alone, and rifled a blistering drive into the cords. The goal marked the first time during the entire series that the Leafs led their rivals during a game.

Even with their one-goal advantage, the Toronto stick-wielders refused to let up in the second period. They rushed repeatedly and gave the Wings little opportunity to make the play. The visitors showed no eagerness, however, and waited for a break.

Goodfellow Evens Score

One came in 9:55 when Johnny Sorrell flashed down the left lane, and handed a sharp pass to Goodfellow. Goodfellow shot fast, and scored from about eight feet out.

This success spurred the Wings, and they shot through for another in 10:38. Herbie Lewis made the play, guiding the puck almost the entire length of the rink. He ended his rush by sending the disk over the goal mouth, and Barry flipped it in with a backhand thrust.

Following these two quick setbacks the Leafs intensified their aggressive efforts, and near the end of the period came close to bringing about another tie. Bill Thoms broke away, split Detroit's defense, and was in on Smith alone, but the latter turned his shot aside with a sensational save.

The Wings took several chances in the third period, but could not beat or get past Hainsworth until 9:45. Then Kelly took a relay from Lewis, and netted the disk easily. Toronto wasted little time getting the score back, however, for in 10:57 Thoms climaxed a sensational solo rush by scoring on a long, straight shot.

From that point on the Leafs went berserk. They abandoned all defense and crowded tenaciously about Detroit's net. Charley Conacher, the Leafs' hard-shooting scoring star, rapped two resounding drives off Smith's stick, while Primeau almost sneaked one past from an angle.

The fans breathlessly followed the play, with one eye on the clock, but all their cheers could not root their favorites home.

The line-up:

DETROIT (3)		TORONTO (2)
Smith	Goal	Hainsworth
McDonald	Defense	Clancy
Young	Defense	Day
Pettinger	Center	Thoms
H. Kilrea	Wing	Finnigan
Howe	Wing	Boll
Goodfellow	Spare	Blair
Bowman	Spare	Horner
Aurie	Spare	Conacher
Barry	Spare	Primeau
Lewis	Spare	Davidson
W. Kilrea	Spare	A. Jackson
Bruneteau	Spare	H. Jackson
Sorrell	Spare	Pep Kelly
Pete Kelly	Spare	Shill

First Period
1—Toronto, Primeau 18:11
Second Period.
2—Detroit, Goodfellow (Sorrell)......9:55
3—Detroit, Barry (Lewis)......10:39
Third Period
4—Detroit, Pete Kelly (Lewis)......9:45
5—Toronto, Thoms 10:57
Penalties—First period: Horner, Day (2 minutes each). Second period: Goodfellow, Conacher, Howe, Blair (2 minutes each). Third period: None.
Referees—Bill Stewart and Ag Smith.
Time of periods—20 minutes.

April 12, 1936

Center of the Leafs Gets 79 Points in Poll of Hockey Writers—Drillon Second

TORONTO, March 22 (AP).—Sylvanus Apps, Toronto center who stepped into the shoes of the famed Joe Primeau last Fall, was named today as the outstanding rookie of the National Hockey League.

In the third annual rookie poll, conducted by The Canadian Press, the 21-year-old Paris (Ont.) player, who tied for sixth place in the Olympic pole vault last Summer as a member of Canada's team, received more than three times the point total of his team-mate and closest rival, Gordon Drillon.

On the basis of three points for a first-place selection, two for second and one for third in the votes cast by twenty-eight hockey writers, Apps received 79 points, just five short of the highest possible total. Drillon, who was brought up from Syracuse when Chuck Conacher suffered a pre-season wrist injury, got 25 points. Others listed were Ray Getliffe, Boston; 17; Neil Colville, New York Rangers, 16; George Brown, Montreal Canadiens, 13; Walter Broda, Toronto, 8, and Jimmy Fowler, Toronto, 5.

Apps was the second highest scorer for the league season, making 45 points, one less than Dave (Sweeney) Schriner of the New York Americans, who was the best rookie of the 1934-35 season. Last year Mike Karakas, Chicago goaltender, was named the season's leading recruit.

Norm Smith of the Detroit Red Wings was hailed as winner of the Georges Vezina Memorial Trophy today, first of the official league awards. The cup, named in honor of the famous Canadiens' net minder, is given annually to the goalie who has the fewest goals scored against him during the full season. Smith was nicked for 102 tallies, the highest total ever scored against a cup winner.

March 23, 1937

Wings Win League Hockey Title

Detroit Conquers Canadiens, 2-1, In Third Overtime Period of Final

Hec Kilrea's Goal Ends Game After 1 Hour 51 Minutes, Sending Wings to Stanley Cup Last Round—McKenzie of Losers Ties Score Near End of Regular Time—Goodfellow Counts First

By The Canadian Press

MONTREAL, Friday, April 2.—Hec Kilrea, veteran speedster who made Detroit forget the loss of Larry Aurie, slashed home a goal early today to beat the Montreal Canadiens, 2—1, after fifty-one minutes of thrill-packed overtime action in the fifth and deciding game of the National Hockey League championship play-off.

Thus the gallant Canadiens went out of the Stanley Cup fight after one of the greatest comebacks in the history of trophy play. They were put out after tying the score late in the third period when the Red Wings were less than six minutes away from victory in regulation time.

Kilrea's goal, his third of the series, came as the near-exhausted teams skated toward the close of the third overtime period. It gave Detroit the series, three games to two, and a place in the Stanley Cup final against either the Rangers or Maroons. In all, the first-place rivals battled 1 hour 51 minutes in the final game.

Lewis and Barry Assist

The veterans Herb Lewis and Marty Barry, who drew Kilrea as a linemate only because Aurie broke his leg near the close of the season, started the play leading to the winning goal. They carried the puck into the Canadiens' defensive zone, and Barry whipped a shot past the right side of Wilf Cude's net.

The disk came out on the left and Kilrea, parked at the side, slashed it into a far corner before Cude even moved.

The teams went into overtime after Ebbie Goodfellow lashed a twenty-five shot past Cude early in the second period, and Bill McKenzie, just a couple of minutes after he was sent on the ice for the first time, sent a rising backhand shot past Normie Smith at 14:56 of the third period.

It was the pudgy Smith, back in goal after missing half of the third game and all of the fourth, who shared the hero's rôle with Kilrea.

The Line-Up.

DETROIT (2)		CANADIENS (1)
Smith	Goal	Cude
Goodfellow	Defense	Siebert
Bowman	Defense	Buswell
Barry	Center	Haynes
Lewis	Wing	Joliat
H. Kilrea	Wing	Gagnon
Gallagher	Spare	McKenzie
McDonald	Spare	Lorrain
Howe	Spare	Miller
W. Kilrea	Spare	Brown
Sorrell	Spare	Lepine
Pettinger	Spare	Mantha
Bruneteau	Spare	Desilets
Kelly	Spare	Blake
Mackie	Spare	Mondou

First Period
No scoring.
Second Period
1—Detroit, Goodfellow 4:41
Third Period
2—Canadiens, McKenzie..............14:56
First Overtime Period
No scoring.
Second Overtime Period
No scoring.
Third Overtime Period
3—Detroit, H. Kilrea (Barry, Lewis)..11:49
Penalties—First period: Bowman, 2 minutes. Second period: Gallagher, Siebert. Hec Kilrea, 2 minutes each. Third period: Gagnon, Gallagher, 5 minutes each. Overtime periods: None.

Smith was in with an injured left arm but couldn't have been better with two strong ones.

He made fifty-two stops to thirty for Cude before the last overtime period started. And he saved the game for the Wings soon after that

session opened with a thrilling leg stop on a close-in smash by Paul Haynes. He had been almost as brilliant on a half dozen other Canadien rallies in the second overtime period.

Open Hockey the Order

With so much at stake, the teams played surprisingly open hockey. The Canadiens, who would have made hockey history by winning a third straight, outshot the world champion Wings in every period after the first, but couldn't pass Smith save for the late third period goal by McKenzie.

Twice the Canadiens had the advantage of penalties but couldn't do a thing. There were six penalties in all, including majors to Johnny Gallagher and Johnny Gagnon for a brief fighting flurry.

But the teams stuck to hockey in the overtime and they skated through the 51 minutes 49 seconds of extra play without a banishment.

It was the second game of the series in which Kilrea had played a leading rôle. He shot two goals in the 4-0 victory the Red Wings scored in the first game at Detroit.

April 2, 1937

14,000 See Detroit Retain Stanley Cup by Beating Rangers

RED WINGS SUBDUE RANGERS BY 3 TO 0

Win Final Contest of 5-Game Series for World Hockey Title on Own Ice

BARRY MAKES TWO GOALS

Sorrell Tallies Other in Hard-Fought Battle—Score by Pratt Is Disallowed

By JOSEPH C. NICHOLS
Special to THE NEW YORK TIMES.

DETROIT, April 15.—The gallant bid of the New York Rangers for the Stanley Cup failed tonight. Detroit's Red Wings, holders of the trophy and the world hockey championship that it symbolizes, repulsed the Manhattan skaters in the fifth and deciding game of the series by 3 to 0.

An enemy goal in each of the three periods encompassed the defeat of the Blue Shirts who were aspiring to bring the championship to New York for the first time since 1933.

A deliriously happy crowd of 14,-000 persons, packing the Olympia to capacity, saw the Wings, led by Marty Barry, settle the issue definitely.

Barry, whose goal in the fourth game of the series enabled the local forces to beat the Rangers Tuesday night, 1 to 0, came through with two counters tonight, the opener in the first period, and the final in the third chapter. Sandwiched between was a brilliant tally by Johnny Sorrell, the Red Wings' sharpshooting left wing.

Goalie Shares in Victory

Barry and Sorrell may have been the scoring heroes, and their tallies certainly were of the greatest importance. But there is no gainsaying the fact that the result could well have been a different one had it not been for the brilliant work of Earl Robertson in the Detroit nets.

Robertson, a rookie goalie who received his big chance when Normie Smith, the Red Wings' regular goalie, was hurt in an earlier series, played an inspired game.

Beset by the hard-driving Ranger snipers from the opening minute, Robertson was called on to work almost continuously, and the job must have been a nerve-racking one.

But he met his assignments readily, to register his second straight shut-out against the visitors.

Good as his performance was, however, Robertson did allow one shot to get past him, though it will never show in the records. In the second chapter, with the Wings leading, 1 to 0, Walter (Babe) Pratt, Ranger defense stalwart, banged the rebound of a shot into the Detroit cage and thought he had a score.

But, to his chagrin and that of his team-mates, the tally was disallowed by Referee Mickey Ion, who maintained that he had blown the whistle before the shot, to assess a holding penalty against Herb Lewis.

Cooper Penalty Costly

This ruling, naturally, came as a hard blow to the Rangers, since it forced them to maintain an incessant attack in an endeavor to draw on even terms with their foes.

It was through a penalty called against Joe Cooper of the Ranger defense, late in the opening chapter, that Barry was able to make the initial goal. Cooper was detected holding Herbie Lewis near the Ranger net and was sent off for two minutes. Taking advantage of this break, the home stick-wielders launched a heavy charge, practically their first heavy one of the game, and succeeded in beating Davey Kerr.

Syd Howe set the play in motion, by rapping a sizzling shot off Kerr's stick. The New York goalie could not control the rebound which fell at Barry's feet, and the latter had little difficulty lifting the rubber into the cords to give the Wings the lead, at 19:22.

Although they had set the pace from the very start of play, the Rangers found themselves obliged to intensify their charges after yielding this tally. For the Wings were committed definitely to a safety first policy, had been, in fact, with the first whistle.

Shibicky Shoots Wide

New York's intense rushes came close to bearing fruit early in the second period, when Alex Shibicky, after taking a pass from Neil Colville, had an open net in front of him, only to shoot wide.

Forced to commit themselves to a persistent offensive, the Rangers were unable to afford Kerr much protection. Out of a scramble near the Ranger net, Barry and Hec Kilrea came up with the puck and set it up perfectly for Sorrell, deep in Ranger ice. As easy as he had things, Sorrell had to shoot three times to score, his first two drives being splendidly blocked by Kerr. The third, though, went past him,

at 9:36 of the second period.

Practically the same situation obtained in the third frame, when Sorrell broke away with a clear field ahead of him, to hand a sharp pass to Barry, who counted easily at 2:33.

The line-up:

DETROIT (3)		RANGERS (0)
Robertson	Goal	Kerr
Gallagher	Defense	Coulter
McDonald	Defense	Heller
Pettinger	Center	Boucher
Bruneteau	Wing	Dillon
Lewis	Wing	Patrick
Goodfellow	Spare	N. Colville
Bowman	Spare	M. Colville
Barry	Spare	Shibicky
Sorrell	Spare	Watson
H. Kilrea	Spare	Murdoch
W. Kilrea	Spare	Keeling
Sherf	Spare	Pratt
Kelly	Spare	Johnson
Howe	Spare	Cooper

First Period
1—Detroit, Barry (Howe)............19:22
Second Period
2—Detroit, Sorrell (Barry, H. Kilrea). 9:36
Third Period
3—Detroit, Barry (Sorrell)..........2:33
Penalties—First period: Sorrell, Coulter, Sherf, Pettinger, Coulter (2 minutes each). Second period: Lewis, Cooper, W. Kilrea, Coulter (2 minutes each). Third period: Coulter, Gallagher (2 minutes each).
Referees—Bill Stewart and Mickey Ion. Time of periods—20 minutes.

April 16, 1937

League Takes Full Control of American Six; Goalie Robertson Sold to the New York Club

By The Associated Press.

DETROIT, May 8.—The Red Wings sold Earl Robertson, their amazing goal tender, to the New York Americans today in the only deal announced at the Spring meeting of the National Hockey League.

Detroit will receive $7,50⁰ cash and the contract of Red Doran, defense man, in return for the goalie who came up from the Pittsburgh Hornets to take the place of the injured Normie Smith in the Stanley Cup series.

The National League assumed full ownership of the Americans when W. V. Dwyer, original owner, failed to exercise his option to reclaim the club. The league took over control of the club last season because of its financial difficulties.

Unless a buyer should take the franchise to some other city in the interim, the Americans will play in New York again next season.

Frank Calder, re-elected president of the league at the meeting, announced that major league hockey last season enjoyed its most prosperous year since 1930. The eight teams of the National League played to 1,628,785 spectators, which was 125,000 more than in the previous season. The seventeen games of the Stanley Club play-offs drew 314,000 spectators, the largest attendance since the present league was organized.

Although there had been talk of moving the Montreal Maroons' franchise to Cleveland or St. Louis, no such effort was made at the meeting. Frank Ruppenthal, president of the St. Louis Flyers of the American Association, said he did not believe St. Louis was ready for another major league venture. Al Sutphin of Cleveland was at the meeting but there was no outward effort to transfer a National League franchise to the Ohio city.

May 9, 1937

Black Hawks Beat Maple Leafs and Take Stanley Cup Series, 3 Games to 1

17,204 SEE CHICAGO SCORE 4-1 TRIUMPH

Rapid-Fire Goals by Voss and Shill in Second Beat Leafs for World Hockey Title

DAHLSTROM NETS IN FIRST

But Drillon of Toronto Evens Count—Hawks' Victory Caps Post-Season Upsets

By The Associated Press.

CHICAGO, April 12.—The indomitable Chicago Black Hawks, one of the longest long shots in all sports history, scored in every period tonight to defeat the Toronto Maple Leafs, 4 to 1, to win the Stanley Cup and world hockey championship before 17,204 spectators at the Chicago Stadium.

The Hawks, who had finished only third in the American Division and lost their last three games of the regular National Hockey League season, defeated the Leafs, holders of the league title, on sensational second-period goals by Carl Voss and Jack Shill. The tallies, which broke a 1-1 deadlock, indirectly led to an additional counter in the final period to clinch a third victory for the Chicagoans in four starts against Toronto in the final series.

Winning their second Stanley Cup, the Hawks trounced the speedy Leafs with a dogged fighting spirit. Taking the lead within six minutes on Cully Dahlstrom's counter, the Hawks saw the high-geared Leafs, overwhelming favorites to win the cup before the series, roar back for the tying goal, scored by Gordon Drillon, with help from Jimmy Fowler.

Voss Steals Disk

Undaunted, the Chicagoans battled the Leafs evenly through three-quarters of the second stanza and then counted twice in 1 minute 13

Wired Photo—Times Wide World

BLACK HAWKS CELEBRATE VICTORY OVER TORONTO SEXTET
Players around Manager Bill Stewart after winning final Stanley Cup game in Chicago last night

seconds. Voss, a veteran obtained from Montreal's Maroons, stole the puck from Defensemen Fowler and Reg Hamilton and rifled a ten-foot shot past Goalie Walter Broda to put the Hawks in front.

A few plays later Shill drove a counter which will take its place in hockey's "book." Obviously on the defense, he idly lifted the puck into the air toward the Leaf net, flicking the disk from a spot fully 110 feet from the Toronto cage. Broda came out, dropped confidently to his knees for what appeared a routine stop, and then saw the rubber bounce over his stick and into the twine.

The goals forced the Leafs to open up in the third and this aided

Chicago to a score by Mush March, diminutive forward. Taking a pass from Doc Romnes, March rifled a shot from right wing to beat Broda with less than four minutes of play remaining.

During the entire final stanza Chicago, led by Goalie Mike Karakas, fought off desperate Leaf bids which had the crowd in a constant uproar. While the attendance was capacity, it did not approach the 18,496 overflow throng that had set a league record last Sunday.

An Outstanding Feat

The outcome made the Hawk manager, Chunky Bill Stewart, one of the year's outstanding sports figures. In his first year as a major league hockey pilot Stewart led his players through an uphill, incredible climb comparable to the 1914 climb of baseball's Boston Braves from last place to the world title.

The Hawks accomplished close to the same feat. During the regular season they beat Toronto only once in six games. They won only fourteen of forty-eight games and had forty-two more goals scored against them than they could notch. They qualified for the play-offs only because Detroit's Red Wings, Stanley Cup holders the previous two seasons, collapsed.

Reaching the play-offs, Chicago lost a game to Montreal's Canadiens, but then won two straight.

They lost another series opener to the New York Americans, but again advanced by winning the next two games. They won the opener from Toronto, lost the second with Rookie Paul Goodman in the nets and came from behind Sunday to win and qualify for the opportunity to scale the heights they reached tonight.

The victory, worth more than $1,000 to each Chicagoan, climaxed one of the dizziest seasons in the league's history. Not expected to defeat Boston's Bruins, Toronto took the league title in three straight games. Then the Hawks, with Manager Stewart at the reins, galloped to their amazing triumph in the sport's world series.

Only Five Penalties

The deciding game, while rough, was not as vicious as previous encounters, although the first period was enlivened by several "wrestling" matches. Only five penalties in all were assessed, none a major. After the final whistle, as the cup was presented the almost hysterical Hawks, the Leaf personnel congratulated the victors.

Some wag, after the game, dubbed the Hawks the "Election Electrifiers." During the day voters balloted in the Illinois primary and Chicago's last and only other cup victory was achieved during an election. On April 10, 1934, Chicago defeated Detroit for the world title, winning the fourth game in overtime.

The line-up:

TORONTO (1)	CHICAGO (4)
Broda ....Goal.......... Karakas
Horner ....Defense........ Mackenzie
Fowler ....Defense........ Levinsky
Apps ....Center........ Romnes
Davidson ......Wing.......... Thompson
Drillon ....Wing.......... March
Hamilton ......Spare......... Wiebe
Thoms ....Spare......... Shill
Boll ....Spare......... Gottselig
Armstrong .....Spare......... Trudell
Jackson ....Spare......... Voss
Kets ....Spare......... Dahlstrom
Kelly ....Spare......... Jenkins
Parsons ....Spare......... Seibert
Kampman ....Spare......... Palangio

First Period
1—Chicago, Dahlstrom (Trudell, Shill) 5:52
2—Toronto, Drillon (Fowler) 8:26
Second Period
3—Chicago, Voss (Gottselig, Jenkins).16:45
4—Chicago, Shill (unassisted).........17:58
Third Period
5—Chicago, March (Thompson, Romnes) 16:24
Penalties—First period: Davidson, Drillon, Parson, Jenkins, 2 minutes each. Second period: None. Third period: Davidson, 2 minutes.
Referees—Mickey Ion and John Mitchell.
Time of periods—20 minutes.

April 13, 1938

MAROONS DROPPED FROM HOCKEY LOOP

Year's Suspension Granted—St. Louis Bid to Transfer Franchise Is Rejected

---

7 TEAMS IN THE CIRCUIT

Action Is Taken by Board of Governors of the National League at Meeting Here

---

The fate of the Montreal Maroons was decided for one year, at least, when the Canadian outfit was granted a year's suspension from the National Hockey League at a meeting of the loop's board of governors at the Hotel Commodore last night.

Earlier in the day a proposition to transfer the Maroons' franchise to St. Louis was formally rejected by the board of governors. President Frank Calder declared that the board would have favored an outright sale of the franchise to St. Louis sportsmen, but did not like the option agreement that was proposed.

This proposal provided that the Reconstruction Investment Company of St. Louis would take over the Maroons with the option of purchasing the franchise in three years. President Calder stated that the offer did not show much promise, since no cash was forthcoming nor was there a guarantee that the team would be continued in operation for the stated time.

As a result of the action, the National Hockey League will operate as a seven-team circuit during the 1938-39 season. The competing teams will be the New York Rangers, New York Americans, Toronto Maple Leafs, Montreal Canadiens, Boston Bruins, Detroit Red Wings and Chicago Black Hawks.

It will mark the first time since the 1925-26 campaign that the league will operate with seven teams.

The Maroons had made an application for a one-year suspension of the franchise at the annual meeting of the league last June. It was felt that the suspension would be the best solution to the difficulties of the team, which finished in the International Division cellar position last Winter. The Maroons won only twelve games, lost thirty and tied six during the 1937-38 season. They have had poor support at home for two years, losing money steadily.

President Tommy Gorman announced last night that he would rent the players on his squad to the highest bidders. Gorman, besides being president of the Maroons, is also general manager of the Montreal Forum, home rink of the Maroons and the Canadiens.

August 26, 1938

Letters

Asks Origin of Hockey Term

To Sports Editor of The New York Times:

Lately I have noticed the very frequent use of the term "hat trick" to designate the scoring of three goals by one player in a hockey game.

I understand that this same term also is employed with the same meaning in soccer.

What I have been unable to find out, though, is the origin of the term. I wonder if you, or any of your readers, could enlighten me?
A. TYRO.
New Haven, Conn., Dec. 14, 1938.

Editorial Note: If the correspondent had referred to Webster's New International Dictionary, he would have found enlightenment in this definition of "hat trick," with reference to cricket: the performance of a bowler who dismisses three batsmen with consecutive balls, a feat sometimes rewarded with a present of a new hat. Webster also takes cognizance of the term in its application to Association football (soccer), noting, in this case, that the three goals of the "hat trick" do not necessarily have to be consecutive.

December 17, 1938

Eight Major Penalties Called for Fighting as Rangers Win to Prolong Series

15,692 SEE RANGERS STOP BOSTON, 2 TO 1

Lynn Patrick's Second-Period Tally Wins After Mac Colville Counts in First

---

FREE-FOR-ALL AT GARDEN

By JOSEPH C. NICHOLS

The New York Rangers earned a reprieve last night. Carrying a slam-bang, reckless, teeth-rattling attack to their rivals, the Blue Shirts conquered the Boston Bruins, 2 to 1, in a nerve-tingling battle that produced just about every variety of thrill found in hockey.

By their triumph the New York skaters kept alive their chances of winning the Stanley Cup and its attendant honor, the championship of the world. These chances, though, are slim indeed, with the Bruins still having a tremendous edge. The teams are engaging in a four-out-of-seven game playoff, and Boston already has three games tucked away in the win column, while last night's conquest was the first effected by the New Yorkers.

A wild-eyed crowd of 15,692 left Madison Square Garden after a struggle in which the rival teams tore at each other with a savagery that eclipsed, by far, anything produced in the three previous meetings. The tension which the athletes had been under the past week snapped with a crackling suddenness in the first period and a general fist fight occurred that had all the skaters on the ice at the time engaged. This outbreak set the pitch for the rest of the encounter, played under an electric atmosphere until the final buzzer.

Bruins Lose Little Time

The Rangers had to come from behind, a feat that they accomplished with goals by Mac Colville and Lynn Patrick. The Bruins, prepared to meet a last-stand resistance, lost little time getting the first goal, which is always of tremendous psychological importance. The game was only 49 seconds old when Milt Schmidt batted the puck out of a scramble in front of the Ranger cage for the tally which the Bruins hoped would lead them to a fourth straight victory.

But the Rangers were not at all prepared to succumb supinely. Instead they risked all in a bitter offensive that netted the tying tally in the first period and the winning one in the second.

Even when they had the lead the New Yorkers did not hesitate to attack. They were out to "do or die," and they wanted with all their hearts to score as many goals as possible against young Frank Brimsek.

But Boston accorded its goalie excellent protection, and there was no further scoring. With thirty-one seconds left in the third period, Manager Art Ross pulled Brimsek from the nets, so that his team might attack with six skaters, but so prone were the New Yorkers to rush that Ross had to put Brimsek back with eight seconds left after Neil Colville had fired a disallowed goal from a face-off deep in Ranger ice.

Goalies Are Brilliant

Both goalies, Brimsek and Bert Gardiner, played excellently. Both were called on several times to make almost impossible saves and they came through expertly, on the whole.

The mass fist-fight, which broke out shortly after the midway mark of the first period, with the score tied at 1-all, developed from a situation that seemed mild enough. Phil Watson of the Rangers and Jack Portland, Boston guard, were pushing each other to the boards when suddenly they started swinging.

In a trice the other skaters rushed and blows were exchanged freely. Watson, Murray Patrick and Dutch Hiller did most of the fighting for the New Yorkers, while Eddie Shore, Portland and Gordon Pettinger were the Boston champions.

For some time matters were completely out of hand, but at length the officials managed to restore order and sent the six leading belligerents to the penalty box on majors of five minutes apiece. The deferred penalty rule, providing for substitutes to replace the offending players to insure at least four men from each team on the ice, had to be invoked.

When the game began the Rangers rushed, Hiller skating down the left alley with the disk. He lost it to Milt Schmidt, who quickly carried over New York's line down the center.

Coulter's Stick Breaks

Schmidt set the rubber up for Bobby Bauer and Woody Dumart, each of whom fired. Gardiner blocked these shots well enough, and Art Coulter was about to clear when his stick broke, whereupon Schmidt batted the puck into the cords.

This quick tally, of course, was not at all to the Rangers' liking, and they went berserk trying to reach Brimsek. They did so, finally, after a beautiful passing advance made by Bill Carse and Alex Shibicky.

Carse advanced along the center alley and relayed to Shibicky on the left. The latter then flashed a pass back to the center to Mac Colville, who lifted the rubber into the cords in 8:56.

The New Yorkers mantained the offensive and tested Brimsek repeatedly, but with no success. Then occurred the fistic flare-up that threw the Garden into an uproar and resulted in the wholesale banishments. During the absence of most of the belligerents the Rangers led in the rushing and came close to breaking the tie when Clint Smith stick-handled his way to the Boston net, where he was stopped by Brimsek.

Shortly before the end of the period Babe Pratt and Jack Crawford became embroiled in a fight. They, too, received major vacations.

In the second period the Rangers were handicapped by a penalty called on Bryan Hextall. The Bruins could do nothing with this advantage, however, despite their heavy charges.

Then George Allen replaced Hextall in the penalty box and the Bruins attacked again. This strategy did not turn out to their liking, for Clint Smith and Ott Heller worked their way into Boston ice and gave the rubber to Lynn Patrick, who bounced it off Dit Clap-

AS RANGERS DEFEATED THE BRUINS LAST NIGHT

Times Wide World

Players engaging in fight which brought six major penalties in the first period of game

per's skate into the cords in 10:02.

For the rest of the period the Patrickmen rushed determinedly, sending many drives at Brimsek's stick. The Boston goalie was alert, however, and turned back everything.

At the start of the third frame the Rangers kept up the same swift, aggressive pace, but they gradually had to give way to the desperate Bruins. Gardiner certainly had his work cut out for him during these closing minutes, but he rose to the occasion manfully.

Shore's Play Brilliant

Eddie Shore, whose work on the Boston backline was truly sensational, suffered most in the fist fighting. His nose was broken, but that did not keep from returning to the game. He was the spearhead of the third-period attack and almost beat Gardiner twice on short drives.

While Brimsek was out of the cage in the last minute, Neil Colville faced off against Shore deep

in Ranger ice. The Ranger center got the puck and shot in one motion, and the disk slid the length of the rink into the empty cage. No score was allowed, howaver, because of an offside move by Murray Patrick.

Eighteen penalties in all were called, ten against the Rangers. The total time assessed against the New Yorkers was 32 minutes and against the visitors 28.

The teams will play the fifth game of the series tomorrow night in Boston. The sixth, if necessary, will be here on Saturday, and the seventh on Sunday in Boston.

In the second period, while the Rangers were conferring among themselves, Linesman Danny McFadyen faced the puck for Gordon Pettinger, who had no one playing against him. The Blue Shirts sprang out of their huddle to spill Pettinger just as he was about to shoot.

The line-up:

RANGERS (2)		BOSTON (1)
Gardiner	Goal	Brimsek
Coulter	Defense	Shore
M. Patrick	Defense	Portland
Watson	Center	Schmidt
Hextall	Wing	Bauer
Hiller	Wing	Dumart
Heller	Spare	Clapper
Shibicky	Spare	Getliffe
M. Colville	Spare	Welland
N. Colville	Spare	Conacher
L. Patrick	Spare	Cowley
C. Smith	Spare	Pettinger
Pratt	Spare	Hollett
Molyneaux	Spare	Hamill
Allen	Spare	Hill
Carse	Spare	Crawford

First Period

1—Boston, Schmidt (Bauer, Dumart).. 0:49
2—Rangers, M. Colville (Shibicky, Carse) 8:56

Second Period

3—Rangers, L. Patrick (Smith, Heller).10:02

Third Period

No scoring.

Penalties—First period: Heller, Hill, Portland (2 minutes each); Shore, Portland, Pettinger, Watson, Hiller, M. Patrick, Pratt, Crawford (5 minutes each). Second period: Hextall, Allen, Pratt 2, Shore, Hamill (2 minutes each). Third period: M. Patrick (2 minutes).

Referee—Mickey Ion. Linesman—Don MacFadyen. Time of periods—20 minutes.

March 29, 1939

Bruins Gain Cup Finals by Downing Rangers in Overtime

HILL'S GOAL WINS FOR BOSTON, 2 TO 1

Marker After 48 Minutes of Overtime Puts the Rangers Out of Play-Offs, 4-3

By JOSEPH C. NICHOLS

Special to THE NEW YORK TIMES.

BOSTON, Monday, April 3.—The Boston Bruins eliminated the Rangers from the National Hockey League play-offs by defeating the courageous band from New York, 2 to 1, in a stirring overtime strug-

gle that thrilled a capacity crowd of 16,981 wild-eyed fans.

The battle came to an end at 12:40 t' s morning after the teams had pounded each other steadily and without mercy through three periods of regulation play and exactly 48 minutes of overtime, or 108 minutes in all.

Sharp-eyed Mel Hill, who once tried to join the Rangers, came through with the winning tally with the assistance of Bill Cowley and Roy Conacher, and in so doing displayed his "sudden-death" virtuosity for the third time during the series.

Amazing Form Reversal

The Bruins and the Rangers, who finished one-two in the regular National League race, were engaging in a best four-out-of-seven game play-off for the right to meet the Toronto Maple Leafs for the Stanley Cup, emblematic of the world championship. The Bruins went

into a top-heavy lead by setting back the New Yorkers in the first three games, but the Rangers countered with an amazing reversal of form that enabled them to square the competition at 3—all before Hill dashed their title hopes with his precise drive.

In the first two clashes between the sextets it was Hill who brought the Bruins success by slipping the puck into the Ranger net in "sudden-death" play.

The stroke that finally blasted the Rangers' chances came with electric suddenness, and interrupted a period of play which was marked by extreme caution on both sides. Conacher had carried the rubber into the New York corner on the right alley, and Bryan Hextall fought him for possession. Hextall momentarily got the puck but the eel-like Cowley tricked him out of it and flashed a relay to Hill, who was standing alone about ten feet out of the Ranger cage.

Bert Gardiner, who did an excellent job in the Ranger nets since he was conscripted from the Philadelphia Ramblers after the first game of the series, had no protection at all as he got set for Hill's shot. But Hill found the wide-open spot on Gardiner's right and blasted the rubber safely into the cords. The time was 8:00 of the third twenty-minute overtime period.

To effect their triumph the Bruins had to fight off an inspired, confident team that felt it was certain to earn the right to play for the Stanley Cup. Confident as they were, however, the Rangers took no unnecessary chances until the second period, after Ray Getliffe had converted a pass from Gordon Pettinger into the first Boston goal. On yielding this score, the New York skaters charged full strength, and in less than two minutes drew even with their opponents.

Murray Patrick, younger son of the Rangers' manager, Lester Pat-

Wired Photo—Times Wide World

A RANGER SAVE IN FIRST PERIOD AT BOSTON LAST NIGHT

Gardiner stopping a drive by Pettinger in final game of play-off series between the rivals

rick, scored the goal that knotted the count. He took a pass from Mac Colville just inside the Boston blue line and released a blazing shot that flew past the blocked-off Frank Brimsek, Boston's sterling net guardian, into the cage.

After creating this tie, the New Yorkers continued to charge the Boston team all through the third period, and they had several chances to score, each of which was muffled by Brimsek.

Bruins Take Command

When the teams went into the first overtime period the Bruins forcibly took command of the situation. They harried the Ranger puck-carriers from all sides, and gave the visitors little opportunity to organize their advances. At the same time the home skaters vigilantly watched for scoring chances, and frequently bored in on the Blue Shirts' cage, where Gardiner held them off masterfully.

In the second overtime the Bruins followed rather the same policy. They seemed inexhaustible as they sent wave after wave into Ranger ice and the crushing body checks they handed out to the Ranger rushers seemed to be delivered by men who were quite fresh.

The Rangers moved into the aggressive somewhat in the third extra frame, and almost took the honors when Bill Carse skated in on Brimsek, after taking a pass from Neil Colville. But Carse fired squarely at the Boston goalie's pads and the New Yorkers' biggest chance went awry. It was shortly afterward that Hill, the opportunist, brought the grueling game and series to an end.

Boston will have little time to rest before tackling the Leafs. This final series will start here tomorrow night, and the Toronto team, refreshed by its rest since Saturday night, will have the edge on the local skaters in the matter of condition.

Show Passing Skill

Although they did not figure in the scoring, the Bruins' far-famed "sauerkraut line" of Milt Schmidt, Bobby Bauer and Woody Dumart caused the Rangers no end of trouble. They passed their way skillfully into New York ice innumerable times, and their persistence in the vicinity of the Blue Shirts' cage frayed the Rangers' nerves considerably.

On the Boston back line there was no denying the brilliance of Eddie Shore. The bruised and scarred veteran hoisted the opposition carriers heavily but cleanly, and his presence on the ice had very much to do with Brimsek's good showing.

In losing the Rangers' glory was undimmed. Manager Patrick's charges played with an undying will that certainly must have pleased their gray-haired pilot.

Particularly must Patrick have been impressed by the excellent showing made by Ott Heller, Art Coulter, Clint Smith and Neil Colville, not to mention Gardiner.

When the game got under way the Bruins made the first rush, but they were easily repulsed, and the game took on a tinge of cautious play until Heller was sent to the penalty box.

Shot Grazes Goal Post

The Boston skaters tried to rush, but they lost the disk to Alex Shibicky, who twice came close to beating Brimsek on short attempts. Shortly after Heller returned the Bruins lost Hollett, who was sent off for holding Smith. During Hollett's absence the New Yorkers had only one good chance at Brimsek, a drive by Carse which grazed a goal post.

Near the end of the session Red Hamill, Shore and Pettinger each had chances at Gardiner, but each was turned back.

The "Kraut Line" bothered the Rangers a good deal in the second

period, but Gardiner held them off. The Bruins then lay back and awaited their chance, which came finally when Pettinger scurried across the Ranger border and handed a pass to Getliffe. The latter, just outside the goal, swung quickly and the rubber bounced off Gardiner's leg into the cage in 15:52.

Immediately the Rangers cast aside all caution. They swarmed across their foes' line five-strong, with Mac Colville doing some fine stick-handling. He handed a sharp pass to Murray Patrick on the left alley inside Boston's border, and Patrick let fly with the shot that knotted the count in 17:45.

Through the third frame there were many close calls for each team, but the rival goalies played their posts well and kicked out everything that came their way.

Skates In on Gardiner

Matters seemed certainly at an end late in the first overtime period when Conacher skated in on Gardiner alone, to hit the post with one shot and to miss an open cage

with his rebound drive.

The pace seemed to tell on the Rangers as the second overtime wore on, and their rushes slowed somewhat. The situation remained tense, however, and the fans excitedly followed every move on the ice.

Bauer laced a sizzling shot at Gardiner to open the third extra frame, and soon afterward Shore almost crashed the puck past the visiting goalie's stick. Hill and Murray Patrick were sent off for roughing, and while they were out Carse had the chance which he was unable to convert.

When Hill and Patrick returned to the ice, the Boston team sent Conacher ahead on the first manoeuvre of the advance that ended the game. Hextall tried hard to keep the rubber from Cowley, but the latter feinted the Ranger out of his way and placed the puck squarely on the line for Hill's winning shot.

Two New Yorkers Hurt

The Rangers were quite beaten physically, Shibicky suffering a wrenched shoulder and Neil Colville a cut face.

On each of his three "sudden-death" scores in the series, Hill took the immediately contributing pass from Cowley.

The attendance tied the all-time Boston mark set by the same teams here March 26. The total attendance for the four games in this city was 67,073.

The line-up:

BOSTON (2)		RANGERS (1)
Brimsek	Goal	Gardiner
Shore	Defense	Pratt
Portland	Defense	Heller
Schmidt	Center	Watson
Bauer	Wing	Hextall
Dumart	Wing	Hiller
Sands	Spare	Kerr
Clapper	Spare	Coulter
Getliffe	Spare	Shibicky
Weiland	Spare	M. Colville
Conacher	Spare	N. Colville
Cowley	Spare	Dillon
Pettinger	Spare	L. Patrick
Hollett	Spare	Smith
Hill	Spare	M. Patrick
Crawford	Spare	Molyneaux
Hamill	Spare	Allen
	Spare	Carse

First Period

No scoring.

Second Period

1—Boston. Getliffe (Pettinger)........15:52
2—Rangers, M. Patrick (M. Colville)..17:45

Third Period

No scoring.

First Overtime Period

No scoring.

Second Overtime Period

No scoring.

Third Overtime Period

3—Boston. Hill (Cowley. Conacher)....8:00
Penalties—First period: Heller 2. Hollett, Clapper (2 minutes each). Second period: None. Third period: None. Overtime period: M. Patrick. Hill (2 minutes each).
Referee — Mickey Ion. Linesman — Don MacFadyen. Time of periods—20 minutes. Overtime periods—20 minutes each.

April 3, 1939

Boston Wins Stanley Cup by Downing Toronto in the Fifth Contest

16,891 SEE BRUINS CONQUER LEAFS, 3-1

Annex Title Hockey Series, 4 Games to 1, for First Time in Ten Years

CONACHER'S GOAL DECIDES

Hollett Adds to Lead in Last Minute—Calder Presents Trophy After Game

By The Associated Press.

BOSTON, April 16.—The determined Boston Bruins ended a 10-year struggle for the Stanley Cup, professional hockey's world championship emblem, by gaining their third straight victory over the Toronto Maple Leafs, 3 to 1, before a hysterical crowd of 16,891 at the Boston Garden tonight.

When the fifth game of the series ended in the Bruins' fourth victory —the Leafs managed to win the second contest—the prized trophy was handed to Captain Cooney Weiland by President Frank Calder of the National Hockey League, on the ice. However, the latter's presentation speech was drowned by the cheering crowd and the explosions of widely scattered fire-crackers.

Before Weiland, who shares the distinction of having played on the last Boston Stanley Cup champions with Eddie Shore and Dit Clapper, accepted the battered silver bowl, his team-mates scored in each of the three periods against the Leafs, who battled courageously from start to finish.

Penalties Prove Costly

The first period, which saw both teams take advantage of penalties, included goals by Mel (Sudden Death) Hill and Bingo Kampmann. The Hill counter came while Gordon Drillon was on the fence and kept the Bruins for seven minutes. Then Hill was sent off and Kampmann tied the score by firing a 55-foot shot which was deflected into the net by one of Clapper's skates.

The deadlock lasted for more than 17 minutes, until Roy Conacher, whose pair of goals had given the Bruins a shutout victory at Toronto on Thursday, restored their lead by beating Goalie Turk Broda with a 10-foot counter in the second period. Bill Cowley and Shore assisted.

Before that clincher, the Leafs' outstanding threats, Gordon Drillon and Syl Apps, had missed close-up tries by narrow margins in attempting to beat the cool Frankie Brimsek.

After they had regained the lead the Bruins settled down to tight defensive play that ruined all of the Leafs' frantic efforts, which were redoubled when Shore drew his sec-

ond penalty of the game with two minutes to go. Don Metz, recruited from the amateur ranks on Wednesday as a replacement for the injured Busher Jackson, killed the Toronto hopes, however, by drawing a penalty and evening the sides.

Goal in Last Minute

As the pair rested on the fence Bill (Flash) Hollett doubled Boston's margin by tallying with the assistance of Jack Crawford and Milt Schmidt, 37 seconds before the final bell clanged.

Before gaining their second Stanley Cup title—the first was gained

by beating the New York Rangers in 1929—the Bruins had suffered the humiliating experience of being knocked out of four first-round play-offs by the Maple Leafs.

The line-up:

BOSTON (3)		TORONTO (1)
Brimsek	Goal	Broda
Portland	Defense	Horner
Shore	Defense	Kampmann
Pettinger	Center	Romnes
Getliffe	Wing	Chamberlain
Hollett	Wing	Marker
Schmidt	Spare	Apps
Bauer	Spare	Davidson
Dumart	Spare	Drillon
Clapper	Spare	McDonald
Crawford	Spare	Church
Cowley	Spare	M. Metz
Hill	Spare	D. Metz
Conacher	Spare	Hamilton
Hamill	Spare	Langelle
Weiland	Spare	Heron

First Period

1—Boston, Hill (Cowley, Conacher)....11:40
2—Toronto, Kampmann (Romnes)....18:40

Second Period

3—Boston, Conacher (Shore, Cowley)..17:54

Third Period

4—Boston, Hollett (Crawford, Schmidt).13:23

Penalties—First period: Shore, Drillon, Hill (2 minutes each). Second period: None. Third period: Hamilton, Shore, D. Metz, Kampmann (2 minutes each).

Referee—Mickey Ion. Linesman—Rabbit McVeigh. Time of periods—20 minutes.

April 17, 1939

RANGERS TOP LEAFS IN OVERTIME BY 3-2 TO WIN STANLEY CUP

14,894 See Hextall's Shot in 2:07 of Extra Play Decide World Hockey Finals, 4-2

NEIL COLVILLE, PIKE TALLY

New York Third-Period Goals Nullify Scores by Apps and Nick Metz at Toronto

By JOSEPH C. NICHOLS
Special to THE NEW YORK TIMES.

TORONTO, April 13—The Rangers won the Stanley Cup and the hockey championship of the world by subduing the stubborn Maple Leafs tonight, 3 to 2. Two goals behind with only twelve minutes left of the regulation time, the Blue Shirts squared matters and sent the battle into overtime. After 2 minutes 7 seconds of extra play Bryan Hextall, New York right wing, fired the puck past Turk Broda for the score that decided the series, 4 games to 2.

Hextall's climactic drive brought disappointment to 14,894 observers, Leaf fans almost to the last man and woman. The home-team sympathizers, led to expect a decisive triumph by the ease with which the Toronto skaters flashed into the lead by two goals before the game was half over, almost refused to believe their eyes when the winning goal flew home.

Sylvanus Apps gave the Leafs their first goal in 6:52 of the opening period. He was followed by Nick Metz, who beat Davey Kerr

in the New York nets in 4:51 of the middle chapter.

Rangers Persist in Efforts

Toronto, following the puck closely, gave the Rangers little opportunity to organize their speedy advances through the first two periods, and there were visions of a second shut-out for Broda in this series. The Rangers, despite the tremendous odds against them, persisted in attempting to move forward, nevertheless, and their efforts began to meet with some success in the third period.

They finally broke Broda down at 8:08 when Neil Colville beat him and then scored a second time in 10:01, when Alfie Pike drilled a shot into the cords.

These fast goals, important in giving the Ranger skaters new life, also earned for them a psychological advantage that, apparently, was what carried them to success. For, much as they had been outplayed up to the time the score was tied, so they outplayed the Leafs in the minutes that followed.

They put "lift" into their offensive drives, and swept in on Broda time after time on rushes that failed only because of the brilliance of the Toronto net guardian. When the game went into overtime the Rangers, helped by a rest of twenty minutes, massed themselves about the Leaf goal and, though the home skaters sent two fast "breakaway" rushes into New York ice, the Blue Shirts maintained the edge.

Dutch Hiller and Phil Watson had a large part in the winning goal. The alert Hiller swooped on the puck in Toronto's territory as Gordon Drillon and Jack Church of the Leafs collided with each other and went to the ice.

Watson Passes to Hextall

Hiller immediately pushed the puck forward to Watson, who just as quickly whipped it across the rink to Hextall, standing in the right center alley. Hextall, a dead shot from that position, fired seemingly without aiming, but the drive was true, the red light flashed, and the rival skaters immediately forgot their professional differences and pounded their erstwhile opponents

on the back in the time-honored gesture of friendliness that marks the end of every hockey play-off series.

The clash was the sixth of the post-season play-offs between the teams, competing on a four-out-of-seven basis. The Rangers won the first two games in New York, but were set back twice in a row when the series was transferred to Toronto. However, they went into the lead again by scoring an overtime triumph here on Thursday and settled the championship tonight.

Although the Rangers were 5-to-8 pre-game favorites, the Leafs paid little attention to this and lost no time carrying the play. As the game got under way Apps worked across the New York line and was almost in on Kerr before Hextall took the puck away from him. Hextall dashed to Toronto ice, followed by the other four Ranger skaters, but none was able to get a line on the cage.

When Art Coulter and Bingo Kampman were sent off for roughing, the Rangers had a good chance, Mac Colville breaking out of a mid-ice scramble and firing a sharp shot at Broda, who covered well. With the sides even in man power, Clint Smith had a loose puck in front of Toronto's goal, but lost it to Bobby Davidson before he could shoot.

Davidson transferred the rubber to Apps, who made a splendid center-alley rush that carried him between New York's defense to a point over the Rangers' penalty-shot line. From there he got off a fast shot that Kerr had no chance of stopping. The rest of the period saw the Rangers rush time and again, but the Leafs hounded them without let-up, so Broda had little to fear.

Toronto continued to harry the New York puck carriers in the second frame, while the Blue Shirts fought desperately to get near the goal. Hextall succeeded, once, in skating close to Broda, but Sweeney Schriner stole the disk and flew to New York's line. There he transferred to Nick Metz, whose straight shot eluded Kerr and lodged in the cords.

Horner Is Penalized

The Rangers received an advantage in the third period when Red

Horner was sent to the penalty box. Horner's absence did not result in a goal, but it did enable the Blue Shirts to carry the puck into Toronto's ice effectively.

After Horner's return, the Rangers were grouped in Leaf territory when Alex Shibicky came up with the disk and flashed it to Neil Colville on the right alley. Neil released a short backhander and the rubber flew home.

This tally was followed by penalties called against MacColville and Schriner for roughing. While the sextets were minus a man apiece, the Blue Shirts struck for their second goal, which was set up for Pike by Clint Smith.

Just before the regulation time ended the Rangers scored again, but the presence of a New York skater in the goal crease nullified the marker by Watson. The Rangers were chagrined at the ruling, but their chagrin was transformed to boundless joy when Hextall came through for them with his "sudden-death" counter.

History Repeats Itself

It was in Toronto that the Rangers last won the Stanley Cup. In 1933 the New Yorkers beat the Leafs in a series conducted on the basis of three out of five games.

In all, the Rangers were able to put twenty-three shots on Broda's stick, while the Leafs reached Kerr twenty-four times.

The Rangers replaced the Bruins as Stanley Cup champions. Boston retained the National Hockey League title during the regular season, but was eliminated by the New Yorkers, 4 games to 2, in the post-season series between the first and second-place clubs.

April 14, 1940

HOCKEY'S GOVERNORS MOVE TO CURB FIGHTS

Will Fine Players Responsible for General Outbreaks $25

In an effort to curb the general outbreaks of fighting among players, which have been getting out of hand recently, the board of governors of the National Hockey League, at a meeting at the Hotel Commodore yesterday, passed a rule that will bring about an automatic fine of $25 to responsible players.

Any third player or additional ones mixed up in a melee will be so penalized in the future. It is felt that the officials are capable of handling disputes between two players, but when one or more others insert themselves in a fight the situation develops into a rousing free-for-all.

The board announced that attendance figures for the first half of the hockey season show a nice increase, particularly for games played at Detroit and Montreal.

President Frank Calder and Major Frederic McLaughlin of the Chicago Black Hawks will act as a committee to meet with American Hockey Association representatives at Chicago on Sunday to discuss the continuance of the interleague agreement, which expires on Saturday. The agreement with the American Hockey League, which expired last Saturday, will be discussed on Jan. 24.

Rules interpretations also were clarified and it was decided that attacking teams will be permitted to score from the crease, if a loose puck is available. Also, the referees will be instructed to blow their whistles instantly when a player hits the disk with his stick above his shoulder.

A dispute between the Garden and the Boston Bruins concerning Angus Cameron, a junior amateur on the reserve list of the Philadelphia Ramblers, Ranger farm, was decided in favor of the Garden. The Bruins objected to Cameron's place on Philadelphia's list.

January 16, 1941

Boston Vanquishes Detroit, 3-1, And Sweeps Stanley Cup Series

Bruins First Team in Hockey History to Win Four Straight Games in Final—Victors Tally Three Times in Second Period

By The Associated Press.

DETROIT, April 12—Boston's bruising Bruins etched hockey history in Detroit Ice tonight by capturing the prized Stanley Cup with a 3 to 1 victory over the Red Wings, their fourth consecutive triumph in the best of seven final series.

Before 8,125 spectators, one of the smallest crowds in National League play-off history, the Bruins carved out their victory along a familiar pattern. Spotting Detroit the first goal, Boston scored three times in 12 minutes of the second period to gain possession of the cup for the second time in three years.

By closing out the series in minimum time, Boston became the first team to win four straight games in the final series, six years ago the Montreal Maroons blanked the Toronto Maple Leafs when the hockey trophy series was decided on a best of five basis.

Bauer's Shot Decides

Little Bobby Bauer connected with what proved to be the winning goal while Jimmy Orlando, Detroit defense man, was sitting out two minutes for holding. Orlando had barely found a comfortable seat when Bill (Flash) Hollett fired home the tying goal on a face-off pass from Milt Schmidt.

A minute later Bauer poked Schmidt's rebound into the nets and Eddie Wiseman flicked home a fifteen-footer before the period ended. Detroit took the lead in the first period when Carl Liscombe beat Goalie Frank Brimsek with a whistling forty-footer.

For most of the game Brimsek was under pressure, however, making twenty-eight saves to seventeen by Goalie Mowers.

Fondling the Stanley Cup in a wild dressing room demonstration, Manager Art Ross was quick to proclaim his Bruins as the greatest hockey team ever assembled.

If not the greatest, the Bruins should qualify as the least super-

The Line-Up

BOSTON (3)		DETROIT (1)
Brimsek	Goal	Mowers
Clapper	Defense	Orlando
Smith	Defense	Stewart
Schmidt	Center	Grosso
Bauer	Wing	Wares
Dumart	Wing	Abel
Hollett	Spare	Motter
Cain	Spare	Liscombe
Crawford	Spare	Howe
Wiseman	Spare	M. Bruneteau
Conacher	Spare	Giesebrecht
Hill	Spare	Brown
A. Jackson	Spare	Whitelaw
Reardon	Spare	H. Jackson
McReavy	Spare	Jennings

First Period
1—Detroit, Liscombe (Howe, Giesebrecht)...........10:14
Second Period
2—Boston, Hollett (Schmidt)..........7:42
3—Boston, Bauer (Schmidt)..........8:43
4—Boston, Wiseman (Conacher, McCreavy)..........19:32
Third Period
No scoring.
Penalties—First period: Reardon, Orlando (2 minutes each). Second period: Orlando (2 minutes). Third period: Smith, Liscombe, McReavy (2 minutes each).
Referee—Frank Clancy. Linesman—Bill Chadwick. Time of periods—20 minutes.

stitious of athletic teams. Tonight's game was the thirteenth straight in which they have gone unbeaten against Detroit.

By closing out the series, the Bruins deprived hockey tills of an estimated $18,000 in revenue had the series gone the full seven games.

Brimsek saved brilliantly twice on close drives by Howe in the first five minutes of the opening session. Reardon was sent off for high sticking, and the Red Wings attacked viciously, scoring at the 10:14 mark when Liscombe whipped home a long shot on passes from Howe and Giesebrecht.

Howe, skating superbly through the Boston defense, had a hard shot at Brimsek in the second period. The Red Wings peppered the Bruin goalie with shots from every angle, but he weathered the storm. While Orlando was in the penalty box Hollett tied the score by whistling a shot home at 7:42.

Bruins Take Lead

Just 61 seconds later Bauer connected from close in to put the Bruins in front, 2 to 1. Schmidt drew assists on both plays. The

Bruins outskated Detroit the remainder of the period, taking the pressure off Brimsek for the first time in the game.

During the last minute of the session Boston increased its margin to two goals when Wiseman skated in from the boards and flicked the disk into a high corner.

April 13, 1941

LEAFS TRIP WINGS; TAKE STANLEY CUP

16,218 See Toronto Six Win 4th in Row, 3-1, and Final Series by 4-3 Margin

By The Associated Press.

TORONTO, April 18—Staging a brilliant third-period rally, Toronto won the Stanley Cup, which had evaded the team for ten years, by defeating the Detroit Red Wings, 3—1 at Maple Leaf Gardens tonight.

The largest crowd in Toronto hockey history—16,218—saw the Leafs surge from behind to gain the world title. The Red Wings took the lead early in the second period and were less than thirteen minutes from the championship when the Leafs broke loose.

The triumph gained a place in the record books. The Leafs became the first team in history to win the cup after dropping the first three games of a four-out-of-seven series. The Wings were strong favorites after they had set back the Leafs in the opening games.

Dave Schriner, clever left winger, was the hero of Toronto's fourth straight victory in the final series, although Center Pete Langelle fired what proved to be the winning goal. Schriner scored the first and third Toronto markers on plays with his line-mates, Billy Taylor and Lorne Carr.

After the Wings, short-handed two men, had held the Leafs out, Syd Howe sent Detroit in front early in the second period on a play with Sid Abel and Jimmy Orlando. There were five passes before Howe let go his backhand shot from the right.

Orlando had just stepped on the ice after serving a penalty when Schriner scored from a power play. The puck did not leave the ice and Goalie Johnny Mowers was watching Taylor.

Puck Flies Into Air

Two minutes later Johnny Mc-Creedy was checked and the puck flew fifteen feet into the air. It came down on Langelle's stick and the little center just had to shove the puck across the goal line.

The Wings tried desperately in the closing minutes but they were obviously tired. Carr set up the final counter when he checked Howe to the ice. Schriner picked up the

loose puck and Mowers had no

chance to stop his shot from close range.

After the game the Stanley Cup was presented by President Frank Calder of the National Hockey League to Captain Syl Apps of the Leafs. Apps was flanked by Coach Happy Day and Major Conn Smythe, former Toronto manager, now on active duty in the Canadian Army.

The line-up:

DETROIT (1)		TORONTO (3)
Mowers	Goal	Broda
J. Stewart	Defense	Kampman
McCaig	Defense	Stanowski
J. Brown	Center	Langelle
Carveth	Wing	McCreedy
Liscombe	Wing	Davidson
Orlando	Spare	Dickens
Motter	Spare	Goldham
Grosso	Spare	Apps
Wares	Spare	D. Metz
Abel	Spare	N. Metz
Howe	Spare	Taylor
Bruneteau	Spare	Carr
Giesebrecht	Spare	Schriner
	Spare	G. Stewart

No scoring.

First Period

Second Period

1—Detroit, Howe (Abel, Orlando)...... 1:44

Third Period

2—Toronto, Schriner (Carr, Taylor)... 7:46
3—Toronto, Langelle (Goldham, Mc-
Creedy)............................ 9:43
4—Toronto, Schriner (Taylor, Carr)...16:13
Penalties—First period: Schriner, McCaig,
Orlando (2 minutes each). Second period:
McCaig 2, Dickens, Davidson, Bruneteau
(2 minutes each). Third period: Orlando,
N. Metz (2 minutes each).
Referee—Bill Chadwick. Linesmen—Aurel
Joliat and Archie Wilcox. Time of periods
—20 minutes.

April 19, 1942

Hockey League Abolishes Overtime for Duration

By The Associated Press.

MONTREAL, Nov. 20—There will be no more overtime play in the National Hockey League until after the war.

President Frank Calder announced today that due to war-

time travel conditions games in which the score is tied at the end of the regulation sixty minutes will be regarded as draws and no overtime will be played. He did not elaborate, but presumably the action was being taken so that traveling clubs would catch the trains they were scheduled to take.

Calder also announced a meeting of the board of governors in Boston Monday to discuss problems of vital importance to the league, including reconsideration of a proposal to reduce the number of players on each club.

It has been proposed that each club's roster be reduced to twelve players instead of the present fifteen.

November 20, 1942

Detroit Beats Boston for 4-0 Sweep
of Stanley Cup Hockey Finals

MOWERS SHUTS OUT BRUINS AGAIN, 2 TO 0

Goalie Blanks Boston Second Night in Row as Red Wings Win World Hockey Title

CARVETH, LISCOMBE TALLY

Detroit, Playing a Defensive Game, Counts on Solo Rushes Before 12,954 Hub Fans

By JOSEPH C. NICHOLS
Special to THE NEW YORK TIMES.

BOSTON, April 8—The Detroit Red Wings are the new hockey champions of the world. The fast-skating, fast-checking crew managed by Jack Adams took possession of the Stanley Cup tonight by shutting out the Boston Bruins, 2 to 0, for a 4-0 sweep of the final series.

The Bruins' willingness to force the going made for a struggle that thrilled 12,954 spectators. It thrilled them, but it didn't please them, for the enthusiastic Boston supporters were sadly disappointed.

This disappointment was brought about mainly by the brilliant work of Goalie Johnny Mowers. Credited with a 4-0 shut-out last night, Mowers faced a much heavier bombardment and chalked up an-

other whitewashing.

Goalie Dooms Boston Cause

The Wings went into the lead in the first period on a goal by Jack Carveth and extended this margin in the second, when Carl Liscombe tallied after a fine solo rush. After Liscombe's marker the Bruins rushed recklessly, firing at Mowers from all angles. When Mowers handled everything, the Boston cause was doomed.

As the game drew to a close the Bruin fans seemed resigned to this and when it was all over they generously applauded the little goalie. Mowers made 30 saves while Frankie Brimsek, goalie for the Bruins, turned back 18 shots.

Even more emphatically than last night Boston had the territorial edge.

One of the first Detroit moves proved successful. It was launched by Carveth, who stole the puck from Bill Cowley at midice, slid into Boston territory and flipped a ten-foot shot past Brimsek in 12:09 of the first period.

In the second period Liscombe seized the puck near his backboard after a Boston rush. He skated well over the Boston line and let fly a twenty-five-foot drive past Brimsek in 2:45.

Fans' Protest Delays Game

In the third period a fan, dissatisfied with an official ruling, hurled a bottle to the ice, while others threw papers and other debris. Time was called while the ice was cleared.

Boston was the last team to win the cup finals in four contests. The Bruins turned the trick against the Wings in 1941.

The line-up:

DETROIT (2)		BOSTON (0)
Mowers	Goal	Brimsek
Stewart	Defense	Hollett
Orlando	Defense	Clapper
Abel	Center	Cowley
Liscombe	Wing	A. Jackson
Fischer	Wing	DeMarco

Spares
Detroit—Harold Jackson, Simon, Grosso,
Wares, Howe, Carveth, Douglas, Brown.
Boston—Shewchuk, Crawford, Gallinger,
Guidolin, Schmidt, Harvey Jackson, Boyd,
Chamberlain.

Scoring
First period—1, Detroit, Carveth (unassisted), 12:09. Second period—2, Detroit, Liscombe (unassisted), 2:45. Third period—
None.
Penalties—Stewart 4, Harvey Jackson,
Harold Jackson, Orlando 2, Guidolin 3, Gallinger, Carveth, Grosso, Chamberlain (2 minutes each).
Referee—Bill Chadwick. Linesmen—Sam
Babcock and Bob Hedges. Time of periods
—20 minutes.

April 9, 1943

AN OLD FAVORITE RETURNS TO THE ICE

Frank Boucher, former star and for the past five years coach of the Rangers, gets back into action tomorrow night against the Chicago Black Hawks at Madison Square Garden.

BOUCHER TO PLAY FOR RANGERS AGAIN

Because of the player shortage, Frank Boucher, one of the great hockey centers of all time, will don his skates again tomorrow night when the Rangers meet the Black Hawks in the opening game of the home season at Madison Square Garden.

Announcement of Boucher's return to the ice as an active player was made yesterday by Lester Patrick, vice president of the Garden in charge of hockey and manager of the Rangers, in the course of a luncheon for the hockey writers at Toots Shor's restaurant.

A member of the famous Boucher-Cook brothers line that won two national league championships, Frank, now past the 40-year mark, quit active service five years ago to serve as coach. Boucher was "bought out" from the famous Northwest "Mounties" by the Ottawa Senators in the 1921-22 season. After playing with Ottawa and Vancouver, he came to the Rangers in the 1926-27 season.

Boucher, explaining his return to the ice, said that he felt his presence in the line-up would help stabilize some of the newcomers, many of whom had never seen a professional hockey rink before this year.

He will play in the line with Jack McDonald and Billy Gooden. The former, a 6-footer weighing 200 pounds, is regarded as a second Charley Conacher. Gooden has been acclaimed a skating "fool."

McDonald, who has been in the Ranger system for four years, is a powerful shot, according to Boucher. He was a commercial pilot but was rejected by the Royal Canadian Air Force for physical reasons. Gooden, who weighs 150 pounds and stands 5 feet 8 inches, was with the Rangers for their last ten games last year. He and McDonald both are under 20 years old.

November 5, 1943

Howe Sets League Record With Six Goals as Red Wings Crush Rangers Again

By The Associated Press.

DETROIT, Feb. 3—The veteran Syd Howe punched in six goals tonight for a National Hockey League record as the Detroit Red Wings defeated the New York Rangers, 12 to 2, before 8,147 spectators at the Olympia Stadium. The Wings thus seized sole possession of second place, breaking their tie with the idle Toronto Maple Leafs.

Howe got his tallies in pairs as Detroit scored three times in each of the first two periods and gathered six goals in the third. The 32-year-old center counted 18 seconds apart in the first period, 62 seconds apart in the second, and within 57 seconds in the final period.

Lead Mounts to 9—0

Carl Liscombe got two goals and Don Grosso, Cully Simon, Mud Bruneteau and Flash Hollett one each for Detroit. The Rangers did not connect until Detroit had a 9-0 margin.

With six minutes remaining, Bucko McDonald flipped in the first Ranger goal against Detroit in three games. Fernand Gauthier made another a few minutes later.

Grosso had six assists and a total of seven points, in each instance equaling a league record. Moreover, Bruneteau's goal was his twenty-sixth for a Detroit production record.

The scoring splurge, following Detroit's record 15-to-0 triumph over the Blue Shirts a fortnight ago, raised the Wings' total to 50 goals in seven games against New York this season. When McDonald counted, it was the first New York goal in 170 minutes against Detroit.

McAuley Has 39 Saves

All except three of Detroit's thirteen skaters figured in the scoring. Ken McAuley handled 39 chances in the Rangers' nets compared with 21 saves by Connie Dion, who has lost only once in nine starts for Detroit since his medical discharge from the Canadian Army.

Howe smashed a record of five goals originally established in 1917 by Harry Hyland of the Montreal Wonderers and equaled eight times by such notables as Howie Morenz, Charley Conacher, Pit Lepine and a year ago by Ray Getliffe of the Montreal Canadiens.

The line-up:

DETROIT		RANGERS
Dion	Goal	McAuley
Simon	Defense	Heller
Hollett	Defense	W. McDonald
Howe	Center	K. Macdonald
Bruneteau	Wing	Hextall
Liscombe	Wing	Hiller
Jackson	Spare	Mahaffy
Quackenbush	Spare	Dill
Armstrong	Spare	Damore
Brown	Spare	Gauthier
Carveth	Spare	Aubuchon
Kilrea	Spare	J. McDonald
Grosso	Spare	De Marco

First Period

1—Detroit, Liscombe (Hollett, Kilrea). 7:15
2—Detroit, Howe (Grosso) 11:27
3—Detroit, Howe (Jackson, Grosso)..11:45

Second Period

4—Detroit, Howe (Simon) 17:52
5—Detroit, Howe (Grosso) 18:54
6—Detroit, Simon (unassisted) 19:36

Third Period

7—Detroit, Bruneteau (unassisted)... 3:03
8—Detroit, Howe (Bruneteau, Grosso). 8:17
9—Detroit, Howe (Bruneteau, Grosso). 9:14
10—Rangers, W. McDonald (K. Macdonald, Hextall) 13:57
11—Detroit, Grosso (Jackson, Carveth) 15:45
12—Rangers, Gauthier (Aubuchon, Ma-
haffy) 16:09
13—Detroit, Hollett (Armstrong)...18:36
14—Detroit, Liscombe (Grosso, Carveth) 19:22
Penalties—First period: Hollett (2 minutes). Second period: None. Third period: None.
Referee—Bill Chadwick. Linesmen—Stan McCabe and Orville Roulston. Time of periods—20 minutes.

February 4, 1944

CANADIENS SWEEP PRO HOCKEY FINALS

Blake's Goal Tops Chicago in 9:12 of Overtime, 5-4, to Clinch Stanley Cup

MONTREAL, April 13 (AP)—The Montreal Canadiens, National Hockey League champions, won the Stanley Cup and world professional title tonight by defeating the Chicago Black Hawks, 5 to 4, in a "sudden death" period at the Forum to sweep the final play-off series in four straight games.

Hector (Toe) Blake, veteran winger, settled the issue after nine minutes 12 seconds of overtime when he slapped in Butch Bouchard's pass for the winning goal.

The Canadiens, trailing 4—1 after the second period, rallied to tie the count in the third when Maurice Richard scored twice in the last four minutes. Blake figured in every Montreal goal, passing to Elmer Lach for the first two and then to Richard for the tallies that enabled the Flying Frenchmen to carry on into overtime.

Richard's first goal was a remarkable shot. Turned completely around ten feet from the net as he skated in after taking Blake's pass, the young winger completed his spin and let fly a backhand shot that beat goalie Mike Karakas. When he scored again a minute later the game was delayed while the ice was cleared of missiles tossed by the fans.

George Allen was Chicago's chief threat as the Black Hawks scored three times in the second period. After his first-period goal, Allen aided on a counter by Johnny Harms and then tallied again to make the score 3—1. Doug Bentley shot Chicago's final goal halfway through the second period.

The line-up:

MONTREAL (5)		CHICAGO (4)
Durnan	Goal	Karakas
Lamoureux	Defense	Seibert
Bouchard	Defense	Cooper
Lach	Center	Smith
Richard	Wing	Mosienko
Blake	Wing	Bentley

Spares

Montreal — Harmon, McMahon, Getliffe, Chamberlain, Watson, Filion, Majeau.
Chicago—Wiebe, Purpur, Allen, Harms, Dahlstrom, Johnson, Toupin.

Scoring

First period: 1, Chicago, Allen (Dahlstrom). 5:12; 2, Montreal, Lach (Blake), 8:45. Second period: 3, Chicago, Harms (Dahlstrom, Allen), 7:30; 4, Chicago, Bentley (Smith), 9:12; 5, Chicago, Bentley (Smith), 10:09. Third period: 6, Montreal, Lach (Blake), 10:02; 7, Montreal, Richard (Blake), 16:05; 8, Montreal, Richard (Blake, Bouchard), 17:20. First overtime period: 9, Montreal, Blake (Bouchard), 9:12.
Penalties — McMahon, Getliffe, Blake, Watson, Mosienko, Richard, Johnson, Lamoureux, Harms (2 minutes each).
Referee—Bill Chadwick. Linesmen—Jim Primeau and Eddie Mepham. Time of periods—20 minutes.

April 14, 1944

RICHARD SETS MARK AS CANADIENS WIN

TORONTO, Feb. 17 (AP) — The Montreal Canadiens and their star right-winger, Maurice Richard, both cracked season-long National Hockey League jinxes tonight. For the first time this season the Canadiens defeated Maple Leafs on Toronto ice, 4—3, and Richard got his first goal of the year in Toronto to set a modern goal-scoring record for the circuit.

Richard's goal, his forty-fourth of the season, came late in the game when the score was tied at 3—all. The fleet winger took a pass from Elmer Lach in the center zone, rounded the Toronto defense and went right in on Goalie Frank McCool, who partially blocked the shot and spilled Richard, although the puck rolled past him into the nets.

The Montreal winger has made his forty-four goals in forty games. The previous record was set by Cooney Weiland of Boston, who notched forty-three goals in the forty-four-game season in 1929-30. Richard's mark equaled the all-time league record of forty-four goals, shot by Joe Malone in twenty-two contests in the 1918 season.

The 14,922 fans, one of the largest crowds of the season, saw a hard-fought game. The Canadiens had a 2-1 edge in the second period on goals by Lach and Fernand Gauthier. Nick Metz got the Toronto score.

The Leafs went into the lead in the second period on scores by Mell Hill and Art Jackson, but Glen Harmon tied the score with an unassisted goal before Richard fired his jinx-defying counter.

Lach collected two points with a goal and an assist to tie Richard in the league point-getting race. Each now has 65, Lach with 20 goals and 45 assists and Richard with 44 goals and 21 assists.

The line-up:

MONTREAL (4)		TORONTO (3)
Durnan	Goal	McCool
Eddolls	Defense	Pratt
Harmon	Defense	Johnstone
Lach	Center	Kennedy
Richard	Wing	Hill
Blake	Wing	Davidson

Spares

Montreal—Lamoureux, Bouchard, Hiller, Mosdell, O'Connor, Gauthier, Getliffe, Chamberlain.
Toronto—Hamilton, Stanowski, Bodnar, Carr, Backor, Jackson, McCreedy, Metz.

Scoring

First period. None. Second period: 1, Montreal, Lach, 0:36; 2, Toronto, Metz (Bodnar), 4:03; 3, Montreal, Gauthier (Bouchard), 18:06. Third period: 4, Toronto, Hill (Kennedy, Pratt), 7:16; 5, Toronto, Jackson (Pratt), 13:25; 6, Montreal, Harmon, 15:47; 7, Montreal, Richard (Lach), 15:10.
Penalties—Bouchard, Hill, Hamilton, Metz (2 minutes each).
Referee—King Clancy. Linesmen—Jim Primeau and Eddie Mepham. Time of periods—20 minutes.

February 18, 1945

LEAF SIX WINS, 2-1, TO TAKE PLAY-OFFS

Downs Wings for Stanley Cup Laurels at Detroit Before Record Crowd of 14,890

PRATT CLINCHES VICTORY

Scores in 12:14 of 3d Period After Armstrong Fires Goal to Offset Hill Counter

DETROIT, April 22 (AP)—The Toronto Maple Leafs captured hockey's Stanley Cup tonight by defeating the Detroit Red Wings, 2 to 1, in the seventh and deciding game of the play-off series.

Walter (Babe) Pratt, Toronto defenseman, drove the winning goal with eight minutes to play—a rebounder from no more than three feet away.

The championship game tonight was played before 14,890 fans—largest hockey crowd ever to see a game in the Olympia Arena.

The Red Wings who had taken the three straight victories after falling behind, three games to none, thus found their hopes dashed after carrying the series to its ordinary limit of seven games.

Hammers Home Rebound

Toronto scored first tonight after less than six minutes of play in the opening period, Mel Hill hammering in a rebounder from eight feet on an assist by Ted Kennedy.

Detroit tied it up in the third when Murray Armstrong fired a fifteen-footer into an empty net after Toronto Goalie Frank McCool had been pulled out to save on Bill (Flash) Hollett's shot but the score was deadlocked for only four minutes.

The Wings lost center Syd Howe for high sticking Gus Bodnar and nineteen seconds later, at 12:14, Pratt made the winning goal.

Toronto, on Pratt's goal, averted a "reverse" repetition of its cup victory in 1942 when Detroit took the first three games and Toronto came back for four straight and the championship.

The Stanley Cup and its companion runner-up trophy, the O'Brien Cup, were presented at center ice in post-game ceremonies.

Third Triumph Since 1932

Toronto's victory was its third in cup play since 1932.

Harry Lumley, who had blanked the Leafs in the fifth and sixth games of the final series, had less work in the Detroit nets tonight than he did in recording his 1-to-0 overtime shutout Saturday.

Lumley turned aside just 14 Toronto shots tonight—three of them in the final period. McCool, Maple Leaf goalie, had 15 saves.

Detroit had a last desperate chance to tie it up when Leaf defenseman Elwyn Morris served a hooking penalty for the final 1¾

minutes but couldn't capitalize on Toronto's short-handed outfit.

The line-up:

TORONTO (2)		DETROIT (1)
McCool	Goal	Lumley
Morris	Defense	Seibert
Pratt	Defense	H. Jackson
Kennedy	Center	Armstrong
Hill	Wing	M. Bruneteau
Davidson	Wing	McAtee

Spares

Toronto—Bodnar, D. Metz, A. Jackson, Stanowski, N. Metz, Schriner, Carr, Hamilton.
Detroit—Quackenbush, E. Bruneteau, Lindsay, Carveth, Howe, Purpur, Liscombe, Hollett.

Scoring

First period: 1, Toronto, Hill (Kennedy), 5:38. Second period: None. Third period: 2, Detroit, Armstrong (Hollett), 8:16; 3, Toronto, Pratt (N. Metz), 12:14.
Penalties—Schriner, Purpur, Howe, Morris (2 minutes each).
Referee — Bill Chadwick. Linesmen—George Gravel and Sam Babcock. Time of periods—20 minutes.

April 23, 1945

CANADIENS WIN, 6-3, TAKING STANLEY CUP

League Champions Top Bruins in Finals for World Hockey Title by 4 Games to 1

BLAKE'S GOAL IS DECISIVE

Canuck Captain Snaps 3-3 Tie in Closing Period Before 13,000 at Montreal

MONTREAL, April 9 (AP) — The Montreal Canadiens stormed through Boston's defenses for three goals in the final period at the Forum tonight to defeat the Bruins, 6—3, and regain the Stanley Cup, emblematic of the world professional hockey championship.

It was the Canadiens' fourth victory in the four-out-of-seven final series of the National Hockey League play-offs. The Bruins scored their only triumph Tuesday night after the flying Frenchmen had swept the first three contests.

Sweeping to their fifth Stanley Cup triumph since the league was organized in 1917 and their second in three years the Canadiens captured eight of their nine play-off games. The league champions eliminated the third place Chicago Black Hawks in the semi-finals in four straight contests. The Bruins, second place club during the regular season, advanced by whipping Detroit's fourth-place Red Wings, four games to one.

Although they won the league pennant the last three years, the Canadiens were eliminated in the first round of the cup play-offs last year.

Bitterly Fought Contest

The closing contest was bitterly fought. Tempers flared in the final session as the players of both sides dealt out heavy body checks.

With the score 3—all, Toe Blake, Canuck captain, playing despite an ailing back, drove in the winning goal at 11:06 when he fired a high angle shot past Goalie Frank

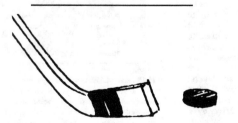

Brimsek. The Boston defenses fell apart thten. and the fleet, hard-driving Canadiens sewed up the contest and the championship with two more tallies.

Three minutes after Blake's clincher, Murph Chamberlain stole the puck from Pat Egan and beat Brimsek with a shot that never left the ice. The final goal went to Dutch Hiller, who took Elmer Lach's pass and drilled the rubber past Brimsek at 17:14.

Twice the Bruins went to the front in the opening period only to have the Canadiens surge back. Bill Cowley, Boston forward, broke the scoring ice at 5:42 on a low

back-hander while Montreal's Butch Bouchard was in the penalty box. Bobby Filion evened the count at 9:55 by converting a goal-mouth pass from Hiller.

Bauer Puts Bruins Ahead

Bobby Bauer, who played a magnificent game, sent the Bruins into a 2-1 lead at 14:01 by converting a rebound off the stick of Porky Dumart. Lach made it 2—2 at 15:51 and Kenny Mosdell sent the Canadiens into the van for the first time when he deflected Teammate Glenn Harmon's drive into the net at 18:28.

The Canadiens lead didn't last long as plucky Milt Schmidt, play-

ing in spite of neck and shoulder injury, snared a loose puck and drilled it into the Montreal net at 7:15 of the second session.

Play in the last session had to be halted for five minutes when the capacity crowd of 13,000 showered the ice with missiles of all sorts. Johnny Crawford's hard check of Lach aroused the fans.

The line-up:

MONTREAL (6)		BOSTON (3)
Durnan	Goal	Brimsek
K. Reardon	Defense	Egan
Bouchard	Defense	Henderson
Reay	Center	Schmidt
Peters	Wing	Bauer
Chamberlain	Wing	Dumart
Lamoureux	Spare	Crawford
Harmon	Spare	Church
Eddolls	Spare	Cain
Lach	Spare	T. Reardon

Blake	Spare	Cowley
Richard	Spare	Gallinger
Mosdell	Spare	Guidolin
Filion	Spare	Shill
Hiller	Spare	McGill
O'Connor	Spare	Smith

First Period
1—Boston, Cowley (unassisted) 5:42
2—Montreal, Filion (Hiller) 9:55
3—Boston, Bauer (Dumart) 14:01
4—Montreal, Lach (Eddolls) 15:51
5—Montreal, Mosdell (Harmon) 18:28
Second Period
6—Boston, Schmidt (unassisted) 7:15
Third Period
7—Montreal, Blake (Lach) 11:06
8—Montreal, Chamberlain (unassisted) ...14:05
9—Montreal, Hiller (Lach) 17:14
Penalties—First period: Bouchard, Bauer (2 minutes each). Second period: Peters, T. Reardon (2 minutes each). Third period: none.
Referee — King Clancy. Linesmen — George Gravel and Sam Babcock.

April 10, 1946

Targets of the Deadly Puck

Hockey goalkeepers are tough and courageous; their job is to stop a hard rubber disk that travels with fury.

By HAROLD KAESE

A HOCKEY fan once approached Harvey Jackson, one of the foremost left-wingers when he played for the Toronto Maple Leafs, and asked: "Will you help me get a goalie's stick for my son? If he doesn't get one he'll have a headache."

Jackson was shocked. "Well," he said, after a pause, "he'll certainly have a headache if you do get him one."

Most hockey players are convinced that fathers who allow their sons to become goalkeepers are as guilty of neglect as fathers who let their offspring play with bowie knives and loaded revolvers. Keeping goal to the average hockey player is in a class with being a live tackling dummy for the Chicago Bears, a sparring partner for Joe Louis or an African dodger at a carnival.

But life for a tackling dummy, a sparring partner and a dodger is relatively simple compared with that of a goalkeeper. The goalie's trust is a target measuring six feet by four; his job is to keep this target from being penetrated by the puck, a hard rubber disk one inch thick and three inches in diameter, which is often propelled at a speed of 100 miles an hour, even more.

To keep his trust inviolate the goalie can use his hands (protected by gloves), his legs (encased in ten-inch mattresses), his body (covered by pads and aprons) or his forehead, chin, nose or Adam's apple, which have no protection at all.

Speed, poise and courage—these are the qualities of great goalkeepers. No man without a stout heart will make a target of himself or dive head first into a whirlwind of steel blades and wooden sticks to cover a puck. These things the goalies do again and again. For hockey is rough and fast—some say the fastest game of all. It is all action. No dull moments, but plenty of thrills for spectator and player alike. Action gives good account for its popularity in the snow-belt cities, where hockey is largely centered. The game, always fast, has been speeded up still more by new rules in recent years, so that the goalkeeper's job has become more difficult than ever. In five or six

seconds goalies, facing each other only 200 feet apart, may both have to make spectacular stops, so quickly does the play go from end to end.

A goalkeeper is the most important player on the team of six—the backbone of the club. He adds nothing, or nearly nothing to the attack, but he is the last line of defense. The defenseman can save the forward, the goalie can save the defenseman, but no one can save the goalie. He just reaches around and fishes the puck out of the net whenever he makes a mistake. He is too often blamed unjustly by teammates, fans and his manager, yet nobody can offer him much good advice.

"A goalie is on his own," said Frank Boucher, coach of the Rangers. "He learns to play by himself, and the only way you can tell a good goalie from a poor one is by the results. You can't measure his speed or judge his form. You rate him off what he produces."

"There's no trouble like goalie trouble," said another coach. Indeed, when a goalie goes to pieces, his team goes to pieces.

IT requires about $125 to clothe a goalkeeper in style. The heavy leg pads, reaching from ankle to above the knee, cost $50; gloves, $20; boots and skates, $30; chest protector, padded underwear, uniform and wide goalie stick come to at least $25.

Goalkeepers' equipment is fundamentally alike, but all goalies have their own pet innovations. Chuck Rayner straps special pads over the toes of his boots. Frank Brimsek ties a heavy felt pad to the back of his right glove. So he could fall comfortably, Tiny Thompson used to tape a little rubber pillow to one thigh.

Despite their armor, goalkeepers are often hurt. Most of their injuries are about the head. Occasionally an "ouch" is wrung from spartan lips by a shot that hits on the side of a foot below the pad, or by an unusually hard drive by a powerful shooter. Goalkeepers, however,

are not a mass of black-and-blue blotches, as many spectators fear. They seem to develop a resistance to bruises, as certain insects do to poisons.

Moreover, they have a philosophical attitude toward injury. While lathering his face one evening, Lorne Chabot, goalkeeper for the Maple Leafs, remarked casually: "I always shave before a game. I seem to stitch better when my skin is smooth."

GOALKEEPERS come big, small and medium. Bill Durnan of the Canadiens stands 6 feet 1. Harry Lumley of Detroit weighs 195 and looks like a football tackle. Connie Dion, formerly of Detroit, stands only 5 feet 5. Roy Worters, an ace with the old New York Americans, weighed only 125 pounds.

Brimsek of Boston is stocky and muscular. Turk Broda of Toronto is pudgy. Paul Bibeault of Chicago is slender and pliant, like a reed. Many are round and soft and do not look like athletes. But Brimsek is a good baseball player. Durnan is a star soft-ball pitcher and Lumley excels at lacrosse.

Goalkeepers are inclined to be nervous. Theirs is a nervous profession. All six regular goalies now in the National Hockey League are cigarette smokers, but none of them is a nail-biter. Of the six, the most high-strung temperamentally seem to be

HAROLD KAESE was a sportsman before he was a sportswriter. He captained the baseball team at Tufts, played basketball, has since reached national finals in squash racquets. He is now a sports columnist on The Boston Globe.

SPEED, POISE, COURAGE make the great goalkeeper.

Bibeault and Brimsek. Bibeault is feline in his movements. Brimsek is moody, savagely quick. Broda is the most easygoing. Whatever their size, shape or temperament, all goalies have one thing in common: they are keen and courageous.

"There is no question that goalies today are much better than they ever were," said Coach Boucher. "They have to be better. They get much more practice than the old goalies, who sometimes didn't have to make a dozen stops a game."

In three successive games during a war season, Ken McAuley of the Rangers made 141 saves. Before the war, Sam LoPresti of the Chicago Black Hawks made 60 stops in a game in Boston, and was beaten by only a 2-1 score. The average stops per game for a National Hockey League goalkeeper are about thirty.

MODERN rules not only have opened up the game, but have increased the importance of luck. About half the goals scored today are lucky goals, because either they are screened or deflected by players between the goalie and the shooter; or they are jammed into the goal during wild scrambles outside the crease, which is the doorstep of the goal and the goalie's private property.

Goals scored on shots they do not see, or on shots that glance past them off a player's leg or skate, are the principal causes of unhappiness in the lives of goalkeepers. The fury of a goalie who has been beaten by a deflected shot exceeds that of a woman whose new dress has

been spattered with mud by a passing taxi.

Team-mates who, during an enemy attack, back in on the goalie, interfering with his vision, get sharp reprimands. Some goalies, assuming the role of quarterback or coxswain, shout salty directions to team-mates: "Get out of my way, you dummy. Move over, will you, so I can see something. If you want to play goal, I'll give you my pads. Hey, cover that guy. Shoot the puck out, shoot it out, I tell you."

Chuck Gardiner of Chicago, first of the modern up-and-down goalkeepers, was an eminent conversationalist. He talked with spectators, goal judges and referees, as well as team-mates, and was sometimes referred to as a skating barber.

NO goalie has yet scored a goal, except against himself, in a National Hockey League game. But Chuck Rayner of the Rangers, then in the Canadian Navy, scored such a goal while playing against an amateur team in Victoria, B. C.

"I stopped a shot and the puck bounced straight out, Rayner recalls. "I skated out to get clear, found myself alone, and went the rest of the way. When I got about fifteen feet from the other goal, I shot and scored."

GOALKEEPERS find it much easier to score on themselves. More than one goalie has caught a shot, then carelessly dropped the puck into his own goal. And in clearing pucks they have stopped, goalies have frequently knocked them into their goal instead of

behind it as they intended.

Fluke goals are not uncommon. Ridiculously easy shots half the length of the ice have somehow slipped through goalkeepers. A long hard shot went high over the Toronto cage, bounced off a screen, hit Lorne Chabot on the back as he stood before the goal and fell into the cage. Goals have been awarded on shots that have sped through the mesh; others on shots that never entered the cage, like one given to the Black Hawks against Boston early this season.

ANYONE who suggests that the goal be widened six or eight inches in order to increase scoring immediately becomes an enemy of all goalies. They would rather see legislation passed to keep players farther from the goal mouth and to disallow goals deflected off legs and skates.

The more pressure put on them, the more resourcefulness do the goalies show. But though their technique improves steadily, they are still goalkeepers and targets every night. As Brimsek said a few weeks ago after being cut on the face by a team-mate's

stick, "What a hell of a way to earn a living!"

January 19, 1947

Rangers Are Beaten by Canadiens in Garden Hockey as Players and Fans Riot

BLUE SHIRTS LOSE TO MONTREAL, 4 TO 3

Free - for - All Player Brawl Marks Wild Finish of Fight for Hockey Play-Off Berth

WINNING GOAL BY PETERS

Habitant Winger Nets Late in Third Frame After See-Saw Struggle for 2 Periods

By JOSEPH C. NICHOLS

The grandest mass riot in the local history of the National Hockey League took place at Madison Square Garden last night as the Canadiens of Montreal beat the New York Rangers 4 to 3. With only thirty seconds of play remaining, and with the Canadiens leading by what turned out to be the final score, the tense feeling that had existed between the teams all night broke out with sudden fierceness.

As Kenny Reardon of the Canadien forces was being led to the Rangers first-aid room to be patched up after having been hit flush in the face by Bryan Hextall's stick, he exchanged hot words with a player on the New York bench.

Reardon rushed at the player and the commotion attracted the attention of all the other skaters, who started for the scene of the action. Since all were bottle-necked at the entrance to the Ranger bench, every combatant, bunched as they were, immediately grappled with his nearest man, much to the delight and satisfaction of most of the 15,925 spectators on hand.

Skaters Wrangle on Ice

In a trice the ice was a mass of wrangling players, many of whom did not hesitate to use their sticks on exposed noggins. The referee, George Hayes, and the linesmen, together with a number of the Garden's special policemen, stepped in to try to restore order, but they could do very little. Miss Gladys Gooding at the organ tried to quell the disorder by playing "The Star-Spangled Banner" but gave up after the first few bars fell on deaf ears.

The standout bout in the battle royal, one that occurred several minutes after the original action began, took place between Maurice Richard of the Canadiens and Bill

HALTING A RANGER DRIVE ON THE MONTREAL GOAL

Kenny Reardon (left) of the Canadiens body checking Ab DeMarco in the second period at Garden

The New York Times

Juzda of the Ranger defense.

Skating around behind Juzda, who was kneeling on the ice. Richard brought his stick down on Bill's head, the weapon snapping into two pieces.

Juzda was dazed, shook his head, got to his feet, seized Richard around the waist, and hurled him to the ice.

Meanwhile, near the Ranger bench, a sparsely-cropped fan took a punch at a Montreal player, a fool-hardy action indeed. For the player had a stick in his hand and he promptly brought it down on the spectator's head, and rendering said spectator decidedly pacific.

After ten minutes or so of battling the pace told on the athletes, who are hockey players and not fighters. Action gradually sagged, until presently there was not a blow being struck.

Blows Whistle on Referee

At length Referee Hayes blew his whistle, separated the combatants and looked about for the prime culprits. He could have thrown a handful of sand and hit a guilty man—goalies included—so he decided to apply penalties to Juzda and Richard. He fined them each a 10-misconduct and the sen-

tence found disfavor in the mind of Murph Chamberlain of the visitors. Murph rushed at the referee with upraised hand, said something, and promptly received a ten-minutes himself.

The fight was the resounding climax to a hard, bitter contest in which the Rangers tried with all their might to stave off elimination from the post-season play-offs. Able as they might have been in the pugilistic department, the New Yorkers could not cope with the Canadiens on skates.

Buddy O'Connor put the visitors ahead in 1:03 of the first period, and the Rangers got the goal back in 8:05 when Church Russell tallied while Montreal was short-handed. In 17:27, with the sides at full strength, Ab De Marco put New York in the van with a short shot.

Montreal scored twice in the second, O'Connor in 3:25 and Toe Blake in 11:06, before Edgar Laprade brought about a tie in 13:18.

This deadlock obtained until 16:29 of the third. At that time Jimmy Peters skated through for the deciding goal. The Rangers struck back at a furious pace, and

toward the close pulled goalie Chuck Rayner out of the nets. It was on one of these high-powered excursions that Hextall cracked Reardon and started the riot on the ice. Reardon had ten stitches taken in a cut just under his lower lip.

The line-up:

RANGERS (3)		MONTREAL (4)
Rayner (1)	Goal	Durnan (1)
Colville (6)	Defense	Reardon (17)
Juzda (19)	Defense	Bouchard (3)
Laprade (10)	Center	O'Connor (10)
Warwick (9)	Wing	Richard (9)
Leswick (18)	Wing	Blake (6)
Laycoe (2)	Spare	Lamoureux (4)
Trudell (4)	Spare	Fillion (5)
Watson (7)	Spare	Macey (11)
Hextall (12)	Spare	Chamberlain (12)
Cooper (11)	Spare	Reay (14)
De Marco (15)	Spare	Allen (15)
Russell (16)	Spare	Mosdell (18)
Gardner (17)	Spare	Peters (19)
Bell (20)	Spare	Leger (21)
Moe (21)	Spare	

First Period

1—Montreal, O'Connor (Richard, Blake)...1:03
2—Rangers, Russell (Trudell)...8:05
3—Rangers, De Marco (Watson)...17:27

Second Period

4—Montreal, O'Connor (Bouchard)...3:25
5—Montreal, Blake (O'Connor, Reardon)...11:06
6—Rangers, Laprade (Warwick, Laycoe)...13:18

Third Period

7—Montreal, Peters (Mosdell, Chamberlain)...16:29

Penalties—First period: Allen, Hextall, Richard (2 minutes each). Second period: Richard, Juzda, Chamberlain (10 minutes misconduct each); Trudell, Reardon (2 minutes each). Referee—George Hayes. Linesman—Doug Young and Stan McCabe. Time of periods—5 minutes.

March 17, 1947

LEAFS TAKE SERIES, TOP CANADIENS, 2-1

Toronto Annexes Stanley Cup Hockey Finals, 4 Games to 2 —Rally Thrills 14,546

By The Associated Press.

TORONTO, April 19—The Toronto Maple Leafs won the Stanley Cup, emblematic of the world hockey championship, by defeating the defending world champion Montreal Canadiens, 2 to 1, before 14,546 partisan fans at Maple Leaf Gardens tonight. The Leafs captured the final series by four games to two.

The Leafs, youngest team ever to capture the Stanley Cup, had to come from behind. With the game twenty-five seconds old, the veteran Canadiens skated into the lead. Butch Bouchard passed to Buddy O'Connor at his blue line, and the diminutive Montreal center dashed down-ice, split the defense, drew Goalie Turk Broda out of position and fired into an open net.

The Canadiens held the edge the rest of the opening period, but the home club scored the equalizer at 5:34 of the middle period in a scramble. After Goalie Bill Durnan of Montreal had cleared Howie Meeker's shot, Vic Lynn skated in to score.

The Leafs put on most of the pressure in the third period with the tiring Canadiens seemingly content to get rid of the puck. The break occurred at 14:39 just after Bouchard had gone off with an injured shoulder. Meeker passed to Ted Kennedy, who was circling twenty feet in front of the Montreal twine, and Kennedy converted.

The clean but hard-fought and penalty-free third period ended with the despairing Canadiens pulling Durnan from the nets and using six attackers in the final 38 seconds.

The deliriously happy crowd shouted "We want the cup!" for minutes after the game as the tired Canadiens congratulated their conquerors. The "mug" was not forthcoming, being locked in a safe at the Montreal Forum.

The game climaxed the first all-Canadian cup finals in twelve years. The Canadiens won the first game, 6—0, but then dropped three in a row. In Montreal Thursday they triumphed to force a sixth contest and were 7-to-5 favorites tonight.

The line-up:

```
MONTREAL (1)              TORONTO (2)
Durnan ..........Goal............ Broda
Reardon ........Defense.......... Boesch
Bouchard .......Defense.......... Barilko
O'Connor .......Center........... Kennedy
Richard ........Wing............. Meeker
Blake ..........Wing............. Lynn
                 Spares
Montreal—Reay, Chamberlain, Peters, Allen,
McKay, Fillion, Eddols, Harmon, Leger, Gra-
velle.
Toronto—Apps, Ezinicki, Watson, Poile, D.
Metz, Klukay, Stewart, Bodnar, Thomson,
Mortson.
                Scoring
First period: 1, Montreal, O'Connor (un-
assisted) 0:25. Second period: 2, Toronto, Lynn
(Kennedy, Meeker) 5:34. Third period: 3, To-
ronto, Kennedy (Meeker) 14:39.
Penalties—Mortson, Meeker, Leger 2, Thom-
son, Chamberlain, Kennedy, Bouchard, Ezinicki
(2 minutes each).
Referee—Bill Chadwick. Linesmen—Sam Ba-
bcock and Harold (Mush) March. Time of pe-
riods—20 minutes.
```

April 20, 1947

Players' Pension, Savings Plan Approved by Hockey Governors

National League Groups Work Out Details of Program Here—First All-Star Game to Be Played Oct. 13 on Toronto Rink

A players' pension and savings plan, described by President Clarence Campbell as "exceptionally progressive," was approved yesterday by the National Hockey League's Board of Governors in the concluding session of a two-day meeting at the Hotel Commodore.

The program, already accepted by 90 per cent of the league's 1946-47 players and ratified by their three-man committee at the meeting, calls for each player to contribute $900 from his salary each year.

The league will turn over to the fund two-thirds of the proceeds from an annual all-star game, the first of which will be staged in Toronto on Oct. 13, plus twenty-five cents on every paid admission to all post-season championship play-off games. Revenue from these sources is expected to net about $60,000 annually.

Eligible at Age of 45

Players will be eligible to apply for pension benefits on reaching the age of 45, or at any interval of five years thereafter. Payments will be based on length of service. Group insurance coverage will be extended to all subscribers to the plan.

President Campbell emphasized that the plan is in line with the league's new liberalized policy of player awards, which includes bonus payments for trophy winners and members of the official All-Star squad. "It is designed to make hockey a better business for the men in the game," he said.

In the All-Star game, which fits nicely into the picture as a major source of revenue for the new fund but actually was conceived before the pension plan, the Stanley Cup champions—this year the Toronto Maple Leafs — will meet the league's official All-Star squad.

The game will be rotated around the six cities of the league, with the 1948 contest due to be staged in Chicago on a date as yet unspecified.

In the initial game, the All-Stars will be able to present an unbroken starting array, for by coincidence, no Leaf player was named on the first sextet. A minimum of three players from each league club will be on the All-Star squad. The Oct. 13 date was selected because that is Canada's Thanksgiving Day.

Local charities will receive the remaining third of the All-Star game proceeds.

New Constitution Drafted

The league officials ratified a 1947-48 schedule calling for each club to play sixty games, including six meetings with each other club both at home and away. The regular season will get under way on Oct. 15 and continue through March 21.

A new constitution, complete terms of which will not be made public but which binds the six league clubs to "play together in perpetuity," was drafted and, among other new by-laws and rules, a provision to increase the waiver price from $5,000 to $7,500 was adopted.

Governors in attendance were Art Ross, Boston; W. J. Tobin, Chicago; James Norris Jr. Detroit; William Northey, Montreal; Brig. Gen. John Reed Kilpatrick, New York, and Connie Smythe, Toronto.

Syl Apps of Toronto, Glenn Harmon of Montreal and Sid Abel represented the players in the discussion of the pension plan and were reported by President Campbell to have "enthusiastically endorsed" the final agreement.

September 5, 1947

ALL-STAR SEXTET DOWNS LEAFS, 4-3

Doug Bentley's Goal in Final Period Decides Before 14,318 —Mosienko Badly Hurt

TORONTO, Oct. 13 (AP)—Scoring twice in the last period, the National Hockey League All-Stars came from behind to defeat the Stanley Cup champion Toronto Maple Leafs 4-3, tonight in the loop's first official all-star game. The attendance was 14,318.

Maurice (the Rocket) Richard of Montreal received credit for the tying goal when during the first half minute of the final period the puck was deflected into the nets by the Toronto defense. Seconds later Doug Bentley of the Black Hawks pushed home the winning marker while Gus Mort-

son was serving a penalty.

Harry Watson netted the Leafs' first goal late in the first period and both sides scored in the middle frame with Wild Bill Ezinicki and Syl Apps accounting for the Toronto tallies and Max Bentley of Chicago and Grant Warwick of the Rangers for the All-Stars.

Mosienko Breaks Ankle

During the middle period Bill Mosienko, Black Hawk star, suffered a broken left ankle from a check by Defenseman Jim Thomson. Mosienko was removed to a hospital and it was feared he might be lost for the rest of the season.

Bill Durnan of the Canadiens started in the nets for the stars and gave up all three Toronto goals. Frank Brimsek, Boston, took over midway of the second period and frustrated the Leafs the rest of the way.

Toward the end of the game play became rougher with Ezinicki and Butch Bouchard engaging in a pitched battle for which each received minor penalties. Vic Lynn of the Leafs suffered a cut on the head on a headlong rush in the final minute.

President Presents Gifts

Before the start of the game, Clarence Campbell, league president, presented miniature gold pucks to members of the All-Star first team which consists of Durnan, Bouchard, Ken Reardon, Milt Schmidt, Richard and Doug Bentley.

Gold pucks also were presented to former and present Leafs who were members of All-Star teams selected by hockey writers in the past. The 1946-47 team was selected by managers and coaches of the Loop's six teams.

Proceeds of the game will be shared by the circuit's player pension fund and the Toronto Community Chest Campaign.

The line-up:

```
ALL-STARS (4)            TORONTO (3)
Durnan, Montreal ..Goal.......... Broda
Reardon, Montreal .Defense....... Goldham
Bouchard, Montreal Defense....... Stanowski
Schmidt, Boston ...Center........ Apps
Richard, Montreal .Wing.......... Ezinicki
D. Bentley, Chicago Wing......... Watson
                 Spares
All-Stars—Brimsek, Boston; J. Stewart, De-
troit; Quackenbush, Detroit; M. Bentley, Chi-
cago; Mosienko, Chicago; Warwick, New York;
Laprade, New York; Lindsay, Detroit; Dumart,
Boston, Bauer, Boston; Leswick, New York.
Toronto—Mortson, Thomson, Barilko, Ken-
nedy, Meeker, Lynn, Pile, Mackell, G. Stewart,
D. Metz, Klukay.
                Scoring
First period: 1, Toronto, Watson (Ezinicki),
12:29. Second period: 2, Toronto, Ezinicki
(Apps, Watson), 1:03; 3, All-Stars, M. Bent-
ley (Reardon), 4:35; 4, Toronto, Apps (Wat-
son), 5:01; 5, All-Stars, Warwick (Laprade),
17:35. Third period: 6, All-Stars, Richard,
0:28; 7, All-Stars, D. Bentley (Schmidt, Rich-
ard), 1:27.
Penalties—Mortson 3, Ezinicki 3, Leswick,
Bauer, Lynn, Pile, Bouchard, Reardon, Schmidt (2
minutes each), Reardon (5 minutes).
Referee—King Clancy. Linesmen—Jim Primeau
and Eddie Mepham. Time of periods—20 min-
utes.
```

October 14, 1947

Hockey Expels Taylor of Rangers and Suspends Gallinger of Bruins

PENALTIES FOLLOW GAMBLING INQUIRY

National League Ousts Taylor for Alleged Hockey Wager Through Paroled Thief

By WALTER W. RUCH
Special to THE NEW YORK TIMES.

LANSING, Mich., March 9—Denouement of the strange case of what happened, when, to whom and where gained new stature today in the National Hockey League when William (Billy) Taylor of the New York Rangers was banned for life and Don Gallinger of the Boston Bruins was suspended indefinitely by the president of the circuit, Clarence S. Campbell.

Nobody, according to Campbell, "fixed" anything anywhere. To some followers of the sport that seemed irrelevant, inasmuch as no one had made such an accusation.

On the other hand, anyone possessing even casual acquaintance with the league did not drop dead in surprise at the findings, caused by re-arrest of James Tamer, paroled bank robber found to have been in contact with some hockey players. Two of those, according to Campbell, were Taylor and Gallinger.

He reported that to Governor Kim Sigler, who in turn stated: "I like the way you do things." The Governor gave assurance of all possible aid by the State in further investigation planned by Campbell.

A Betting Boomerang

The game in question, according to Campbell, was between the Chicago Black Hawks and the Boston Bruins in Chicago on Feb. 18. The Black Hawks, although favored heavily until a few hours from game time, dropped the match, 4 to 2.

The outcome was of dismal nature to Taylor, who, according to Campbell, had placed a bet through Tamer to the tune of $500. Gallinger was accused by Campbell of associating with Tamer, and the last named has been charged with having close association with gamblers in Chicago, Buffalo and New York.

No other player or club in the league was involved "in any manner in gambling on this or any other N. H. L. game," Campbell declared. Nor had there been any "fix" or attempted "fix" of any hockey game, he said.

Confronted with evidence police had obtained by listening to Tamer's telephone conversations, Taylor admitted having talked to Tamer, Campbell said, but he denied having made the bet. The

HOCKEY PLAYERS EXPELLED, SUSPENDED IN GAMBLING PROBE

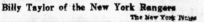

Billy Taylor of the New York Rangers
The New York Times

Don Gallinger of the Boston Bruins
Associated Press Wirephoto

player made no statement to Campbell as to what action, if any, he would take to fight the expulsion.

Taylor, center for the Detroit Red Wings last season before he was traded to Boston and subsequently to New York, had told a newspaper here he would "sue the league" if he were suspended or expelled.

Aid Asked and Promised

Investigation of Gallinger's associations with gamblers might go on "for years," Campbell told the Governor. He asked Sigler for further assistance by Michigan law enforcement agencies.

"I can say frankly I like the way you do things," the Governor replied. "There is no compromise with crookedness. You may rest assured the law enforcement agencies of Michigan will be available to help you clean up this situation."

Gallinger's action against hockey ethics, the league president said, consisted of associating with Tamer.

"Can you confirm that Gallinger

did not bet?" he was asked.

"No," Campbell replied.

Campbell, who was an Allied prosecutor of German war criminals, interviewed Tamer at the state prison of southern Michigan and talked with both offending players.

The New York and Boston clubs will play out the season with holes in their squads, Campbell said. The league has a rule that after Feb. 15 no players may be brought up from the minors.

Asked whether he would waive that rule this season, Campbell said: "Absolutely not."

Campbell told the Governor he had not immediately suspended the affected players when he received the evidence a week ago. "It would have jeopardized this inquiry and might have been unfair to the players affected if that evidence had not first been verified and corroborated," he pointed out.

"I am sure that these considerations completely justified allowing Taylor and Gallinger to remain on the active rosters of their teams

for a matter of seven more days," he added. Campbell assumed responsibility for permitting them to play the last seven days, but said their clubs now had instructions to put the disciplinary action into effect.

"The National Hockey League will not tolerate gambling on hockey games by any of its personnel," Campbell declared, "nor will it tolerate their knowingly association with gamblers or other such undesirable characters."

League rules provide for expulsion, suspension and fines of $500 for a player and $2,000 for a club official for conduct which is "dishonorable, prejudicial to or against the welfare of the league or the game of hockey."

Further, the rule says: "A player betting on or being interested in any pool or wager on the outcome of any N. H. L. championship or play-off game, whether or not the player has any connection with such game, will be deemed to come under this section."

March 10, 1948

Leafs Keep Stanley Cup With 4-Game Hockey Sweep Against Wings

14,043 SEE TORONTO WIN AT DETROIT, 7-2

Maple Leafs Gain Hockey Title Third Time in Four Years With a Swift Attack

KENNEDY NETS TWO GOALS

Watson Also Scores Twice as Lumley Wilts Under Worst Bombardment of Season

DETROIT, April 14 (AP)—With three goals in each of the first two periods at Olympia tonight, the Toronto Maple Leafs swept their fourth straight game from the Detroit Red Wings, 7 to 2, and retained the prized Stanley Cup, emblematic of world professional hockey supremacy.

By sweeping the final series after whipping Boston, four games to one, in the opening play-off round, the Leafs attained their third cup triumph in four years and their fourth in eight years under their clever coach, Clarence (Happy) Day. Altogether it marked the sixth time the battered old trophy was won by Toronto.

The brilliant Leafs, gaining momentum all the way through the final series, pumped seven goals past Detroit's big red-cheeked netminder, Harry Lumley, in the final game for one of the most decisive climax cup victories in history. Not in sixty regular season games and nine play-off clashes had so many shots eluded the 21-year-old goalie, who stopped only fourteen shots.

Capacity Crowd Present

The capacity crowd of 14,043 was chilled quickly, and so were the Red Wings' dying hopes, when the Leafs turned on the steam for two goals in the first five minutes. One of them was Ted Kennedy's rebound effort and the other occurred on a break-away by Defenseman Garth Boesch.

When Harry Watson caromed a shot off Detroit Defenseman Bill Quackenbush midway through the opening period to make it 3—0 the Leafs were in.

Eight of the sixteen men in maple leaf uniforms took a hand in the scoring spree. Kennedy and Watson, a former Detroiter, cashed two goals each and the veteran Max Bentley had a pair of assists. The rest of the scoring was spread down the line with Boesch, tall Syl Apps and Rookie Les Costello getting the other Toronto goals.

Trailing, 3—1, at the outset of the second stanza, Detroit made its bid to get back into the game when Leo Reise tipped in the first Red Wing goal. A minute and a half later Toronto regained the three-goal margin on Apps' solo sprint and before the middle period was over Kennedy and Watson scored for the second time each to make it 6—1.

Horeck Ends Scoring

Detroit's second score was made 72 seconds from the end when Pete Horeck tipped in rookie Lee Fogolin's long one. Costello had thumped a close-in shot between Lumley's legs earlier in the period.

Walter (Turk) Broda, Toronto's stout-hearted goalie, kicked out twenty-six shots with another brilliant performance.

This marked the first time since Day took the reins that the Leafs captured both the National Hockey League championship and the Stanley Cup.

The line-up:

TORONTO (7)		DETROIT (2)
Broda	Goal	Lumley
Boesch	Defense	Quackenbush
Barilko	Defense	Stewart
Apps	Center	Abel
Ezinicki	Wing	Howe
Watson	Wing	Lindsay
N. Metz	Spare	Reise
Bentley	Spare	Gauthier
Kennedy	Spare	Horeck
Meeker	Spare	McFadden
Lynn	Spare	Conacher
Klukay	Spare	Pavelich
Thomson	Spare	Kelly
Costello	Spare	Bruneteau
Selmis	Spare	Fogolin
Stanowski	Spare	McNab

First Period

1—Toronto, Kennedy (Bentley) ... 2:51
2—Toronto, Boesch (unassisted) ... 5:03
3—Toronto, Watson (unassisted) ... 11:13

Second Period

4—Detroit, Reise (Pavelich, Horeck) ... 2:41
5—Toronto, Apps (Thomson) ... 4:26
6—Toronto, Kennedy (Lynn) ... 9:42
7—Toronto, Watson (unassisted) ... 11:38

Third Period

8—Toronto, Costello (Bentley) ... 14:37
9—Detroit, Horeck (Fogolin) ... 18:48
Penalties—First period: Horeck, Metz, Fogolin, Barilko (2 minutes each). Second period: Howe, Lynn (2 minutes each). Third period: Fogolin (2 minutes).
Referee—Bill Chadwick. Linesmen—Sammy Babcock and George Hays.

April 15, 1948

TORONTO'S SEXTET KEEPS STANLEY CUP

Takes Honors for Third Year in Row—Beats Wings by 3-1 for a Four-Game Sweep

By The Associated Press

TORONTO, April 16—The Toronto Maple Leafs won the Stanley Cup, professional hockey's highest award, for the third straight year tonight, beating the Detroit Red Wings, 3 to 1, to sweep the best-of-seven series in four straight games.

The triumph marked the first time since professional clubs began contesting for the coveted cup in 1917 that one team has won the silverware three consecutive years.

Toronto finished fourth during the regular National Hockey League season while the Wings won the pennant. The Leafs disposed of the Boston Bruins in the semi-final round while the Wings took the measure of the Montreal Canadiens.

Lindsay Scores Goal

The Wings took a 1-0 lead during the first three minutes of play tonight with Left Winger Ted Lindsay shoving the puck home after passes from George Gee and Gordie Howe.

Young Ray Timgren tied it up for the Leafs shortly after the halfway mark of the second period when he batted home Max Bentley's rebound. Fiery Cal Gardner shoved the Leafs ahead when he netted with only fifteen seconds of play remaining in the middle session. Bentley sent home the final marker during the last five minutes of play with Timgren setting him up.

A crowd of 14,544 fans, six short of the capacity for Maple Leaf Gardens, went wild with joy as the final whistle sounded. After the game the cup was brought on the ice and League President Clarence Campbell presented the trophy to the Maple Leaf captain, Ted Kennedy.

Only in the first period and in the opening minutes of the second were the Wings really in the game against the seemingly tireless Toronto crew. The Wings had five shots on the goal in the first to Toronto's six. But in the last two periods the Leafs had a 25-10 margin and only Harry Lumley's spectacular work in the nets kept down the score.

Referee Bill Chadwick imposed nine penalties—five on Wings and four on Leafs. There were six in the first period, three in the second but none in the third when the Wings were slowing down under the Toronto pressure.

The Leafs, who played listlessly during the regular season, came to life in the play-offs during which they looked like the champions they were last season when they won everything in sight.

Toronto opened up the final round on Detroit ice and took the first game, 3—2, in overtime. They annexed the second, 3—1, and were never headed. They took the third game last Wednesday night, also by a 3—1 count, and came up with the lucky count again tonight.

The Wings, who won the flag by nine points, apparently were worn out in their hard-fought semi-final round against the Montreal Canadiens which went the full seven games.

Detroit's top line of Lindsay, Howe and Sid Abel, which starred against Montreal, played hard against the Leafs but it wasn't enough. The Leafs, abounding in reserve strength, wore out the Wings' No. 1 trio.

The Stanley Cup victory is the fifth for the Leafs since Clarence (Hap) Day took over as coach of the club in the 1940-41 season. They won it in 1942 and 1945 before starting the three-straight string. It was the third time they had beaten the Red Wings in the final—1942, last year and this.

The line-up:

DETROIT (1)		TORONTO (3)
Lumley	Goal	Broda
Stewart	Defense	Boesch
Quackenbush	Defense	Barilko
Abel	Center	Bentley
Howe	Wing	Klukay
Lindsay	Wing	Timgren
Kelly	Spare	Thomson
Reise	Spare	Morison
Fogolin	Spare	Juzda
Reid	Spare	Gardner
Couture	Spare	Ezinicki
Podolsky	Spare	Watson
McFadden	Spare	Kennedy
Horeck	Spare	Mackell
Fido	Spare	Smith
Gee	Spare	Lynn
Pothe	Spare	Dawes

First Period

1—Detroit, Lindsay (Gee, Howe) ... 2:59

Second Period

2—Toronto, Timgren (Bentley) ... 10:10
3—Toronto, Gardner (Thomson, Ezinicki) ... 19:45

Third Period

4—Toronto, Bentley (Timgren) ... 15:16
Penalties—First Period: Boesch, Fido, Ezinicki 2, Reid, Lindsay (2 minutes each). Second Period: Horeck, Juzda, Howe (2 minutes each). Third Period, None.
Referee — Bill Chadwick. Linesmen—Ray Getliffe and Butch Keeling.

April 17, 1949

HOCKEY ACE FINED $1,000

Reardon Penalized Because of Statements in Article

MONTREAL, March 1 (AP)—Ken Reardon of the Montreal Canadiens has been fined $1,000 because of statements attributed to him in a magazine article, the National Hockey League announced today.

In the article Reardon was quoted as threatening to see that Cal Gardner of the Toronto Maple Leafs gets fourteen stitches in his mouth—the same as Reardon received after an affair with Gardner in a game several seasons ago.

In announcing the fine, Clarence Campbell, president of the league, at the same time said that Reardon at the end of his playing days in the N. H. L. could petition for a refund.

Campbell said that the fine is not so much a penalty as a personal

cash bond for Reardon's future good conduct.

March 2, 1950

LINDSAY HOCKEY LEADER

First Detroit Player to Pace Scorers Tallied 78 Points

Ted Lindsay is the first player in Detroit history to lead the National Hockey League in scoring.

The talented left-winger rolled up 78 points for the champion Red Wings, including a record-breaking fifty-five assists. Lindsay broke the former mark of fifty-four assists set by Montreal's Elmer Lach in 1944-45. Lindsay scored twenty-three goals.

The leading scorers:

	G.	A.	Pts.
Ted Lindsay, Detroit	23	55	78
Sid Abel, Detroit	34	35	69
Gordon Howe, Detroit	35	33	68
Maurice Richard, Montreal	43	22	65
Paul Ronty, Boston	23	36	59

G Goals. A Assists. Pts. Points.

March 28, 1950

Detroit Beats Rangers in 2d Overtime Period and Wins Stanley Cup

TALLY BY BABANDO TOPS NEW YORK, 4-3

End of Long Struggle Comes After 28:31 of Overtime Play on Detroit Ice

LESWICK IS RANGER STAR

Wings Wage an Uphill Battle After Rivals Lead Twice —Rayner Is Injured

By JOSEPH C. NICHOLS
Special to The New York Times.

DETROIT, Monday, April 24—The Detroit Red Wings won the Stanley Cup and the hockey championship of the world this morning.

Coming from behind in the regulation three periods of play and forcing the game into sudden death overtime, the local skaters gained the victory in the seventh and deciding game of the best four-out-of-seven series on a goal by Pete Babando, whose counter at 8:31 of the second overtime session gave the Red Wings the verdict by the score of 4 to 3 over the New York Rangers. The total sudden death play was 28:31.

It was a dramatic denouement to the hockey campaign for the Detroit players, who gained first place in the regular National

A RED WING CHARGE THWARTED BY THE RANGERS

Rayner, New York goalie, has just cleared a drive by Gee (right) of Detroit in final game. The others are Couture (left), Red Wing forward, and Kyle, defense man for the Blue Shirts. *Associated Press Wirephoto*

League campaign and who were favored to romp through the playoffs to bring this city its first ice championship since 1943.

All the favoritism that existed for Detroit was dissipated, though, by the sturdy Rangers, as the series plowed its way down to the very final game and—considering the overtime—beyond.

Given little chance to survive even its first round of play against

the Montreal Canadiens, the New York team surprised the hockey world by sweeping that set, 4 to 1, and by forcing the Detroit team to the limit in the final series.

Rangers in Early Lead

In the game that ended this morning, though, the Red Wings were back in the favored role, but for a good part of the early going it appeared as if the Rangers were on the way to registering an up-

set. For Lynn Patrick's crew went into a lead of 2 to 0 in the first period, and indications were that, this time, the advantage would stand up. The New Yorkers had the same advantage early in Saturday night's game, but they blew it, and also blew the contest.

The early deficit did not discourage the Red Wings in this seventh battle. They made it up within twenty-one seconds in the middle period when the Rangers' Allan Stanley was sitting out a penalty.

The Rangers pulled ahead again in the same frame, on a goal by Buddy O'Connor, but Jimmy McFadden scored to knot the count before the session ran out, and the teams finished the second period each with three goals.

They battled through a scoreless third period, and through one overtime sudden death chapter. In the second one of these added frames the Detroit team continued the aggressiveness it showed through most of the game, and this aggressiveness bore fruit in 8:31 when Babando beat the Ranger goalie, Charley Rayner, on a straight line shot, after taking a pass from George Gee.

Abel Leads in "Blitz"

For Babando, the goal was his second of the game. He also tallied in the Red Wings' second period blitz while Stanley was out. The other Detroit player to score in the quick sequence was Sid Abel, the Red Wings' captain whose dynamic play in the entire Ranger series was probably the greatest single skater's contribution to the local team's titular achievement.

The New York first-period goals were scored by Stanley and Tony Leswick, each counter occuring while the Blue Shirts were favored through the presence of Detroit men in the penalty box. The second period scores came with each team at full strength.

Although the Rangers went into the lead as early as they did, there was no denying that the Detroit team deserved the victory. Off to a start in which they seemed to stress power rather than skill, the local puck chasers settled down to pure hockey when the score went against them, and for the greater part of the game they had a decided territorial edge.

Although he let one shoddy goal get by him, the drive with which McFadden evened the count, Rayner on the over-all played a sizzling game in the New York net, piling up a total of 39 saves as against only 26 for Harry Lumley in the Detroit cage. In the first overtime, particularly. Rayner was at his best.

His defense slowed down and allowed the Red Wing forwards to "walk in" pretty much as they pleased. The Ranger attack, on the other hand, failed to function smoothly in these late stages, and Lumley had a comparatively soft time of it. Rayner was hurt in the first overtime, but stayed in the game.

In the opening stages of the game the Rangers' slippery passing attack puzzled the Detroiters, and enabled the visitors to acquire a couple of penalty advantages. One of these banishments came when Edgar Laprade and Ted Lindsay roughed it up, Laprade drawing two minutes and Lindsay four, two for fighting and two for slashing.

It was while Lindsay was sitting out his second penalty that the Rangers struck for their initial score.

Before Lindsay returned, he was joined by Marty Pavelich, who was sent out for slashing. This set-up gave the Rangers a 6 to 4 advantage in manpower for 51 seconds, and at the precise expiration of Lindsay's exile the Blue Shirts scored, Leswick caging the disk

The Line-Up

RANGERS (3)		DETROIT (4)
Rayner	Goal	Lumley
Stanley	Defense	Stewart
Egan	Defense	Reise
Raleigh	Center	Abel
Lund	Wing	Lindsay
Slowinski	Wing	Carveth
Eddolls	Spare	Martin
Shero	Spare	Kelly
O'Connor	Spare	Gee
Laprade	Spare	Peters
Mickoski	Spare	McNab
Fisher	Spare	Babando
McLeod	Spare	Pavelich
Kyle	Spare	McFadden
Lancien	Spare	Couture
Kaleta	Spare	Black
Leswick	Spare	Dewsbury
Smith	Spare	Pronovost

First Period

1—Rangers, Stanley (Leswick) 11:14
2—Rangers, Leswick (Laprade, O'Connor) ..12:18

Second Period

3—Detroit, Babando (Kelly, Couture) 5:09
4—Detroit, Abel (Dewsbury) 5:30
5—Rangers, O'Connor (Mickoski) 11:42
6—Detroit, McFadden (Peters) 15:57

Third Period

No scoring

First Overtime Period

No scoring

Second Overtime Period

7—Detroit, Babando (Gee) 8:31

Penalties—First period: Pavelich 2, Lindsay 2, Laprade, Slowinski, O'Connor (2 minutes each). Second period: Stanley (2 minutes). Third period: Kyle, Dewsbury (2 minutes each). First Overtime period: None. Second Overtime period: None.

Referee—Bill Chadwick. Linesmen—Hugh McLean and George Hayes.

with the help of Laprade and O'Connor.

Detroiters Move Fast

The Red Wings moved fast in the second period. Stanley, baffled in an attempt to clear the puck, interfered with Jerry Couture and drew a banishment. Detroit capitalized on the setup, and did so beyond the expectations of the most rabid fans in the crowd of 13,095. Red Kelly and Couture set up the disk for Babando, who scored with a sliding shot in 5:09.

Wasting no time at all, Detroit was right back in New York ice and Abel sped in to release a 20-foot drive that eluded Rayner in 5:30. The New Yorkers played a strictly defensive game. A break came when Nick Mickoski broke away to fire at Lumley. The goalie blocked, but O'Connor poked the rebound home in 11:42.

This goal fired the Red Wings to carry the play. Trying to clear quickly, Stanley put the rubber on McFadden's stick and McFadden fired away. The shot looked like an easy one for Rayner, but he lost it in flight, and the puck hit the cords in 15:57.

The third period saw each team draw a penalty, but no harm was done. The Red Wings simply overwhelmed their foes in the first overtime, and only Rayner's dexterity prevented the game from ending much earlier than it did.

April 24, 1950

Red Wings Rout All-Star Six, 7-1, As Lindsay Performs 'Hat Trick'

DETROIT, Oct. 8 (AP)—Ted Lindsay and Terry Sawchuck combined their talents tonight to give the Detroit Red Wings a lopsided 7—1 decision over the National Hockey League's All-Star squad before 11,058.

It was the first time in the four-year history of the All-Star game that the All-Stars were beaten and they really were whipped tonight. Lindsay's three goals and an assist marked the first time in the series a player had turned hockey's coveted "hat trick."

He slammed in the first goal of the night just 19 seconds after the game started and added another one at the 17:12 mark of the first period. The little Detroit forward was the key man in the third goal as he feinted Goalie Turk Broad badly out of position to clear the way for Gordie Howe to score.

That tally upset the All-Stars badly and Jimmy Peters, Marty Pavelich and Metro Prystai added goals before Lindsay wrapped up the Wings' scoring for the night by banging in this third goal at 14:28 of the final period to make it 7—0.

The All-Stars, pressing to avert a shut-out, finally tallied as Toronto's Sid Smith slipped a shot past Sawchuck just one minute and 33 seconds before the game ended. That made it 7-1 but the margin was sufficient to satisfy even the most goal-thirsty Red Wing supporters.

Detroit thus completed the first grand slam in the history of professional hockey — winning the league title, the Stanley Cup play-offs and the All-Star game.

The 21-year-old Sawchuck, making his debut as Detroit's regular goal tender, racked up twenty-five saves, some of them among the most brilliant ever seen on Detroit ice.

October 9, 1950

First Negro in U. S. Hockey

ATLANTIC CITY, Nov. 15 (AP)—The first Negro to enter organized hockey in this country was signed today by the Atlantic City Seagulls of the Eastern Amateur League. He is Arthur Dorrington of Canada. Seagull Coach Herb Foster announced the signing of Dorrington and two white players, Roy McPhee and Hugh Douglas. Foster said it is believed Dorrington is one of four Negroes in organized hockey, three of whom play in Canadian leagues.

November 16, 1950

Attack on Referee Costs Montreal's Richard $500

By The United Press.

MONTREAL, March 12—Maurice (The Rocket) Richard, whose goal-scoring ability is matched only by his quick temper, was fined $500 today by National Hockey League President Clarence Campbell for an attack on Referee Hugh McLean in a New York hotel on March 4.

The attack followed the Canadiens-Detroit game here in which Richard maintained he had been unfairly penalized by McLean. His protest during the game brought him a misconduct penalty and a $50 fine.

In his ruling, Campbell said that the original accounts of the incident had been exaggerated. "No blows were landed on any of the participants," he said.

"The league officials are entitled to full protection and to be free of molestation of any kind from players and others associated with the clubs, and that applies on and off the ice," Campbell said.

March 13, 1950

LEAFS VICTORS, 3-2, GAIN HOCKEY TITLE

Beat Canadiens on Barilko's Goal in Overtime to Win Cup Play-Offs by 4-1

By The United Press.

TORONTO, April 21—The Toronto Maple Leafs won the Stanley Cup tonight as they defeated Montreal, 3 to 2, in overtime on Bill Barilko's "sudden death" goal at 2:53. The Leafs won the series, four games to one.

The curly-haired defenseman cinched the contest on a 20-foot shot when he converted Howie Meeker's setup. Meeker started the "big play" by firing a shot that goalie Gerry McNeil kicked aside. Harry Watson spun the disk back to Meeker who placed it on Barilko's stick for the crusher.

The tally capped one of the most grueling Stanley Cup finals in history, which saw the rivals go into sudden death overtime in every one of the five games.

The victory marked the fourth time in five years that Conn Smythe's Maple Leafs have won the cup. Their streak was broken last year when the Detroit Red Wings beat the New York Rangers.

An hysterical, jampacked crowd of 14,577 saw the Canadiens take the lead twice only to have the Leafs come back to tie the game.

It was a heartbreaking loss for Coach Dick Irvin and the Canadiens. First they took a 1-to-0 lead after a scoreless first period when Maurice Richard shook loose for a typical breakaway, faked Jimmy Thomson out of position and beat Goalie Al Rollins from close in at 8:56.

But rookie Tod Sloan, who has been bad medicine for the Canadiens in this series, tied the game about three minutes later when he took a pass from Ted Kennedy at the blue line and flashed between Doug Harvey and Bud Macpherson to flip the disk over Gerry McNeil as the rookie netminder fell prone.

Ted Lindsay (#7), who was a mainstay of the great Detroit teams of the early '50s, is seen here scoring against Toronto in 1955. His temper earned him the nickname of "Terrible Ted."

Montreal again forged to the lead in the final period and seemed to have the game wrapped up until the closing seconds when the Leafs again deadlocked the score.

Paul Meger gave the Canucks a 2-to-1 edge at 4:47, backhanding home a pass that Doug Harvey slipped between the feet of Toronto's Joe Klukay.

As the crowd stood and stamped in a frenzy, Coach Joe Primeau derricked Rollins from the nets and the Leafs went after McNeil in a six-man surge that paid off. Smith whipped the disk to Max Bentley and he shot it across McNeil's doorstep to Sloan, who slapped it into the net before McNeil could switch sides.

The game ended on a glum note for the Canadiens in more than one way as Center Bobby Dawes was taken off the ice with a broken leg in the second period.

The line-up:

TORONTO (3)		MONTREAL (2)
Rollins	Goal	McNeil
Mortson	Defense	Harvey
Thomson	Defense	MacPherson
Kennedy	Center	Dawes
Sloan	Wing	Masnick
Smith	Wing	Meger

Spares

Toronto—Watson, Barilko, Bentley, Klukay, Meeker, Flaman, Mackell, Gardner, Juzda, Lewicki, Timgren, Hassard. Montreal—Bouchard, Lowe, Geoffrion, Curry, Richard, Johnson, MacKay Reay, Olmstead, Lach, Mosdell, Mazur.

Scoring

First period: None Second period: 1. Montreal, Richard (Harvey), 8:56; 2. Toronto, Sloan (Kennedy), 12:00. Third period: 3. Montreal, Meger (Harvey), 4:47. 4. Toronto, Sloan (Smith, Bentley), 19:28. Overtime period: 5. Toronto, Barilko (Meeker, Watson), 2:53. Penalties—Dawes, Barilko 2, Johnson (2 minutes each), Reay (misconduct), 10 minutes. Referee—Bill Chadwick. Linesmen—Bill Morrison and Sam Babcock.

April 22, 1951

LATE HAWK RALLY BEATS RANGERS, 7-6

Mosienko Sets Record With 3 Goals in 21 Seconds—Red Wings and Bruins Win

By JOSEPH C. NICHOLS

Bill Mosienko led the Chicago Black Hawks to victory over the New York Rangers at Madison Square Garden last night in the final game of the regular National Hockey League season. The right wing scored three goals in record-breaking time as the cellar-dwelling Hawks subdued the fifth-place New York sextet, 7 to 6.

Mosienko's hat trick came in the third period, and he required only 21 seconds to tally the three markers. He made his first in 6:09, his second in 6:20 and his third in 6:30. The previous record for a triple was one minute and four seconds, established by Carl Liscombe while a member of the Detroit Red Wings in 1938.

In addition, Mosienko's performance eclipsed a team-record for the speedy scoring of three goals. The Montreal Maroons of 1932 whipped home that number in a game in 24 seconds.

The crowd of 3,254 cheered Mosienko with a volume that seemed to come from twice that number when the record-breaking accomplishment was announced. Little thought was paid to the fact that the goals were made against a rookie net-minder, Lorne Anderson. A member of the Rovers all season, Anderson played in the Blues' cage the last three games of the season.

Bodnar a Big Help

Anderson might have stopped Mosienko on the Hawk star's first shot, an open thrust from the center alley. But the second and third shots were neatly executed, and could have fooled any goalie in the league. Gus Bodnar assisted on all three tallies and George Gee collaborated on Mosienko's third one.

The result was rather an anticlimax to a game in which neither team suffered a penalty. The Rangers yielded the first tally to Bodnar in the opening session, but scored three in a row on efforts by Frank Eddolls, Don Raleigh and Ed Slowinski before Pete Horeck came through for Chicago. In the second period, the Rangers counted twice, and in the third they added to their lead on another marker by Slowinski.

Then came Mosienko's effort. A pair of goals by Sid Finney in 13:50 and 19:22 capped the rally and enabled the Hawks to pull out the victory.

Before the game, Hy Buller, Ranger defenseman, was honored by the West Side Association of Commerce for having been selected the team's most valuable player. Buller received a trophy and a war bond in a presentation in which Harry Williams and Harold McGraw of the West Side organization participated.

The line-up:

RANGERS (6)		CHICAGO (7)
Anderson (1)	Goal	Lumley (1)
Ross (15)	Defense	Gadsby (4)
Stanley (6)	Defense	Raglan (19)
Laprade (10)	Center	Bodnar (12)
Sinclair (21)	Wing	Mosienko (8)
Kullman (19)	Wing	Gee (17)
Eddolls (2)	Alternate	Fogolin (3)

Evans (3)	Alternate	Dewsbury (5)
Buller (4)	Alternate	Hucul (3)
Conacher (5)	Alternate	Horeck (11)
Raleigh (7)	Alternate	Peters (14)
Ronty (9)	Alternate	Finney (15)
Dickenson (14)	Alternate	Guidolin (16)
Stewart (16)	Alternate	McFadden (16)
Hergesheimer (18)	Alternate	....
Slowinski (20)	Alternate	....

First Period

1—Chicago, Bodnar (Gadsby, Mosienko).. 0:44
2—Rangers, Slowinski (Eddolls)........ 4:50
3—Rangers, Raleigh (Stewart, Stanley).. 11:12
4—Rangers, Slowinski (Raleigh, Stewart).18:35
5—Chicago, Horeck (Finney, Hucul)......18:47

Second Period

6—Rangers, Stewart (Slowinski).........13:19
7—Rangers, Dickenson (Ronty, Hergesheimer)...........................15:55

Third Period

8—Rangers, Slowinski (Raleigh)......... 3:37
9—Chicago, Mosienko (Bodnar)......... 6:09
10—Chicago, Mosienko (Bodnar)........ 6:20
11—Chicago, Mosienko (Bodnar, Gee)... 6:30
12—Chicago, Finney (Hucul, Fogolin)....13:50
13—Chicago, Finney (Gadsby)...........19:22
Penalties—None.
Referee — George Gravel Linesmen — Doug Davis and Dom Saolto.

March 24, 1952

WING SIX WINS, 3-0, GAINS STANLEY CUP

Sweeps Canadien Series for Record of 8 Games in Row —Sawchuk Ties Mark

DETROIT, April 15 (UP)—Metro Prystai scored two goals and assisted on another tonight as the Detroit Red Wings swept to the Stanley Cup with a 3-0 victory over the Montreal Canadiens before 14,090 fans.

The Red Wings thus became the first team in history to sweep eight straight games without a loss in cup competition.

Terry Sawchuk, Detroit goalie, equaled a play-off record with his fourth shutout of the series. He blanked Toronto twice and the Canadiens twice. Frank McCool of Toronto and Dave Kerr of New York also had four play-off shutouts in the past. McCool needed thirteen games and Kerr nine.

The Red Wings beat Toronto in the minimum of four games in the semi-finals and handed the Canadiens four successive setbacks.

Just About Everything

The victory gave Detroit just about everything the National Hockey League has to offer. The Red Wings won the regular season championship with a 22-point edge over the runner-up Canadiens, and

now have their second Stanley Cup in three years.

Prystai blazed in his first goal at 6 minutes 50 seconds of the first period, a 25-footer from in front, with Goalie Gerry McNeil well screened. Alex Delvecchio and Johnny Wilson drew assists on the first goal. Maurice Richard was serving a Montreal penalty for holding at the time.

Detroit widened its lead with only 21 seconds remaining in the middle period and again Prystai played a major role. He fired a blazing shot from the corner and Glen Skov tapped the rebound past McNeil from five feet out.

Prystai Scores Unassisted

With Montreal trying desperately to get back into the game, and playing five men up, Prystai sneaked behind the defense to pick up a loose puck at center ice and dash in to beat McNeil unassisted. The time of the goal was 7:35 of the final period.

Sawchuk stopped twenty-six Montreal shots during the game and was mobbed by his teammates when the final buzzer sounded. His work was reminiscent of his regular National Hockey League net-minding. He led the league in shutouts with twelve, and walked off with the Vezina Trophy as the top goalie in professional hockey.

The line-up:

DETROIT—Goal, Sawchuk: defense, Goldham and Pronovost; center Skov: forwards, Pavlich and Leswick: alternates, Woit, Kelly, Reise, Lindsay, Howe, Prystal, Abel, Delvecchio, Wilson, Stasiuk.
MONTREAL—Goal, McNeil; defense, Bouchard and MacPherson: center, Richard; forwards, Moore and Mazur: alternates, Harvey, Geoffrion, Curry, Johnson, Reay, Olmstead, Lach, Meger, Long, Masnick.
FIRST PERIOD—Detroit. Prystal (Delvecchio, Wilson) 6:50. Penalties: Bouchard (0:24), Leswick (11:09), Richard (14:39), Masnick (14:28), Leswick (18:10).
SECOND PERIOD—2, Detroit, Skov (Prystal) 19:39. Penalties: Delvecchio (9:35), Moore (11:45).
THIRD PERIOD—3, Prystal (unassisted) 7:35. Penalties: None.
Referee—Bill Chadwick. Linesmen—Bill Morrison and George Hayes.

April 16, 1952

Record Set by Sawchuk

DETROIT, April 17 (P)—Another record has been chalked up for Terry Sawchuk, the Red Wings' goal tender. Sawchuk was unscored on for 277 minutes and 54 seconds of consecutive play on home ice at the end of the season—including four Stanley Cup play-off games. The previous mark was 270 minutes.

April 18, 1952

Richard Sets Hockey Scoring Record as Canadiens Triumph Over Black Hawks

MONTREAL, Nov. 8 (UP)—After being frustrated for three games, Maurice (Rocket) Richard finally established a new National Hockey League scoring record when he rapped in the 325th goal of his career tonight as the Montreal Canadiens whipped the Chicago Black Hawks, 6 to 1.

The Canadiens' speedy star had tied Nels Stewart's old record of 324 goals on Oct. 29 and then was blanked in his next three games. The record-breaker was a typical Richard goal. The Rocket, playing his eleventh season in a tempestuous, injury-studded career, blasted a low shot past Al Rollins at 10:01 of the second period. The shot came just 30 seconds after Elmer Lach, who holds the N.H.L. total points record, had netted the

200th goal of his thirteen-season career.

The victory, before a crowd of 14,562, gave first place to the Canadiens. They had been in a three-way tie with Chicago and the Toronto Maple Leafs for the lead.

Gamble, Curry Score Twice

Richard has won many honors while with the Canadiens, but tonight's thrill was probably his greatest. He holds the league record for most goals in one season and most goals in Stanley Cup play-offs. He won the Hart Trophy as the league's most valuable player for the 1944-45 season.

As for the game itself, Dick Gamble scored twice and Floyd Curry and Paul Meger once each for the Canadiens as they rifled a total of forty-one shots at the harried Rollins. George Gee, Jim McFadden, Fred Glover and Al Dewsbury of the Hawks flipped the rubber past young Hal Murphy, who was playing with Ste. Therese in the Quebec Provincial League only ten days ago. Murphy was substituting for the injured Gerry McNeil, out with a fractured cheek bone.

Butch Bouchard, Richard's team-mate for his entire N. H. L. career, set up the Rocket's record-breaking goal. He flipped Richard a pass about 18 feet out in front of Rollins and Richard's shot was low and to the corner. Rollins covered the shot, lost it, and the disc skidded in. Richard dived in to retrieve the puck as the crowd showered the ice with programs.

The line-up:

MONTREAL—Goal, Murphy; defense, Bouchard, Johnson; center, Lach; wings, Richard, Olmstead. Alternates: Harvey, Curry, Masnick, McCormack, St. Laurent, MacPherson, Geoffrion, Gamble, Reay, Mosdell, Meger.
CHICAGO—Goal, Rollins; defense, Mortson, Gadsby; center, Abel; wings, Feters, McFadden. Alternates: Fogolin, Mosienko, Hucul, Glover, Gardner, Dewsbury, Conacher, Bodnar, Couture, Gee.
FIRST PERIOD—1, Montreal, Gamble (Masnick, Johnson), 11:25; 2, Chicago, Gee (unassisted), 17:49. Penalties—Couture (7:24), Olmstead (15:42).
SECOND PERIOD—3, Chicago, Glover (unassisted), 2:36; 4, Montreal, Curry (Mosdell),

3:12; 5, Montreal, Lach (Richard, Harvey), 9:29; 6, Montreal, Richard (Bouchard), 10:01; 7, Chicago, McFadden (Dewsbury), 11:46; 8, Montreal, Gamble (Curry, Harvey), 19:12. Penalties—Gee (4:47), Richard (5:02), Fogolin (10:14 and 17:59).
THIRD PERIOD—9, Montreal, Meger (McCormack), 15:46; 10, Chicago, Dewsbury (Mortson, Raglan), 19:54. Penalties—Johnson (7:14), Lach (12:01), Harvey (13:50).
Referee—Red Storey. Linesmen—Jim Primeau and Frank Udvari.

November 9, 1952

RANGERS DEADLOCK CANADIENS' SIX, 4-4

Richard, Montreal, Clips Mark With 629th Point

MONTREAL, Jan. 8 (UP)—Maurice (Rocket) Richard broke a National Hockey League point-scoring record tonight as the Montreal Canadiens and the New York Rangers staged a lively 4-4 draw before 14,110 fans in the Forum.

Richard assisted on Bernie (Boom Boom) Geoffrion's first-period goal and then scored himself in the final period to send his lifetime point total to 629, one more than the previous record held by Line-mate Elmer Lach.

Rocket broke Nels (Old Poison) Stewart's goal-scoring record of 324 earlier this season. His fifty goals in the 1944-45 season set a record for a single year.

The goal was No. 332 for Richard in regular season play and No. 379 in his life-time season and play-off total. He has tallied 249 assists in both regular and play-off games since he began his pro career twelve years ago.

A costly penalty to Paul Masnick midway through the final period enabled the Rangers to flash two quick goals and earn the tie.

Paul Ronty took a pass from Wally Hergesheimer and Neil Strain to fire the first goal during Masnick's penalty. Ninety-three seconds later, Defenseman Hy Buller ripped one home from a Hergesheimer-Ronty play-making combination and the game was knotted.

The line-up:

MONTREAL—Goal, McNeil; defense, MacPherson, Johnson; center, Lach; Wings, Richard, Olmstead. Alternates: Harvey, Geoffrion, Curry, Gamble, Masnick, McCormack, Mosdell, St. Laurent, Meger.
RANGERS—Goal, Worsley; defense, Kraftcheck, Stanley; center, Mickoski; wings, Stoddard, Kullman. Alternates: Howell, Buller, Raleigh, Ronty, Kukulowicz, Haworth, Prentice, Hergesheimer, Slowinski, Strain.
FIRST PERIOD—1, Montreal, Geoffrion (Richard) 1.41; 2, Montreal, Curry (Gamble) 3:30; 3, New York, Prentice (unassisted) 10:59; 4, Rangers, Strain (Hergesheimer, Raleigh) 16:05. Penalties: Stoddard (1:24), Richard (2:15), Masnick (10:03), Slowinski (12:18), Mickoski (5-minute major, 19:12), Johnson (5-minute major, 19:12), Ronty (19:50) Olmstead (19:50).
SECOND PERIOD—No scoring. Penalties: Meger (5:50), Prentice (13:12). Saves: Worsley 16, McNeil 7.
THIRD PERIOD—5, Montreal, Richard (Gamble), 5:29; 6, Montreal, Meger (Geoffrion),

Masnick, 8:16; 7, Rangers, Ronty (Hergesheimer, Strain), 12:32; 8, Rangers, Buller (Hergesheimer, Ronty), 14:05. Penalties—Masnick (11:27). Saves—Worsley 14, McNeil 6.
Referee—Bill Shadwick. Linesmen—Sammy Babcock and Doug Davies.

January 9, 1953

HOWE NETS NO. 201 IN 4-TO-1 TRIUMPH

Red Wing Star Tallies Twice Against Hawks at Chicago— Bruins Nip Montreal, 1-0

CHICAGO, Feb. 15 (UP)—Gordie Howe scored his 200th and 201st National Hockey League goals tonight as the Detroit Red Wings dropped the Chicago Black Hawks into fifth place by beating the Hawks, 4—1.

The game drew a sell-out crowd of 16,518, the largest Chicago Stadium hockey attendance in three seasons. The victory was Detroit's seventh over the Hawks in ten games this campaign.

Howe's two tallies ran his season's total to forty-one and he became the first player in league history to score forty or more goals in each of three seasons.

He also became the twenty-fifth player to reach the 200-goal mark and the eighth now active. Others sharing the mark now playing are Bill Mosienko, Elmer Lach, Maurice Richard, Ted Lindsay, Max Bentley, Milt Schmidt and Woodie Dumart.

The line-up:

DETROIT—Goal, Sawchuk; defense, Kelly, Goldham; center, wings, Lindsay, Howe. Alternates—Pronovost, Wolt, Leswick, Prystai, Skov, Sinclair, DelVecchio, Wilson, Bonin, Hay.
CHICAGO—Goal, Rollins; defense, Mortson, Gadsby; center, Gardner; wings, Peters, McFadden. Alternates—Mosienko, Lynn, Finney, Hucul, Dewsbury, Fogolin, Abel, Raglan, Couture, Gee.
FIRST PERIOD—1, Detroit, Howe (Lindsay) 1:04; 2, Detroit, Leswick (Kelly) 7:48; 3, Detroit, Leswick (Skov, Bonin) 8:08. Penalties: Dewsbury (2:57), Gadsby (5:32). Favelich (12:30). Saves: Rollins 13, Sawchuk 9.
SECOND PERIOD—4, Chicago, Mosienko (Mortson, Raglan) 4:21. Penalty: Fogolin (5:57). Saves: Rollins 12, Sawchuk 9.
THIRD PERIOD—5, Detroit, Howe (Lindsay, Kelly), 7:47. Penalties: Mortson (19:47), Bonin (19:47). Saves: Rollins 10, Sawchuk 16.
Referee—Red Storey. Linesmen—Mush March and George Hayes.

February 16, 1953

Wings Crush Rangers as Howe Surpasses His Own Scoring Record

DETROIT DEFEATS NEW YORK SIX, 7-1

Howe's 2 Goals and 3 Assists Against Rangers Help Set 90-Point Season Record

DETROIT, March 5 (UP)—Gordie Howe and Ted Lindsay each scored twice tonight as the Detroit Red Wings defeated the New York Rangers, 7 to 1, at Olympia to move within three games of their fifth straight National Hockey League championship.

In addition to his pair of goals Howe picked up three assists to break the league season scoring record. The 5 points lifted his total to 90, 4 more than he scored in each of the past two seasons for the record.

One of Howe's goals came on a rare penalty shot in the second period. It was the first such shot at Olympia in seven years.

Lorne Worsley, the New York goalie, and Terry Sawchuk, Detroit's net minder, both were superb in the opening period; which was scoreless. Worsley stopped three shots and Sawchuk a dozen.

Five Goals in Second Period

But the Red Wings treated the 10,663 fans to a five-goal outburst in the middle period to wrap up the game. Lindsay connected for his thirtieth goal of the season at the 47-second mark. Johnny Wilson notched his twenty-first at 4:01 and Red Kelly followed fifty-eight seconds later with his eighteenth. Howe assisted on the goals by Lindsay and Kelly.

After Alex Delvecchio increased the margin to 4-0 at 13:12, Howe received his penalty shot. The Red Wings were short-handed, with Delvecchio serving a holding penalty when Howe started a breakaway. He was tripped from behind by Hy Buller and Referee Red Storey awarded the gift shot to Howe.

With only Howe and Worsley on the ice, the Detroit right wing skated in and blazed a 15-footer past the New York goalie in 15:36.

The Rangers were two men short when Howe connected for his second goal of the night and his forty-fifth of the season at 2:01 of the final period. He now needs to cage the puck six times in nine remaining games to break the season goal-scoring record held by Maurice Richard of Montreal.

Aldo Guidolin spoiled Sawchuk's bid for a shutout at 9:01 of the third stanza while Tony Leswick was serving a Detroit penalty.

Lindsay got that one back at 19:06 by batting in Howe's rebound. It was the eighth goal in three games for the Wing captain.

The line-up:

DETROIT—Goal, Sawchuk; defense, Goldham, Kelly; center, DelVecchio; wings, Prystai, Wilson. Alternates: Pronovost, Wolt, Lindsay, Leswick, Howe, Pavelich, Skov, Sinclair, Bonin, Hay.
RANGERS—Goal, Worsley; defense, Howell, Reise; center, Mickoski; wings, Stoddard, Cullman. Alternates: Buller, Kraftcheck, Raleigh, Stanley, Ronty, Murphy, Guidolin, Prentice, Hergesheimer, Strain.
FIRST PERIOD—No scoring. Penalties: Guidolin (11:25), Howe (17:53). Saves: Sawchuk 12, Worsley 13.
SECOND PERIOD—1, Detroit, Lindsay (Kelly, Howe) 0:47; 2, Detroit, Wilson (Prystai, DelVecchio) 4:01; 3, Detroit, Kelly (Prystai, Howe) 4:59; 4, Detroit, DelVecchio (Wilson, Prystai) 13:12; 5, Detroit, Howe (unassisted) 15:36. Penalties: Howell (3:31), DelVecchio (14:02). Saves: Sawchuk 5, Worsley 11.
THIRD PERIOD—6, Detroit, Howe (Lindsay, Pavelich) 2:01; 7, Rangers, Guidolin (Raleigh, Buller) 9:01; 8, Detroit, Lindsay (Howe, Pavelich) 19:06. Penalties: Mickoski (0:54), Howell (1:57), Leswick (8:23). Saves: Sawchuk 11, Worsley 15.
Referee—Red Storey. Linesmen—Jerry Olinski and Doug Young.

March 6, 1953

CANADIENS WIN, 1-0, TAKE STANLEY CUP

Beat Bruins on Lach's Goal in 1:22 of Overtime and Annex Series, 4 to 1

MONTREAL, April 16 (UP)—Elmer Lach scored at 1 minute 22 seconds of a "sudden-death" overtime period tonight to give the Montreal Canadiens a 1-0 victory over the Boston Bruins and the National Hockey League's Stanley Cup.

Lach's goal tore into the net like a bullet. Maurice Richard had given his pivot man the puck in the Bruin end zone and Elmer turned and fired. When it swept by the startled Sugar Jim Henry, over his right shoulder, Richard grabbed Lach and threw him into the air. Both crashed to the ice as the 14,450 fans started clambering over the sideboards.

The Canadiens thus wrapped up the championship in five games. By coincidence, the last Montreal cup victory came in 1946 in five games against the Bruins.

Irvin's Third Champion

It was the twenty-third appearance in Stanley Cup play-offs for the colorful Canadiens and gave Dick Irvin, at 60 the oldest coach in the National Hockey League, his third world champion club. The Canadiens won the cup in 1930, 1931, 1944 and 1946. Irvin coached

them in their last two victories. He also led Toronto to the cup in 1932.

Lach's goal meant a $1,000 bonus to each of the eighteen regulars on the roster. The defeated Bruins earned $500 each for chasing the Canadiens to the wire.

The climactic game was colorless until Lach's goal. For three periods, the Bruins and the Habitants had checked one another into the ice, afraid to open up. The shots on goalid told the even territorial play: Henry stopped twenty-four in the three regulation periods, Gerry McNeil twenty.

Brilliant Goal-Tending

Brilliant goal-tending by Henry and McNeil kept the game scoreless. Richard, the greatest play-off scorer of them all, tried at least three times to beat the steel-nerved Henry but Sugar Jim was in a blue-chip game and making no mistakes.

McNeil, meanwhile, had the Bruin forward, Ed Sandford, leading scorer of these play-offs with eight goals, whizzing around him twice in the third period, but was prepared for every move.

The Stanley Cup, bought for $50 by Lord Stanley when he was Governor General of Canada sixty years ago, was presented to the Canadien team captain, Emile (Butch) Bouchard, in a ceremony at center ice immediately after Lach's goal.

The line-up:
MONTREAL—Goal. McNeil; defense. Bouchard, Johnson; center. Lach; wings. Richard, Mazur; alternates. Harvey, Mackay, Geoffrion, Curry, Masnick, Moore, Reay, Olmstead, Mosdell, St. Laurent, Davis.
BOSTON—Goal. Jim Henry; defense. Quackenbush, Godfrey; center. Schmidt; wings. Dumart, Klukay; alternates. Armstrong, Sandford, Mackell, Laycoe, Labine, Creighton, MacIntyre, Toppazzini, Martin, Peirson, Chevrefils.
FIRST PERIOD—No scoring. Penalties: None. Saves: Henry 9, McNeil 7.
SECOND PERIOD—No scoring. Penalties: Moore (11:58). Saves: Henry 9, McNeil 6.

THIRD PERIOD—No scoring. Penalties: None. Saves: Henry 6, McNeil 7.
OVERTIME PERIOD—1, Montreal, Lach (Richard), 1:22. Penalties: None. Saves: Henry 2, McNeil 1.
Referee—Bill Chadwick. Linesmen—Bill Morrison and George Hayes.

April 17, 1953

Moore Sets 2 Records

MONTREAL, March 25 (UP)—Dickie Moore set two scoring records tonight as the Montreal Canadiens took a 2—0 lead in their four-out-of-seven Stanley Cup semi-final playoff with an 8—1 victory over the Boston Bruins. The game also established a mark for penalties.

A crowd of 14,464 saw Stanley Cup play-off records fall and fists fly as the Bruins fought desperately against the defending Stanley Cup champions.

Moore, a native of Montreal whose National Hockey League career has been plagued with serious injuries since his rookie season of 1951-52, had his best night as he rapped three goals past Sugar Jim Henry and picked up three assists for 6 points.

Moore's performance broke the record of 5 points in a single play-off game that was held jointly by his team-mate, Maurice (Rocket) Richard; Joe Blake, a former Canadien; Eddie Bush, formerly with Detroit, and Don Metz, an ex-Toronto wing.

Moore, a left wing, set a mark for the fastest goal in a play-off game when he opened the scoring at the ten-second point. This clipped five seconds off the record set by Sid Smith of Toronto in the first game of the cup final between the Maple Leafs and the

Canadiens in Toronto in April, 1951.

Referee Jack Mehlenbacher called twenty-three penalties, including eight majors for fighting, and three misconducts to break the record of twenty-one handed out by Red Storey March 3, 1951, when Boston and the Maple Leafs met in a semi-final at Toronto.

The line-up:
MONTREAL—Goal. Plante; defense. Harvey, St. Laurent; center. Beliveau; wings. Geoffrion, Moore. Alternates: Bouchard, Curry, Richard, Johnson, Davis, Olmstead, McCormack, Mosdell, Meger, Masnick, Mazur.
BOSTON—Goal. Henry; defense. Armstrong, Quackenbush; center. Schmidt; wings. Sandford, Peirson. Alternates: Godfrey, Mackell, Gardner, Brown, Lumart, LaBine, Creighton, Bodnar, Mohns, Martin, Klukay.
FIRST PERIOD—1, Montreal, Moore (Beliveau, Geoffrion), 0:10; 2 Montreal, Geoffrion (Moore), 5:57; 3, Montreal, Geoffrion (Beliveau, Moore), 6:28; 4 Montreal, Mazur (Mazur, McCormack), 16:41; 5. Montreal, Moore (Beliveau, Johnson), 18:10. Penalties: Davis (10:04), Mackell (13:35), Labine (19:05). Saves: Plante 7, Henry 7.
SECOND PERIOD—6, Montreal, Beliveau (Moore, Geoffrion) 1:10; 7, Boston, Mackell (Sandford, Martin) 13:07. Penalties: Mackell (1:37), Mosdell (1:37), Johnson (2:27), Harvey (4.17), Labine, Schmidt, Johnson, Mazur (5 minutes each, fighting) (14:10). Saves: Plante 11, Henry 5.
THIRD PERIOD—8, Montreal, Meger (St. Laurent), 5:03; 9, Montreal, Beliveau (Geoffrion, Moore), 13:38. Penalties: Labine and Olmstead (3:26), Labine and Olmstead (five minutes, 3:26), Labine, Schmidt and Johnson (five minutes fighting and automatic misconduct, 3:26), St. Laurent (11:13), Brown (13:23), Harvey (16:51). Saves: Plante 10, Henry 10.
Referee—Jack Mehlenbacher. Linesmen—Bill Morrison and George Hayes.

March 26, 1954

Red Wings Beat Canadiens in Overtime Hockey Game and Win Stanley Cup

15,792 SEE LESWICK DECIDE FINALE, 2-1

Detroit Goal on a 40-Foot Shot at 4:29 of 'Sudden Death' Halts Montreal

DETROIT, April 16 (UP)—Tony Leswick brought the Stanley Cup to Detroit tonight with a dramatic goal after 4 minutes 29 seconds of a "sudden-death" overtime period. His 40-foot shot sailed into the Montreal net to lift the Red Wings into a 2-to-1 hockey victory before a record crowd of 15,792 at Olympia.

Leswick, who generally confines himself to checking high-scoring opponents, took a pass-out from Glen Skov. He waited for Skov to skate out in front of

Goalie Gerry McNeil and provide a screen.

The puck sailed over McNeil's shoulder to settle the issue and enable the National League champions to take the trophy, emblematic of the world professional title, for the third time in five years.

The goal occurred at a time when the Red Wings appeared to be tiring and victory seemed unlikely.

Canadiens Score First

Montreal's Stanley cup defenders scored first in the seventh game of the four-out-of-seven series. Floyd Curry, whose two goals had helped Montreal even the series in the sixth game, scored from 50 feet at 9:17 of the opening period. His shot bounced over the stick of Goalie Terry Sawchuk.

Detroit pressed for most of the first two periods and tied the score at 1:17 of the second stanza. With Paul Masnick of Montreal off for hooking, Ted Lindsay found Defenseman Red Kelly alone at the left of the

Montreal goal. Lindsay's pass was quickly converted by Kelly.

The Red Wings continued to press in an effort to claim the lead. They tired, however, at the start of the third period when Montreal staged a strong rally.

Sawchuk was at his best as he stopped Gaye Stewart on a breakaway and turned aside several other threatening shots.

Goal Is Disallowed

At the 16-minute mark of the third period Maurice (Rocket) Richard picked up a loose puck in his hand and threw it into the Detroit net. Referee Bill Chadwick promptly disallowed the goal.

Had Richard left the puck on the ice a team-mate, Elmer Lach, was in position for a possible goal.

Detroit earned the Stanley Cup for the sixth time. Montreal had stopped the Boston Bruins in five games in the finals a year ago.

The line-up:
DETROIT—Goal, Sawchuk; defense, Graham, Pronovost; center, Prystai; wings, Wilson, Dineen. Alternates: Kelly, Holt,

Lindsay, Leswick, Howe, Pavelich, Skov, Delvecchio, Allen, Peters, Dube.
MONTREAL—Goal, McNeil; defense, Harvey, St. Laurent; center, Masnick; wings, Curry, Olmstead. Alternates: Bouchard, Beliveau, Geoffrion, Richard, Johnson, Moore, Davis, Lach, Mosdell, Mazur, Stewart.
FIRST PERIOD—1, Montreal, Curry (Masnick), 9:17. Penalties: Harvey (14.20), Skov (17:11). Saves: Sawchuk 4, McNeil 12.
SECOND PERIOD—2, Detroit, Kelly (Delvecchio, Lindsay), 1:17. Penalty: Masnick (0:20). Saves: Sawchuk 5, McNeil 12.
THIRD PERIOD—No scoring. Penalties: None. Saves: Sawchuk 12, McNeil 6.
OVERTIME PERIOD—3, Detroit, Leswick (Skov), 4:29. No penalties. Saves: Sawchuk 1, McNeil 1.
Referee—Bill Chadwick. Linesmen—George Hayes and Bill Morrison.

April 17, 1954

RICHARD IS BANISHED AS CANADIENS BOW

BOSTON, March 13 (UP)—The Boston Bruins defeated the Montreal Canadiens, 4—2, tonight before 12,000 at Boston Garden. The game was marked by a fight in the third period and the banishment of Maurice (Rocket) Richard.

The outburst started when Hal Laycoe of the Bruins high-sticked Richard. The Rocket, with blood streaming down his face, smashed Laycoe across the shoulders with his stick. Then he struck Linesman Cliff Thompson with his fist.

After one more stick-wielding attack by Richard, order was restored and both players were led to their dressing rooms.

Richard was handed a match penalty which calls for an indefinite suspension, a fine of $100 and an investigation of the incident by the league president.

The line-up:

BOSTON—Goal, Henderson: defense, Flaman, Godfrey; center, Mackell; wings, Laycoe, Sandford. Alternates: Quackenbush, Armstrong, Bodnar, Smith, McKenney, Chevrefils, LaBine, Ferguson, Mohns, Costello, Bolvin, Gardner.
MONTREAL—Goal, Plante; defense, St. Laurent, Harvey; center, Mosdell; wings, Mackay, Curry. Alternates: Beliveau, Geoffrion, Olmstead, Johnson, Bouchard, Ronty, Marshall, Richard, Moore.
FIRST PERIOD—1, Montreal, Moore (Leclair Johnson), 13:04. Penalties: Mosdell (0:29), Laycoe, (4:45), Ferguson (15:16), Mosdell (15:16), Armstrong (17:37), Olmstead (17:37), Bouchard (18:31). Saves: Henderson 6, Plante 7.
SECOND PERIOD—2, Boston, Chevrefils Ferguson, Bolvin), 1:37; 3, Boston, Mackell (Sandford, Armstrong), 7:08; 4, Boston, Sandford (Mackell, Godfrey), 16:00. Penalties: Beliveau (7:54), Flaman (7:54), Richard (12:22), Ferguson (14:05), Geoffrion (15:16), Saves: Henderson 6, Plante 4.
THIRD PERIOD—5, Boston, Sandford (Costello), 2:12; 6, Montreal, Johnson (Mackay, Mosdell), 19:55. Penalties: Godfrey (13:34), Richard (match penalty, 15:11), Laycoe (five minutes and misconduct, 15:11). Saves: Henderson 8, Plante 9.
Referee — Frank Udvari. Linesmen — Sam Babcock and Cliff Thompson.

March 14, 1955

Richard Barred Rest of Season, And Also From Hockey Play-Offs

Ban for Boston Fight Likely to Cost Ace Scoring Title, Hurt Montreal in Race —Fans Threaten League Head

MONTREAL, March 16 (UP)—Maurice (The Rocket) Richard was banned today from all remaining National Hockey League games this season. He was also barred from the post-season play-offs for the Stanley Cup.

The fiery Montreal Canadien star was suspended by Clarence Campbell, the league president. His action stemmed from a fight during last Sunday night's game in Boston. Richard had been charged with punching Linesman Cliff Thompson and attacking a Boston Bruin player, Hal Laycoe, with a hockey stick.

The penalty stunned the Canadiens. They are engaged in a close race with the Detroit Red Wings for first place in the regular-season play.

Campbell's decision is almost certain to cost Richard the league scoring title. It was in his grasp for the first time in his thirteen seasons with Montreal.

Montreal fans reacted angrily. The switchboard at the league office was swamped with calls. Many threats were made against Campbell's life.

Campbell's ruling followed a hearing this morning. He said the Canadiens could appeal the case to the league's board of governors.

An appeal could be carried to the governors before the start of the play-offs. There was no possibility, however, that Richard could play in the final three games of the regular season.

Richard is the most heavily fined player in hockey history. But he did not suffer a direct financial penalty today. However, the suspension could cost him several thousand dollars.

The league scoring champion receives $1,000. Each player on the N. H. L. championship team also receives $1,000. There are bonuses for victory in the cup play-offs.

Richard, with 74 points, has a two-point lead in the scoring race. His team-mates, Bernie Geoffrion and Jean Beliveau, have 72 and 71 points, respectively.

Campbell held a 3½-hour hearing in his office.

"The time for probation or leniency (for Richard) is past," he ruled.

Campbell also referred to a fight in Toronto three months ago. He said, "the pattern of conduct by Richard was almost identical, including his constant resort to the recovery of a stick to pursue his opponent, as well as his flouting of the authority of the official."

Richard was fined $250 as a result of the Toronto incident.

March 17, 1955

Hockey Fans Riot in Montreal; League Head Attacked at Game

By The Associated Press.

MONTREAL, March 17—Thousands of spectators took over the Forum tonight in a frenzied demonstration against Clarence Campbell, president of the National Hockey League. They were furious over the suspension of their idol, Maurice (the Rocket) Richard.

Campbell was assaulted and pelted with fruit and overshoes before the game between Montreal and Detroit was forfeited to the visiting Red Wings.

At first, it was reported that police had fired over the heads of the crowd. But this was later denied by Police Chief T. O. Leggett.

Throughout the riot, Richard sat in a seat at the end of the Forum. The Montreal team's high-scoring star was set down yesterday for the rest of the regular league season and the post-season Stanley Cup play-offs.

Campbell arrived midway in the first period of the game. He was greeted by catcalls and assorted epithets by the crowd, which was getting out of hand even then.

For the next quarter-hour the fans' pent-up emotions grew louder until they reached a fever pitch.

At the intermission, with the Red Wings ahead by 4—1, a smoke bomb exploded and hundreds of the spectators, along with Campbell, made their way to the exits.

It was at this point that Fire Chief Armand Pare ordered the game halted for the "protection of the people." Fearful of a full-scale panic Pare ordered his men from the building, explaining that the sight of firemen by the 14,000 persons might lead to a stampede.

Although there were no immediate reports of serious injuries, many of the spectators who made their way to the exits were coughing. Their eyes and throats were filled with the acrid smoke of the bomb.

Campbell was greeted with a barrage of programs, peanuts and eggs when he arrived at the home rink of the Canadiens' sextet. But he kept his composure through violent threats until the bomb went off.

He was pelted with overshoes, rubbers and oranges all through his stay and finally was assaulted by a man who slipped through police lines on the pretext of being a friend of the

ASSAULTED: Clarence Campbell, National Hockey League president, at last night's game in Montreal.

Associated Press Wirephoto

league head. Campbell did not appear to be injured, but he made his way from the arena.

Police said the man—who was not immediately identified—walked up to Campbell and offered his hand before punching him.

Richard was suspended by the league president for a fight with Hal Laycoe of Boston last Sunday night. Laycoe suffered a cut on the head, as did Richard. The Montreal ace also punched Linesman Cliff Thompson twice.

At least a half-dozen demonstrators, some with blood streaming down their faces, were hauled away by police. The man who assaulted Campbell put up a battle against the police. He was dragged away, kicking, punching and screaming.

The spectators poured from the Forum after the bomb went off. They fell over one another.

Outside, other demonstrators, equally furious, threw rocks, frozen snow and bottles at police, street cars and automobiles. Some overhead wires of the trolley lines were pulled down, too.

An aerial ladder truck, a smaller fire truck and several emergency vehicles were dispatched to the scene. Where Campbell was no one could learn. The crowd tried to break into the office of the heavily guarded Forum, but was turned back by police.

Even in the afternoon there were indications of trouble, for

Campbell received many threatening telephone calls. But he announced he would be at the game.

Police on Patrol

Outside the Forum, before Campbell's arrival thousands of persons milled around. Dozens of police were on roaming patrol. The lobby was packed long before game time and for a while the crowd appeared to be in fairly good spirits. Later the fans became surly and tried to break into the Forum. They were turned back by police.

Most of the spectators who were bleeding said it was caused by being hit by missiles. Only the calm of the spectators in the upper seats, who were unaffect-

ed by the fumes, prevented a mob scene at the exits.

Montreal is perhaps the most rabid hockey city in North America. The suspension of Richard would be the equivalent of Baseball Commissioner Ford Frick suspending Willie Mays of the New York Giants in the middle of the pennant drive and adding that he couldn't play in the world series either.

According to the rules, the league president "shall issue instructions pertaining to records, etc., of a forfeited game."

The forfeit victory gave the Red Wings sole possession of first place in the circuit standing. They hold a 2-point margin over the second-place Canadiens.

The Montreal sextet is sched-

uled to play the New York Rangers next, at Montreal on Saturday. On Sunday the Canadiens will close the regular league season at Detroit.

The line-up:

DETROIT—Goal, Sawchuk; defense, Goldham, Kelly; center, Reibel; wings, Howe, Wilson. Alternates: Pronovost, Wolt, Leswick, Delvecchio, Pavelich, Skov, Hillman, Dineen, Hay, Stasiuk, Bonin.
MONTREAL—Goal, Plante; defense, Bouchard, Johnson; center, Beliveau; wings, Geoffrion, Olmstead. Alternates: Harvey, Curry, LeClair, Mackay, Moore, Ronty, Mosdell, St. Laurent, Marshall, Lamirande.
FIRST PERIOD—1. Detroit, Kelly (unassisted), 5:05; 2. Detroit, Reibel (Howe) 11:60; 3. Detroit, Kelly (Pavelich) 12:58; 4. Montreal, Mackay (Mosdell) 15:18; 5. Detroit, Reibel (Wilson, Delvecchio) 13:23. Penalties: Johnson (1:17), Moore (3:42), Wilson (11:17), Olmstead (18:04). Saves: Plante 9, Sawchuk 15.
Referee—Red Storey. Linesmen—Doug Davies and Bob Roberts.

March 18, 1955

Rocket Is Symbol to His Followers

Richard, Ace Hockey Scorer, Is the Idol of French-Canadians

By JOSEPH C. NICHOLS

"Why, they'd pay a buck a head just to watch him go fishin'."

That, in perhaps the most eloquent way to put it, describes the tremendous admiration that the French-Canadian sports fan in the Province of Quebec holds for Maurice Richard.

The fishing reference was offered in a quasi-serious manner by an experienced and knowing sports columnist, Dink Carroll of The Montreal Gazette, on the occasion of the Canadiens' last visit to this city.

It is almost impossible for the sports follower in this country to realize the hold that Richard, graphically nicknamed The Rocket, has on his compatriots.

Still fiercely nationalistic despite more than two centuries as subjects of the British Empire, the French-Canadians regard the fiery right wing of the Canadiens of Montreal as more than a man.

He is a symbol of their race. The fact that he is as good as any ice hockey player who ever lived serves merely to burnish that symbol with a golden brightness.

The applause that has been Willie Mays' due ever since he thrilled the sports world with his fine performance in baseball's world series and the praise that has gone up for Dusty Rhodes' batting in the same event are lukewarm compared with the joyful reaction among the hockey fans of Montreal when The Rocket soars.

Stewart Next Best

And, this year, he has been soaring frequently. He has played a little more than twelve seasons with the Canadiens, and his total output of goals is 422.

This production is almost a hundred more than the next best total, made by Nels Stewart, who campaigned with the Mon-

Associated Press Wirephotos

Maurice Richard as he watched Canadiens play the Red Wings Thursday night.

treal Maroons, the Boston Bruins and the New York Americans almost a generation ago. Stewart's total was 324.

Every time the Rocket scored a goal in the last two years, he was adding to a record. Every time he scored one of these goals in his home rink, the Montreal Forum, the cheers, shrieks, plaudits and such were just about as noisy and spontaneously erupted as the exploits of Mays and Rhodes.

It didn't matter that the goals were becoming almost commonplace. They were part of a record string, and they were scored by the Rocket.

Richard, always motivated by the burning urge that sets the champion apart from the also-ran, is aware of the chauvinistic regard that the French-Canadian fans have for him. He is proud of that regard.

The Rocket, who was born in Montreal on Aug. 4, 1921, did not know any language but

French until he was well along on his career as a professional hockey player.

It was said of him that he was surly off the ice, in the early days, and that this attitude was the result of his inability to talk or understand English. The Rocket realized that a knowledge of English was necessary to a person of his status in his profession and he made it a point to learn it.

Facile in Two Languages

He is now facile in both tongues, and the "surliness," off the ice, has given way to a confidence and ease that make him an agreeable companion—again, off the ice.

On the ice, The Rocket is always eager. He has been that way since he started to play the game as a boy. Richard learned to skate early, as do most kids in Canada. He took his place, normally, with neighborhood and school teams while he was growing up.

He became a professional in 1940, joining a team on the bottom rung of the Canadiens' farm-system ladder. After two seasons of schooling, he was brought up to the Canadien team and took part in sixteen games, scoring five goals.

He blazed the following season when he tallied thirty-two times in forty-six games. It was the next season, though—1944-45—that The Rocket really went up. He played every game of the fifty-game campaign, and scored fifty goals, a record for a single season's output that still stands, although the teams now play seventy contests a season.

In subsequent campaigns, The Rocket has struck for as many as forty-five, forty-three and forty-two in a season, and he became the most feared of skaters by rival goaltenders. It was said of him that he was only a "one-way" player—that is, a player who does well on the offensive, but is almost valueless on the defense.

Conn Smythe, the sharp general manager of the Toronto Maple Leafs, said of him a few years back, "he's just a one-way player, but I'll give $100,000 for

him. If he could play two ways, I'd give $200,000."

Needless to say, so integral a part of the French-Canadian culture—civic as well as athletic—was not sold to Toronto, that British citadel of all the things that the French-Canadian considers inimical to his nationalistic interests.

114 Minutes on 'Fence'

Two-way or no two-way, Richard was a competitor. Everybody found that out. He has been a frequent visitor to the penalty box, one season serving 114 minutes on the "fence."

It is part of the strategy of the game to goad a star player, and Maurice has been goaded beyond patience by inferior players, whose aim is to carry him to the penalty box with them.

These goadings have been responsible for many of Richard's flareups. But he also has lost his temper often purely in the course of play.

His present difficulty stems from an altercation in Boston last Sunday with Hal Laycoe, Boston defenseman, with whom Maurice exchanged vigorous whacks with the stick. When Linesman Cliff Thompson sought to separate the players, The Rocket dealt him a punch.

It was after an investigation of this affair, conducted by the league president, Clarence Campbell, in Boston on Wednesday, that Richard became a cause célèbre.

Campbell barred The Rocket from the remaining games in the league race, and from the post-season Stanley Cup competition that starts on Tuesday. The Stanley Cup play is for the championship of the world.

Richard had his first brush with Campbell in April, 1947, for cracking a couple of Maple Leaf players over the head with his stick. The fine was $250.

In January, 1948, Maurice was fined $75 for hurling two sticks from the penalty box onto the ice. In March, 1951, he had a scuffle with a referee named Hughie McLean in the lobby of a New York hotel the day after a game against the Rangers. In this game Richard was banished on a "match penalty" for fighting. This time he was fined $500.

The Rocket used to conduct a sports column in a Montreal French language paper. He accused Campbell in print of being a dictator and dared the league head to bar him from hockey. On talking things over Richard apologized.

The 5-foot, 10-inch Richard, who weighs 175 pounds, has made Montreal fans forget the late Howie Morenz, an idol of another day. His people love The Rocket and take up collections for him whenever he is fined. They also buy him presents and send him cash offerings, but these he turns over to charity.

The Rocket is well off. He doesn't need or want this indulgence. All he wants is a chance, through his performance with the Canadiens, to bring glory aux Habitants de Québec.

March 19, 1955

151

Detroit Keeps Stanley Cup Hockey Title, Beating Montreal in Seventh Game

Associated Press Wirephoto

GOAL ATTEMPT FAILS: Alex Delvecchio extreme left, of the Detroit Red Wings sending the puck toward the Montreal Canadiens' net in the first period of last night's game. Two players down on the ice are Jacques Plante, left, Montreal goalie, and Butch Bouchard, who blocked puck as he fell. At extreme right is Canadiens' Don Marshall.

DELVECCHIO CAGES TWO IN 3-1 VICTORY

Howe Also Scores Goal for Red Wings—Curry's Tally Averts Canadien Shutout

DETROIT, April 14 (UP)—The Detroit Red Wings won the Stanley Cup, emblematic of the world professional hockey championship, with a 3-1 victory over the Montreal Canadiens tonight.

Alex Delvecchio scored two goals for the National Hockey League titleholders, who took the final series from the runner-up team by four games to three.

The victory, before 15,141 fans, ended a grueling championship round. Each team had scored three victories on its own ice before the decisive battle.

Delvecchio, who lost his job as center for the high-scoring Gordie Howe and Ted Lindsay at mid-season because of his inability to collect goals, opened the scoring at 7:12 of the second period. He trapped an attempted

Montreal pass out at the blue line and skated within twenty feet of Goalie Jacques Plante before firing a short backhander that skidded past the netminder's leg pads.

Howe increased Detroit's edge to 2—0 with 11 seconds of the middle period remaining. Marcel Pronovost fired a shot from the sideboards which Howe deflected into the net.

Plante Beaten at 2:59

Delvecchio's second goal clinched the victory. Don Marshall, a Canadiens' rookie, dropped a blind pass in the Detroit zone which Delvecchio picked up to skate the length of the rink and beat Plante at 2:59 of the final period.

Although three goals behind, Montreal didn't let up and finally spoiled Goalie Terry Sawchuk's shutout bid at 14:25 while Bob Goldham was serving a tripping penalty. Floyd Curry picked up a loose puck near the Detroit net and tucked the disk into the corner before Sawchuk could stop it.

It marked the second straight year that the Red Wings and the Canadiens battled seven games in the fight for Lord Stanley's trophy. The Red Wings won it last year on a dramatic overtime goal by Tony Leswick.

Unlike the 1954 cup wind-up, the Canadiens skated out en masse to congratulate the Red

Wings at the final buzzer. Not one Montreal player offered a handshake last year.

Oddly, it was the second show-down battle between the two teams this season on Detroit ice. The Red Wings ripped Montreal, 7—0, in the final game of the regular season to edge out the Canadiens by two points for the National League championship. It was Detroit's seventh straight league title.

Home Ice Big Advantage

That victory played an important part in the Stanley Cup finals, for Detroit received the advantage of home ice for four games by finishing ahead of Montreal. And this was strictly a home ice series.

The National Hockey League president, Clarence Campbell, ruled that the Red Wings could not use two rookies recalled yesterday from Edmonton.

The Red Wings brought up a center, Bronco Horvath, and a left wing, John Bucyk, believing that the two forwards would be eligible since they had completed the Western League play-offs. Howeve., Edmonton still must face the winner of the Quebec League play-offs.

Campbell said the National League had an agreement with the two minor leagues stipulating that players competing in the inter-league series would not be eligible for Stanley Cup competition.

The line-up:

DETROIT—Goal, Sawchuk, defense, Goldham, Pronovost; center, Reibel; wings, Lindsay, Howe. Alternates: Kelly, Wolt, Leswick, DelVecchio, Pavelich, Skov, Wilson, Dineen, Hay, Stasiuk, Bonin.
MONTREAL—Goal, Plante; defense, Harvey, St. Laurent; center, Mosdell; wings, Curry, Mackay, Alternates: Bouchard, Beliveau, Geoffrion, Lec'air, Johnson, Moore, Ronty, Olmstead, Marshall, McAvoy, Gamble.
FIRST PERIOD — No scoring. Penalties: Lindsay (1:12), Bouchard (5:16), Harvey (7:19), Pavelich (11:51), Howe (19:34), Bouchard (19:34), Sa... Sawchuk 5, Plante 7.
SECOND PERIOD — 1, Detroit, Delvecchio (Kelly), 7:12; 2, Detroit, Howe (Pronovost), 19:49. Penalties: Leswick (7:44), Marshall (9:30), Mosdell (15:25). Saves: Sawchuk 8, Plante 16.
THIRD PERIOD—3, Detroit, Delvecchio (unassisted), 2:59; 4, Montreal, Curry (Geoffrion and Beliveau), 14:35. Penalties: Stasiuk (3:36), Mosdell (10:23), Johnson (11:36), Dineen (12:28), Goldham (14:09). Saves: Sawchuk 8, Plante 7.
Referee—Bill Chadwick. Linesmen—George Hayes and Bill Morrison.

April 15, 1955

Into Each Professional Hockey Player's Life Some Penalties Must Fall

But a Little 'Stretch in the Cooler' Can Do a Lot of Good

By JOSEPH C. NICHOLS

As is the case with all sports, enthusiasts for hockey avail themselves of every possible opportunity to serve as missionaries for their pet pastime.

They grasp every lapel within reach when the subject comes up. They beam when their listeners are sympathetic. They shake their heads in bafflement when their audience pays them little heed.

When a listener goes beyond the point of sympathetic agreement and says, "Oh, yes. The game is all right. But it's got too many rules that I can't understand," he's in for it. His preceptor can rattle off items of defense for his chosen sport at a speed that defies interruption.

The gist of these defenses is "Why there's nothing to it. F'r instance, take the penalties—." And that's just it, penalties. Among those who regularly attend hockey games, long-time observers as well as this year's neophyte, the different violations of the rules and the application of the punishments quite often arouse wonder.

Punishment Is Varied

There are more than twenty penalties that can be called to rule a player off the ice for two minutes. There are some half-dozen offenses that carry with them banishment for five minutes. Also, there are graver penalties that carry with them exiles for ten minutes or for the unexpired part of a game.

The one most often applied is the two-minute banishment, called the minor penalty. A five-minute exile is a "major," a ten-minute one is a misconduct, and the unexpired game's enforced absence is a match penalty. Among the most common minors are tripping, cross-checking, holding, interference and hooking.

It only stands to reason that a game played at so fast a pace, a game in which jarring body-contact figures so prominently, should cause a participant to "blow his top" easily.

To govern these low boiling points, the referee must be vigilant, must know his book of rules, and must have sufficient strength of character to ignore the raves and rants of (a) the home-town rooters and (b) the coaches and players of both teams.

Olinski Shows Courage

A referee in New York last Sunday night, Jerry Olinski, dared the wrath of the visitors' bench when he made a "brave" call such as has not been made here in two years. On a breakaway toward the Toronto Maple Leaf net, Larry Popein of the New York Rangers was tripped from behind by Gerry James of the visitors.

Because Popein was in the open and would have had a clear shot at the cage, Olinski ruled a penalty-shot foul against James. This marked the first instance such a punishment had been ordered in this city in two years and it brought out a cry of "homer" from the Toronto bench against Olinski.

A penalty shot is one in which a member of the offended team may skate without opposition to the opposing net and shoot—in an attempt to score. In the instance in question the Ranger player failed to make good, but the Leafs were not assuaged. They continued the cry of "homer against Olinski all through the game, which they lost, 4 to 1.

Because it is called so infrequently, the "penalty shot" is the least of the referee's worries. What he has to concern himself with most is preventing the spread of fist-fighting when the tempers explode.

Although there are rules in the National Hockey League that call for automatic cash fines against players joining fights that do not concern them originally, the skaters have a habit of joining these scraps anyway.

Referee Makes Decision

In the same game in which the penalty rule was invoked, there were four outbursts of fist fighting, but the participants drew nothing more than two minutes each for "roughing." It is up to the referee to determine between fighting and roughing.

Olinski did call one major, though. That one was against Lou (Rocky) Fontinato, the one-man riot squad who operates at a defense position for the Rangers.

Fontinato brought his stick down on the head of the same Gerry James.

To correct a general fallacious belief, Fontinato was not banished for drawing blood, per se. There is nothing in the book of rules that refers specifically to the "letting of gore."

The regulation applying to Fontinato's major reads: "When a player carries or holds any part of his stick above the height of his shoulder so that injury to the face or head of an opposing player results, the referee shall have no alternative but to im-

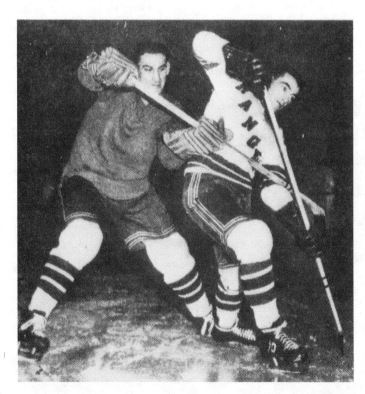

The Rangers' Lou Fontinato, in dark shirt throughout series, committing a hooking foul against team-mate Guy Gendron at Iceland rink. The penalty is a minor one, but becomes major if the player hooked is injured.

The New York Times (by Meyer Liebowitz)

A holding penalty (minor) shall be imposed on a player who holds opponent with hands or stick or in any other way.

This cross-checking foul is one of several ways of invoking a board-checking penalty. At the discretion of the referee—based on degree of violence—penalty may be minor or major.

Here the foul being demonstrated is tripping. A minor penalty is imposed on any player who places his stick (as in this case), his knee, foot, arm, hand or elbow in a manner causing opponent to trip or fall.

penalized must at once proceed to the penalty bench but may be replaced by a substitute until such time as the penalty time of the penalized player shall commence." And a referee does not need a law degree to hold down his job!

A lot of fans wonder why the goalie is never penalized, because they never see him go to the penalty box. The goalie is subject to penalties just as much as a skating player is. However, the goaltender is permittted to remain in the game, while a member of his team goes off the ice to sit in the penalty box.

There is one real protection for the goaltender, though. He is not allowed to fight. Any player who leaves the net to join a fight loses at once. He suffers an automatic fine of $50, a most effective deterrent to a professional athlete.

December 25, 1955

HOWE GETS 300TH AS WINGS WIN, 3-2

DETROIT, Feb. 7 (UP)—Gordie Howe scored twice to enter the 300-goal circle tonight as he led the Detroit Red Wings to a 3—2 victory over the Chicago Black Hawks in a National Hockey League game before 10,420 fans at Olympia.

The victory snapped a three-game losing streak for the Wings and thwarted the Hawks' bid to strengthen their grip on fourth place in the standings.

Howe's milestone tally was scored on a Detroit power play with Chicago's Norm Corcoran sitting out a penalty. The Detroit forward teamed with Ted Lindsay, who rifled a shot into the boards that rebounded in front of the Chicago net. Howe netted a slap shot.

He scored his second marker of the night and his thirtieth of the season on the same set-up play in the second period. This time he teamed with Earl (Dutch) Riebel, picking up the rebound from five feet out and sending his shot past Goalie Al Rollins.

The Detroit right wing now enters the select company of the retired Nels Stewart (324) and Maurice (Rocket) Richard (449), both of the Montreal Canadiens, as the only players in N. H. L. history to pass the 300-goal mark.

DETROIT—Goal Hall: defense, Pronovost, Hillman; center, Reibel; wings, Lindsay, Howe. Alternates: Goldham, Kelly, Godfrey, Delvecchio, Prystal, Ferguson, Ullman, Dineen, Hollingsworth, Costello, Pavelich.
CHICAGO—Goal, Rollins; defense, Sullivan, Mortson; center, Ciesla; wings, Litzenberger, Wilson. Alternates: Pilote, Fogolin, Watson, Wolt, G. Sullivan, Leswick, Mickoski, Sandford, Skov, La Lande, Corcoran.
FIRST PERIOD—1, Detroit, Howe (Lindsay), 6:33; 2, Chicago, Leswick (Mortson, Watson), 9:40. Penalty: Corcoran (6:17). Saves: Hall 2, Rollins 8.
SECOND PERIOD—2, Detroit, Howe (Riebel, Hillman), 12:55. Penalties: Corcoran (6:40), Mortson (14:24). Saves: Hall 10, Rollins 12.
THIRD PERIOD—4, Detroit, Ferguson (Dineen) 5:25; 5, Chicago, G. Sullivan (Mortson, Leswick) 16:03. Penalties: None. Saves: Hall 4, Rollins 5.
Referee—Red Storey. Linesmen—Bill Roberts and Doug Davies.

February 8, 1956

pose a major penalty on the fending player."

In many instances, it is up to the referee's discretion to extend minor penalties into majors, if the "assessed" player complains too loudly or too long against the application of the lesser ruling. It is under this heading that the misconduct penalty normally comes.

The misconduct role calls for the banishment of a player for ten minutes, but his team is permitted to replace him. In other words, its effectiveness is that it can deprive a team of a star player, permitting an inferior performer to take his place.

The penalty is called mostly against a player acting contrary to gentlemanly standards, mainly in the matter of inelegant language.

The "match" penalty has a number of variations. It involves the suspension of a player for the balance of a game, with a substitute permitted after ten minutes. It is called for such offenses as deliberately injuring an opponent and carries an automatic fine of $100.

A rather involved occurrence in the rink sport is the deferred penalty. Here is its main rule:

"If a third player of any team shall be penalized while two players of the same team are serving penalties, the penalty time of the third player shall not commence until the penalty time of one of the two players already penalized shall have elapsed.

"Nevertheless, the third player

154

Canadiens Beat Wings and Win Stanley Cup Hockey Finals

MONTREAL VICTOR, 3-1, BEFORE 14,152

Canadiens Win Stanely Cup Play-Off Series With Red Wings, 4 Games to 1

MONTREAL, April 10 (UP)—The Montreal Canadiens completed the downfall of hockey's greatest dynasty tonight. They beat the Detroit Red Wings, 3—1, to take the final National League play-off series by four games to one and capture the Stanley Cup for the seventh time.

The triumph ended Detroit's two-year grip on the trophy, emblematic of the world professional hockey championship.

A crowd of 14,152 roared with delight when the buzzer sounded ending the game and signaling a new era in the league in which the colorful Canadiens figure to reign supreme.

The Canadiens, who failed in two previous years to halt the great Detroit club in the finals of the Stanley Cup series, made no mistake about it this year. They beat the Wings in the first two games here, split two in Detroit and then took tonight's hard-fought fifth contest.

After the game, players and photographers streamed over the fence to mob the Canadiens, and especially the goalie, Jacques Plante. The acrobatic netminder handled twenty-five of twenty-six shots, many of them of the spectacular variety, as he turned back the hard-skating Red Wings time after time.

It was an even struggle until the Canadiens broke it open with their famed power plays in the second. Until then the Red Wings hardly looked like a team facing sudden elimination.

The defending cup champions were slightly outplayed in the first period, as the Canadiens outshot the Wings 11—7. But Detroit dominated the play in the early minutes of the middle period.

Montreal wasted three man-power advantages before Marcel Pronovost of Detroit got the gate for tripping Maurice Richard at 12:50. Twenty-six seconds later Montreal notched its first goal.

Floyd Curry carried the puck deep into Detroit ice and passed behind him when Gordie Howe tied him up. Jean Beliveau took the relay in the clear and flipped it over Goalie Glenn Hall's outstretched leg into the far corner.

Fifty-two seconds later Mau-

rice Richard grabbed a loose puck out of a goal-mouth scramble, skirted the pack and back-handed the puck behind Hall before the latter could cover.

Both teams were at full strength when Bernie Geoffrion pounced on Beliveau's rebound and punched it past Hall when the third period was only 13 seconds old.

Alex Delvecchio streaked in on Plante 22 seconds after Geoffrion's counter and beat the Montreal goalie with a wide-angle drive from 25 feet out for Detroit's score.

MONTREAL (3) — Goal, Plante; defense, Harvey, Turner; center, Beliveau; wings, wings, Geoffrion, Olmstead. Alternates: Bouchard, Curry, Leclair, M. Richard, Johnson, Moore, H. Richard, Talbot, Mosdell, St. Laurent, Marshall, Provost.
DETROIT (1)—Goal, Hall; defense, Goldham, Pronovost; center, Reibel; wings, Lindsay, Howe. Alternates: Kelly, Arbour, Delvecchio, Pavelich, Ferguson, Hillman, Ullman, Dineen, Hollingworth, Bucyk, Melnyk, Burton.
FIRST PERIOD—No scoring. Penalties: Hillman (2:48), Pronovost (6:42), H. Richard (9:35), Howe (10:47), Harvey (10:47). Saves: Hall 11, Plante 7.
SECOND PERIOD—1. Montreal, Beliveau (Curry, Harvey), 14:16; 2. Montreal, M. Richard (Geoffrion, Beliveau), 15:08. Penalties: Harvey (0:42), Lindsay (6:30), Beliveau (6:30), St. Laurent (9:56), Pronovost (13:50). Saves: Hall 6, Plante 10.
THIRD PERIOD—3. Montreal, Geoffrion (Beliveau, Olmstead), 0:13; 4. Detroit, Delvecchio (Lindsay), 0:35. Penalties: Kelly (7:07), M. Richard (12:50). Saves: Hall 19, Plante 8.
Referee—Frank Udvari. Linesmen—George Hays and Bill Morrison.

April 11, 1956

HOCKEY RULE CHANGED

Player Serving Minor Penalty to Return if Rivals Score

MONTREAL, June 4 (AP)—The National Hockey League's rules committee today adopted a regulation providing for immediate return to the ice of a player serving a minor penalty if the opposing team scores a goal.

It was the only major change made in the rules and will be put into effect next season in all professional leagues.

Under a long-standing rule the penalized player sat out his minor penalty for the full two minutes.

June 5, 1956

Campbell Criticizes Canadiens Following Near Riot at Montreal

President of League Puts Blame on Club Owners for Refereeing Problem, but Montreal Plans Udvari Protest

MONTREAL, Jan. 11 (UP) — Clarence Campbell, president of the National Hockey League, today lectured club owners who criticize referees. His action followed a near riot over the officiating of Frank Udvari at the Forum last night.

Udvari aroused Montreal Canadiens fans with his work during the local club's 2-1 victory over Toronto. He and Campbell required police protection to leave the Forum.

Udvari so enraged Maurice Richard, Montreal's temperamental star, that the Rocket kicked in the door of the team's dressing room after Udvari had banished him with a misconduct penalty.

General Manager Frank Selke of the Canadiens said a protest against Udvari would be made to Referee in Chief Carl Voss, blaming Udvari for inciting the fans over what they considered his refusal to penalize the Maple Leafs for their "clutch and grab" tactics. Selke also demanded that Udvari be banned from officiating in Montreal's home games.

Breaking Contract Doubted

Campbell said bluntly that the refereeing problem lay with the club owners.

"I don't see where Voss or anyone else can break a refereeing contract we have with Udvari," Campbell said. "As for Selke's plan for having the referee barred from officiating at all remaining home games of the Canadiens, it is inconceivable to think that anyone would

'go for a deal like that

"If a man isn't competent enough to referee in one building it follows that he should be barred from refereeing in all other buildings. Acceptance of a proposal like that would push us to the point where league owners would be selecting officials they want for their home games."

Montreal fans, aroused by mixed emotions of jubilation at their team gaining first place in the league for the first time since early in the season, and anger at Udvari, staged an exhibition reminiscent of the St. Patrick's Day riot of 1955.

On that occasion fans pelted Campbell with fruit and overshoes because of a Richard suspension. They later carried their demonstrations into the streets and hurled rocks at policemen, automobiles and street cars.

Police Protection Needed

Last night they threw programs and fruit at both Udvari and Campbell after the game, forcing Forum attendants and policemen to supply protection.

The outburst was sparked by Udvari's penalty against Richard for high-sticking Jim Morrison. While the Rocket sat out his penalty the Leafs tied the score and Richard rushed off the bench eyes ablaze, heading straight for the referee and swinging his stick.

Udvari threw him out. Richard banged the sideboards with his stick and lunged off the ice in a rage.

Then Donnie Marshall won the game for the Canadiens with

only six seconds left and the hubbub turned into a tumult.

Udvari Not Resigning

KITCHENER, Ont., Jan. 11 (AP)—Frank Udvari said today he had no intention of resigning over criticism leveled at him by General Manager Frank Selke of the Montreal Canadiens.

Udvari said he had received encouragement from the league president, Clarence Campbell of Montreal, who telephoned him at his home.

"I'll admit I never felt more like quitting, but I feel a lot better since I heard from Mr. Campbell," said the referee.

"I only did my duty, but it makes you wonder how long you can put up with this sort of thing. Why does it only happen in Montreal?"

January 12, 1957

National League Hockey Players Organize, Name Lindsay Head of Association

ATHLETES PLEDGE TO ASSIST SPORT

Hockey Players Aim to Make Pro Game More Popular— No Complaints Are Cited

The National Hockey League players, after five months of preparation and discussion, yesterday formed a players' organization "to promote and protect the best interests" of the players.

Ted Lindsay, one of the forwards on the Detroit Red Wings, was elected president. The group, the National Hockey League Players Association, retained the services of J. Norman Lewis and Milton Mound as attorneys and announced the formation of the association in the lawyers' offices.

Lewis has been serving for the past few years as legal adviser for the major league baseball players' organization.

In addition to Lindsay, the following officers were elected for two-year terms:

Doug Harvey, Montreal Canadiens, first vice president; Fern Flaman, Boston Bruins, second vice president; Gus Mortson, Chicago Black Hawks, third vice president; Jim Thomson, Toronto Maple Leafs, secretary; Bill Gadsby, New York Rangers, treasurer.

Officers Govern Body

The officers also constitute the executive committee, the governing body of the association. The officers held their first meeting yesterday in the office of Lewis and Mound, whom they have retained for a two-year term.

All the new player-officers were present as Lindsay conducted a press conference. He said the N. H. L. association probably would be patterned after the baseball group. However, he emphasized that it was not out to "make trouble."

"This association will be news to the N. H. L. owners, I believe, but we get along fine with them," Lindsay said. "We are very happy, but we want to make the league so popular that youngsters in both Canada and the United States will want to grow up and play professional hockey."

Lindsay said the players first talked about an association after playing together in the annual All-Star game at Montreal last October.

"We were just sitting around talking after the game and the subject came up," he said.

PLAYERS' CHOICES: Ted Lindsay, left, of the Detroit Red Wings, who was chosen president, and Doug Harvey of the Montreal Canadiens, who was elected first vice president, of new National Hockey League Players Association.

One Player Holds Out

Lindsay said each N. H. L. player had contributed $100 to the association. Only one player whom he refused to identify, had not yet joined.

Lindsay emphasized that the players had "no complaint such as the professional football players have."

Lewis said, "There isn't anything in the nature of ill will or any particular demand that is on an unpleasant basis. It hasn't been decided as yet when we will meet with owners or in what manner — separately or collectively."

N. H. L. players already have a minimum salary of $6,500, which is $500 above big-league baseball's minimum salary. In addition, N. H. L. players have a pension plan that will be ten years old this fall.

Players must be in the league two years to participate in this pension. They can begin to collect their pension at 45 or leave it in until they are 65. A ten-year player who waits until 65 to draw his pension will receive $300 a month.

Each player puts $900 a year into the pension fund. Two-thirds of the All-Star game take goes into this fund, along with 25 cents from every ticket sold for the Stanley Cup play-offs.

"Of course, each of us might have individual problems, but we have no group complaint right now," Lindsay said. "Maybe we might try to make the pension so inviting that more and more boys would want to play hockey, but we have no such plan at present. We aren't going to try to change the league."

Third Group Involved

The skaters are the third professional player group to organize or threaten to organize in recent months.

The National Basketball Association players threatened to join an industrial-type of union last month, but agreed to hold off when Maurice Podoloff, the president of the circuit, asked for three months to set up machinery for settling grievances with the owners.

The National Football League players organized last December. The N. F. L. owners refused to recognize their association early this month during their annual meeting in Philadelphia. The football players, who have hired Creighton Miller of Cleveland as their attorney, said last week they had the support of 370 of approximately 403 players in the league and said they planned to discuss joining an industrial-type of union.

In Montreal, Clarence Campbell, the president of the league, told the United Press that he could not voice approval or disapproval of the newly-formed association.

Campbell said that the comment made by Lindsay "represents about as fine a public relations statement as the National Hockey League could hope to have. Because it is quite evident that the officials of the new association are completely satisfied with the treatment they have received from the member clubs of the N. H. L. both individually and collectively."

February 12, 1957

Canadiens Rout Bruins for Second Stanley Cup Hockey Title in Row

MONTREAL VICTOR AT FORUM, 5 TO 1

MONTREAL, April 16 (AP)—The Montreal Canadiens won the Stanley Cup, symbol of National Hockey League supremacy, for the second consecutive year tonight, defeating the Boston Bruins, 5—1. It was a rugged battle that wrapped up the final best-of-seven play-off series for the Frenchmen, four games to one.

The Canadiens, denied a four-game sweep by a Bruin comeback that snared a 2-0 victory in Boston last Sunday, made no mistake on this one, building a 5-0 lead within two periods.

It was a furiously fought game, with numerous penalties and a free-for-all breaking out just before the first period came to a close.

The injuries almost matched the goals as Montreal claimed its eighth Stanley Cup championship.

Rocket Is Injured

Maurice (The Rocket) Richard went off the ice under his own power in the third period; bleeding from a head wound suffered when he was slammed to the ice after being checked by Boston's Doug Mohn.

Earlier, a Boston defenseman, Bob Armstrong, was taken to a hospital for X-rays of his ankle, injured when he slammed off his own goalie, Don Simmons, and crashed into the end boards.

And Boston's John Peirson

The best against the best: Montreal goalie Jacques Plante has just deflected a shot by Chicago's Bobby Hull (#7). Plante won the Vezina Trophy seven times. Hull's slap shots were feared by all N.H.L. goalies. In 1966, he set two new records, scoring 54 goals and accumulating 97 points.

An N.H.L. goalie in the 1950's would have been terribly unhappy to see these three Montreal Canadiens skating toward him. From left to right: Bernie "Boom Boom" Geoffrion, Jean Beliveau and Maurice "The Rocket" Richard. Geoffrion twice led the league in scoring; Beliveau was named to 10 all-star teams and was twice the M.V.P.; Richard is generally considered to be one of hockey's immortals.

suffered a head cut as the result of some high-sticking by Montreal's Dollard St. Laurent.

René Pronovost opened the scoring for the Canadiens, beating Simmons with a shot just outside the goal crease at 18:11 of the first period.

Dickie Moore counted for Montreal when the second period was only 14 seconds old.

Geoffrion Gets Goal

Bernie Geoffrion scored at 15:12 of the period, which saw a major handed out to St. Laurent for drawing blood in the stick job on Peirson. In the first

period, the Bruins' Fern Flaman and Montreal's Bert Olmstead got majors for their part in the free-for-all.

Leo LaBine finally got a shot in for the Bruins at 13:43 of the final period, but it was no more than a token challenge by Boston. The Bruins entered the game faced with the improbable share of becoming the second team to win the cup after losing the first three games of the final series.

Don Marshall and Floyd Curry wrapped it up for the Canadiens, who were rooted along by a hoarse and frenzied crowd of

15,286 in the Forum. Marshall counted at 18:31. Moore assisted on both goals.

Simmons finished with twenty-nine saves, turning away twelve shots in the final period. Jacques Plante saved twenty-seven shots at the Montreal goal, thirteen of them in the first period.

MONTREAL (5)—Goal, Plante; defense, Johnson, Talbot; cent. Beliveau; wings, Geoffrion, Olmstead. Alternates: Harvey, Curry, M. Richard, Turner, Moore, Provost, H. Richard, St. Laurent, Goyette, Marshall, Pronovost, Broden.
BOSTON (1)—Goal, Simmons; defense, Mohns, Flaman; center, McKenney; wings, LaBine, Chevrefils. Alternates: Armstrong, Boone, Stasluk, Mackell, Gardner, Bionda, Caffrey, Bolvin, Toppazzini, Peirson, Regan

FIRST PERIOD—1, Montreal, Pronovost (Marshall, Provost), 18:11. Penalties: LaBine (6:56), H. Richard (2:44), Boone (11:24), St. Laurent (11:24), Harvey (13:20), LaBine (19:18), Flaman (5 and 2 minutes, 19:18), Olmstead (5 and 2 minutes), 19:18. Saves: Simmons 7, Plante 13.
SECOND PERIOD — 2, Montreal, Moore (Geoffrion, Harvey), 0:14; 3, Montreal, Geoffrion (Olmstead, Johnson), 15:12. Penalties: Bionda (2:20), Pierson (7:52), St. Laurent (5 minutes, 7:52), Flaman (9:26). Saves: Simmons 10, Plante 7.
THIRD PERIOD—4, Boston, LaBine (Bolvin), 13:43; 5, Montreal, Marshall (Moore, Curry), 17:38; 6, Montreal, Curry (Moore, Broden), 18:31. Penalties: H. Richard (2:20), Mackell (10:50), Pronovost (10:50). Saves: Simmons 12, Plant 6.
Referee—Frank Udvari. Linesmen—Georges Hayes and Bill Morrison.

April 17, 1957

Canadiens Down Bruin Six to Capture Stanley Cup, 4 Games to 2

GEOFFRION STARS IN 5-TO-3 TRIUMPH

Tallies Twice as Canadiens, by Defeating Bruins, Win Cup Third Year in Row

BOSTON, April 20 (UP)—The Montreal Canadiens won their third straight Stanley Cup championship tonight as Bernie (Boom Boom) Geoffrion scored twice in a 5-3 victory over the Boston Bruins at the Garden.

A capacity crowd of 13,909 saw the Canadiens strike for two goals less than two minutes after the opening face-off. These provided the victory margin as Montreal took the National Hockey League play-off, four games to two.

Geoffrion scored at 0:46 of the first period and again just before the end of the middle period. Montreal's other scorers were Maurice Richard, Jean Beliveau and Doug Harvey.

Don McKenney, Norm Johnson and Larry Regan tallied for the Bruins. Boston scored twice in the last period in a desperate bid to tie it, but Montreal got a cushioning goal after the Bruin goalie, Don Simmons, had been withdrawn for a sixth skater.

Richard's goal was his eleventh of the play-offs, one less than the league record the Rocket shares with Beliveau.

Simmons made a good stop on the first shot of the game, a forty-footer by Beliveau from the left board. Then Geoffrion converted another shot by the Montreal wing from the identical spot. The Canadiens had a two-goal lead little more than a minute later when Richard put a twenty-footer between Simmons' legs at 1:54.

McKenney got his ninth goal of the play-offs at 18:35, using

Associated Press Wirephoto

MONTREAL SCORES: Bernie Geoffrion, left, of the Canadiens swings away from net after driving puck past Don Simmons, Bruins' goal tender, in play-off game in Boston.

a defenseman, Doug Mohns, at the crease as a screen on his twenty-five-footer. The Montreal goalie, Jacques Plante, brought Simmons to the blue blocked it but the puck fell to the ice and dribbled into the net.

In the second period Beliveau took passes from Geoffrion and Harvey at 6:42 and fired a fifty-footer past Simmons, Geoffrion picked up his sixth goal of the play-offs at 19:26, gunning a twenty-five-footer past Simmons.

The Bruins, who won the second and fourth games of the

series, emerged from their sluggishness in the third period. Johnson slapped in Larry Regan's rebound at 5:20 and Regan converted Fernie Flaman's rebound at 13:41.

The Bruin coach, Milt Schmidt, brought Simmons to the blue line with 1 minute 31 seconds remaining, then took him out for a sixth skater a few seconds later and Harvey scored.

MONTREAL (5)—Goal, Plante; defense, Turner, Harvey; center, Beliveau; wings, Geoffrion, Olmstead. Alternates: Curry, M. Richard, Moore, Provost, H. Richard, Talbot, Bonin, Goyette, Langlois, Marshall, Pronovost, Broden, T. Johnson.
BOSTON (3)—Goal, Simmons; defense,

Stanley, Bolvin; center, N. Johnson; wings, Regan, LaBine, Alternates: Horvath, Stasluk, Mackell, Bucyk, Flaman, McKenney, Mohns, Toppazzini, Hillman, Peirson, Boone.
FIRST PERIOD—1, Montreal, Geoffrion (Beliveau, Olmstead), 0:46; 2, Montreal, M. Richard (Moore), 1:54; 3, Boston, McKenney (Mohns), 18:35. Penalties: Goyette (1:59), Bucyk (7:38). Saves: Simmons 12, Plante 13.
SECOND PERIOD—4, Montreal, Beliveau (Geoffrion, Harvey), 6:42; 5, Montreal, Geoffrion (unassisted), 19:26. Penalties: N. Johnson (0:35). Saves: Simmons 18, Plante 7.
THIRD PERIOD—6, Boston, N. Johnson (Regan), 5:20; 7, Boston, Regan (Flaman, LaBine), 13:41; 8, Montreal, Harvey (unassisted), 19:00. Penalties: None. Saves: Simmons 11, Plante 11.
Referee—Frank Udvari. Linesmen—George Hayes and Bill Morrison.

April 21, 1958

CANADIENS KEEP STANLEY CUP

MONTREAL DOWNS TORONTO SIX, 5-3

Canadiens Take Stanley Cup Fourth Straight Time by Winning Play-Offs, 4-1

By United Press International.

MONTREAL, April 18—The Montreal Canadiens, flashing championship hockey form, won a record fourth consecutive Stanley Cup tonight as they defeated the Toronto Maple Leafs, 5-3, and took the four-out-of-seven series, four games to one.

Bernie (Boom-Boom) Geoffrion was the big man for the Canadiens for the second game in a row. He scored twice and assisted on another goal. His rookie lineman, Ralph Backstrom, was just as effective, scoring once and setting up three other tallies.

Tom Johnson and Marcel Bonin, the high scorer in the playoffs with ten goals, got the other Montreal goals.

Pulford-Olmstead Net

Bob Pulford, Frank Mahovlich and Bert Olmstead — a member of this winning Canadiens team just one year ago—were the Leaf marksmen.

The victorious Habitants kept the glittering huge trophy — most coveted in hockey—by scoring three times in the first period and twice more in the middle frame. But the valiant Leafs, who surprised everyone by making the semi-final playoffs, went down fighting.

Trailing 5—1, entering the final twenty minutes, they rallied for a pair of goals late in the period. They pressured the champions relentlessly in the final minutes in a vain effort to score again.

With 2:33 remaining to play, Coach Punch Imlach removed the Leafs' goalie, Johnny Bower, and put six forwards on the ice.

While Dickie Moore completed a hooking minor, the Leafs were playing with a two-man advantage. But the Canadiens' defense, led by Goalie Jacques Plante and Doug Harvey and Tom Johnson withstood the desperation bid by the Leafs.

14,790 Watch Game

With a few seconds remaining, some of the 14,790 fans began pouring over the boards to congratulate their victorious heroes. Within minutes after the final buzzer sounded, the players were engulfed by the cheering mob.

The ice was still a melee of players and fans when Maurice (Rocket) Richard—the 37-year-old Canadiens' captain who had to sit out most of the series with injuries—accepted the newly-polished cup from a former team captain, Dutch Bouchard, and carried it off the ice to the Montreal dressing room.

The National Hockey League president, Clarence Campbell, then presented the cup to Richard again for the benefit of their televiewers in the crowded dressing room.

The Canadiens, who have been in the Stanley Cup finals a record nine straight years, have won it five times during that span. For Montreal's coach, Toe Blake, it was his fourth straight cup in four years. Hap Day is the only other coach to win more Stanley Cups—five with the Leafs.

The Canadiens won their second straight National Hockey League title and third in Blake's four years in a breeze. They went on to eliminate the Chicago Black Hawks in six games and then took on the Leafs who beat Boston in seven games.

MONTREAL (5)—Goal, Plante; defense, Harvey, Turner; center, Goyette; wings, Bonin, Moore. Alternates: Geoffrion, Backstrom, Hicke, M. Richard, Johnson, McDonald, H. Richard, Talbot, Provost, Langlois, Marshall.
TORONTO (3)—Goal, Bower; defense, Horton, Stanley; center, Pulford; wings, Stewart, Olmstead. Alternates: Reaume, Regan, Duff, Armstrong, Brian Cullen, Harris, Ehman, Brewer, Baun, Creighton, Mahovlich.
FIRST PERIOD—1, Montreal, Backstrom Geoffrion (Backstrom, Harvey), 13:42; 2, Geoffrion, Backstrom, Harvey), 13:42; 3, Montreal, Johnson (Backstrom), 16:26. Penalties: Backstrom (1:44), Mahovlich (2:44), Harvey (10:24), Pulford (10:25), Plante 15.
SECOND PERIOD—4, Toronto, Pulford (Armstrong, Brewer), 4:27; 5, Montreal, Bonin (H. Richard, Harvey), 9:55; 6, Montreal, Geoffrion (Backstrom, Johnson), 19:25. Penalties: Harvey (4:10), Brewer (18:29). Saves: Bower 7, Plante 9.
THIRD PERIOD—7, Toronto, Mahovlich (Harris, Ehman), 12:07; 8, Toronto, Olmstead (Ehman), 16:19. Penalties: Harvey (7:03), Baun (15:12), Moore (15:59). Saves: Bower 15, Plante 9.
Referee—Eddie Powers. Linesmen—George Hayes and Art Skov.

April 19, 1959

De Luxe Model Protective Mask Arrives for Paille of Ranger Six

By WILLIAM J. BRIORDY

Marcel Paille, the New York Rangers' goalie, will use his protective mask for the first time this morning during practice at Madison Square Garden.

The mask, made of white fiberglass with a wide plexiglass eye strip, arrived yesterday. Alf Pike, the coach, unpacked it and said: "Paille will look like a knight in armor in that thing."

The mask was made in Toronto by the Brunswick-Balke Collender Company from a mold of Marcel's face. The device appears to be an improvement on the mask worn by the Montreal Canadiens' Jacques Plante, the goalie who broke the ice in the National Hockey League. Don Simmons of the Boston Bruins is the only other major-league goalie wearing one.

Plante wore his mask for the first time in a regular game on Nov. 1 at the Garden after a flying puck caused a severe facial cut. Play was held up for twenty minutes. Plante, the winner of the Vezina Trophy as the league's top cage guardian for four straight years, returned to the ice wearing his mask and helped beat the Blues, 3—1.

Paille has been injured several times by disks and wild sticks. On Dec. 13, he suffered a twelve-stitch cut but returned to beat the Boston Bruins, 3—1. In that game, Simmons wore a mask for the first time.

The masks worn by Plante and Simmons have slits for the eyes, nose and mouth. Paille's mask is probably more advantageous because of the wide eye shield, which is detachable.

Paille will decide after the workout whether to wear it for the game tomorrow night with the Chicago Black Hawks.

Canadiens' Coach Angry

In Montreal, Toe Blake, the Canadiens' coach, voiced another opinion on masks.

"Plante won the Vezina Trophy four years in a row without a mask, and I'm wondering if he needs it now," Blake said. "If the mask is affecting his play, perhaps he should try to do without it."

Of course, Blake was irked by his club's 6—5 loss to the Rangers on Sunday night. The Blues, turning in one of their better games, hit for four goals in the third period.

Blake didn't blame Plante entirely for the defeat. "The whole team isn't pulling its weight," he said. Montreal's pace-setting team has lost only six games this season, three of them to the Rangers.

December 22, 1959

BATHGATE FINED $500

Ranger Penalized by League for Article on 'Brutality'

MONTREAL, Dec. 21 (AP)—Andy Bathgate of the New York Rangers was fined $500 by the National Hockey League today for writing a magazine article alleging brutality in the sport.

Muzz Patrick, general manager of the Rangers, was fined $100 for approving the story.

In announcing the fines, Clarence Campbell, the league president, said, "The sum total effect of the article is definitely prejudicial to the league and the game, and this was not seriously contested by the principals involved."

Regarding Patrick, Campbell said, "It is clear that he did not authorize or approve the article in the form in which it finally appeared but by his failure to consider its possible implications, which were quite plain in the text which was submitted to him, he gave his authorization by default and is responsible under the bylaws."

The article, in which Bathgate was critical of "spearing" in the league, appeared in the Canadian edition of True magazine two weeks ago. Spearing is defined in the league rule book as "the stabbing of an opponent with the point of the stick blade***."

The fine was said to be equal to the sum Bathgate received for collaborating on the article.

December 22, 1959

Canadiens Rout Leafs and Retain Stanley Cup

BELIVEAU IS STAR IN 4-TO-0 VICTORY

His 2 Goals Help Canadiens Complete a 4-Game Sweep for 5th Cup in Row

TORONTO, April 14 (UPI)—Led by Jean Beliveau, the Montreal Canadiens swept to their fifth consecutive Stanley Cup tonight with a 4-0 triumph over the Toronto Maple Leafs.

This was the first time that any National Hockey League team had won the cup five times in a row.

Beliveau, a center, scored twice. Henri (Pocket Rocket) Richard and Doug Harvey counted once apiece as the Canadiens completed a four-game sweep. The Flying Frenchmen also needed only four games to knock off the Chicago Black Hawks in the semi-final round of cup play.

The 1951-52 Detroit Red Wings were the only other squad to win the cup in eight games since the league was founded forty-two years ago.

Rocket Accepts Trophy

Immediately following the game, the league president, Clarence Campbell, handed the cup to the Montreal captain, Maurice (Rocket) Richard.

The Canadiens dominated the action despite the Leafs' frantic efforts to make a contest of it. As they had in the three previous games, the Habs skated to a quick lead and then coasted.

Bernie (Boom Boom) Geoffrion did not score, but the Montreal right winger collected three assists to tie a team-mate, Henri Richard, and Red Kelly of Toronto in the race for the individual point title.

Montreal wheeled in front to stay in the first period, scoring twice on long screened shots from the points.

Beliveau clicked at 8:16, with Junior Langlois and Geoffrion assisting. Then at 8:45, Harvey drove home a long shot that Toronto's goalie, Johnny Bower, could not see. Again, Langlois and Geoffrion assisted.

Brewer Hits Crossbar

The Leafs had three great chances in the middle period; Dickie Duff picked a post and Carl Brewer hit the crossbar behind Jacques Plante, the Montreal goalie. But it was the Canadiens who scored. The Pocket Rocket took the Rocket's pass, worked in close and fooled Bower.

The final period was less than two minutes old when Montreal made it 4-0 on Beliveau's second counter of the game. The husky center took a relay from Geoffrion and Marcel Bonin to beat Bower with an angled shot from 20 feet out.

MONTREAL (4)—Goal, Plante; defense, Langlois, Harvey; center, Beliveau; wings, Bonin, Geoffrion. Alternates: M. Richard, H. Richard, Moore, Pronovost, Goyette, Provost, Marshall, Backstrom, Hicke, Johnson, Talbot, Turner.
TORONTO (0)—Goal, Bower; defense, Horton, Stanley; center, Pulford; wings, Olmstead, Stewart. Alternates: Baun, Brewer, Duff, Kelly, Mahovlich, Edmundson, Wilson, James, Regan, Harris, Armstrong, Ehman.

April 15, 1960

Penalty Record Set

MONTREAL, Oct. 20 (AP)—Reggie Fleming, a rookie defenseman of the Chicago Black Hawks, set a National Hockey League record for penalty minutes during last night's encounter with the New York Rangers. A re-check of the official game statistics today showed that Fleming was assessed thirty-seven minutes in penalties. The old record of thirty minutes was set by Ted Lindsay of Detroit on Oct. 12, 1952.

October 21, 1960

Howe Breaks Record

DETROIT, Dec. 1 (UPI)—Gordie Howe, assisting on Detroit's first goal early in the third period, set a National Hockey League scoring record tonight. However, goals by Don McKenney and Charlie Burns later in the period carried the Boston Bruins to a 3-2 victory over the Red Wings.

Howe's assist, giving him a career total of 1,092 points, broke the record he had shared with Maurice Richard of the Montreal Canadiens. Howe also assisted on Detroit's second goal in the last minute of play to run his total to 1,093.

The history-making point came at 6:23 of the final period and moved the Red Wings into a 1-1 tie. But the Bruins, who dominated the play through the first two periods, charged right back.

BOSTON (3)—Goal, Gamle; defense, Boivin, Erickson; center, Burns; wings, Topazzini, Bartlett. Alternates: Horvath, Stasiuk, D. Smith, Bucyk, Ouellette, Flaman, Labine, McKinney, Tessier, Mohns, A. Pronovost.
DETROIT (1)—Goal, Sawchuk; defense, M. Pronovost, Goegan; center, Oliver; wings, Howe, McDonald. Alternates: Reaume, Godfrey, Ullman, Delvecchio, Aldcorn, Fonteyne, Melnyk, Glover, B. Smith, Johnson, Odrowski, Lunde.

First Period—1, Boston, Bartlett (Boivin, Topazzini), 13:43. Penalty: D. Smith (5:56). Saves: Gamble 7, Sawchuk 6.
SECOND PERIOD—No scoring. Penalty: Goegan (14:46). Saves: Gamble 5, Sawchuk 6.
THIRD PERIOD—2, Detroit, Oliver (Odrowski, Howe), 6:33; 3, Boston, McKenney (Fleman), LaBine, 10:55; 4, Boston, Byrnes (A. Pronovost, Boivin), 15:31; 5, Detroit, Delvecchio (Howe, Godfrey), 19:03. Penalty: LaBine (18:32). Saves: Gamble 10, Sawchuk 9.
Referee—John Ashley. Linesmen—Neil Armstrong and Ron Wicks.

December 2, 1960

CANADIENS DOWN BLACK HAWKS, 3-1

Geoffrion Equals Record— Wings Tie Leafs, 4 to 4

By The Associated Press.

MONTREAL, Dec. 24—Bernie (Boom Boom) Geoffrion equaled a National Hockey League record tonight by scoring in his ninth consecutive game as the Montreal Canadiens defeated the Chicago Black Hawks, 3—1.

Geoffrion's goal went into an open net at 18:49 of the third period after Glenn Hall, the Hawk goalie, has been taken out for an extra forward.

The league-leading Canadiens spotted Chicago a goal by Reg Fleming in the second period, then struck swiftly early in the third period with goals by Marcel Bonin and Jean Beliveau.

By scoring in nine straight games, Geoffrion equaled the record made in the 1944-45 season by Montreal's famed Maurice (Rocket) Richard, now retired. Referee Frank Udvari called eighteen penalties, including a major against Fleming for intent to injure in highsticking Tom Johnson of the Canadiens in the third period.

The seventeen minor penalties—ten against the Hawks—embraced tripping, hooking, holding, highsticking, elbowing and spearing.

Doug Harvey, the Montreal defenseman, had to leave the game in the second period because of an injured shoulder. Stan Mikita, a Hawk center, suffered a two-stitch cut over the left eye.

The victory gave Montreal a 7-point lead in the league standing over the second-place Toronto Maple Leafs.

The triumph was the Canadiens' eleventh in the last twelve games.

Chicago's goal came at 19:12 of the second period when the puck, fired by Pierre Pilote, went into the net off Fleming's skate.

Bonin deflected Dickie Moore's shot past Hall at 1:57 of the final period. Beliveau hit the far side of the net with a 15-foot backhander at 3:10.

Hall was taken from the net with 1 minute 35 seconds of the game left. Geoffrion finally broke loose from the Montreal end and was almost blocked out by a Chicago defenseman, Dollard St. Laurent. But he carefully fired a backhander into the net as St. Laurent lunged for him.

Geoffrion then retired the puck as a souvenir while the crowd showered the ice with papers and programs. It was Geoffrion's twenty-fifth goal of the season.

MONTREAL (3)—Goal, Hodge, defense, Johnson, Talbot; center, Beliveau; wings, Geoffrion, Gendron. Alternates: Harvey, Blackstrom, Hickey, Turner, Moore, Provost, H. Richard, Bonin, Langlois, Goyette, Tremblay, Marshall.
CHICAGO (1)—Goal, Hall; defense, Pilote, Vasko; center, Sloan; wings, Nesterenko, Murphy. Alternates: Arbour, Evans, Fleming, M. Balfour, Hay, McDonald, Wharram, St. Laurent, E. Balfour, Mikita, Hicks.
FIRST PERIOD—No scoring. Penalties: Fleming (2:28), Pilote (12:44), Beliveau (12:58), Nesterenko (4 minutes, 16:30), Bonin (16:43). Saves: Hall 8, Hodge 8.
SECOND PERIOD—1, Chicago, Fleming (Pilote), 19:44. Penalties: Turner (5:36), Hay (8:58), Beliveau (9:40), St. Laurent (14:33), Pilote (17:13). Saves: Hall 3, Hodge 5.
THIRD PERIOD—2, Montreal, Bonin (Richard, Moore), 1:57; 3, Montreal, Beliveau (Hicke, Geoffrion), 3:10; 4, Montreal, Geoffrion (Gendron, Talbot), 18:49. Penalties: Fleming (2:50), Fleming (6:28), Johnson (6:28), Mikita (14:28), Gendron (14:28), Pilote (15:37), Backstrom (15:37). Saves: Hall 20, Hodge 23.
Referee—Frank Udvari. Linesmen—George Hayes and Loring Doolittle.
Attendance—13,346.

December 25, 1960

Canadiens Down Leafs as Geoffrion Ties Mark

MONTREAL VICTOR IN 5-TO-2 CONTEST

Geoffrion Gets 50th Goal of Campaign to Tie Maurice Richard's Season Mark

MONTREAL, March 16 (UPI) —Bernie (Boom Boom) Geoffrion scored his fiftieth goal of the season tonight to tie the league record of Maurice Richard as the Montreal Canadiens defeated the Toronto Maple Leafs, 5—2. Montreal moved to within one victory of clinching its fourth successive National Hockey League regular-season championship.

The Canadiens broke a 1-1 tie with a flurry of four goals in the third period.

Billy Hicke, Henri Richard, Ralph Backstrom and Geoffrion beat the Toronto net-minder, Cesare Maniago, in a span of less than ten minutes, beginning at 4:57. Guy Gendron of Montreal got the first goal of the game in the second period. A rookie, Dave Keon, got his twentieth of the season a minute and nine seconds later for Toronto. Eddie Shack got his fifteenth in the third period for the second Toronto goal.

Montreal Increases Lead

The victory lifted Montreal's margin over the second-place Leafs to 3 points, with two games left for each team. A victory against Chicago here Saturday or the Red Wings in Detroit Sunday, the final day of the regular season, would give the Canadiens the title. It would be their fifth in the six years that Coach Toe Blake has handled the team.

Geoffrion, who had missed a wide-open net seconds earlier, pounced on a loose puck just off the corner of the net and shoved it behind Maniago at 14:15 of the third period. The goal widened Montreal's lead to 5—2.

Geoffrion leaped into Jean Beliveau's arms and both tumbled to the ice. The crowd of 15,011, the largest of the season, cheered for several minutes and littered the ice with programs. A photographer picked up the puck and gave it to Geoffrion.

The elder Richard, who holds the mark of 544 goals in eighteen years of regular league play, got his fiftieth during the fifty-game season of 1944-45.

Geoffrion Gets Assist

Earlier, Geoffrion picked up an assist on Gendron's goal and the 2 points lifted his total to 95. This is one short of the league record of 96 set by a team-mate, Dickie Moore.

Geoffrion's fiftieth goal completely overshadowed a league record set by Beliveau. The big center set up two goals. His two assists increased his season total to fifty-eight. This is two more than the record he had shared with Bert Olmstead, formerly with the Canadiens and now with the Leafs.

MONTREAL (5)—Goal, Plante; defense, Johnson, Talbot; center, Richard; wings, Provost, Marshall. Alternates: Harvey, J. C. Tremblay, Beliveau, Geoffrion, Backstrom, Hicke, Turner, Gendron, Bonin, Langlois, Goyette, G. Tremblay.
TORONTO (2)—Goal, Maniago; defense, Horton, Stanley; center, Keon; wings, Nevin, Mahovlich. Alternates: Regan, Duff, Stewart, Harris, Olmstead, Brewer, Pulford, Baun, Hillman, Shack, McMillan.
FIRST PERIOD — No scoring. Penalties: Shack (2 minutes and 5 minutes, 5:13), Bonin (5 minutes, 5:13), Talbot (served by Goyette, 5:47), Brewer (8:06), Hicke (8:44), Pulford (9:30), Richard (9:30). Saves: Maniago 8, Plante 10.
SECOND PERIOD — 1, Montreal, Gendron (Beliveau, Geoffrion), 13:35; 2, Toronto, Keon (Olmstead, Stanley), 14:14. Penalties: Baun (12:05), Talbot (14:00), Harvey (19:46). Saves: Maniago 13, Plante 10.
THIRD PERIOD—3, Montreal, Hicke (Bonin, Backstrom), 4:57; 4, Montreal, Richard (Marshall), 7:33; 5, Toronto, Shack (Duff, Harris), 8:42; 6, Montreal Backstrom (Bonin, Hicke), 9:02; 7, Montreal Geoffrion (G. Tremblay, Beliveau), 14:15. Penalties: Beliveau (11:02), Brewer (11:31), Shack (19:29). Saves: Maniago 10, Plante 11.
Referee—Frank Udvari. Linesmen—George Hayes and Patty Pavelich.
Attendance—15,011.

March 17, 1961

Hawks Turn Back Red Wings and Win Stanley Cup Play-Offs

CHICAGO SKATES TO 5-TO-1 VICTORY

Hawks Score 2 Goals in 2d Period and 3 in 3d to Win First Cup in 23 Years

DETROIT, April 16 (UPI)—The Chicago Black Hawks capped one of hockey's greatest success stories tonight when they won their first Stanley Cup championship in twenty-three years by walloping the Detroit Red Wings, 5—1.

The Black Hawks, who scored two goals in the second period and three more in the third, thus polished off the Red Wings, four games to two. Earlier they had eliminated Montreal in six games in the semi-finals.

It was only the fourth time in national hockey league history that a team that had finished third in the regular season went on to win Lord Stanley's trophy.

Third Time for Hawks

The last time was in 1945 when the Toronto Maple Leafs accomplished the feat. It also was only the third time in history that the Black Hawks had won professional hockey's biggest prize.

The Red Wings dominated the play through the first period and in the early moments of the second. Parker MacDonald gave Detroit a 1-0 lead at 15:24 of the first period.

The Black Hawks battled back to take a 2-1 lead in the second period on goals by Reg Fleming and Ab McDonald. Then the roof caved in on the Red Wings in the third period as Eric Nesterenko, Jack Evans and Ken Wharram fired shots past Hank Bassen, the goalie.

It was an especially great moment for Evans, whose goal was his first in two full seasons of play.

Hicks Is Penalized

The turning point of the game came during the seven-minute mark of the second period when a rookie, Wayne Hicks, was penalized for hooking. The Red Wings, leading by 1—0, formed a power play in the hope of getting a second goal.

Fleming crossed them up when he broke up the pattern, followed the play down to the Detroit end and stole the puck there from a defenseman, Pete Goegan. He then raced in alone on Bassen and fired over the goalie's stick into the net.

The trying goal, coming while they were short-handed, fired up the Black Hawks and they were unbeatable thereafter. Conversely, the Red Wings seemed to collapse as the second period progressed and appeared to be a defeated club when they came out for the final period.

It was the first time in five play-off games that Detroit had lost on home ice. In this series, in fact, both teams went into this game with undefeated records at home. The Hawks had taken three at Chicago and the Wings two at Olympia.

CHICAGO (5) — Goal, Hall; defense, Pilote, Vasko; center, Litzenberger; wings, Hay, Hull. Alternates: Arbour, Evans, Fleming, Sloan, Murphy, McDonald, Nesterenko, Wharram, E. Balfour, Mikita, Hicks, Hillman.
DETROIT (1) — Goal, Bassen; defense, Goegan, Godfrey; center, Delvecchio; wings, Howe, Stasiuk. Alternates: Pronovost, Young, Ullman, LaBine, Fonteyne, Melnick, Glover, MacGregor, Johnson, Odrowski, MacDonald, Lunde.
FIRST PERIOD—1, Detroit—McDonald (Delvecchio, Howe), 15:24. Penalties: Howe (7:17), Evans (11:16), Arbour (13:34). Saves: Bassen 4, Hall 7.
SECOND PERIOD—2, Chicago, Fleming (unassisted), 6:45; 3, Chicago, McDonald (Mikita, Hull), 18:49. Penalties: Goegan (1:24), Hicks (6:05), Sloan (14:17). Saves: Bassen 8, Hall 8.
THIRD PERIOD — 4, Chicago, Nesterenko (Sloan, Pilote), 0:57; 5, Chicago, Evans (unassisted), 6:27; 6, Chicago, Wharram (unassisted), 18:00. Penalties: MacGregor (3:28), MacGregor (10:55), Sloan (18:23). Save, Bassen 8, Hall 6.
Referee—Eddie Powers. Linesmen—George Hayes and Bruce Sirs.

April 17, 1961

Hull of Hawks Ties Scoring Mark With 50th Goal

By WILLIAM J. BRIORDY

The New York Rangers beat the Chicago Black Hawks, 4—1, at Madison Square Garden last night before a crowd of 15,618 that was less interested in who won or lost than in who scored the goals.

With a Ranger berth in the Stanley Cup play-offs already clinched, interest centered in the duel between Andy Bathgate of New York and Bobby Hull of the Hawks for the National Hockey League scoring championship.

This was a stand-off. Each player entered the game, the

last of the regular season, with 83 points. Each finished with 84, tying for the league title on the strength of first-period goals. Neither had an assist.

Hull's goal, his fiftieth of the season, tied the league goal-scoring record set by Maurice (Rocket) Richard for the Montreal Canadiens in fifty games during the 1944-45 season and equaled last season by Bernie Geoffrion of the Canadiens in seventy games.

Each to Get $1,000

Bathgate and Hull will receive $1,000 apiece from the league as a bonus for their point tie. But Hull will get the Art Ross Trophy, emblematic of the league scoring championship, for having scored more goals than Bathgate.

Hull collected his points during the seventy-game season on fifty goals and thirty-four assists. Bathgate, the Ranger captain, made twenty-eight goals and fifty-six assists.

Chicago's big club, particularly Reg Fleming and Eric Nesterenko, did everything possible to stop Bathgate from passing Hull in the scoring race. Their defensive measures included obvious holding violations in the closing minutes.

Hull was the first to earn the plaudits of the crowd. Fleming set up the goal Bobby's forty-first in the last forty-seven games.

Fleming intercepted a pass by Al Langlois and fed to Hull, who back-handed a shot past Gump Worsley at 4:58 of the opening period.

Bathgate scored at 10:19. Earl Ingarfield beat Hull to the puck and whipped it to Bathgate, who drilled a ten-footer past Glenn Hall.

Rangers Stage Rally

After a scoreless second period, Ingarfield, Andy Hebenton and Ted Hampson hit for third-period Ranger goals.

STICK SWIPING: As game between Chicago and New York drew to a close, Chicago players tried to prevent Andy Bathgate from scoring and thus winning point championship. Reg Fleming has taken Bathgate's stick and is sitting on it. Glenn Hall is goalie.

Bill Hay hooked Doug Harvey, the Rangers' player-coach, at 7:21. Then Pierre Pilote was sent off for board-checking Hampson at 18:29. With forty-eight seconds left, Nesterenko held Bathgate. His penalty was a delayed one. Still, the Rangers couldn't help their captain to another point.

In the waning seconds Fleming held Bathgate. It was a flagrant infraction. But time ran out. Hull congratulated Bathgate and then Fleming skated over and apologized to the Ranger star.

"I just had to do it under the circumstances," Fleming said.

Andy took it in gentlemanly style. He and Hull skated on many lines. Andy was on the ice for 34 minutes 2 seconds, Hull for 33 minutes 15 seconds.

As the game progressed, the fans kept chanting "Put Bathgate on." Some urged more duty for Hull. Hull skated for 12 minutes 21 seconds in the first period, Bathgate for 11 minutes 57 seconds. Normally, a hockey player works seven minutes in a period.

Hull had five shots on goal, Bathgate three in the first period. It was one shot for Hull in the middle period and none for Bathgate. Each had one shot in the last period.

RANGERS (4)		CHICAGO (1)
(1) Worsley	....Goal	Hall (1)
(2) Harvey	...Defense	Turner (2)
(3) Bacon	...Defense	St. Laurent (19)
(6) Hannigan	....Center	Hay (11)
(16) Wilson	....Wing	Horvath (9)
(16) Wilson	....Wing	Hull (7)
(5) Howell	....Alternate	Pilote (3)
(5) Cahan	...Alternate	Vasko (4)
(7) Gendron	....Alternate	Evans (5)
(9) Bathgate	...Alternate	Fleming (6)
(11) Hadfield	...Alternate	Balfour (8)

(12) Hebenton	....Alternate	Melnyk (12)
(15) Spencer	....Alternate	McDonald (14)
(16) Wilson	....Alternate	Nesterenko (15)
(17) Prentice	....Alternate	Mikita (21)
(21) Henry	....Alternate	
(22) Hampson	....Alternate	

First Period

1—Chicago, Hull (Fleming) 4:58
2—Rangers, Bathgate (Ingarfield, Prentice) 10:19

Second Period

No scoring.

Third Period

3—Rangers, Ingarfield (Prentice, Harvey) 2:05
4—Rangers, Hebenton (Prentice, Harvey) 6:36
5—Rangers, Hampson (Hebenton) 14:44
Penalties—First Period: Melnyk (10:50), Henry (14:37), Prentice (15:40), Nesterenko (15:46), Third Period: Mikita (5:01), Cahan (9:12), Balon (17:06), Hay (17:21), Pilote (18:29), Nesterenko (15:12).
Saves—First Period: Worsley 13, Hall 7. Second Period: Worsley 11, Hall 7. Third Period: Worsley 6, Hall 4.
Referee—Frank Udveri, Linesmen—Neil Armstrong and George Hayes.
Attendance...15,618.

March 26, 1962

Leafs Beat Hawks With Rally and Take Stanley Cup First Time Since 1951

TORONTO WINS, 2-1, ON CHICAGO'S RINK

Goals by Nevin, Duff in Last 10 Minutes Decide After Hull of Hawks Scores

CHICAGO, April 22 (UPI)—Goals by Bob Nevin and Dick Duff in the last ten minutes tonight enabled the Toronto Maple Leafs to beat the Chicago Black

Hawks, 2—1, for their first Stanley Cup championship since 1951.

Duff's winning goal, which gave the Leafs hockey's most prized trophy for the eighth time, came only forty-seven seconds after Eric Nesterenko of the Hawks had been penalized for hooking.

The tally resulted from a nifty piece of teamwork. Tim Horton intercepted a Chicago pass in mid-ice and passed to George Armstrong, who carried into Hawk territory. Armstrong then passed back to Horton, who set up Duff on the opposite side of the Chicago cage for a shot that Glenn Hall could not obstruct.

Bobby Hull had put the

Hawks ahead, 1-0, earlier in the third period.

The victory gave Toronto the final four-of-seven-game series, four games to two. It was the first triumph for the Leafs away from home in the playoffs. In the semi-finals against New York all the Toronto victories came at home. And its previous victories in the final series also had been on home ice.

Hall Impressive in Goal

Except for Hall, the Hawks would have been blasted from the rink long before Duff's score. The Chicago goalie was under constant pressure. He had to make thirteen saves in the first period and fourteen in the

second to prevent a Toronto tally. Simmons, in the Toronto cage, had only twelve for the same two periods.

The Hawk goal, which brought about the biggest pile of litter on Chicago ice this year, was scored at 8:56. It came on a short flip by Hull that bounced off a Toronto player over Simmons into the cage.

The capacity crowd, announced at 16,666, threw about two dozen hats, red ink, raw eggs, beer cans and cups, oranges, shoes and paper of very description on the ice.

But their heroes could not hold their margin for two minutes. Nevin's goal tied the score at 10:29 and Duff's goal, at 14:14, ruined the Hawks' hopes of retaining the cup they won last season.

Each Leaf Gets $4,250

The victory brought each Maple Leaf player $2,000. With their semi-final prize of $1,500 each, and $750 for finishing second in the National Hockey League race, they earned a total bonus of $4,250 apiece.

Each Chicago player received a total of $3,000, including $500 third-place money. $1,500 for the semi-final victory over Montreal and $1,000 as the loser's share in the final series.

Tonight's triumph gave Toronto's coach, Punch Imlach, his first Stanley Cup in four tries. Hall finished with thirty-five saves, compared to twenty for Simmons, a stand-by goalie who got into action when

Johnny Bower suffered a pulled muscle in his thigh in the fourth game.

TORONTO (2)—Goal, Simmons; defense, Brewer, Baun; center, Pulford; wings, Nevin, Olmstead, Alternates: Mahovich, Kelly, Horton, Shack, Stanley, Arbour, Duff, Armstrong, Stewart, Keon, Harris.

CHICAGO (1)—Goal, Hall; defense, Pilote, Vasko; center, Mikita; wings, McDonald, Warram, Alternates, Turner, Evans, Hull, Balfour, Hay, Melnyk, St. Laurent, Horvath, Marcetta, Fleming, Nesterenko.

FIRST PERIOD—No scoring. Penalties: Evans (2:57), Hull (6:08), Pulford (12:09). Saves

Hall 13, Simmons 4.
SECOND PERIOD—No scoring. Penalties: Fleming (5:19), Nesterenko (7:42), Baun (11:46), St. Laurent (18:07). Saves: Hall 14, Simmons 8.
THIRD PERIOD—1, Chicago, Hull (Hay, Balfour), 8:56; 2, Toronto, Nevin (Mahovlich, Baun), 10:29; 3, Toronto, Duff (Horton, Armstrong), 14:14. Penalties: Horton (14:30), Nesterenko (13:27), Horton (14:02). Saves: Hall 8, Simmons 8.
Referee—Frank Udvari, Linesmen—Neil Armstrong and Matt Pavelich.
Attendance—16,666.

April 23, 1962

Leafs Beat Wings, 3–1, and Take Stanley Cup, 4 Games to 1, on Late Goals

KEON HITS TWICE AND SHACK ONCE

2 Goals in Last Period Win Cup for Leafs— Delvecchio Scores for Wings

By WILLIAM J. BRIORDY

Special to The New York Times

TORONTO, April 18—George (Punch) Imlach, who had been "supremely confident" that his Maple Leafs would keep the Stanley Cup, professional hockey's No. 1 prize, made good his boast as Toronto beat the Detroit Red wings, 3—1, tonight.

A capacity crowd of 14,403 roared its approval as the Leafs won the Stanley Cup for the ninth time and second in a row. Dave Keon, a hero in this city, and Eddie Shack, a former New York Ranger, were the key men as Toronto took the fifth contest and won the four-of-seven-game National Hockey League final playoff series, 4 games to 1.

Shack, skating furiously, deflected a sizzling shot by Kent Douglas at 13 minutes 28 seconds of the third period to break a 1-1 tie that had lasted 33 minutes. The ever-present Bob Pulford also assisted on the goal that was to prove the clincher.

Keon scores Two Goals

While Shack got the tie-breaking goal, Keon, a center, easily became the No. 1 citizen of Toronto by scoring two goals.

Clarence Campbell, the president of the N.H.L., presented the Stanley Cup to George Armstrong, the Leafs' captain, but the fans wanted Keon. They roared "We want Dave." Keon had to skate onto the ice before the crowd was satisfied. Shack also received a share of the crowd's approval.

Keon put the Leafs ahead at

17:44 of the first period, but Alex Delvecchio, a standout player, scored for the wings 49 seconds after the second period began.

After Johnny Bower, the Leafs' goalie, had thwarted Gordie Howe, Shack came up with his goal by tipping in Dougals's drive.

When Bob Pulford of the Leafs was banished for holding at 18:07 of the tense third period. Imlach's crew supplied the crusher.

Sid Abei took the Wings' goalie, Terry Sawchuk, out of the nets with a minute remaining. Then Keon, taking feeds from Armstrong and Alan Stanley—another former, Ranger—whipped the puck into the open Detroit net at 1955.

To say that the Leafs were delirious in their dressing room following the game would be putting it mildly. Champagne seldom seen here in the staid Maple Leaf Gardens—flowed freely.

Said Imlach: "I told you we'd take 'em, didn't I?"

Shack's goal was his second of

the playoffs, while Keon picked up his sixth and seventh. Imlach said that Keon "is one of the finest hockey players I've ever coached."

Toronto had to go all-out to win this one, and did it in the stylish fashion that has marked its play all season. The Wings gave Toronto and Bower fits often, but the Leaf skaters managed that extra something in solid hockey that brings victory.

Sawchuk stopped Dick Duff late in the final period and also thwarted the energetic Shack.

When Pulford held Delvecchio at 18:07, the Toronto fans groaned—and justifiably so. But Keon had his supporters shouting when he made it 3—1.

The Leafs were short handed in the first period when Keon put them ahead. Stanley was in the penalty box at 17:13 for an elbowing infraction called by the referee, Frank Udvari. Taking a relayfrom Armstrong at his own blue line, Keon skated around Delvecchio to beat Sawchuk. He got the goal at 17:44.

TORONTO (3)		DETROIT (1)
(1) Bower	Goal	Sawchuk (1)
(2) Brewer	Defense	M. Pronovost (2)
(21) Baun	Defense	Goegan (18)
(4) Kelly	Center	Delvecchio (10)
(12) Stewart	Wing	P. MacDonald (20)
(27) Mahovitch	Wing	Howe (9)
(7) Horton	Alternate	Gadsby (6)
(8) MacMillan	Alternate	Bailey (5)
(9) Duff	Alternate	Ullman (7)
(10) Armstrong	Alternate	MacDonald (8)
(11) Nevin	Alternate	Stasiuk (11)
(14) Keon	Alternate	Faulkner (12)
(15) Harris	Alternate	Jeffrey (14)
(19) Douglas	Alternate	A. Pronovost(15)
(20) Pulford	Alternate	MacGregor(16)
(22) Hillman	Alternate	Smith (19)
(23) Shack	Alternate	Fonteyne (19)
(25) Litzenberger	Alternate	Joyal (21)
(26) Stanley	Alternate	Odrowski(32)

FIRST PERIOD
1, Toronto, Keon (Armstrong) 17:44
SECOND PERIOD
2—Detroit, Delvecchio (Howe, M. Pronovost) 0 : 49
THIRD PERIOD
3—Toronto, Shack (Douglas, Pulford) . . 13:28
4—Toronto, Keon (Armstrong, Stanley) 19:55
Penalties—First period: Faulkner 10:49, Pulford 10:49, Odrowski 11:01, P. MacDonald 14:09, Stanley 17: 13. Second period: Smith 8:35, Shack 11:35, Jeffrey 3:59. Third period: Howe 9:18, Steward 9:18, Smith 15:33.
Saves—First period: Bower 5, Sawchuk 9. Second period: Bower 7, Sawchuk 4. Third period: Bower 14, Sawchuk 12.
REferee—Frank Udvard. Linesmen—M. Pavelich and Ron Wicks.
Attendance—14,403. April 19, 1963

Behind Plante's Mask: 'Man Alone'

By ROBERT LIPSYTE

Jake the Snake loves his work. Three nights a week he crouches in front of a hockey goal, loose and agile on skinny steel blades, peering down the ice through the eye-slits of a plastic mask. He seems to say, "I am Jacques Plante, the greatest goalie in the business, and I dare you to get one past me."

And of course they try, bursting through Plante's New York Ranger teammates, a swirl of colors and flung ice roaring down toward the goal, thousands screaming as the stick cracks against a frozen rubber disk that becomes smaller and harder as it hurtles, 100 miles an hour, at Jacques Plante's throat.

Slap. Time stands still and thousands catch their breaths as

Plante's big glove flicks out and kills the puck in its leather folds. Plante sinks to his knees, drawing out the last bit of emotional suspense. Then, as the breaths explode in a mighty whoosh, he disdainfully flips the puck away and watches the mad scramble start again.

"You must be born a goal tender, a man alone," says the 34-year-old Plante. "Even the rule book says you are not a hockey player, that a team is made up of 17 hockey players and a goal tender. You are a man who can prevent defeat, but you cannot win a game.

"The eyes are upon you, you are the target of the game. When a goal is scored, play stops and people talk. They say how you missed the puck, how you made a mistake. They do not talk of all the mistakes that were made before the opposing player took his shot. They say it is your mistake alone."

Plante, who joined the Rangers this year after nine successful seasons with the Montreal Canadiens, looks like a man born to accept such responsibility. His face is strong and angular with deep hollows beneath the scarred cheekbones and quick mobility around the eyes and mouth.

During a game, the face, which bears the marks of several hundred stitches, is covered with a 10-ounce, padded plastic mask. He introduced the mask to the National Hockey League four years ago because, he admits freely, he was tired of seeing his blood on the ice.

"During the game itself there is little time to be afraid. Once you are afraid in a game you are through," he said in a clipped accent with traces of his French mother tongue.

"But I was not sleeping at night, replaying each game in my head, the pucks I stopped and the ones that missed my

United Press International
Jake the Snake displays mask he uses to protect him from 100-mile-an-hour shots.

The New York Times
Jacques Plante in action in Ranger net during a recent game at Madison Square Garden

head by an inch, thinking about more stitches and going back to the hospital—and wasn't four times enough for one nose to be broken?"

He began wearing a mask in practice sessions in 1950, while he was with the Canadiens. On Nov. 1, in New York, Andy Bathgate, now a Ranger teammate, backhanded a shot into the left side of Plante's nose. Jake the Snake went down like a tree in the night.

Puts On the Mask

Twenty minutes and seven stitches later (hockey games are held up when a team's only goalie net is emergency repairs) Plante skated out with a ghoulish, Plexiglass mask.

The controversy has waxed ever since. Originally, the Montreal coach said Plante might wear the mask until his nose healed. But Plante, impervious to catcalls from the safe seats, refused to take it off. And the Canadiens won their next 11 games.

"I am the best goalie in the league," Plante has said, "And with the mask I am even better. I can laugh at getting hit in the face. I can use my face to stop pucks."

Barefaced or masked, Plante has statistical support for his contention. Since he broke into the N.H.L. as a regular in 1954, he has won six Vezina Trophies, a record, the last two with a covered face. The trophy annually goes to the goalie who was least scored upon.

Just as the mask is becoming standard equipment for younger goalies throughout Canada, Plante's other innovation—wandering—is widely copied. He moves around, plays the angles instead of the net, skates out to make saves and pass the puck, and shouts instructions to the defensemen.

Breathing a Problem

For all his activity, agility and grandstanding, Plante's biggest problem is breathing. Plante was raised in Shawinigan Falls, Que., and severe asthma kept him from competitive athletics until he was in his teens. The son of a machinist, Jacques was the oldest of a large family. He diapered, sewed and cleaned for the brood.

Until he was 14 he slept sitting up, coughing all night, falling asleep at dawn when he was too tired to cough any longer. At 14, the asthma disappeared

and Jacques began playing hockey. He became winded too quickly to skate very long, so he played at goal.

The asthma still bothers him. Last week, he flew to Montreal to receive emergency treatments for it. But he never uses it as an excuse. He just admits he's a little bit crazy to continue playing (even with the mask he still gets sliced up now and then) with a wife and two boys in Montreal, a newspaper column, an off-season job with a brewery and such peaceful interests as oil painting and knitting.

"I worked very hard to get to the top, and now that I'm here I want to enjoy it, to taste it," he says.

"And there are the nights I go home and I tell my wife I don't know how they could score, I filled the net tonight, I blocked it all and every time they shot I scooped up the puck and laughed 'Aha, look what I found' and it is nights like that keep me going, nights like that I know I love what I do."

November 3, 1963

Howe's 545th Goal for Record Helps Wings Beat Canadiens

DETROIT, Nov. 11 (UPI) — Gordie Howe scored his 545th goal on a spectacular play with Detroit a man short tonight to finally break Maurice Richard's career goal-scoring record as the Red Wings defeated the Montreal Canadiens, 3—0.

Terry Sawchuk, the Detroit goalie, tied a record as he turned in the 94th shutout of his career. George Hainsworth, a Montreal goalie, held the mark.

Howe's goal at 15:06 of the second period gave him a "grand slam" of hockey's biggest records. He has scored more points (1,221), and more assists (676) and played in more games (1,132) than any other player in National Hockey League history.

Howe's goal was the third

for the Wings in the second period. Bruce MacGregor got the first at 4:49 of the period and Alex Faulkner tallied 47 seconds later.

Not so long ago, Howe said that his only goal in hockey was to play 20 years. He is now in his 18th season. The only other National Hockey League player to attain 20 years as an active player was Dit Clapper of Boston.

Last season, Howe won the Hart Memorial Trophy for the sixth time. He polled 111 of a possible total of 180 points in taking the trophy that goes annually to "the player adjudged the most valuable to his team."

No other player in history has won the Hart Trophy so many times as Howe. He won it pre-

Gordie Howe

viously in 1951-52, 1952-53, 1956-57, 1957-58 and 1959-60. The great Eddie Shore won it only four times.

Last season was a banner one for Howe. He picked up an extra $5,000 from the league for outstanding individual achievements.

Aside from winning the Hart Trophy, he also collected the Art Ross Trophy as the league's leading scorer. Howe, who has played in 14 All-Star games, topped the 1962-63 scorers with 38 goals and 48 assists for 86 points.

Howe was born on March 31, 1928, to Katherine and Albert Howe of Floral, Sask. He was the sixth of nine children—five boys and four girls.

It is said that Gordie Howe began skating at the age of 4. At 14, he was a star on local teams. At 15, he was invited to his first N. H. L. tryout camp, that of the Rangers at Winnipeg. The Rangers will never live down their mistake. They sent him home.

Then the late Fred Picknev, a Detroit scout, saw Howe performing in juvenile hockey in

Saskatoon. Howe was sent to the Detroit training camp in Windsor, Ont., in 1944.

At 19, Gordie suddenly became a major leaguer, getting his first big-league goal in his ... game on Oct. 16, 1946. Three seasons later, this shy, muscular young man blossomed into a star respected by all.

DETROIT (3)—goal, Sawchuk; defense, M. Pronovost, Gadsby; Center, Delvecchio; Wings, Howe, P. MacDonald. Alternates: Ingram, Barkley, Ullman, L. MacDonald, Faulkner, Jeffrey, A. Pronovost, MacGregor, Geogan, McNeill, Joyal.
MONTREAL (0)—Goal, Hodge; Defense, La-Perriere, Talbot; Center, Richard; Wings, Russo, Harper. Alternates: Tremblay, Bel-

veau, Geoffrion, Backstrom, Provost, Balon, Ferguson, Berenson, Hicks, Watson, Rose.
FIRST PERIOD—No scoring. Penalties: A. Pronovost (3:54), Harper (7:40), Barkley (7:40). Saves: Sawchuk 12, Hodge 8.
SECOND PERIOD—1, Detroit, MacGregor (A. Pronovost, Ullman), 4:40; 2, Detroit, Faulk-ner (L. MacDonald), 5:36; 3, Detroit, Howe (McNeill), 15:06. Penalties: Harper (6:43), Howe (7:54), Ferguson (8:19), Balon (10:25), Faulkner (five minutes, 13:57). Saves: Sawchuk 14, Hodge 9.
THIRD PERIOD—No scoring. Penalties: A. Pronovost (0:39), Howe (2:17), Balon (3:45), Ullman (3:45), Tremblay (6:18), Talbot (10:03), Watson (11:03), Howe (16:50). Saves: Sawchuk 13, Hodge 8.
Referee—Frank Udvari. Linesmen—George Hays and Bill Clements.
Attendance—15,027.

November 11, 1963

They Call Him The Greatest on Ice

By WILLIAM BARRY FURLONG

NOWHERE are the dark forces that impel a man toward athletic self-destruction more clearly definable than in a hockey player—indeed, the hockey player—named Gordon Lowe. Howe, who this season set a record for goals scored during total years of play — breaking Maurice Richard's record of 544 — has a medical history that would turn Blue Cross green. In one hockey accident he suffered a fractured skull, a brain concussion, a fractured cheekbone, a fractured nose and deep cuts upon his right eyeball. Only emergency surgery saved him. He lost his front teeth in his first year in the National Hockey League; has had his ribs broken three times; suffered several broken toes and shoulder dislocation, and had both knees operated on.

Some years ago he played 15 games with his broken right wrist in a cast and still led the league that season in goals and assists. The skin over the bridge of his nose has been sewed so often that it is now difficult to get a needle through it. He estimates that he has had 300 stitches in his face. "I had 50 stitches on my face one year—that was a bad year," he said a while ago. "I had only 10 stitches taken last year that was a good year."*

Most hockey players last an average of 6.6 years in the National Hockey League (hockey's only major league). Howe, who is 35, is now in his 18th season and his ambition is to pursue this masochistic history into its 20th year. Why? "Well," he says engagingly, "the hours are good and the pay is excellent."

But the season is long — 70 games from early October to late March. It is also demanding. At his peak, Howe played at least 45 of the 60 minutes—more than two 20-minute periods—in every game. Indeed, it might be said by any but the most reverent baseball

followers that Howe is more valuable to his employers — the Detroit Red Wings—than Mickey Mantle is to the New York Yankees. For baseball is a comparatively somnolent pastime, especially in centerfield. Thus Mantle — when he plays at all—need work only at a leisurely pace except during those widely separated moments when he is directly involved in the action of the game.

Howe, on the other hand—except for those few moments of respite on the bench—is *always* involved in the action of the game. Moreover, his involvement is furiously and unceasingly muscular. This is partly because of the breakneck pace of hockey and partly because the pattern of Detroit's game —on both offense and defense—focuses on the superb skills of Gordie Howe.

Howe, who plays right wing for Detroit, has missed only 40 games in his entire big-league career. It is this defiance of destiny that contributes to his special appeal. For hockey is a harsh game, a cruel game. It is a game of sticks and stitches, of slashes and gashes—and this is its attraction to its fans. Howe emerges as a hero who never shirks the violence of the game.

LAST year was a big one for him. He was the highest paid player in the league, earning in the neighborhood of $25,000, plus bonuses of $9,500. He led the league in points—a figure arrived at by adding goals and assists—for the sixth time. He was elected the most valuable player in the league for the sixth time and was named to the league's all-star team for the 14th time. With the acquisition of the goal-scoring record this season, he now holds virtually every career record in history. "The thing you've got to know about Howe," says a player on a rival team, "is that he can do everything better than anybody else." He is, in short, the greatest hockey player who ever lived.

There are, to be sure, certain of the faithful who would dispute this. They

favor Maurice (The Rocket) Richard, who retired from the Montreal Canadiens in 1960. Richard himself has gone on record that Howe's latest goal-scoring record should be recorded, like Roger Maris's home run record in baseball, with an asterisk because it took Howe 149 games more than Richard played to break Richard's record. "I missed 169 games because of injuries," said Richard. "If I hadn't been hurt that often, I would have scored 100 more goals."

Richard was, without doubt, the most exciting shot-maker in hockey history. He had the drama, the high style, the élan to raise a game to an art. "Richard used to come up on you with his eyes lit up like 200-watt bulbs," said Glenn Hall, goal-keeper for the Chicago Black Hawks. "You couldn't miss him because he was so dramatic."

Howe's art is more subtle and comprehensive. His skating is so beautifully controlled, his shot so carefully disguised, his command of the pattern of play so easy that you have to understand hockey—its pace, its feel, its very texture—to appreciate him.

SEVERAL years ago, the six coaches then in the National Hockey League defined, in a poll, the ultimate differences between Richard and Howe. They named Richard as having the most accurate shot in the league and as the game's best man on a breakaway. They selected Howe as the smartest player, the best passer, the best play-maker and the best puck-carrier.

Howe's impact on the game goes much beyond scoring records or medical records. "He's rewritten the entire game," says one of his admiring opponents. The rewriting has come in everything from a particular shot—"That wrist slap shot you see so often was his"—to an entire pattern of play. The pattern worked

WILLIAM BARRY FURLONG is a sports columnist turned freelance writer whose articles have appeared in many magazines.

*The reason hockey players do not wear face-protectors, helmets or thicker padding than they do is that they need to skate fast and have quick reactions. "The player cuts his safety margin to a thin line in the interest of speed," Howe said not long ago.

165

out under Howe's leadership has the forwards sweeping down the ice in a criss-cross design, hunting for "opportunities of the moment," instead of relying on the historic, position-play game.

"He's got a super body for hockey—absolutely no shoulders and long arms," says one of his rivals. He also has grace and great balance. "He's very hard to knock off his feet," says a player who has made a career of trying.

MENTALLY, Howe is a master of the game. "Every team has a pattern and he reads the pattern better than anybody else," says one adversary. He knows, for instance, that the New York Rangers are a passing team with a minimum of contact; that the Toronto Maple Leafs are a tight-checking team that will labor to protect a one-goal lead; that the Montreal Canadiens play a wide-open game and expect to trade a lot of goals in order to win. He also knows how to protect himself—and it is a characteristic, more than anything else, that hockey players speak of.

"Howe is everything you'd expect the ideal athlete to be," says one of his more articulate adversaries. "He's soft-spoken, deprecating and thoughtful. He's also the most vicious, cruel and mean man I've ever met in a hockey game."

Retaliation, for Howe, is protection. And at this, as with everything else in hockey, he is a master. One of his opponents asserts that the number of injuries Howe has suffered is surpassed, perhaps, only by the number he has inflicted.

HE offers no imprecations when he is assaulted. "But he always knows who it is and he pays back his debts quietly," says a member of the New York Rangers. "The trouble is that he knows how to shade the rules," says a member of the Chicago Black Hawks. "You do something to him, he won't let on you got to him. But in the next melee, you've got four or five stitches you don't know how you got."

Howe is thought to perform in this area with such exquisite skill that not even the officials notice it. "He never gets a penalty," Rudy Pilous, former coach of the Black Hawks, has observed. Once Vic Stasiuk of Boston approached Howe aggressively and emerged spurting blood from a six-stitch cut. "No penalty for Howe," says Pilous. Another time Lou Fontinato, then of the New York Rangers, somehow escaped from a skirmish with Howe with a 12-stitch gash

around his left ear. "No penalty for Howe," says Pilous. "So the fans think he's an angel."

It is difficult to separate legend from fact in these matters. Certainly Howe knows all the damaging tricks of the trade — spearing or jabbing with his stick, hacking a player on the back of the legs. "But if you play hockey," says one enemy player, "he'll play hockey. I don't think he ever really tries to ruin a player."

Some players recall that Howe once charged in on Gump Worsley, then goalkeeper for the Rangers, when Worsley was lying helpless on the ice with the puck loose in front of his face. Many a player would have slashed at the puck with decapitating force, letting Worsley bleed for himself. Howe dashed in to protect the puck from other players, then held off to allow Worsley to reach out and smother it. Howe passed off the incident without notice. Worsley got to his feet and muttered, "Thanks, bud." Howe shrugged. "I'll still get a few goals off you; you'll still stop a few," he said. "So consider us even."

It is this paradox—the ruthless protection of his own rights minus a "killer instinct" where others might be hurt—that marks much of Howe's career. "If Gordie has ever had a fault," says Sid Abel, coach of the Red Wings, "it is his tendency not to shoot as much as we'd like. He'd rather pass off to somebody else."

LAST year Howe's sense of justice stood in the way of his earning a little more money. He was to get a $1,000 bonus from the Red Wings if he scored 35 goals and an extra $100 a goal for everything over 35. Yet three times he went to the scorekeeper and insisted that goals credited to him were really scored by his teammates. (He finished with 38 goals and $1,300 in bonus money from the Red Wings. The rest of his bonus boodle came for winning various awards—$1,500, for example, for the most valuable player award — and for playing in the Stanley Cup Playoffs.)

On another occasion two seasons ago, Howe learned that one of his teammates, who had 14 goals, would get a bonus for scoring 15. When he got into the game with the player, Howe maneuvered until he could rush down the ice with the puck, muscle aside the defenders, fake the goalie out to the side, then pass off to his teammate bang in front of the net and watch him tick in his 15th goal. Then, in one of those rare and exhilarating moments

that reflect his change from a shy and diffident boy to a self-assured man, Howe skated past his own bench and inquired, "Anybody else looking for bonus money?"

HIS basic shyness cost the New York Rangers a chance to land Howe. He was, from his boyhood, endowed with an exceptional skill. He grew up in Floral, Saskatchewan, on the outskirts of Saskatoon where playing outdoors could only prepare the youth for life-long masochism. The temperature sometimes dropped to 50 below.

"We had to play with a tennis ball instead of a puck," Howe has recalled. "The ball would get so hard we'd have to get new ones all the time. A woman next door used to warm them up in an oven for us. His mother has said, "He used to practice at night under the street lamps by the hour. I'd put papers on the kitchen floor so he wouldn't have to take his skates off while he ate."

At 12, Howe scored 13 goals in a schoolboy game on a rink in his home town. At 15, he was invited to a tryout camp by the New York Rangers. It was his first trip away from home; indeed, it was his first exposure to the formalities of hockey equipment and he didn't know how to put on the pads and protectors. "I just dropped the gear in front of me and watched the others," he has said. The older players heckled him and, being shy, anyway, he soon yielded to homesickness and quit the camp to go

home. There he was promptly "discovered" by a Detroit Red Wing scout and two years later he was in the big leagues.

IT took him three years to "mature." In that time he scored a total of only 35 goals, or as many goals as he scored in his fourth year alone. Since then, he's maintained a scoring pace close to that figure.

In his younger days he "threw concrete" on construction projects during the summer—activity that helped build his massive forearms. Now his summertime activities are not quite so strenuous. He likes to work out from time to time with the Detroit Tigers. Or play golf. Or frolic with his four children. During the season, his favorite relaxation is solving crossword puzzles, particularly when time drags on interminably with the team on the road.

Over the years he's felt, as well as seen, the change in hockey defense, especially as regards physical contact. "They seem to hold more and hit less than in the old days. Maybe it just seems that way because I've learned to slip a lot of hits, but I do think I used to be ridden out of a lot more plays on body-checks." On offense, he's noticed the swift increase in the use of screen shots: "I can remember when just a few players like Max Bentley and Richard had the knack for snapping off a shot just as they passed a defenseman, using him for the

NET PLAY—Gordie Howe brakes after firing the puck past a Toronto goalie, Johnny Bower. Howe holds the record for total goals scored.

screen. Now a lot of guys are doing it."

Howe's temples are gray now and his hairline is receding. This season he's been playing only 30 to 35 minutes a game—"About a period and a half," says Sid Abel. Howe is perhaps more critical of his own flaws than his rivals. "I'd say the only thing that's changed is that he's lost a little speed," says one enemy player. Says Howe: "I think I play a lot more bad games than I used to."

TODAY Howe is an assistant coach—as well as a player — of the Red Wings. He is a citizen of the United States, a resident of Detroit and owner of an ice rink there called "Gordie Howe's Hockeyland." He is wonderfully unaware that hockey has been a punishing way of making a living. "It really isn't that bad," he says softly. Then he blinks—a periodic wink that is a legacy of his fractured skull—as he considers the future. Only one player, Dit Clapper, ever played 20 years in the National Hockey League and Howe would like to match his record. Why not go for 21years and a new record? "You've got to last through 20 first, he says.

February 23, 1964

MAN UNDER PRESSURE: Tim Horton of Toronto on ice under teammate, Johnny Bower, after they blocked a shot by Floyd Smith, right, of Wings during Stanley Cup game.

United Press International Telephoto

LEAFS WIN BY 4-0 FOR 3D CUP IN ROW

Beat Wings in 7th Game of Hockey Series—Bower Is Standout in Goal

By WILLIAM J. BRIORDY
Special to The New York Times

TORONTO, April 25 — Andy Bathgate scored in the first period and his Toronto teammates added three goals in the third as the Maple Leafs beat the Detroit Red Wings, 4—0, tonight and captured the Stanley Cup for the third straight season at Maple Leaf Gardens.

Bathgate got the first goal of the game at 3:04 of the first period and then the favored Leafs wrapped it up with three power in the third period on goals by Dave Keon, Red Kelly and George Armstrong.

This was the first shutout of the four-of-seven-game series that went the limit before the tired and somewhat battered

Leafs won, 4 games to 3. Coach Punch Imlach's Leafs won the hard way. They had returned here after squaring the series with a 4—3 "must" victory in Detroit Thursday night.

Johnny Bower, the long-time goalie for the Leafs, turned in a tremendous job in blanking the Wings. He was mobbed by his teammates as the game ended.

Clarence S. Campbell, the president of the National Hockey League, made the trophy presentation. The Leafs won the Stanley Cup for the 10th time, tying the Montreal Canadiens for the most cup triumphs.

Playing with two injured men, Bob Baun and Kelly, the favored Leafs couldn't have performed more stalwartly.

This has been a great final series, and the goalies have been tops. Bower couldn't have been more alert tonight. Bathgate's first-period goal looked like a mightly slim edge until the Leafs turned on the power in the final period.

Baun, bothered by an ankle injury, and Kelly, hampered by a leg injury, certainly didn't appear to be hurting as the Leafs continued to carry the attack to the Wings, who also were tired.

Baun had delivered the goal at 1:43 of the sudden-death overtime period Thursday night to keep the Leafs alive.

Billy Harris was halted on a two-on-one break early in the third period, and that seemed to be the spark that carried the Leafs to their goal-scoring spree.

Bathgate, who had supplied

the goal that won the fourth game of the series by a 4-2 score, thrilled the crowd of 14,-571, largest in three seasons, when he broke away to beat Terry Sawchuk from 10 feet out.

Toronto kept pressing and had Sawchuk working overtime. In the scoreless second period the Leafs continued to pepper Sawchuk. Bathgate, Ron Stewart, Carl Brewer and Keon tested Sawchuk.

Two Goals Quickly

The Leafs got two goals within a space of 1 minute 27 seconds. Keon posted his seventh goal of the playoffs when he sent a 30-foot slap shot past Sawchuk at 4:26. At 5:53 Kelly made it 3—0. The Leaf supporters roared when he hit on a short shot to cap a play engineered by Frank Mahovlich. That was Kelly's fourth goal in the playoffs.

Then Armstrong, notching No. 5 of the playoffs, completed the scoring at 15:26. Armstrong rapped in a rebound of a shot by Mahovlich.

Bower had 33 saves in achieving his shutout. Sawchuk also had 33 stops.

DETROIT (0)		TORONTO (4)	
(1) Sawchuk	Goal	Bower	(1)
(2) A. Langlois	Defense	Brewer	(2)
(3) M. Pronovost	Defense	Kelly	(4)
(7) Ullman	Center	Bathgate	(9)
(14) Jeffrey	Wing	Pulford	(20)
(17) Smith	Wing	Shack	(23)
(5) Barkley	Alternate	Ehman	(8)
(8) Martin	Alternate	Armstrong	(10)
(9) Howe	Alternate	Stewart	(12)
(10) Delvecchio	Alternate	Keon	(14)
(11) Spencer	Alternate	Harris	(15)
(12) MacMillan	Alternate	Pappin	(18)
(4) Gadsby	Alternate	Horton	(7)
(15) A. Pronovost	Alternate	Baun	(21)
(16) MacGregor	Alternate	Hillman	(22)
(18) Miszuk	Alternate	Litzenberger	(25)
(19) Henderson	Alternate	Stanley	(26)
(20) MacDonald	Alternate	Mahovlich	(27)
(21) Joyal	Alternate		

FIRST PERIOD
1—Toronto, Bathgate (unassisted), 3:04.

SECOND PERIOD
None.

THIRD PERIOD
2—Toronto, Keon (Harris) 4:26
3—Toronto, Kelly (Mahovlich, Stanley).. 5:53
4—Toronto, Armstrong (Mahovlich)...15:26
Penalties — First period: Horton (5:05), Joyal (6:34), Harris (8:51) Gadsby (8:51). Second period: Harris (4:00), MacMillan (15:29). Third period: A. Pronovost (11:41), Horton (15:36), Brewer (18:44).
Saves—First period: Bower 8, Sawchuk 12. Second period: Bower 12, Sawchuk 10. Third period: Bower 13, Sawchuk 11.
Referee — John Ashley. Linesmen — Neil Armstrong and George Hayes.
Attendance—14,571.

April 26, 1964

The Hockey Official: 'A Man With Iron in His Soul'

Road to Top Lonely One of Movies and Hotel Lobbies

By ROBERT LIPSYTE
Special to The New York Times

MONTREAL, Dec. 26 — It usually starts on a frozen pond, in British Columbia or Saskatchewan or Ontario, when a boy on skates realizes he will never be as quick and strong as his friends. So he offers to referee their games. And if someone doesn't jam a stick in his belly after the first decision or, worse, ignore it, the boy may set out on the long, perilous and lonely road of a professional hockey official.

He will referee games for a dollar, five in one night to pay for his gas, he will referee Peewee events where he will have to look down to see where the abuse is coming from. There will be nights in the provinces when he has nothing to do but brood over the decisions he blew. Then one day he might get a letter from the National Hockey League offices here: We have had good reports on your work, it will say, would you like to come in for a try-out?

"It's a hell of a job," says Clarence Campbell, the N.H.L. president, who once held it himself for four years. "A man has to have iron in his soul, the will to command. And he can't be a drinker—he'll have thousands of hours with nothing to do." Campbell will tell the prospect about Bill Chadwick, a referee who made the Hall of Fame. Chadwick used to bite his nails so much that his fingers bled continually from October to March.

Campbell, who is also a lawyer, will tell the prospect about the rules. No fraternizing with the only other people who understand you—hockey players and club personnel. No drinking in public, only alone or with other officials. No drinking the day of an assignment (although Campbell looks benevolently upon "relaxing spirits" after a game, which he remembers did wonders for his pleurisy). Refrain from habits of gambling and immorality—which is very easy in some of the towns an official must go to.

And then there are some rules that must be explained, such as never, even as a sentimental gesture, throw the puck into the crowd. A referee once did, at Madison Square Garden, and a boy in the balcony fumbled it. The boy followed the puck out of the balcony and into a lower deck where he fell on a woman and broke her leg.

Jesting and wisecracking with the players on the ice is forbidden. Seventeen years ago, when George Hays was a referee, a prominent player skated by with a bleeding mouth.

"Look here, George," mumbled the victim.

"What did ya do, bite yaself?" jested George. He felt very badly later when he learned the player had just lost three teeth. It may also have been one of the reasons why he decided to become a linesman, which he still is.

If the prospect is young, he will probably become a linesman first. There are two in each game, watching for the more mechanical infractions, and breaking up fights. Linesmen, who often get knocked down as mediators, earn $50 per game in the N.H.L., less in the minors. Referees make between $125 and $225 per game in the N.H.L.

There are five full-time N.H.L. referees and four linesmen, all of whom travel alone in a rotating, cross-league schedule they rarely know more than two weeks in advance. There is at least one four-week trip a year to the Western Hockey League, on the Pacific Coast, and constant shuttling among the N.H.L., the American League and the Central Professional League.

The mark of an official's considered worth and the size of his annual salary depends on how many N.H.L. games he is assigned. More than 50 N.H.L. games of a total of 75 or 80 assignments is considered good, and a referee can make anywhere between $9,000 and $16,000 for seven months work.

There are fringe benefits: a pension, a $20,000 life insurance policy (no official has yet earned one on the job) and first class plane and rail travel.

"But we get to alot of places every year we'd never see otherwise," says Bill Friday, in his fifth year as an N.H.L. referee. "New York, Chicago, San Francisco, Vancouver."

They also see a great many

The excitement of hockey sometimes draws an official like George Hayes, a linesman, perilously close to action. Hayes, once a referee, earning between $125 and $225 a game, took the lesser paying linesman job "to sleep nights."

The speed of hockey is interrupted only occasionally. One of those times is when referee, Art Skov, in this instance, signals a penalty. Pressure on referee calls for "iron in his soul." Reflection at right is caused by protective glass wall.

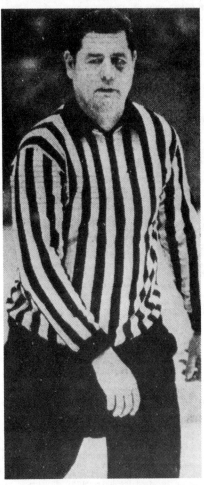

The New York Times (by Barton Silverman)
Wearing a dark badge of his profession, Hayes emerges from arbitration session.

movies and hotel lobbies Friday, a 31-year-old, was on ice in Montreal two years ago when his fifth child was born And he remembers a Christmas not too long ago, far from his home in Hamilton, Ont., when he bought himself a shirt, had it gift-wrapped, and put it under his hotel bed for Christmas morning. He didn't even fool himself.

The loneliness is offset, according to Matt Pavelich, a 30-year-old linesman, by hard-core hockey fans who are passed from official to official — a businessman in Springfield who loves to talk to officials and will drive them around, a Greek restaurant owner in Quebec, an elderly couple in Minneapolis.

"The real big problem is rabbit ears," says Friday. "You skate past the bench and a guy says 'Boy, are you having a bad night' and if you say, 'Be quiet,' he'll say 'I wasn't talking to you,' and then you're in for it.

"Or you pick up a scrap of paper off the ice," says Pavelich, "and some fan yells 'Garbageman, you're getting good practice for your next job.' You better not look up."

Because officiating is a "personality job," according to Campbell, referees and linesmen usually do well after their hockey days. Bill Chadwick, the nail-biter, is a New York executive, King Clancy is assistant general manager of the Toronto club, others are insurance salesmen, construction supervisors, public relations men. But many drop out after a few years; the demands of a family, the loneliness, the need to stay in shape for 60 minutes of skating at least three times a week, through a winter of drafty or overheated public places.

"But then comes springtime," says Pavelich, who has seen nine N.H.L. springtimes, "and the league tells you that you did a good job, and you feel satisfied inside yourself, and you realize you really had a good time. And somehow the summer never goes fast enough."

December 27, 1964

CANADIENS GAIN STANLEY CUP

By GERALD ESKENAZI
Special to The New York Times

MONTREAL, May 1 — The Stanley Cup was captured for a record 11th time tonight by the stylish Montreal Canadiens.

Gliding over the shimmering smooth rink at The Forum, cheered by a National Hockey League season-record crowd of 15,740 and outplaying its opponents, the Montreal club won the cup by defeating the Chicago Black Hawks, 4-0.

All the scoring came in the first period in this, the seventh and deciding test which gave the Canadiens the series, four games to three. The game virtually ended for the Hawks 14 seconds after play began as Jean Beliveau kicked in a shot past Glenn Hall.

After that, it was the final buzzer that the fans waited for. Screaming the last 60 seconds of the game away, tearing newspapers and throwing them on the ice, skimming fedoras through the air, the crowd made The Forum a bedlam at the end.

6th Cup for Blake

The players mobbed Lorne (Gump) Worsley, who had turned in his second shutout of the series after missing three games.

Then the cup was wheeled onto the ice. Gump was hoisted

169

on the Canadiens' shoulders and everyone in The Forum was standing and stomping.

For Coach Hector (Toe) Blake, who paced behind the Canadiens' bench during the final minutes, the cup victory was his sixth, setting a coaching mark.

The festivities started early for the fans, most of whom are French-Canadian After Beliveau's goal, Dick Duff scored on a fine pass from Beliveau. The fans began chanting "Les Canadiens sont là" (the Canadiens are there, adapted from a war song).

Duff's goal was followed by a brilliant score by Yvan Cournoyer, who skated through the Hawks' defense, faked Hall out of position and sent the puck home. Henri Richard tallied what proved the final goal as he slapped in a center pass from Ted Harris.

At the game's end, with fans singing and jumping for joy, Beliveau was announced as the first winner of the Connie Smythe Trophy. The award, worth $1,000, is to be given annually to the playoffs' most valuable performer.

The 6-foot-3-inch Beliveau, a gazelle on ice, scored five goals during the seven-game series. Tonight his passes were on the mark, his skating effortless, his defense superb. He was the consummate player playing for the biggest hockey prize.

The Hawks, who are supreme at home, perhaps because of the Chicago Stadium's slower ice surface, could not keep up with the fast Canadiens on the fast ice here. Montreal checked and slammed the Chicagoans into submission from the early minutes of the second period.

$3,500 Each for Winners

The Canadiens will receive $3,500 a man for winning the series. Perhaps as important is that the names of the winners will be engraved on the 25-inch silver base that supports the nine-inch high Stanley Cup. The Hawks must be content with $2,500 each.

Montreal, second in the final regular-season standing,

United Press International Telephoto

THE BLACK HAWKS THWARTED: Gump Worsley, Montreal Canadiens' goalie, blocks scoring attempt by Phil Esposito in first period of final playoff game in Montreal.

reached the cup final by turning back the Toronto Maple Leafs in a six-game semi-final series. But it was the Hawks who apparently were the ones to watch in the final series. They finished third during the season, but defeated the league leaders, the Detroit Red Wings, in a seven-game semi-final playoff.

The Hawks' great player, Bobby Hull, had slammed in eight goals against the Wings. But during this series, he scored only twice, both goals coming in one contest.

Blake, whose great Canadiens of the late nineteen-fifties won the cup in his first five years, ending in 1960, surpassed Clarence (Hap) Day, whose Leafs had also took five cups.

Modern Stanley Cup competition dates back to 1926, when it was put up to decide supremacy in the league.

Chicago won the cup in 1961,

and then the Leafs held it for three consecutive years. Last season, the Canadiens dropped the deciding seventh game to Toronto at The Forum.

There was no chance of that happening tonight.

Shutout Gained by Hodge

After stunning the Hawks, the Canadiens were intent on keeping the puck in friendly territory. The bruising Chicagoans couldn't get untracked. They took only six shots in the second period at Worsley, who was to turn in the third Canadiens' shutout of the series. Charlie Hodge did the trick while Gump was nursing a strained thigh muscle.

The pudgy Worsley, who was used tonight, said Blake, "because I thought he'd be less nervous," turned in several brilliant saves when the Hawks were able to reach him.

Worsley had only five saves in the final period. It was his

easiest as the Hawks cracked under the pressure and the Canadiens gleefully skated through the Chicago defense.

MONTREAL (4)—Goal, Worsley; defense, J. C. Tremblay, Harris; center, Beliveau; wings, Duff, Rousseau. Alternates: Backstrom, Larose, Cournoyer, Provost, Richard, Talbot, Harper, Balon, Ferguson, Berenson, Gauthier, Roberts.

CHICAGO (0)—Goal, Hall; defense, Nohns, Vasko; center, Mikita; wings, Pilote, Wharram. Alternates: Ravlich, Stanfield, Esposito, Henry, R Hull, D. Hull, Hal, Nesterenko, Maki, MacNeil, Jarret.

FIRST PERIOD — 1, Montreal, Beliveau (Duff, Rousseau), 0:14; 2, Montreal, Duff (Beliveau, Rousseau), 5:03; 3, Montreal, Cournoyer (Duff, Rousseau), 16:27; 4, Montreal, Richard (Harris), 18:45 Penalties: Harris (7:55), Pilote (16:08), Esposito, Henry, R. Hull, D Hull, Hay, 10 minutes, 19:56). Saves: Hall 11, Worsley 9.

SECOND PERIOD—No scoring. Penalties: Nesterenko (7:11), Jarrett (17:42). Saves: Hall 12, Worsley 6.

THIRD PERIOD—No scoring. Penalties: Vasko (4:03), Richard (4:03), Mikita (6:16), Mohns (9:16), Beliveau (17:29), Henry, 8 (18:36), Provost (19:27). Saves: Hall 8, Worsley 5.

Referee — John Ashley. Linesmen — Matt Pavlich and John D'Amico.

May 2, 1965

Big League Hockey Adding Six Teams

The National Hockey League granted six new franchises to United States cities yesterday, extending major league hockey from coast to coast for the first time.

The league, which includes teams in Canada, awarded on a conditonal basis franchises to Los Angeles and San Francisco-Oakland on the West Coast, Minneapolis-St. Paul and St. Louis in the Midwest and Pitts-

burgh and Philadelphia in the East.

Major league baseball, football and basketball already have expanded, with lucrative national television contracts as part of the rewards.

The additional hockey teams will double the size of the professional circuit, which now consists of New York, Boston, Chicago, Detroit, Montreal and Toronto.

The cost of each new franchise is $1-million and each new club owner must provide a satisfactory playing arena seating at least 12,500.

The New York Times · Feb. 10, 1966

Map shows league expansion plan for the 1967-68 season

Coast-to-Coast Hockey Means Ear-to-Ear Smiles

Organized in 1917

The National Hockey League was organized in 1917 as a purely Canadian operation. It extended to the United States in 1924 with the founding of the Boston Bruins.

The New York Rangers, Chicago Black Hawks and Detroit Red Wings date to 1926. In the early nineteen-thirties the league had grown to 10 teams. It settled into a six-team form in 1942.

When the National Football League expanded to Atlanta recently, the franchise cost more than $8-million. Miami got an American Football League franchise for $7.5-million. The price to a Chicago group for a National Basketball Association franchise last month was $1.6-million.

In baseball's expansion, which took place in 1961 and 1962, the new teams bought players from existing teams instead of paying for franchises.

A formula for stocking the new hockey teams has not yet been worked out, but each new team probably will be allowed to select players from the existing squads, which will be permitted to "freeze" a certain number.

The new teams are expected to begin playing in the 1967-68 season. They will all be in one division, playing 10 games against each opponent in their division and four against each of the six older clubs in the other division for a total of 74.

No Bid From St. Louis

The $12-million in entrance fees will be divided among the present six teams, whose principal owners are Weston Adams, Boston; James Norris, Chicago; his brother, Bruce Norris, Detroit; David Molson, Montreal; the Madison Square Garden Corporation, New York, and Stafford Smythe, Toronto.

A franchise was granted to St. Louis even though there was no bidder from that city. The grant was in the nature of an accomodation to James Norris, who owns the St. Louis Arena. A condition for operating a new team there would be the purchase or rental of the arena from Norris.

Stan Musial and his partner in the restaurant business, Biggie

Clarence Campbell, center, president of National Hockey League, congratulates George Fleharty, left, and Gordon Ritz, after the league granted them franchises. Fleharty represents San Francisco-Oakland, while Ritz is head of the Minneapolis-St. Paul group.

Garagnani, are expected to apply for the St. Louis franchise.

If no suitable St. Louis applicant comes forth by April 5, the date of the league's next meeting, Baltimore will get the sixth franchise. Baltimore was named an alternate in the event any newcomer could not fulfil its promises.

Jack Kent Cooke, who has interests in many sports organizations, acquired what was believed to be the best new franchise — Los Angeles. He said on the Coast yesterday that he would build a $7-million arena seating 16,000 for his basketball team, the Los Angeles Lakers of the N.B.A., and the hockey team.

Jerry Wolman, the president of the Philadelphia Eagles of

the N.F.L., is a principal in the Philadelphia group. This is headed by William Putnam, a former vice president of the Morgan Guaranty Trust Company of New York in charge of sports financing.

Art Rooney, the president of the Pittsburgh Steelers of the N.F.L., will be a minor investor in his home town's major league hockey team. Jack McGregor, a state senator, is the principal in a 31-member syndicate and the team wil play in the Civic Arena, which will increase its seating capacity from 11,500 to 12,800.

Barry Van Gerbig of New York, a former Princeton goaltender, and George Fleharty of the Shasta Corp., which owns the Ice Follies, are the principals in the San Francisco-Oakland group, which has sup-

port from Bing Crosby. This team will play in the Alameda Coliseum, which is under construction and will be part of the sports complex being built in Oakland.

Gordon Ritz, a former Yale hockey star, heads the Minneapolis-St. Paul group. It has promised the N.H.L. to build an arena adjacent to the baseball-football stadium at Bloomington Minn.

Cities shut out in this expansion move were Vancouver, B.C. which had arena and financing problems, and Buffalo, which had no appeal in spite of adequate financing from Yale's Knox brothers, Seymour Jr. and Northrup.

February 10, 1966

Hull Tops Record With His 51st Goal

By United Press International

CHICAGO, March 12—Bobby Hull scored his 51st goal tonight, breaking the National Hockey League record for goals in one season, as he led the Chicago Black Hawks to a 4-2 victory over the New York Rangers.

Hull's record goal came on a deliberate 40-foot, straight on

slap shot at 5:34 of the final period, tying the game at 2-2.

The Hawks, who had just caught fire on the first of Chico Maki's two goals, were on the prowl with a power play. Red Hay and Lou Angotti got assists on the historic score. Cesare Maniago, the lanky Ranger goalie, was partially screened by Eric Nesternko when Hull shot.

Four times, twice by Hull, N.H.L. players had scored 50 goals. Maurice (Rocket) Rich-

ard of the Montreal Canadiens first did it in the 50-game campaign of 1944-45 and a teammate, Bernie (Boom Boom) Geoffrion matched it over the 70-game route of 1960-61.

Hull hit for 50 in 1961-62 and then did it again earlier this season. His record 51st came in Chicago's 61st game, but it was only the 56th for Hull who missed five with knee injuries.

Maki started the Hawks rolling at 2:57 of the final period, hitting the corner of the net with a rising 35-foote. It was Chicago's first goal in 228 min-

utes 55 seconds—more than 11 full periods.

Hull followed with the tying marker while Harry Howell was in the penalty box. Chicago steamed ahead as Maki cashed Hull's pass for the winner at 7:25. Doug Mohns added an insurance goal at 18:41.

FIRST PERIOD No scoring. Penalty: Stapleton (9:10). Shots on Goal: Chicago 13, Rangers 10.
SECOND PERIOD—1, Rangers, Marshall (Hickey), 2:50; 2, Rangers, Hickey (Ingarfield, Selling), 13:08. Penalties: Wharram (0:57), Fleming (7:23), Mikita (7:23), Howell (9:26). Shots on goal: Chicago 11, Rangers 12.

March 13, 1966

Hull's Success Understandable: Skates Fastest, Shoots Hardest

His blond hair contrasting with his blood-red jersey, his thick, gloved hands curled around the stick, Bobby Hull is electrifying as he skates down the ice faster than any man in hockey. He shoots at 120 miles an hour the hardest slapshot in the sport.

There is little doubt among his opponents and fans that Robert Marvin Hull is the most exciting player in the National Hockey League. With last night's goal, he surpassed Maurice (The Rocket) Richard and Bernie (Boom Boom) Geoffrion as the greatest goal scorer in a single N. H. L. season.

Hull's 51st goal broke the record he had shared with the former great stars of the Montreal Canadiens. Hull, however, did ita against defenses rigged especially for him and against the game's toughest players who were given only one job each time they faced the Chicago Black Hawks' left wing: Stop Hull.

Hull is frank about his life's ambition. He says in his biography, "Bobby Hull," which will be published March 31, "I want to make a million dollars and retire to a ranch."

From the loneliness of a 14-year-old living 150 miles away from home to play junior hockey, Hull has traveled the long road to acclaim, wealth and stardom.

His public image is carefully nurtured. The 5-foot-10-inch 195-pounder speaks graciously to his fans and accommodates screaming teen-agers after each game with his autograph.

He even speaks publicly as if he were a storybook hero, which to Chicagoans he is. He describes his house as "nine rooms, resting on top of a knoll,

overlooking a lagoon."

Hull, now 27, lives on an island in southeastern Ontario with his wife, Joanne, and their three children—Bobby Jr., 5; Blake, 4, and Brett, 20 months. The island is not far from his 600-acre ranch that he reaches in an 18-foot runabout.

As a youngster, he had the same ambition as every other boy in Point Anne, Ont.—to play hockey. He was barely into his teens when he went away to play for a junior team.

Hull's Goal Record

Goal No.	Date	Opp. Goalie
1,	Oct. 23	Bower, Toronto
2,	Oct. 23	Bower, Toronto
3,	Oct. 23	Bower, Toronto
4,	Oct. 24	Johnston, Boston
5,	Oct. 28	Crozier, Detroit
6,	Oct. 28	Crozier, Detroit
7,	Oct. 30	Worsley, Montreal
8,	Oct. 30	Hodge, Montreal
9,	Nov. 7	Sawchuk, Toronto
10,	Nov. 7	Sawchuk, Toronto
11,	Nov. 7	Sawchuk, Toronto
12,	Nov. 13	Worsley, Montreal
13,	Nov. 17	Giacomin, Rangers
14,	Nov. 17	Giacomin, Rangers
15,	Nov. 20	Sawchuk, Toronto
16,	Dec. 4	Pare, Boston
17,	Dec. 5	Giacomin, Rangers
18,	Dec. 15	Cheevers, Boston
19,	Dec. 15	Cheevers, Boston
20,	Dec. 15	Cheevers, Boston
21,	Dec. 15	Cheevers, Boston
22,	Dec. 19	Crozier, Detroit
23,	Dec. 19	Crozier, Detroit
24,	Dec. 22	Simmons, Rangers
25,	Dec. 25	Simmons, Rangers
26,	Dec. 25	Sawchuk, Toronto
27,	Dec. 25	Sawchuk, Toronto
28,	Dec. 31	Crozier, Detroit
29,	Jan. 2	Johnston, Boston
30,	Jan. 5	Worsley, Montreal
31,	Jan. 5	Worsley, Montreal
32,	Jan. 9	Sawchuk, Toronto
33,	Jan. 16	Maniago, Rangers
34,	Jan. 16	Maniago, Rangers
35,	Jan. 16	Maniago, Rangers
36,	Jan. 16	Maniago, Rangers
37,	Jan. 20	Johnston, Boston
38,	Jan. 23	Worsley, Montreal
39,	Jan. 26	Hodge, Montreal
40,	Jan. 26	Johnston, Boston
41,	Jan. 29	Crozier, Detroit
42,	Jan. 29	Crozier, Detroit
43,	Feb. 2	Giacomin, Rangers
44,	Feb. 2	Giacomin, Rangers
45,	Feb. 12	Worsley, Montreal
46,	Feb. 16	Giacomin, Rangers
47,	Feb. 20	Johnston, Boston
48,	Feb. 26	Crozier, Detroit
49,	Feb. 27	Parent, Boston
50,	Mar. 2	Bassen, Detroit
51,	Mar. 12	Maniago, Rangers

He would cry nights and look forward to the weekends when his parents would be able to visit him.

"You have to bear burdens like that," says Hull. "It's part of growing up in Canada if you want to make the N. H. L."

Four years later Hull was on the Black Hawks. By the time he was 20 he led the league in scoring and two years later he scored 50 goals in a season.

Now in his ninth N. H. L. campaign, Hull already holds the Hawks' record for career goals. Many have zipped past opposing goaltenders because of his custom-made stick, which he uses much like a jai alai player uses a cesta.

Hull curves the blade of the stick, and it gives him more whip (at one time he used to bend the blades under a door, but now he has convinced manufacturers to make them curved).

March 13, 1966

BRUINS WIN, 4-2; HULL SETS RECORD

Hawk Star Gets 97th Point of Season on an Assist

BOSTON, April 3 (UPI)—The Boston Bruins ended a record five-year residency in the National Hockey League cellar tonight with a 4-2 victory over Chicago in their final game. The victory moved them into fourth place in the league standings, ahead of the New York Rangers.

Ron Stewart scored twice and John McKenzie and Ron Schock once each to give the Bruins their fourth victory of the season over the Black Hawks.

Bobby Hull, the Chicago star, set a season scoring record with a first-period assist.

Hull, who had set a record of 54 goals in a season earlier, brought his point total to 97 with his 43d assist to shatter the record of 96 points set in the 1958-59 season by Dickie Moore of Montreal.

The Bruins spent most of this season in the league basement after finishing last in the previous five seasons.

FIRST PERIOD—1, Chicago, Mikita (Hull), 1:01; 2, Boston, Schock (McKenzie, Doak), 16:33. Penalties: Mohns (3:18), Jarrett (11:20). Shots on goal: Boston 13, Chicago 9.

SECOND PERIOD—3, Boston, Stewart (Bucyk, Oliver), 10:24. Penalties: Westfall (4:16), Esposito (9:13), Kennedy (14:13), Mikita (17:58), Kennedy (17:58). Shots on goal: Boston 8, Chicago 13.

THIRD PERIOD—4, Chicago, Angotti (unassisted), 0:21; 5, Boston, McKenzie (Oliver, Shock), 2:09; 6, Boston, Stewart (Oliver, Bucyk), 2:38. Penalties: Jarret (five minutes, 6:27), Kennedy (five minutes, 6:27), Pollte (11:55), Chicago bench (11:55), Mohns (18:51). Shots on goal: Boston, Chicago 8.

Goalies—Boston: Johnson. Chicago: Dryden. Attendance—13,909.

April 4, 1966

Canadiens Top Wings, 3-2, in Overtime and Win Stanley Cup, 4 Games to 2

DETROIT BEATEN 4TH TIME IN ROW

By GERALD ESKENAZI
Special to The New York Times

DETROIT, May 5—As hundreds cheered and thousands sat mute, Henri Richard slid into the Detroit net tonight, carrying the puck with him for a 3-2 Montreal victory goal as anti-climactic an ending as the National Hockey League's Stanley

Cup playoffs have produced in 40 years.

The roly-poly Richard, who had failed to score during the series, was tripped by a Red Wing defenseman, slipped and fell on Dave Balon's pass, then rolled into the crease after 2 minutes 20 seconds of a sudden-death overtime period.

Roger Crozier, in the Detroit nets, was stunned, most of the capacity crowd of 15,154 at the Olympia Stadium was shocked and even the goal judge hesitated before flashing the red light.

Then the realization set in that one of the great comebacks in N.H.L. history had been

snuffed out and the crowd began to applaud quietly as the 83-inch-high Stanley Cup was wheeled out for the Canadiens' pleasure for the second year in a row.

Only once before had an N.H.L. team dropped the first two games and gone on to win the cup—the 1942 Toronto Maple Leafs. And only once had a team finished fourth during the regular season and won the cup—the 1949 Leafs.

4 Straight for Montreal

The Red Wings had finished fourth this time, but had won the first two games at the Forum in Montreal. Then the Canadiens suddenly came to life

and flashed to victory with four straight victories.

The Red Wings had been all but written off when they took the ice tonight. Their 38-year-old defenseman, Bill Gadsby, had a broken big right toe, which he "froze" before the game started. Their other great 38-year-old, Gordie Howe, had scored only one goal in the series. And their fine young goalie, Crozier, with a badly bruised left leg, had looked bad during a 5-1 rout on Tuesday.

Yet the Wings were flashier and faster—and rougher—than the classic Flying Frenchmen for most of tonight's game. Detroit had everything to lose, and everything to gain, and the

Wings roared back to cheers of "Go, go, go!" After being behind by 2-0, they tied the game and forced the first overtime period in Stanley Cup play in two years.

Crozier was the surprise winner of the Conn Smythe Trophy as the playoff's outstanding performer (worth $1,000 and a Ford Mustang). He insisted after the shouting died down that Richard had slapped the puck in, an illegal maneuver.

Richard described the goal that gave the Canadiens the cup for a 12th time this way:

"It just hit my leg and went in. I didn't even know I had scored a goal until I heard everyone screaming."

"Yes, we got a break," admitted Coach Toe Blake while staring at his seventh Stanley Cup, "but we'll never give it up."

"If he had just shot the puck," moaned Coach Sid Abel of the Wings. "Sliding along on his body . . . sliding along on his body . . . slapping it with his hand." He forced himself to relive the weird moment, repeating his story, certain his team had lost on a "fluke," his facing showing his ulcer trouble and his defeat.

The man most observers had expected to win the Conn Smythe Trophy for the second year in a row—Jean Beliveau of the Canadiens—opened the scoring midway through the first period. Two minutes before he had been racked up by Dean Prentice and Bert Marshall—one hitting him high, the other low—but it didn't stop him.

When Floyd Smith tied the game with less than 10 minutes to play, the fans tossed bouncing balls and garbage onto the ice, holding up play for five minutes.

The monetary difference between winning and losing the Stanley Cup is $2,000 a man—$3,500 to the victors, $1,500 to the losers. The payoff has nothing to do with the length of the series. Prize money is determined in advance.

DETROIT (2)		MONTREAL (3)
Crozier	Goal	Worsley
Gadsby	Defense	J. C. Tremblay
Bowen	Defense	Harris
Selvecch	Center	Beliveau
Prentice	Wing	G. Tremblay
Howe	Wing	Provost
Ullman	Forward	Backstrom
Fontaine	Forward	Duff
MacGregor	Forward	Cournoyer
MacDonald	Forward	Rousseau
Smith	Forward	Richard
Watson	Forward	Balon
Henderson	Forward	Ferguson
Bathgate	Forward	Rochefort
	Forward	Roberts
Marshall	Defense	Talbot
Bergman	Defense	Harper
Godfrey	Defense	Price
Bassen	Goal	Hodge

FIRST PERIOD — 1, Montreal, Beliveau (Provost, G. Tremblay) 9:08. Penalties: Watson (11-25), Balon (15:04). Shots on goal: Detroit 10, Montreal 5.
SECOND PERIOD—2, Montreal, Rochefort (Richard, Balon) 10:11; 3 ,Detroit, Ullman (Selvecchio, Howe) 16:42. Penalties: Bowen (0-23), Marshall (7:13), Harris (10:42), Roberts (misconduct, 11:55), Watson (12:18), McDonald (16:42). Shots on goal: Detroit 10-9, Montreal 5.
THIRD PERIOD—4, Detroit, Smith (McDonald, Bergman), 10:30. Penalties: none. Shots on goal: Detroit 10, Montreal 9.
OVERTIME PERIOD—5, Montreal, Richard (Balon, Talbot), 2:30. Penalties: none. Shots on goal: Detroit 1, Montreal 2.
Attendance—15,154.
Referee—Frank Udvari. Linesmen—Matt Pavelich and John D'Amico.

May 6, 1966

Bent Sticks Suit Hawks' Shooters

Hull and Mikita Use Biggest Hooks on Their Blades

On the Chicago Black Hawks, the trend to bend hockey stick blades began accidentally.

About four years ago, Stan Mikita's blade split from top to bottom during practice. But he continued to use it, and found he could control the puck better on forehand and get his shot off quicker and harder with the cracked stick.

"I told Bobby Hull about it," Mikita recalled the other day. "He tried mine and liked it, and then we started bending them under doors overnight. We tried them in practice for a couple of days, and then used them in games."

Great Variety of Hooks

That started it. Now all the Black Hawks use the hooked sticks except three defensemen, John Miszuk, Matt Ravlich and Pat Stapleton.

The degree of the hook varies from the exaggerated ones favored by Hull (it resembles the profile of a spoon or a jai-alai cesta) and Mikita (the drastic bend starts a third of the way from the heel of the blade) to those with the slightly discernible curves preferred by Billy Hay, Eric Nesterenko and Doug Mohns.

Nonetheless, the Hawks have made a shambles of the National Hockey League race since their five-week unbeaten streak between Jan. 12 and Feb. 18. The Hawks are in Toronto tonight, and then come into Madison Square Garden Wednesday for the next-to-the-last time this season to face the Rangers.

Hull credits his scoring rampage in the last two years to his hooked blade. When Hull used a straight blade his shot used to "slice off, just like a golf ball.

"Now I can pull the puck in and shoot it all in one motion. The hook cradles the puck, and I can get a little action on it. It'll drop or rise, and I know which way it's going by the way I follow through."

Hull's assessment of a "little

The New York Times

Nick Garen, Hawks' trainer, shows the difference in blades

action" on his slap shot seems a modest one.

"From center ice, Hull overpowers you," says the Ranger goalie, Ed Giacomin. "His slap shot comes in on you good and fast, and if the puck is rolling right when he shoots, it'll be fluttering. I've had it drop as much as a foot."

Giacomin has noticed that the hooked blades place some limitations on the Hawks' offense. Other teams still predominately using straight blades may have taken the drawbacks into consideration.

"It's amazing that sometimes Hull can't get the backhander up," Giacomin recalls. "I remember a game Christmas night when we won, 1-0. I was down, and Hull had a terrific opportunity to score on the backhand. But he couldn't get it up over me, and it went right into my pads. I'd like to see Bobby Hull on a backhand shot 90 per cent of the time he's on the ice," he said with a smile.

He's more wary of Mikita, however, when the little center gets around the net. "He can get the puck up, and even over the net from two feet out."

Whatever the drawbacks, an official at the Northland Ski Manufacturing Company in St. Paul, which makes sticks for four of the six N.H.L. teams, says the Hawks have "revolutionized hockey sticks."

March 12, 1967

Leafs Win, 3-1, and Take Stanley Cup

By DAVE ANDERSON
Special to The New York Times

TORONTO, May 2 — Old Eyes and young legs provided the Toronto Maple Leafs with victory and the Stanley Cup playoff championship tonight.

In a classic game decided by a fluke goal, the Maple Leafs defeated the Montreal Canadiens, 3-1. The triumph eliminated the defending champions, 4 games to 2, in the four-of-seven-game series for the Cup, symbolic of the world professional hockey title.

The Old Eyes belonged to Terry Sawchuk and George Armstrong, the young legs to Ron Ellis and Jim Pappin.

Sawchuk, the 37-year-old goaltender who has repeatedly stated that this would be his final campaign, accumulated 40 saves. He performed spectacularly throughout the first two periods, then held the fort after Dick Duff's goal had narrowed the Maple Leaf lead to 2-1 early in the final period.

Old Order Prevails

Armstrong, who is 36, clinched the victory with the Leafs' third goal from mid-ice into a corner of an empty net with 47 seconds to play. Moments earlier Red Kelly, whose eyes are 39 years old, swooped in to pick up a loose puck following a standoff faceoff between Jean Beliveau and Allan Stanley to Sawchuk's left.

Ellis, who is 22, had broken the scoreless tie early in the second period. The right wing swatted Kelly's rebound over a sprawling Gump Worsley.

In the final minute of the second period, however, Pappin was credited with the goal that proved to be decisive. Shooting blindly from the left corner, the 27-year-old right wing's shot deflected off the angular body of Jacques Laperriere, who was locked with Pete Stemkowski in front of the net.

Worsley, who contributed 33 saves, never had a chance to stop the ricochet into the far corner of the net. The chubby goalie had been chosen by his coach, Toe Blake, to replace the rookie, Rogatien Vachon, who had sparked his team to a 16-game unbeaten streak through the opener of the series as the Canadiens sought their third straight Stanley Cup.

For Worsley, who underwent knee surgery shortly before mid-season, it was his first complete game since March 11, his second since Dec. 7.

Sawchuk Dominates Play

Although Worsley performed gallantly, Sawchuk was the game's dominant player. The only Montreal goal occurred on a brilliant effort by Duff. The little left wing, once a Maple Leaf, swerved around Tim Horton and, skating with the defenseman virtually on his back, swatted a backhander past Sawchuk's stick.

Duff's goal deflated the capacity crowd of 15,977, but it did not disturb Sawchuk and his teammates.

In the ceremony at mid-ice following the final buzzer, Armstrong, as the team captain, accepted the gleaming Stanley Cup from Clarence Campbell, the president of the National Hockey League. The Maple Leafs have now won the Cup 11 times, three short of the record held by the Canadiens.

For George (Punch) Imlach, the triumph represented the fourth Cup won during his regime as both general manager and coach. The late Lester Patrick of the New York Rangers and Jack Adams of the Detroit Red Wings were the only others to have held dual jobs as the major domos of three Cup champions.

During the mid-ice celebration, Stemkowski lifted Imlach's fedora and tossed it high in the air. If the Stanley Cup wasn't old hat to Imlach before this, it is now.

MONTREAL (1)		TORONTO (3)
Worsley	Goal	Sawchuk
Laperriere	Defense	Hillman
Harper	Defense	Pronovost
Backstrom	Center	Stemkowski
Larose	Wing	Pappin
Ferguson	Wing	Pulford
Beliveau	Forward	Keon
Rousseau	Forward	Armstrong
G. Tremblay	Forward	Mahovlich
Richard	Forward	Kelly
Rochefort	Forward	Ellis
Balon	Forward	Conacher
Cournoyer	Forward	Walton
Duff	Forward	Shack
Roberts	Forward	Marcetta
Harris	Defense	Horton
J. C. Tremblay	Defense	Stanley
Talbot	Defense	Baun
Vachon	Goal	Bower

FIRST PERIOD
No scoring.

Second Period
1—Toronto, Ellis (Kelly, Stanley)......6:25
2—Toronto, Pappin (Stemkowski, Pulford)......19:24

Third Period
3—Montreal, Duff (Harris)......5:28
4—Toronto, Armstrong (Pulford, Kelly) 19:13
PENALTIES—First Period: Conacher (2:30), Backstrom (5:16), Beliveau (10:21), Conacher (13:25), Ferguson (18:50). Second Period: Harper (3:05), Stemkowski (7:14), Stanley (13:43), Rousseau (14:34). Third Period: Pappin (11:46). SHOTS ON GOAL—First Period: Montreal 17, Toronto 11. Second Period: Toronto 16, Montreal 14. Third Period: Montreal 10, Toronto 9.

Toronto	0	2	1—3
Montreal	0	0	1—1

Referee—John Ashley. Linesmen—Neil Armstrong and Matt Pavelich.
Attendance—15,977.

May 3, 1967

CANADIENS TAKE HOCKEY CUP

BLUES BEATEN, 3-2

Canadiens Rally in 3d Period of 4th Game to Sweep Series

By GERALD ESKENAZI
Special to The New York Times

MONTREAL, May 11 — The Montreal Canadiens, with their controlled madness, unleashed a final-period drive that enabled them to catch, and defeat, the St. Louis Blues, 3-2, today and win the Stanley Cup in four straight games.

A goal by J. C. Tremblay that rattled off the posts gave the Frenchmen their 15th cup, and their eighth in the 13 years they have played under the volatile coach, Hector (Toe) Blake.

Minutes after the victory, Blake, who had said this was the "toughest and longest of them all," went on Canadian television and announced his retirement.

So the first series played between an expansion team and an established club ended under conditions more dramatic than had ever been expected. In sweeping the four-of-seven-game National Hockey League series, the Frenchmen never won a game by more than one goal and were forced into overtime twice.

Always Faithful Fans

The Blues played it for the breaks today, rarely risking a too-deep commitment of their outmanned forces. The Canadiens bolted out of the opening face-off with their classic forward-motion attack, bringing guttural French cries from the 15,505 fans at the Forum.

But they have played better than they did in the first two periods, and after a few opening minutes of electricity they disappointed the crowd as they were continuously hamstrung by the prodding sticks and heavier blocks thrown by the Blues.

Dick Duff gave the Canadiens the lead late in the opening period on a play that should have shown United States fans, viewing the game on network television, what the Montreal legend was all about.

Duff stole the puck deep in his own end, and set sail. He was joined by Jacques Lemaire, with the Blues' Barclay Plager stationed between them and St. Louis's goalie, 37-year-old Glenn Hall.

Lemaire took Duff's pass and in the same motion shoveled it back. Just as it appeared Duff would bypass the goal, he stuffed it in.

Then the Blues took charge, and their spurts finally reached a peak in the second period when they scored twice in a 57-second span. First, Craig Cameron scored following a behind-the-net pass, and then Gary Sabourin, while his club had a man advantage, lined a 30-footer past Gump Worsley.

But the Canadiens know the route to the 3-foot-high Cup by heart, and in the final 20 minutes they were perfect. J. C. Tremblay, who plays the game, "cute," almost poked fun at the futilities of opponents who tried to stick-handle past him. He played his defensive position so perfectly and got off passes to his forwards so deftly that the Canadiens began driving.

They hit Hall eight times in the first five minutes, and the great goaltender began to juggle some of the shots. Tremblay finally spotted Henri Richard, and the small chunky center pushed the disk past Hall. Fewer than five minutes later, Tremblay rocketed in a 30-footer. Now the Canadiens were in full control and the Blues began to show their age and inexperience. They had been bulwarked in the road to the finals by the play of 43-year-old Doug Harvey on defense, and 37-year-old Dickie Moore. Both are former Canadiens' stars.

The final buzzer sounded and the air was filled with flying newspapers, balloons and hats. A red carpet was rolled onto the ice and the Cup was hauled out, followed by Jean Beliveau, the Canadiens' captain. His right foot was in a cast and he hobbled on crutches (he broke an ankle bone last week).

The Cup continues to be more than a symbol of hockey supremacy for the predominantly French-Canadian fans. It helps solidify their Gallic feelings and when Beliveau addressed them in French, they applauded wildly.

Florida Trip on Blues

In a few days, as a reward for gaining the final, the Blues will send 81 persons—players, wives, children, and the club's organist Norm Kramer — to Florida for a vacation, all expenses paid.

Lynn Patrick, the Blues' general manager, was boasting before the game of how Kramer had sneaked in jibes at the officials after a "bad" call against St. Louis.

Organists around the league have been forbidden to play "Three Blind Mice," which some did after a decision went against the home club. Kramer, however, played the theme song of "The Three Stooges."

Bill Gadsby, the former longtime star of the Rangers and Detroit Red Wings, is expected to be named the Wings' coach this week. Sid Abel currently handles the coaching and general manager duties.

MONTREAL (3)		ST. LOUIS (2)
Worsley	Goal	Hall
Laperriere	Defense	Harvey
Harper	Defense	Arbour
Backstrom	Center	Berenson
Ferguson	Forward	Roberts
Duff	Forward	St. Marseille
Larose	Forward	Schock
Provost	Forward	Sabourin
Rousseau	Forward	Moore
Richard	Forward	Ecclestone
Grant	Forward	Veneruzzo
Redmond	Forward	Keenan
Lamaire	Forward	Crisp
	Forward	Cameron
J. C. Tremblay	Defense	Picard
Harris	Defense	Bob Plager
Savard	Defense	Barclay Plager

May 12, 1968

Blood And Ice

The best defenseman in the most savage sport outside of bullfighting

By BILL SURFACE

THE other night at the Boston Garden, a frozen rubber puck ricocheted so violently off the rink's sideboards that a typical, improvised play developed before most spectators realized what was happening. The Montreal Canadiens' three-man offensive line glided at about 25 miles an hour toward the Boston Bruins' end of the rink. Claude Provost, the right wing, caught the puck with the tip of his curved hickory

BILL SURFACE is the author of "The Poisoned Ivy" and "Inside Internal Revenue."

stick and began zigzagging and shaking his head to confuse the Bruins.

But a tall blond Bruin with the number 4 on his white and gold jersey swerved in front of Provost and zigzagged backward, watching Provost's hands. Suddenly Provost swung his stick downward; by the time it reached the ice there was nothing for it to hit. No. 4 had maneuvered his stick so swiftly and gracefully that Provost was left to curse in French as the puck slid toward one of the Boston forwards.

Most of the fans were shouting by this time as the Bruins' line skated

toward the Canadiens' tense, masked goalie. As usual, the play of No. 4—defenseman Bobby Orr—was forgotten; perhaps it was just too fast to be noticed. But this type of defensive move is, in essence, the name of the game in professional hockey and the reason that Bobby Orr, a friendly, heavily muscled young man with a bump on his nose as a result of multiple breaks, is considered the best defenseman of them all. Opposing coaches call him the Bruins' "meal ticket." An even more laudatory opinion comes from the New York Rangers' Harry Howell, a first-

ICE CAPER—Bobby Orr of the Boston Bruins, left, checking Reggie Fleming of the Rangers. Orr's job as a defenseman requires the callousness of a mugger and a disregard for personal disfigurement with sticks, skates or fists. "When we see blood or one of our guys getting hurt," he says, "we're like a bunch of animals."

rate defenseman himself for 17 years: "Only one great hockey player comes along every 10 or 20 years, and Orr is that man for these 10 years."

Although Orr is only 20 years old, his skating has made veteran players envious. In 1967, he was voted the National Hockey League's rookie of the year. Last season he was selected the league's best defenseman despite injuries that kept him out of 26 games. This season, opposing players insist, Orr, who dominated the All-Star game two weeks ago, is better than ever and is a principal reason that the Bruins, who once customarily finished at the bottom of the N.H.L., have been in first place for most of last month.

The Bruins may be the roughest, brawlingest team in a sport so fast and furious that it precludes the use of scientific plays like those designed for football. Seldom are more than three or four goals scored by both teams during a game's 60 minutes of play. Even these goals usually occur after the puck has bounced off a lunging goaltender; in the split second before the entangled defenseman and goalie recover, a player slaps the puck into one of the cage-like nets at each end of the rectangular, 85 by 200-foot rink. It is, moreover, a game in which scoring is so difficult that the league's six new teams, created largely with expendable substitutes, either defeat or tie the superior East Division teams in a surprising 40 per cent of the games. By contrast, new pro football teams almost *never* beat first-rate clubs.

The presence of the new teams is an indication of the unprecedented popularity of hockey, a sport whose major-league practitioners include 213 Canadians, two Americans, one Pole, one Czech and one Scot. Refined from the European sport of bandy, it was adopted in Canada's colder areas in the eighteen-eighties, and in 1917 teams from four Canadian cities formed the National Hockey League. The sport gained increasing acceptance in the mid-thirties following rule changes that speeded up the game and innovations by men such as Conn Smythe, owner of the Toronto Maple Leafs. He is credited with taking the game away from rednecks and barroom brawlers by prohibiting the use of whisky before or during a game and seeking superbly conditioned athletes. Since 1947 the Toronto Maple Leafs and the Montreal Canadiens haven't started a home game with a single ticket unsold. In more recent years the Boston Bruins, New York Rangers, Chicago Black Hawks and Detroit Red Wings have played before crowds which averaged 96 per cent of their arenas' capacities and last

season moved the N.H.L. to add teams in Los Angeles, Minnesota, Oakland, Philadelphia, Pittsburgh and St. Louis.

WHAT such crowds usually see is a sustained sport in which organized savagery is unmatched outside the bullring. Orr's face epitomized that brutality after a recent game when he slumped on a bench and reached for two paper cups of icewater. He emptied both cups on his face and hair, and, as the water dripped off his bloody, Vaseline-smeared and blackened face, he pondered a question. "Rough?" he mused, then managed to smile. "In about the first game I'm in, Joe Watson, one of our players then, comes over to the bench with his mouth bleeding like he's been shot. Danny, the trainer, says: 'It'll be O.K., Joe. Just rinse it out.' Joe rinses his mouth all right, and eight or nine teeth come out with the water. But nobody's too concerned."

Defensemen like Orr, more than goalies and glamorized shooters, make pro hockey intense. They are, from a game's outset, continuously knocking men down — and being knocked down — amid sharpened skates, slashing sticks and flying elbows. Take, for example, a typical two minutes of work for Orr. It be-

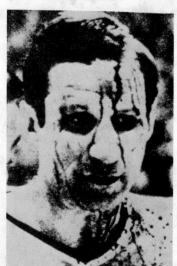

CASUALTY — The battered face of a player suggests the extent of "organized savagery" in major-league hockey.

gan in a recent game against the New York Rangers when he leaped over a skate behind his goal to push the puck to teammate Glen Sather. Sather moved between two Bruins and skated toward the Rangers' goal. But, within six seconds, the Rangers' two defensemen had elbowed the puck loose from Derek Sanderson, a Bruin forward, as soon as he touched it. Suddenly, two Rangers skated quickly toward Orr and Dallas Smith, another defenseman, who had been crouching near the blue line designating the Bruins' end of the rink. Smith, on cue, skated forward but only slowed down the two Rangers. As the Rangers approached the goal Orr skated sideways without deliberately charging into them, then pivoted and, still obeying hockey's liberal interpretation of the rule on "checking," skated so forcibly into Rod Gilbert's shoulder that the momentum carried both of them against the unpadded sideboards.

After they bounced off the boards, Orr recovered the puck and, though about to fall, passed it to Sanderson. By the time Orr recovered, the Rangers had again separated the Bruins from the puck and were skating toward Boston's net. The puck went to Dennis Hextall, who was instantly slammed against the boards by Orr. Spinning around, Orr passed the puck to his forwards, who were once more stopped by the Rangers. Again, Gilbert skated toward Orr, who poked his stick under Gilbert's arm and stole the puck, then skated until accidentally colliding with the Rangers' Larry Jeffrey. Though Jeffrey fell, Orr continued to skate until hit hard by Brad Park, a Ranger defenseman. Orr knocked the puck to Sanderson while lying on his back.

Though the Bruins substituted defensemen (few hockey players can skate effectively for longer than two or three minutes without resting), Orr got less than 25 seconds off the ice instead of the usual few minutes. Two Bruins were sent to the penalty box for unnecessarily fouling the Rangers. Not unexpectedly, most of the fans in Madison Square Garden cheered as enthusiastically as if New York had scored. It seemed highly probable that the Rangers would do so soon; they would have five men skating against three Bruins. But, it turned out, not against just *any* three Bruins. "We need —— ——body work," snapped Harry Sinden, the Bruins' peppery little coach, as he tapped Orr's right shoulder.

Orr, still breathing heavily, leaped over the rink's sideboards and stationed himself in front of the Bruins' goalie for the face-off, in which a referee drops the puck between two opponents. A Ranger knocked the puck toward Boston's net, but Orr kicked it away. Another Ranger passed the puck, only to have it intercepted by Orr. Then, since the Bruins wanted only to stall until they were again at full strength, Orr skated in circles with the puck while two Rangers pursued him for about 10 seconds. Faking left, he passed to a teammate, who quickly returned the puck. Orr skated sideways, but found himself trapped behind his own goal by three Rangers. There was no way for him to knock the puck out of the area or to a Bruin. Instead of surrendering the puck, he hit it against the rink's sideboards and sent it ricocheting 200 feet to the Rangers' zone. Within 10 or 12 seconds he had recovered the puck.

SUCH work is not as easy as the fast, agile Orr makes it appear. Most forwards are remarkably skilled skaters who can glide like ballet dancers through the narrowest openings while steering the puck and, without even raising an arm, send it flying toward the goal. Each forward, furthermore, has such a distinct style of skating, passing and shooting that, Orr maintains, "you try stopping one the same way as the other and you'll be flat on your back and he'll be heading down your goalie's throat."

To be sure, Orr has convinced opponents that he can react to each style. Consider, for example, how he frequently plays against the Rangers' Bob Nevin, Phil Goyette and Donnie Marshall, who pass the puck so skillfully that they have made competent defensemen appear clumsy. "You find out how good this Orr is when the three of us go in on two defensemen," Goyette emphasizes. "I'll go in with the puck and then suddenly leave it behind me for either Nevin or Marshall and continue skating into the defenseman to block him out of the play. This leaves two guys against one defenseman. You might eliminate yourself from the play, but you don't eliminate Orr too often. He's so fast that he's almost never too far away to block a shot."

If Orr uses speed against the Rangers, he has found that brawn succeeds most often against the Chicago Black Hawks' Bobby Hull, the league's most feared offensive player. Hull not only has exceptionally strong shoulders that enable him to push most defensemen away, but also is the league's fastest skater and has the fastest shot (118.3 miles an hour). Orr, however, similarly exploits his exceptional 5-foot-11-inch, 180-pound physique. Once he senses that Hull will get the puck he usually skates forward and uses his muscular legs (which have, from years of skating instead of walking, developed out of proportion to the rest of his body) to hit Hull somewhat like a football player throwing a body block. If Orr isn't satisfied with the first collision, he hits Hull again. "You also got to have some surprises for him," Orr says, "but mainly it's tight checking."

Hull calls Orr's "checking" something else. "Running into Orr," he tells you, "is like getting hit by a pickup truck."

Orr has a logical reason for bumping Hull even before Hull approaches the Bruins' net. He is not hesitant to admit it: "I have to make him realize that he's got to shoot from the blue line or else," Orr says. "That 'else' is me. Hull's shot rises so fast that, if you're 10 feet away and try to block it with your knees, it'll rise up and take your head off. You'd better believe it'll kill you. Eddie Johnston, one of my roommates, got hit in the head with a puck that wasn't going nearly as fast as Hull's shot. He got a blood clot on his brain and didn't even remember the first 15 days in the hospital. Hull? You can't be bashful about checking him."

Orr is seldom bashful about blocking pucks that have been shot by other forwards. Even when he is several feet from the shooter it is not uncommon for him to lunge and deflect a shot with his thick gloves. It is more common for Orr to use his skates or legs to knock down a shot by a forward he is guarding, push him to the ice with one hand and guide the puck with the other—all before his opponent has landed. Before 10 seconds of a period elapsed against the Rangers, Orr had stolen the puck from Arnie Brown and scored so easily that the Rangers were seemingly demoralized for the rest of the game.

It is usual for Orr to slide almost effortlessly across the ice to intercept a puck before it reaches the forward who expected to shoot. "In fact, Bobby is at his best when he anticipates where the puck will go," says Sinden, the Bruins' coach. "Sure, you can be a guesser and make a few lucky steals of the puck and have the crowd cheering like you're a hero. Then you guess wrong and get burned enough times and you'll be back in Saskatchewan looking for a job. But when Orr goes for a pass, he has the uncanny knack of being there and gone with the puck."

ORR is equally adept at getting a loose puck when he and a forward are fighting for it with their sticks. One reason that he occasionally exasperates forwards into swinging at him is that, unlike most defensemen, he maneuvers his stick as skillfully as some offensive players. As the Rangers' Phil Goyette points out: "Most defensemen can't do much with the puck even when they take it away from you—and that's why they're playing defense. But Orr handles the puck well enough to be a forward, and if he gets a chance to shoot he's extremely accurate."

Orr creates so many opportunities to shoot that, though he is a defenseman, he had, by last week, scored 13 goals this season—only 17 fewer than the total scored by Phil Esposito, the Bruins' leading offensive man. Many of Orr's goals, moreover, come in such tense situations as the one that occurred late in a bitterly fought game with the Montreal Canadiens. With the score tied, he knocked two Canadiens loose from the puck, skated at three-quarter speed while passing to forward John McKenzie, then suddenly increased his speed as the puck was returned to him; he glided past a defenseman and into Montreal's zone. Then, calculatingly, he swerved and faked right in order to force the Canadien goalie, Tony Esposito (Phil's younger brother), to move in that direction. When the goalie moved, Orr swung left-handed and drove the puck past Esposito's shoulder for the goal that won the game.

Few defensemen could have outskated forwards in a similar situation. But Orr has the ability to do almost anything expected of him, and that is why he is rated above such outstanding defensemen as J. C. Tremblay and Jacques Laperrière of Montreal; Tim Horton of Toronto; Pat Stapleton of Chicago; Harry Howell and Jim Neilson of the Rangers, and Gary Bergman of Detroit. All of them do *many* of their jobs well. But Orr, hockey coaches maintain, does them *all* exceedingly well.

Orr cannot, of course, intercept, steal or block more than half of the attempted shots. In a typical game, the Bruins' opponents manage about 35 times to knock the puck toward the goalie, who, on the average, kicks, catches or deflects all but 2.5 of the shots. Goalies are almost singularly credited with a team's success in this area. But, while no team can win without a competent goalie, there is no such thing as an outstanding goalie who is not supported by first-rate defensemen. Even when Orr doesn't block shots, he usually causes them to be so hurried that they are too wide or too close to the goalie instead of the net's vulnerable corners. Just how effective goalies would be without defensemen like Orr is underscored whenever a defenseman chases a puck too deeply into the other team's zone and an opponent gets the puck and skates unchallenged toward the goalie. Although a mere 7 per cent of the shots harassed by defensemen score, 50 per cent or more of the "breakaway" shots are successful.

Shots that are deflected or blocked frequently bounce into a corner of the rink, the

66His nose, which now slants right, has been broken six times; the edges of his mouth have been cut five times.99

scene of much of hockey's combat and much of Orr's work. "The corners are just a survival of the fittest," Orr maintains, shaking his head for emphasis. "My job is to dig that puck out of the corner and feed our wings."

To dig out the puck requires both the callousness of a mugger and a virtual disregard for personal disfigurement by sticks, sharpened skates and fists. In essence, Orr—like other Bruin defensemen—is attracted by blood; he is not reluctant to admit it. "We're just like a bunch of animals," he volunteers. "When we see blood or one of our guys getting hurt digging out the puck, we're in that corner like a bunch of animals."

ORR hurts men in those corners and is himself injured despite his youth and the protective equipment worn on his hands, shoulders, thighs and knees. When, for example, he attempted to skate between Marcel Pronovost of Toronto and the rink's boards, his right knee was hit so forcibly that it repeatedly stiffened. When the same knee was hit a second time in Toronto and again in Montreal, it slipped from a socket and locked. Time after time he would bite on a glove while Danny Canney, the Bruins' trainer, pulled the knee back into its socket. The clicking sounds in the knee grew more ominous and it became more and more difficult to unlock. Last season Orr underwent surgery on the knee to repair torn cartilage. He returned for the last 10 games of the 1967-68 season, but needed another operation after the season ended.

Orr also suffered the usual multitude of injuries to his upper anatomy. Players have driven sticks and knees so violently into his back that on one occasion his left shoulder was fractured and on another his right shoulder was separated. His nose, which now slants right, has been broken six times, and the edges of his mouth have been cut five times, deeply enough to require 22 stitches in all (which he received without anesthesia). Twenty-two stitches for five gashes, though, is below average for professional hockey players. "Stitches like mine are just Band-Aid stuff so far," he says, knocking on a wooden table. "You know I've still got all of my teeth. But I don't want anybody to think I'm bragging about it."

Why doesn't Orr preserve

those teeth — and his face — by wearing a mouthpiece and helmet? Like most professional hockey players, Orr finds the use of such equipment so unnatural, and so uncommon, that it would affect his play. Young members of Canada's junior leagues wear helmets, and those who advance to the N.H.L. in eight or ten years are likely to continue doing so. Some goalies wear masks, and several N.H.L. players wore helmets briefly last season after Bill Masterton of the Minnesota North Stars died from brain damage — though nobody is certain how it occurred — and became major-league hockey's first fatality in modern times.

Scarred though he is, Orr is not the Bruins' so-called "enforcer," the man who provokes fights and punishes dirty players on opposing teams with a zeal approaching sadism. To volunteer for such a role would increase both Orr's chances of being injured by other "enforcers" and his chances of being banished from the game for penalties of two, five or ten minutes. As it is, Orr's aggressiveness makes him one of the Bruins' most penalized players and a target of hatchet men. The team "enforcer" is usually a more expendable (or at least less valuable) player.

DIVISION OF OPINION—*Orr, right, battles a Detroit Red Wing. While hardly shy on the ice, he is disciplined and usually leaves such jobs to the "enforcer," the man who punishes dirty opponents.*

And another of the Bruins' defensemen, stocky Ted Green, fills that role so well that he is called the "Boston Rangler" and is so despised that some teams have a standing reward for any player who "puts him out of the game."

Just how such "enforcers" help protect players like Orr was vividly illustrated in a game against the Rangers. A few minutes after play began, Reggie Fleming, the Rangers' self-appointed enforcer, brought his forearm so viciously under Orr's chin that Orr was knocked about five feet into the air before somersaulting and landing on his face. Players with less discipline would have retaliated and, as a result, been ejected from the game for at least two minutes. Instead Orr let Green retaliate.

Two minutes later Green slammed Fleming into the rink's sideboards so hard that from the opposite side of the glass wall Fleming's nose seemed flat. No more than a minute elapsed before Green, sensing that the nearest official's vision was partly blocked, elbowed Fleming under the ear and kicked him with his skates. Infuriated, Fleming began beating Green in the face. Green and Fleming were penalized two minutes for fighting.

Still, Orr was repeatedly struck, gouged and kicked by Fleming; after seven minutes of the second period, he didn't wait for Green. Orr skated fast to the center of the ice and threw his body into Fleming. His left knee went into Fleming's groin, his left elbow into Fleming's nose and mouth. Fleming was hurled forward, mucous and blood squirting from his nose. Orr was, of course, penalized for two minutes.

He has, feeling that he was unnecessarily fouled, twice knocked down Montreal's Ted Harris, one of the league's best fist fighters, and seemingly stunned Brian Conacher of the Toronto Maple Leafs and Gary Dornhoefer of the Philadelphia Flyers. Orr also has pounded the faces of players he was holding down. Incongruously, he has not even struck others. "There are some guys who don't try to hurt you when they have you down," he said recently. "Then there are others who have a mean streak in them and try to break every tooth in your mouth." He treats them accordingly.

BUT hockey is not all that grim for Orr. A friendly, polite and modest man away from the ice, Orr lives like the handsome, *single* star athlete that he is without antagonizing lower-salaried teammates. He usually wears turtle-neck shirts, cardigan sweaters and a black windbreaker decorated with a large Bruins emblem. And, along with some of his buoyant teammates, he can be found often enough at the "singles bars" to uphold the contention that professional hockey players have never done anything to harm the saloon business. Unlike many such hockey players, however, he is not known to have broken a chair, bottle or nose in a barroom brawl.

Similarly, Orr has learned how to live comfortably at minimum expense. Like other hockey players, he pays reasonable rents during the mid-October to mid-April hockey season in semiwinterized summer homes that may be too frigid for their owners but are no colder than the homes in Canada's subzero plains, where he huddled around oil heaters. Orr shares a four-bedroom, ocean-front house in Nahant, Mass., with Gary Doak, another defenseman; Ed Johnston, a goalie, and John (Frosty) Forristall, the team's

The Bruins spent less than $2,500 to sign Orr for the rest of his hockey-playing days

assistant trainer. All four roommates initially agreed to share the cooking, but most of that responsibility was assumed by Forristall when Orr let four steaks disintegrate under a broiler while he slept.

Nonetheless, Forristall maintains, "Bob does more than his share around the house in other ways." The roommates ride in Orr's automobile, since he receives it and the gas with the compliments of a dealer Of greater interest is Orr's ability to provide his roommates — as well as some other teammates—with dates. He upholds his nickname, "Lover," by referring to a small black address book whenever a Bruin asks: "What do you have in mind for an all-around hockey player?"

Some of the Bruins are impressed by the way Orr can persuade young women who idolize star athletes to do things for him. "He could have women in here cooking and cleaning for free," volunteers Forristall. "He just told this girl who's a vet or works for a vet that we needed a good, mean-looking watchdog. Well, a week later she's out here with a Labrador retriever that actually smiles trying to show off his teeth. Bob said that was fine but we still need a monkey to open the door for us. She said to give her two weeks and she'd have it."

Although Orr was bashful when he joined the Bruins, he may now be their best practical joker. One afternoon, for example, he telephoned a teammate with an injured jaw, and, pretending to be a reporter, asked such flattering questions that the other player answered, despite the pain.

Orr does not neglect the almost ritualistic training routine that keeps him psychologically and physically prepared for the Bruins' 76-game schedule. He invariably attends a movie the evening before a game to relax before getting "psyched up." Since the Bruins usually play three times a week, he and other players sometimes see movies that even the critics might have ignored. His alertness against possible illness was typified the other afternoon when Sinden, the coach, sauntered into the Bruins' dressing room to announce: "This Hong Kong flu's going all over the place, and I want you guys to watch out for these puddles and things like that."

"I'm already fighting it off," Orr said softly as he finished his third one-pint container of orange juice in 10 minutes.

"That stuff fights it off, huh?" he was asked.

"I don't have the flu, do I?" Orr replied, knocking on a wooden bench.

IT is understandable why Orr is so serious about preparing for a game. Hockey has been his life since he was 5 years old. He follows a little-known, little-discussed pattern of some outstanding athletes: his father "could've made it big in the pros" but missed his chance and transferred his stunted ambition to his well-coordinated son. Bobby's father, Doug Orr, outskated and outshot two boyhood acquaintances who later earned good salaries as professional hockey players in Canada. Doug, a muscular, tatooed man who works in the shipping room of a chemical manufacturing company, joined the Canadian Navy in 1942 to "see the world." Upon his return, he found that the expense of marriage and children prevented him from playing in the competitive junior hockey program.

But he didn't let Bobby, the third of five children, forget what he might have been or how hockey should be played. By the time Bobby was 3 he was stumbling on skates in the back yard of their large old house on the Tower Hill — or poorer — side of Parry Sound, Ont., a small fishing and vacation community about 120 miles north of Toronto. Before he was 4, Bobby was skating on the frozen Parry Sound, and at 5 he was swerving between other children in the Minor Squirt League. He advanced through the Peewee and Bantam leagues of Canada's highly competitive juvenile and amateur hockey before he was noticed by pro scouts as a skinny 12-year-old.

The discovery was accidental. Wren Blair, then coach and general manager of the Bruins' minor-league team in Kingston, Ont., asked Lynn Patrick, then the Bruins' general manager, to meet him in Sault Ste. Marie to scout two boys playing against Parry Sound. Blair, though, was soon distracted by Orr. "See that skinny No. 2 out there making monkeys out of these older kids?" he asked Patrick.

To obtain contractual rights to Orr, the Bruins spent $900 to subsidize and befriend the Parry Sound team. Then, by the time Bobby was 14, the Bruins' representatives sat down at the Orrs' kitchen table and promised to "fix up and stucco the house" and give Bobby and his father "a chunk of money." The Bruins spent less than $2,500 to sign Bobby to a "Junior A Card" that obligated him to them for the remainder of his hockey-playing days.

Under the system then in effect in Canada, the Bruins owned Orr but didn't have to pay him. They assigned him to play for the Oshawa Generals, a "Junior A" team — the highest amateur category — 140 miles from home. Under the rules, he could not receive more than $60 a week for room, board, transportation, education and salary. "I got a $10 bill every weekend," he recalls.

Before he was 16 and weighed 120 pounds, Orr outskated and outshot 18-year-old and 20-year-old players. Sensing that he had a potential star, Bucko McDonald, the Oshawa coach, told Orr: "Look kid, you'd be better off on defense 'cause forwards are a dime a dozen." Defensemen like Orr were not so plentiful. By the time he was 17, Orr had quit high school, had won recognition as Canada's best amateur player and had begun to cause unexpected trouble for the Bruins' management. Instead of accepting the nominal salaries offered by the National Hockey League clubs, Orr threatened to play for the Canadian Olympic team and, in time, hired Alan Eagleson, who negotiates salaries for about 20 good hockey players, to represent him.

The result was a three-year contract that Orr calls "something I'm happy with." Though sportswriters term it a "$100,000-a-year pact," he has been paid about $26,500 a season during his three years in the N.H.L. As inequitable as such a contract may now appear, it was so far above any ever given a rookie that it impelled many star hockey players to demand the salaries that are paid standouts in other pro sports. Orr immediately proved that he was worth all he was paid; the Bruins did not have to wait for him to develop into an outstanding player. "I'd like to read that Orr developed under my steady coaching during the three years we've been together," volunteers Harry Sinden. "But he had it by the time they played the national anthem."

Orr also had, even as an impressionable, oft-praised rookie, the foresight to sense that he needed more than exceptional ability to do well against men who prolong their careers by intimidating young players. Orr blushed as he described his first days with the Bruins. "I couldn't believe all the things people said about me," he recalled, drinking another container of orange juice. "People were saying that I was as cool as a cucumber and had fulfilled a lifetime ambition by playing with the Bruins. I love Boston now, but the reason I signed with the Bruins is that they were just the worst team going and looked like the easiest place to play.

"I was having trouble, too. Look, I was coming out of our end with the puck right here in Boston and, about the time I see two Rangers in front of me, one of our guys whispered from behind me: 'Bob baby, I got a clear shot.' I give the puck to my teammate. But he turns out to be Vic Hadfield of the Rangers and he scores easy. I got embarrassed."

IT was not long before Orr's skating, finesse and awesome "checking" embarrassed his opponents and, more often than not, motivated reporters to pose questions like that asked the other night outside the Bruins' dressing room: "Would you say that Orr played an unusually great game?"

"No, I wouldn't want to say he played an *unusually* great game," Sinden replied slowly. "I don't recall that Bobby Orr ever played anything but a great game." ■

February 2, 1969

Canadiens Down Blues, 2-1, to Retain Stanley Cup With Four-Game Sweep

HARRIS, FERGUSON TALLY FOR VICTORS

Score in 3d Period After Gray Gives Losers Lead —Vachon Has 32 Saves

By DAVE ANDERSON
Special to The New York Times

ST. LOUIS, May 4—Despite a gallant effort by the St. Louis Blues to obtain a stay of execution, the Montreal Canadiens did today what they usually do at this time of year. They won the Stanley Cup.

With goals by Ted Harris and John Ferguson within a span of 2 minutes and 20 seconds early in the final period, the Canadiens rallied for a 2-1 victory and a four-game sweep of the final playoff round before a noisy, hand-clapping assembly of 16,126 devotees in the arena.

For the Club de Hockey

Canadien, the triumph represented its 16th Stanley Cup conquest in its glorious 52-year history.

Of the other national hockey league teams, only the Toronto Maple Leafs are close to the Canadiens in total number of playoff championships. The Maple Leafs have won 11, while the New York Rangers have won three, the last in 1940.

40th Time in Playoffs

To appreciate how the Canadiens and the Stanley Cup are interlocked, consider that they have won it nine times in the last 14 years, and that they hold the records for most years in the playoffs, 40; most consecutive years, 21, and most times in the championship final, 20.

But for two periods in the 81-degree warmth of the nationally televised matinee finale, the Canadiens were outskated, and more important, outscored by the Blues.

Midway in the second period, Terry Gray, a member of the Canadiens briefly five seasons ago, swooped in to whack a point-blank shot past Rogatien Vachon, the tiny sideburned goal-tender. When the red light flashed the adoring crowd demonstrated its affec-

tion for the Blues. Paper littered the milk-white ice. With the arena's organist, Norm Kramer, booming out the notes, the people sang "When the Blues Come Marching In," but when their crowd's roar subsided, the Blues discovered that affection was not enough to prevent a Canadiens' rally.

Hall's Efforts Fail

For the remainder of that period Glenn Hall, the 37-year-old goal-tender, thwarted several Montreal shots with spectacular saves. But in the opening minute of the third period, Harris drilled a screened 50-foot shot past Hall, then Ferguson flicked in a 10-foot goal.

Suddenly, the Canadiens were in command. Vachon preserved the triumph, making a total of 32 saves.

Vachon, a stand-in for Gump Worsley, was the Montreal goal-tender throughout the final series. He replaced Worsley when the former Ranger incurred a broken small finger on his left hand during the East Division final with Boston and played the last three games of that series.

In eliminating the Rangers in four games, the Bruins in six, and the Blues in four, the Canadiens won the silver mug for

the second consecutive season. But it took them 14 games, compared to 13 a year ago. As a reward, they will split $204,750 in bonus money as world champions.

MONTREAL		ST. LOUIS
Vachon	Goal	Hall
Savard	Defense	Arbour
Laperriere	Defense	B. Plager
Beliveau	Center	Berenson
Cournoyer	Wing	Sabourin
Duff	Wing	McCreary
Richard	Forward	Schock
Redmond	Forward	Gray
Lemaire	Forward	Keenan
Backstrom	Forward	Ecclestone
Rousseau	Forward	Cameron
Ferguson	Forward	McDonald
Bordeleau	Forward	Crisp
Grenier	Forward	St. Marseille
Harris	Defense	W. Plager
Tremblay	Defense	Roberts
Harper	Defense	Talbot
Hillman	Defense	Picard
Esposito	Goal	Plante

First Period

No scoring

Second Period

1- St. Louis, Gray (St. Marseille, Crisp) 10:50

Third Period

2- Montreal, Harris (J. C. Tremblay, Duff) 0:43
3- Montreal, Ferguson (Backstrom) 3:03
Montreal Canadiens .... 0 0 2—2
St. Louis Blues .... 0 1 0—1
PENALTIES—First period: Savard (0:25), Talbot (4:40), Ferguson (6:42), Ferguson (9:07), Sabourin (14:03), LeMaire (14:03), St. Marseille (16:14), Savard (19:34), McDonald (19:34). Second period: Roberts (3:36), Berenson (14:37), J. C. Tremblay (14:37), LeMaire (14:45), W. Plager (14:45), Ecclestone (16:06), Savard (16:06), McDonald (19:59), Laperriere (19:59). Third period: Arbour (5:25).
SHOTS ON GOAL—Montreal: 8, 14, 9—31; St. Louis: 13, 12, 8—33.
Referee—Buffey. Linesmen—Pavelitch and Der.
Attendance—16,176.

May 5, 1969

Green of Bruins Is Sidelined Indefinitely by Skull Fracture From Stick Fight

STAR DOING WELL AFTER OPERATION

Defenseman, Hurt in Battle With Wayne Maki, Given Hope of Full Recovery

OTTAWA, Sept. 22 (UPI)— Ted Green, the aggressive defenseman of the Boston Bruins, who suffered a fractured skull in a stick fight, may be able to return to action before the end of the season, doctors said today. He has a "reasonable chance" of avoiding permanent damage.

Dr. Ashby Moncur of Massa-

chusetts General Hospital in Boston reported that Green had suffered brain damage during a stick-swinging melee last night with Wayne Maki of the St. Louis Blues. Green was experiencing a weakness of the grip in his left hand and a muscular weakness on the left side of his face.

Following the injury, which occurred in the first period of an exhibition game won by St. Louis, 5-1, a team of doctors inserted a permanent plate in Green's skull. He was listed in satisfactory condition.

Green's Life Not in Danger

Green suffered "a compound comminuted, depressed skull fracture with a dural laceration and a brain laceration," Moncur, the Bruin team physician, said. "The dura is the thick covering on the brain. Bony fragments went through this thick covering and

into part of the brain itself."

Moncur said the 29-year-old defenseman was "as good as could be expected." His life is not in danger.

"There is a reasonable chance that he will be as good as ever, a possibility that he could play the last month or two of the season with a helmet."

Green will be hospitalized for two weeks.

In his reaction to the incident, Scotty Morrison, the referee-in-chief of the National Hockey League, said that he would instruct officials to "rule with an iron hand" to prevent stick-swinging fights. He said any player who swings at another player—even from a distance—would be evicted immediately, fined and forbidden to play pending a review by Clarence Campbell, the league president.

Campbell said that he was

awaiting a report from Referee Ken Bodendistel before taking any action. Green and Maki were given match misconduct penalties at the time of the fight that call for automatic fines of $100. There is also an automatic fine of $200 for stick-swinging.

The trouble last night started, it was reported, when Maki appeared to spear Green in the stomach. Green responded by hitting Maki on the head with his stick and Maki retaliated with a full swing at Green's head.

The rugged defenseman dropped to the ice, and after examination in the dressing room, was taken to the hospital. The operation was performed by a team of surgeons, led by Dr. Michel Richard, a neurosurgeon.

The incident was the second involving the Bruins over the weekend. Saturday night in

Ranger goalie Ed Giacomin awaits Boston defenseman Bobby Orr's shot in a 1969 game. Orr's career was tragically cut short by a knee injury. He was certainly the best defenseman in the history of the game and possibly the greatest all-around player.

Phil Esposito, then with the Boston Bruins, whoops it up after scoring his 450th career goal in 1974.

Montreal, Dick Duff of the Canadiens and Jim Harrison of the Bruins tangled. In both games players left the benches to join in the scuffling. Campbell said that all members of the teams—with the exception of those on the ice at the time—would be fined $50 each for jumping to the ice. Green was to get a $75 fine for arguing a minor penalty on Saturday night.

September 23, 1969

Hockey Brawl Draws $5,775 Total in Fines

MONTREAL, Nov. 27 (AP)—Clarence Campbell, National Hockey League president, suspended John Ferguson, Montreal Canadiens left wing, for six games tonight and handed out $5,775 in fines to two clubs and their players.

The action was the result of a stick-swinging battle between Ferguson and Gary

Sabourin of the St. Louis Blues at St. Louis Nov. 15, which was followed by a general melee.

The St. Louis club was fined $2,000 and Montreal $1,000 for failing to stop their players from joining in the fight Ferguson was fined $325 and 11 players from each club were fined a total of $2,540.

November 28, 1969

National Hockey League Takes in Vancouver and Buffalo

EXPANSION ADDS 13TH, 14TH CLUBS

Both Will Begin Play Next Season if Conditions Are Met—$6-Million Entry

By AL HARVIN

To show how inflation has set in since the National Hockey League doubled its size from six to 12 teams at the start of the 1967-68 season, the league awarded conditional franchises to Vancouver and Buffalo yesterday for $6-million each, three times the former entry fee.

The Vancouver franchise went to Medicor, a Minneapolis-based company whose principal stockholder is its president, Tom Scallen, a lawyer.

The Niagara Frontier Hockey Corporation, a group headed by Seymour and Northrup Knox, Buffalo bankers and Woolworth heirs, received the Buffalo franchise.

Each will be allowed to select 18 players and two goalies from the existing clubs and begin play next season.

Placed in East Division

Both will join the East Division with New York, Boston, Montreal, Detroit and Toronto. The Chicago Black Hawks, now in the East, will move to the West.

"The reason for that is that we wanted the three Canadian teams to play in the same division, and we thought geograph-

ically Chicago was the farthest west of the other teams," said Clarence Campbell, the league president, who made the announcement of the new franchises at the Hotel Warwick here.

As to the Vancouver conditions, Medicor must execute a lease with the Pacific Coliseum that is acceptable to the league. That arena is owned by Pacific National Exhibition. The condition for the Buffalo franchise also involves a satisfactory lease with the city, which owns War Memorial Auditorium, and increasing its capacity to 15,000.

All conditions must be met by Dec. 20.

Must Give Up Interest

In addition, the Knox brothers must divest themselves of their 20 per cent interest in the Oakland Seals, which they

had obtained in hopes of moving that team to Buffalo. The league squashed that move.

The agreement calls for each new team to pay 25 per cent or $1.5-million down and the remainder in five equal payments of $900,000 for five years.

However, Vancouver will get in at a slight discount because the money is payable in the currency of the country involved. According to the latest rate of exchange, the Canadian dollar is worth 92.5 cents, which means a saving of 7.5 per cent or $450,000 in American money.

The selection of Vancouver was in reaction to a protest from Canadian interests that no Canadian cities had been added in the last expansion.

December 3, 1969

Bruins Beat Blues in Overtime, 4-3, and Gain First Stanley Cup Since 1941

ORR'S GOAL WINS FINAL SERIES, 4-0

By GERALD ESKENAZI
Special to The New York Times

BOSTON, May 10 — Although unable to leap over buildings with a single bound, Bobby Orr flew through the air in overtime today, rapped home Derek Sanderson's pass and gave the Bruins their first Stanley Cup since 1941.

The symbolism was perfect.

The goal was scored by the young man who made the Bruins the offensive threat that they are, and the pass came from the pug-nosed scrapper who helped to make them one of the National Hockey League's most ferocious teams.

Orr's goal, after 40 seconds of the sudden-death period, lifted the Bostonians to a 4-3 victory over the St. Louis Blues and completed a sweep of the four-of-seven game series. It was eight months ago today that the training season started for Boston and now their fans can return to outdoor sports.

The obligatory champagne splattered over the dressing-

room walls. The players tapped one another over the head with the three-foot high Stanley Cup, and they chug-a-lugged champagne from the chalice.

Coach Harry Sinden got into a squirting match with John McKenzie and Ted Green, a tough defenseman who missed the whole season because of an injury in a fight, took off his street clothes, put on an undershirt, and ran around the dressing room getting doused.

The Bruins began their new era in 1967—for seven of the previous eight years they had finished last. Then Milt Schmidt, the general manager, told the scouts looking for promising

players: "If they can fit through the door, I don't want them."

In winning, the Bruins again demonstrated the East Division's stranglehold as the superior division. Since expansion, the West Division has never won a Stanley Cup game against the East. The Blues have been the expansion division's sole representative—and they have dropped 12 straight in the final round.

Rick Smith Scores First

Scoring in today's game, the only close one of this series, started with Rick Smith of the Bruins getting a rising shot past Glenn Hall, underneath a.

Orr's Goal in Sudden-Death Overtime Brings the Bacon to Beantown

Bobby Orr raises his stick after he scored on Glenn Hall, Blues' goalie. Derek Sanderson received an assist on play.

sing that read, "Happy Mother's Day Mrs. Orr."

This was for Bobby's mother who had come from their home in Canada.

Red Berenson tied the score late in the opening period. Gary Sabourin of St. Louis and Phil Esposito traded goals in the second session. Esposito's was his 13th, breaking the play off series record set by Maurice Richard of Montreal in 1944 (in nine games) and tied by Jean Béliveau of the Canadiens in 1956 (in 10 games). This was Esposito's 14th playoff game.

The pressure was on the Bruins in the waning minutes of the third period, after Larry Keenan gave the Bules a 3-2 edge in the first minute. The Bostonians wanted to win it at home, before 14,835 fans and a national television audience. It was John Bucyk, who has been with the Brunins since 1957, longer than any of his team-mates, who forced the game into overtime with a tip-in at 13:28.

As soon as Orr took Sanderson's pass, in the overtime period he was rapped by Keenan and went sailing. But he knocked the disk past Glenn Hall. Then a crepe paper shower strated, and because of the heat the colors ran, tinting the ice orange, yellow and blue. Children dashed past unconcerned special police and mobbed the Bruins. The fans

remained standing and cheering. Then the cup was wheeled out.

BOSTON (4)		ST. LOUIS (3)
Cheevers	Goal	Hall
Orr	Defense	R. Plager
Awrey	Defense	Picard
Sanderson	Center	Berenson
Carleton	Wing	McCreary
WestHall	Wing	Roberts
Esposito	Forward	St. Marseille
Hodge	Forward	Goyette
Bucyk	Forward	Sabourin
Cashman	Forward	Crisp
Stanfield	Forward	Ecclestone
McKenzie	Forward	Keenan
Lorentz	Forward	McDonald
Marcotte	Forward	Boudrias
	Forward	Gray
R. Smith	Defense	Fortin
D. Smith	Defense	Talbot
Speer	Defense	W. Plager
Doak	Defense	
Johnston	Goal	Wakely

Boston Bruins . . . . 1 1 1 1—4
St. Louis Blues . . . . 1 1 1 0—3

First Period
1—Boston, R. Smith (1) (Sanderson) . . . 5:28
2—St. Louis, Berenson (7) (Ecclestone, R. Plager) . . . 19:17
Second Period
3—St. Louis, Sabourin (5) (St. Marseille) 3:22
4—Boston, Esposito (13) (Hodge) . . . 14:22
Third Period
5—St. Louis, Keenan (7) (Goyette, Roberts) . . . 0:19
6—Boston, Bucyk (1) (McKenzie, R. Smith) . . . 13:28
Overtime
7—Boston, Orr (9) (Sanderson) . . . 0:40
PENALTIES—First period: Sanderson (0:40), Fortin (4:41), Picard (4:41), Ecclestone (4:41), Orr (4:41), McKenzie (4:41), McKenzie 7:13), Picard (8:07), Stanfield (12:58), Awrey (16:04), Boudrias (18:36), Stanfield (18:36). Second period: Sanderson (4:21), Berenson (6:32), McKenzie (11:55), D. Smith (18:52). Third period: Esposito (6:15), Fortin (6:15), R. Plager (8:25). Overtime: None.
SHOTS ON GOAL—Boston: 10, 6, 13, 1—32. St. Louis: 14, 7, 10, 0—31.
Referee—Bruce Hood. Linesmen—Matt Pavelich and Ron Ego.
Attendance—14,835.

May 11, 1970

HULL SCORES TWICE AND PASSES RICHARD

CHICAGO, Feb. 14 (UPI)— Bobby Hull got his 35th and 36th goals of the season and moved into second place among N.H.L. career scorers tonight as the Chicago Black Hawks defeated the Vancouver Canucks, 3-1.

The goals were the 545th and 546th of Hull's career, putting him two ahead of Maurice (Rocket) Richard, retired Montreal great. Gordie Howe of

Detroit is in first place.

Vancouver Canucks . . . . 0 0 1—1
Chicago Black Hawks . . . . 2 0 1—3
FIRST PERIOD—1, Chicago, Pappin (14) (R. Hull, Campbell) 10:16. 2, Chicago, R. Hull (35) (Campbell, Pinder) 15:43. Penalties—Magnuson, Chicago (1:21); Corrigan, Vancouver, (9:03); Tallon, Vancouver, (13:49); Nesternko, Chicago, (16:53); Corrigan, Vancouver, (17:15).
SECOND PERIOD—No scoring. Penalties—D. Hull, Chicago (0:08); Koroll, Chicago (10:05).
THIRD PERIOD—, Vancouver, Taylor (Tallon) 7:35; 4, Chicago, R. Hull (36) (Pappin, White) 11:40. Penalties—Corrigan, Vancouver (1:07); Nesternko, Chicago (15:11).
Shots on Goal—Vancouver: 13, 8, 5—26; Chicago: 11, 9, 14—34.
Goalies—Hodge, Esposito.
Attendance—19,000.

February 15, 1971

Bruins Win as Esposito Sets Mark of 60 Goals

INGLEWOOD, Calif., March 11 (UPI)—Phil Esposito scored two goals and an assist to shatter three records tonight and Bobby Orr added 4 points to set two more marks as the Boston Bruins crushed the Los Angeles Kings, 7-2.

Esposito's goals gave him 60 for the season, two more than Bobby Hull's National Hockey League mark established two seasons ago. The total was also

one more than Jean Béliveau of Montreal scored for a season, including the playoffs, in 1955-56.

The 3 points gave the 29-year-old center 128 points for the season, breaking his own milestone of 126 set in 76 games two seasons ago. Esposito has played in 67 games this season.

Orr assisted three times to surpass by one his mark of 87

183

assists for a season established last year.

The 22-year-old Orr has 122 points for the season, 2 more than the record he established in 1969-70 for a defenseman. Orr also contributed a second-period goal to increase his record goal production by a defenseman to 35.

The assault on the record book enabled Boston to register its 50th victory and increase its point total to 107, already a league standard. The seven goals brought Boston's total to 339, another mark.

Los Angeles enjoyed a brief lead, scoring first on Bob Pulford's rebound shot just over three minutes into the contest.

But Esposito broke Hull's goal record four minutes later

FIRST PERIOD — 1, Los Angeles, Pulford (15) (Byers, Lonsberry) 3.04. 2 Boston, Esposito (59) (Green, Hodge) 7:03. 3. Boston, Bucyk (46) (Orr, Esposito) 19:48. Penalties—Awrey, Boston, (13:51) Marotte, Los Angeles (18:17).
SECOND PERIOD—4, Boston, Carleton (13) (Orr, Walton) 12:04; 5, Boston, Esposito (60) (D. Smith, Hodge) 15:40; 6, Boston, Westfall (23) (Carleton) 16:24; 7, Boston, Orr (35) (McKenzie, Stanfield) 17:49. Penalties—Orr, Boston (0:19); R. Smith,

Boston, (4:28); Lonsberry, Los Angeles (5:16).
THIRD PERIOD—8, Boston, Bucyk (47) (McKenzie, Orr) 6:11; 9, Los Angeles, Backstrom (9) (Hoganson, Cahan) 10:09. Penalties—Howell, Los Angeles, (6.05); Lemieux, Los Angeles (10:39); Awrey, Boston (16:40).
Shots on goal—Boston: 20, 15, 7—42. Los Angeles: 12, 12, 14—28.
Boston Bruins 2   4   1—7
Los Angeles Kings 1   0   1—2
Goalies—Johnston, Delordy and Norris.
Attendance—14,316.

March 12, 1971

Canadiens Win Stanley Cup, Beating Hawks, 3-2

Richard Notches Tying, Winning Goals in Rally

By DAVE ANDERSON
Special to The New York Times

CHICAGO, May 18 — With spectacular goaltending by a rookie, Ken Dryden, and two dramatic goals by a gray-haired star, Henri Richard, the Montreal Canadiens won the Stanley Cup tonight with a 3-2 victory over the Chicago Black Hawks.

In the seventh and last game

of the championship playoff, Dryden, who had never played a National Hockey League game until two months ago, held the fort with 31 saves while Richard supplied the tying and winning goals after the Black Hawks had taken a 2-0 lead midway in the second period.

The winning goal by the 35-year-old Richard, younger brother of the legendary Maurice, early in the final period completed his scenario. He had criticized Al MacNeil, the Canadiens' coach, as "incompetent" following a 2-0 loss here last Thursday in the fifth game. But tonight they embraced during the Canadiens' celebration on the ice.

Cast as Underdogs

"Let's forget about what I said," Richard told reporters. "This was the biggest goal of my life and of the 10 Stanley Cup winners I've been on, this is the best because we were the underdogs."

MacNeil, a 35-year-old rookie coach who replaced Claude Ruel on Dec. 3, also minimized Richard's criticism.

"I'm really happy for Henri," said MacNeil, his beige suit splashed with champaign in the dressing room. "He's a pro and I am, too."

Dryden was selected for the Conn Smythe Trophy as the most valuable player of the entire playoff. He also won a

Dodge Charger awarded by Sport Magazine to the outstanding performer in the title series.

"It's the greatest thrill of my life," said the 23-year-old McGill University Law student who had been an all-America performer on Cornell's hockey team. "But it's difficult to articulate something like this."

Suffered Broken Bone

Another drama involved Jacques Laperriere, the tall defenseman. He disclosed that he had played with a broken bone in his left forearm since the second game of the final series.

It was the Canadiens' 16th Stanley Cup since the formation of the N.H.L. in 1917 and

United Press International

Keith Magnuson, right, of Chicago and Jacques Lemaire of the Canadiens, left foreground, being held off by officials during an argument near the end of the first period of the final Stanley Cup game in Chicago last night.

their 11th in the last 19 years. It was the 31st time that a team representing Montreal had won the cup since it was donated by Frederick Arthur, Lord Stanley of Preston, in 1893. Each member of the winning team received $7,500 against $6,000 for each losing player.

The return of the Canadiens to hockey supremacy followed their failur to qualify for the playoffs a year ago for the first time in 20 years. They were placed fifth in the East Division when the New York Rangers were awarded fourth on two more goals scored.

For the first time in the final series the visiting team won. However, the Canadiens, who finished third in their division during the regular season, completed their previous playoff triumphs on the road—in the seventh game of the opening series at Boston and the sixth of their semifinal at Minnesota.

In his 20th playoff game, after only six regular-season games, the 6-foot-4-inch Dryden kept the Canadiens alive with at least eight spectacular saves in the first period alone. He was like a giant spider.

But it was the Hawks who produced the first goal late in the period during a power play. Bobby Hull's slap shot from the blue line sent Dryden, protecting against a deflection, to the ice. Rebounding off the boards, the puck came to Dennis Hull, who drilled it in off the scrambling Dryden.

During the second period small patches of fog hung above the ice in the corners not far from Dryden as a result of humidity generated by the sellout crowd of 21,000 and the 80-degree heat in Chicago Stadium. The Candadiens put pressure on Tony Esposito, the Hawk goalie, who had 223 saves, but a sudden goal by Danny O'Shea gave the Hawks a 2-0 lead.

With their pride and tradition at stake, the Canadiens attacked in desperation. Jacques Lemaire's shot from the blue line got past Esposito for a score with about six-minutes remaining in the period. Four minutes later, Lemaire whipped a pass into the goal mouth and Richard swatted the disk by Esposito for the tying goal.

Early in the final period Richard swooped in front of Esposito and lifted a 15-footer into the net for the winning goal.

Dryden preserved the lead with remarkable poise for a rookie. When the siren sounded ending the game, the puck was in his glove. He held it high as if it were a torch of triumph.

For the Canadiens, the Stanley Cup is a traditional spring rite. This time an Ivy Leaguer had led them.

MONTREAL (3)   CHICAGO (2)
Dryden.......... Goal ...... Esposito
Laperriere...... Defense ....White
Lapointe........ Defense ....Stapleton
Beliveau........ Center ....Mikita

Cournoyer......	Wing	...........Koroll
F. Mahovlich...	Wing	..........D. Hull
P. Mahovlich...	Forward	.........Martin
Houle..........	Forward	.........Pappin
Ferguson.......	Forward	.........B. Hull
Lemaire........	Forward	...........Maki
Richard........	Forward	......Nesterenko
Tardif.........	Forward	.........Pinder
Roberto........	Forward	........Angotti
Roohefort......	Forward	.........O'Shea
Larose.........	Forward	........Jarrett
Harper.........	Defense	........Jarrett
Tremblay.......	Defense	......Magnuson
Bouchard.......	Defense	.........Foley
Murdoch........	Defense	.........Shmyr
....	Defense	.........Korab
Vachon.........	Goal	..........Brown

First Period

1—Chicago, D.Hull (7) (B.Hull, Koroll) 19:12.

Second Period

2—Chicago, O'Shea (2) (Martin) 7:33
3—Montreal, Lemaire (9) (Laperriere)..14:16

4—Montreal, Richard (4) (Lemaire)....18:20

Third Period

5—Montreal, Richard (5) (Houle, Lapointe) 2:34.

Montreal Canadiens 0   2   1—3
Chicago Black Hawks..... 1   1   0—2
PENALTIES — First Period Harper (1:22), Lemaire (4:09), Magnuson (4:09), D. Hull (17:35). Second Period Magnuson (1:49), P. Mahovlich (3:20), Nesterenko (3:20), Chicago bench (too many men on ince, served by Angotti, (4:14), Magnuson (12:32), Tremblay (13:07), Jarrett (17:54), Ferguson (18:11). Third period: Harper (5:32), P. Mahovlich (7:37),
SHOTS ON GOAL — Montreal 6, 9, 10—25. Chicago: 12, 9, 12—33.
Referee—Ashley. Linesmen—Pavelich and D'Amico.
Attendance—21,000.

May 19, 1971

Hockey League Formed In Rivalry With N.H.L.

By GERALD ESKENAZI

The prospect of a major rival to the National Hockey League, which has not been seriously threatened since it was formed in 1917, has arisen with the formation of the World Hockey Association.

The president of the association is Gary Davidson, who was the first commissioner of the American Basketball Association. The A.B.A., formed as a rival to the established National Basketball Association in 1967, succeeded in forcing the N.B.A. to agree to a merger, which has not yet been completed.

Davidson, a lawyer, said yesterday from his office in Santa Ana, Calif., that his league planned to begin operating next year, with groups from 14 cities having agreed to back franchises.

He indicated that a bidding war for players was likely.

Will Meet With Shea

He said he had backers in Los Angeles and San Francisco, which are N.H.L. territories. Later this week, in a significant move by the three-month-old league, its representative will meet with William A. Shea to discuss a franchise for the new Nassau Coliseum in Hempstead, L.I.

Shea is the lawyer who brought the Mets to New York by threatening to start a rival baseball league. Shea Stadium was named in his honor. He was retained by the Coliseum to bring major league basketball and hockey to the arena, which is expected to open within six months.

Shea would like to get an N.H.L. franchise for the Coliseum. He has said that New York could support two hockey teams easily. The Rangers are entrenched in Madison Square Garden.

Last night Shea commented: "Sure, I'll meet with this new league. I don't have to be smart to know that the key to any

league is the Coliseum."

William Jennings, president of the Rangers, has said that he would want an indemnification fee of more than $5-million to allow a team into Ranger territory. That would be in addition to the probable $6-million or $7-million a new team would have to pay the N.H.L.

Neither Jennings nor any N.H.L. official was available for comment last night.

Davidson conceded that Shea "probably was using leverage against the N.H.L. by talking to us." But he added:

"Any investor who pays the kind of money the Rangers and the National Hockey League are asking would have to be crazy. It would be impossible to survive the debt. Any potential hockey owner is better off coming into our league. The cost to enter is nominal."

He would not disclose how much it had cost to form the league or what a franchise would cost.

Associated with Davidson in the new league were Michael O'Hara of Los Angeles and Dennis Murphy, a Floridian. O'Hara is a former vice president of Art Linkletter Enterprises, and was the first general manager of the Texas Chaparrals when that team entered the A.B.A. Murphy was general manager of the A.B.A. Floridians.

O'Hara has been in New York the last few days attempting to find backers for a hockey team in the Coliseum. He is the one who will meet with Shea.

Virtually all the players in the N.H.L. are Canadian. In recent years most have been chosen from the annual amateur draft. The amateurs are under the aegis of the Canadian Amateur Hockey Association,

which receives more than $1-million a year from the N.H.L.

Davidson did not believe it would be difficult to get players from the amateur ranks. The bidding war he hinted would be the kind that forced the pro football merger and the pending basketball merger.

"We've talked to the amateur association," he said. "That draft is not a locked-in draft—the N.H.L. still has to sign the players."

Was he thinking about a merger with the N.H.L.?

"No," he said. "They haven't been flexible in the past. A number of years will go by before we have cooperation."

The new league has granted franchises to Milwaukee, Baltimore, Long Beach, Calif., and Honolulu.

September 14, 1971

NEW HOCKEY LOOP PICKS CLUB SITES

Shayne Is Given New York Franchise—10 Others Are Awarded for '72 Play

By GERALD ESKENAZI

The World Hockey Association, a fledgling group that is going to attempt to compete with the National Hockey League, awarded 11 franchises to major North American cities last night and declared its intention to begin play Oct. 1, 1972.

At a meeting in Los Angeles, the association granted its prestigious New York franchise to Neal Shayne, a lawyer from Woodmere, L. I., who said he was "a dynamite roller hockey player as a kid."

Fourteen groups made bids for franchises. Each group that has been accepted will have to post a $100,000 bond and show a bank account with a minimum of $2-million.

Pat Brown Heads Group

Perhaps the most famous new owner is Pat Brown, the former Governor of California, who is the chairman of the Los Angeles entrant's organization.

The other cities given franchises are: Miami, Dayton, Ohio; Chicago, Milwaukee, St. Paul, San Francisco, Winnipeg, Manitoba; Calgary, Alberta, and Edmonton, Alberta. One other franchise will be awarded—either to a group from the

185

Washington-Baltimore area or from Atlanta. There is a possibility that Carolina, Albuquerque, N. M., or Indiana also will receive franchises.

The association will hold its next meeting in New York in early November, when it will disclose its plans to acquire players. The league probably will attempt to spirit some players away from the N. H. L., but most likely will get most of them from the minor leagues and the United States college ranks.

League officials have spoken of the hockey boom that would take place on the collegiate level in this country if the graduating athletes knew they could get jobs on professional teams. Virtually all the players in the N. H. L. are Canadians.

The N.H.L.'s president, Clarence Campbell, said the other day that he was "delighted to know hockey has so much appeal." But Campbell added that if the W.H.A. attempted a player raid, "We will man the ramparts."

The N.H.L. had not planned to expand further before the 1974-75 season. However, it is virtually certain that the league will be forced to take in at least two clubs before 1974. The most likely sites would be Long Island, where a new Coliseum is being built in Hempstead, and Atlanta—both prime markets.

Shayne said, "We'd like to play in the Coliseum—and I think we should. If the Rangers allow an N.H.L. club to come into the Coliseum, they'll want an indemnity. But the Coliseum would be in competition with Madison Square Garden, which owns the Rangers. That's not a good situation. The Rangers are asking $5-million indemnity. If they reduce it to keep us out, then I think we've got an anti-trust action."

September 25, 1971

N.H.L. Fund Earnings Dip as Brawl Market Declines

By GERALD ESKENAZI

The frenetic, often violent, world of hockey has been in a state of virtual tranquility this season following stiffer rules and public outcries against its brutality.

With the first third of the National Hockey League campaign just ended, the Players' Emergency Fund — stocked from fines levied against fighters—is down considerably. It collected only $6,500 this season—compared with $20,000 at the same stage last year.

It had been accepted as unsubstantiated truth that most fans like to see a brawl in hockey. While Clarence Campbell, the league's president, has admitted that fights between two players are a "good safety valve," he deplored the mass exodus of players from the bench over the last few years.

Most major fights in hockey start after teammates pile in to rescue one of their own. However, this season two new rules have been put into effect: The third man into a fight automatically is ejected. And the first player to leave the bench to join a fight also is automatically ejected. In the event of a bench-clearing situation, the team suffers a double two-minute penalty.

As a result, major penalties have gone down about 30 per cent—from 185 last season, to 134 this campaign.

Meanwhile, game misconducts (ejections) have more than doubled—from seven last year to 15 this season. Eleven of this year's ejections were kicked out under the new rules.

In the first two months of play, only one bench emptied —that occurred in Pittsburgh's first home game. But fans have noticed the substantial decline of group hitting.

"We hear very little from the public this season about the violence, so that must be a good sign," said Brian F. O'Neill, the league's executive director. "Of course, we've got to realize the first half of the year isn't nearly so rough as the second half, when clubs are battling for position."

O'Neill pointed out that the number of high-sticking and cross - checking infractions has lowered considerably, "probably tying in with the players' general attitude toward fighting."

"There seems a conscious effort of the players to keep others out of a fight," said O'Neill. "And there also appears to be less incidence of players antagonizing one another—they know that now they can't be rescued."

That's fine as far as the linesmen are concerned. The linesmen are the generally faceless officials whose major job is calling offsides' infractions. But linesmen also are critically important to peace and order on the ice.

The referee-in-chief, Scotty Morrison, runs a preseason camp for linesmen—and referees — in which, among other duties, they're taught how to handle brawls.

"We give the linesmen a little hand wrestling on the ice," said Morrison. "One guy squares off against the other. And then we also simulate fighting, one official wrestling with another. Then two linesmen practice breaking it up."

The reason referees rarely get involved as peacemakers is quite simple: They have to watch the action to determine who gets penalized.

"We tell our linesmen that they should never go into a fight alone. And you never grab just one guy, especially from behind. This leaves the player's opponent free to pummel him."

To prepare for the long season, the linesmen attend camp for a week. Every day before breakfast they run half a mile, then do calisthenics, then run

RESTRAINED: Bruins' Derek Sanderson held by Ken Hodge from Bob McLaren (20) and Matt Pavelich Wednesday in Los Angeles. Sanderson was penalized for tripping and berating official and ejected for leaping out of penalty box.

another half mile. After lunch they work on the ice for 2½ hours.

Linesmen are instructed that if two players are fighting to let them go at it for a few seconds. Generally, the players then are looking for someone to break it up.

"We say something soothing to them," said Morrison. "Something like, 'O.K., you've had your fun.'"

December 12, 1971

Bruins Trounce Rangers, 3-0, And Capture Cup in 6 Games

By GERALD ESKENAZI

It was over suddenly for the Rangers last night, quick and clean, as the Boston Bruins captured the Stanley Cup with a 3-0 victory before a Madison Square Garden crowd that gave the New Yorkers a final 50-second standing ovation for the try that failed.

In capturing the National Hockey League's most prized trophy—and $15,000 a man—the Bruins took the four-of-seven-game series by 4-2 for their second championship in three years.

There was a difference between the clubs, and it's spelled Orr. The remarkable defenseman was not at his best. His surgical left knee still bothered him and often he was content to let someone else bring the puck up over the soft ice.

Still, Orr blasted home a first-period score, rapped a liner that was deflected home for goal 2 in the final session, and did what he had to do to preserve the victory.

As a result, Orr won the Conn Smythe Trophy as the playoffs' top performer (worth $1,500) and took home a Dodge Charger donated by Sport Magazine as the top player in the final series.

Wayne Cashman got two third-session goals, both times aided by Phil Esposito, his center, who failed to get a goal in the six Ranger games. But the man he was pitted against often, Walt Tkaczuk, only got one.

The Rangers, of course, skated with Jean Ratelle, their leading scorer, at less than full efficiency, and without Jim Neilson, a key defenseman.

"We never alibied," said Coach Emile Francis, "because we knew the other guys would have to come along to pick up the slack. And that's what they did."

The Bruins never expected the series to go this far. They had sailed through the regular season the easy winner of the East Division. They lost only one game in their first two playoff series. They had trounced the Rangers in the

last five regular-season meetings between the clubs.

Bruins at Their Best

And last night they did what they do better than anyone else—hit and take advantage of the breaks.

On their first goal, Orr nearly lost the puck to a pressing Bruce MacGregor. Instead, Orr pirouetted away, zeroed in on Gilles Villemure, and slid the disk past a tangle of players and the goalie.

On Cashman's first goal in the final period, Francis had unsuccessfully attempted to replace Tkaczuk with Pete Stemkowski for a face-off against Esposito. But Referee Art Skov ruled Stemkowski off since the puck was ready to be dropped. Esposito won the face-off, and dropped it perfectly behind him to Orr, who fired. On the first two goals, the Bruins had a man advantage.

Throughout the long, quick, bruising game the Rangers had their chances in front. Shots

The New York Times/Donal F. Holway

VICTORY IN SIGHT: Bruins rushing to Wayne Cashman, right, after he scored second goal in third period. From left: Phil Esposito, Bobby Orr, Dallas Smith, Ken Hodge.

sailed wide or thudded into Gerry Cheever's pads. The Bruins' goalie who had yielded 10 goals to the New Yorkers in his two other appearances this final series received help from his teammates, who swarmed around the man with the puck just when it appeared a Ranger would get off a good shot.

Most of the fans in the crowd of 17,250 applauded the Bruins when the Cup was carried out by Lefty Reid, the custodian of the Hockey Hall of Fame in Toronto. But John Bucyk, the Bruins' captain, didn't take the Cup on its customary victory lap. He skated only a few feet with the 3-foot trophy.

"I was afraid I'd get hit in the head," he explained later.

The millions of fans who saw the game over national television were seeing two teams who used to share the cellar until the late 1960's. Last night, they saw the sport's two best

teams, who talk openly of their dislike for each other but also of their respect.

"I guess Orr was the difference," said Esposito. "That and the hitting. The two games we lost we didn't hit."

RANGERS (0)		BOSTON (3)
Villemure	......Goal......	Cheevers
Park	...Defense...	Orr
Doak	...Defense...	Smith
Tkaczuk	...Center...	Esposito
Fairbairn	...Wing...	Hodge
Stemkowski	...Wing...	Cashman
Sather	...Forward...	Bucyk
Gilbert	...Forward...	Walton
Goyette	...Forward...	Bailey
Hadfield	...Forward...	Sanderson
MacGregor	...Forward...	Stanfield
Ratelle	...Forward...	Westfall
Carr	...Forward...	McKenzie
Rousseau	...Forward...	Marcotte
Irvine	...Forward...	Roberts
Rolfe	...Defense...	Green
Dorey	...Defense...	Vadnais
Seiling	...Defense...	Awrey
Giacomin	...Goal...	Johnston
Boston Bruins		1 0 1—3
New York Rangers		0 0 0—0

First Period
1—Boston, Orr (5) (Hodge, Bucyk)....11:18
Second Period
No scoring.
Third Period
2—Boston, Cashman (3) (Orr, Esposito) 5:10
3—Boston, Cashman (4) (Hodge, Esposito)................18:11
Attendance—17,250.

PENALTIES — First Period: McKenzie (2:32), Hodge (7:07), Tkaczpk (10:25), Hodge (minor, major) (13:06), Hadfield (minor, major (13:06), Cashman (14:46), Orr (10-minute misconduct) (14:46), Doak (14:46). Second Period: Vadnais (3:45), Hadfield

(3:45), Sanderson (minor, major) (4:33), Gilbert (major) (4:33), Marcotte (4:33), Carr (9:16), Cashman (12:0.), Doak (12:05), Cashman (major) (16:01) Tkaczuk (major) (16:01), Third Period: Rolfe (3:20), Smith (10:36).

SHOT ON GOAL—Rangers (9, 11, 13—30): Stemkowski 5, Park 3, Selling 3, Gilbert 3, Hadfield 3, Tkaczuk 3, Rousseau 3, Rolfe 2, Fairbairn 2, MacGregor 2, Daok, Ratelle, Carr, Irvine. Boston (8, 9, 10—27): Esposito, 6, Orr 3, Walton 3, Smith 2, Awrey 2, Hodge 2, Cashman 2, Sanderson 2, Westfall 2, Vadnais, Bailey, McKenzie.

Referee—Art Skov. Linsmen—Natt Pavelich and Neil Armstrong.

May 12, 1972

Bobby Hull Shifts Hockey Leagues for $2.5-Million

Associated Press

Bobby Hull and son leave car that took them from airport to St. Paul office for signing

By GERALD ESKENAZI

In a deal of such magnitude that it had to be consummated in two countries, Bobby Hull jumped from the National Hockey League to the World Hockey Association yesterday for a package worth at least $2.5-million.

Hull, a left wing for the Chicago Black Hawks, with more goals than any other active player in the N.H.L., first received a check from the W.H.A. in St. Paul for $1-million as his bonus. Then he took off in a chartered plane for Winnipeg, Manitoba, where, on Portage and Main Streets, he signed a 10-year contract to play and coach the Winnipeg Jets.

Hull will receive $200,000

a year for five years as the club's player-coach. If he retires as a player after that time, he'll receive $100,000 for five additional years as either a coach or front-office official. However, if he plays in any of those next five years, he will receive $100,000 extra for each season.

The 33-year-old blond, known as the Golden Jet, becomes the first superstar to leave the established N.H.L., where he was perhaps its most dramatic player, to join the recently organized W.H.A. The money in his new contract is believed to be far greater than any similar deal offered to basketball or football players to change leagues and also makes Hull one of the

highest salaried athletes in the sports world.

Hull presumably received his $1-million bonus in the United States because of a highly favorable tax break. Under a new income tax provision for 1972, the maximum tax on earned income for an individual in the United States is 50 per cent. In Canada, it is between 80 to 90 per cent. Thus Hull stands to keep at least $500,000, and possibly more, depending on whether he has losses in other businesses.

An Immediate Problem

His signing presented an immediate problem for the N.H.L. —to sue or not to sue. Hull's contract with the Hawks contains the controversial reserve clause, which, in effect, gives the club a lifetime option on his services.

The Hawks' general manager, Tommy Ivan, said from Chicago after the signing, "We've made our decision on what we want to do about Bobby. We've turned the matter over to the N.H.L.'s legal committee, which will meet on the matter on Thursday. This whole thing involves other clubs."

The legal committee was recently empowered to investigate court action against any players that might jump from the N.H.L. To date, it hasn't taken any. Ivan, however, indicated that he would like it to.

Printed on Cardboard

Hull's million-dollar outsize check, printed on cardboard, came from the W.H.A.'s "properties" division, which will seek to get endorsements for W.H.A.-related products. In a sense, the million dollars is an advance against any royalties Hull would receive.

His bonus was collected from the 12 member clubs of the W.H.A., which considered his presence essential to give the league a flying start. Until Bobby Orr of the Boston Bruins came along to share the spotlight, Hull was hockey's most dynamic star, a remarkably muscled athlete whose booming slapshot sped goalward at 108 miles an hour, or 50 feet in less than half a second.

Over the years he has been the sport's biggest drawing card as he became the first man to hit the 50-goal plateau more than once. His 604 career goals over 15 seasons include five campaigns of 50 or more goals. Only Gordie Howe of Detroit, who played 25 seasons and scored 786 goals, surpasses him in career production.

The man who convinced Hull to leave his $150,000 salary at Chicago was Ben Hatskin of Winnipeg, a 54-year-old hockey buff who made his money in the corrugated-box business.

Hatskin is the president of the Winnipeg Jets. Like most of the owners in the new league, he was unable to afford an N.H.L. franchise, which costs $6-million. So far, his start-up costs for the Jets have been about a quarter-of-a-million dollars, not counting salaries.

'I Growl and Yell'

Many observers laughed when Hatskin, in what seemed like a publicity move at the time, "drafted" Hull last winter from Chicago.

"I'm mean," said Hatskin yesterday. "I growl and yell. When I have to talk my way through a business deal, I can talk. If I have to push my way through a deal, I push."

If there was much pushing and yelling in the negotiations, Hull stepped aside to permit Harvey Wineberg, a Chicago certified public accountant, to.

bear the brunt of it. Wineberg, acting as Hull's agent, dealt long and hard with Winnipeg and the Hawks. He got the Hawks to increase their offer to $200,000 a year to keep Hull, a figure never received by an N.H.L. player.

Hull, of course, smiled throughout his long day yesterday. He was whisked from the Minneapolis airport to a St. Paul hotel in a Rolls-Royce. His blond hair transplants were in place. After steadily losing his hair several years ago, he underwent the transplants and was rewarded last year with a hair-grooming commercial.

Still smiling, Hull said he didn't believe the Hawks would go to court to prevent him from jumping.

"I think they'll consider this a business transaction," he said. Clarence Campbell, the N.H.L.'s president, was traveling to Washington and was un-

available for comment. Campbell, however, warned the W.H.A. in its infancy that if it raided N.H.L. players, "we will fight them from the ramparts."

June 28, 1972

Canada Beats Soviet Six, Wins Series

Henderson Nets Deciding Goal in 6-5 Game

By THEODORE SHABAD
Special to The New York Times

MOSCOW, Sept. 28 — With 34 seconds to go the Canadian professional ice hockey team scored a dramatic goal tonight and won the deciding game in the series against the Soviet Union, 6-5.

Paul Henderson, a left wing for the Toronto Maple Leafs, slipped the disk into the net for the deciding score of what looked like a virtual tie in the tension-charged eighth game of the series.

The series ended with four victories for Canada, three for the Soviet Union, and one tied game.

Din filled Moscow's Luzhniki Sports Palace at the close of play. About 3,000 boisterous Canadian fans, for whom the series had been a matter of national honor, began to chant off the last few seconds of the game while the Russians battled desperately to even the score.

But time ran out and the triumphant Canadians, waving their red and white Maple Leaf flags, loosed cheers that reverberated through the brightly lighted arena. A capacity crowd of 14,000 was in attendance.

Parise Ruled Off Ice

True to the entire emotion-filled half of the eight-game series played here, tempers flared again tonight. In the first period, Jean-Paul Parise of the Minnesota North Stars was expelled for the rest of the game after he had apparently threatened a West German referee with his stick over a penalty call.

Parise appealed for support to his teammates, and while the Canadians conferred, play was delayed for more than 10 minutes. The incident, combined with frequent arguments over penalties dragged out the first period to 65 minutes.

With the fortunes of the game surging back and forth, there was bound to be tension between the players. Each team scored twice in the opening period, with the Soviet Union going ahead twice. Its first goal was matched by Phil Esposito of the Boston Bruins, and its second by Brad Park of the Rangers.

But in the second period, the Soviet Union scored three times to one Canadian goal, by Bill White of the Chicago Black Hawks. Team Canada thus had to gain control of the play in the final period to draw even.

In the third period, Yevgeny Mishakov, a Russian forward, and Rod Gilbert, a New York Rangers right wing, came to blows. They wrestled on the ice as their teammates clustered around. Each was sent to the penalty box for five minutes.

As excitement mounted in the closing minutes, after Esposito netted his second goal to make the count 5-4, Yvan Cournoyer of the Montreal Canadiens equalized the score. However, the red signal light

behind the Russian cage failed to flash, apparently because of a malfunction.

It appeared, momentarily, that the goal was not being granted and the Canadian players suddenly raced to one side of the rink with sticks raised high. They were going to the aid of Alan Eagleson, their player association head, who had got into an altercation with policemen. The incident soon subsided, however. The goal was allowed with about seven minues left to play.

Tensions engendered by the hotly contested four games here along with the presence of the vocal Canadian fans, who came on charter flights, had raised questions among some Russians whether sports, in fact, did help to bring nations closer together.

"I am for better relations between the United States and the Soviet Union," one Muscovite said the other day, "and I can tell you I am glad that it is a Canadian team and not an American team our players are battling out there on the ice."

Henderson's deciding goal

Gary Bergman, of Team Canada, raising his arms after teammate, Paul Henderson, scored deciding goal in Moscow

came on a rebound of a shot by Esposito which the Russian goalie could not clear quickly enough. Henderson slapped it into the net and for the third time notched the final goal of a game. His shot won Sunday and again on Tuesday with about two minutes to play.

At a news conference after tonight's game, the coaches of the two teams insisted that the experiment of matching stars of the National Hockey League against the Soviet national ice hockey team had been worthwhile.

The Scoring

| Team Canada | 2 | 1 | 3—6 |
| Soviet Union | 2 | 3 | 0—5 |

First Period
1—Soviet Union, Yakushev (2)
  (Maltsev, Lyapkin) 3:34
2—Canada, P. Esposito (1) (Park) .. 6:45
3—Soviet Union, Lutchenko (1)
  (Kharlamov) 13:10
4—Canada, Park (2) (Ratelle, Hull) ... 16:59

Second Period
5—Soviet Union, Shadrin 0:21
6—Canada, White (2) (Gilbert, Ratelle) 10:32
7—Soviet Union, Yakushev 11:43
8—Soviet Union, Vasilyev 16:43

Third Period
9—Canada, P. Esposito (1)
  (P. Mahovlich) 2:27
10—Canada, Cournoyer (2)
  (Park, P. Esposito) 12:56
11—Canada, Henderson 19:26
Shots on goal—Canada: 12, 10, 9—31;
Soviet Union: 13, 10, 9—32.

"Such games undoubtedly enrich Soviet hockey, said Boris Kulagin, the team's second coach. "We will be happy to meet the Canadians again after the results of this experience have been digested."

Harry Sinden, the Canadian coach, said the series had demonstrated "to our professional hockey players that hockey is being played as well—or almost as well—in many parts of the world, particularly in the Soviet Union."

Referring to the contrasting styles of play between the two teams, Sinden added that the games had exposed the Canadians to "a manner of puck-handling and passing that we don't see much in the National Hockey League."

Actually, the Russian team outscored the Canadians 32 goals to 31 in the eight games. They got a big bulge with a four-goal edge with a 7-3 victory in the first game.

September 29, 1972

CANADIENS DOWN BLACK HAWKS, 4-3

MONTREAL, March 28 (UPI)—Jacques Lemaire and Frank Mahovlich scored in the third period tonight to lead the Montreal Canadiens to a 4-3 victory over the Chicago Black Hawks.

The triumph helped set a Na-

tional Hockey League record for the fewest losses in a season. With only two games remaining in the regular schedule, the Canadiens have dropped only 10 games while winning 50 and tying 16. The old record of 13 losses was established two years ago by the Boston Bruins.

Lemaire's goal broke up a 2-2 tie between the two division champions. The Montreal wing shot the puck from the side of

the net at 5:33, and it rebounded into the cage off the leg of the Chicago goalie, Gary Smith. Less than three minutes later, Frank Mahovlich made the count 4-2, when he scored his 38th goal of the season on a breakaway.

Guy Lafleur opened the scoring for Montreal at 6:48 of the first session but Chicago tied it up later in the same stanza as Stan Mikita scored a power-play goal while Guy LaPointe was in the penalty box.

| Chicago Black Hawks | 1 | 0 | 2—3. |

Montreal .... 1 1 2—4.
FIRST PERIOD—1, Montreal, Lafleur (28)
(Tardif, Houle) 6:48. 2, Chicago, Mikita
(25) (Hull, Martin) 13:25. Penalties—Korab
Chicago (10:14); P. Mahovlich Montreal
(16:43); Lapointe Montreal (12:16).
SECOND PERIOD—3, Montreal, Lapointe (19)
(F. Mahovlich, Lafleur) 14:03. Penalties—
Russell, Chicago and P. Mahovlich, Montreal (5:41); Russell, Chicago (19:10).
THIRD PERIOD—4, Chicago, Korab (12)
(Angotti) 3:27. 5, Montreal, Lemaire (42)
(Murdoch, Lafley) 5:33. 6, F. Mahovlich
(35) (Lapointe) 7:49. 7, Chicago, Martin
(29) (Hull, Pappin) 10:07. Penalties—
Savard, Montreal, (11:55).
Shots on goal—Chicago: 6, 6, 13—25; Montreal: 16, 11, 8—35.
Goalies—Smith, Plasse.
Attendance—16,796.

March 29, 1973

Whalers Take First W.H.A. Title

Boston Defeats Jets, 9-6, on Five Goals in First Period

BOSTON, May 6 (AP)—Larry Pleau scored three goals and Tommy Webster contributed two today as the New England Whalers defeated the Winnipeg Jets, 9-6, for the first World Hockey Association championship.

The Whalers, who won nine consecutive playoff games at home, took the four-of-seven game series, four games to one, in capturing the Avco World Cup.

Pleau, who was born in the Greater Boston area and who formerly played with Montreal, crushed Winnipeg's last hopes by completing his three-goal performance with a pair of goals within two minutes after the Jets had gained a 6-5 edge.

New England got off to a quick start as Webster took a pass from Tommy Williams and scored his 11th playoff goal with the game only 21 seconds old.

The Whalers then went on to a 5-2 lead in the first period as Pleau, Guy Smith, Rick Ley and Tim Sheehy scored. Danny Johnson and Norm Beaudin tallied for the Jets, who were frustrated much of the time by Al Smith, the Boston goalie.

Webster increased New England's lead to 6-2 by cashing another pass from Williams after 15 seconds of the second period. Then the Jets began their comeback.

Pleau Scores 2 More

Beaudin scored his 10th playoff goal on a power play at 3:15 and Milt Black tallied at 4:02. Bob Woytowich cut the deficit to a single goal at 4:59 of the third period and the Whalers appeared to be hanging on.

However, Pleau tallied at 5:44 and then connected again after a tremendous effort by Sheehy at 7:31, pulling the Whalers out of danger. It was Pleau's 12th playoff goal.

Bobby Hull, the player-coach of the Jets, gambled and lost, when he pulled the goalie, Joe Daley, for a sixth skater with nearly 3½ minutes remaining to play.

The strategy backfired as New England's Mike Byers slid a 120-foot shot into the open net.

Immediately after the game Howard L. Baldwin, the president of the New England club, issued a challenge to the eventual National Hockey League champion to meet in a one-game playoff on neutral ice for the Stanley Cup. The trophy is considered symbolic of world hockey supremacy by the N.H.L.

| Winnipeg Jets | 2 | 2 | 2—6 |
| New England Whalers | 5 | 1 | 3—9 |

FIRST PERIOD—1, New England, Webster
(11) (Williams, Ley) 0:21. 2, New England,
Pleau (10) (unassisted) 4:46. 3, Winnipeg,
Johnson (4) (Sutherland) 7:07. 4, New
England, G. Smith (2) (Webster, Williams)
11:47. 5, New England, Ley (3) (unassisted)
15:43. 6, Winnipeg, Beaudin (12) (Hull)
17:53. 7, New England, Sheehy (9) (Pleau,
Webster) 18:41. Penalties—Green, New
England 3:04); Asmundson, Winnipeg
(8:37).
SECOND PERIOD—8, New England, Webster
(12) (Williams, Green) 0:15. 9, Winnipeg,
Beaudin (13) (McDonald, Bordeleau)
3:15. 10, Winnipeg, Black (11) (Shmyr), 4:02.
Penalties—Green, New England (1:41; Asmundson, Winnipeg (5:49); Shmyr, Winnipeg (9:53); Green, New England (19:34).
THIRD PERIOD—11, Winnipeg, Woytowich
(1) (Asmundson, Swenson) 4:59. 12, New
England, Pleau (11) (Sheehy, French)
5:44. 13, Pleau 12) (French, Sheehy) 7:31.
14, New England, Byers (6) (Green, Williams) 17:20. 15, Winnipeg, Asmundson (1)
(Cuddie, Swenson) 18:10. No penalties.
Shots on goal—Winnipeg: 17, 12, 13—42.
New England: 11, 6, 10—27.
Goalies—Daley, Smith.
Attendance—11,186.

May 7, 1973

Canadiens Capture Cup in 6 Games, 6-4

By GERALD ESKENAZI
Special to The New York Times

CHICAGO, May 10—It didn't matter that 20,000 hostile fans screeched for the Black Hawks, and it didn't matter that the Canadiens were playing for their fourth coach in six years. Montreal won the Stanley Cup anyway tonight.

With a 6-4 victory, after trailing by 2-0, the Frenchmen returned the National Hockey League's cherished award to Canada by taking the finals, 4 games to 2.

"Their mystique?" asked Stan Mikita. "It didn't do bad things for us. But it did wonders for them."

Although playing for the four different leaders, the Canadiens won the Cup for the fourth time in the six years—and for the 18th time over all.

There was a bounce or two in the Canadiens' favor. There was a break or two in front of the Hawks' goalie, Tony Esposito.

"Sometimes, it was meant to be," said Chicago's Cliff Koroll.

He wondered about Yvan Cournoyer's goal in the final period, a record score on two counts. "It really wasn't a good shot," said Koroll.

Cup Scoring Runneth Over

But it counted, and it lifted the visitors to a 5-4 lead and there was the feeling that the season really was over. The goal was the little, muscular Cournoyer's 15th in only 17 playoff games—and broke the record set by his teammate, Frank Mahovlich, in 20 games in 1971.

It also was the 55th goal of this four-of-seven-game series, the most goal-filled playoffs since the N.H.L. took over the Cup in 1927. The previous mark of 54 was set during the Montreal - Boston seven - game slugfest two years ago.

For his scoring, and his scurrying and general mischief-making, Cournoyer was named the Conn Smythe Trophy winner as the playoff's most valuable performer. It is worth $1,500. He also took home the Dodge Charger donated by Sport magazine.

At first, the Hawks sent out an eager rookie named John Marks to shadow the elusive Cournoyer, and other Hawks were sent to chase the Frenchmen's spiritual leader, Henri Richard. Although Richard repeatedly was slammed and tripped and cross-checked, Cournoyer was more fortunate. He escaped.

But the Chicagoans' pressing tactics dulled Montreal in the opening period and the Hawks took a 2-0 lead when Pit Martin scored twice within 56 seconds.

The Canadiens went nowhere, and only last-second lunges for passes in front of their goalie, Ken Dryden, prevented more goals.

Yet, within 12 seconds remaining in the session, they cut the score to 2-1 when Richard's shovel-shot bounced off Pat Stapleton's stick and found an air space behind Esposito.

The Canadiens, buoyed by this gift, scored three times in the second session. First, Pete Mahovlich tied the score and Rejean Houle put them ahead. Dave Kryskow tied it for the Hawks, on a disputed goal in which the goal judge pressed the red-light button late. The Canadiens thought the play was dead and the protesting Cournoyer hopped like a rabbit.

Then Frank Mahovlich, shaking off Bill White, rapped home a short shot on the power play, but Martin tied it with his third goal of the game.

The Canadiens played most of the period without Claude Larose, who broke his right leg after sliding into the goalpost.

Cournoyer's record goal in the final period was followed a few minutes later by a score from Marc Tardif.

The underdog Hawks didn't stop, though. But they had nowhere to go. The Canadiens were in command now, flicking off frustrating little passes that ate away the clock, and suddenly the game was over and the Canadiens were richer by $15,000 a man. The Hawks skated past each Frenchman and shook hands, consoled by $10,000 as the loser's share.

Richard lifted the Cup, a replica down to the tiniest scratches of the one that stands in the Hockey Hall of Fame in Toronto, and took a victory lap. Perhaps it is hislast. He wouldn't say. He is 37 years old and has played 18 seasons.

There was champagne later in the dressingroom, but the television cameras were barred. The league didn't want people to see its athletes drinking.

Mikita, who one day will be voted into the Hall of Fame with Richard, was cryptic about his future. He may jump to the World Association.

When someone mentioned money, Mikita said, "I could be richer. Make of that what you will."

```
Montreal Canadiens    1  3  2—6
Chicago Black Hawks    2  2  0—4
FIRST PERIOD—1, Chicago, Martin (8)
(Mikita, Stapleton) 10:35. 2, Chicago,
Martin (9) (Pappin) 1:31. 3, Montreal,
Richard (6) (F. Mahovlich) 19:48. Penal-
ties—Roberts, Montreal (3:40); Korab,
Chicago (3:40); Martin, Chicago (8:21);
Roberts, Montreal (10:43); Wilson, Mon-
treal (12:29).
SECOND PERIOD—4, Montreal, P. Mahov-
lich (4) LaParrier, Lefley) 5:02. 5,
Montreal, Houle (3) (P. Mahovlich, Lefley)
6:37. 6, Chicago, Kryskow (2) (Back-
strom, Maki) 8:32. 7, Montreal, M. Mahov-
lich (9) (LaPointe, Cournoyer) 10:54. 8,
Chicago, Martin (10) (Hull) 17:05. Penal-
ties—White, Chicago (2:25); Russell, Chi-
cago (10:20); Korab, Chicago (10:26);
Roberts, Montreal (16:58).
THIRD PERIOD—9, Montreal, Cournoyer (15)
(Lemaire) 8:13. 10, Montreal, Tardif (6)
(Cournoyer, Lemaire) 12:42. Penalty—
Russell, Chicago (11:29).
Shots on goal—Montreal: 7, 15, 11—33.
Chicago: 9, 14, 4—27.
Goalies—Dryden and Esposito.
A—16,666.
```

Associated Press

Puck rebounding past Pete Mahovlich of the Canadiens after his shot was blocked by Black Hawks' goalie, Tony Esposito, in Stanley Cup action in Chicago last night.

May 11, 1973

GORDIE HOWE GETS $1-MILLION PACT

Aeros Sign Former Detroit Ace for 4 Years and Also Provide Job for Wife

By SAM GOLDAPER

The World Hockey Association, grappling for recognition and box-office dollars, reached into the National Hockey League's past yesterday for Gordie Howe.

The former Detroit Red Wing, the most prolific scorer in N.H.L. history, signed a four-year, $1-million contract with the Houston Aeros, bringing him out of retirement.

Since the deal included a

job for Howe's wife, Coleen, who may become a consultant for amateur hockey, there will be four members of the family working for the Aeros.

Houston recently signed Howe's sons, Marty, 19, and Mark, 18, to four-year contracts that were reported to be worth $400,000 apiece.

The 45-year-old Howe said it was always his dream to be able to play on the same team with his sons. Howe is expected to be on the same line with Mark, a left wing. Marty is a defenseman.

Paul Dineau, the Aeros' owner, turned to Howe at the signing and said, "And I want to thank you and Howe, and Howe and Howe."

The N.H.L. Hall of Famer said, My only regret, and I have only one, is that I'm sorry I'm not the Gordie Howe I was 10 years ago so I could go out and fulfill what the Aeros want of me and repay them for what they're doing for me. In the realm of finances alone, they've put my projected plan six to 10 years ahead.

"I'll give 100 per cent on the ice, and if anyone takes a shot at one of my sons, I'll be a protective father. I like to be sure the Howes are all even. In fact, I like to be one-up against the opponents.

"If anyone gets a Howe then he's going to hear from me. I won't go after him then, but if I get a shot at him, I'll take it."

During his 25 seasons with the Red Wings, in which Howe played 1,687 games, scored 786 goals and got 1,023 assists, all N.H.L. records, he established a reputation as one of the most feared fighters in the league.

Howe retired on Sept. 9, 1971, and one of the reasons he gave was a nagging wrist injury.

"Although my golf scores don't indicate it, the wrist is fine," he said. "It doesn't hurt even when I hit a bad shot. I'm sure it might hurt if it gets in the way of someone's chest.

Campbell Is Disappointed

In Montreal, Clarence Campbell, the president of the N.H.L. reacted with disappointment to the signing.

"He was obviously unhappy with his position in Detroit," said Campbell. "I hope he won't suffer the fate of other people who have played too long. It would make me sick if instead of applause, he was greeted by boos. I'd be sorry to see him in that position."

Howe resigned as vice president of the Red Wings last week, when negotiations began with the Aeros. He had expressed unhappiness with his position because, "they weren't listening to me."

In an apparent last-ditch effort to keep Howe from jumping to Houston, the N.H.L. was

Gordie Howe

reported to have offered him a $500,000 contract to act as league public relations ambassador for the next five years.

"I feel we made him a generous offer," said Campbell," not competitive with Houston, but generous. Basically, Howe has been well taken care of during his N.H.L. career, commanding a top salary. But you can't go bribing a man to stay."

In Detroit, Red Wing officials said no one would argue with Howe's decision to jump to the Aeros.

"There certainly is no animosity whatsoever," the spokesman said." The Wings still regard Howe as 'Mr. Hockey.' We can never forget his countless great moments with this club and wish him every success and happiness."

June 20, 1973

Hockey Leagues In Tune

By GERALD ESKENAZI

Without officials of either league ever having sat at the same bargaining table, the National Hockey League and World Hockey Association formally ended their differences yesterday.

The peace treaty took place in Philadelphia, where Federal Judge Leon A. Higginbotham allowed the rivals to settle out of court.

In a sense, both sides won. For $1.75-million, the N.H.L. persuaded the W.H.A. to drop its $50-million law-

suit, which charged restraint of trade and monopoly practices.

The indemnity is a fraction of the wealthy N.H.L.'s treasury, a cheap price to pay to get the upstart league off its back, observers noted.

Now, they said, the N.H.L. can sit back and wait for the W.H.A. to sink under the weight of high salaries and poor attendance.

But the W.H.A. gained several victories with the decision. First, virtually all its demands were met by the N.H.L. The key demand, perhaps, was for interleague exhibition play. There will be 15 such games next fall. If a game is not played, the N.H.L. will pay the W.H.A. $10,000.

Other terms of the settlement, as reported in The New York Times on Jan. 15, call for the leagues to recognize each other's player contracts and for he N.H.L. to make its arenas available for W.H.A. play.

The agreement was arranged between lawyers. "I have never sat down with the W.H.A.," Clarence Campbell, N.H.L. president, emphasized at his Montreal office.

The 68-year-old Campbell has been president since 1946, the longest tenure for the head of a major professional sports league. With the settlement, it is likely that he will be ready to end his reign.

He noted some time ago, "I guess I'm the most qualified person in the league to have in the antitrust litigation." Since he had been active so long, he was able to answer most of the questions dealing with antitrust investigations of his league's complex association with the minor and amateur leagues.

"I thought of retiring for some time," he admitted yesterday. "But since 1965 there has been a steady series of near crises."

That year the league agreed to expand from six teams. There are now 16, with two more to be added in the fall. The W.H.A., in its second season, has 12.

The N.H.L. Players Association is not happy over the end of the warfare. Since the formation of the W.H.A. salaries in the N.H.L. have jumped from an average of $30,000 to $44,000. Now the association contends that the exhibition games will be a prelude to merger.

To keep the players happy, Campbell said the N.H.L. would contribute up to $150,-000 to the players' pension fund. The W.H.A. insisted on that to insure the exhibition games. There was talk that the N.H.L. players would

boycott the exhibitions.

Campbell stressed that the agreement was not a merger, nor a prelude to one. "That can be done only by Congressional approval," he said.

One bit of unfinished business remained. The group that took over the New York franchise of the W.H.A. last year and changed the name from Raiders to Golden Blades did not take part in the settlement. It was ousted from the league this season, and the league took over the franchise and moved it to New Jersey.

The Golden Blades group still may sue. If it does and wins, the W.H.A. has agreed to pay the cost to the N.H.L.

February 20, 1974

Islanders Shut Out By Parent

PHILADELPHIA, April 4 (UPI)—Bernie Parent recorded his 12th shutout in goal and set two National Hockey League records tonight as the West Division champion Philadelphia Flyers achieved their 49th triumph, beating the New York Islanders, 4-0.

Ross Lonsberry scored his 30th and 31st goals of the season. He put Philadelphia ahead after 9 minutes 32 seconds of the first period with a 50-foot backhander and got the final goal at 17:25 of the third period.

The Islanders stymied the Flyers until 2:34 of the third period when Tom Bladon shot a 40-footer from the right boards. Philadelphia then scored on a power play at 8:25 with Bill Barber making the goal from 15 feet.

It was Parent's 46th victory against 13 losses and 12 ties and he now has a goals-against average of 1.89. It was his 72d start—a season record—and a record number of minutes played at 4,254.

The loss assured the Islanders of last place in the East Division for the second straight season.

The Flyers' victory pushed their point total to 110, only 1 behind Boston. The overall point champion gets the home-ice advantage should each division leader reach the Stanley Cup final.

New York Islanders	0	0	0—0
Philadelphia Flyers	1	0	3—4

Shots on Goal—N.Y. Islanders 7, 13, 10—30; Philadelphia 13, 13, 14—40.
Goalies—Smith and Parent.

April 5, 1974

Flyers Capture Stanley Cup by Beating Bruins, 1-0

Championship First For an Expansion Club in N.H.L.

By PARTON KEESE
Special to The New York Times

PHILADELPHIA, May 19—The Philadelphia Flyers arrived today.

With a remarkable 1-0 shutout of the Boston Bruins at the Spectrum, the National Hockey League's West Division champions turned back the East Division champions, 4 games to 2, and became the first expansion team to win the Stanley Cup and the league title.

Nothing better typified a championship victory for the Flyers in their seventh season of existence than a shutout, a tribute to Bernie Parent their goalie. Although it was the first time he held the high-scoring Bruins scoreless, Parent's sensational performances in the six games earned him the Conn Smythe Trophy as the outstanding player in the series.

The deciding goal today was scored by Rick MacLeish in the first period. MacLeish scored 13 goals in the playoffs to lead all players. However, none could have been more important to his and his team than the last one, on which he barely saw the puck and had little to do except to be in the right spot at the right time.

André (Moose) Dupont, a Flyer defenseman, had received the puck at his position on the right point from MacLeish, who won the faceoff from Gregg Sheppard on Philadelphia's first and only power play in the opening period. Dupont skated inside the blue line to the center and let go a soft shot at Gilles Gilbert, the Boston goalie.

MacLeish, in the meantime, was battling Dallas Smith and Carol Vadnais, Boston defensemen, for position in front of the net. The puck struck Rick in the upper leg, deflected off his stick and slithered past Gilbert into the goal.

"Aw, I saw that lousy shot by Dupont," said the 24-year-old Gilbert. "But when a puck bounces off somebody on the way, you don't know if it's going high or low, right or left."

"I thought six of their eight shots in the first period

could have gone in," Gilbert added. "And this was probably my best game, too."

The Bruins doubled the Flyers' number of shots-on-goal in the opening period as the teams abandoned the pushing-shoving, tying up-slugging brand of hockey of the previous two contests.

"This was a game for skating and scoring goals," said Dave Schultz, the Philadelphia penalty-record holder. "We left all that rough stuff in Boston on purpose."

As a result, today's total of 34 minutes for 17 penalties called by Referee Art Skov left the two teams 16 minutes and three penalties short of the records for a playoff series.

When Bobby Orr, Boston's superstar, was sent off the ice by Skov for tackling Bobby Clarke on a breakaway with just 2 minutes 22 seconds left, it signaled the end of the game for all intents and purposes. Orr sat disconsolately in the penalty box and watched the Flyer fans create bedlam until the final buzzer sounded.

Then, with Parent and Bobby Clarke leading the

way, the Flyers skated round the rink carrying the Stanley Cup as hundreds of fans swarmed on the ice. Those in the stands clapped and yelled and cried.

The ending was almost as emotional as the beginning. First the rink crew wheeled in an organ, then they laid down a 30-foot carpet. And out stepped Kate Smith, in person, the good-luck "charm" of the Flyers. A recording of "God Bless America" by her had been "good luck," for the Flyers had won 36 of the 40 games at which it was played.

Kate gave it everything she had. She waved passionately to the roaring crowd. She threw punches in the air, and the fans screamed louder. With a spotlight on her, she aimed her hand pistol-like at the Bruins, and then started singing "God Bless America."

The rafters resounded, everybody joined in, and when she finished, the famous singer left in a tumult. But not before Orr and Phil Esposito stopped her to shake hands, haping, perhaps, some of the luck would rub off.

"We just had to prove we had the ability to win the

cup," said Clarke in the madhouse dressing room afterwards.

Esposito, philosophical as always, put this series well behind his top thrills—his first cup victory and the Team Canada games with the Soviet.

"By the way," Esposito said, "I haven't been offered one stinking penny from the other league. I haven't even talked to them." Thus he dispelled a report that he would jump to the World Hockey Association next season.

"When we beat the Rangers in the semifinal, we got no credit," Clarke reminded the well-wishers. "All they said was the Rangers choked. When we led the Bruins, 3 to 1, in games, they didn't call it talent but rather that we were hungrier.

"Along with this biggest thrill of winning the cup, I think I'm happiest knowing that we showed them we did have the ability."

Boston Bruins .... 0 0 0—0
Philadelphia Flyers ...... 1 0 0—1
FIRST PERIOD—1. Philadelphia, MacLeish (13) (Dupont) 4:45. Penalties—Dupont, Philadelphia (0:32), Clement, Philadelphia (10:18), Forbes, Boston (10:18), Cowick, Philadelphia .10:18, O'Reilly, Boston (12:58), Orr, Boston (14:22) Clarke, Philadelphia (14:22).
SECOND PERIOD—No scoring. Penalties—Dupont, Philadelphia (0:40), Hodge, Boston (1:15); Sims, Boston (5:44); Joe Watson, Philadelphia (9:22), Joe Watson, Philadelphia (15:03), Vadnais, Boston (17:46).
THIRD PERIOD—No scoring. Penalties—O'Reilly, Boston (3:12); Schultz, Philadelphia (11:15); Bucyk, Boston (14:54); Orr, Boston (17:38).
Shots on goal: Boston: 16, 9, 5—30; Philadelphia: 8, 14, 4, 26.
Attendance—17,007.

May 20, 1974

N.H.L. Gives Franchises To Denver, Seattle for '76

Rangers Obtain Sanderson— Officially

By PARTON KEESE
Special to The New York Times

MONTREAL, June 12—The National Hockey League filled the rosters of its two new teams today, the New York Rangers officially acquired Derek Sanderson from the Boston Bruins and Denver and Seattle were named as the expansion clubs for 1976. The league business all went without a hitch, as everyone expected.

As soon as the Washington Capitals and Kansas City Scouts had completed drafting 24 players each from the unprotected lists of the 16 established clubs, Emile Francis, the Ranger general manager, was free to announce what nearly everyone already knew: Sanderson, the colorful and eccentric center, had

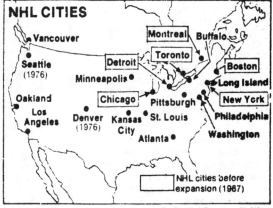

NHL CITIES

Vancouver · Seattle (1976) · Oakland · Los Angeles · Denver (1976) · Minneapolis · Chicago · Kansas City · St. Louis · Atlanta · Detroit · Toronto · Montreal · Buffalo · Pittsburgh · Long Island · Boston · New York · Philadelphia · Washington

☐ NHL cities before expansion (1967)

The New York Times/June 13, 1974

been traded to New York for Walt McKechnie.

Earlier, Clarence Campbell, the N.H.L. president, announced that the Buffalo Sabres' claim of McKechnie had been overruled by the board of governors, and it was only a matter of waiting until the expansion teams had completed their rosters before it was legal to announce the trade.

Denver and Seattle currently hold franchises in the Western Hockey League. The price of each franchise was $6-million.

The Denver group was represented by Ivan Mullenix while Vince Abbey represented Seattle.

The addition of the two teams will bring the N.H.L. to a four-division, 20-team league in 1976. It also will put an end to the Western Hockey League as an entity the same year, with several of the clubs possibly moving to the Central Hockey League.

San Diego also had applied for an expansion franchise but was rejected.

June 13, 1974

Violence in Hockey: Blood Over Finesse

By STAN FISCHLER

"Canadian hockey isn't breeding men of character and future leaders, it's breeding a stable of animals. It's an outrage."
—*Arthur Maloney, Toronto lawyer.*

"When people call me an animal, it gets to me. But the guys on our team tell me, 'We know what you are, what you're doing. Just don't worry about it.'"—Dave Schultz, Philadelphia Flyers

Big-time professional hockey prepares for the 1974-75 season more schizophrenic than Dr. Jekyll and Cinderella combined.

National Hockey League and World Hockey Association leaders can't seem to make up their collective minds whether they want their product hyped as a refrigerated second coming of D-Day or an athletic ballet on ice.

At the moment, blood holds a slim lead over finesse, but gore threatens to score heavily in the months to come. There are some who fear that the new season will be dirtier than "Deep Throat."

No wonder. The Philadelphia Flyers won the Stanley Cup last spring on a platform of consummate skill, unplanned violence and specifically calculated intimidation, and not necessarily in that order of importance.

The Flyers' "Mean Machine" attracted such notoriety, and filled so many rinks, that three full-length books on hockey violence will appear this season. Obviously, blood-on-the-ice not only sells, it also threatens to sell out the non-belligerent masters of stickhandling.

While skill has not exactly been banned this year, such pacifists as Jean Ratelle and Rod Gilbert must be wondering whether there still is room for

Stan Fischler is New York correspondent for the Toronto Star, columnist for the Sporting News, co-editor of Action Sports Hockey Magazine and author of more than 40 books about hockey. He examines blood on the ice in his autobiography, "Slapshot!," as well as the soon-to-be published critique of hockey, "Slashing!" (Thomas Y. Crowell.) As an amateur player, he received two misconduct penalties in a 14-year career.

law and order in the contemporary game.

Consider these episodes:

¶In a W.H.A. playoff game last spring, Mike Curran, the Minnesota Fighting Saints' goalie, punched Referee Bob Sloan to the ice. The league office waited four months before announcing a penalty to the goaltender—a short suspension and a fine likely to be paid by his team.

¶In a Philadelphia-Atlanta Stanley Cup game last April, Dan Bouchard, the Atlanta goalie, assaulted Referee Dave Newell. Instead of banishing the intemperate goaltender, the N.H.L. let him off the hook with a misconduct penalty, not even a suspension.

¶Bill White, the Chicago Black Hawk defenseman, put a headlock on Referee Ron Wicks after a questionable call last March. Clarence Campbell, the N.H.L. president, called it one of the worst cases of manhandling an official he had seen, yet White escaped with a five-game suspension.

When hockey's system of law and order disintegrates, vigilantes replace the enforcement officers. Nowadays, goon squads are popping up all over the place to maintain decorum.

In Pittsburgh, the Penguins hired burly Steve Durbano and Battleship Kelly as an antidote to the Flyers. "Once we got them," said Manager Jack Button, "the Flyers didn't push

us around anymore." Better still, the Penguins' home attendance climbed by almost 2,000 a game.

Even the Montreal Canadiens, once revered as a collection of Nureyevs on ice, have vowed to come out swinging this year, confirming that violence is de rigueur from the oldest established team to the newest expansion club.

Headline Tells It All

A headline in The Washington Post last summer said it all: "ANDERSON VOWS ROCK 'EM, SOCK 'EM HOCKEY."

The story went on: "Washington hockey fans were promised yesterday that while they are waiting for their expansionites to mature into possible champions, they will be treated to blood and guts."

Coach Jimmy Anderson added: "I like to work with young kids who like to hit."

No doubt Anderson's accent on bop has helped sell tickets, but it also has angered purists such as Burling Lowrey, an English professor at Montgomery (Ala.) College.

Lowrey suggests that a dirty hockey game be X-rated and banned just like "Deep Throat" on the ground that it is pornographic.

"The offense of assault and battery," says Lowrey, "which can result in a stiff jail sentence if committed on the street, is permissible on a hockey rink, where it is euphemistically called 'hitting hard.'"

Nobody suggests that legal hitting be eliminated from a robust body contact sport such as hockey. What is terribly disturbing, however, is that violence and fighting have become strategic techniques in winning, techniques glorified above and beyond all reason.

The Boston Bruins launched the trend in the late nineteen-sixties and pro-

duced Stanley Cup championships in 1970 and 1972. Then came Coach Fred Shero and the Flyers, who embellished Boston's battle plan.

Philadelphia introduced Dave Schultz as hockey's "designated hitter," sort of a smart bomb on skates. Schultz is a modestly skilled player assigned to pick a fight with one of the enemy's key players. When the star fights back, both are penalized and, in a sense, Schultz's assault is rewarded.

Schultz had made no bones about his role as hit man: "It makes sense to try and take out a guy who's more important to his team than I am to mine. If I take out Brad Park, that's not a bad trade, is it?"

Sure it is, because the customers, except for the usual number of cretins in any crowd, are being cheated out of artistry and, instead, are being fed a brand of ersatz machismo.

Hockey leaders normally would yawn deeply over criticism of ice savagery, but last August the Province of Ontario crosschecked the N.H.L. with a withering indictment of the big-leaguers and their negative influence on kids.

The fuss started with a terribly bloody amateur game last April that required 14 police officers to restore order, and ended with a Provincial white paper on violence in amateur hockey.

The investigation was conducted by a Toronto attorney, William McMurtry. He is an associate of Alan Eagleson, the director of the N.H.L. Players' Association and one of the game's most influential leaders.

McMurtry heard testimony from more than 50 witnesses, including Campbell; Scotty Morrison, the N.H.L. referee in chief, and Pit Martin, president of the N.H.L. Players' Association.

Some of McMurtry's conclusions in

the 47-page report were devastating. "The N.H.L. was told," said Jim Proudfoot, sports editor of The Toronto Star, "that its product is considered unsavory, even evil." The report singled out the N.H.L. as the strongest influence contributing to increased violence in amateur hockey in Ontario. It charged that violence has become a tactical weapon [Schultz-Flyers] to achieve victory in the N.H.L. McMurtry said:

"When the evidence strongly indicates that there is a conscious effort to sell violence in hockey to enrich a small group of show-business entrepreneurs at the expense of a great sport [not to mention the corruption of an entire generation's concept of sport], then one's concern grows to outrage."

By contrast, there was Campbell's testimony about the main purpose of his league: "We must put on a spectacle that will attract people. . ."

N.H.L. club owners are working on two false premises—that hockey needs gore to be salable in the United States, and that curbing violence will turn hockey into an uninteresting pantywaist sport.

The fallacy of these theories was underlined by the 1972 and the current Team Canada-Soviet games, which have featured good, robust hockey without Dave Schultz-type "hit" men beating up on the enemy superstars.

Time and again, these international games have demonstrated that speed, skill and legitimate sock are enough to sell the sport anywhere and at any time.

Given a choice between a bloody game and an arty game, I'll take art any time. Or, as a Torontonian recently put it, "Would you rather have your hockey-playing child be a Dave Schultz or a Jean Ratelle?"

October 6, 1974

Rangers Lose, 6-2

By NEIL AMDUR
Special to The New York Times

ST. LOUIS, Dec. 14—A wild 15-minute free-for-all in the final period that led to two National Hockey League records for penalty minutes and left blood on the ice overshadowed the Rangers' 6-2 loss to the St. Louis Blues tonight.

No players appeared seriously injured, other than a few scraped noses, after the brawling finally ended. But so many penalties were administered that only eight players were left on the arena ice on both teams to complete the final 3 minutes 12 seconds.

A total of 180 penalty minutes was handed out for the fight alone, which began with Claude LaRose of the Blues and Greg Polis of the Rangers swinging at each other.

The total number of pen-

alty minutes for the third period was 186, a league record. So was the game total of 246, which surpassed the early season brawl between the Philadelphia Flyers and California Golden Seals.

Even the two goalies, Ed Giacomin and John Davidson, left the nets and burrowed into the swinging, which delayed the game for 27 minutes until officials could restore order and quiet the crowd of 18,203.

Giacomin, perhaps frustrated by the Blues' assault, was charged with a game misconduct penalty as the third party in the fight. It was the first time the Ranger goalie had been ejected from an N.H.L. game.

The only consolation for the Rangers, who had their undefeated string of five snapped, was the failure of the Blues' center, Garry Unger, to score a goal in his eighth consecutive game.

The free-for-all had been preceded by individual sparring sessions in the first period between LaRose and Derek Sanderson and two lively second-period scraps between Steve Vickers and Doug Palazzari, and Sanderson and Bob Plager.

Plager emerged as the heavyweight champion, throwing his right hand like a hammer while holding Sanderson's long hair with his left hand.

The early fighting appeared to take the Rangers' mind off their primary task—skating, particularly after Vickers, their leading scorer, was banished for seven minutes in the second period.

Vickers had scored the first goal at 6:25 of the opening period, before the Blues rebounded for a 3-1 lead after two periods.

Initially, the LaRose-Polis fight seemed isolated, until players on both sides started closing in. Suddenly, after Giacomin tried to pry them apart, both benches emptied, and players were grabbing and swinging all over the ice.

Bob Cassoff lost a fight

with Bill Fairbairn, as his bloodied nose testified. Brad Park, the Ranger defenseman, found himself squared off first against Barclay Plager and then against Floyd Thomson.

New York Rangers .... 1 0 1—2
St. Louis Blues .... 1 2 3—6
FIRST PERIOD—1, Rangers, Vickers (12) (Ratelle, Mamtte), 6:52. 2, St. Louis, LaRose (2) (Unger, Gassoff), 10:40. Penalties—Plant 6, (9:13); Butler (9:13); Butler, (13:25); Sanderson, (major), (15:41); LaRose, (major), (15:41); Bednarski, 19:20).
SECOND PERIOD—3, St. Louis, Lefly (5) (Thomson, Plante), 3:47. 4, St. Louis, Plante (10) (Lefley), 14:17. Penalties—Bailey, (1:08), Palazzari, (major-minor), (8:12); Vickers, (major-minor), (8:12); Sacharuk, (game misconduct), (8:12); R. Plager, (double minor), (19:49); Sanderson (19:49).
THIRD PERIOD—5, Rangers, Ratelle (9) (Park, Vickers), 2:30. 6, St. Louis, Palazzari (7) (Merrick, B. Plager) 2:59. 7, St. Louis, Patrick (6) (Unger, Hess), 4:01. 8, St. Louis, Merrick (11) (Unger, LaRose), 16:22. Penalties—Park, (6:48); Unger, (12:43); Park, (12:43); Polis, (double major, minor, game misconduct), (16:48); Butler, (major, misconduct), (16:48); B. Wilson, (major, misconduct), (16:48); Park, (major, misconduct), (16:48); Giacomin, (game misconduct), (16:48); LaRose, (major, misconduct), (16:48); Gassoff, (double major, misconduct, games misconduct), (16:48); Bailey, (major, misconduct), (16:48); Thomson, (major misconduct), (16:48); R. Wilson, (double minor, game misconduct), (16:48); Davidson, (16:48).
Shots on goal—Rangers 12, 9, 11—32. St. Louis 10, 12, 16—38.
Goalies—Giacomin, Villemure and Davidson.
Attendance—18,203.

December 15, 1974

Women Reporters Break the Ice
Special to The New York Times

MONTREAL, Jan. 21—History was made tonight at the National Hockey League All-Star game, but it had nothing to do with the outcome. Two women reporters entered the hockey players' dressing room for postgame interviews in what was probably the first time at a professional sports event.

Robin Herman, a reporter from The New York Times, and Marcelle St. Cyr of Radio CKLM in Montreal accepted the open-door invitation from both coaches to talk to the players as they prepared to take their showers.

"I was more embarrassed by all the attention my presence in the locker room made than by the nakedness," said the 22-year-old Miss Herman, a graduate of Princeton.

Miss St. Cyr said about entering the dressing room: "I'm glad I did it. It proves women can do it with no problems.

January 22, 1975

Islanders Oust Penguins on Late Goal, 1-0

By ROBIN HERMAN
Special to The New York Times

PITTSBURGH, April 26—The tortuous road that brought the New York Islanders back from a three-game deficit in their four-of-seven-game quarterfinal series with Pittsburgh ended in pure joy tonight as the Islanders shut out the Penguins, 1-0.

The game had been a standoff until Ed Westfall's goal on a high backhanded shot after 14 minutes 42 seconds of the final period.

The startling four-game sweep, only the second such playoff comeback in National Hockey League or major pro sports history, was a tribute to Glenn Resch. The little goalie, who had started in all four victories, played an outstanding game and gained the shutout by stopping 30 shots.

"It couldn't have been a more fitting way for the whole team to come back," said Resch. "Any time you get a shutout in the other team's rink you know you're getting some help."

Tonight's shutout enabled the Islanders to duplicate a feat achieved by only one team. The Toronto Maple Leafs, in 1942, were the first to win a playoff series after losing the first three games.

Now the Islanders meet the defending champions, the Philadelphia Flyers, in the semifinals beginning Tuesday night in Philadelphia. "We can take Philly if we play tough," said Resch, grinning.

The intense game was the best of the series as each team played in its distinctive style — the Islanders working as an integrated defensive unit, killing penalties superbly, and the Penguins

Associated Press

Penguins' Dennis Owchar sailing over Gary Inness, teammate, and Islanders' Billy MacMillan in the first period at Pittsburgh.

dancing around in the Islanders' zone, taking pretty shots and chasing rebounds.

"The first two periods were probably our worst two periods of the series," said Al Arbour, the Islander coach. The Penguins were swarming in New York's zone, pushing the Islanders' defensive line farther and farther back. The pressure forced the defense to stop Penguin shots while in retreat instead of standing up at the blue line or interrupting plays in mid-ice as the club had done in the previous three games.

Nonetheless, an Islander usually was there to make the belated stop and when shots got through, Resch was quick, well-positioned or lucky in stopping them.

"We were written off in the New York series," said Arbour. "We were down three here and they wrote us off. Which just proves what great players we have. They never heard of the word quit."

The 26-year-old Resch kept his team safe while the players regained their poise in the offensive zone. "The two best saves I made," he said, "were with my head." In the first period Jean Pronovost and Syl Apps both fired shots off Resch's mask on the same shift. And Resch's "lucky" goal post came into play twice on other shots by the two Pittsburgh forwards.

The Islanders followed precisely their offensive game plan of dumping the puck into the corners and following up with muscle along the boards instead of taking straight shots at Gary Inness, the Penguins' goalie (he had only 17 Islander shots to

stop). But unlike their play in previous games, the Penguins fought furiously to clear the puck quickly.

The strategy finally paid off with Westfall's goal. The line of Westfall, J. P. Parise and Judge Drouin—with Bert Marshall and Dave Lewis, the Islander defensemen, on the ice—took their time setting up the play. Marshall, who was stalwart in this series, ended up with the puck on the boards in the corner and fed to Westfall who put it past Inness.

The Penguins failed to get another shot on goal after the Islanders scored.

"This was worse than the Rangers series I think," said Bill Torrey, the Islanders' general manager, whose nerves

took a beating tonight as they had when the Islanders-Rangers series also went the full distance. "But we didn't make a bad mistake defensively," said Torrey, "and nobody lost their cool."

Joy and Sorrow

A few people did lose their cool—after the game. At the buzzer Resch leaped out of his cage and danced like a marionette across the ice to his teammates who swamped him with adulation. Moments earlier, with 1:25 remaining, the Pittsburgh fans lost their cool, throwing debris on the ice that delayed the game while attendants swept it up.

The Islanders' season has had its amazing moments. Before facing the Rangers in the final weeks, the Islanders had never won a game in

Madison Square Garden, yet they took the final game of the season on the Ranger's ice and went on to beat them twice in the playoffs there.

Similarly, the 3-year-old Islanders had never beaten the Penguins in Pittsburgh until they took two games from them in the Civic Arena to win this series. Never say never, the Islanders say.

NY Islanders   0 0 1 —1
Pittsburgh   0 0 0 —0
First Period—None. Penalties—Paradise, Pit, 5-min., fighting, 2:44; Gilies, NY, 5-min., fighting, 2:44; Burrows, Pit, 3:48; Lewis, NY, 6:06; Westfall, NY, 7:27; Owchar, Pit, 11:17; Lewis, NY, 17:25; Kelly, Pit, 17:25; Campbell, Pit, 18:07; St. Laurent, NY, 18:07; Hart, NY, 20:00; MacDonald, Pit, 20:00.
Second Period—None. Penalties—Pronovost, Pit, 1:11; J. Potvin, NY, 3:11; Arnason, Pit, 15:35.
Third Period—1, NY Islanders, Westfall 4 (Mashal), 14:42. Penalties—Howatt, NY, 5:48.
Shots on goal: New York 5-6-4—17. Pittsburgh 14-11-5—30.
Goalies: NY Islanders, Resch. Pittsburgh, Inness. A: 13,404.

April 27, 1975

Flyers Capture Seventh Game, 4-1, and Foil Islander Comeback

By ROBIN HERMAN
Special to The New York Times

MacLeish's 3 Goals Put Cup Defenders in Final

PHILADELPHIA, May 13—The inspiring saga of the three-year-old New York Islanders came to a close tonight as the Philadelphia Flyers finally let out the tiger and roared into the Stanley Cup finals with a 4-1 victory.

After having held a lead in games in the semifinal series, it took the defending National Hockey League champions four more games to subdue a team that passionately believed in itself. The Flyers thus earned the right to meet the Buffalo Sabres in a four-of-seven-game final round beginning here at the Spectrum Thursday night.

The Islanders' comeback dreams ended with Rick MacLeish's empty-net goal with 68 seconds to play. It gave the brilliant Flyer forward a three-goal hat trick and caused the faces of 20 Islanders to fall in unison.

The Islanders had survived eight other critical playoff contests in which a loss would have meant elimination. They had rallied twice from three-game deficits and they had won two playoff games in overtime. They had, in short, done far more than could have been predicted for a third-year expansion club carrying nine

players 23 years old or younger.

But they could not cope when the Flyers finally decided to play with some verve and hunger.

Flyers Dominate

The game was really decided in the first seven minutes, when the Flyers exploded to a 3-1 lead. Behind so early, the Islanders could not afford to play their usual conservative style. In the end, the Flyers' domination was spelled out in the shots-on-goal advantage: 35-15.

Although the Islanders' captain, Ed Westfall, had presented flowers to Kate Smith before she sang "God Bless America", and each member of the New York team had shaken her hand, the mollifying gestures failed to dampen the revival spirit that surged through the crowd and the Flyers.

As the 17,077 fans responded to Miss Smith's song with tumultuous cheers, the Flyers responded by blitzing the Islanders. They pounded Glenn Resch with nine shots in the space of 2½ minutes, scoring a goal on Gary Dornhoefer's shot just 19 seconds into the game.

MacLeish tipped in a 55-foot shot by Bill Barber 2 minutes, 8 seconds later on a power play. The Flyers had failed to score on the previous 18 power plays in this series.

MacLeish added a power-play goal at 7:11 of the period. It offset the Islanders' only tally, by Jude Drouin, also on a power play at 5:02.

First Goal Is Key

"I can't stress enough the importance of that first goal," said Resch, who led the Islanders through 10 of their last 11 contests. "It changes your whole game plan. The thing that frustrates me is that I got a piece of it. You should be able to stop the ones you get a piece of."

Dornhoefer's clean 40-foot shot beat Resch on the gloved side.

"The whole secret to winning this game was to shut the door in the first period," Resch explained, "and give us time to regroup. We're slow starters. We never got the chance."

From the drop of the puck the Flyers were skating with the dynamism of old and seemed to be wherever the puck wandered. The Island-

ers couldn't move out of their zone, and the few times they did, Flyer defensemen stood at the blue line to stop them.

Resch's hardest saves in the first period came during Islander power plays, when he had to stop Ross Lonsberry and Bill Barber on dangerous breakaways. He would have had to face a third breakaway during the last Islander power play of that period, but Denis Potvin hooked MacLeish, drawing a penalty to stop the fluid-skating center.

After a scoreless second period, the Flyers were able to alter their strategy in the third period, taking fewer risk-filled rushes in order to protect their lead.

"It's good to get the lead," said New York's Clark Gillies, "You can tighten up a little and get careful. When we got down, we had to pull out all the stops and go after them. We were bound to leave a few positions open. They stormed us in the first period. Everyone on their team was hustling."

A Glowing Future

Although the Islander locker room was solemn, the players found a lot of which to be proud. They also realized that the team's prospects for next year are golden.

"We proved a lot to ourselves," said Gillies "This extra month that we played

The Philadelphia Flyers' Rick MacLeish scored 13 goals in the Stanley cup Playoffs in 1974.

Flyer's goalie Bernie Parent blocks a shot with his knee pads in this 1975 game against Vancouver. He was voted the M.V.P. in the 1974 and 1975 playoffs.

is going to give us extra experience for next year. We have it in our heads that we can get all the way in."

Bert Marshall, a 31-year-old defenseman, said he had learned this season that, "Every guy on this team can do the job in the season and the playoffs. I have to take my hat off to them all. Many of them are young guys who hadn't experienced before the lifestyle changes that come with the playoffs. There's definitely a future for this team."

Andre St. Laurent spoke in a choking voice.

"Nobody really expected us to go this far, what the heck.

And it'll be so much better for next year. We know we can do it and a lot more teams in the N.H.L. will have respect for ours."

First Period — 1, Philadelphia, Dornhoefer 3 (Jim Watson), 0:19. 2, Philadelphia, MacLeish 8 (Barber, Clarke), 2:27. 3, New York, Drouin 6 (D. Potvin, Westfall), 5:02. 4, Philadelphia, MacLeish 9 (Goodenough), 7:11. Penalties — Hart, NY, 1:40; Jim Watson, Phi, 4:09; Dupont, Phi, 4:56; D. Potvin, NY, 6:08; Schultz,

Phi, 8:12; D. Potvin, NY, 8:12; Joe Watson, Phi, 12:29; Saleski, Phi, 15:27; Van Impe, Phi, 17:34; D. Potvin, NY, 18:28. Second Period — None. Penalties — Marshall, NY, 8:02; Leach, Phi, 13:04; Drouin, NY, 13:22; D. Potvin, NY, 18:35. Third Period — 5, Philadelphia, MacLeish 10 (Saleski), 18:52. Penalties — Dupont, Phi, 1:50; D. Potvin, NY, 9:43. Shots on Goal: New York 4-5-6 — 15. Philadelphia 15-11-9 — 35. Goalies: New York, Resch. Philadelphia, Parent. A: 17,077.

May 14, 1975

Flyers Defeat Sabres by 2-0 For 2d Straight Stanley Cup

By PARTON KEESE
Special to The New York Times

BUFFALO, May 27—Casting off the label of "lucky team," the Philadelphia Flyers captured their second straight National Hockey League championship tonight by beating the Buffalo Sabres, 2-0. The defense-oriented Flyers won the coveted Stanley Cup just as they had last year, 4 games to 2.

"This second Cup is more satisfying than the first," said Bernie Parent, Philadelphia's goalie, who won the award as the most valuable player in the playoffs for the second consecutive year. "We proved something this time, that we were no fluke champion."

While Parent was turning away 32 shots, Philadelphia's Bob Kelly and Bill Clement went from unsung heroes to men of the hour. It was Kelly's goal at the 11-second mark of the third period that proved the Cup-winning tally, while Clement's score clinched the crown with 2 minutes 48 seconds remaining.

Kelly, who is called Hound by his teammates, usually plays about two out of three games as Coach Fred Shero mixes his third line. Clement had been benched the last two contests.

The "biggest goals" of their careers came against Roger Crozier, who started his first playoff game in the Buffalo net. The 33-year-old, balding Crozier won a Conn Smythe Trophy for best playoff performer in 1966, but he has experienced serious stomach problems the last few years. He replaced Gerry Desjardins, who went from brilliant to shaky as the Sabres advanced to the final series.

Crozier was nearly as sensational as Parent today as he held the Flyers scoreless for the first two periods. Then, as the final period began, Kelly emerged from a pile-up behind the Sabre cage and beat Crozier with a quick shot in front.

Squirting champagne at Ed Snider, the Flyers' chairman of the board, the exuberant Kelly was asked to describe his Stanley Cup goal. "It just went in, that's all," he said, and then drowned his words in champagne.

In the quiet Sabre dressing-room, the name "Parent" was repeated often. "Some people say Parent is lucky," said Jocelyn Guevremont, a Sabre defenseman. "But that's not luck the way he plays."

"They gave the trophy to the right guy," said Richard Martin, the Sabre left wing who probably came the closest to beating the Flyer goalie when his shot banged

Philadelphia Flyers' Bernie Parent, left, and Bobby Clark carry the Stanley Cup off the ice at Buffalo last night.

off both of Parent's skates and then caromed off the post as the goalie turned, expecting to see the puck in the net.

The shutout was Parent's fourth of the playoffs, but it was the fifth for the Flyers, breaking a playoff record. Wayne Stephenson, No. 2 goalie, recorded one of them against the New York Islanders when Parent was injured.

For Coach Shero, the triumph was a sign of toughness as well as maturity for his team. "Nobody likes a winner, really," he said.

"After you win, they look for flaws or a weakness and lay for you every game, hoping to knock you down.

"What they didn't realize was that we didn't want to lose."

For Floyd Smith, the Buffalo coach, the game "ended too abruptly." Then he added: "But I have no complaints. We played pretty well. We couldn't get any breaks and really put anything together.

"This is our first shot. We'll be back."

For Ted Harris, the 39-year-old defenseman, the

game was the last of his career. This was his fifth Stanley Cup winner (the first four with Montreal), and he noted:

"Going out on top, that caps a perfect career. A lot of guys play their whole lives without being on a Cup winner. I feel very fortunate."

Ed Van Impe, the Flyers' oldest defenseman, became 35 years old today, and the Cup was the "best birthday present" he's ever had. But Parent kidded him, saying, "That Van Impe is getting too wide to play. I can't see around him any more."

Then Parent hugged his teammate and added: "We're going to take the Cup a third time now. Why not?"

```
Philadelphia ................. 0   0   2—2
Buffalo ..................... 0   0   0—0
FIRST PERIOD — None. Penalties — Korab,
Buf, 2:19; Clement, Phi, 8:53; Dupont,
Phi, 11:41; Van Impe, Phi, 14:19; Robert,
Buf, 15:24; Schultz, Phi, 19:21.
SECOND PERIOD—None. Penalties—Korab,
Buf, 5:19; Harris, Phi, 7:39; Guevremont,
Buf, 13:53.
THIRD PERIOD—1, Philadelphia, Kelly 3
(Leach, Jim Watson), :11. 2, Philadelphia,
Clement 1 (Kindrachuk), 17:13. Penalties
—Martin, Buf, 1:11; Carriere, Buf, 3:35;
Kindrachuk, Phi, 10:32.
Shots on goal: Philadelphia, 6-12-13—31.
Buffalo, 13-13-6—32.
Goalies: Philadelphia, Parent. Buffalo,
Crozier. A: 15,863.
```

May 28, 1975

Salaries in Hockey Drying Up Minors

By ROBIN HERMAN

For every extra $30,000 that Bobby Orr can extract from the Bostons Bruins by the end of his multi-million-dollar contract talks, "some minor league player has paid for it with his job," according to Richard Sorkin, a player representative.

Sorkin is one of the agents who have been watching with concern as minor league hockey in North America withers year by year, leaving increasing numbers of their player clients unemployed.

Franchises once would sign 40 or more players in order to supply a major and minor league team with at least 20 players apiece. For economy's sake now, most franchises have joined hands in minor league operations so that each partner need supply but 10 players to a farm club.

"They're spending money on proven players and saving money on the guy who isn't

going to make it," said Sorkin.

It has become common practice for franchises to rid themselves of surplus long-term obligations to less-talented players by buying up the remaining years of a player's contract —offering cash on the line equivalent to between 30 and 60 per cent of what the player would have earned.

Bob Woolf, a Boston lawyer who represents Derek Sanderson among other players, said that some of his clients seeking contract renewals had received half-price "take it or leave it" offers from their employers.

"And they're serious," Woolf said. "I've had people who made $50,000 to $60,000 and are getting contracts for $25,000."

At one time, every club in the 18-team National Hockey League ran its own minor league affiliate. But now only Chicago, Toronto

and California operate minor league clubs without partners. The trend is toward having skeletal farm operations in the manner of a taxi squad.

In the extreme, Houston of the World Hockey Association went through last season with just one minor league player in reserve, Bill Prentice, who was placed on the Tulsa club, which is shared by Vancouver and Atlanta of the N.H.L. Fortunately, Houston went through an injury-free season, but this season the Aeros will carry four or five minor leaguers.

"The minor leagues are slowly being destroyed," said Woolf. "This isn't what the athlete was seeking. He wanted a reasonable living. Let other sports take warning. I think we [player representatives] really have to be concerned with the health of the industry rather than

any individual. I always thought it important that athletes earn a good living, but not so much that they strangle the franchise.

"Calgary [formerly Vancouver of the W.H.A.] got rid of $1,200,000 in contracts," said Woolf. "It's almost like Derek. Remember we got a million [from the W.H.A. Philadelphia Blazers] not to play hockey. These are a series of little Dereks."

One "little Derek" is Pat Price, a rookie defenseman with the New York Islanders, who had been signed to a five-year, $1-million contract with Vancouver of the W.H.A. He played one unhappy and unproductive season, then won his release and was waived through the league. The Islanders picked him up at the "bargain" price of about $60,000 a year.

September 21, 1975

Compensation Rule Key to N.H.L. Pact

By PARTON KEESE

The National Hockey League Players Association negotiated a five-year agreement with the N.H.L. owners yesterday that acknowledges the right of a team to be compensated when a player plays out his option year, becomes a free agent and then signs with another club.

The hockey players' decision to accept the "right to equalization or compensation" clause is directly opposite the stand taken by the National Football League Players Association. The football union is suing to eliminate a similar clause, known as the Rozelle rule.

A key difference between the two free-agent rules is that the N.H.L. agreed to an impartial arbitrator, Judge Edward Houston, to determine the compensation if the two teams cannot agree. In the N.F.L., Commissioner Rozelle settles the case when a deadlock develops. The football players have charged that Rozelle, as the representative of the owners, is a barrier to the movement of a free agent.

Pit Martin of the Chicago Black Hawks, president of the N.H.L. players' group, defended the acceptance of the compensation clause:

"One big reason is that hockey has another league [World Hockey Association] while football hasn't. This gives an N.H.L. player still another alternative, jumping to the W.H.A., if he is not satisfied with his contract. The pro football player has no such bargaining power."

Another important part of the agreement states that in the event of a merger between the N.H.L. and the W.H.A., the players are entitled to terminate the agreement and to reopen negotiations in regard to equalization and free agents.

"The players' association

has fought such a merger and will continue to fight a merger," asserted R. Alan Eagleson, executive director of the N.H.L. Players' Association. "A merger would only bring salaries down. When the American Football League merged with the N.F.L., average salaries went down from $40,000 to $28,000."

Other provisions of the agreement, which is retroactive to Sept. 15 aid is in effect until Sept. 14, 1980, include:

A dual option permitting teams and players to negotiate contracts with option clauses. At the end of such contracts, the players become free agents.

A 50 per cent increase in pension benefits from $500 per year of service to $750 per year of service.

An equal split with the N.H.L. of proceeds from international hockey games, such as the upcoming eight-game series with the Soviet Union.

And an increase of nearly $500,000 in league prize money.

Though the Rozelle rule has seldom been invoked in the 12 years it has been in effect in the N.F.L., testimony by football players has pointed to its threat in restricting their movement from one club to another. The players contend that teams are reluctant to sign free agents and expose themselves to possible arbitration by Rozelle. Such a reluctance, they claim, works a hardship on free agents selling their services.

In the National Hockey League, however, this was the first year that players were permitted to play out their options and sign with another team. The most celebrated case was Marcel Dionne of the Detroit Red Wings, the league's third highest scorer, who signed a contract with the Los Angeles Kings. The Wings were compensated with Terry Harper and Dan Maloney, the players agreed upon by both clubs.

If the owners had not been able to agree, they probably would not have completed the deal, although the N.H.L. had the arbitration services of Judge Houston available.

In a byplay to the Dionne move, Harper has challenged the league and the Kings in court, charging fraud in the trade and that the deal was a violation of antitrust laws. A hearing on Harper's request for a restraining order was scheduled to be heard today in a Los Angeles court.

Reactions from other sports embroiled over freedom of players appeared to differ. An official of the N.F.L.'s Management Council praised "hockey people and hockey players for succeeding in settling the issue in collective bargaining."

Terry Bledsoe, assistant executive director of the council, said that "collective bargaining is where this should be all along. This is too critical an issue to bargain around."

But Larry Fleisher, general counsel of the National Bas-

ketball Association Players, said that basketball players would not accept the agreement that the hockey players had accepted.

"We're not privy to all of the factors involved in hockey's collective bargaining," Fleischer added, "but we understand that a major factor in the agreement was the requirement that there be no merger between the two leagues or all bets are off.

"I also understand there are numerous other aspects totally unrelated to professional basketball. We have

indicated all along that a rule that inhibits a player from exercising his free right of choice after his contract expires is unacceptable even if we have no merger agreement.

"The basketball players have strongly felt the entire system of college drafts, tied together with the reserve clause and a form of compensation such as the Rozelle rule, violates the antitrust laws, and we have proceeded accordingly in the Federal courts."

October 7, 1975

Canadiens Defeat Flyers, 5-3, Sweep Series for Stanley Cup

By ROBIN HERMAN
Special to The New York Times

PHILADELPHIA, May 16—Hoisting hockey's glistening prize, the Stanley Cup, on their shoulders, the Montreal Canadiens returned the National Hockey League championship north of the border tonight.

The Flying Frenchmen defeated the defending champions, the Philadelphia Flyers, 5-3, and swept the final series, 4-0, before a frenzied, capacity crowd in the Spectrum. The Flyers had held the cup the last two years.

It had taken just 13 games for the Canadiens to complete three playoff rounds and forge the quickest Stanley Cup conquest since the league expanded. They had beaten the Flyers by a single goal in each of the first three games, but tonight the Canadiens' most high-powered line broke a 3-3 deadlock with 5:42 to go on a goal by Guy Lafleur. Then Peter Mahovlich scored for the two-goal victory.

"I think there's a lot of happy faces out there because we lost," said the Flyers' Bill Barber. "More than if we won. I don't think too many people were happy the last two years that we won it. Because of this violence thing. It was blown out of proportion."

But he added: "We lost to a hell of a team that's got the depth of no other team in the league, and I think that hurt us."

The level of hockey skill in tonight's game and in the entire series was remarkable, and this game never became violent. Philadelphia left that tactic behind in Toronto when several of its players were indicted after a quarter-final game there.

But when the hard-working Flyers came close to Montreal's incredible pace, the Canadiens, coached by Scotty Bowman, simply sharpened their play to match them.

"You must remember," said Fred Shero, Philadelphia's coach, "Montreal's such a great club; if we

would have played better, maybe they would have played even better."

Of his plans for next season, Shero said, "I imagine we have to make some decisions quickly about trades and strengthen the team."

Bob Gainey, one of Montreal's outstanding new brand of defensive-minded wings, credited the regular-season point race with Philadelphia for keeping Montreal sharp. The Canadiens lost only 11 games this season and amassed a record 127 points in 80 games.

"I don't think anyone wins the Stanley Cup in just the playoffs," said Gainey, shouting over the din of his exultant teammates and the popping of champagne bottles in the locker room. "It's the whole year. I think if you look, it's the team that's been there the whole year that's there in the end."

In such a desperate situation, down 3 games to none, the Flyers began by introducing Kate Smith, who wore a

flouncy, lime-colored dress and waved her arms about as she sang "God Bless America," the Flyers' good-luck song.

Then, with 41 seconds ticked off the clock, Reggie Leach electrified the sellout crowd of 17,077 by scoring on the game's first shot. He thus set a season and playoff goal-scoring record of 80. He had a record 19 goals in 16 playoff games and won the league's Conn Smythe trophy as the playoffs' most-valuable player.

"I don't know, it's just unbelievable," said Leach of his magic touch, shaking his head and acting as if it had been someone else who upset so many goaltenders this season.

But after Leach's score came a succession of power-play goals for both sides. Steve Shutt of the Canadiens beat Wayne Stephenson while Don Saleski was in the penalty box, and then, with Barber off the ice Pierre Bouchard shot through a crowd and past the screened Flyer goalie. Before the first period was over, Tom Bladon of the Flyers helped tie the score by sending a shot from the point during a power play that hit off Barber and eluded Ken Dryden.

The Flyers, who had sagged in the middle periods of the series' previous games, remained tenacious as they opened the second period in a 2-2 tie. And when Andre Dupont popped in a rebound for another power-play goal, a spotlight caught the Moose doing a prolonged version of his knee-pumping celebration dance.

But less than five minutes later the Canadiens evened the score again. Stephenson pushed away a rolling shot across the crease, but Yvon Cournoyer lifted the puck over the prone goalie for Montreal's third power-play goal.

Thus the teams faced the

third period locked in a 3-3 tie and knowing that whichever scored the next goal in the difficult game probably would be the winner.

After a number of tremendous stops by Stephenson, whose work had been admirable in each game, the Canadiens' highest scoring regular-season line of Lafleur, Mahovlich and Shutt claimed the game and the cup for the Canadiens.

Philadelphia had just killed off a penalty to Larry Goodenough and then failed to score on a power play when the Mahovlich line tore into the Flyers' end.

On the line's second playmaking attempt of the drive, Lafleur knocked in a pass from Mahovlich to make it 4-3, and 58 seconds later the pair reversed the order and Mahovlich scored the fifth goal.

"In the last four games," said Leach, "they never used to play that line that much. They come up with Doug Jarvis and those guys [Montreal's checking line], Cournoyer and the rest didn't get much ice time. They have so much bench strength."

So strong were the Canadiens in talent that Scotty Bowman, their coach, devised 31 combinations of forward lines tonight while the Flyers were sending out 17.

Considering the Canadiens' depth, do the Flyers stand much chance of beating them next season?

"Put it this way," said Leach. "Montreal had the same team last year, but lost out to Buffalo [in the semi finals]. They just put everything together this year and we didn't."

"It's hard to believe," said Stephenson. "I sat in my

locker a long time. I couldn't believe it was over. We'll think it over the summer and when we come back next season we'll be that much hungrier to get the cup back in Philadelphia."

Montreal   2 1 2—5
Philadelphia   2 1 0—3

First Period—1, Philadelphia, Leach 19 (Bridgman), :41. 2, Montreal, Shutt 7 (Cournoyer, Mahovlich), 5:35. 3, Montreal, Bouchard 2 (Risebrough), 11:48. 4, Philadelphia, Barber 6 (Bladon, Dupont), 19:20. Penalties—Schultz, Phi, double minor, :29; Savard, Mon, :29; Saleski, Phi, 4:20; Barber, Phi, 9:54; Lapointe, Mon, 17:32.

Second Period—5, Philadelphia, Dupont 2 (Barber, Clarke), 13:59. 6, Montreal, Cournoyer 3 (Robinson, Lafleur), 19:49. Penalties—Gainey, Mon, :21; Clarke, Phi, :21; Lapointe, Mon, 12:43; Lemaire, Mon, 17:20; Dornhoefer, Phi, 17:53.

Third Period—7, Montreal, Lafleur 7 (Mahovlich, Shutt), 14:18. 8, Montreal, Mahovlich 4 (Lafleur, Shutt), 15:16. Penalties—Goodenough, Phi, 9:03; Gainey, Mon, 11:26.

Shots on goal: Montreal 11-7-12—30. Philadelphia 7-9-8—24.

Goalies: Montreal, Dryden. Philadelphia, Stephenson. A: 17,077.

May 17, 1976

Orr Joins Hawks, but His Knee Is Doubtful

Associated Press

Alan Eagleson, agent for Bobby Orr, pats Tommy Ivan, Black Hawks' general manager on the shoulder as they prepare to announce deal with Orr at Montreal news session.

By PARTON KEESE
Special to The New York Times

MONTREAL, June 9—Bobby Orr agreed today to accept the terms offered by the Chicago Black Hawks' hockey team.

Though the financial arrangements and other details will not be released until Orr officially signs the contract, his agent said the agreement covered several years, concerned business and hockey employment and was not

conditional on Orr's being able to play.

Early in the negotiations, William A. Wirtz, president of the Black Hawks, had been reported saying he was prepared to offer Orr $3 million on a multiyear contract. But

neither Paul A. Mooney, president of the Boston Bruins, nor Alan Eagleson, Orr's agent, would comment on the figure agreed on.

"Whether it's six years for $3 million or three years for $6 million," Eagleson said, "I'm not here to discuss the money Orr will get. You'll be told everything when Bobby signs the pact soon in Chicago."

The 28-year-old Orr, who became the game's most acclaimed defenseman in a 10-year career with the Bruins and achieved free-agent status last week, flew here last night to complete lengthy negotiations This morning he left for Toronto General Hospital, where he was to undergo examination of his damaged left knee and learn whether he would be able to play again.

According to Eagleson, the Bruins made a last-ditch effort to bring Orr back to Boston, but Orr said that new business interests he had in the Midwest precluded such a move.

"Since our last offer near the end of 1975 was declined by the Bruins," Eagleson said, "Bobby has developed major business interests which require him to be located in the Midwestern section of the United States.

"But Bobby asked me to say for him that he hates to leave Boston, where he spent the best 10 years of his life and where he will always feel in debt to the fans, his coaches and former teammates."

Eagleson said the Bruins reneged on an agreement reached in September 1975 by which he said Orr would have been paid $295,000 a year for five years, plus a lump sum of $925,000 to be paid in June 1980. As an alternative, he said, Orr was to have taken an 18.6 percent ownership in the team.

A few days later, Eagleson said, he asked the Jacobs brothers (owners of the Bruins) to amend the lump-sum figure as $185,000 a year for five years. They agreed, he said, but 48 hours later, according to him, the brothers called to say there had been a misunderstanding, and the deal was off.

The agreement between Orr and the Hawks also specified that compensation for Boston would be worked out between the teams in collective bargaining, and that the National Hockey League's arbitration procedures would be waived.

The N.H.L. requires a team signing a free agent to compensate his former team in a mutually satisfactory way through players, cash or both.

Tommy Ivan, the Hawks' general manager, said that compensation would be worked out after the medical report on Orr, which might lead to a sixth operation on his knee. But no players will change hands, he added, until Orr "plays for us and we see what kind of an Orr we're getting."

"There will be no deferment of compensation, though," asserted Eagleson. "It's cash on the barrelhead. If Bobby plays in Chicago as if he were 100 percent, then compensation would have to be three, four or five players of high caliber.

"But if he doesn't turn out to be the Orr of, say, 1974 or earlier, then the position of compensation would adjusted accordingly."

Ivan said: "We'll take one step at a time. If he can't play, we'll find something for him to do."

Eagleson: "But if Orr can't play, he won't take anybody's money under false pretenses. He's that kind of guy."

Ivan: "But we're obligated to pay him regardless, no matter what he says."

Eagleson: "Bobby will be the ultimate person to decide that."

Then Eagleson was asked: "How many games will it take to decide how much Orr Chicago is getting?"

"That's also up to Bobby, who is honest and would tell the truth," the agent replied. "But he is different than a guy who has a heart murmur, say, and wants to come back. Orr keeps recovering. Didn't he play pretty well last year between his fourth and fifth operations, even if it was just for 10 games?"

Orr had to be summoned here yesterday from his hockey camp in Orillia, Ontario, Eagleson said, when the negotiations began to touch

on things that only Bobby could answer.

"Chicago is buying a pig in a poke and paying a very high price for it," said the agent.

Meanwhile, Denis Potvin of the New York Islanders and Brad Park, the former New York Ranger now with the Boston Bruins, were named defensemen on the N.H.L. All-Star team. Glenn Resch of the Islanders was named goalie on the second team.

Others on the first team were Bobby Clarke, Philadelphia Flyers, center; Guy Lafleur, Montreal Canadiens, right wing; Bill Barber, Flyers, left wing, and Ken Dryden, Canadiens, goalie.

The second team included Guy Lapointe, Canadiens, and Borje Salming, Toronto Maple Leafs, defensemen; Gil Perreault, Buffalo Sabres, center; Reggie Leach, Flyers, right wing, and Rick Martin, Sabres, left wing.

June 10, 1976

Canadiens Oust Bruins, 2-1, For 2d Straight Cup Sweep

By PARTON KEESE
Special to The New York Times

BOSTON, May 14—An overtime goal by Jacques Lemaire tonight not only gave the Montreal Canadiens a 2-1 victory over the Boston Bruins, the championship of the National Hockey League and the Stanley Cup, but also may have proved what people have been saying all along: The Canadiens are the best hockey team in the world.

When Guy Lafleur passed the puck to his linemate, Lemaire, for the sudden-death goal at 4 minutes 32 seconds —they combined for the first goal in the same way, too—it represented Montreal's second straight league crown, the second straight time the Canadiens had swept the final series in four games and quite possibly the start of another awesome dynasty.

And for Lafleur—they now call him SuperFleur—the Conn Smythe Trophy for the most valuable player in the playoffs was awarded to him, as well as a new car from Sport magazine for his 26 points in 14 playoff games. Lafleur came within 1 point of tying the record for most points in a playoff season.

Bobby Schmautz led the Bruins in honors, scoring his 11th goal of the playoffs tonight, the highest total for an individual player, though Gerry Cheevers, Boston's goaltender, also starred in a losing cause.

"They're certainly a good club," Schmautz said of the Canadiens, "and over the year they've proved how good. Eighty games and eight defeats, that tells the story pretty well."

Schmautz had given Boston a 1-0 lead at 11:38 of the first period when his 40-foot shot surprised Ken Dryden, Montreal's goaltender, who had been demasked a few seconds before by a collision in front of his cage.

But the Canadiens, taking advantage of the only poor moment the Bruins had in the game, tied the score when Lemaire converted Lafleur's pass from the slot at 1:34 of the second period. Boston looked hapless in trying to clear a puck that just wouldn't be cleared.

In the scoreless third period, the Bruins were outshooting the Canadiens, 10 to 8, while Cheevers was making spectacular saves, particularly on Murray Wilson and Lafleur, probably the two fastest skaters on the Montreal club.

In the overtime, the first one of this final series, the Canadiens kept the pressure on virtually the whole 4 1-2 minutes, taking four shots, to none for Boston. Cheevers continued to sparkle until Lafleur grabbed a loose puck behind the net and passed quickly to Lemaire at the corner of the net. Cheevers had no chance, and the season ended with a flash of Lemaire's stick.

"Lafleur is so quick and in both ends," said Mike Milbury, the Boston defenseman who had been automatically suspended for the third game because of acquiring two game-misconducts. "He forces mistakes out of you, and he can anticipate as fast as he skates."

The Canadiens' Secret

But nearly everyone agreed that Lafleur wasn't the only reason Montreal was so far ahead of other N.H.L. teams. Harry Sinden, the Bruins' general manager, claimed their secret lay in their checking.

"In most areas we're equal to Montreal," Sinden asserted, "but their ability to check is superior to any other team. They check you every inch of the ice. In that respect, they're champions, and I congratulate them."

Guy Lapointe, one of the three big and mobile Montreal defensemen a lot of people considered the difference, said:

"At Montreal they teach you only one way: win, win, win. If you don't, they're right on top of you, putting pressure on you and won't let you relax. So you can't do anything but work at winning or you're out."

Larry Robinson, another of Montreal's Big Three defense, said: "A season like ours doesn't come easy. We had to work very, very hard. There had to be a lot of dedication. We had to sweat it a lot, too. What it amounted to was 80 games of work."

Then Robinson added: "I think Bobby Schmautz put it best when he said, 'The Bruins have a hard-working team, but the Canadiens have a talented team that works hard. Maybe that was the difference.' "

Montreal .... 0 1 0 1—"

Boston .... 1 0 0 0—1

FIRST PERIOD—1, Boston, Schmautz (11) (Park), 11:38. Penalties—Wensink, Boston (4:25); Lemaire, Montreal (9:32); Mahovlich, Montreal (18:17).

SECOND PERIOD—2, Montreal, Lemaire (6) (Lafleur, Robinson), 1:34. Penalties—Robinson, Mon (7:53); Shepoard, Bos (8:19); Montreal, bench, served by Mahovlich (10:25); O'Reilly, Bos (13:07).

THIRD PERIOD—No scoring. No penalties.

OVERTIME—3, Montreal, Lemaire (7) (Lafleure) 4:32. No penalties.

Shots on goal—Montreal: 4, 12, 8, 4—28. Boston: 8, 8, 10, 0—26. Goalies—Dryden and Cheevers. Attendance—14,597.

May 15, 1977

Ken Dryden, Canadiens' goalie, looking over his shoulder as shot by Bruins' Bobby Schmautz got by him for a goal last night in Stanley Cup playoff game in Boston. Dryden had his face mask knocked off moments earlier.

N.H.L. Governors Turn Down Merger With 6 W.H.A. Teams

By ROBIN HERMAN

After five years of being simultaneously wooed and wounded by the World Hockey Association, the National Hockey League's 18-member board of governors yesterday rejected a merger with the rival W.H.A. The actual rejection came in the form of a vote against expansion.

Said John Ziegler, president-elect of the N.H.L.:

"After very careful and due consideration, the proposed plan of expansion was put to the governors and it failed to receive the requisite [three-fourths] majority for approval, and thus any possible expansion for the

1977-78 season has gone by the board at this point."

Following six weeks of negotiation with the W.H.A. teams, the governors cast secret ballots late yesterday afternoon. Ziegler did not reveal the vote count to the governors or to the press.

The six teams hoping to join the N.H.L. were the Cincinnati Stingers, New England Whalers, Houston Aeros, Quebec Nordiques, Winnipeg Jets and Edmonton Oilers. Presumably the six teams will continue to play next season as the W.H.A. with the Birmingham Bulls and the Indianapolis Racers, both of whom had not applied for membership in the N.H.L.

Until yesterday, the N.H.L. board had

never voted on a new expansion. When support for merger seemed more firm six weeks ago, the board had empowered a fact-finding committee to negotiate the possibility of expansion, or de facto merger with the W.H.A. Opposition to such an accomodation had been staunch throughout the summer-long meetings. The Boston Bruins, Toronto Maple Leafs and Los Angeles Kings were the most vocal opponents.

Harold Ballard, president of the Maple Leafs, left the meetings and said, "Am I happy! Nothing like a winner. There will be no expansion this year."

Bill Torrey, general manager of the New York Islanders expressed calm satisfaction. "I think at this time it's the proper decision," he said.

Ziegler informed the W.H.A. representatives of the vote at 6 P.M. yesterday. Nelson Skalbania of Edmonton, Harrison Vickers of Houston, Howard Baldwin of New England and Bill De-Witt of Cincinnati had been waiting for the N.H.L.'s decision in their suite at the Waldorf Astoria, where the meetings had been taking place.

Baldwin, who as a member of the W.H.A. merger committee, served as a prime mover in the ill-fated effort, was the most visibly angered by the news. His words signaled a continuation of the five-year "war" between the leagues that has seen the average base salary of an N.H.L. player inflate from $31,118 in 1971-72 to $96,319 last season mostly because of competition for personnel.

'Getting Aggressive'

Later last night, Baldwin added: "Let the N.H.L. come to us in the future. We are going ahead with plans for an eight-team league that includes Edmonton, Winnipeg, Quebec, New England, Cincinnati, Houston and perhaps Birmingham and Indianapolis. John Bassett, the owner of Birmingham,

just called to confirm his intention to play."

"Remember what the general said. 'And the blood will let in the streets.' Well, the red ink will let in the streets. They made a very unbusiness-like decision," Baldwin said. "There isn't a league in pro sports that has had an application like mine. The decision was made by a small group of emotional men, not in the best interest of hockey. We're not going out of business. Now maybe we'll concentrate on getting aggressive."

"They weren't dealing in good faith because the decision, on a business-like basis, was so incredibly simple that it's almost impossible to reject it," Baldwin said. "It's a sad thing that you have four or five people in the N.H.L. that are little thinkers.

"We did feel it was in the best interest of hockey. And I still do. But I wouldn't want to try to kid anybody. I'm bitterly disappointed.

What about future merger possibilities?

"I have been going so hot and heavy for six months, for me to think of future merger—other then getting together with my wife and kids after

six months—is impossible," Baldwin concluded.

Jacques McKeag of the Winnipeg Jets said, "We believe that the N.H.L. was afraid of the high caliber of our on-ice product . . . we opened our books to them . . . what has happened here today has turned us off completely."

DeWitt was another stunned man in the 15th floor suite at the Waldorf, saying I think they acted as if they would do it [merge] all along. They didn't turn down any individual applications, only the idea that they were going to expand."

David Weinstein, the W.H.A.'s lawer, repeatedly asked Ziegler why the governors apparently had changed their minds, "but he refused to give an explanation," Weinstein said.

Since negotiations began in earnest in June, the W.H.A. had extended a legal agreement releasing the N.H.L. from any liability in the event the merger was not consumed. Some governors expect the W.H.A. to sue, however, charging a lack of good faith in the negotiations.

August 10, 1977

Canadiens Win, 4-1, and Take 3d Straight Stanley Cup

By PARTON KEESE
Special to The New York Times

BOSTON, May 25—Neither the tenacious Boston Bruins, the cozy Boston Garden rink, 14,602 mostly hostile fans nor the coaching of Boston's Don Cherry could prevent the Montreal Canadiens tonight from capturing the Stanley Cup for the third consecutive time.

By a score of 4-1, the Canadiens snuffed out the Bruins, four games to two, and once again captured the championship of the National Hockey League.

The only other club besides the Canadiens to win the cup as many as three straight years was Toronto, which twice accomplished the feat—from 1947 to 1949 and from 1962 to 1964. Montreal won five cups in a row, from 1956 to 1960—and has now won 21 championships since the league was formed in 1917. The next best record is Toronto, with 11.

"They're worthy champions," said Cherry, who only yesterday was blatantly criticizing both the Canadiens and the refereeing. "They beat us in our own building, so you can't take anything away from them."

Robinson Most Valuable

Larry Robinson, the Canadiens' 6-foot-3-inch defenseman, was awarded the Conn Smythe Trophy as the most valuable player in the playoffs. With two assists tonight, Robinson completed the 15-game stretch with 21 points, which tied him with his teammate, Guy

Lafleur, as the point leader in the playoffs.

After all the previous charges and countercharges concerning penalties, plus the fighting of the last two games, tonight's contest could have won a peace award. Referee Andy van Hellemond called only five penalties, three against the Bruins, none in the final period.

With rough stuff a thing of the past, the players were able to concentrate on pure hockey.

Mario Tremblay was one player who rose to the occasion. Without a goal until tonight, and having appeared in only four previous games, the 21-year-old Tremblay came through with two scores against Gerry Cheevers, the Bruin goalie, to lead Montreal's attack.

Pierre Mondou, another unsung youngster, set up two goals, while Rejean Houle, who hadn't scored in the last five games, picked up the final goal for Montreal.

"That's one of the secrets to our success," said Robinson. "We always seem to have someone to step in for somebody else and take up the slack."

Mondou was able to skate a regular shift for the first time because Doug Risebrough came up with an injured back in the first period.

The lone Boston scorer was Brad Park, who finished second in the balloting for most valuable player. Four minutes 5 seconds into the game, On the first shot, Park did what the Bruins had said all along was so important for them to do—score the first goal.

For Park, it was a record-tying ninth

goal for a defenseman in playoff action. Bobby Orr also scored nine times for Boston in 1970.

Boston lost its 1-0 lead less than three minutes later, at 7:01, when Steve Shutt put his own rebound into the cage, and the Bruins were able to take only seven more shots in the first two periods as they lost control of the game.

"Our defense won it," said Yvon Lambert, a large Montreal forward who excelled in screening Cheevers's view near the crease. "All our guys played well, but they don't call Robinson, (Guy) Lapointe and (Andre) Savard the Big Three for nothing. They bottled up Boston completely."

Besides the accolades for the defense, the talk centered on the new breed of Canadiens—the Mondous, Tremblays and Pierre Larouches.

"I didn't expect to score and I didn't even expect to play," said Tremblay. "But when things aren't going right, Bowman [Coach Scotty Bowman] likes to change things around. Mondou, Larouche and I were fresh, and so he puts us in to give the team a lift.

"It is the happiest day of my life since I was born."

Mondou, 22, was also ecstatic, saying: "This was my greatest game. I'm so happy that I was able to help. Last year I did nothing."

Cherry considered the Canadiens' depth a prime factor in their victory.

Canadiens' Scoring

Montreal Canadiens .... 2 2 0—4
Boston Bruins .... 1 0 0—1
FIRST PERIOD—1, Boston, Park 9 (Marcotte, Sheppard), 4:05. 2, Montreal, Shutt 9 (Mondou, Robinson), 7:01. 3, Montreal, Tremblay 1 (Mondou, Robinson), 9:20. Penalties—Nyrop (3:43); O'Brien (4:54).
SECOND PERIOD—4, Montreal, Tremblay 2 (Lambert, Nyrop), 13:37. 5, Montreal, Houle 3 (Jarvis), 17:46. Penalties—Jonathan (4:34); Jarvis (7:09); Wensink (8:43).
THIRD PERIOD—No scoring. No penalties.
Shots on goal—Montreal: 8, 9, 7—24. Boston: 4, 4, 8—16.
Goalies—Montreal, Dryden. Boston, Cheevers. A—14,602.

"They're the strongest team in the league," he said. "Where I had to use the same guys to kill penalties as I used on power plays, they could put in fresh players from their bench.

"But we made it a little bit closer than last year," Cherry said, alluding to the Canadiens' four-game sweep in 1977. "Let them get stronger. We'll get stronger, too, and we'll win more games next season."

May 26, 1978

North Stars, Barons Merge in N.H.L.

By PARTON KEESE
Special to The New York Times

MONTREAL, June 14—The Cleveland Barons and Minnesota North Stars have agreed to combine their starting teams for the 1978-79 season, the National Hockey League governors announced today. As a result, the N.H.L. will be reduced to 17 teams.

In the agreement, a special dispersal draft will be held tomorrow morning, preceding the regularly scheduled amateur draft, to stock the new combind team. As per agreement, the new Minnesota North Stars team will be allowed to protect 10 skaters and two goalies from the combined rosters of about 60 players. Following that, the Washington Capitals and the St. Louis Blues will each be allowed to draft one player each from the remaeining list, followed by Minnesota adding one more player to its protected list.

Next in line in this dispersal draft will be Vancouver and Pittsburgh, which will also draft one player each from the leftover players. Then Minnesota will add one more to its protected list before the Colorado Rockies get a chance to draft one player.

Whatever players are left will then be placed on the new Minnesota squad. The new team will also be paid $30,000 for each player drafted by another club.

The combined Minnesota-Cleveland team will be situated in Minneapolis, with the management to be formed from both clubs. It will play home games at Bloomington, Minn. The team will play in the Adams Division with Boston, Buffalo and Toronto.

The reason given for five other clubs being allowed to draft from the combined Minnesota-Cleveland list was to improve the chances of the weaker clubs. Neither Washington, St. Louis, Vancouver or Pittsburgh qualified for the playoffs last season, though Colorado did. That's why the Rockies were placed last in the final drafting position. Minnesota had the worst record in the league last season, although it was in a prime hockey area. Cleveland reportedly lost $3.5 million last year.

Unofficially, the new team is expected to protect the following players, according to Lou Nanne, current general manager of the North Stars:

Al MacAdam, right wing; Dennis Maruk, center; Rick Hampton, defense; Mike Fidler, left wing; Greg Smith, defense, and Gilles Meloche, goalie, all of Cleveland, and Glenn Sharpley, center; Tim Young, center; Brad Maxwell, defense; Bryan Maxwell, defense; PerOlov Brasar, left wing, and Pete LoPresti, goalie, all of Minnesota.

Players left unprotected would include Kris Manery, Dave Gardner, Bob Murdoch, J.P. Parise and Jean Potvin, all of Cleveland, and Ron Zanussi, Kent Andersson, Steve Jenson, Don Palafous, Nick Beverly and Harvey Bennett, all of Minnesota.

Islanders, Canadiens Cited

The governors enjoyed one break in their hectic day, the annual N.H.L. awards luncheon. Enjoying it most were the Montreal Canadiens and New York Islanders, who dominated the first and second all-star teams.

The islanders placed three players on the first all-star team, Denis Potvin, defense; Bryan Trottier, center, and Clark Gillies, left wing. Montreal had two, Guy Lafleur, right wing, and Boston Bruins' Brad Park filled the other defense post.

Mike Bossy of the Islanders was named right wing on the second all-star team, giving the Islanders four all-stars, which equaled their total number for the previous five seasons.

June 15, 1978

Canadiens Beat Rangers for
4th Stanley Cup in Row

Gainey Is Given Smythe Trophy

By GERALD ESKENAZI
Special to The New York Times

MONTREAL, May 21 — The dream stopped at the Forum tonight for the Rangers, as it has for so many other clubs. The Stanley Cup again was captured by the Canadiens, this time in five games, by a 4-1 score.

They won their fourth Cup in a row by defeating the New Yorkers, those upstarts who had finished in third place only to tear through three playoff rounds and reach the final for only the third time since 1940.

But the Rangers did not have the presence under pressure acquired from playing for the Cup, and that was a major reason the Canadiens won.

Since the Rangers last won it in 1940, the Canadiens have taken it 18 times.

Yet, this was special. For the Canadiens had not won it at the Forum since 1968, taking six Stanley Cups after that on the road. So the crowd stood for the final half-minute, and dozens others crowded near the entrance to the rink, where the Cup would be hidden (because of superstitious players) until the closing seconds.

And then it appeared at game's end, a gleaming, silvery symbol that, to Canadians, transcends the Super Bowl or World Series.

The players mobbed Ken Dryden, their goalie who played only because the man who was supposed to replace him in Game 2, Michel (Bunny) La-rocque, was conked on the head by a teammate's practice shot.

Suddenly, they started throwing pieces of their equipment, like roses, to the adoring crowd. A glove flew. Applause. Then a stick. More screaming. Finally, a white helmet.

Gainey Also Gets New Car

On the rink's other end John Davidson, the ninth-grade dropout who had been battered almost twice as often as Dryden, a lawyer, in this series, was surrounded by his teammates. They knew one of the reasons they had come this far was their big goalie, who played his best six weeks of hockey of a previously mediocre career.

Perhaps if it had lasted another game Davidson might have received the Conn Smythe Trophy as the play-offs' most valuable performer. Instead, it went to Bob Gainey, who also deserved it. The hard-working Canadien forward batters people with his clean checks, and unnerves goalies with his cruises goalward.

Gainey also won the Sport magazine award as the most valuable player in the final series. For his prize he will get a new car.

Only two months ago, Dryden admitted, he thought the Canadiens were done for, that they could not sustain the intensity for another run at the 35½-inch trophy that has enough room on the base for rosters of Cup teams until 1992.

"But it's all passé now," he said in the locker room.

He was a virtual spectator the final two periods when the crowd, and players, sensed victory. The Canadiens strc:ed 22 shots at Davidson while Dryden was tested only seven times.

The New Yorkers rarely followed their battle plan: to ram the puck behind Dryden and then to pounce on it, or hit a defenseman and prevent him from making or o of those miraculous outlet passes that result in so many of the Canadiens' classic rushes.

Canadiens Take Charge

But the Canadiens were buoyed by a Madison Square Garden-style 90-second ovation when they took the ice. They took command and rarely returned it. In the first 7 minutes they outshot the Rangers by 5-0.

Midway through the opening session they got lucky when Rick Chartraw's shot bounced off someone in front of Davidson and went into the net.

Yet, this appeared to give the Rangers a strange sort of lift and they put together their best — and virtually only — sustained effort of the game. They somehow lost their intensity in Game 2, after winning the opener, when they blew an early 2-0 lead.

Some of it returned late in the opening period tonight when they tied the game on Carol Vadnais's deflected backhander. The Rangers now needed to protect Davidson, who disclosed that he had stretched ligaments in his left

Rangers Scoring

Rangers .... 1 0 0—1
Montreal Canadiens .... 1 3 0—4
FIRST PERIOD — 1. Montreal, Chartraw 2 (Houle, Lambert) 10:36. 2. Rangers, Vadnais 2 (Murdoch) 16:52. Penalty — Dave Maloney, Rangers 19:59.
SECOND PERIOD — 3. Montreal, Lemaire 10, 1:02. 4. Montreal, Gainey 6 (Jarvis, Houle), 11:01. 5. Montreal, Lemaire 11 (Houle) 18:49. Penalty — Langway. Mon. 6:41.
THIRD PERIOD — No scoring. Penalties — Napier, Mon, 18:12; Greschner, Rangers, 19:41.
Shots on goal — Rangers: 8,3,4—15. Montreal: 9,14.8—31.
Goalies — Rangers, Davidson. Montreal, Dryden. A—18,076.

knee and had played with pain after Game 1.

But the Canadiens began the second period with a power play left over from Dave Maloney's penalty with 1 second remaining in the first period, and Jacques Lemaire, with a 130-foot rush and a 60-foot slap shot, beat Davidson with the first of his two goals.

"That was the only bad goal I allowed in the whole playoffs," admitted Davidson, who said he had been playing with strained ligaments in his left knee since the Islander series. "My leg just wouldn't go down on that shot. It was the only time."

The New York Times / Barton Silverman

Yvon Lambert skates past John Davidson of the Rangers after Rick Chartraw scored Canadiens' first goal of the game during the first period.

In all, the Canadiens got three scores in the period, outshooting the New Yorkers by 14-3, and it was virtually over.

Gainey, moving down the middle, shot home a Doug Jarvis pass and then Lemaire swooped down alone on Davidson, brought him out of the cage and spun in a backhander.

So the final period became a succession of little star turns. There went Guy Lafleur, the city's uncrowned king, and the crowd applauded wildly his low shot that Davidson juggled.

Mark Napier leaped over a fallen Ranger and it was like an aria. The crowd bellowed for more.

"They were flying. I don't think I've seen a team that fast in my life, even the Russians," said the Ranger coach, Fred Shero, later.

"Yes, I was pleased with the year's performance," said Shero, "but it's not easy losing.

"What will we have to do to catch the Canadiens? Pick up some speedier players, I guess. Especially, fast and mobile defensemen. That's the trend of hockey today. At least I hope it is."

Not many people beat the Canadiens once they have come this far. This marked the 26th time since 1926 they were in the finals. Only two clubs — the

Detroit Red Wings and the Toronto Maple Leafs, who did it three times apiece — have taken the Cup from them over that span.

This was not the Rangers' night. Their inexperience showed. They are a team whose players averaged 1.05 playoff appearances to the Canadiens' 4.2. Next year's Rangers will have doubled their playoff experience.

It was Serge Savard, the acting captain for the injured Yvan Cournoyer, who took the big trophy for the victory lap after the traditional handshaking ceremony.

To show what the Rangers were up against, Savard captured the Smythe Trophy 11 years ago.

Yet, the Rangers bumped off the Kings in two straight games. Then they faced the Flyers, who had finished ahead of them in the Patrick Division. The Flyers fell in five. Next came the Islanders, who had finished atop the division with hockey's best mark.

The Islanders fell in six.

And next came the legend as well as a team. Their names go on the cup. Again.

May 22, 1979

SOCCER. The most popular sport in the world. Organized soccer is played in 140 nations, with nearly 16 million players participating. The final match of the 1978 World Cup, in which Argentina defeated the Netherlands, was televised around the world and attracted an estimated billion viewers. Soccer stadiums such as the Maracana Stadium in Brazil, which has held crowds of more than 200,000, are built to accommodate the multitudes of spectators who enjoy the game. The sport experienced extraordinary growth in the United States in the 1970's.

The essence of soccer is its simplicity. Known as "football" in much of the world, it is still a game for the masses, speaking a language that knows no international barriers. The object of the game is to get the ball, by any means except using the hands, into the rectangular goals at each end of the field. The team scoring the most goals is the winner. Often, the games end in ties.

Soccer, which evolved from centuries of different ball games, did not always allow only the goalkeepers, or goalies, to use their hands to touch the ball. Formal rules and distinctions among players did not emerge until the late 19th century. Rugby and U.S.-style football developed out of the division that came with decisions to prohibit certain actions in soccer, such as handling the ball, tackling with the arms, and hacking.

COMPETITION

The playing dimensions of soccer fields must conform to certain limitations, but need not be uniform. The length may vary from a minimum of 100 yards to a maximum of 120 yards (91–110 meters). The width of the field must never exceed the length. The field is divided in half crosswise by a center line. At the middle of this line is the center spot, where the game is initially started and then restarted following goals. The center circle has a radius of 10 yards (9.1 meters) from the center spot. The field is bordered by touchlines on the sides and by goal lines on the ends.

At each end of the field is a goal 24 feet (7.3 meters) wide and 8 feet (2.4 meters) high, consisting of two uprights joined by a crossbar. In front of each goal are two rectangular boxes. The smaller box, measuring 20 yards by 6 yards (18.3 by 5.5 meters), is the goal area, in which the goalkeeper cannot be charged and where the ball is placed for goal kicks, which are taken by the team defending the goal area. The larger rectangle, measuring 44 yards by 18 yards (40.2 by 16.4 meters), is the penalty area. It designates the area where the goalkeeper may use his hands to touch the ball without being penalized, and within which any one of the nine direct-free-kick offenses committed by a defensive player will result in a penalty kick. A penalty kick is a free shot at the goal from the penalty spot, 12 yards (11 meters) from the center of the goal. All players except the shooter and goalkeeper must be outside the penalty area and at least 10 yards from the penalty spot. The penalty area has an arc at the top to maintain the 10-yard distance. In each corner of the field are arcs, 1 yard (0.9 meter) in radius from the corner, which are used for corner kicks.

Players and Equipment. Teams have 11 players, with one player, the goalkeeper, readily distinguishable by uniform from his teammates and the opponents. Under international rules, only two substitutions are allowed, with no resubstitution. In the United States, National Collegiate Athletic Association (NCAA) regulations allow five substitutes on an unlimited basis.

All players are equipped with approved shoes, calf-length socks, shorts, and either long- or short-sleeve shirts. Shin guards are optional. The game is played with a spherical ball that must have an outer casing of approved material, usually leather. It must be 27 to 28 inches (69–71 cm) in circumference and weigh between 14 and 16 ounces (396–454 grams).

Under international regulations one referee and two linesmen officiate. The referee's primary responsibility is to control the game with the assistance of the linesmen, who notify the referee when the ball is out of play; when a team should be awarded a throw-in, corner kick, or goal kick; and when a player is offside. The referee makes the final decision in all disputes.

Rules, Penalties, and Scoring. The game of soccer is governed by a set of 17 "laws" devised and enforced by the Federation of International Football Associations (FIFA), soccer's international governing body, in order to bring conformity to the rules of the game and to enhance international competition. The first six laws pertain to the field, equipment, players, and officials, and the remainder are discussed below.

A game consists of 90 minutes and is divided into two 45-minute periods, although the length of the game may be shortened. U.S. colleges play four 22-minute quarters. Youth-level teams throughout the world have adjusted the length of their games to meet the varying physical abilities of their players.

Every game begins with a kickoff in the center of the field, with the flip of a coin determining which team will kick off. The other team kicks off to start the second half, when the teams exchange sides of the field. Following each goal, the game is restarted with the scored-upon team kicking off. At kickoffs each team must position itself in its defensive half of the field, and the defensive team must keep out of the center circle, at least 10 yards from the ball, until the ball is kicked. The kicking team must move the ball forward at least its circumference before it is in play, and the player who first plays the ball is not allowed to touch it again until another player on the field touches it.

The ball is out of play when it wholly crosses a goal line or touchline, or when the game is stopped by the referee. When the ball crosses the touchline, the team that touched it loses possession, and it is put back into play by a throw-in by an opposing player. When the ball crosses the goal line, it is put back into play by either a goal kick or corner kick, depending on which team last touched the ball. If the defensive team last touched it, a corner kick is taken by the offensive team from the corner on the side on which the ball went out. If the offensive team last touched the ball, the defensive team restarts play with a goal kick, taken from within the goal area. The ball must completely clear the penalty area before it is considered in play.

A goal is scored when the entire ball pases over the goal line. It must pass betwen the posts and under the crossbar, and it must not have been thrown, carried, or propelled by the hand or arm of an attacking player.

Offside is the only rule in soccer that is difficult to understand, and it is confusing only because of its varying ramifications. Fundamentally, a player is offside if he is nearer his opponents' goal than the ball at the moment the ball is played, unless (a) he is in his defensive half of the field, (b) there are two opponents between him and the goal line, (c) the ball was last touched or played by an opponent, or (d) he receives the ball directly from a goal kick, a corner kick, or a throw-in. An offside results in an indirect free kick by the opposition.

A player who intentionally attempts to or actually kicks, trips, jumps at, violently charges, charges from behind, strikes, holds, or pushes an opponent, or intentionally handles the ball is penalized by the awarding of a direct free kick to the opposing side. A direct free kick is one from which a goal can be scored without the ball touching another player. If any one of the nine direct-free-kick offenses is committed by the defending team in its own penalty area, the offensive team is awarded a penalty kick. Only the player taking the shot and the goalkeeper are allowed inside the penalty area during a penalty shot.

For less flagrant violations, such as offside, dangerous plays, obstruction, or "ungentlemanly conduct," an indirect free kick is awarded to the opposing team. An indirect free kick is one that cannot lead directly to a goal. It must touch another player before entering the goal. In the case of all free kicks the opposing players must be at least 10 yards from the ball at the time the kick is attempted. The player who first plays the ball may not play it again until it is touched by another player.

Play and Tactics. The basis of well-played soccer is control of the ball, primarily with the feet, but also with the head and body. Players "trap" the ball (bring it under control) with a foot, a leg, or a part of the upper body. Then the player passes or dribbles—runs with the ball at his feet—using the instep or the inside or outside of the foot. For hard, power kicking, the instep is normally used. The head is used to intercept balls in the air, to pass, and to shoot the ball at the goal. Good players time their jumps and snap their heads forward to strike the ball with their foreheads and propel it with great power and accuracy.

When one player has the ball, all the other players constantly shift their positions—the offensive players seeking space in which to receive a pass; the defensive players trying to intercept, to cover opponents, or to "tackle" the man with the ball. Hard physical contact is permitted in soccer only when the primary purpose of the players coming into contact is to kick or head the ball.

With the exception of the earliest years of modern soccer—when teams lined up their 11 players in a formation with 8 forwards, 2 fullbacks, and a goalkeeper—the positional arrangement of players has consisted of varying combinations of forwards, halfbacks, and fullbacks, in addition to the goalie. The forwards are the attacking players who do most of the

scoring. The halfbacks are linkmen who coordinate the play between the forwards and fullbacks. The fullbacks are defenders whose primary assignment is to prevent the opposing team from scoring and to feed the ball to the halfbacks to initiate the attack.

By the late 1870's teams had begun the trend away from all-out offensive play by using 6 forwards, 2 halfbacks, and 2 fullbacks, plus the goalkeeper. In 1883 one forward was moved back into the halfback line to produce the conventional 2-3-5 system, which evolved slowly into the most popular formations in use today—the 4-2-4 and 4-3-3 formations. In each case the back line of defense has 4 players. The changes are between 2 or 3 players in midfield and 4 or 3 players in the forward line. The modern formations although they are more defensively inclined, also give defensive players room and opportunity to move forward as offensive players.

Soccer's main attraction is that players must be prepared to use their skills instantly and their own initiative within certain basic patterns. The speed of the game demands improvisation and limits the use of set "plays."

National and International Competition. One of soccer's outstanding characteristics is its international flavor. The supreme achievement in soccer is capturing the World Cup championship. More than 100 national teams compete every four years for the World Cup. After two years of regional eliminations, 16 teams qualify for the final round of competition, which is held over a period of three weeks in one country.

In Mexico City in 1970, Brazil, led by the incomparable Pelé, won its third World Cup title. This earned the Brazilians the right to keep the Jules Rimet Trophy and necessitated the provision of a new trophy. Italy, Uruguay, and West Germany have each won the tournament twice.

Each year since 1956 the league champions of each of the European nations have qualified to compete for the European Cup, symbol of the club championship of Europe. The tournament has been dominated by the famed Real Madrid team of Spain.

In even-numbered years when there are no World Cup finals, the Olympic Games provide a competition for national amateur teams. Two years of eliminations precede the tournament, which ranks second only to track and field in spectator appeal at the games. Western European and South American countries took most of the early titles, but eastern European nations, particularly Hungary, have dominated the competition since 1952.

Other national and international competitions include the European Championship (formerly, European Nations Cup), held in Olympic Games years since 1958. In addition to a league competition, each nation conducts a separate National Cup competition, which consists of an elimination tournament involving the country's amateur and professional teams. Each year the Cup champions of Europe compete in the Cup Winners Cup. English teams have dominated the event. Africa, Asia, and the Conacaf (North America, Central America, and the Caribbean countries) also hold yearly continental club championships for league and cup winners.

Soccer in the United States. After nearly a century in which it was lost in the shadow of its own outgrowth—American football—soccer experienced a renaissance in the 1960's and a boom in the 1970's. Considered from the number of both spectators and participants, soccer has become firmly established on the American scene as a big-time sport.

Improved world communications, providing needed exposure, and the advent of a professional league have helped to develop this rather sudden and growing interest in soccer in the United States. The recruitment of Pelé and other great foreign stars by U.S. professional teams stirred the interest of the fans, who began turning out by the thousands at league games. In addition, the marked growth of soccer has been aided by the low cost of organizing and maintaining the sport and, most importantly, the lack of emphasis on special physical requirements to be a successful player. for example, Pelé in his playing career stood only 5 feet 9 (175 cm) and weighed about

165 pounds (75 kg), and most professional players are under 6 feet (183 cm). Many parents have encouraged their children to participate in the sport because if offers a much lower risk of injury than does football.

Soccer is the fastest-growing sport at both the secondary-school and collegiate levels. It is estimated that more than a million young people, from elementary school to college, are playing the game, compared with only 50,000 in the 1960's. Youth leagues have sprung up around the country so rapidly that it has become a problem to find enough coaches andplaying sites to accommodate all the youngsters who want to play. Unlike many other team sports, soccer attracts large numbers of women and girls. In some youth leagues as many as 40% of all competitors are girls. Women make up about 40% of the attendance at professional games.

Soccer has become a popular intercollegiate sport. The NCAA reports that 430 of its members are fielding soccer teams and that many other schools have club teams. Collegiate soccer received a major boost in 1971 when the NCAA championships were moved to the Orange Bowl in Miami, Fla.

Bibliography

Arnold, Peter, and Davis, Christopher, *Hamlyn Book of World Soccer* (Hamlyn 1976).
Bradley, Gordon, and Toye, Clive, *Playing Soccer the Professional Way* (Harper 1973)
Glanville, Brian, *Soccer: A History of the Game* (Crown 1968).
Toye, Clive, *Soccer* (Watts 1968).
Universal Guide For Referees (Federation of International Football Associations, annually).

Center. To pass the ball from a sideline to the center of the field.

Charging. Knocking an opposing player off balance legally by making contact with the shoulder; contact from behind is illegal; referee determines whether contact is excessively rough and subject to penalty.

Corner Kick. A kick from a corner arc by an attacking player, putting the ball back in play after it has been sent over the goal line by a defending player.

Cross. A ball kicked from one side of the field to the other.

Dribble. To move the ball along the ground by short taps with the feet.

Free Kick. An unchallenged kick awarded for a personal foul; a *direct free kick* may result directly in a goal; an *indirect free kick* must be touched by another player before entering the goal.

Goal Kick. A kick by the defending team that puts the ball in play after it has been kicked over the goal line by the attacking team; the goalie usually kicks it out.

Hacking. Kicking an opposing player deliberately.

Hands. Intentionally touching the ball with the hands or arms; a rule violation for all except the goalie.

Heading. Passing or scoring by hitting the ball with the head.

Marking. Guarding an opposing player.

Obstructing. Blocking by taking a position in the path of an opposing player; a rule violation for which an indirect kick is awarded.

Offside. Being within 35 yards of the opponent's goal line at the instant the ball is passed, unless two defenders are nearer their goal line than the attacking player; a rule violation for which an indirect kick is awarded.

Penalty Area. A rectangular area, 44 yards wide and 18 yards long, in front of the goal, within which the goalie may use his hands without penalty and penalty kicks are taken.

Penalty Kick. A free kick awarded to the attacking team following a major foul by the defending team inside its own penalty area; the kick is attempted from 12 yards in front of the goal, and only the goalie may defend against it.

Save. A defensive maneuver by a goalie that prevents a score.

Screen. To protect the ball by keeping one's body between it and an opposing player.

Tackling. A defensive maneuver with the feet to steal the ball from the player dribbling or about to kick it.

Trap. To control the ball by stopping its flight with one's foot, chest, or thigh.

Volley. Kicking the ball while it is in flight; a half volley is done off one bounce.

HOCKEY is played on an ice surface, or rink, with six players on a team. Each player has a bladed stick that he uses to advance a disk, called a *puck,* toward the opponents' end of the rink. The object is to hit the puck into a netted cage and score a goal (point), the winner being the team with the most goals at the end of the game. Each team has three players on a forward line (right and left wingmen and a center), a right and a left defenseman, and a goaltender. The game is played in three 20-minute periods, with 10-minute intermissions between periods.

The Rink. A regulation rink is 200 feet long and 85 feet wide, with rounded corners of 15-foot radius. The entire surface is enclosed with 4-foot-high wooden boards. Red lines across the rink and 10 feet from the backboards are called goal lines. Posts for a goal cage in the center of each goal line are 4 feet high and 6 feet apart; they are connected at the top by a horizontal bar. Usually there are two circular arcs extending 22 inches to the rear from the base of each post. The posts, crossbar, and arcs are attached to a net that extends back at least 17 inches from the top and down to the ice. In front of the cage is a rectangular area 4 feet deep by 8 feet wide, called the *crease.* This is the goaltender's domain, where he has certain privileges that other players do not. No opposing player can stay in or score from the crease.

Blue lines across the rink divide the surface between the goal lines into three zones. The middle area is the neutral zone. The space from one team's goal line to its blue line measures 60 feet and is that team's defensive zone and the opponents' attacking zone. In professional hockey, a red line divides the rink in half; this center line is not used in amateur games.

On the professional rink there are eight red spots (circles 12 inches in diameter) designating where the game can be restarted after a whistle stoppage, and a center spot where the game is started. Two of the 8 spots are in each end zone, each 15 feet out from the goal line and midway between the sideboards and the nearer goalpost. These spots and the center spot are surrounded by 2-inch-wide circles of 10-foot radius, called face-off circles. The official starts and restarts the game by a face-off—that is, by dropping the puck between the sticks of two opponents who stand opposite each other and outside the red spot, with stick blades flat on the ice. No player may be within 10 feet of the two players facing off. The four other red face-off spots are in the neutral zone, one in each corner, and are not surrounded by circles. These spots do not appear on the amateur rink.

The rink includes a seating area and a penalty box (space) for each team. The penalty box must be large enough to hold 10 persons—penalized players, timekeepers, and scorer.

Equipment. The puck is a vulcanized black rubber disk 1 inch thick and 3 inches in diameter; it weighs between 5½ and 6 ounces. The stick has a handle, or shaft, about 1-¼ inches wide by ¾ inch thick and a 3-inch-wide blade. The goaltender's stick has a 3½-inch-wide blade. Sticks measure no more than 55 inches (professional) or 53 inches (amateur) in length from the heel to the end of the handle, and 12½ inches from the heel to the tip of the blade. Some sticks have curved blades. In this case, the stick's widest curving point is limited to ½-inch from an imaginary perpendicular line drawn between the handle and the tip of the blade. Most blades have a slight bevel in one or the other direction; accordingly, the sticks are right-handed or left-handed. Sticks that are not beveled are called "neutral."

An ice hockey skate is made of tubular aluminum, has a narrow steel blade, and is permanently attached to a heelless boot. To aid maneuverability, the blade generally is "rockered"—that is, only about 4 inches of its edge is flat on the ice. The goaltender's skate has a completely flat edge.

For body protection players wear shoulder, hip, and elbow pads, gauntlet-type gloves, and shin and knee guards. In addition to the regular equipment, goaltenders wear 10-inch-wide leg pads and chest protectors. Collegiate and other amateur players must wear protective helmets; and goaltenders, face masks. Some professional players favor such equipment. The average weight of a player's equipment is 20 pounds. Goaltenders wear about 40 pounds.

Skills and Fundamentals. Every hockey player must be an expert in skating, puck handling, shooting, and checking.

In skating, a player must use short, fast, forceful strides, keeping his knees bent and flexible. He must start quickly from a dead stop and gain full momentum almost immediately. To outwit an opponent, he must change pace constantly.

Successful puck handling—that is, maneuvering the puck down the ice and past the opponents—is largely a matter of deception. An experienced player never looks at his stick or puck during the game; he keeps his eyes on his opponents. When he maneuvers the puck, he must keep the blade of his stick flat against the puck, or else the puck will roll or bounce. In receiving a pass, he should let his blade "give" a little as the puck hits it, so that the puck will not rebound out of reach.

Players must know how to shoot from every angle, with both forehand and backhand. The best spot from which to try for a goal is 10 to 15 feet in front of the goaltender; this angle offers more open goal to shoot at. Also, as the shooter follows his shot, he may have another try if the puck rebounds in his path. A fast sweeping motion or a quick snap of the wrist will lift the puck off the ice and make the shot considerably more difficult for the goaltender to handle.

Checking is principally a defensive skill. It is accomplished by using the body to throw the opponent off balance and cause him to lose control of the puck or by using the stick (poke checking) to break up an opponent's attack before he gets underway.

Responsibilities of Players. An ideal forward line has a smooth-skating, speedy, good stick-handler at center, flanked by one wingman who is aggressive and able to battle for the puck in the corners of the rink, and another who can deliver a hard, accurate shot.

The center is the playmaker, the key man on offense and defense. He carries the puck up the ice, sizes up the defense, and sets up the play. He must be a good poke checker, a master at body checking, and the best shot.

Wings should follow the puck in with every shot on offense. On defense they should keep inside and toward the boards, ready to receive a pass and start an attack. The right wingman is responsible for the right side of the ice, and the left wingman handles the left side, both offensively and defensively. Wings seldom enter a sector assigned to another player unless a plan of interchanging positions has been prearranged.

Forwards, after a rush up ice, skate back toward their own goal and cover opposing players to prevent them from gaining an advantageous attacking position. This defensive play is called *backchecking*. In *forechecking,* the forwards guard the opponents closely to make them work hard to get the puck out of their defensive zone.

The sole job of the goaltender is to keep the puck out of his team's net. He stops the shot for goal with feet, legs, body, hands, or stick, and clears the puck to the side or behind the goal, attempting to get it to a teammate. Though often called on to defend the goal by himself he usually can depend on help from the two defensemen and three forwards on the ice with him. Goaltenders must have lightning reflexes.

The Squad. A regulation hockey squad usually has 11 forwards, 5 defensemen, and 2 goaltenders. Because it is impossible for players to stay in the game continuously, due to the strain on the legs from rushes up and down the rink and from sudden stops and starts, coaches substitute frequently to maintain a team's overall speed. Substitutes may be sent in either when play has been halted or while the game is in progress.

Because of frequent substitutions, players practice and play as partners, in units or "teams." For example, a squad usually has three offensive units (three forward-line teams of three players each, with two "spares") and two units of two defensemen each, with one spare. Coaches try to put together forward and defense units in which the individual talents of the players complement one another for a cohesive attack. Ordinarily one of the squad's two goaltenders plays the entire game. The second goalie may replace the starter at any time, but a coach usually substitutes only if the starting goalie is injured.

Conduct of the Game. There are three officials for each game: a referee and two linesmen. The referee is in charge of the game, and he rules on penalties and goals. He drops the puck at center ice face-offs at the start of each period and after goals. Linesmen rule on infractions, handle all face-offs other than those at center ice, and break up fights among players. In amateur hockey, fighting results in expulsion from the game.

At the start of the game the puck is put into play in the center ice spot by a face-off between the opposing centers. They try to get possession of the puck and send it out of the wings. Play then moves up and down the ice until either a goal is scored, an infraction is called, or a penalty is assessed. After any halt in play action restarts with a face-off.

Two important infractions are offside and icing. A player is offside if he precedes the puck over the blue line into the attacking zone. Players may pass the puck ahead to teammates in the same zone but not ahead to teammates in another zone. Icing is hitting the puck the length of the ice from the defending side of the center red line (professional) or from inside the defensive blue line (amateur). This is a maneuver defenders use to relive the pressure in their defensive zone. After an icing infraction the puck is returned to the defensive zone of the team that iced it, for a face-off. A team is permitted to ice the puck without the face-off if it has fewer players in the game than the opponents.

Penalties are classified according to the severity of the offense, and the offender must remain in a penalty box for a stated number of minutes or, in rare cases, leave the game. When a player is penalized, his team must play shorthanded while the opponents maintain a full complement of five skaters. This situation offers an excellent opportunity for the team at full strength to set up a power play—that is, to use five of its best shooters to try to score. If a team scores as a result of a penalty, the penalized player returns to the ice. Otherwise, he must stay in the box until he has served full penalty time.

Major penalties that draw 5-minute suspensions include fighting and such dangerous play as charging a player from behind. Two-minute suspensions are assessed for minor penalties such as tripping, holding, interference, and high-sticking (striking a player with one's stick above shoulder level).

A player's total points in scoring, at the end of a season, includes both goals made and assists. An assist is one point credited to a player other than the scorer of a goal for a maneuver that results in a goal; no more than two players may receive assists on any one scoring play. Thus, a player may lead the league or his team with, for example, a total of 70 points—30 goals and 40 assists.

Origin and Organization of Hockey. Ice hockey is Canada's national sport. The first organized game of hockey was played in Kingston, Ontario, in 1855, between teams from the Royal Canadian Rifles. It soon spread to other towns.

Much of the game's early development can be traced to Montreal, where students at McGill University in 1875 proposed a code of conduct familiarly called the McGill Rules, and formed a league with the Victoria Club of Montreal and a club from Quebec. In 1885 the Amateur Hockey Association (AHA) of Canada, the country's first national hockey association, was formed and comprised teams from Montreal, Quebec, and Ottawa.

In 1893 the governor-general of Canada, Lord Stanley of Preston, donated a cup to be presented to the amateur hockey champions of the country. It was won by the Montreal Amateur Athletic Association, the winner of the AHA title. By 1896 teams were playing in the New York area, which led to the formation of the American Amateur Hockey League. In 1899, U.S. and Canadian teams competed for the first time.

In 1909 the National Hockey Association (NHA), comprising teams from Toronto and Ottawa and two teams from Montreal, was organized in eastern Canada; and in 1911 the Pacific Coast Hockey League (PCHL), embracing teams from Canada and the United States, was formed in the West. The two leagues conducted a playoff in 1912, after which the Stanley Cup became the symbol of professional hockey supremacy rather than amateur. The first U.S. team to win the cup was the Seattle Metropolitans of the PCHL, which defeated the Montreal Canadiens in 1917. In that same year the NHA disbanded, and the National Hockey League (NHL) was formed. This league started with the original four NHA teams and added Quebec in 1919; in 1924 Boston gained the first U.S. franchise. By 1926 most PCHL players had joined the NHL, and the Stanley Cup henceforth became the exclusive possession of the NHL. Since the 1930–1931 season, All-Star first and second teams have been selected by a ballot of three hockey writers from each league city.

In 1942 the NHL included six teams: Boston, Chicago, Detroit, Montreal, New York Rangers, and Toronto. Six more teams were added in 1967—California, Los Angeles, Minnesota, Philadelphia, Pittsburgh, and St. Louis—and an additional six by 1974—Atlanta, Buffalo, Kansas City, New York Islanders, Vancouver, and Washington.

A new professional league, the World Hockey Association, was formed in 1972. In its first season of play, the WHA comprised 12 U.S. and Canadian teams in two divisions: *East*—Cleveland, New England, New York, Ottawa, Philadelphia, Quebec; *West*—Alberta, Chicago, Houston, Los Angeles, Minnesota, Winnipeg. Since that time, however, there have been a number of franchise shifts and realignments.

The Ligue Internationale de Hockey sur Glace (International Ice Hockey Federation) was founded by governing organizations in Britain, France, Belgium, Switzerland, and Bohemia in 1908. This federation conducts a tournament each year (except in Olympic Games years) to determine the world amateur champion. The Amateur Hockey Association of the United States, formed in 1937, became a member of the Ligue in 1947. The international rules are applicable to most of the more than 30 affiliated countries in the federation, with slight variations in the rules followed in Canada, Britain, and the United States. Hockey has been an Olympic sport since 1920.

Bibliography

Further Reading: Beddoes, Richard, and others, *Hockey: The Story of the World's Fastest Sport,* 3d rev. ed. (Macmillan, N.Y., 1973); Eskenazi, Gerald, *Hockey,* (Follet 1971); Sullivan, George, *Face-Off: A Guide to Modern Hockey* (Van Nostrand-Reinhold 1968).

GLOSSARY OF HOCKEY TERMS

Attacking Zone. The area from an opponents' blue line to the goal line; also called *offensive zone.*

Backchecking. Falling back after an attack to check an opponent in the player's defending zone.

Blocking. Throwing the body in the way of either the puck or an opposing player.

Blue Lines. Two lines, one at each end of the rink, and 60 feet from the goal line, which define the attacking zone. Used to determine offside.

Boarding. Body checking or causing in any other way a player to fall heavily into the wallboards.

Body Checking. Using the body to block or hit an opponent. Legal only when the player hit has the puck or was the last one to have touched it.

Center Ice. The area between the blue lines.

Charging. Running or jumping at, or taking more than three strides toward, a player before checking him. Illegal and calls for a minor penalty.

Checking. Stopping, blocking, or hitting an opponent. See also *Body Checking, Cross Checking, Poke Checking.*

Crease. A rectangular area marked off in front of the goal net; it is the goaltender's domain.

Defending Zone. The area from a team's goal line to its blue line; also called *defensive zone.*

Elbowing. Hitting an opponent with the elbow. Illegal and calls for a minor penalty.

Face-off. The dropping of the puck between two opposing players to start the game, and to restart play after each whistle stoppage and after each period.

Forechecking. Checking an opponent in his own zone.

Headmanning. Advancing the puck to the skater farthest up ice.

High-sticking. Carrying the stick above shoulder level. Calls for a penalty if one player strikes another with it, or a face-off if no other infraction occurs.

Holding. Using the hands on an opponent or his equipment. Illegal and calls for a minor penalty.

Icing. Shooting the puck from behind the center red line across an opponent's goal line. Illegal and calls for a face-off in the defensive zone of the team that shot the puck; also called *icing the puck.*

Interference. Body contact with a player not in possession of the puck or who was not the last one to touch it. Illegal and calls for a minor penalty.

Kneeing. Using the knee to check an opponent. Illegal and calls for a minor penalty.

Neutral Zone. Center ice.

Penalty Killer. The player who uses up time while his teammate serves time in the penalty box. He tries to hold onto the puck and prevent the opposing team from scoring as a result of its manpower advantage.

Playmaker. A player, usually the center, whose skating and puck-handling ability enable him to set up or make a play that can lead to a goal.

Poke Checking. Thrusting the stick at the puck. Illegal if this causes the opponent to trip and fall and calls for a minor penalty.

Power Play. A play in which the attacking team tries to exploit its advantage in numbers as a result of a penalty to the opposing team. Usually four forwards and one defenseman will be used to increase the team's scoring potential.

Red Line. The line that divides the rink in half. Defending teams may clear the puck out of the defensive zone up to this line without incurring an offside.

Save. Prevention of a goal by the goalie.

Slap Shot. A shot in which a player winds up and slaps his stick at the puck; usually his fastest shot.

Slashing. Swinging the stick at an opponent. Illegal and calls for a minor penalty.

Spearing. Using the stick like a spear. Illegal and calls for a minor penalty.

Stick Handling. The art of propelling the puck with the stick; also called *puck handling.*

NORTH AMERICAN SOCCER LEAGUE CHAMPIONS

1967	Oakland Clippers
1968	Atlanta Chiefs
1969	Kansas City Spurs
1970	Rochester Lancers
1971	Dallas Tornado
1972	New York Cosmos
1973	Philadelphia Atoms
1974	Los Angeles Aztecs
1975	Tampa Bay Rowdies
1976	Toronto Metros
1977	New York Cosmos
1978	New York Cosmos

THE WORLD CUP

YEAR	CHAMPIONSHIP FINAL
1934	Italy 2, Czechoslovakia 1
1938	Italy 4, Hungary 2
1950	Uruguay 2, Brazil 1
1954	West Germany 3, Hungary 2
1958	Brazil 5, Sweden 2
1962	Brazil 3, Czechoslovakia 1
1966	England 4, West Germany 2
1970	Brazil 4, Italy 1
1974	West Germany 2, Netherlands 1
1978	Argentina 3, Netherlands 1

STANLEY CUP WINNERS

1893–94	Montreal A. A. A.	1918–19	No decision[2]	1948–49	Toronto Maple Leafs
1894–95	Montreal Victorias	1919–20	Ottawa Senators	1949–50	Detroit Red Wings
1895–96	Winnipeg Victorias	1920–21	Ottawa Senators	1950–51	Toronto Maple Leafs
1896–97	Montreal Victorias	1921–22	Toronto St. Pats	1951–52	Detroit Red Wings
1897–98	Montreal Victorias	1922–23	Ottawa Senators	1952–53	Montreal Canadiens
1898–99	Montreal Victorias	1923–24	Montreal Canadiens	1953–54	Detroit Red Wings
	(February)	1924–25	Victoria Cougars	1954–55	Detroit Red Wings
1898–99	Montreal Shamrocks	1925–26	Montreal Maroons	1955–56	Montreal Canadiens
	(March)	1926–27	Ottawa Senators	1956–57	Montreal Canadiens
1899–1900	Montreal Shamrocks	1927–28	New York Rangers	1957–58	Montreal Canadiens
1900–01	Winnipeg Victorias	1928–29	Boston Bruins	1958–59	Montreal Canadiens
1901–02	Montreal A. A. A.	1929–30	Montreal Canadiens	1959–60	Montreal Canadiens
1902–03	Ottawa Silver Seven	1930–31	Montreal Canadiens	1960–61	Chicago Black Hawks
1903–04	Ottawa Silver Seven	1931–32	Toronto Maple Leafs	1961–62	Toronto Maple Leafs
1904–05	Ottawa Silver Seven	1932–33	New York Rangers	1962–63	Toronto Maple Leafs
1905–06	Montreal Wanderers	1933–34	Chicago Black Hawks	1963–64	Toronto Maple Leafs
1906–07	Kenora Thistles	1934–35	Montreal Maroons	1964–65	Montreal Canadiens
	(January)	1935–36	Detroit Red Wings	1965–66	Montreal Canadiens
1906–07	Montreal Wanderers	1936–37	Detroit Red Wings	1966–67	Toronto Maple Leafs
	(March)	1937–38	Chicago Black Hawks	1967–68	Montreal Canadiens
1907–08	Montreal Wanderers	1938–39	Boston Bruins	1968–69	Montreal Canadiens
1908–09	Ottawa Senators	1939–40	New York Rangers	1969–70	Boston Bruins
1909–10	Montreal Wanderers	1940–41	Boston Bruins	1970–71	Montreal Canadiens
1910–11	Ottawa Senators	1941–42	Toronto Maple Leafs	1971–72	Boston Bruins
1911–12	Quebec Bulldogs	1942–43	Detroit Red Wings	1972–73	Montreal Canadiens
1912–13	Quebec Bulldogs[1]	1943–44	Montreal Canadiens	1973–74	Philadelphia Flyers
1913–14	Toronto Ontarios	1944–45	Toronto Maple Leafs	1974–75	Philadelphia Flyers
1914–15	Vancouver Millionaires	1945–46	Montreal Canadiens	1975–76	Montreal Canadiens
1915–16	Montreal Canadiens	1946–47	Toronto Maple Leafs	1976–77	Montreal Canadiens
1916–17	Seattle Metropolitans	1947–48	Toronto Maple Leafs	1977–78	Montreal Canadiens
1917–18	Toronto Arenas			1978–79	

[1] Victoria defeated Quebec in challenge series. No official recognition.
[2] Playoff between Montreal Canadiens and Seattle Metropolitans not completed because of influenza epidemic in Seattle.